Also by Mark Arax

West of the West

The King of California (with Rick Wartzman)

In My Father's Name

THE DREAMT LAND

THE DREAMT LAND

Chasing Water and Dust Across California

Mark Arax

Alfred A. Knopf
New York
2019

THIS IS A BORZOI BOOK PUBLISHED BY ALFRED A. KNOPF

www.aaknopf.com

Portions of this work originally appeared, in slightly different form, in *The California Sunday Magazine*: "Singed" first appeared as "Dry" on January 4, 2015. "Kingdom of Wonderful" first appeared as "A Kingdom from Dust" on January 31, 2018.

Library of Congress Cataloging-in-Publication Data
Names: Arax, Mark, author.
Title: The dreamt land : chasing water and dust across California / Mark Arax.
Description: First edition. | New York : Alfred A. Knopf, 2019. | Includes bibliographical references and index.
Identifiers: LCCN 2018048481 (print) | LCCN 2018057714 (ebook) | ISBN 9781101875216 (ebook) | ISBN 9781101875209 (hardcover)
Subjects: LCSH: Water resources development—California—History. | Water-supply—California—History. | BISAC: NATURE / Natural Resources. | HISTORY / United States / State & Local / West (AK, CA, CO, HI, ID, MT, V, UT, WY). | POLITICAL SCIENCE / Public Policy / Environmental Policy.
Classification: LCC HD1694.C2 (ebook) | LCC HD1694.C2 A24 2019 (print) | DDC .91009794—dc23
LC record available at https://lccn.loc.gov/2018048481

Jacket art courtesy of Matthew Brandt
Jacket design by Janet Hansen
Map by Mapping Specialists

Manufactured in the United States of America
Published May 21, 2019

Reprinted Two Times
Fourth Printing, December 2019

Where eyes become the sunlight, and the hand
Is worthy of water: the dreamt land
Toward which all hungers leap, all pleasures pass.

—from Richard Wilbur's "A Baroque
Wall-Fountain in the Villa Sciarra"

CONTENTS

Part Four Children of the Desert (2016–2017)

THE DREAMT LAND

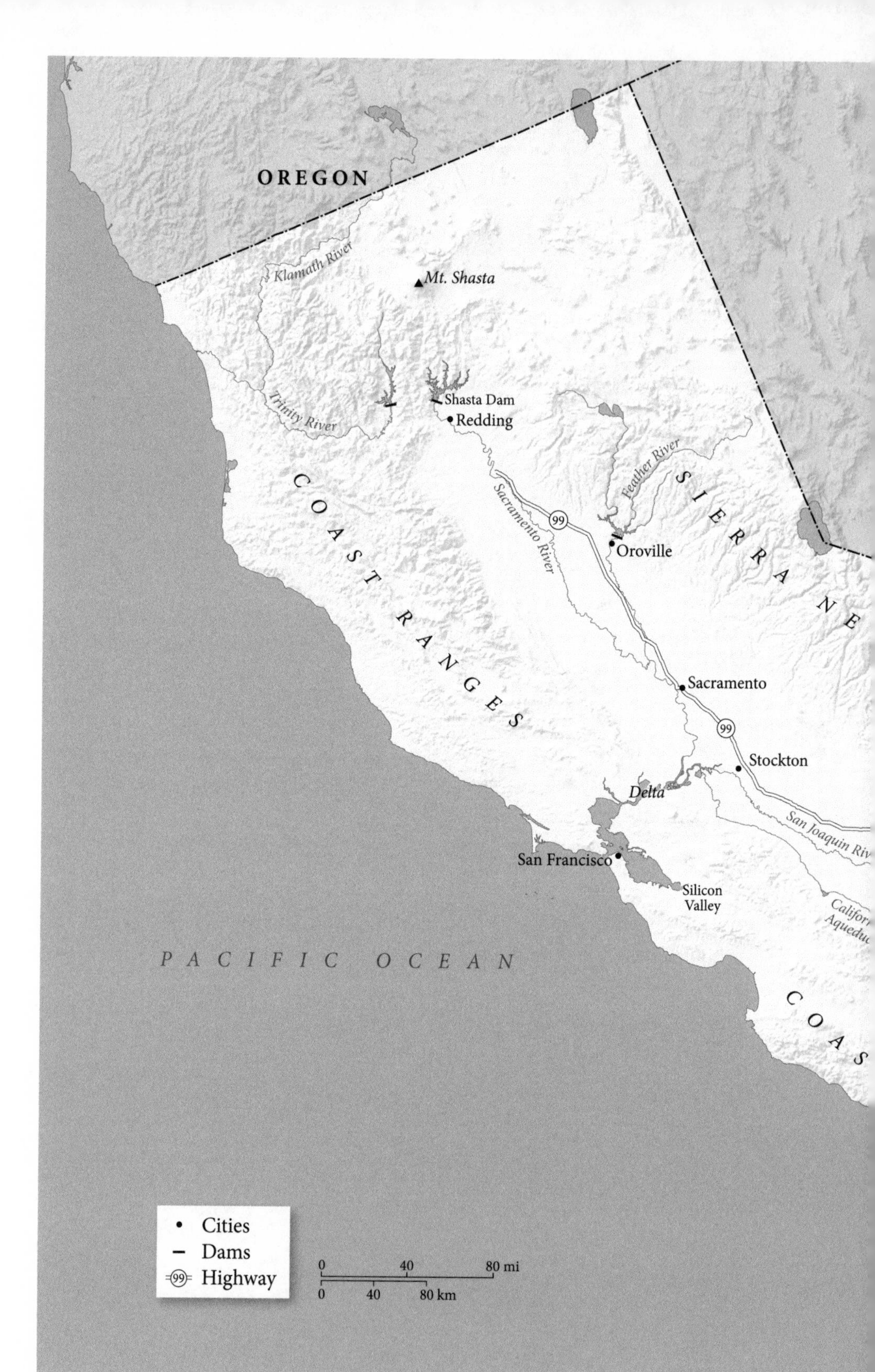
OREGON
Klamath River
Mt. Shasta
Trinity River
Shasta Dam
Redding
COAST RANGES
Sacramento River
Feather River
Oroville
Sacramento
Stockton
Delta
San Francisco
Silicon Valley
PACIFIC OCEAN
Cities
Dams
Highway
99
0 40 80 mi
0 40 80 km

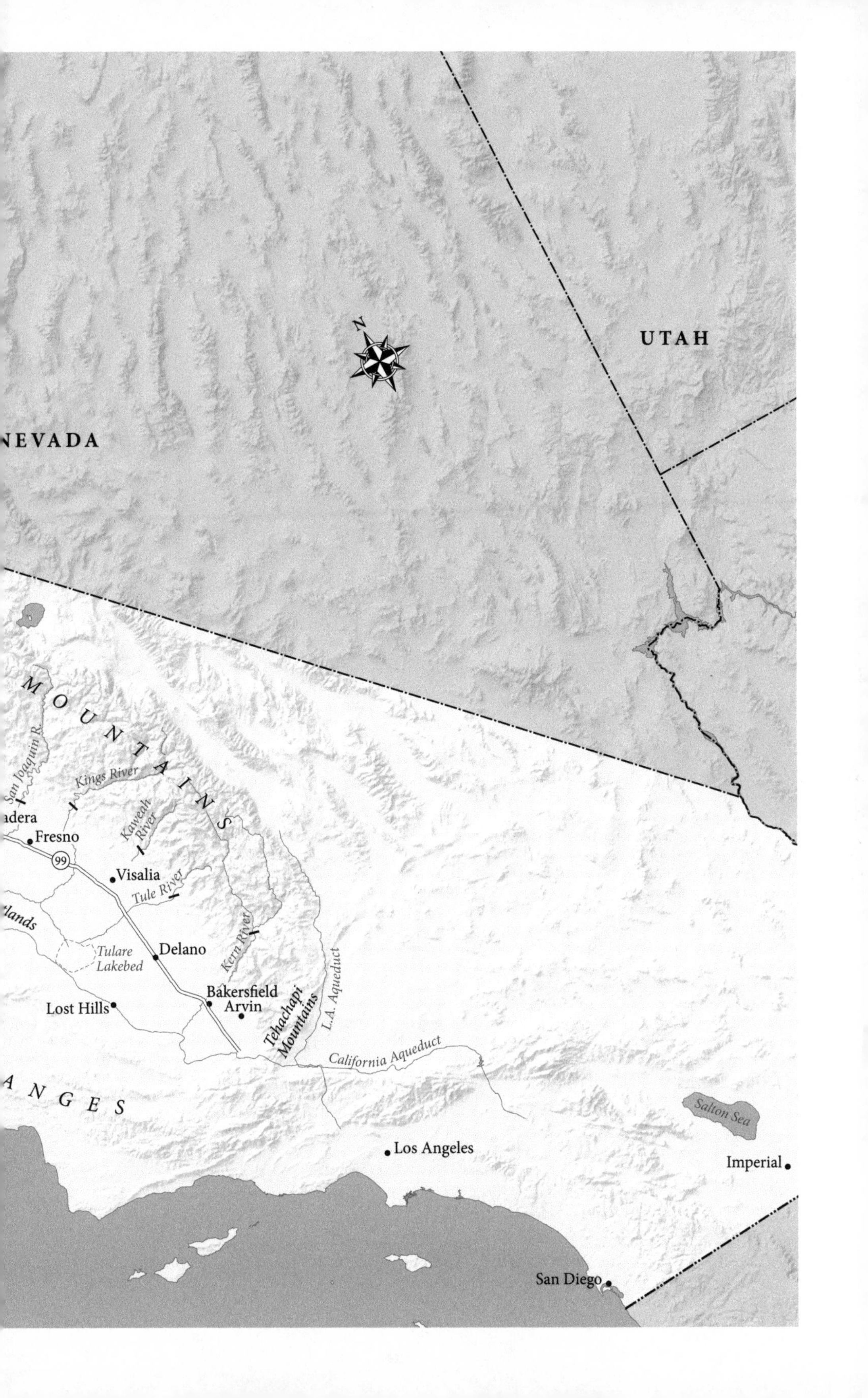
UTAH
NEVADA
N
MOUNTAINS
San Joaquin R.
Kings River
Kaweah River
adera
Fresno
99
Visalia
Tule River
lands
Tulare Lakebed
Delano
Kern River
Bakersfield
Arvin
Lost Hills
Tehachapi Mountains
L.A. Aqueduct
California Aqueduct
ANGES
Salton Sea
Los Angeles
Imperial
San Diego

PROLOGUE
(SUMMER 2016)

Kern River, dry as a bone, slices through Bakersfield

On a summer day in the San Joaquin Valley, 101 in the shade, I merge onto Highway 99 past downtown Fresno and steer through the vibrations of heat. I'm headed to the valley's deep south, to a little farmworker town in a far corner of Kern County called Lost Hills. This is where the biggest farmer in America—the one whose mad plantings of almonds and pistachios have triggered California's nut rush—keeps on growing, no matter drought or flood. He doesn't live in Lost Hills. He lives in Beverly Hills. How has he managed to outwit nature for so long?

The GPS tells me to take Interstate 5, the fastest route through the belly of the state, but I'm partial to Highway 99, the old road that brought the Okies and Mexicans to the fields and deposited a twang on my Armenian tongue. Ninety-nine runs two lanes here, three lanes there, through miles of agriculture broken every twenty minutes by fast food, gas station and cheap motel. Tracts of houses, California's last affordable dream, civilize three or four exits, and then it's back to the open road splattered with the guts and feathers of chickens that jumped ship on the slaughterhouse drive. Pink and white oleanders divide the highway, and every third vehicle that whooshes by is a big rig. More often than not, it is hauling away some piece of the valley's unbroken bounty. The harvest begins in January with one type of mandarin and ends in December with another type of mandarin, and in between comes everything in your supermarket produce and dairy aisles except for bananas and mangoes, though the farmers here are working on the tropical, too.

I stick to the left lane and stay ahead of the pack. The big-rig drivers are cranky two ways, and the farmworkers in their last-leg vans are half asleep. Ninety-nine is the deadliest highway in America. Deadly in the rush of harvest, deadly in the quiet of fog, deadly in the blur of Saturday nights when the fieldwork is done and the beer drinking becomes a second humiliation. Twenty miles outside Fresno, I cross the Kings, the river that irrigates more farmland than any other river here. The Kings is bone-dry as usual. To find its flow, I'd have to go looking in a thousand irrigation ditches in the fields beyond.

There's a mountain range to my left and a mountain range to my right and in between a plain flatter than Kansas where crop and sky meet. One of the most dramatic alterations of the earth's surface in human history took place here. The hillocks that existed back in Yokut Indian days were flattened by a hunk of metal called the Fresno Scraper. Every river busting out of the Sierra was bent sideways, if not backward, by a bulwark of ditches, levees, canals and dams. The farmer corralled the snowmelt and erased the valley, its desert and marsh. He leveled its hog wallows, denuded its salt brush and killed the last of its mustang, antelope and tule elk. He emptied the sky of tens of millions of geese and drained the eight hundred square miles of Tulare Lake dry.

He did this first in the name of wheat, then beef, milk, raisins, cotton and nuts. Once he finished grabbing the flow of the five rivers that ran across the plain, he used his turbine pumps to seize the water beneath the ground. As he bled the aquifer dry, he called on the government to bring him an even mightier river from afar. Down the great aqueduct, by freight of politics and gravity, came the excess waters of the Sacramento River. The farmer commanded the distant flow. The more water he took, the more crops he planted, and the more crops he planted, the more water he needed to plant more crops, and on and on. One million acres of the valley floor, greater than the size of Rhode Island, are now covered in almond trees.

I pity the outsider trying to make sense of it. My grandfather, a survivor of the Armenian Genocide, traveled seven thousand miles by ship and train in 1920 to find out if his uncle's exhortation—"The grapes here are the size of jade eggs"—was true. My father, born in a vineyard outside Fresno, was a raisin grower before he became a bar owner. I grew up in the suburbs where our playgrounds were named after the pioneers of fruit and irrigation canals shot through our neighborhoods to farms we did not know. For half my life, I never stopped to wonder: How much was magic? How much was plunder?

I'm going to Kern County, just shy of the Tehachapi Mountains, to figure out how the big farmers, led by the biggest one of them all, are not only keeping alive their orchards and vineyards during the worst drought in California's recorded history but planting more almonds (79,000 acres), more pistachios (73,000 acres), more grapes (35,000 acres) and more mandarin oranges (13,000 acres). It's a July day in 2016, five years into the dry spell, and the delirium that has gripped the growers, by far the biggest users of water in the state, shows no sign of letting go. Even as the supplies of federal and state water have dropped to zero one year and near zero the next year, agriculture in Kern County keeps chugging along, growing more intensive. The new plantings aren't cotton, alfalfa or carrots, the crops a farmer can decide not to seed when water becomes scarce. These are trees and vines cultivated in nurseries and put into the ground at a cost of ten thousand dollars an acre to satisfy the world's growing appetite for nuts and fruits.

Agriculture in the south valley has extended so far beyond the provisions of its one river, the Kern, that local farmers are raising nearly one million acres of crops. Fewer than half these acres are irrigated with flows from the Kern. The river is nothing if not fickle. One year, it delivers 900,000 acre-feet of snowmelt; the next year, it delivers 300,000 acre-feet. To grow, Big Ag needed a larger and more dependable supply. So beginning in the 1940s, Kern farmers went out and grabbed a share of not one distant river but two: the San Joaquin to the north and the Sacramento to the north of that. The imported flow arrives by way of the Central Valley Project and State Water Project, the one-of-a-kind hydraulic system built by the feds and the state to remedy God's uneven design of California. The water sent to Kern County—1.4 million acre-feet a year—has doubled the acres of cropland. But not even the two projects working in perfect tandem can defy drought. When nature bites down hard, and the outside flow gets reduced to a trickle, growers in Kern turn on their pumps and reach deeper into the earth.

The aquifer, a sea of water beneath the clay, isn't bottomless. It can be squeezed only so much. As the growers punch more holes into the ground chasing a vanishing resource, the earth is sinking. The choices for the Kern farmer now come down to two: He can reach into his pocket and purchase high-priced water from an irrigation district with surplus supplies. Or he can devise a scheme to steal water from a neighbor up the road. I now hear whispers of water belonging to farmers two counties away being pumped out of the ground and hijacked in the dead of night to irrigate the nuts of Lost Hills.

I roll past Tulare, where every February they stage the biggest tractor show in the world, even bigger than the one in Paris, France. Past Delano and the first vineyards that Cesar Chavez marched against. Past McFarland and the Mexican boy runners who won five state championships in a row in the 1990s. Past Oildale and the boxcar where Merle Haggard grew up. Past Bakersfield and the high school football stadium where Frank Gifford and Les Richter, two future NFL Hall of Famers, squared off in the Valley Championship in 1947 in the driving rain. And then it hits me when I reach the road to Weedpatch, where my grandfather's story in America—a poet on his hands and knees picking potatoes—began. I've gone too far. The wide-open middle of California did its lullaby on me again.

I turn back around and find Route 46, the road that killed James Dean. I steer past Wasco to the dust-blowing orchards and vineyards that rise out of the desert in Kern County, the densest planting of almonds, pistachios, pomegranates and grapes on earth. Down this road are the baronies of Marko Zaninovich, who once was and may still be the nation's largest table grape grower, and the Assemi brothers, Farid and Farshid and Darius, who plant cherries and nuts when they're not planting houses, and Freddy Franzia, who grows and bottles more wine grapes than anyone except the Gallos. His most popular brand, 450 million bottles and counting, is Charles Shaw, "Two-Buck Chuck," which sells for $1.99 at Trader Joe's. Up ahead is the kingdom of Stewart Resnick, the richest farmer in the country and maybe the most peculiar one, too, whose 120,000-acre empire of fruits and nuts is called Wonderful. His story is the one I've been carting around in my notebook for the past few decades, sure I was ready to write it after five years or ten years, only to learn of another twist that would lead me down another road.

I park the car and start walking. The sun's brutal beat reminds me of my grandfather pouring salt on his watermelon, an old farmworker trick to ward off sunstroke. I keep walking until I find myself straddling one of those divides that happen in the West, and maybe only in the West. Behind me, the hard line of agriculture ends. In front of me, the hard line of desert begins. In between wends the concrete vein that funnels the snowmelt from one end of California to the other. I have found Lost Hills, it would seem, but like so many other optical illusions I've followed along the thousand-mile path of bent water and reborn dust, the hills are not hills.

Part One

CRACKS IN THE EARTH (2014–2016)

The Aqueduct, California's concrete river, ships water north to south

One

APRICOT'S LESSON

Winter 2014

I look out the window on a late January day and see blossoms on my apricot trees. What to call this new season? In the confused heat, the buds turn into white flowers, pink-eyed. The fruit sets three weeks ahead of its usual clock, and heavy, and I can't help thinking it's going to be one of those bumper-crop years. I'll be eating apricots off the tree all June and still have plenty of leftover fruit to make sun jam in July. But I know a lot can go wrong between now and summer. My father and his father were farmers who couldn't hold on to the farm. They got rid of our last orchard a couple years before I was born. There were two versions of the story, one my grandfather told and one my grandmother swore was truer. That ranch beside the San Joaquin River, its entrance limned in pomegranates, became a faraway picture to me.

In the city where we grew up, not ten miles removed from the farm belt, we stayed dumb to our place. What kid in the Fresno suburbs knew we had built the grandest reclamation project in the world, and all it took was transporting water from where it was abundant to where it was scarce? Canals and ditches filled with snowmelt in spring, and they ran like veins through our subdivisions, but we never thought to ask—and our elders never thought to tell us—where the flow was going and to whom and by what rights. The summer before turning seventeen, I went to work at a packinghouse in Selma, the raisin capital of the world, and got to know a man named Amos Margosian who farmed stone fruit to the east out of Yettem, which means Eden in Armenian. Margosian was just about the darkest Caucasian I had ever seen. He sported a white felt cowboy hat and was famous for picking his plums a little green to catch the early market's big money. He would come in immaculate from the fields and stand on the cull line and watch the sorter reject his fruit right and left. Too early, too green. Too early, too green. He would grow madder by the minute and storm up to the second-floor office, where he'd cuss out the packinghouse boss, who was an even darker-skinned Armenian than he was. And then he'd return the next day with his plums a little less green. By the end of summer, I figured out that the farmer who wasn't a fool didn't count his fruit in the box until it was in the box.

I wait until mid-March and let the nubs grow into something capable before I even say the word "fruit" or guess how many Mason jars I'll need to handle the load on my three apricot trees. So many babies suck on each little branch that I have a choice to make. To make big fruit, you take your thumb and index finger and pinch off two of every three offspring. There are no runts in the litter to make the job less cruel. The kill is purely arbitrary. Man, not nature, selects what lives and dies. Thinning fruit is routine on the farm. Absent the drain of siblings, the chosen ones have a chance to size up and sell for a premium to the wholesale houses. Thinning fruit makes less sense in the backyard. Here, I'm compelled by a different greed. Each Blenheim apricot and Elberta peach and Santa Rosa plum and Mission fig and Page mandarin and Washington navel and Thompson Seedless grape that fights its way to suburban ripe is a thing to behold. And so I put off thinning.

Then one April morning, nothing particularly eventful about the night before, I walk outside and am confronted by a lineup of trees that suddenly appear weightless. As I draw closer, I can see hundreds of apricots, firm and green, sitting in a pile at trunks' feet. I survey each branch sure I have missed something. But not a single fruit has held. Only a trespass of some persistence can explain such a mass shedding, and I begin to curse the squirrel, the rat, the opossum, the jaybird, the sixteen-year-old son. Then I think better. They'd be after sugar, and sugar is two months away.

I call my old friend the nut grower. He's always been kind to my observations, no matter how silly it is to compare my quarter-acre ranch house in Fresno with his big-acre ranches out in the country, where all can go wrong in an endless monoculture and all can be righted with the infinite manipulations at his disposal.

"Brad, there's not a single apricot left on my trees."

"Let me show you my pistachios," he says.

He drives up in a battered white Chevy truck, and I climb aboard. He's a tall man in his mid-fifties with a little round gut just starting to protrude. He isn't wearing Wranglers or a cowboy hat. The only thing farmer about him is his checkered, button-down short-sleeved shirt and the dust on his Georgia wedge boots. He has blue eyes that gaze out kindly from wire-rimmed glasses and a full head of graying brown hair feathered back. The creases the sun has put on his face come from golfing, not farming. He started off in agriculture as a certified public accountant, and now he grows crops on his own land and land he custom-farms for Brentwood investors residing in $10 million houses. Brad himself doesn't live on the farm. He lives in a condo in Fresno and a house in Pebble Beach.

We drive out from the suburbs and into the valley. "The country," my mother used to chant, as if its never-ending earth were an elixir. "Let's take a drive out in the country," she would tell my father, and he'd go to the edge of the river, to the Fig Garden Golf Course, and not beyond. Once again, drought is encroaching on the land, and the big-city journalists are parachuting in, looking for California apocalypse, a new "Dust Bowl." I know how a good story works. I used to be one of them. They're recalling Mark Twain's quip that out here "whiskey is for drinking and water is for fighting over." The quip isn't Twain, it turns out, but the fighting is real, and it's been going on for a while.

Our capture of the rivers began in 1868 when John B. Sweem dug the valley's first ditch, tapping into the main stem of the Kings River to power his gristmill near the town of Centerville. We've scraped out tens of thousands of miles of ditches and canals in the years since, and they seem of the simplest linear design when encountered on the ground. Only from the window of an airplane can one appreciate the complexity of alignments, grades, cross sections, conduits, weirs and checks and begin to grasp the challenge of persuading a people downright hostile to government to put aside their mistrust long enough to create such a system. By its very fulfillment, we were able to reinvent ourselves and then reinvent the land. Drought and flood would throw their tantrums but neither would bring us to our knees again, or at least that's how the chamber of commerce version went. I still haven't figured out my version. I'd get close and then the valley would mock me with another of its convolutions.

Outsiders see it as one shared landscape, the Great Central Valley, four hundred and fifty miles long and sixty miles wide, pinched by the cathedrals of the Sierra Nevada to the east and the less dramatic Coast Ranges to the west. If they take Interstate 5, the new road, they traverse almost nothing but farmland from Kern County on the bottom to Shasta County at the top. If they take Highway 99 straight up the heart, they'll come upon a half dozen farm towns desperately seeking to be city towns. Each one is trying to get there the same way, sprawl and then bust, sprawl and then bust, so that Bakersfield looks no different than Tulare and Tulare looks no different than Fresno and Fresno looks no different than Modesto, and only when they hit Stockton, where the great rivers of the north meet, does the land let out a breath, and only when they come upon Sacramento, its gilded capitol stabbing at sky, do they feel they have arrived, somewhere.

If they've been paying attention, this is where they might understand that the Central Valley is two different valleys, the Sacramento and the San Joaquin, each named after a river discovered in the mid-1700s by Spanish explorers, if you don't count the natives whose discovery came ten thousand years before. No other river roars out of the Sierra with the ferocity of the Sacramento, and even after everything that man has done to tame it, the river still has the capacity for great flood. One-third of California's water comes from the Sacramento and its offshoots. The rivers of the San Joaquin Valley, by comparison, are meek, and their taking by agriculture amounts to a death. But there's another difference in the two valleys that has come to matter more: the well-drained soils deposited long ago by the Kern, Kings and San Joaquin Rivers produce crops like no other place, 250 varieties of vegetables and grains and fruits and nuts with a year-round abundance that puts the farms of the Sacramento Valley to shame. And so this is how it came to be that the contradiction of California was in the land, and the fix was in the water.

Brad steers a course along the San Joaquin River, east to west, across not one kind of place but at least three kinds of places, each with its own variety of soil and each with its own relationship to water. These differences aren't inconsequential but amount to differences of culture and ways of living and ways of extracting that have enabled east side to become the Eastside and west side to become the Westside and the middle land to become its own place, too. We follow the river to the spot where its flow becomes a trickle and then sinks abjectly into sand. This is one of the oddest deaths of any river in America. The San Joaquin has been dammed six times in its upper reaches and one more time for good measure here below. The streambed goes dry 250 miles shy of its ocean journey. When the water picks up again downriver, it blends fresh snowmelt with the salts, selenium and petrochemicals that drain off the farm fields. A giant blue heron alights from a spit of sand, and I trace its flight up and over the new green of a vineyard until it, too, becomes a figment.

Across the vast flattened earth, farmers in Fresno County have planted whole sections of almonds, pistachios, grapes, alfalfa, cotton, corn, tomatoes, garlic, cantaloupes and bell peppers. It's as if each crop is a township, and this doesn't count the dairies with their five and ten thousand Holsteins apiece. If you know how to read them, the fields tell you in a glance what the world is eating and drinking at this moment. Consumers change their tastes and the farmer jumps to change what he is growing. It's gotten to be a reflex. A farmer of stone fruit in the tradition of his grandfather for fifty seasons straight suddenly becomes a farmer of nuts without shedding a tear. The good ones are soothsayers. They see the turn not only before other farmers but before grocery shoppers even realize their tastes are about to change. The ones who jump aboard too late and find themselves on the wrong side of a trend learn all over again the cruelty of farming. A grower planting, say, newfangled subacid peaches in 1998 only to bulldoze the same orchard of subacid peaches in 2005 happens more than anyone cares to admit, or wishes to remember.

As for my friend Brad, he has farmed the last decade and a half on the right side of the gamble, watching his almonds and pistachios triple in price. He talks about his success in the manner of pure observation. "I've been pretty fortunate," he says. "Who would have ever guessed when I started planting nuts in 1989 that they'd be selling for four and five dollars a pound."

There is no sign on the highway but thirty minutes into our drive the land suddenly switches up. We enter the realm of the west side where the roads are public roads and each 640-acre section is a parcel, and each parcel is listed on the county tax collector's rolls, but the farms have no farmhouses. This is a province, vast and annealed, that belongs unto itself. Out here, the decision of what to plant isn't only a response to consumer fickle. It's how a farmer chooses to accept or to fight the character of his dirt and his water. One type of soil fans out for miles and keeps running and then stops all at once and another soil type takes over; sandy loam gives way to clay and clay gives way to alkali. Because dirt that suits cotton doesn't necessarily suit grapes, it would seem that a farmer on the west side would be stuck with his lot. But if he's generous with his applications of gypsum and smart with his applications of water, he can turn cotton ground into vineyard ground, and this is how the land has changed over time.

"This was all cotton. And this was alfalfa and barley and row crops, melons and tomatoes and maybe sugar beets," Brad says as we whiz by one field and then another. "It's almost all almonds now."

If we keep on westward, we will go to where the farmland finally peters out and salt brush runs into the Coast Ranges and the hills are rattlesnake dry. Beneath the three rocks where the bandit Joaquín Murrieta was shot dead in 1853, his head pickled in a jar of gin, the creek known as Cantua hasn't carried water in five years. But Brad steers south and heads through the cultivated fields in a more or less straight line toward the town of Huron and his pistachio orchard. We cross the California Aqueduct, filled with snowmelt, though none of that water will be stopping here, not in this third year of drought. "We're dry," Brad says, passing fallowed grain fields only to come upon another new planting of nuts. "We just don't know it yet." We don't stop in Huron, known as "Knife-Fight City," a clump of Mexican shanties that becomes the poorest place in California whenever the lettuce crop goes to hell.

Brad turns off the asphalt road and takes a dirt trail deeper into one of the most disputed regions in America. This is the territory called Westlands, where big farmers have carved out the largest district devoted to irrigated agriculture in America—one thousand square miles—in the shape of a giant beached whale. Westlands came rather late to the game, drawing its boundaries as a public water district in 1952 under California law and waging a two-decade-long battle to drink from the federal project. The water lawyers love it because no one can figure out what the land truly is or how much subsidized crops and water it deserves. The ground was ocean in another age; it is desert by measure of rainfall. If you stand on one end, where a shallow clay layer prevents irrigation water from percolating deep into the earth, it is a land made dead by salt. If you stand on the other end, where Brad has planted 260 acres of pistachios, it is the most fertile farm dirt in the West as soon as water hits it, a deep loam called Panoche that sits upon this part of the valley like a many-layered German chocolate cake.

Brad jumps out of his truck, grabs a pistachio stick off the ground and heads into his orchard. I run to catch him. He's jousting with a pistachio's gray branches, which resemble the antlers on a big buck. Unlike a walnut grove, tall and leafy and throwing out so much shade that it draws you into its tranquillity, the pistachio orchard has been grooved for industry. Not a weed pokes out of a crack. Not an animal scurries into a burrow. Wood and leaf follow sharp pruned lines. The orchard has been laid out with the same exactness. For every twenty-four females, a single male has been planted within a patterned radius. There is no mistaking the males: their trunks are painted rooster red. I joke to Brad that this is agriculture's version of a harem, but he's in no mood for humor as he walks from male to male, reaches back with his stick and gives a hard spank to the hanging flowers. No green-brown pollen comes puffing off.

"In all my years growing pistachios, I've never seen this happen. The females are ripe and ready, but the males are nowhere near. The whole orchard is out of sync."

"What do you think it is?"

He stares down at the toe of his boot scuffing dirt, then looks up. "Global warming," he says. "Climate change."

Brad and I have known each other since the seventh grade and over the course of our adult lives—mine as a writer, his as a grower—he has often served as my voice of agrarian reason. He's never been afraid to take on the role of heretic, but no other big farmer I know dares speak those words out loud.

"You sure?"

"We haven't had a winter in two years. You need chill to make nuts. There's no chill."

I think back to my grandpa Arax, not quite poet, not quite farmer, who settled in this valley during the 1920s when heat in a corporeal form baked the soil and the rivers turned to sand. He believed that every piece of fruit wore in its flesh the acts of nature and man: drought, flood and hail and the vex of pests and the wise and not-so-wise cuts of pruning shears. But it was the apricot, the one fruit that truly belonged to us, *Prunus armeniaca,* that was especially attuned to the handoff between winter and spring. Any stressor out there, he said, would show up first in the apricot. What Brad is seeing in his pistachios is no different than what I had witnessed in my backyard an hour away. Without winter's hibernation, the fruit aborts in spring. The apricot has to touch death to know to hold life.

"No winter chill, no summer jam," I say.

The calculation in Brad's head dwarfs mine. His company is farming close to twelve thousand acres of pistachios and almonds. In a good year, after paying off all the costs to raise the crop, he and his investors can net $30 million. If that doesn't sound like ma and pa farming, it's because growing nuts is a lucrative business. At the end of each season, it dares him to plow a sizable chunk of his profits back into more agricultural production. This is how Brad has become the part owner of a rather large nut-processing plant. With $80 million in financing from the banks, every crop for Brad is make or break. The pistachio is an alternate bearer: heavy producer one year and lighter producer the next. This year, the clock is set to heavy. "With this kind of bloom on the females, you're looking at a heck of a crop right here," he says. "But the males just aren't ready. And I can't afford to wait any longer."

On a path alongside the orchard, two men have driven up in their four-by-four truck. I don't pay attention to what they're unloading until I hear a full-throttle whine. They're now seated atop dune buggies, zipping up and down the rows, and for a second I think that the sport of off-road racing has come to the nut orchards of California's middle. But from the end of a gardener's blower, they're shooting harvested male pistachio pollen into the waiting limbs of the females. Brad is paying the semen spreaders one hundred dollars an acre to mend the mismatch. He'll find out in ten days if the ladies are keen. "Pollinating every pistachio orchard I've got isn't the problem," he says, climbing back into the cab of his truck. "It's water. Where in the hell am I going to find the water?"

Brad Gleason tends to his almond orchard on
Fresno County's west side

Growing pistachios in jackrabbit country isn't the same as growing almonds. The pistachio tree, like its fellow ancient the pomegranate, is a diehard. Let it live, and it can live to more than two hundred years old. Whereas the almond tree is fussy and throws off all sorts of rank growth when deprived of water, the pistachio gets by fine with less water, and among the abuses it can take are long stretches of absolute thirst. This is important to Brad because no river courses through his land. He relies instead on the 710-mile-long system of federal and state canals that ships High Sierra snowmelt to California's farms and cities. But that concrete and hydraulic conveyer, for all its monumental fabrication, now must pick and choose among the places to deliver its flow. The Westlands Water District, which didn't link its pipes to the system until the mid-1960s and holds only junior contractual rights, stands as the last suitor in line. This year, last year, the year before, the feds have slashed Brad's water to a dwindle.

"It's zero," he says. "How am I supposed to farm with zero?"

The look on Brad's face is grim, but I'm not sure how grim. He picks up his cell phone and fingers the number to a middleman from San Diego who at this moment is scouring the state on his behalf, looking for any large blocks of water for sale. The broker is knocking on the doors of rice farmers in the far north, in the Sacramento Valley, who have more water at their disposal than any other growers in the state, enough water to flood their rice paddies and ship what's left to nut growers two hundred miles south. There's just one hitch. Any export of water from north to south has to be pumped through the California Delta, the state's hydraulic heart, where our two biggest rivers, the Sacramento and the San Joaquin, meet and push their waters, the waters we don't take, into the San Francisco Bay and out to sea.

The delta, battered by a century and a half of man's meddle, teeters on the point of collapse. It can no longer furnish the ecosystem that the Chinook salmon and delta smelt, its two most imperiled species, need to survive, much less deliver a full supply to cities and farms. And the drought is only making the wheeling of water through dams, pumps, aqueduct, canals and pipes infinitely more challenging. Five state and federal agencies, more or less operating together, regulate the flows in and out of the delta down to the hour, to the precise needs of the fish. To the dismay of west side farmers like Brad, it is the federal biologists and not the federal and state water managers who hold the law of ultimate consequence in their hand. Under the guardianship of the U.S. Endangered Species Act, the delta pumps—built sixty years ago in the name of irrigated agriculture—have been shut down.

"It's a bottleneck," the deep voice of his water broker intones. "We've got willing sellers north of the delta and desperate buyers south of the delta. Farmer to farmer. But the law won't let the water get through."

What does a man who farms twelve thousand acres of nuts do? He stakes out the far western edge of Fresno agriculture, where everything beyond him is tumbleweeds and salt grass, and plants another three hundred acres of pistachios on an even drier slab of old cotton ground. This is the outpost known as Pleasant Valley, a public water district that has no public water be it a wet or a dry year. In older times, three creeks came alive here and gouged a cleft into the earth. I had witnessed the wake of one flash flood in the spring of 1995, when the waters of the Arroyo Pasajero Creek came roaring down the Coast Ranges from three thousand feet high and slammed into the moorings of Interstate 5 just as Martha Zavala and Linda Muniz, two eighteen-year-old college students, were driving home to Huron on a Friday night. The bridge collapsed, and the two lanes of the freeway fell into a hole that swallowed up the girls and five others buried inside their cars. Rescuers searched nearly a week before they found Zavala's body. She had been propelled so far down the creek that she had come to rest in a cotton field next to her home. "It's over," her grandmother Mercedes Ruiz kept muttering. Twenty years have gone by and the creek has returned to rock and stone and pebble and salt and spinescale and kit fox.

"There it is," Brad says, pointing straight ahead. "My million-dollar hole."

A drill rig and its monumental platform rise before us as if we've happened upon a Texas oil field. The rig is boring a hole a third of a mile deep into the alluvium of the dry creek. We climb down from his truck and walk to where the driller is tapping not so gently into the aquifer. The well's giant casing slices through seashells deposited before the Coast Ranges rose up in one epoch or another. The water shooting out of the pipe—who knows how far back it dates—tastes like the sea. But it matters not to the pistachio, which tolerates salt and boron and arsenic. Over the years, Brad has dug eleven other holes in the ground of Pleasant Valley, holes that stopped at one thousand feet. This hole reaches down eight hundred feet deeper. "There's so many holes being drilled across the valley right now that it's a one-year wait for a well digger," he says. "I was lucky to find this contractor in Southern California."

To be precise, the farmers have dug 2,500 wells across the San Joaquin Valley in this rainless year alone, the highest number on record. More than 600 of these wells, the deepest ones, are out here on the west side. The lesson of decades of courtroom battle over what the government owes to the west side farmer and what the west side farmer owes to the fish boils down to this: File a lawsuit to get the giant turbines in the delta pumping again; in the meantime, ride out the warmest winter on record by planting more pistachios and drilling more holes to water them. As president of the Pleasant Valley Water District, Brad knows that the unremitting pumping of groundwater cannot be maintained forever. We're extracting eight million acre-feet of water a year out of the earth in California, more than twice the amount stored behind Shasta Dam. One acre-foot, 326,000 gallons, is enough to sustain two to three suburban families for a year.

To keep the vast underground lake from petering out, the state has decided to govern groundwater pumping for the first time in its 164-year existence. Waiting that long to regulate a precious resource doesn't sound right to anyone who knows California. We were the first state to equip every car with a device that reduced smog, the first state to mandate cutting greenhouse gases by a third. Businesses are leaving California in droves because of environmental constraints, or at least that's what we're being told by those who don't want the protections. Yet pumping the aquifer remains a farmer's inalienable right. When you consider the size of the farms here, that notion isn't so quaint. In fact, California is one of the last remaining states still committed to a carte blanche notion of groundwater.

Brad believes the new law is necessary to bring sanity to pumping, but he's sure happy its implementation is a decade, if not two, away. A new legal fight about the water beneath us now dares to dwarf the old legal fight about the water above. Brad's new well, lucky for him, will be flowing long before the law clamps down, pouring out at 1,800 gallons a minute, which is enough to keep 41,000 trees producing heart-healthy pistachios from one year to the next.

"It's salty," he says, running his hands through liquid that a moment before had gurgled many hundreds of feet below the ground. "It's not like the people can drink it. It's not like I'm watering surplus cotton. It's going to make food."

A hint of peevishness sticks in his throat, and that's when I notice the look in his eye. That's when I begin to realize that Brad Gleason, a good man who makes a yearly pilgrimage to Calcutta as part of a church mission to help the poor, who plans to pass on his orchards to his three grown children but first they have to earn paychecks that don't bear his name, has contracted the same fever that once gripped James Henry Carson. Carson had journeyed west from Virginia in 1846 and was the first man to envision that this desert-and-marsh valley, with big rivers dammed and liberally portioned out, could rise as the greatest of agricultural gardens. The crops would have to wait, though, for there was gold in the hills of Calaveras that Carson was compelled to fetch. "A frenzy seized my soul. Unbidden, my legs performed some entirely new movements of Polka steps," he wrote in one of the first published accounts of early California. "Piles of gold rose up before me at every step; castles of marble dazzling the eye; thousands of slaves bowing to my beck and call; myriads of virgins contending with each other for my love. The Rothschilds and Girards and Astors appeared to me but poor people." Gold's riches would elude Carson as they did so many others. He would die at the age of thirty-two of a fungal disease known as valley fever, believing at the end that agriculture would be California's great salvation.

"You're mining water, Brad," I say. I'm smiling, trying not to come off like a scold.

"I know, Mark," he replies, his flat voice flatter. "But what am I going to do? The water's down there."

Where rainfall isn't routine and the land shifts between drought and flood, people might be forgiven for seeing nature's volatility as the rhyme and reason of their own actions. The native Yokut who lived on the valley floor once recorded the year of the great tule fire as the year the long drought broke. When the long drought came a second time, the Yokut along Tulare Lake waited again for nature's fire. When it didn't come, they rationally took it upon themselves to set fire to the tules, the bulrushes that clotted the marshland. They watched the cloud of smoke ascend and the rain start to fall once more. This is how superstition was born. This is why storytelling began.

The idea that man's earthly actions could please or displease the spirits and change the sky did not die with the native culture. "Rain follows the plow" became a dictum of the arid West declared emphatically by farmers every bit as earnest as Brad. There was no science behind it besides the science that the virtuous acts of man get rewarded. In the early 1880s, one booster of dry farming claimed that irrigation would never be necessary as long as the farmer kept striking at the earth with his implements. "Since the country has been cultivated," he noted, "the rainfall has perceptibly increased, and there is a fair prospect that the dry years will almost entirely disappear." When the plows of farming failed to vanquish California drought, the pomologist in his booster's hat came along to spread the notion that his planting of fruit trees would. He offered no testimony other than an orange or a peach was God's sweetest design and He would provide all that was necessary, abundant water included, to make the fruit flourish. Never mind that man himself came to every sort of silly end. The makers of such myths invariably hailed from the lush landscapes of the East. Humidity in their minds was nature's being. Aridity of the Western ilk was an aberration that needed to be placated first and then, if that didn't work, beaten into submission. Before we decided to domesticate our snowmelt by feat of dam, aqueduct and pump, however, we had men among us who could intervene on a parched community's behalf and make the clouds turn one way or the other.

Such a man was Charles Hatfield, a sewing machine salesman with a homespun manner who moonlighted as a "moisture accelerator" at the turn of the last century. In the winter of 1915, by a four-to-one vote, the city council of San Diego hired Hatfield to fill Lake Morena with rain. Like every other newspaper reader in California, the residents of Mission Valley had been following the fantastic feats of Hatfield the Rainmaker. The strange Quaker seemed stricken with the powers of a wizard, summoning a series of drought-busting storms across California in the early 1900s. From city to farm to desert, he had wrung rain from skies that had forgotten how to make clouds. In Los Angeles, he produced eighteen inches of rainfall in the first four months of 1905. Out in Riverside County, in the little boomtown of Hemet, he pledged to fill the half-empty reservoir for a fee of four thousand dollars. He precipitated a downpour of such proportions that eleven inches of rain promptly fell, raising the water behind the dam by twenty-two feet. He then packed his gear and headed to the San Joaquin Valley. The farmers of dry dirt were so grateful for his rainmaking that they brought him back for eight straight years. He became the first folk hero of the arid West, the stories of his storm whispering rivaling the tales of Paul Bunyan and Pecos Bill. While Hatfield was not altogether sociable, and never revealed the secrets of his conjuring, his mother did tell the newspapers once that God and Science together worked through her diligent son. That was as good an explanation as any for the primitive cloud seeding he practiced. "I do not make rain. That would be an absurd claim," he explained. "There are times when the clouds need tickling. If one knows how to tease or coax them a trifle, the results are often pleasing."

The boomers of San Diego weren't asking Hatfield to end a drought. The rain, without tickling, had come back to the city that winter. More than fourteen inches had fallen in 1915, four inches beyond the average.

But nature's drought had given way to man's drought. San Diego was hosting the Panama-California Exposition to promote its role as the first U.S. port of call for ships passing through the newly built canal. To woo the fat-cat investors attending the expo, the city had to show them that it possessed a steady supply of water. Lake Morena, for one, sat two-thirds empty. So much of the river's flow was being siphoned off by ranchers and local real estate promoters that even wet years weren't enough to cover San Diego's ambition. Ten billion more gallons of water had to be brought forth in quick fashion and stored behind the dam to fuel the growth that was San Diego's destiny.

Hatfield, unfailingly polite, didn't beat around the bush. Traveling from one parched region to the next, he had held out the same enticement: "Four inches of rain for four thousand dollars. No rain, no pay." When it came to San Diego, however, he was pledging something more biblical: fifty inches of rain by the end of summer. This was in the universe of one man taking the desert and turning it into a rain forest. On a handshake, the city fathers agreed to pay him ten thousand dollars, knowing full well it would be a miracle if he delivered even half that amount. Ten grand went a long ways in 1916, about as far as $230,000 goes today. But Hatfield wasn't motivated entirely by money. His salary at the New Home Sewing Machine company in Los Angeles was a respectable $125 a month. Rather, it was the miracle that moved him.

While he never talked of such things, those who saw him in action recalled the chemicals he discharged into the sky from atop his twenty-foot-tall wooden towers. The concoction smelled terrible and not by accident, they believed. As far back as the ancients, it was postulated that the stench of bodies decomposing after a major battle triggered rain. When artillery fire became a feature of war, Benvenuto Cellini, the sixteenth-century Florentine writer and sculptor, surmised that it was the explosions of gunpowder that had caused the skies to open in deluge. The theory that nature felt compelled to wash away man's reek explained the storms that crippled the Spanish Armada, the mud that mired Napoleon at Waterloo, and two hundred instances of precipitation that fell upon the putrefaction of the Civil War battlefield and Native American massacres in the West. Bad odor is how the Great Chicago Fire drenched itself.

In the first week of January 1916, Hatfield and his brother headed into the mountains east of San Diego and erected a few wooden towers on a slope next to Lake Morena. A wisp of a man with a pointy nose and a pointy chin, Hatfield wore a meticulously pressed suit, fresh linen and a broad Quaker hat. His pale white skin, an eerie translucence, made his blue eyes even more piercing. From the vantage of a few onlookers, it wasn't easy to discern what he was doing atop the towers. He grabbed one black bottle and another, mixed a cocktail of many chemicals and poured it into a series of shallow iron pans. Vapors floated into the heavens. One eyewitness said it smelled as if a "Limburger cheese factory has broken loose." Others said he employed a metal device to shoot the chemicals into the sky, little bombs that spewed flames and smoke and touched the cumulus clouds. One scoffer, a county bee inspector, quipped that Hatfield "could talk more and say less than anyone I had ever known." The bee inspector noted that the rain already had begun to fall days earlier, when Hatfield was purchasing the lumber to build his towers. "I wish I was out under this rain with my apparatus," Hatfield told the man. "You may get three inches from this storm. I could give you three and a half."

The insinuation that Hatfield's gift was merely a matter of impeccable timing did not begin to explain what happened in the days, weeks and months that followed. On January 10, the rain commenced to fall, and it kept falling in such torrents that even the doubters started to wonder. "Let's pay Hatfield $10,000 to quit," one property owner forced into a rowboat wisecracked. Over the next five days, an incredible seventeen inches of rain poured down. Was this God? Was this Hatfield? As the water behind Morena Dam kept rising to levels never seen, Hatfield himself picked up the telephone at the dam site and called the *San Diego Union*. "I understand the newspapers are saying I didn't make the rain. All I have to say is that Morena has had seventeen and a half inches of rain in the last five days and that beats any similar record for the place that I have been able to find."

The San Diego River, reduced to a trickle by the diversions of farmers and subdividers, found its old fury. The river leaped past its banks, washed out roads and bridges, lifted railroad tracks, gouged hillsides and flooded houses and farms across Mission Valley. To the south, the Tijuana River set upon the utopian community of Little Landers, leveling crops and carrying away its dreamers. A wall of water forty feet

Hatfield the Rainmaker

high hurdled the stone dam on Dulzura Creek, roaring with a thunder that residents had never heard before. The damage to the region's backcountry was "unbelievable." Near the mouth of the Otay River, a colony of Japanese fishermen had been swept into the San Diego Bay. As the Japanese community searched for its dead, a group of white men talked of organizing a party to ride to Morena Dam to lynch the wizard.

What they didn't know was that Hatfield was already gone, fording streams and climbing in and out of mud-filled gullies. He was hiking back to San Diego to collect his ten grand for the simple reason that he had made good on his spectacular promise. The dam at Lake Morena was holding rain at its absolute rim. The reservoir had surpassed fifteen billion gallons of water for the first time. By the time Hatfield's storms were done, San Diego had recorded more than fifty inches of rain.

The good men of the city council were in no mood to honor their handshake, however. For one, the handshake had never become a signature, they argued. Two, the county coroner was estimating that as many as fifty people had perished in what they were calling "Hatfield's Flood." Three, Hatfield now had a choice. If it was God's work, the city owed him nothing. If it was his work, then he owed the city millions for the property damage his rain had wrought. Hatfield sued San Diego for breach of promise, and the matter bounced around the courts in one form or another for the next twenty years. The city never paid him a dime.

When Carey McWilliams, one of the first and most enduring chroniclers of the California myth, landed in Los Angeles in 1922, he was immediately drawn to Hatfield as metaphor. Municipalities across the sprawling basin were still signing contracts with Hatfield to make rain. As the newspapers counted down the number of days left for him to fulfill one of his pledges, thousands of Southern Californians, scanning the skies, would speculate on whether "Hatfield was going to make it." McWilliams mused in his book *Southern California Country* that this belief in the extraordinary powers of one man to save a community from doom grew out of an odd feeling of impermanence. "Even newcomers are vaguely aware that the region is semi-arid, that the desert is near, and that all the throbbing, bustling life of Southern California is based on a single shaky premise, namely, that the aqueduct life-lines will continue to bring an adequate supply of water to the region," he wrote. "The exotic has been superimposed on this semi-arid land; it is not native."

J. B. Priestley, an English novelist who had visited California long enough to write *The Doomsday Men*, an apocalyptic fantasy set in the Mojave Desert, sensed something disturbing about this strange corner of America, a vague fear that for all of man's contrivances, none more than the movement of water, it would all be for naught. God was going to smite California in the end, and that would be soon. "A sinister suggestion of transience" is how Priestly described it. "There is a quality hostile to men in the very earth and air here. As if we were not meant to make our homes in this oddly enervating sunshine . . . California will be a silent desert again. It is all as impermanent and brittle as a reel of film."

The founding president of Stanford, Professor David Starr Jordan, was intent on poking holes in the legend of Hatfield. The myth of rainmaking in modern California could be traced at least as far back as the summer of 1833, when residents of Santa Barbara, mystified that the skies had turned stingy, asked the holy fathers at the mission to parade through town holding an image of the Blessed Virgin Mary and praying for her intercession. In the name of science, Professor Jordan determined that Hatfield was neither a magician waving a hazel wand nor a practitioner of the "science of pluviculture." Rather, he was a diligent student of weather charting. As such, Hatfield would bide his time until December or January, when an absence of winter rain would turn Californians to despair, and appear on the doorstep of a city or farm. With or without the Limburger cheese smell, the rain was patterned to come.

The professor's debunking was quite thorough, but Hatfield's fame only spread. From Texas to the Klondike, from Canada to Central America, he'd show up to where the ground was dry and the people were willing to pay him ten grand. In the Mojave Desert near Randsburg, he produced forty inches of rainfall in three hours. "I do not doubt," Hatfield said, "that my methods would have saved all the tremendous losses of the Dust Bowl had they been called into play." The last anyone in San Diego heard of Hatfield, he was mixing his secret concoction in the jungles of Honduras, trying to save the country's banana crop from conflagration. He would return to the public eye a final time to attend the Hollywood premiere of *The Rainmaker,* the 1956 movie based loosely on his life that starred Burt Lancaster and Katharine Hepburn. He died two years later, taking the secret of his recipe to the grave.

Had meteorology been able to call upon radar and satellite in 1916, the acts of God trotted out in *Hatfield v. San Diego* would have implicated the phenomenon known today as the "atmospheric river." When Californians pray for drought-curing rain, they are praying for the return of an immense band of moisture that blows in from the tropics during so-called El Niño years. Be careful what you wish for, because the most potent of these heavenly rivers can stall over watersheds prone to flooding and dump rain for days. The drops—big, fat and windblown—strike the earth at pickax angles. Hatfield's Flood, most likely, was the product of not just one atmospheric river but two, back to back, in the same month. I witnessed a similar phenomenon in the winter of 1996–97 when a series of cold storms draped the Sierra Nevada in snow only to be followed by a series of warmer storms, dubbed the Pineapple Express, that melted the snowpack in a flash. The combination of rain and snowmelt at once overwhelmed the rivers and creeks. California's middle became marsh again.

A few days into the storm, the phone in my office rang. It was one of my colleagues at the *Los Angeles Times* who worked out of our Sacramento bureau.

"Don't know if you've heard," he said, "but Tulare Lake has come back to life."

"Tulare Lake?" I grabbed the map from a desk drawer and traced my index finger across the west side of the valley between Kettleman City and Corcoran, where the California Aqueduct ran. There was a Tulare Lake all right, and it was even painted blue. But the mapmaker had drawn it in the shape of a perfect square.

"The square lake?"

"Yeah, that's it," he said. "It's a phantom, a ghost that vanishes for years and years and then suddenly comes back in flood."

The next day, I hopped into my car and sped fifty miles across the smoothened expanse of Kings County, past vineyards and orchards, dairies and alfalfa fields, to where the cottonwoods edged the rushing river's bank. The road quit at the base of a huge earthen wall. Never in my life had I seen a dike or a levee, and I parked the car and rushed up the muddy embankment. As I neared the crest, I could feel the air change and hear the sound of water. Standing on the levee crown, gaping at the lake's big belly, I felt dizzy. Was this the middle of California cotton country or the New Jersey shore? The wind whipped whitecaps past telephone poles stained by the high-water marks of previous floods. The lake was brown in one part and pure blue in another, and the speed with which nature had found its old self was a wonder. The sun glinted off flocks of mud hens, pintails and mallard ducks, giant blue herons and white egrets. Pelicans far from the coast were scooping up catfish.

The lake, maybe one-twentieth of its native size, had come back. Bordered on all sides by the hard lines of levees, it had come back square. The lake bottom once fished by four tribes of Yokut now belonged to J. G. Boswell, the biggest farmer in the world at the time and the last of California's land and water barons. The Boswells had been chased out of the Georgia cotton fields by the boll weevil in the early 1900s. They'd landed in Kings County along with a handful of other southern transplants and proceeded to drain the largest body of fresh water west of the Mississippi. They straitjacketed the four rivers that fed into Tulare Lake and installed a series of pumps that made the Kings River run backward. On the drive home, the idea for a book came to me. I teamed up with a close friend, and we dug into the soil and its people and the dams that subdued the four rivers in all but the Pineapple Express years. The U.S. Army Corps of Engineers had perversely declared the inland sea a flood zone so that it could dam the Kings River.

That was my baptism into western water, and I learned, if nothing else, that superstition as much as science explained California's defiance. The measure of rain in the Great Central Valley did not matter as long as there was enough snow in the Sierra; the desert was not desert when five good rivers ran through it; last year's weather meant almost nothing as a guide when the occurrence of drought and flood were recorded in the books thusly: the droughts of 1851, 1863–64, 1870–71, 1876–77, 1898–99, 1917–21, 1923–24, 1929–34, 1946–49, 1976–77, 1987–92, 2007–09; the floods of 1849–50, 1852, 1861–62, 1867–68, 1878, 1907, 1909, 1933–34, 1937, 1938, 1950, 1955, 1964, 1969, 1982, 1986, 1995, 1997. When the book on Boswell was finished, six years after the flood of 1997, I vowed never again to touch the subject of water. Everything I had learned about rivers and dams I thankfully purged from my brain.

Now the worst drought in the history of white man's California has me dwelling on the capture of water again, only this time about a system that extends beyond Tulare Lake to the whole of the state and its history. Extraction was how California was conceived in myth by sixteenth-century Spain and then born as a real place. Each taking of a resource—the body of the native, river, mineral, element, soil—allowed for the next taking. In the continuum of reinvention, if I dug down, I could spot my own family's story: the ranch as a rebirth out of genocide, the lopping off of farm to embrace suburbia, the premature end of a rural life, for which my grandfather never forgave America because it took the life of my father, and so on. This is the way it always begins, at least for me: the searching out of one's own story in the larger story, the personal a means to find the communal, and vice versa, so that each might have a chance to keep honest the other, though who knows where it might go after that. My assumptions at the outset are few. Water binds us and pulls us apart. A land this crazy makes people crazy. One hundred million acres takes a while to screw up. Highest mountain, lowest desert, longest coast, most epic valley, riparian forest, redwood forest, Douglas fir forest, wetland, grassland and inland sea. The rain falls 125 inches a year in one place and 7 inches a year in the other place. When the lines of latitude cover ten degrees and the topographical regions number eleven, what are a people to do? They can honor the distinctions and allow each region to exist within its own plentitude and limit. Or they can draw a line around the whole, count it as one state and begin their infinite tinkering to even out the differences.

Amid the stacks of books on California that bunker my desk—the constructions of history by H. H. Bancroft, Josiah Royce, Bernard DeVoto and Kevin Starr, the plunging into reclamation by Donald Worster and Marc Reisner, the piercing of the myth by Carey McWilliams and Joan Didion—sits a thin volume bound in a thick green cover that my father left me years ago. *The Central Valley Project* it is titled, written by the California Writers of the Work Projects Administration in 1942. He had lifted it from the library at Pasadena City College on his way to a football scholarship at USC before he came back to the family farm along the San Joaquin River. On the first blank page, jotted in pencil, is the phone number of my mother, Flora Mekhitarian, the priest's daughter, along with the numbers of a Florence and Betty Mae. I can recall the first time I opened the book, twenty years after his murder, and encountered the curious phrase "misplaced rain" on page 8. It meant "too much in the wrong places and too little in the right places and never in the right season." And so it became the herculean job of the Central Valley Project to move that water to the land that nature had shorted. In my later readings, I could see that the writers of the WPA had struggled to fashion a narrative that wasn't too subservient to the postwar promotions of the U.S. Bureau of Reclamation. They didn't always succeed, but the story was nonetheless full of supernatural details witnessed in real time. They captured the conquering of the Sacramento River and the building of Shasta Dam, right down to its forty million sacks of cement, fifteen million tons of aggregates and one man working a pneumatic drill. "What are you doing?" he was asked. He looked up from his drill and answered, "Mister, I'm moving the rain."

We've been moving it ever since.

Two

AGRARIAN REVOLT

The rain stopped falling, and now winter is gone, too. What to blame on man-made global warming? What to blame on the arid West? You can check the diaries of John Sutter, the first of our reinvented men, or go back to the tree rings in the redwood forest. Drought is California. Flood is California. One year, our rivers and streams produce 30 million acre-feet of water. The next year, they produce 200 million acre-feet. The year we hit near average, 72.5 million acre-feet, is an aberration. The greatest daily flow of our watersheds surpasses the least daily flow by five hundred times. Here in California, Mother Nature doesn't need man to deliver climate change. She does a swell job all by herself. Start with the most recent ice age and move forward through the eleven thousand years of human civilization, and then find the time period, right next to ours, when a five-hundred-year drought erased the great agricultural tribes of the Southwest, the Pueblo and the Anasazi, who employed dams and the gravity of canyons to direct rainwater from mesa to field.

Since my packinghouse days, I've counted five distinct droughts in California. The headlines of one read like the headlines of another, and where I've mistakenly clipped off the dates, I can't tell if it is the drought of 1992 or 2007 or 2009 that I'm reading about. I'd be inclined to greet this one wearily, too, with the awareness of California returning to form, but the UC scientist is calling it "the worst drought in five hundred years," and I have to admit that I can't remember dry times ever being so devious. The air in the valley, already the nation's worst for smog, has turned into bits and pieces I can touch, taste and smell. Not only the usual cow shit mixed with sinus-plugging alfalfa curing into hay but a blanket of smoke that creeps down from the burning Sierra. Wildfires blot out the sun, and the pallid sky starts to rain. Not water but ash. For three days, heavenly gray soot floats down upon the choked valley. In my backyard, across from the barren apricot trees, the vegetable garden has fizzled out six weeks early. The Armenian cucumbers have balloons for bellies; the purple eggplants never turned purple. Chickenshit, the last of my hens, is rendered eggless. In a hunt for moisture, cockroaches by the hundreds, Chinese and American breeds, invade my kitchen and bathrooms. Vacuum cleaner in hand, I hunt each one down. The hose with its angled attachment makes the perfect sucking sound. Up and into the clear middle receptacle they tumble. Round and round they crawl, climb, flip, compress their bodies by half—all the usual cockroach tricks—to no avail. Death by suffocation takes a full day.

Outside, I can hear the hydraulic tribes of California's north, middle and south warring again over water's spoil. In my lifetime alone, the population of California has nearly quadrupled to forty million, and the constituencies have only grown more adamant in their claims to the snowmelt. The impulse to water warring, for all I know, may be a congenital trait. When it came time to populate the one thousand miles of our nation-state, we planted 70 percent of the people at the southern end where only 30 percent of the water was made. This wasn't misplaced people, we told ourselves. This was misplaced rain. In our resolve to move those molecules of water to where the crops and houses grew, California pulled off the ultimate sleight of hand. Naturally, performing magic of that kind, people have come to believe that all manner of diversions are possible. The hydraulics we created is an engineer's delight. So how can a system of such infinite gesture now be turning against us? Rural activists in the north are resurrecting an old plan to split California into two. "WELCOME TO JEFFERSON—THE 51ST STATE," reads their banner. It is no coincidence that the twenty counties comprising their proposed union are the sodden ones. At home, an agrarian revolt is sweeping across the farm towns. In a few days, it will reach Fresno. The growers and their congressmen are preparing to gather downtown at city hall for a rally and then a field hearing of the House Natural Resources Committee. They vow to keep shouting until the switches on the federal and state pumps are turned on full bore in the delta and California's "man-made drought" is no more.

In a valley of vast farms and vast suburbs that used to be farms, Fresno stands out as the region's one true city. Our urban experiment hasn't gone nearly as well as our farming experiment. Fresno houses more gang members per capita than any other city in the United States. On the south side of town, the acid of deprivation eats away at the structure of life. What remains in the hollow is the nation's highest concentration of poverty. The school district is such a disaster that an entire exiled community of mostly white people—the cowboy town of Clovis—has risen to the north and east. But Clovis is no longer considered far enough away. Now the gentry are fleeing across the San Joaquin River into Madera County and right up into the golden hills. Left behind in Fresno's crater are mostly poor Mexicans who, understandably, want no part of the fields that brought their parents and grandparents to their knees. Yet in their liberation from the farm, too many of them have found no other sustaining life. One BBC documentary—*The City Addicted to Crystal Meth*—tells of a despair we care not to look in the face even as it gets passed on to the next generation. No county in California delivers more babies with syphilis than Fresno County. The community jail, just down the block from the community maternity ward, has devolved into a chamber of torture. The head psychiatrist is denying mentally ill defendants the medications prescribed to them by their outside doctors—medications needed to keep them sane. In an attempt to cut down on drug costs, the jail is triggering psychotic episodes in schizophrenics. Their prolonged mental breakdowns are forcing them to languish in isolated confinement for years. Inmates in the throes of delusions have slashed their throats with county-issued razors. One man lost eighty pounds while sitting in an isolated cell for five months. He turned his sock into a sponge so he could drink water from the hole where he relieved himself. County judges have begun transferring these inmates to state facilities, where medications are dispensed to make them mentally fit to stand trial. But as soon as they are brought back to Fresno, the jail yanks their meds, and they fall into madness again.

I park my car across from the courthouse named for B. F. Sisk. That would be Bernice Frederic Sisk, the cotton picker from Texas who sold tires in Fresno and became our congressman for the sole purpose of delivering cheap federal water to his cotton-growing friends. I recall one line from the memoir he self-published at the end of his life. "In the West," he said, "a man would rather trust another man with his wife than with an acre-foot of his water." Halfway up the steps of city hall, I can hear the banging of a drum and the chants of a man: "Water. Water. Water. Water." A crowd of three hundred people has assembled in a kind of practiced formation, holding up signs they've held up before: "FEDERAL WATER THEFT" and "NO WATER, NO WORK, NO LIFE." Scores of them have taken up a position along a grassy knoll, and the rest are huddled on the flat ground beneath the magnificent sweep of the metal-clad city hall. Its construction two decades earlier marked our boldest attempt to project an image beyond the raisin. The booms and busts of the shriveled-up Thompson Seedless grape, chronicled with such gusto by our most famous son, author William Saroyan, defined Fresno's first century. The modern edifice lands on downtown like an immense stainless steel UFO. The jut and fall of its blinding rooftop are supposed to represent Sierra and valley, snowmelt and fruit.

The crowd listens closely as a bald man in his mid-seventies, a grower of pistachios, almonds, grain and cotton, rails at the environmentalists. They won't be content, he says, until the valley has reverted to desert. Big-city politicians, distant judges, President Obama in Washington, D.C., have chosen a tiny cucumber-fragrant fish—the delta smelt—over the farmer. The same forces stealing government water from our canals are now aiming to steal private water from under our feet. As demographics go, most of the protestors are white and dressed in a style of California rural, which is to say a style no different from Iowa rural or New York rural. I pick out a half dozen of the least angry faces and ask about their connection to the land.

Glen Martin farms 180 acres of navels, Valencias, grapefruits, Minneolas, blood oranges and lemons on the far east side of the valley, a region known as the citrus belt. In the 1960s, as the last of Southern California's groves were plowed under for suburbia, his father came up and over the mountain and planted his oranges in the heavy dirt of Terra Bella. For the past sixty years, the quilted hills of the east side have relied on imported water from the Central Valley Project. This year, the feds have announced that not a drop of the water will be delivered to Martin's farm or any other farm along the 160-mile-long Friant-Kern Canal. Because Terra Bella never had groundwater to speak of, no backup well can save Martin's orchard. His father once instructed him that if he pruned the limbs on his citrus trees way back and gave up any hope of fruit for a season, the orchard might ride out a year on the thinnest of water. "I'm about to find out if that's true," he says.

Next to a public fountain shooting water high and low, a dozen Latinos in ball caps stand in silence, holding up protest signs lettered in Spanish. They have been sent here by the farms that employ them. Hopping from rally to rally, they've become props in a mobile production put on by the California Latino Water Coalition, a front for the big growers who have decided that the best way to plead their story of "stolen water" is by displaying the brown and weathered faces of their workers. No one would dispute that these are the men and women who will lose their jobs if the land goes dead. But for 150 years, the plight of the farmworker rarely has been a concern here. Now the suffering of the Mexicans on account of the delta smelt is a million-dollar PR campaign funded by the growers. The campaign's talking points avoid any mention of how the machines that harvest the nut orchards, and put more profits in the pockets of growers, are an even bigger job killer than the fish.

On the face of it, the Latino Water Coalition is one of the screwiest political amalgamations to emerge in California as a reaction to drought. It is one part Mexican field hands who cross the border without papers, speak no English and fear nothing more than the public spotlight. It is another part lathered-up white men and women who parade around in T-shirts that depict President Obama—"THE MARXIST, THE COMMUNIST"—as Adolf Hitler. It is yet another part rich growers, plain dirt farmers and hip young men and women who have graduated from agronomy programs at Cal Poly and UC Davis and come home as enlightened agriculturalists. The coalition's mouthpiece, of all people, is a comedian named Paul Rodriguez, who has morphed into a grower himself after helping his family purchase a ranch in the citrus belt. Water is his new bit. "The only water this field has seen is our sweat," he cries. "This used to be almonds. Now it's firewood."

Five years ago, during the last drought, Rodriguez brought Fox News host Sean Hannity to the valley to see how President Obama had turned the most productive farmland in America into a "Dust Bowl." Hannity devoted an entire live broadcast to what he called "The Valley

Hope Forgot." Standing in an open field in Huron, thousands of agitated rural folk surrounding him, he held up a giant photo of the tiny delta smelt. It might as well have been a great white shark. News footage depicted orchards uprooted, fields fallowed and equipment spoiling to rust. Never mind that the same dirt Hannity was standing on had produced a bounty of tomatoes only the day before. One hundred feet away, beyond the camera's frame, acre after acre of irrigated green fields awaited harvest. "I never saw an issue where it was so simple," Hannity said. "Just turn the water on." The whipped-up audience began to shout, "Turn on the pumps! Turn on the pumps!" Overnight, the Huron chant became an agrarian battle cry. The farmers, if not Hannity, surely knew that the delta pumps already had been turned on. For two and a half months, they'd been moving water to these fields and beyond.

Now descends the drought of droughts. The farmworkers clutching their signs eye my approach warily. Their crew boss, a man who speaks "not too much English," steps forward and shakes my hand. These same men, he tells me, held up the same signs at a free-lunch rally the day before in the west side town of Firebaugh. That agrarian protest drew one thousand people demanding that another dam be built on an already dried-up river. The farmworkers who come from south of the border, he says, know little about the issues at play. Drought in their land has always been a matter of the sky. They're here today because the big boss told them to be here. They're being paid for their time the same as if they were sweating in the field.

"Hey, asshole," a voice shouts from the knoll. I look up. "Yeah, you. I can smell you. You smell like shit. You smell like Senator Feinstein. Like one of those Commie environmentalists."

He's a burly man with wild hair and a gray beard sheared off at the chest. He is staring at me mad-eyed, waiting for a response. I can tell right away he's a Russian from the west side who belongs to the tribe of Molokans, an ethnic religious sect whose surnames run along the lines of Nazaroff, Podsakoff and Kochergan. Like the Amish, the Molokans are devoted to the old ways. No outsider can step foot in their church; no son who marries outside the flock gets to stick around, either. The Russian doesn't like it that I'm asking questions of the farmworkers. He likes it even less that I'm writing down their answers. I don't appreciate that he's showering down obscenities and complicating my work.

I march to the top of the knoll, thinking it might get heated. When I introduce myself, the anger in his face melts away. He sticks out his hand. "It's a pleasure to meet you," he says. My brother the high school football coach loved his Molokan players over in Kerman. Maybe this is the father of one of them. As it turns out, one of my books sits on his nightstand, he says. As the rally ends and the field hearing begins, the Russian wants me to know that he isn't a farmer anymore. He is leasing his land in Huron to a pistachio grower, who at this moment is drilling a hole two thousand feet into the ground.

Inside city hall, the Republicans from the western states take command of the congressional field hearing. This comes as no surprise. The Democrats on the committee, with the exception of one, saw the stacked deck of planned speakers and chose to stay home. This is just as well because I find myself drawn to two valley Republicans, Devin Nunes and David Valadao, who sit on the committee and, session after session, hustle the same agenda: build more dams; gut the Endangered Species Act and kill efforts to revive the Chinook salmon run on the San Joaquin River. We tend to see and hear Nunes and Valadao as one, the milk-and-cheese twins, sons of a tight-knit community of Portuguese who left the Azores as far back as the 1890s to build their dairies here. In the communities of Tulare and Hanford, where so many Azoreans have settled, Holsteins outnumber humans maybe ten to one. Unlike the nut growers, the dairy families live in castles built on the farm, upwind if they can manage it. The dairy dads don't like talking about the government handouts they get for their surplus crops and surplus milk. Their politician sons don't like discussing the handouts, either. Both prefer taking aim at government entitlements for the poor.

That Congressman Valadao is viewed as the more reasonable twin only speaks to the inexhaustible fanaticism of Congressman Nunes. In contemplating the latter, it should be noted that the Azorean Portuguese, by and large, are a gregarious people. They drink sweet wine and celebrate the pig in an annual blood sausage festival here. At their elaborate bullfights, they step into the ring with swords that don't draw blood but stick to pads of Velcro affixed to the bulls. Two and three generations after their grandparents and great-grandparents came to California, a good many of them still speak their language, marry fellow Azoreans and return to their native islands in the summer to taste the bread and fish of the Atlantic.

Nunes, by contrast, appears incapable of any such felicity. As the hearing opens, his face moves past dour to a wince. In grade school, he raised a Holstein named Gem and won a Future Farmers of America blue ribbon. He was in his early twenties when he hung up his milking boots at the Nunes & Sons dairy and plunged into politics. Term after term, for more than a decade in Congress, he has staked out the most extreme positions on water in the West. Yes, the sky hasn't spilled much rain in three years. Yes, we are facing the hottest and driest spell on record. But it's not nature's drought that bedevils the valley, he assures us. It's a plot hatched by the Communists. His constituents, more than a few of whom share his attachment to conspiracy theories, seem not to care that the water legislation he authors has little chance of influencing debate, much less becoming law. Whether he is a cold and calculating man or a lonely man without moorings or a paranoiac man, they can't be bothered. It is his pandering to their infatuations that counts. Every two years, by ever-wider margins, they vote him back into office.

As Nunes grimly launches into his opening statement, I wonder if he realizes he's doing the farmer no favor by tying the delta smelt to the Communist Party. The environmentalists in their comfortable homes in San Francisco are part of a left-wing conspiracy so vast it boggles the mind, he tells us. They regard our farms as a blight on nature. They're conducting a "guinea pig" experiment to fallow the land, uproot entire rural communities and restore the valley to "some mystical state." The government biologists are working in cahoots with the leftists. The dying smelt and salmon have become their convenient cover to toss away four million acre-feet of water during the drought so far. This was water destined for the valley, water that Congress earmarked for agriculture more than a half century ago, water now wasted on the ocean. "This is not a result of global warming or drought," Nunes chants. "It's the result of government run amok."

The farmers and small-town mayors selected to address the committee speak movingly of being caught in a desperate strait that leaves them no strategy other than to repeat what they are doing. Keep on pumping ancient water from the ground; keep on buying whatever snowmelt they can afford on the open market. The price for river water has shot up from $400 an acre-foot to as high as $1,400. As long as nuts are still selling for three or four bucks a pound, they can hold out.

No one talks, much less testifies, about the hundreds of thousands of people throughout California whose only draw of water to drink and bathe in is water that endangers their lives. It comes out of the ground tainted by arsenic, uranium and nitrates, the latter a remnant of agricultural fertilizers. It comes out of the canal laced with so much organic matter that it combines with the chlorine needed to clean it up and forms a carcinogen. In farm towns up and down the valley, a different chemical, one of the most potent cancer-causing agents in the world, taints the aquifer. It's called 1,2,3-TCP, though it wasn't listed as an ingredient in the pesticides sold to farmers by Dow and Shell beginning in the 1940s. The farmers thought they were buying a simple fumigant to control the nematodes destroying their crops. The formulation killed the root-eating worms all right, but not because 1,2,3-TCP was in it. The chemical was nothing but a junk ingredient, a waste product from the manufacture of plastic. As a convenient way to get rid of it, Dow and Shell threw 1,2,3-TCP into their fumigant. The chemical infiltrated the soil and decades later, it yet lingers, triggering variants of cancer that doctors have never seen.

The hearing ends with no commonsense plan that might better portion out the water to the most fertile soil and fallow the land that's third-rate. The agrarians march out of city hall and back into the foul air knowing that nothing will change. In the short term, federal and state environmental restrictions will continue to choke off their imports from the delta. In the long term, groundwater regulations will tighten the screws and likely force a million and a half acres of valley cropland, if not more, into retirement. Until a new U.S. president more kind to growers gets elected, the federal government seems prepared to never turn on its pumps full blast again.

My father, the lapsed grape grower, used to confide to the men who drank at his bar that he was a Communist and a capitalist, that he admired the big farmers and Cesar Chavez, too. All things must have seemed truly within reach because he knew how far our family had traveled. His father had survived a genocide in Turkey and picked the fruits and vegetables of the valley and saved up enough money during the Depression to buy his own vineyard, where my father, Ara, was born in the late summer of 1931. Grandpa believed that dusting sulfur on grapes was the only agriculture he needed to practice, and he busied himself reading the *New Masses* and writing poetry. Grandma scolded him for being too trusting of nature as she fretted nonstop about the irrigation ditch that ran along the front of their forty acres. The cold mountain water threatened her two little boys with drowning. This was the same awful death that had taken her two-year-old sister Seranoush back in Hartford, Connecticut. It mattered not to my grandmother that her baby sister had fallen into a bucket of scalding water used to clean the floor. Drowning remained the manner of death she feared more than any other.

My grandfather gave up that farm in the late 1930s when the vine hopper bugs became too many, and he moved the family to San Francisco to start over again as a greengrocer. There, he joined the Communist Party and pocketed $250,000 from the sale of his two markets. He befriended a union man turned state senator named George Miller Sr., and the two comrades bought a ranch in Manteca in the late 1940s that allowed my grandfather, grandmother, father, uncle and aunt to return to a life of valley farming. It was a life that lasted until my father met my mother, a pretty Armenian clotheshorse from Marseille, France, who told him she had no intention of living on some dirt farm next to the San Joaquin River. By then, Grandpa and Grandma had purchased a house in Fresno's Fig Garden on a civilized street called Garland, where a large irrigation ditch sliced across the neighborhood. Grandma made me promise I would never go near the ditch, never climb its steep embankment, never gaze into its cold waters, because I would lose my balance and fall in and, like the poor sons of the Mexican farmworkers, no one would hear my screams or be able to save me. The men who ran the irrigation district wouldn't shut off the valve and drag me out until the growing season was over, she told me. When I asked her why, she said the flow of one irrigation ditch meant more to the valley than the body of one silly boy.

I exit city hall and drive in the direction of the river and our last ranch. The farmland outside my window takes up one view; the blue ridges of the Sierra Nevada where 100 million trees are dying of drought, disease and smog take up the other view. The way the mountains catch and

Citrus orchards skirt the Sierra near Orange Cove.

store the snowpack made a settled life possible in the valley, but it did not erase the truth of our condition. "We had acted upon the western landscape with the force of a geological agent," Wallace Stegner, the great chronicler of the West, once wrote. "But aridity still calls the tune, directs our tinkering, prevents the healing of our mistakes; and vast unwatered reaches still emphasize the contrast between the desert and the sown." Aridity and fertility in my valley were a canal apart. We had found a way to calm our paradox. It was our madness and our invention. Except for a few years on the East Coast and a few more in Los Angeles, I have lived all my life here. I've never known the agrarians not to be angry. I've always felt they had a right to be. Wresting crops from the irrigated desert is hard fought, and we all root for them. We still mark time their way. When the grapes ripen early, that is summer. When the pomegranates turn red, that is fall. When the snowmelt courses down the mountain and into the canal, that is last winter's rain. It is manipulation as much as it is nature, we understand, but paradise was lost a long time before we got here.

Years after he left the farm, my father still kept a strange-looking blade in the tool drawer, and only after he died did I ask an older relative about its purpose. He told me it was a "girdling knife," an implement grape growers used to cut gashes into the trunks of vines. The girdle of lacerations forced the vine to hold nutrients longer in its upper reaches and made the grapes grow fatter and bigger, if not sweeter. Where the cuts were made, the trunk sprouted tumorous scars. The knife, he said, was better left in the drawer as an artifact. The vineyardist now sprays his grapes with a synthetic plant hormone called "gib" to make the bunches grow bigger and ripen earlier, with a more vivid color and a stem that holds.

I have read that the Wintu Indians, who lived at the foot of Mount Shasta where the great flow of northern water begins, watched in bewilderment in the 1850s as the white man started to erect his system of moving the rain. The natives could not fathom the pressure the stranger was putting on the land. Demands of this sort would stretch the earth too thin, the Indian warned. Cracks would open up in the ground and swallow up mankind. The spirit of the land would strike back first as drought and then more devastatingly as flood. "When the Indians all die, then God will let the water come down from the north. Everyone will drown. The white people dig deep long tunnels. Eventually the water will come." Be careful what you wish for, the Wintu were telling us.

I live in arid lands in a valley where men and mules, before my time, pulled an army of Fresno Scrapers across the barren west side and east side and acres in between. The scraper, a five-foot-wide hunk of sheet iron invented by a man named James Porteous whose great-grandson was my classmate in high school, revolutionized the movement of dirt throughout the world in the years before the gas-powered bulldozer. The valley in its natural state resembled a rolling savanna not unlike the Serengeti. The scraper reconfigured the land field by field, leveling knolls and filling in gulches, a huge continuous flattening that allowed the waters of irrigation to move like a cue ball across green felt. I grew up here in the years when the system knew no bounds, and we could ignore our temperament without consequence and go on believing that rain truly followed the plow or whatever else we chose to impose on the land. We understood from all that we had been told, and could see, that we were the exception to the laws of aridity because we lived not in the West but in a place west of the West. Our Sierra Nevada wasn't a simple mountain range but one of the most prolific watersheds on earth. It not only mitigated aridity but negated it. I felt sorry for the California doomsayer. Time and again, we had proven him or her wrong with our capacity to invent and reinvent, no more so than when it came to the capture and movement of water.

This time, though, something feels different. We have run out of tricks, or at least the easy ones. A fastening has come undone. The water system that allowed California to be California can no longer keep up with our ambitions. It was designed to withstand five years of drought but most of its parts were built in the 1940s, '50s and '60s, and its plumbing no longer appears sufficient. The people who drink from it number too many. It is a troubling fact, at least to those urbanites who live north and south of us, that eight out of ten drops of captured water go to the farmers. How had such a taking come about? Can a different portioning out among north, middle and south be fashioned a half century after the fact, without risking civil war? Is water pushing out to the ocean in a pulse as old as time really a waste? The colossal bulwark we have put to the task will not see us into a future of more almonds, more houses and more people, that is sure. Something has to give. One thing is certain in the meantime: The tribes of the north, middle and south will keep on warring.

If the positions are hardened, here's why:

In the county of Imperial, near the border with Mexico, the sky offers three inches of rain a year. The earth produces $2 billion in crops. These crops include spinach, potatoes, cauliflower, broccoli, melons and two million tons of hay, the biggest water hog of them all. To keep it going, a new version of the eighty-two-mile-long All-American Canal has replaced the old leaky version known as "the most dangerous body of water in the world." There is no reason to suspect that the new canal will prove any less deadly. Here, more than five hundred bodies, a good number of them Mexican migrants coming to work the fields, have been fished out of the water over the past thirty years. The new All-American Canal guarding our border is made of concrete and delivers 22 billion gallons more water every year than the old earthen one did. The basic plumbing has not changed. There is the Colorado River on one end and 650,000 acres of desert farmland on the other end.

The poverty hasn't changed, either. Even as the salt-laden land pumps out more crops—and these crops command a premium because the Imperial sun ripens everything early, so that Americans might eat their vegetables in winter, too—one-third of the people here still live hand to mouth.

Waterwise, no growers in California sit prettier than the growers of Imperial, many of whom are actually sitting more than a hundred miles away in their summer mansions in San Diego. As irrigation canals go, none carries as much capacity as the All-American. Of the 4.4 million acre-feet of Colorado River water that flows to California each year, the farms of Imperial, five hundred in all, receive more than 3 million acre-feet. The growers tilling their grandpas' land wield so much water that they can raise all the hay they want and still sell 500,000 acre-feet to San Diego and beyond. The growers and non-growers of Imperial, perhaps 180,000 people at most, are controlling 70 percent of the state's total draw of the Colorado River while 20 million other Southern Californians get by with 30 percent. If these numbers seem lopsided, well, that was the beauty of sticking your straw into the Colorado early and often. Inside the Pioneers' Park Museum off Highway 111 near the Super Walmart, it is no coincidence that a framed copy of the front page of the *Imperial Press* dated June 8, 1901, hangs in a prominent spot. This was the year the local farmers engineered their first heist of the magnificent river. "First in time, first in right" was the way the California gold miners had arbitrated their disputes. The courts eventually came up with a special word for that kind of thievery. It wasn't *stealing*. It was *appropriation*. The framed Imperial County newspaper proclaimed its motto, and rightly so: "Water Is King—Here Is Its Kingdom."

On the coastal side of the desert, in the City of Angels, the region's one modest river was contoured and paved like a highway soon after 1938, the last year it got out of hand. For a thousand years, the Los Angeles River provided for each settlement in its streamflow. First the Gabrielino Indians, then the Spanish missions, then the dons of the Pico, Castro, Sepúlveda and Verdugo clans, and then the grain and fruit farmers whose diversions neutered the river except when floods came. The swollen river shooting down the Simi Hills couldn't decide on its course. One flood year it emptied into the Santa Monica Bay. The next flood year it emptied into the San Pedro Bay. The land boomers decided that nature's indecision was no way to build a world-class city. In the wake of the 1938 flood, which took the lives of 115 people, the boomers persuaded Los Angeles voters to approve millions of dollars in bonds. A project to "channelize" the fifty-mile river began. The U.S. Army Corps of Engineers, declaring the watershed a flood zone, lowered the river's bed, widened its main stem and funneled its flow into a "continuous trapezoidal concrete channel" that ushered the river from Elysian Park to Long Beach.

When the job of paving was finished in 1960, the Los Angeles River no longer flooded, but it no longer replenished the ancient aquifer, either. This wasn't considered a problem because the same boomers already had taken care of drought by stealing a river 230 miles away, in the Owens Valley. As the flow of the Owens River ran over the hillside for the first time on November 5, 1913, cascading down a stone staircase into the San Fernando Valley, William Mulholland, son of Belfast, self-made engineer of modern-day L.A., directed the forty thousand people gathered for the occasion: "There it is," he said. "Take it."

In the interior beyond San Francisco, the Sacramento River, traveling south, meets the San Joaquin River, traveling north, in an arrangement far different from their natures. The two rivers still marry in the delta, 1,100 square miles of swamps and tules, bucolic farms and lazy towns, but only until the system of hydraulics revs up its half-million horsepower and grabs the flow. Every year, two giant sets of pumps, one belonging to the feds, the other to the state, hurl more than four million acre-feet of delta water down the valley and over the mountains to Los Angeles. A half century ago, when Governor Pat Brown installed the last piece of plumbing connecting the delta to the mega-farms in Kern County and millions of faucets in Southern California, he said his motivation was to "correct an accident of people and geography." Only later, as that system ended up only adding more people and geography to its service area, did he add this: "I loved building things. I wanted to build that goddamned water project. I was absolutely determined I was going to pass this California Water Project. I wanted this to be a monument to me."

As a circulatory body, the project's intricacy invites comparisons to the human body. What is the delta if not the occluded, still beating heart of an impossibly elaborate water-delivery system? Because ocean tides pulse in from the west, the water is complex in a way that makes the marsh especially vulnerable to drought and flood and the abuse of man. Where seawater sloshes against fresh water, a nutrient-rich zone of its own peculiar blend feeds organisms and fish indigenous to the delta. Several native species, under man-made assault for 170 years, now teeter on the edge of extinction. Thirty-five species of fish, animal and plant life that predated modern man have been listed as endangered under state or federal law. The fate of the Chinook salmon and the delta smelt, in particular, isn't tied to the agricultural pumping alone. Invasive weeds, floor-dwelling clams and predatory bass planted here from New Jersey do their own harm.

As the Sacramento River pushes down through the delta, a flow of treated and untreated sewage pushes down with it. Along its right bank, the Hemly family, pear growers with delta roots six generations back, waits for another menace. The levees of soil and peat, first erected by Chinese hands in the mid-1800s to hold back the water, are sinking. All that dredging and reclamation over a century's span is only a big earthquake away from being erased. The Sacramento–San Joaquin Delta, 430,000 acres of farmland, 500,000 people living in suburban tracts protected by the same levees, sits just east of the Hayward Fault, one of the most perilous earthquake zones in the country. The odds of a major quake striking in the next thirty years and tearing apart the 1,300-mile levee system is better than even. Who knows if the Bartlett and Bosc trees will survive, much less the houses and the system that delivers water to 25 million Californians and a $40-billion-a-year agricultural economy. "If the Big One doesn't get us," pear farmer Cathy Hemly tells me during a break in the harvest, "the Twin Tunnels will."

The Twin Tunnels are California's newest plumbing project, a more politically polite version of the old Peripheral Canal, though not so politically polite that it hasn't created a new battlefront in the long war. In the 1980s, the canal went down to defeat in one of the most bitterly divided votes—North versus South—in California history. The tunnels, stalled in their own endless review, would haul five million acre-feet of water a year straight from the north delta to the federal and state pumps on the south end. As it now stands, the powerful pumps siphon water from the south delta and throw the flow to the nearby aqueduct. But the pumps aren't benign. Throttled up, they cause channels in the delta to run backward. This pulling of water south is what draws the endangered fish into a danger zone, where they become easy prey for birds and bass. By reducing pumping from the south delta, the $20 billion tunnels would lessen the reverse flows and presumably save salmon and smelt. Four stories high and forty feet wide, the tunnels would bore beneath the earth and extend thirty-five miles, dwarfing the tunnel under the English Channel. The California WaterFix, as faraway growers and developers have rechristened it, will allow the snowmelt to flow more reliably to their farms and faucets. Or at least that's their hope. As for the Hemlys, the massive mouth of the tunnels will be built near enough to be considered next door. "It's a fix," Hemly says. "The kind of fix our addicts to the south need to keep their old ways going. More almonds, more pistachios, more mandarins, more McMansions."

She is walking along the riverbank on her island in the marsh, and the setting is so lovely that one can almost forget that this place, too, is among the most engineered landscapes in America. Her pear orchard stands twenty yards away. Her perfectly restored historic house sits even closer. There are no thousand-foot holes in the ground where her husband and son have had to drill to look for irrigation water. Their water-sucking pump sits submerged a few feet down in the Sacramento River itself. The river, she says, actually went dry during a drought in the 1860s. Family lore has it that their ancestor Josiah Greene, an abolitionist from Virginia who came to California to prospect for gold and ended up planting vegetables and fruit trees, walked across the riverbed one summer day in his bare feet. The delta, in other words, doesn't need modern man's dams, ditches or pumps to be in peril. It is never far from peril on its own. "How much more of man's fussing can the delta stand?" she asks. "We're tired of playing savior to the rest of California."

Geographically speaking, I find myself in the middle, surrounded by the top four agricultural counties in the nation and by farmers, including members of my own family, who believe they perform miracles with the water California entrusts to them. As the principal beneficiaries of the system, they harbor no doubt that they are bearing the brunt of the system's breakdown. The list of culprits imperiling the delta is long, they say, yet government regulators have targeted the state and federal pumps as the No. 1 bad guy. "Why go after invasive species and urban pollution when they can simply shut off the pumps and pretend to reduce the kill of the fish?" they groan. The farmers in my part of the valley have a point, but they're just about the worst tellers of their own story. Their collective mutter now takes on the sound of a threat. The water we're being denied from the northern rivers, we're gonna take from the ground beneath us, they vow. They know the ground is sinking and turning to salt. They know that history has dealt harshly with every civilization built on irrigation before ours. And yet they believe that science and technology will somehow deliver them, and us, a different fate. Until then, what choice but mining the aquifer do they have?

My friend Brad, shortly after we tour his orchard of libido-challenged pistachios, answers a call from a pair of radio assassins named Ken and John who host a talk show in Los Angeles and want to invite him on. I advise Brad not to do it. The shock jocks, a duo of snarling demagogues, are taking a break from their usual skewering of minorities to go after the state of California for imposing water limits on cities. Ken and John aren't keen on restricting their morning showers to five minutes or seeing front lawns in L.A. go brown so agriculture in Fresno can grow more nuts. It is going to be an ambush, I am sure. But Brad thinks urban California needs to hear the voice of a farmer.

Ken and John frame the segment with their researched numbers: 80 percent of the water used by humans in California is going to agriculture; 10 percent of that water is going to the almond growers alone. California's economy is running at $2.3 trillion. Almonds account for less than 1 percent of this engine. Why should city residents be rationing their water to prop up a nut that takes so much and gives back so little?

"Because we're producing food, and we're producing food efficiently," Brad says.

"You're producing almonds," Ken shoots back. "And you're using more water than all the people in L.A. and San Francisco combined."

Brad tries to offer some context. The Central Valley Project was built in the 1940s in the name of agriculture, and nearly the entirety of its flow was intended to go to farms in the San Joaquin Valley. The State Water Project was built two decades later, with 30 percent of the water going to valley farms and 70 percent going to houses and industries in Southern California. The farmers aren't stealing someone else's water. The water belongs to rivers that run through farmland. Ken's numbers are a perversion of that history.

"No, no, no, no. You're not going to pull that crap," Ken says. "You're one of these industry lobbyist buffoons who tries to shovel horse crap at people. You're taking thirty times the water you deserve."

"Listen," Brad says, "the thing with water—"

"You know what? I'm done with you!" The line goes dead. The last of Brad's voice drifts off into the ether between Fresno and Burbank. Ken keeps on frothing, telling his listeners that Governor Brown is protecting guys like Brad. "This is why we're getting water meters. This is why we're getting lectured and scolded. We got to take shorter showers. We can't water our lawn. This is BS!"

"This guy's making trail mix and taking ten percent of our water," John adds. "He sounded constipated with almonds. He was a nut."

Ken and John were sitting in a studio in a city where practically every drop of water has been pilfered from hundreds of miles away. Los Angeles almost went dry a century ago. To keep paving over its farmland with houses, the city shoved its spigot first into the Owens Valley, then into the Colorado River, then into the rivers that fed the delta. Yet Ken and John have a point. The almonds are using a lot of water. For all its virtues—high protein content and more—the almond crop is mostly being shipped beyond the borders of California, beyond the borders of the United States. With every nut that heads to Asia, a slug of our water goes with it. Maybe the time has come to consider their advice and create a different formula for bestowing water. But giving a bigger portion of river, snowmelt and aquifer to those who produce more dollars in the economy is probably not the formula. If water flowed in the direction of economic prowess, Ken and John's San Fernando Valley, the dwindling porn capital, might find itself high and dry, too.

This is where our civil discourse has landed us. We have labs working to create artificial intelligence, yet we cannot manage to get the farm and the city to see water as anything but yours or mine. This is nothing new, of course. Our water wars began 150 years ago, at least. What's changed is our old nemesis drought has been joined by the new nemesis of climate change—and thirty million more people. Our experiment out West always has been premised on snowpack and not mere rain, but the "snowpack" our governor is photographed standing on for winter's annual measurement has never looked paltrier. Is this clearing of mostly rock and dirt in the High Sierra the same spot where the heaviest snowfall in the continental United States was recorded the year my youngest son was born? Each of my children has chosen to stay in California and so have my sister and brother and their children. When we argue over our water-guzzling ways, we don't talk about leaving, unless it is leaving the valley for the coast. We keep our lawns green and our swimming pools filled even as our farmers are crying for more water because they are the ones who feed us. But many of the farmers themselves don't live on their farms. They live in the same suburbs where we live and keep their lawns green and their swimming pools filled, too. As summer turns to fall, to the "big El Niño rain" that might rescue us all, I drive past the San Joaquin River and our old ranch and steer toward the cracks in the earth that the Wintu saw coming. The cracks are the truest thing, and if all goes according to plan I'll follow them from one end of California to the other, from drought to flood to wildfire to mudslide, for that is our natural order of things. I'll start in the middle because this is where I know the land and its tribes best, and then I'll move outward to regions north and south because every piece of the system we have built relies on another piece, and what the system takes from one place it gives to the other place, and no place but the mountaintop has a claim to the righteous.

Three

SINGED

The old skinny preacher, the one they're accustomed to seeing in his black Stetson, black vest, black jeans, black cowboy boots, doesn't know what more to tell them. He knows that their water has gone dry and they're measuring now whether to stay or leave. He can sense in their song that they've come together this Sunday, in their little country church, the Galilee Missionary Baptist, in the colony of Fairmead, for something to hold on to. As a man of the cloth, Reverend R. L. Walker can't help but see what's happening to the valley as biblical. Paradise is burning. The orchard is going back to dust. Faucets are pouring out sand. When nature's having its fit, only a whisper in God's ear has the power to stop it. In the meantime, get used to fetching water in a barrel the way they did when they came here a long time ago.

The Coopers, Annie and Lawyer, sit in the third pew from the front singing "I Keep on Toiling." It's better than crying, which Lawyer did at the board of supervisors a few weeks ago. The Coopers, too, would like to believe that what they're enduring in this patch of Madera County, alongside Highway 99, is just another of drought's thefts. No need, then, to assign any human blame. Shake your fist at the solemn sky and be done with it.

Only this isn't the way the water went dry in Fairmead. No disrespect to the reverend, but the way it went dry is that one day last June, Annie Cooper was looking outside her kitchen window at yet another orchard of nuts going into the ground. This one was being planted right across the street. Before the nursery trees even arrived, the big grower—no one from around here seems to know his name—turned on the pump to test his new deep well, and it was at that same hour,

Annie says, when the water in his plowed field gushed like a flood, that the Cooper's house went dry. The kitchen faucet, the fancy bathtub, the washing machine, the toilet—all drew back into themselves. A last burble. Her husband of fifty-five years told her what she already knew: Their old domestic well, sitting 280 feet deep, could no longer reach the plummeting aquifer, could no longer compete with the new farm wells sunk hundreds of feet deeper.

"I thought we were just alone, and then you get to talking and it's the whole community," Annie says, standing in the kitchen. "We're all drying up. The orchards are draining everything. We've changed our whole way of living. Hauling water in the back of a truck. Not being able to cook. Not being able to take a decent bath. Driving your clothes five miles to the wash house."

Two dozen homes in this community of fourteen hundred residents—those on private wells nearest to the nut orchards—have come up dry since summer. A few families have already left. Just packed up and walked away. No "FOR SALE" signs. No good-byes. Scores of others, black families like the Coopers, white and Latino ones, too, who share a fickle community well system, are thinking of doing the same. "Outside is so dusty. So dusty. The wind picks up at night, and it just blows right on through these little cracks," Annie says, pointing to the windows. "I sweep and sweep and look in the dustpan. It's shocking how much dirt. If I didn't have plastic coverings on the living room furniture, the couches and chairs would be black. No kidding." She looks over at her husband, his gray head bowed, silent. "I told Lawyer, 'We got to go. We got to go.' But this land, for him, ain't so easy to leave."

In case it matters, the black families of Fairmead were here before the almonds and the pistachios. They arrived when the land was barren, when their great migration bypassed Detroit and Chicago and Los Angeles and Oakland and came to a stop in the San Joaquin Valley. They were looking for a land of no-mores. No more lynchings or biting their tongues or drinking from separate fountains. No more sharecropping. They were looking to keep alive their rural souls, and if that meant picking cotton for just a while longer, this ground was as good as any. All through the Depression and beyond, they kept trickling in—cousins and uncles and aunties. What they didn't know was that the dream of Fairmead as a place of agrarian ideal was already behind it. The high-water mark had come and gone.

Rev. R. L. Walker and his Galilee Missionary
Baptist Church in Fairmead

"Fairmead Colony," proclaimed the 1912 ads in the *Los Angeles Times* and *Pacific Rural Press.* "Fourteen thousand acres in small farms just placed on the market. Deep, rich sandy loam. Abundant and cheap WATER SUPPLY." What made Fairmead a colony and not a town? That was the genius of land speculators who controlled entire swaths of the San Joaquin Valley from their offices on Spring Street in Los Angeles and Market Street in San Francisco. No need for sidewalks and gutters, sewer and water systems if the place wasn't incorporated. The soil alone was sufficient.

The dreamers of small farming took the bait, first among them the German Mennonites. Here rose fields of alfalfa, a Fairmead Mercantile, a Fairmead Inn, the *Fairmead Herald.* The Mennonites built a church. The Presbyterians built a church. The dairymen built a cheese factory. The German kids attended the local Munich School, at least until the First World War broke out and the community was forced to change the name. They renamed it the Dixieland School, of all things. The abundant water, pulled up from the ground by windmill-driven pumps, stayed abundant, at least for a while. Then the bad droughts of the 1920s struck, and the water table plummeted, and the whole experiment withered. The wells, the farms, the dairies, the businesses. The ground returned to gophers and horned toads. The federal government, looking to save the desert from itself, drew up a list of places worthy of a great California irrigation project. Fairmead didn't make the list. The soil was too shallow, the groundwater too scant.

"What isn't parched earth?" is how the black families from Oklahoma, Arkansas and Texas greeted Fairmead. If they had an idea of living in a nearby city, it got squelched by real estate covenants that locked them out of towns up and down Highway 99. There was one man, a Jewish farmer named Jacob Yakel, who paid no mind to local codes. He let it be known that he would sell his extra acres in Fairmead to white, brown or black. First came the Ameys in the 1920s and then the Wheelers, the Wards, the Bells, the Whittles, the Mitchells. They dug their wells deeper and hooked up their pumps to a new electrical grid. The Williams family, fleeing Louisiana in a school bus, bought eighty acres and set to work building the largest black-owned dairy in California. By midcentury, the African-Americans of Fairmead neared four hundred strong. There were two gas stations and a restaurant and three little juke joints—"country clubs," they called them—where you could dance to rhythm and blues all night long.

"It was just open pasture, with maybe a few cows," Lawyer Cooper says, describing his land when he first set eyes upon it as a young boy in the 1940s. He had driven out with his grandmother Elizabeth Miller, in her brand-new 1942 Lincoln-Zephyr, all the way from Frenchman Bayou, Arkansas. "She was quite a lady, uh-hum," Annie says. "She knew what she wanted. She saw Los Angeles and wanted no part of it."

Grandma Miller bought five acres and raised cows, sheep, rabbits, peacocks and chickens that she sold to the slaughterhouse. "Evenings would come and I'd shout, 'The peacock is gone, Momma,'" Lawyer recalls. "'Nah, it ain't,' she'd say. 'Look up there, Lawyer.' It was just roosting on the telephone pole." When her own well started acting up and her five-horsepower pump died, Grandma Miller jury-rigged a system with a new pump and tank and a garden hose hooked up to the farmhouse. Right there, she opened Miller's Store and made a small fortune until the white folks who owned a nearby market burned it down. The sheriff in Madera wasn't curious in the least about the fire. By that time, Lawyer had gone to live in Alameda with his parents, who had landed decent jobs in the Bay Area. "I'd come back every summer. From 1945 to 1958. My uncles Patrick and Tommy Miller bought twenty acres in Fairmead. Raising cows."

The country life got into Lawyer's blood. That year he spent in Vietnam, those years working as a telephone-equipment operator at the Naval Air Station in Alameda, he kept thinking about this place. How it felt. Annie hadn't lived on the land since she'd left Lexington, Mississippi, when she was five. She was an Oakland girl through and through. Lawyer, though, kept pestering her. He retired early because of seizures from Agent Orange, one of the "rainbow" herbicides the U.S. military dropped on the rice paddies of Vietnam to starve out its peasants. He felt the rural pulling on him. When it came time for Annie to retire in 2001, after years working in the legal department at Bechtel Corporation and operating a daycare, she felt the itch, too. If Fairmead wasn't the Promised Land, it was something.

"I never even knew what a well was. Until we moved into this house," she says. "I never even knew what a propane tank was. Until we moved in this house. I never even knew what a cesspool was. . . ." She enjoys jabbing Lawyer this way. She considers him her best friend. That's why she takes so long finding him the right birthday card. "To my husband—and best friend," it has to say. They've got four children and a whole gallery of grandchildren whose framed photos adorn the wall. They planted roses and Saint Augustine grass, a Mississippi magnolia and a weeping willow to civilize the yard for their family reunions.

"This yard right here was beautiful. Oh God, you should have seen

Empty house in Fairmead after well runs dry

it. Just like a park," Annie says. Lawyer is standing off to the side, shaking his head. It's all singed now. Like some fire hit it. The nectarine and apricot and Santa Rosa plum, its sweet and sour hitting your tongue in the same burst, dried up months ago. "Look at the weeping willow. It's almost gone, too."

We're standing not twenty yards from the new orchard going in across the beaten road. The trees have yet to be planted. Almond or pistachio, Annie and Lawyer figure. It's a good guess, given the stampede of farmers willing to satisfy the world's appetite for nuts. California almonds are going to India, where the nut is regarded as a builder of smart brains. Breakfast for Indian children includes six or seven almonds with their skins removed because the skins are thought to cause the body to heat up. In China, supermarkets go wild for almonds kept in the shell and salted. In Japan, almonds are roasted, salted and covered in the finest chocolate. When someone in Asia presents you with the gift of California almonds or pistachios, it means they truly savor your friendship. What this all means in Madera County is the land that surrounds Fairmead looks much different than it did a decade ago. In Madera alone, the land planted to almonds and pistachios has tripled since the mid-1990s—to 170,000 acres. "It's just nuts, nuts, nuts," Annie says, laughing at her double meaning.

To our left and right, across the valley, farmers and hedge fund capitalists and investors from India and China are adding more acres to the already one million plus of almonds, a race to one crop that hasn't been seen since the grape boom of the 1990s. The Nut Rush. It's true that nowhere else on the globe do nuts grow with the fecundity and flavor they achieve here. It's true, too, that if you're going to spend hundreds of thousands of dollars sinking a new well more than a thousand feet deep, you might as well do it in the name of a crop that can turn you into a multimillionaire. If the orchard is fertile, the math is simple: Each acre of almonds produces three thousand pounds of crop. Each pound sells for more than three dollars. It takes but one hundred acres to make a million-dollar harvest every year. So farmers have pulled out cotton and stone fruit and grapes to plant almonds. They've bought poor hog wallows and coached up the ground to plant almonds. They've gone into wetlands and the rolling hillsides, simply because drip irrigation lines can take them there, to plant almonds. It's as if the middle of California has undergone a change of civilizations.

The trucks rattle on by day and night, kicking up that crazy dust, Annie says. "Almond harvest is a mess. I have to get a shot every fall for my sinus." The trucks bear names, but they're not the names of the farmers. "We don't know who they are," Lawyer says.

When it comes to farm fields and wells, Madera County officials aren't able to provide much information. Yes, the number of new ag wells has nearly doubled in the past few years. But where those wells are being drilled, how deep and by whom, the county cannot say, because it doesn't keep those records. A farmer looking to turn open ground into orchard needn't fret that the government will say no, because no agency regulates such things. Not even when the water a farmer pulls from the ground is draining his neighbors dry. The spoils here go to the one with the deepest hole, the highest horsepower. "Like the rest of California, we're in the dark ages in terms of the groundwater," Jill Yaeger, the county's director of environmental health, tells me.

The young executive director of the Madera County Farm Bureau, Anja Raudabaugh, couldn't stand seeing Lawyer Cooper break down in tears in front of the board of supervisors. She immediately went to some of her member farmers and persuaded them to donate bottles of water to the Coopers and twenty-five or so of their neighbors whose wells have gone dry, too. "It's a heartbreaking story, what's going on in Fairmead," Raudabaugh says. The farm bureau chief blames the drought, first and foremost. She blames Madera County because it receives federal and state funds to oversee Fairmead and it hasn't done nearly enough to fix the broken water system. She blames, too, the farmers whose bottom line, and greed, drives them deeper and deeper into the ground for water. "The farmers have a moral obligation to help. We want that community to stay intact," she says. "But my growers are private guys. They've got big hearts, but they just don't want their names in the paper."

Deep in the county pesticide report, the names appear. There's Cavalletto Ranches, Campos Brothers Farms and L. G. Merriam. There's the California Prison Authority and its 350 acres of almonds outside the women's penitentiary just south of town. There's James Maxwell and his various farming entities and partnerships with the Mormon Church, which may rank as the largest agricultural enterprise in the world, raising almonds and walnuts in California, potatoes in Idaho, cattle in Florida, cherries in England and grapes in Australia. And there's big Russell Harris, who grew up in nearby Chowchilla and watched his father, who could lay it on thick, go bust in one farming fiasco and another. The son now grows twelve thousand acres of nuts along the highway, and in case anyone mistakes this fact, he's planted a fancy palm tree at the end of every fifth row. "These are Russell Harris's almonds," the palms shout. His father, the original braggart, suffered a stroke near the end of his life and lost the ability to talk. He wanted in the worst way to tell his friends that his son had become one of California's almond kings. Russell printed a card attesting to the $6.1 million he netted in that first boom year and stuffed the card in his dad's shirt pocket. The old man, born on a wooden wagon in 1924 as the family migrated from Alabama to California, only needed to pull out the card to show his buddies that the Harris Almond Company had, indeed, swelled from four employees to four hundred. Russell now has a nursery where he raises acre upon acre of baby trees and a mammoth plant where he processes more than 100 million pounds of almonds a season. The nuts grown by him and his growers make up 5 percent of the state's haul.

The Coopers have never met the farmers who are sucking dry their aquifer. Harris, for one, doesn't live anywhere near Fairmead or his orchards on the Madera side of the San Joaquin River. He and his wife live thirty miles to the south in a river-bluff estate on the Fresno side. Their Moroccan mansion, which took three years to build and cost $15 million, is so fantastic that the subcontractors can't quit gossiping about it: ten thousand square feet of main quarters, four thousand square feet of guest house and maid's quarters, five kitchens, his and hers dressing rooms fit for Broadway stars, an authentic movie theater, a Las Vegas–style poker club and a backyard fire pit and waterfall. To get back at his wife for the inlaid walnut floors she picked out from Dubai, Russell bought himself a $10 million Cessna XLS+ jet.

Raudabaugh, the farm bureau chief, now wonders if at least some of the anger felt by the Coopers and their neighbors isn't resentment. "If we're pinning the blame for those houses going dry," she tells me, "let's not forget the people of Fairmead. If ag finds itself in an unsustainable and indefensible situation, what about the residents? They purchased those houses knowing the wells were old and shallow." A 280-foot well isn't exactly shallow, Lawyer says, but he understands her point. Unlike some of his neighbors, he can afford to dig deeper, to six hundred or seven hundred feet if need be. Heck, he could even sell Annie's 2006 Mercedes to help pay for a new well. But he sees the $30,000 price tag as a poor gamble. He would need to dig a lot deeper to compete with the farms surrounding him. And how long would a new well last? Five years? Ten years? A better bet, as heartaching as it would be, would be to sell the house and its 8.9 acres of empty dirt and move back to the city. So many black folks have died or otherwise departed over the years, no one would even notice them gone. But what buyer is going to want a stucco-and-brick ranch house in the middle of nowhere with no water? Lawyer has a hunch. Farmers are already making offers to some of his neighbors. They'll tear out his house and yard and turn the whole thing into another almond grove.

In the meantime, he's set up a water system in his front yard, built with tanks and rubber hoses and a two-horsepower sump pump, not unlike the contraption his grandmother had going all those decades ago. Every other day, he fills it up with water he's fetched from a relative's house across the fields. "I don't know how he does it," Annie says. "Dragging that water. He's got diabetes, and his legs aren't good. He fell off the truck the other day. He's worn out, and there's nothing I can do to help him."

Lawyer trudges to the canal that separates his land from his uncle's old farm. The local irrigation district constructed it years ago, taking a full acre from his uncle in a show of supreme domain. The canal is where his cousin drowned when she was eight years old. In good times and bad times, the water flows right on by. It goes to farmers whose daddies and granddaddies were farmers before them. Out back stands the dead well next to Lawyer's idled tractor, and the chicken pens with no chickens and an Arabian horse named Sunshine who's there to keep the grass down, if only they had any. He knows now why a grown man could cry at a board of supervisors meeting. "I thought about no runoff from the mountain, and the farmers are still getting all this water from the earth. I thought about the people who are doing without, just for someone to get rich. I thought about the rivers going dry and the lakes and everything. I thought about the fish, the cities and the small farm. I thought about those things, and it hurt. For us to come and try to live a decent life here . . . It's not our fault the water's going dry."

Lawyer stares at his land. "Dry," he says. Then he gazes across the torn road at the orchard. "Water," he says. "Dry," he repeats. "Water." Back and forth his head moves. "Dry . . . water." Pretty soon, the two words become one in his throat. *Drywater.*

On the way out, I spot a pomegranate tree standing all alone. The ancient fruit, like this land, is hard to love. The beauty of its shape and color come with a thorn that draws blood. Its outside is red leather, its inside a catacomb of waxy white that hides so many little rubies. My grandfather once told me that every pomegranate holds 840 seeds, no more, no less, and I wondered how that could be. He said the fruit, bitter and sweet, was a metaphor for our rebirth. One of the first acts that Armenian families committed in the new land was to plant a pomegranate tree in the front yard. As a kid, I could ride my bicycle through the streets of south Fresno and tell you every house that belonged to an Armenian just by spotting the tree. My uncle Mike Mamigonian's mother, who looked like a Cherokee survivor of the Trail of Tears, had the patience to work past the thorns, the leather and the wax. After dinner, she'd bring to the table, as if it were an offering, a giant bowl piled high with sparkling fruit. It must have taken her hours to clean. There wasn't a speck of red rind or white membrane to be found. We'd devour the rubies, their crunch spitting out a juice that stained tablecloth and shirt.

The first pomegranate trees to grow in the valley were planted in the 1880s, not for their fruit so much but because they grew like bushes and nothing could kill them, especially not drought, and they were so thick with branches that no better windbreak could be found. One of my favorite Saroyan short stories captures the predicament of his uncle Melik, who had spent years trying to grow twenty acres of pomegranates—for their fruit—in the dry earth not far from Fairmead. With no good water, he had a helluva time. He finally raised a single crop that he sent with great pride to the produce houses in Chicago. When he heard not a word for a month, he placed a long-distance call. The produce man told him that no one knew what his fruit was. It wasn't an apple or a peach. It wasn't an orange or a grapefruit. He couldn't sell the pomegranates for any more than a dollar a box, if he could sell them at all. A dollar a box? Uncle Melik shouted. "What kind of businessman are you? There is no other fruit in the world like the pomegranate. Five dollars a box isn't half enough." The produce man shipped all eleven boxes back without a single sale. Uncle and nephew spent the rest of the winter eating pomegranates and not saying a word to each other, "because there was such an awful lot to say, and no language to say it in."

Four

SINKING

The photograph of the man standing next to the telephone pole is making its rounds again. Every drought, as the water table plummets, it gets dusted off and recirculated. Every drought, as the San Joaquin Valley sinks a little more, the ghost of Joe Poland returns to point his finger. Poland understood better than anyone the granular nature of subsidence and the do-nothing of government when confronted by its hidden force. Steady, sedate, he was a geologist's geologist. Yet at the end of his long career, he could not help wondering if his cautiousness as a scientist had been a mistake. More and more, he found himself captivated by the idea of turning the quiet of subsidence into a drama. The sinking of the earth was like a termite that ate from the inside at the structure of things. You didn't feel the foundation crumbling. You didn't see the meticulous ravage until it was too late. But what if he could wake up the public to its destruction? What if those years of measuring the earth's downward creep could be rescued from his files and turned into a provocation?

Thus was born the iconic photograph

Joe Poland shows how much the land has sunk on Fresno County's west side

of the man—Poland acting as his own droll model—standing in the baking sun next to the telephone pole. For the longest time I pondered the inspiration for his stunt. Then it occurred to me that Poland was a child of the Roaring Twenties and must have been a fan of *Ripley's Believe It or Not!,* a regular cartoon in the newspapers of the day. His photo might not carry the same capacity for marvel as the African with the foot-long horn growing out of his head or the six-inch mummified body of Atta Boy that Ripley himself held in the palm of his hand, but it does tell a story that's not easy to believe.

On a summer day in 1977, in the midst of a then-record drought, Poland drove out Panoche Road toward the farm town of Mendota and stopped at the edge of a vineyard where a utility pole reached arrow-straight into the pale blue sky. In the company of a photographer, he chose the spot with scientific care. He was the world's foremost expert on soil subsidence, the arcanum of how the earth loses elevation when too much groundwater is taken by man. A geologist trained at Harvard and Stanford, Poland was revered in Venice, Italy, where he had figured out why the floating city was sinking and how to make it stop. He was less revered in the San Joaquin Valley, where he had spent thirty-five years in the uniform of the U.S. Geological Survey documenting the most dramatic alteration of the earth's surface in human history. More than 5,200 square miles, an area nearly as large as Connecticut, had sunk at least a foot on Poland's watch.

What is the duty of a geologist when the earth beneath the people is collapsing? Where to tread when agriculture, a people's bread and butter, is extracting water from the ground at a rate far beyond what snowmelt and rain can replenish? For three decades, Poland answered the question with an inch-by-inch, season-by-season, tracing of subsidence in the valley. The stacking of scientific data, he presumed, would make its own case. But the pumping went on, and no amount of earthfall was enough to persuade the state of California to regulate agriculture's bleeding of the aquifer. So Poland, taking a page from Ripley, set out to turn one telephone pole along a vineyard road into a marker of the worst subsidence in the world.

At the age of sixty-nine, his thin left arm leaning against the wood, Poland appears in the photograph as the furthest thing from a government scientist looking to make a subversive statement. He's wearing a gentleman's hat and a plain white short-sleeved shirt with his eyeglass case stuck in the breast pocket. His belt cinches an old man's paunch and what looks to be a calculator of the early Texas Instruments variety. He did his measurements well in advance. Near the top of the pole is a sign that reads "1925." Halfway down is a second sign painted with "1955." At the bottom, where Poland's clunky shoes touch the ground, a third sign says "1977." It takes a second to figure out, but the pole is the geologist's yardstick. In a half-century span, the land here has sunk almost thirty feet—right down the length of the wood. It's a strange visual effect, as if Poland is standing at the bottom of a mine shaft with no way to climb out, while at the same time he's standing on top of the open earth. From here to there, we can see that it's a long ways down but we don't quite believe our eyes. We are left to ponder how it can be that the pole, the vineyard and the road have all sunken in unison, and valley earth has settled pancake flat again.

Forty years later, on a drive through Mendota, I try to locate the pole. If Poland were with me—he died in 1991 at the age of eighty-three, eulogized as "Mr. Soil Subsidence"—he would point out that the earth's sinking isn't short-lived. Once the land compacts, it never finds its old elevation, no matter how many floods might come to fill the aquifer back up. The earth is a human face, I imagine him telling me, and the farmer has sucked out all the collagen. Young ground has been turned into old ground before its time. I drive up and down Panoche Road, but the utility poles lined up along the vineyards all look the same. There's no marker saying, "Here's the most famous utility pole in the West." Like the record of a crime expunged, the sign with its dates is long gone. Only the sinking remains.

Farmers are poking so many holes in the ground, sucking out so much water from prehistoric depths, that the earth is pulling away, first by inches and now by feet. The earth doesn't sink alone, of course. It takes with it roads, bridges, dams and canals. In another part of the United States with a different history, the situation might cause a reaction. It might even provoke the kind of alarm that would curtail, if not stop altogether, the pumping. But this is the land of the Big One, and shifts of ground that don't register on a Richter scale don't register. So the extraction of groundwater accelerates at a magnitude rarely seen before.

Farmers in the Westlands Water District are pumping 660,000 acre-feet of groundwater a year to grow their crops in drought. Los Angeles, by comparison, consumes only 587,000 acre-feet of water a year. As the water table gets drawn down, it is dog eat dog. The almond farmer digs a 1,200-foot well and dries up the alfalfa farmer. The alfalfa farmer digs a 1,600-foot well and dries up the grape farmer. No farmer dares to go deeper than cotton king J. G. Boswell, who has drilled fifty-two wells in the bottom of old Tulare Lake, seven of these wells to a depth of 2,500 feet. That's a hole the length of one Empire State Building stacked on top of another. And so on and on it goes, in a rush to the nethermost.

On a windy March morning after a good rain, I find Michelle Sneed twenty miles north of Poland's pole, where she's come to a bend in the Delta-Mendota Canal to survey subsidence anew. This is one of those plains of solitude in the valley traversed by farmers and their Mexican crew bosses—men and more men. If nothing else, it makes for a straightaway spotting of Sneed. A good-sized woman with a sturdy swimmer's frame, she wears her brown hair tied in a ponytail, jeans rolled up and boots caked in mud. In the event her snooping around raises any suspicion, she's made sure to put on her green USGS T-shirt over a longer-sleeved one. Geologists refer to this part of the valley, where the San Joaquin River stops its westward run and heads north to the delta, as Oro Loma. A lone metal shed in the shadow of the giant canal marks the location. The shed houses a gauge made of aircraft cable that runs down a hole a thousand feet deep and is used to measure subsidence. Outside the shed are two more holes that Sneed plumbs to track the depth of the water table.

Half a dozen students and two teachers from a high school in the Bay Area have driven down to take a tour of the land and watch Sneed gather her data. The students signed up for a course that integrates photography and California water, and they step down from the van with their cameras, real ones, clicking away. As visuals go, there's none more telling of a sinking landscape than this. Here along Russell Avenue, it's not only earth that is falling. The infrastructure of California, its roads and bridges and canals big and small, is sinking inexorably, too.

"Where's the weird canal where the water runs higher than the road?" one of the students asks.

"It's a little ways down," Sneed says with a teacher's patience. "That will be our grand finale."

The teens from Danville understand the basics. In years of good snowmelt, when the rivers are flush, cities and farms in California draw a third of their water from the ground. In drought, when the rivers run low, the farmers here on the west side depend almost wholly on water lifted from deep beneath the earth. Other states, even some as prone to drought as California, passed laws long ago to limit the mining of groundwater. In California, the legislature has debated the merits of groundwater regulation for more than a century. Still, the land sinks. "Because it's happening by degrees, we can pretend that it's not happening at all," Sneed says. "Unfortunately, it's not like a giant sinkhole that appears out of nowhere. You have to know where to look to find it."

Sneed has been on the subsidence watch for twenty years, most of that time operating under the presumption that the valley was no longer sinking because farmers were flush with the state and federal water shipped in from the delta. With imports plenty, they didn't need to tap the earth anymore. "We thought we had subsidence licked and stopped taking measurements," Sneed tells the group. "From 1983 to 2009, we put our resources elsewhere. So we've got a big data gap. Then the last couple droughts hit and showed us we were wrong. We started measuring again, and we were shocked at what we found."

She hands out a packet of fact sheets and photos that chart the measurements in Oro Loma, hit and miss, since 1935. The groundwater depth is a blue line. The elevation of earth is a red line. The blue line rises and falls with great variability. In dry periods, the water table drops hundreds of feet. In wet years, it fills up but not nearly all the way. In a century's time, the cumulative overdraft of the aquifer—the difference between what man takes and what nature makes—is more than 122 million acre-feet in the Central Valley. That's equivalent to draining Lake Tahoe dry. The hydrology on the valley's west side makes for a strange desert. The rainfall, four to seven inches a year, doesn't stretch very far. But the San Joaquin River, as it swings north to the delta, recharges some of the aquifer in flood years. And the irrigation canals that move delta water south to these farms replenish the groundwater as well, because they leak from their bottoms. So the blue line of the aquifer, dry year to wet year, goes up and down like an erratic heartbeat. But the red line, the line charting the sinking of the earth, shows a one-way trajectory down. The spot where we're standing has sunk thirteen feet since 1935. Not quite Joe Poland–dimension subsidence but still alarming. “The hot spots have moved. There’s more of them,” Sneed says. “As agriculture has expanded into new areas, subsidence has traveled.”

Satellite images see the earth’s elevation with centimeter accuracy. There is California. There is the San Joaquin Valley. The ground on which we’re standing is painted a crazy red on the map, as if a wildfire were burning. This is the color that NASA uses to designate the worst subsidence. Two of the hottest spots are located ninety miles due south of here. One is near the town of Corcoran in the bottom of old Tulare Lake, and the other is just outside a place called Pixley. A third hot spot, the worst of them all, sits nearby in Red Top. Across a 1,200-square-mile swath of the valley, a landmass that can hold two L.A.s, the earth is sinking nearly a foot a year, rivaling the greatest rate of subsidence ever recorded. Flat roads that Joe Poland drove on in the 1970s now roll out in undulations. Erect wooden poles carrying electricity from irrigation pump to irrigation pump tilt nearly sideways. A husband and wife sitting on the porch of their farmhouse can no longer see the postman coming from up the street. “As far as impacts go,” Sneed says, “we’re in uncharted territory.”

Some of the bigger growers, tired of waiting for overbooked well diggers to schedule their jobs, have spent millions of dollars buying their own drilling rigs. As new wells go in right and left, who knows if they’re even bothering to get permits. Out in the middle of old Tulare Lake, where not even a quasi-government agency supervises the J. G. Boswell Company’s mining of groundwater, the main levee protecting the town of Corcoran from flood has dropped more than a foot in only eight months. Not surprisingly, no one at the local city hall wants to blame Boswell’s pumps for causing the earth to sink so dramatically or to speculate what damage the next flood might bring.

It would be one thing if the Boswells needed the water to irrigate their own crops. But they and other big growers in Tulare Lake are selling a portion of their supply for tens of millions of dollars to irrigation districts that have depleted their own aquifers. To shore up the sinking levee and keep the town of Corcoran dry when the lake returns, the residents and the local state prison have to pony up more than $10 million in extra taxes. One disillusioned homeowner, a third-generation farmworker, sent me a letter wondering why no newspaper had investigated the situation and no agency of the county or state had intervened to stop the pumping for profit. "This is water that has flowed from the beginning of time into Tulare Lake. This is our water," he wrote. "How can they keep drilling new wells, pumping more water, sinking our houses, churches, businesses and the prison and then make us pay for it? This is criminal."

Why is subsidence causing Corcoran to sink so fast and leaving another town fifteen miles away relatively unscathed? The answer, Sneed says, is geology. The San Joaquin Valley is a great structural trough, a downwarp in the earth's crust carved out sixty million years ago. The rivers washed down clay, sand, silt and gravel as they poured their snowmelt into a vast bay connected to the Pacific. Then two million years ago—during the Pleistocene Epoch or great ice age—the Sierra Nevada to the east lifted higher. This tilt raised the alluvial fans, and the steepening made the rivers flow with even greater erosive force. This is how deposits of mountain sediment kept shallowing out the bay until its waters dried up, creating the valley as we know it. As the rivers lost their direct path to the ocean, the snowmelt had few places to go but down. Sinking into clay, sand and gravel, the water created a second vast lake, this one reaching thousands of feet below ground. In the mid-1940s, the amount of water stored in the aquifer's upper strata alone was estimated at 100 million acre-feet. Then came the boom of groundwater extraction with its ever more powerful pumps. As the water table sank, so did the earth. The pattern of valley subsidence, however, was similar to the blaze of a wildfire. As it struck one place without pity, it left the place just down the road without scar.

The hit and miss, Sneed explains, is a function of the fine clay that came down the mountain when the land was conceived. In those areas where clay wed clay and formed a layer, subsidence is showing its greatest impact. Across the broad west side, clay accumulates in fluctuating degrees of depth. Some layers of clay measure 150 feet in thickness, others less than an inch. One clay layer can sit close to the land's surface, another much deeper down. This means that a farmer on the far west side can sink his well six hundred feet deep and not hit clay. A farmer in the alluvium of the San Joaquin River can punch a hole through the clay layer at two hundred feet. Where clay is, water is. Water can be found in the porous sediments both above the clay and below the clay and also inside the clay layer itself. In fact, clay stores more water per unit than any other sediment. This is clay's gift and its curse. When a farmer digs a well and punctures the clay layer, whether it's sitting shallow or deep, he may have hit the aquifer's mother lode. But as soon as that well—and there are tens of thousands of them across the valley—starts pumping water from inside or below the clay layer, the clay compresses. As it tightens and shrinks down, the clay draws the rest of the earth down with it. There's really no way to dig a well on the west side, pump water through clay and not cause subsidence. The thinner the clay layer, the faster the earth sinks. The thicker the clay layer, the more the earth sinks over time. For every inch an aquifer collapses, its capacity to store water is forever reduced by that inch.

In this epic of expanding agriculture, it is subsidence and not rain that follows the plow. Over the past half century, the footprint of agriculture on the west side has continued to creep outward to the very edge of the Coast Ranges. Alkali ground deemed unsuitable even for pasturage is now nut country. This pattern of sprawl has persisted through drought and pestilence, crop surpluses and recession only to accelerate faster. Planting crops on third-class soils has been made possible, and profitable, by the hoses and emitters of drip irrigation, which can now deliver water and chemicals to a precise root zone. It no longer matters to the farmer today that three generations of his predecessors deemed the earth here unfit for agriculture. The ground is now merely there to physically prop up the tree. The farmer might as well be farming hydroponically. Thanks to drip irrigation, tens of thousands of acres on the west side—ground crusted with salts and unable to drain itself because the clay is impenetrable—are being farmed today. This includes ground inside the irrigation districts and ground outside, which is known as the "white area," agriculture's version of a no-man's-land.

The irrigation districts, for all their expansion into junk lands, at least have access to a supply of water provided by a local, state or federal project. Farmers inside the districts draw surface water from rivers nearby or rivers whose flows are imported from the delta. The white areas, on the other hand, have no rivers to call on. Farmers in these ungoverned zones rely completely on groundwater. Farming's footprint is spreading outward at the same time the intensification of agriculture is shooting upward. Whether on good ground or poor ground, inside an irrigation district or outside, farmers are growing crops they've never grown before. The scarcity of water is as much a consequence of shifts in agricultural practices as it is of drought. Farmers who've known only cotton, wheat, barley, tomatoes, melons and garlic have switched their ground from seasonal crops to permanent ones. In doing so, they've lost the nimbleness to respond to dry times. They're both hardening their water demand and using more water than ever before. Turning up the dial on drip irrigation is irresistible. Do you want to harvest 1,700 pounds of nuts an acre or 3,000 pounds? On a 400-acre ranch, this extra yield can mean the difference between breaking even or pocketing a million dollars. A farmer who plants his seasonal crops in spring or fall can look at his water availability and decide how much ground to plant or to fallow. But a farmer who's converted to permanent crops such as almonds and pistachios operates in a perpetual bind. When drought comes, he's left with only one choice: either dry out his trees or dig a deeper well.

"The situation is no longer sustainable," Sneed warns. "On the supply side, less water is being sent here from the delta because of the needs of fish and the environment. On the demand side, we're seeing a growth of agriculture onto lands that have never been farmed before. And now the farmers are raising crops they've never raised before."

In the past, a decent year of snowmelt meant that farmers inside the irrigation district boundaries would cease their day-and-night pumping. There was ample water from the backyard river or the faraway river to handle the chore. This allowed the aquifer to recharge in wet years, maybe not all the way but close to it. Now, however, the intensification of valley agriculture has created a situation where even a normal year of snowmelt isn't enough to stop the pumping. Even when the rivers are delivering a goodly amount, it doesn't cover the ambition of farmers inside the irrigation districts looking to produce more crops. As for the farmers outside the districts with no draw of river water, they have no operational model other than to keep pumping until the aquifer bleeds out. The entire west side—irrigation districts and white areas—now finds itself in an everlasting state of drought. Not nature's drought, mind you, but farmer's drought. The pumping does not cease, and the ground keeps on sinking.

"What about the new law in California regulating groundwater," one of the high school teachers asks. "Doesn't that change things?"

"That's our hope," Sneed says. "But each local area has to come up with a groundwater management plan. And the state has to review the plans and approve them. The locals have about twenty years to come into compliance. So a lot of damage can be done in the meantime while they're trying to figure this out."

In geological time, the wait is nothing. In career time, Sneed will likely retire before a single farmer pumping water is handed a cease and desist order. "Yes, the new law is a step in the right direction. Baby steps, right? We didn't get into this mess overnight, and we're not going to get out of it overnight, either."

Sneed does an artful dodge. She does not mention that the big farmers sitting on the irrigation district boards are the ones putting together the groundwater management plans. The big lawyers are right behind them, already sounding out arguments that posit that a farmer's past "beneficial" use of groundwater becomes a right to future use. In other words, the more land a farmer plants between now and the time the law goes into effect—and the more water he pumps—the more he'll be allowed to pump into the future.

As it is, the earth of Oro Loma is sinking four inches a year. To demonstrate what four inches means to the infrastructure of California, Sneed leads us on short walk along the Delta-Mendota Canal, which transports river water 116 miles south from the delta to a slough outside Mendota. The canal may look like one splendid gravity-fed ditch moving water across the vast plain, but it is actually a series of twenty giant pools laid out end to end. One pool is separated from the next by a small dam that checks and controls the flow of water. When the canal breaks down in one spot or another, the operators can stop the flow and drain the individual pool without having to dry out the entire canal. Such a closure is a rare occurrence, Sneed says, and it's always a kick to see what has come to rest at the canal's bottom. "In one stretch, fifty cars were found. One of the vehicles was a federal truck."

Where the check dam divides one pool from another, the concrete is buckling. As subsidence messes with the carefully graded banks, it pushes the canal deeper into the earth. When one pool collapses, a whole long section of the canal loses gravity. Water that cannot flow with the same force backs up on itself. The pool truly becomes a pool. To speed up the flow, the canal's operators have raised the check dam and its gates by four feet. But this lifting hasn't been matched by the lifting of the nearby road and bridge. At the spot where the canal and the road across it intersect, the flow of water actually laps the top of the concrete bridge. If a kid on an inner tube dared to ride the canal on a hot summer day, he wouldn't make it very far. His tube would strike hard against the concrete, not to mention the blow that would greet his head. Sneed doesn't know how much of the canal's capacity has been diminished by subsidence. Not far from here, the Sack Dam on the San Joaquin River is sinking six inches a year. The canal that serves the dam is now pushing water uphill at half its old capacity. The fix will cost at least $20 million.

Then there's the California Aqueduct and its fitness to deliver four million acre-feet of water to the farms of the San Joaquin Valley and the faucets and swimming pools of Southern California. The middle leg of the aqueduct—a distance of more than twenty miles—is sinking, too. Because of the loss of gravity flow, state operators must set their pumping stations to "absolute maximum." They are trying to push so much water through the dead spots that the water laps along the very top of the aqueduct's lining. Even at absolute maximum force, pools 18 and 20—each ten miles long—are backing up. Subsidence has so altered the design of the aqueduct that the public is spending tens of millions of dollars a year in extra energy costs. No single system in California consumes as much electricity as the aqueduct. More than 15 percent of its monthly energy bill now reflects the cost of overcoming subsidence. Reengineering gravity back into the stalled pools will cost hundreds of millions of dollars. Building new bridges, roads, dams and levees in each hot spot will cost hundreds of millions of dollars more. What portion of this rebuilding will be borne by the irrigation districts and, by extension, the farmers? What portion will be borne by the state and the feds? These are the questions now being wrestled over.

I hop into my car and follow Sneed to the grand finale a couple miles down the road. We pass the Grassland Bypass Project, a $22 million experiment by the U.S. Bureau of Reclamation that is attempting to clean up the salts and selenium that poison ninety-seven thousand acres of west side agriculture. The same clay layers implicated in subsidence are turning the soil into a bog of contamination. Irrigation water percolates only a shallow ways down, hits the hard clay and bubbles back up. The toxic brew of salt and selenium stunts crops and deforms and kills migratory birds. The farmers used to siphon this polluted water through a system of drains and canals and into holding ponds, but the ponds became their own killing fields. The Grassland Bypass Project was conceived to move the polluted waters onto six thousand acres of land planted in 'Jose' tall wheatgrass, a salt-tolerant feed for beef and dairy cows. The polluted water is filtered once by the wheatgrass and then again by a reverse-osmosis plant next door. The discharge, just about clean, is then sent down the river. The farmers consider the project an unmitigated success, citing the reduced levels of pollutants draining into the San Joaquin. The environmentalists consider it a boondoggle, a taxpayer-funded laundering operation that keeps the worst of California farmland in production.

The kids from Danville are posing for pictures in front of the Outside Canal, which was built in the late 1800s by Henry Miller, the cattle king who controlled a million acres of pasture. This canal, too, has been sinking, and the vexed men who operate Miller's old irrigation system have been building up the sidewalls to keep the water running. A more expensive solution will have to be found. In the meantime, the flow runs brimful as it crosses under the bridge—so high, in fact, that if you look at the whole thing sideways, the water level actually tops the road itself. How the water doesn't spill over and wash out the road is another one of those optical illusions of California's bending. The kids can't believe their eyes.

Red Top sits halfway between Ora Loma and the house in Fairmead where Annie and Lawyer Cooper live. Driving along Highway 152, the road from Fresno to San Francisco, I follow the palm-lined almond orchards that belong to Russell Harris. As his last orchard peters out, there's Red Top sitting three feet lower than it did when the drought began. If Red Top were a town, that much sinking wouldn't be tolerated. But Red Top isn't a town or even a place on the map, no matter how hard Ray Flanagan tried to turn it into one. The Flanagans, who liked to say they were "Irish from their ass both ways," settled in this patch of alkali in the 1890s when the San Joaquin River ran reasonably free. Dig a hole eight feet deep and a fountainhead of artesian water burst out of the ground to the height of a grown man.

Ray was born in 1899 amid nine brothers and sisters who wore garments of green to show their ethnic pride. The whole clan was pigheaded but no one more so than Ray. As a kid, he milked cows and drove tractor and fished in the river. When cotton started to get planted by the tens of thousands of acres in the 1930s, he bought a couple of school buses and contracted Okie, black and Mexican labor for the big growers. He'd fly overhead in his Curtiss Robin and survey his crews trailing their ten-foot sacks, filled with cotton and a few pounds of dirt clods thrown in to offset the boss man's crooked scales. Ray saved enough money to buy himself a twelve-thousand-acre cattle spread. Dairies chased out of Southern California and relocating their herds to the valley were desperate for hay. Ray, a good-sized man with a kind face, timed it right and became an alfalfa grower.

One day in the 1950s, as he hit the sky, Ray looked below and was struck by a new vision. When he came back down, he idled a few sections of his lousier ground and built a market, a café, a cotton gin, a gas station, an airstrip with two hangars and a park with llamas, goats and turkeys. To honor the woman who inspired his dreaming—Suzie Flanagan, his wife with the blazing red hair—he called it Red Top. Ray pestered the U.S. Postal Service into awarding him a zip code, thinking it might help put his little corner of Madera County on the map. When the traffic picked up only a little, he decided he needed a gimmick.

That was how Ray came up with the Museum of Exotic Fish, a glass-enclosed exhibit that wrapped around his Red Top Market and Café and drew passersby who couldn't believe that a piece of ocean had landed smack-dab in the middle of the alkali. They turned off Highway 152 going east or west, pulled up to the café and peered into the warped Plexiglas to study the forty-six different species of deep-sea fish, all bagged by Ray, including five species that could not be seen in any other single location in the world. The smaller fish were mounted on the wall. The bigger ones dangled from the ceiling on chains, moving ever so slightly when a heavy truck rumbled up. Swimming in the waters of space, their death masks became animated. Caught in Peru, Panama, Baja and the Bahamas, each one was a trophy. There was even a 950-pound blue marlin snagged by Ray while fishing the Kona coast off Hawaii. Their perfect iridescence, that wild rainbow gleam, left visitors wondering if the fish were real, like the moose head on the wall, or replicas made out of fiberglass.

I stand outside the café, not sure I want to go in. Ray died about twenty-five years ago. The Okie waitresses that used to serve shit on a shingle are all dead, too. But the fish are as alive as dead fish can be. I try to read the small signs that list the species and weight of each one and where Ray caught them, but the glass is fogged by the breath of too many chicken-fried steaks. The market is a cluttered mess of cobwebbed items that have been sitting on the shelves for years. The café, Mexican now, serves chile verde for $5.50 a plate, cash money only. There's a *Los Angeles Times* article from 1982 plastered on the wall about Ray and his "world famous exhibit." The tables are empty, the lunch counter is idle and the kitchen is quiet. My eyes bite on the bluefin tuna that once weighed 547 pounds and swam in the waters of Bimini before Ray hauled it in with a rod and reel and brought it back to the people of Red Top a half century ago.

Ray's dream of turning Red Top into a thriving community was dashed for all sorts of reasons, not the least of which was the dam built on the San Joaquin River by the Central Valley Project in the early 1940s. The dam sent the snowmelt flowing in an entirely foreign direction, 160 miles south to Bakersfield, by way of the Friant-Kern Canal.

Red Top Cafe and Museum of Exotic Fish

The concrete river took the real river and dumped it three counties away. That stealing, as they still refer to it here, dried up the old San Joaquin as it ran past Red Top. In some flood years, the water had come right up to Ray's market, and the farm kids caught catfish and carp and a wayward salmon or two where the highway runs today. Every twenty years, the old-timers would curse and then forgive another flood. As the dam rose and the flow their way became a trickle, they found themselves missing the fight the river had brought out in them. The San Joaquin that flooded their backyard channels, washed out the salts from the soil and recharged the aquifer was no more.

The damming of the San Joaquin was different from the damming of the Sacramento. The Central Valley Project took only a small portion of the Sacramento and pushed its flow south to our valley. The Sacramento was four times the river the San Joaquin was. Whatever the system had stolen from the north, it at least left behind a river that could still find its old banks. But where to find the San Joaquin? The people in and around Red Top would have to get in their cars and drive two hours south to one of those alfalfa fields in Tulare, where hay was being shoved down the throats of Holsteins, to see what remained of their river. For Ray Flanagan, the stealing was personal. His small canal that drew off the San Joaquin and delivered the freshest water right to his crops went dry, too. With some desperation, he drilled thirty-one new wells in the Red Top ground to replace his flow from the river. He got so carried away with hole punching that he began tapping into the aquifer of a neighbor, who sought an injunction against Ray by filing a lawsuit that alleged "wrongful diversion and exploitation of water."

Exploitation of water. Now, that was a crime of too many in these parts. The morgue in the Madera County library doesn't say how the lawsuit worked out. Safe to assume that Ray had to shut down a few of his offending wells. Like every other farmer with wells poked deep into the earth, Ray wanted to believe that the aquifer was going to last. He and the other growers formed a resource conservation district and met once a month to push for constraints on farming. But no line ever held. Ray and his neighbors went back home, looked their wives and children in the eyes and couldn't bring even themselves to stop pumping.

From the café to the fields is a short walk down Red Top Road. The path leads from one world-famous exhibit to the other, from exotic fish to exotic subsidence. The walk illustrates, in a most heartbreaking way, how land with no water but the diminishing water underground has evolved into a mega-dairy, a mega-vineyard, a mega–nut orchard.

I say heartbreaking because this is one of the places where I've done time. I knew this dirt when it was sugar beets. This is where my high school buddies and I took jobs one summer with a company called Sun Fruit Ltd., which seemed more apropos of a grower of plums and peaches, not sugar beets and cotton. We were paid the minimum wage to wield long-handled hoes and trudge up and down the quarter-mile rows of beets, looking for weeds. The object was to chop down every last stalk of johnsongrass and wild mustard that was stealing nutrients from the crop. We were a poor excuse for farmworkers, though we didn't know it yet. The crew boss let us go at our own pace for a week or two, perhaps thinking we would find our way to usefulness after a suitable period of breaking in. Our third week there, he drove up and unloaded from the back of his truck a bunch of cages holding some kind of species of bird that he let out on the rows next to ours. Weeder geese, he announced. A whole battalion of them.

I never knew such a bird existed. We were in decent enough shape for seventeen-year-old boys, most of us training for our senior year of football. The plan was to work the fields for a month or two and then quit in late August when double-day practices began. What none of us had factored in was the arrival of the geese. They'd been bred with a streak of mean and an appetite for weeds that could not be quenched. That first day, they laid down an immediate challenge. We could either follow their lead or be put to shame by it. We stopped talking, leaned forward into the earth and locked onto each of our rows. It was 105 in the sun and the thick coating of sulfur that dusted the waist-high beets turned into a vapor that made everything smell more rotten than it was.

That first week up against the birds was a blur. This wasn't mowing and edging the front yard and hula-hoeing the courtyard. Field labor took a grit that suburbia had not conditioned us for. Honking and hissing, the geese had no quit. Day after day, our defeat became a mockery. Sulfured faces dripping lines of sweat, we began to plot against the birds. Taking them on at close range was out of the question. They were the perfect size to go right for our privates. Since I played quarterback, the long-distance assault was led by me. The heavy soil of Red Top produced a high-quality dirt clod. One by one we started picking off the birds, not enough to kill or maim them, but enough to let them know that they couldn't get ahead of us without feeling it. When our six weeks of labor was finished and we walked off the sugar beet fields and onto the gridiron at Bullard High, we'd been made better by the birds, or so we thought. Then a 5–5 season made us question how we'd spent our summer and more. In all my drives through the fields in the years that followed, I don't think I ever saw another crew of weeder geese. With the rise of Monsanto's Roundup, I believe the birds finally came to understand the agony of defeat. In the move from row crops to permanent crops, the geese were the first workers to be idled.

I walk out of the café and head south on Red Top Road. Ray's old cotton gin is still here, one of the last ones in the valley still pumping out bales. In the fields behind the gin, Dirk and Case Vlot, sons of a Dutch immigrant, have built themselves a mega-dairy. I count seven or eight metal barns with no sides and pitched roofs that house maybe six thousand Holsteins, who are protected from sun and rain until the 105 of summer hits and scores of them die. The way they bloat is a supplication, backs to the ground, legs ramrod straight into the air. Give the Vlots credit. They didn't build their mansion in the city like so many other farmers. They built theirs on a hill behind gates next to the Holsteins and piles of shit and great mounds of feed under plastic cover that will be converted into more shit and plenty of milk and cheese to add to the nation's surplus of milk and cheese.

Every 160 acres, the Vlots have dug a well that sucks out water to grow their alfalfa and corn on salt land. I follow the whine of the diesel pump, a high-gear sound, a quarter way into the field. Most pumps here can draw two thousand gallons a minute with a 100-horsepower engine. This pump is a 200-horsepower Anderson pulling from an aquifer that's overtapped. The water pouring into the concrete standpipe is considerably less than two thousand gallons a minute. A dairy this size takes an ungodly amount of water to keep its milk flowing. There's the water the cows drink, and the water to wash out the shit from the stalls, and the water that water-guzzling crops like alfalfa require almost year-round. Some of the dairy's effluent gets flushed into lagoons, and the lagoons percolate into the ground and recharge the aquifer. But this is water tainted with nitrates and unfit for human consumption. Needless to say, the dairy's presence on ground that once grew cotton and

San Joaquin River, dried up, near Red Top

sugar beets represents an intensification of agriculture. Plainly, there isn't enough water below the earth here to support such zeal.

I look for the telltale of subsidence. It is happening at a rate in Red Top not seen anywhere else in the world, but I can't discern it. The Vlots have spread sulfur pellets over the topsoil to break the bind between salts and clay. Unhooking the minerals will allow the Vlots to flush the freed alkali down past the root zone, where it can no longer harm their crops. Salt flushing takes a lot of water, too. Maybe this explains why the brothers, who as kids watched their father go bankrupt on the family's 125-cow dairy, are preparing the ground for a new cash crop. They've carved out the rows and ordered the pistachio trees. It is a move in the direction of diversification—and a crop that can tolerate the salt.

Twenty-five years ago, the two brothers drew up plans on a napkin to win back what their father had lost. Besides this dairy, they've built a ranch in nearby Chowchilla where they raise thirty thousand calves to sell to other dairymen. Then they built a second dairy in Smith Valley, Nevada, because who knows what the future of California agriculture is going to bring. The brothers and their wives have nine beautiful children between them, some of whom want to go into farming. Adding nuts to the mix makes napkin sense. Pistachios selling for three dollars a pound to the processor is a return that few crops can match.

But napkin sense doesn't always make community sense. The "tragedy of the commons" tells us that a shared resource—in this case, the aquifer—can withstand many things, but it cannot withstand each individual maximizing what is best for himself alone. The pursuit of a single farmer meets the pursuit of another single farmer until so many singular pursuits steal from everyone the very thing they are pursuing. Unregulated pumping in Red Top is no different from unregulated grazing on a shared pasture in the British Isles. The resource is finite. The greed isn't. During the next drought, the Vlots won't be able to fallow their pistachio ground the way they can fallow their alfalfa ground. The 200-horsepower motors will have to roar for as many years as a pistachio tree can produce a crop—and that's seventy-five years at least. The aquifer doesn't have that long. Red Top doesn't have that long. The pistachio tree is a sturdy customer with deep roots, but those roots are being forced into an earth that's not stable.

I walk over to the other side of the road where one of the world's largest winemakers, the Wine Group, has grabbed three thousand acres of cattle ranch and planted several varieties of grapes. Just to be clear, these aren't Napa Valley vines. These are hardworking industrial grapes that will be crushed and sent to fermentation tanks three stories tall to make cheaper wines. Over the past five years, the Wine Group has invested tens of millions of dollars to develop the ranch. The soil had to be deep ripped, leveled, bermed, fertilized and carpet-bombed with chemicals before a single fruit could be harvested. Converting cattle ground into vineyard requires tapping the aquifer to an extent it has never been tapped before. The failure of Madera County to keep track of how many wells have been dug here makes it difficult to put a magnitude on the extraction now taking place. Farmers in the irrigation district next door tell me that the Wine Group has bored dozens of newer and deeper wells over the past six years, and these wells draw straight from below the clay aquifer. Even though grapes don't require as much water as almonds, the jump in water use from the old cattle days is considerable.

As for subsidence, the farmers don't need a NASA satellite to tell them it is happening in dramatic fashion. Close by these three thousand acres is a natural gas well field that used to belong to Shell. The old gas pipes are anchored vertically into the earth thousands of feet below. For years, the pipes barely peeked out of the ground, their tops painted bright orange to keep tractor drivers from hitting them and triggering another explosion like the one in 1953. Today, after years of the company pumping water to make wine, the orange-topped metal pipes protrude a full two feet out of the ground, a yardstick of how much the earth has sunk in a few years' time.

"Those pipes are a marker that no one can deny," says Jack Fry, an eighty-nine-year-old almond and turkey farmer operating in the irrigation district next door. "Same with the pumps. If you drive around this area and check out the pumps, you'll see that many of them have broken free from the concrete base that holds them to the ground. They're a foot or two in the air. Because of the earth sinking, they've torn themselves loose." He is laughing when he tells me this, and I ask him why. "When I laugh, it's almost like I'm crying. I think about my father, who came to this land in 1918 from Iowa. He died when he was only sixty-three. He'd be laughing and crying, too."

Up ahead where the road dead-ends, a guard station looms. It is a strange bit of architecture for the farm belt, as if a military outpost or a Hollywood studio lay beyond and not almond and pistachio trees. Then again, twenty-one square miles of old rangeland planted end to end in nuts isn't exactly common in Red Top, either, so maybe John Hancock, the farmer in question, has good cause to check the IDs of the curious. The twelve-thousand-acre development, still young enough that the trees have yet to bear a full crop, might be seen by the locals as an epic poaching by East Coast moneymen whose returns are studiously tracked by a horde of faceless investors. But this land hasn't belonged to a local farmer for close to a century now, and for good reason. It's what they call "deep pockets" land. Before the agricultural hand of the John Hancock Life Insurance Company snatched it in 2010, the ground was grazed by Hereford cattle and lorded over by the oddest of ranchers, a short, nattily dressed professor named Grover Dean Turnbow. He had taught at the University of California, Davis, and was known in the academic world as "Mr. Ice Cream." When he wasn't judging college ice cream–making contests up and down the state, he was tinkering endlessly in his lab, bending cow's milk into shapes it had never attained, inventing a half dozen formulations in the 1920s and '30s that he filed with the U.S. Patent Office.

It was Turnbow who created powdered milk, or at least the version of it that tasted like real milk. The first formulations had a horrible burnt flavor. The heating process, akin to incineration, scalded the butterfat. In his search for a truer taste, the professor began with one basic notion: When he stuck his finger on a hot stove, his skin burned. But if he bothered to wet his finger, the molecules of moisture were enough to prevent a burn, at least for a second. He took a mister, filled it with milk and sprayed it through a column of superheated air. As the mist passed through the heat, it landed on the other side not only as milk powder but as powdered milk with the full flavor of butterfat. The conversion into mist had allowed the milk to sneak through the heat as if it wore a protective coating. Flash evaporation left the powder with no scald. The fat was free to remain fat.

His contortions of milk didn't stop there. He discovered a way to stabilize ice cream so it didn't melt on the trip from store to home. He made sherbet taste like the sherbet we know. He wrote the world's first textbook on ice cream, titled simply *Ice Cream,* and then left the university to run Golden State Dairy, the Oakland creamery with the famous gold miner logo that survived the Depression thanks to A. P. Giannini, whose Bank of Italy had become the Bank of America. Several decades later, as World War II ended, American soldiers stationed at U.S. bases across the Pacific grew tired of the insipid taste of the military's brand of powdered milk. Turnbow knew that cows didn't fare well in tropical climes, and countries like Japan had no room for them anyway. With a loan from Giannini, he founded International Dairy Supply and perfected one machine that removed water from milk and a second machine that mixed the water back in and recombined it with the fat. The finished product tasted like milk straight from a cow's teat.

He headed to Asia with enough powder, tanks and agitators to produce thousands of gallons of milk each day, plenty for the troops and plenty for the local villagers. The Japanese had known about cow's milk since the fifteenth century, when Christians had first tried pushing its virtues. But that milk didn't taste like Turnbow's milk. His formulation, it was said, caused peasant children to grow several inches taller than their parents. The emperor's bureaucrats took note and, lactose intolerance be damned, gave milk a place in the national nutrition program. In Thailand, condensed milk furnished by Turnbow led to the first Thai teas. As his International Dairy became a Fortune 500 company, he found himself a wealthy man entertaining an offer from Foremost Dairies to sell his operation for several million dollars.

And that was how Professor Grover Turnbow said good-bye to milk and came to Red Top in 1956 and founded the Triangle T Ranch on thirteen thousand acres once owned by cattle king Henry Miller. Naturally, the professor had done his studies, poring over maps of the land and its water. The Fresno River, a tributary of the San Joaquin, ran straight through the property. So did Ash Slough and Willow Slough. The big federal dam now on the San Joaquin River mostly kept the water from flowing onto his land. When the river did find its old self, floodwaters jumped the banks and filled the old creeks and sloughs, recharging the aquifer.

Every week, the professor made the two-hour trek to the Triangle T from his gorgeous home in the Piedmont Hills above the East Bay. His wife and grown children couldn't care less about his remaking of the ranch, how he had built up his herd of Hereford cattle to seventeen thousand head and bred a stable of quarter horses that became racing champions. Like Ray Flanagan before him, the professor awoke one day seized by a vision to turn rangeland into cropland. He drilled thirty wells, dug a couple hundred miles of ditches and began flooding the ground to drive the salts down into the soil. He planted six thousand acres of alfalfa and cotton as a way to further leach out the salts and left the rest as pasture for the cattle to graze on. Turnbow well knew that he was drawing down the water table, but the 1950s and '60s was a time of floods that saw the river give back a fair share of what he was taking. It helped, too, that the ditches crisscrossing Triangle T were leaking water back into the aquifer.

All this mattered to the professor because he liked to think of himself as a conservationist. A large berm crossed a section of his ranch, and on its far side were several hundred acres of unspoiled earth. The Spanish and their cows had never touched this land. Henry Miller had left it alone, too. The grasses and wildflowers were native; the birds and foxes and lizards were species that had disappeared from the rest of the

Great Central Valley. This was a piece of California in its original form, or very near to it. The professor told his ranchman that neither man nor cattle was to tread there. These acres were to become his version of a wildlife refuge where nothing but water would intrude and drain back into the earth.

The professor died in 1971 before he could convert the entire ranch to farm. His daughter Millie, a Stanford graduate who had married James Wickersham, another Stanford grad, was an accomplished painter and a member of the Piedmont Garden Club. A cattle rancher she cared not to be. The Wickershams did have an oldest son named Grover who was fascinated by his grandfather Grover's life and studied everything the professor had built. He went to law school, took a job as a branch chief for the U.S. Securities and Exchange Commission and became an adviser to a substantial hedge fund. After the death of his parents, he paid his sister and brother $33 million to buy out their shares of Grandpa's cattle ranch. Triangle T, and all the sinking around it, was now his to figure out.

Grover Wickersham is a big man in his late sixties who wears his gray hair long and his gray beard short and considers himself the smartest guy in any room, though not with airs that make him unlikable. He'll admit that he didn't know the first thing about row-crop farming. What he did have was a vision for the place: to finish the job his grandfather had started and maybe pass along his love of the ranch to his distracted son and turn him into a farmer. Wickersham decided to keep the old ranch house with its maid's quarters and library, and the four-hundred-acre farm and feedlot. He kept, too, the horses and stables, five thousand head of Black Angus, Jersey cows and heirloom pigs and the chickens with the baby blue eggs. As for the rest of Triangle T, Wickersham went about developing those 12,500 acres into a full-bore farm with the guidance of one of J. G. Boswell's finest cotton men: Mark Grewal, a.k.a. "the Wild Ass of the Desert."

With Grewal egging him on, Wickersham planted nine thousand acres of alfalfa, cotton and wheat and drilled ten new wells more than one thousand feet deep. The deep water under the clay layer had never been tapped. As soon as the well casing broke through it, the cork popped and water pressurized over the centuries shot up artesian-style.

Most wells initially draw water that's muddy. This water from the old flows of the river came out clear and pure. It boomed out at three thousand gallons a minute and filled up the ditch in no time. When Wickersham and Grewal gazed into the bottom of the ditch, it looked like the bottom of their swimming pools. They installed two dozen giant sprinklers that stood on stilts and were equipped with tires that rolled across the fields. With so much new land under till, the demand for irrigation shot up by a third from the old ranch days. The new Triangle T was using twenty-eight thousand acre-feet of water a year, enough to supply a city of fifty thousand people. "I was making four bales of cotton per acre out there," Grewal recalls without apology. "As you know, that's no joke."

Twelve thousand acres of almonds and pistachios is no joke, either. In 2010, Grover Wickersham sold Triangle T for $78 million. He got back all the money he had paid his siblings and then some. Like a good lawyer, he kept half the water rights that came with the river. He kept the house and its four hundred acres, a dozen Black Angus, the stables and horses and farm animals, too. The rest of Triangle T went to John Hancock. The insurance giant was making a bet that there was enough water left under the ground to grow nuts.

Hancock's men began to level the land and develop the orchards in a manner that Wickersham had never imagined. By the time I reach him, on a December day in 2016, Wickersham sits far away at his house in Portland, Oregon, but close enough to know every alteration Hancock has made to the Triangle T. He rages on the phone. "They took out all the ditches. They took out all the old valley oaks. They took out all the roads. They took out most of the water bank and recharge areas. They piped the whole ranch like it was a house in need of plumbing. Not a drop of that water will replenish the aquifer now. Then they took their tractors onto those four hundred and seventy acres that no one—not Henry Miller, not the Spanish—had messed with. And they nuked that pristine California land and the seven endangered species that lived there. It was fucking criminal. For what? So they could plant twelve thousand acres of almonds and pistachios wall to wall?"

The valley is littered with men who sold the family ranch to distant investors only to regret it for the rest of their days. If you find them on a particularly choleric day, they will go into great and bitter detail about how they sold the ranch too early or too late or to the wrong person or entity. "The Hancock buyer said they were going to be stewards of the land, and I believed him," Wickersham tells me. "I handed over my grandfather's ranch to these guys, and what they did to it just makes me sick to my stomach."

Hancock is naturally sensitive about its development of the ranch and the profound subsidence that has taken place in and around here. How much to blame on Wickersham and Grewal for dialing up the farming in the years they oversaw Triangle T? How much to blame on Hancock for cutting back on recharge even as the company plants every last acre with trees whose thirst will only grow? Hancock's director of corporate communications tells the *Sacramento Bee* that his company has installed "state of the art moisture monitoring and irrigation systems" that will reduce water use by 50 percent. "Water is a business expense," he points out. "We run as efficient an operation as possible and try to use only the water we need. It must be a long-term sustainable resource." The old-timers who've watched this land go from open cattle range to border-to-border farming over the past seventy years scoff at that. When John Hancock's trees hit peak maturity and start to demand the water it takes to make three thousand pounds of nuts an acre, sustainability won't be a factor in their calculations. To produce such yields for their investors, they'll be using more water than the professor and his grandson ever thought possible.

I am standing in the Central California Irrigation District a few miles down from Red Top where the canals, ditches and dams date back to the 1870s and Henry Miller's first capture of the San Joaquin River. Chris White, the district's longtime manager and historian, figures he's seen just about everything the river can give and take here. The system that conveys water to the district's 145,000 acres is now being sorely tested by subsidence. White is trying to persuade the big farmers to limit their groundwater extraction to no more than two hundred feet deep. By tapping only the shallow aquifer, they can avoid the worst of the sinking, he believes. It's not an easy sell, mostly because the shallow aquifer is nearly exhausted in so many places. He's hoping that when the next flood comes and sails down the ancient river channel known as the East Side Bypass, farmers might find a new way to tap into its flow. His idea is to siphon the floodwaters into an underground water bank that will allow farmers to recharge the shallow aquifer. Like Wickersham, he talks with passion about the project. But the last big flood to come through here was almost twenty years ago. And underground water banks aren't cheap to build or immune to a mining of their own.

"There's only one solution, really," Jack Fry, the almond and turkey farmer, says. "That's to stop pumping so much and take the poorer land out of production. But unless the government's forcing you, who's going to do that?" Not long ago, Fry watched one of his wells dry up because of drought and too much pumping by himself and his neighbors. And what did he do? He dug a new well eight hundred feet deep into the antique heart of old Ash Slough. The water flowed out at a beautiful twenty-six hundred gallons a minute. "I got three hundred acres of almonds that need to be irrigated," he says.

The road out of Red Top takes me straight across the East Side Bypass. When the next flood comes, the dry channel is designed to carry the deluge away from the farms and houses of Mendota and Firebaugh. It is supposed to shoot the water twenty miles north to rejoin the middle leg of the San Joaquin River as it pushes toward the delta.

Triangle T Ranch, an expanse of almonds, now farmed by John Hancock Insurance

Trouble is, certain sections of the bypass, plagued by subsidence, have sunk more than five feet. The drop in elevation has altered its pitch and pinched down its capacity by a quarter. The bypass isn't a ditch that has lost the momentum of gravity to carry irrigation flows to farmers. It is a bulwark flanked by levees that has lost the ability to hold back floodwater traveling at a speed of sixteen thousand cubic feet per second. The falling and rising and narrowing of the bypass is not about to be fixed anytime soon. I ask Chris White what the next flood is likely to bring, besides much-needed recharge.

"The channel is five feet lower right there in the middle, and it's going to create a waterfall that will speed up the velocity and carry more debris down the bypass. It will scour in one part and clog with debris in another part." He then describes the water as it roars past the bridge where I am standing. "You're going to see two to three thousand cubic feet of water per second coming over that bridge. The school is right there. The dairy is right there. The cotton gin is right there. The Red Top Market and Café is right there. Highway 152 is right there. . . . It will be a disaster."

Five

UPON DRY LAND

On a late fall afternoon in the fourth year of drought, I turn my car in the opposite direction and roll south to Kern County. For months now, in small-town coffee shops where the growers sit around to commiserate about the dry times and the wet times, I've been picking up stories of big guys stealing water from little guys. Powerful growers in the Panoche Water District, on the west side of Fresno County, are conspiring with the manager to rustle water out of the aqueduct late at night when no one's looking. Two ditch tenders got drunk at a bar in Los Banos and gave away the details. Agents from the FBI and the state of California, who've been working the case for more than a year, confirm the scheme. Whether the purloined federal water was five thousand acre-feet or fifty thousand acre-feet, they're still not sure. In Madera County, one of the biggest almond growers in the state—a leader of the Mormon Church who is known for his charitable giving—is illegally siphoning water out of the main canal. He'll plead "no contest" and pay the local irrigation district eighty thousand dollars in restitution, which is what fifteen million gallons of pirated water can fetch on the drought exchange.

Now come whispers of a plot involving the richest farmer in America, Stewart Resnick, king of the pistachio, almond, mandarin and pomegranate. He's so short of water, I hear, that he's teamed up with a farmer two counties away to pump groundwater from one of the most depleted aquifers in the state and send it by ditch and pipeline to his trees on the dry slope of western Kern. This would be a violation of local ordinances prohibiting groundwater from being shipped from one basin to another, and it may be a breaking of state code, too. Inside a landscape this vast and webbed with ditches, it's almost impossible to ferret out any water that's flowing where it shouldn't be flowing. The man in the Greek restaurant in Bakersfield who passed along the Resnick rumor didn't know the location of the wells or canals used in the grab. The best he could tell me was the water is moving from Pixley to a spot near Blackwell's Corner, the last stop James Dean made before he crashed his Porsche on Highway 46 sixty years ago. That's a fifty-mile stretch of farmland, I replied. What ditch along the way wouldn't be moving water?

I drive in the direction of a giant cardboard cutout of Dean. He's standing eighteen feet tall and wearing blue jeans and a white T-shirt, his perfect hair swept back. He's pointing his finger to the rest stop at Blackwell's. Inside the gift shop and diner, where they make a special "East of Eden" fudge, the proprietor has erected a museum exhibit of the Okie migration to California that delivered us Merle Haggard, Buck Owens and the Okie nose blow. As to the latter, there is no tissue required, just a thumb pressed to one plugged nostril at a time. The exhibit's centerpiece is a Model A pickup, circa 1930, with an old gas-powered Maytag washing machine hitched to the back. "This is how they came to California all through the thirties, forties and fifties," proprietor Kossie Dethloff, who migrated from Texas in 1962, tells me. He traces the history of western Kern back to a man named George Blackwell who bought a piece of land here in the early 1900s and then was jailed on income tax evasion before getting himself killed on a motorcycle.

I ask him if he's ever heard about the five Lazard brothers who arrived long before Blackwell, when this chunk of western Kern was nothing but desert. He says their story isn't familiar to him. The Lazards came to California in 1849 lugging a different idea, I tell him. Finding themselves among tens of thousands of argonauts lured west by the gold rush, the brothers didn't grab the nearest donkeys and head into the hills. They were dry goods salesmen. By 1851, their White House Department Store in San Francisco was stocking more items and doing a brisker trade than any other dry goods store on the West Coast. They opened a bank in the city and then added branches in London, Paris and New York. Brothers Alexandre, Maurice, Elie, Simon and Lazare were soon joined by cousin Alexandre Weill, a financial wunderkind, and they became the first transporters of gold between the United States and Europe.

No bank profited more handsomely from the Civil War than the House of Lazard. As the North and South kept printing greenbacks that became more and more worthless, the Lazard banks stockpiled gold and used their liquidity to make loans at ever-higher interest rates. At the close of the nineteenth century, the brothers owned eight hundred thousand acres of open land in California and the Oregon Territory. More than twenty-five thousand acres, one contiguous chunk, sat on the far western flank of Kern County. This was the land that the Lazards, horrified by the slaughter of their fellow Jews back in Russia, tried to turn into a refuge for those who had escaped. They surveyed and leveled the land. They dug hole after hole in the sandy soil, searching for water. Most of the holes came up dry. Others coughed up black water so high in salts that it was unsuitable for irrigation. Needless to say, their dream of a Hebrew kingdom rising twenty miles west of Lost Hills died aborning.

The Lazards might have saved themselves the trouble had they read the studies from 1878 by Eugene Hilgard, the University of California soil scientist who found that vast stretches of western Kern were too charged with boron to sustain crops or cities. The water, if it could even be found, was "fatal" to grain and vegetables, and no telling what it might do to humans. Then again, Hilgard's own UC agricultural station spent the next century disregarding his warning, enticing farmers to plant cotton in the same unfit ground. By 1920, the growers in Kern were drawing up irrigation districts with no mind to how good or poor the soil was. The growers figured that the bigger they carved out their districts, the more water they could demand from the Kern River and, eventually, whatever government water project got built. Soil experts hired by the state directed the growers to remove thousands of acres of alkali land from inside their boundary lines. That ground didn't rate even rainwater. The growers tried appealing to the state engineer, but he, too, wouldn't budge. He told the farmers that their districts needed to be redrawn in the rational manner the soil experts saw fit.

The worst of the black alkali land—salty and boggy at once—was excluded from the district boundary lines. So were thousands of acres deemed suitable only for livestock grazing. Being patient men, the growers waited for the state engineer to retire. When the districts were being drawn up again in the 1940s, '50s and '60s—to receive flows first from the Central Valley Project and then from the State Water Project—the sons of the desert threw the junk acres back in, and then some. Governor Pat Brown, who believed bigger was better, wasn't about to tell them no. Extending agriculture's footprint onto inferior land has never been regarded as a problem here. Not before the building of the federal and state projects, and certainly not since.

Looking for the artifacts of Kern's gung ho spirit, I came across the September 3, 1951, issue of *Life* magazine, the one featuring the fiery beauty of actress Gina Lollobrigida on the cover. The editors had sent a photographer named Loomis Dean to the San Joaquin Valley to do an essay on the "Shirtsleeve Millionaires" of the soil. Besides their noble sweat, the magazine wondered, what accounted for their wealth? The answer, no surprise, was the deep turbine pump developed by the Harnish brothers of the Peerless Pump Company. Its advent had allowed the farmers to reach as far as twenty-five hundred feet into the earth to lift water to irrigate their crops. "The newest crop of the San Joaquin is the sum of all the others. It is millionaires, dozens of new millionaires," the magazine declared. "They work as industriously as when they began—only now they roam their ranches in Cadillacs and hop from farm to farm, or to the seaside, in private planes."

The shirtsleeve millionaires included Luca Luisi, the smiling grape grower from Italy who stood in his sweaty cotton shirt and wrinkled baggy pants in front of the National Bank of Orosi, which he now owned. And the rugged Rudnicks, four cowboy sons and their cowboy father, Oscar, an immigrant from Russia who sold buttons in New York City and wound up in Bakersfield, where he owned fifteen thousand acres of grazing land, sixty thousand cattle and one hundred thousand sheep. And grape grower Dutch Leonard, who was able to sit in any room of his specially wired house and enjoy concerts from his insane collection of five hundred thousand record albums. And John Lachenmaier, a potato grower who spent half the year hunting big game around the world and the other half in Shafter, where his fellow millionaires poked fun at him for being the only man on the block who didn't own a Cadillac. And Ed Peters, the Mennonite potato king, who held a Bible breakfast every Tuesday for his laborers at the Grange hall in Wasco.

"I thank all the hands for their help this year," he said in prayer. "The potatoes have closed and the price was high. I hope we all hold together as a big family so we can ride through the cotton harvest as successfully as we did this one. Amen."

Here we are sixty-three years later and maybe one of their progeny is farming the fields. Had *Life* done a follow-up story just a decade later, more than one of the shirtsleeve millionaires would have been found flat broke. The sons of the sons of the Kern desert—those who remain in farming today—wouldn't think to trace their water woes to the expansion of hundreds of thousands of acres of marginal scrubland. Not when they continue to plant nut trees on ground better left to cattle and sheep. Not when it's easier to blame a couple species of fish for the fact that the federal and state projects can no longer deliver on their promise of "full" water. From the conception of the irrigation districts onward, the ambition of Kern farmers has exceeded the reach of the water, even as the water has been made to reach from one end of the state to the other. First the farmers grew beyond their own river, the Kern. Then they grew beyond what even their Peerless pumps could extract from the aquifer. Now they've grown beyond what the state project on the west side and the federal project on the east side, pinched by drought and the needs of rivers and fish, can reliably furnish.

Of the nine hundred thousand acres of crops grown across Kern, nearly half are no longer sustainable. The two sides of Kern don't see their world of scarcity the same. The west side farmer who drinks from the state project thinks his draw of the water is more righteous. No farmland existed on the west side before the state of California in the 1960s made a concrete river here. The desert dirt blossomed in the purest expression of reclamation. The east side farmer who drinks from the older federal project thinks the water is meant for him. He didn't need government to create his farm. His guile and ingenuity took it right from the ground. His forebears began tilling the east side soil in the 1850s. Only when he had proved his mettle did the government decide, nearly a century later, that the east side farmer deserved even more water. The faraway San Joaquin River was then dammed in his name.

One righteousness or the other, they're both dry now.

"Can you imagine an Israel right here? Forty square miles. Twice the size of Manhattan Island," the cowboy says. "Today it's the Berrenda Mesa Water District. And they're still punching holes in the ground looking for water."

I'm sitting in the cab of a four-by-four Super Duty Ford truck, listening to Keith Grant trace the history of western Kern back to the 1860s. That's when his grandfather, a Scottish sheepman, came to California and picked up grazing land in the hills beyond Lost Hills dirt cheap. It was dirt cheap for the same reason that no Jews could be resettled here: water. Grant's grandfather did come upon a black goop oozing out of the earth, but who knew what to do with it back then. "My parents bought a house a mile from the Kern County line in a place called Bitterwater Valley. They ran sheep up and down this hillside. My dad was fifty-three years old when I was born. And his dad was an old man, too, when he was born. That's how I can reach back to the 1860s in just two generations." We had met a few weeks earlier when I stopped at a Mexican restaurant on Highway 46 for a bean burrito and spotted Grant sitting alone and struck up a conversation. He had returned to a cowboy life after teaching math and science for thirty years at Wasco High. As we left, he gave me his cell number and said to call him the next time I came through. He'd be happy to give me a tour of western Kern. Not the orchards of fruit and nut but the open rangeland on the other side of the line.

Now he's powering his monster truck up a grade to where the hills are shale and the ocean, aeons ago, wore away at the rock. When he was young, the ranch kids would go hunting up here for remnants of the sea. They'd collect clamshells, sharks teeth and sand dollars. "If they're right about global warming, this might be lakefront property again someday," he says tongue in cheek. He's a handsome man in his early eighties with blazing blue eyes and a face crinkled kindly by the sun. He's wearing Wrangler jeans, a Wrangler shirt and a Silver Belly cowboy hat that a friend gave him twenty-five years ago. His Roper boots are still wet after a morning of moving water from tank to trough to feed his one hundred cows. We cross the big aqueduct at one of its highest points, dividing the hillside into haves and have-nots. "Before the water came down the concrete, the only ones who could make a living off this land were the sheepmen and the cattlemen. This was all salt

Keith Grant in western Kern where the farm gives way to open range

brush and tumbleweeds. In a good rain year, you could put six thousand steers out here and fatten them up," he tells me.

From Cholame to McKittrick, forty miles of skyline, the entire rolling hillside was "squatters' country" back then. Basque sheepmen and American cattlemen engaged in a free-for-all. Young men would arrive from the Pyrenees to tend to flocks of sheep and marry Basque-American spinsters for the paper. Then a big cattle-and-sheep family from Germany, the Twisselmans, bought a huge chunk of the hillside. "They were good livestock people. They had their headquarters next to us in Bitterwater Valley. They bought the skyline." In rainy years, the Russian thistle and Mexican filaree ran up the hill and was as good a feed as alfalfa. The Twisselmans hauled in fresh water, and their cows and sheep got through spring fat and ready for slaughter. Some years, like 1948, when the sky dried up and the wind wouldn't stop blowing, it was hard for even the Twisselmans to make a go of it. Then the duster would turn into rain, and every shepherd and cowboy would be happy again. In his heyday, rancher Ernest Still had twenty-five thousand acres on the hillside where he fed his cattle. A Lebanese millionaire later bought a chunk of it, tried to grow apples and went bust. The Dinsdales, owners of the Bank of Colorado, still graze thousands of head of cattle on their own twenty-five-thousand-acre spread.

"This is some of the best rangeland in the state in a wet or normal year," Grant says. "There's a Mexican man who dry-farms up here and hits a crop of grain every now and then when it rains. But other than that, as you can see, the line between the farm and the range couldn't be more stark."

Green orchard to the left, salt brush and blue belly lizards to the right: the line is made firm by the aqueduct's reach. Where the land heaves and orchards hug the hillsides, the imported water is able to extend to the trees because of the stretch of drip irrigation. The farmer loves to trot out drip as Exhibit A in his efforts to conserve water and help California get through its drought years. The thin black plastic lines can run atop the ground or beneath it and are punctured every several feet by emitters that let out small but steady doses of water for hours at a time. Compared to drip, old-style furrow irrigation—flooding wide rows and letting the water soak into the ground—is made to look like a thief on par with the cattle rustler. But with all its flow, furrow irrigation actually helps replenish the aquifer. The paradox of drip is that for all its precision, it does not save water in the aggregate. Because a drip line can reach anywhere, hundreds of thousands of acres in California—land on hillsides, land with rocks the size of baseballs, land with impenetrable clays and impervious salts—have come under cultivation.

"You couldn't farm this hillside without drip," Grant says. "Furrow irrigation would never be able to work its way up the slope."

"Drip, drip, drip. It's all I hear from farmers and environmentalists," I say. "It's the one thing they agree on. But when you catch the farmer in his bragging moment, he'll tell you he's big on drip because it increases his yields by thirty percent."

Drip irrigation is hardly the first inducement that has taken the farmer beyond river's reach to plant crops in places where crops don't belong. Before drip, the California Aqueduct had already planted the notion that as long as water could go everywhere, the orchards and fields could go everywhere, too. The road that winds in front of us bends a little to accommodate the aqueduct as it banks the hillside on its way to deliver 1.1 million acre-feet of water to the farmers of Kern and 2 million acre-feet to the faucets of Southern California. But in those early years after the State Water Project was completed, in 1968, the flow came upon Kern in such abundance that the farmers didn't know what to do with all of it. For the first dozen years of the state project, the Metropolitan Water District of Los Angeles took nowhere near its full allotment from the delta. With its draw of Colorado River water to supplement what it was siphoning from the Owens Valley, L.A. had plenty of water to grow its suburbs.

This unleashed hundreds of thousands of acre-feet of state water—practically free for the taking—for the cotton, barley and wheat fields of western Kern. Some of this land was the third-rate stuff that the state engineer, back in the late 1920s, had refused to include in the districts. The farmers believed they had reclaimed the alkali and hardpan by adding thirty tons per acre of gypsum and other amendments over decades. The soil deserved the water that Los Angeles couldn't take. "In the 1970s and the '80s, the farmers here were just smoking," Grant says, pointing from the seat of his truck. "When they first broke this ground down, all of it was farmed. But this is tough earth. You can see the alkali bubbled up on the side. It is now back to tumbleweed and salt grass. The sign says, 'CONGRESS INDUCED DROUGHT,' but that's not why. This ground returned to dry long before the recent environmental restrictions."

The farmer is trapped, I tell Grant. He's giving himself no room to maneuver out of drought. In the nearly half century of the State Water Project, the share of permanent crops across Kern County has jumped from 19 percent of the farmland to 60 percent. In the four water districts of western Kern alone, where Stewart Resnick, Marko Zaninovich, Freddy Franzia and the Assemi brothers are dug in, the permanent cropland has tripled to 150,000 acres. Cotton used to cover more than 100,000 acres out here. On this day, Grant and I can't find a single boll. He has no idea how the big growers are keeping their orchards and vineyards alive in the worst of the drought when the aqueduct has flat stopped making its deliveries. He hasn't heard the rumors of a secret supply of water being shunted here in the still of night from two counties away to keep Resnick's kingdom afloat.

"I don't pretend to know what goes on in the head of a big nut grower," he says. "I'm just a cow man. I'm always out here looking for an extra blade of grass. That's my search. Cattle aren't anywhere near as lucrative as these pistachios. But the thing about cattle is it takes that tumbleweed right there and starts chewing on it because it knows it's filled with beneficial oils and nineteen percent protein, which is as good as alfalfa. You have to admit a cow is a wonderful thing. To eat something like a tumbleweed and make a wholesome food out of that. Now, that's an invention."

I picture another cow, the water it consumes, the hillside it denudes, the air it fouls, but I keep my mouth shut. "So it's desert scrub you thank when you're tearing into a juicy porterhouse?" I ask.

"This ain't desert, Mark. This ain't scrub. This is cattlegrass," he chuckles.

Once upon a time in California, droughts created dams. Then they created low-flow toilets. The drought of 1987–92 delivered a concept between a dam to fill and an eco-friendly toilet to sit on and have to flush two times. This concept was called a water exchange. Farmers and cities looking to buy and sell allotments of state and federal water suddenly had a market. Within a few years, no one wielded a bigger stockpile of public water turned private water—water to use, water to sell—than Stewart Resnick and his Paramount Farming Company. He had gained ownership of California's largest water bank, a project jump-started with $74 million in taxpayer money, after a series of secret negotiations between state officials and water contractors. For years, the growers of western Kern had coveted a water bank, an empty space in the aquifer with enough room to park a lake's worth of water and enough soundness to keep it from migrating to another basin. As it so happened, the California Department of Water Resources had acquired a twenty-thousand-acre stretch of old cotton land where the Kern River meets the aqueduct. Looking to add to the state's supply, the department planted some wells and pipes but never stored enough water there to actually create a bank. Geologically speaking, the ground was a wonder. Flat, porous and stingy, it drank and drank and held on to what it drank. The hydraulics were simple: Capture the water that flowed down the river and the aqueduct in wet times and let it percolate deep into the sandy ground so that it could be pumped out in dry times. Send in a flood every five years and the bank could store nearly one million acre-feet of water. Like a dam, only beneath the earth, it tempered our tantrums with magic.

Back in the winter of 2003, I had met up with a young, ponytailed muckraker named John Gibler who was working for Public Citizen, a nonprofit that aimed to expose the state's giveaway of the Kern Water Bank. No journalist had written a word about Resnick's rise as a giant of agriculture, how his grab of the water bank had enabled him to plant millions of trees on ground that had no groundwater. Over a beer in my kitchen, Gibler began to riff: "The water bank was designed by the state. It was supposed to act as a safeguard against drought. But it's being used by Paramount and other mega-farms to grow even bigger." The plutocrats of the loam were so flush with water in Kern County that they were selling some of their imported state supply, at least on paper, to builders of new towns and golf courses in Los Angeles and the Bay Area, he said. "A public resource, the people's water, has been privatized by and for the wealthiest."

Gibler was small, slight and fearless, a leftist not in the mold of my dreamy grandfather but one who believed that the world's inequality allowed for only so much mirth. The plantations of agriculture in the valley needed to be broken up, he argued, and the government's regulation of water was the best avenue to do it. There was no louder exhibit of the subverting of the people's water than Resnick's empire. You didn't have to be a leftist to see that the San Joaquin Valley had veered so far off course from the Jeffersonian ideal of yeoman farmer that it had come to resemble a banana republic. Where Gibler and I parted ways was over the question of inevitability. I happened to think that the valley had been doomed from the get-go by its compulsion to intensify farmland, and it was a life's work to write about the doom. Gibler's pen was an activist's pen.

We joined up forces and began digging—me for the *Los Angeles Times* and Gibler for a Public Citizen report titled "Water Heist." Grabbing the water bank, I discovered, had been a brilliant move initiated by William D. Phillimore, Resnick's right hand at Paramount. Phillimore, naturally, denied playing any role. He pointed out that he hadn't even been in Monterey in December 1994 when the amendments to the State Water Project were spelled out in a hotel room far from the public eye. "The backroom fable, smoke-filled and all, seems to make pretty press," he said. "But we got lucky to get the water bank and worked hard to make it a success."

Most everyone in that room—head honchos from the Metropolitan

Water District of Los Angeles, the Kern County Water Agency, the state Department of Water Resources, the J. G. Boswell Company—recalled Phillimore as a constant behind-the-scenes presence in the negotiations. It was Phillimore who plotted with Tom Clark, general manager of the Kern County Water Agency, to find a way to take more water from the state and bring it home to the farmers of Kern. And it was Phillimore who insisted that a change had to be made to a state law that was forcing Kern County to suffer a disproportionate share of state water cuts during droughts.

This is not to say that Clark played the role of errand boy for Paramount Farming. Five foot seven and balding, a smoker with a perfect potbelly who loved cheeseburgers and pizza, he walked into the room believing that Kern County was getting screwed. Growers were having to idle their land during drought while watching all that water pass by on its way to L.A. If urban contractors didn't agree to share some of that water in times of historic scarcity, Clark had no choice but to bring down a lawsuit of such heft that it would engulf the State Water Project in a civil war. "You're messing with a bunch of junkyard dogs down here," he told the state bureaucrats. "You don't take water from us and not feel the bite."

Clark wasn't above playing the hayseed from Bakersfield whose Okie twang got twangier in the heat of horse-trading. Before one meeting, he stopped off at a grocery store and bought a dozen pacifiers that he kept in a bag until the urban water district directors started whining. "Here, suck on this," he told them, passing out the binkies. On his way back from Los Angeles, he visited a store in Hollywood that sold movie props and filled his bag with Old West pistols. For the next meeting, the boys from L.A. had to drive up and over the Tehachapi Mountains to his office, which put them in a foul mood. He pulled out a half dozen guns and set them down on the Kern County side of the table. "Boys, you're in Bakersfield now," he said. Even the stiff from the Department of Water Resources cracked up. "Tom's greatest skill was his ability to read people," one of his assistants at the water agency recalled. "He wasn't afraid of getting into you. But when he challenged you, it was always with humor first. His stunts totally disarmed them."

Clark walked out of the Monterey Plaza Hotel on December 1, 1994, with every concession he'd been looking for—and even more. In times of drought, the first cuts in state water would no longer be borne by Kern County farmers alone. The water bank and its capacity to store 1 million acre-feet of surplus water now belonged to Resnick and other local growers. As if that wasn't enough, the state would do all it could to encourage water sales from farmer to farmer and farm to city, a big first step toward deregulation and privatization. Water was now truly a liquid asset, a commodity to be bought and sold like lean hog futures. In return for such gifts, Kern County would have to let go of 45,000 acre-feet of state contracted water. To the outsider, this sounded like a lot to pony up. Clark, though, knew this wasn't real water he was relinquishing but paper water that was never coming to Kern County anyway. The system had been built with the intention of delivering 4.1 million acre-feet of water to farms and cities, but most years, California didn't have enough water to make good on this promise. Instead, the state delivered close to 3 million acre-feet, which was just fine with valley farmers and L.A. developers. The 45,000 acre-feet that Kern was "giving up" came out of the mythical 4.1 million acre-feet.

Nine years after that deal was struck, it didn't take a lot of digging for Gibler and me to uncover the documents that spelled out the true owners of the Kern Water Bank: Westside Mutual, a subsidiary of Paramount Farming, owned the largest share, at 48 percent. Another 10 percent share was owned by the Dudley Ridge Water District, whose board president was Joseph C. MacIlvaine, the president of Paramount. Add the two together and Resnick controlled nearly 60 percent of the water in the bank. In a good year, when the bank extracted 250,000 acre-feet of water for its growers, 150,000 acre-feet went to Paramount alone. It was this water, along with Resnick's yearly allotments from the State Water Project, that kept his fruit and nut trees from ever knowing thirst. Paramount Farming was damn near drought-proof.

"He's got some five million almond trees planted in the desert," Gibler said. "Most of the water has gone to create a nut empire."

It was December 2003, and the time had come to reach out to Resnick himself. I dialed the number to Roll International, his Los Angeles–based holding company, and asked for the public relations department.

"We don't have a public relations department," the secretary said. "Who are you with?"

"The *L.A. Times*. I'm doing a story on the Kern Water Bank. Might I talk to Mr. Resnick or maybe one of the managers at Paramount Farming?"

"We don't talk to the press. Good-bye." The phone went *click*.

I drove to Paramount's headquarters in Shafter, a small farm town on the north side of Kern County, and talked my way into the office of Scott Hamilton, Paramount's resource planning manager. He was a tall guy in his forties whose Australian accent made his certainty sound even more assured. "At the time we took over the water bank, it was the biggest white elephant boondoggle that the Department of Water Resources had ever wasted its money on," he said. "There were no recharge ponds, no new wells. We spent $30 million on infrastructure. It's the locals here who built the water bank." A day later, back in my office, I got a call from Phillimore. "The water bank, as it currently exists, is an asset for the entire state," he told me. He was an Aussie, too, or maybe a Brit, and he didn't mind making a show of his contempt for lesser beings. "The problem with these water deals is they are very convoluted and very complicated. Anyone advancing the argument that the benefits are going to one grower hasn't done his homework."

He left it there until the story was published. And then for the next six months he sent letter after letter to my editors, each one demanding the same retraction. "Paramount Farming Co. does not control the Water Bank," he wrote. "To the contrary, the Water Bank is controlled by a joint powers authority." He kept citing the legal structure of the authority as proof that I had made a mistake. But it was the shell of the authority—a front for Resnick—that the story had unmasked. My editor faxed him copies of the joint powers agreement, showing that the joint powers included Paramount's Westside Mutual and Dudley Ridge. Together, they owned 58 percent of the shares in the water bank. Was 58 percent not a majority interest? He wrote back perplexed. "I remain astounded that the *Los Angeles Times* prints articles so full of errors. I feel sorry for the declining standards of what was once a respectable paper. There is little more I can say." As his letters continued to say more, our reader rep began to refer to him as "He Whose Name We Shall Not Utter."

In the late 1960s, more than a half century after the last of the Lazard brothers had died, the men running the House of Lazard thought they'd give farming a shot in western Kern. In the Berrenda Mesa Water District outside Lost Hills, they formed a company called Blackwell, named after the general store on Highway 46 where James Dean made his last stop. They teamed up with farm advisers from the University of California to see if grapes, almonds and pistachios might take in the desert earth. Their seventy-acre test plot produced enough fiber, fruits and nuts that they decided to plant five thousand acres of cotton, three thousand acres of wine grapes, four thousand acres of almonds and thirty-five hundred acres of pistachios. The water was cheap and delivered to their doorstep by the California Aqueduct. The Lazard manager out of New York bought a beautiful home at the most exclusive country club in Bakersfield and waited on the nineteenth hole for the profits to roll in. A freeze on October 29, 1970, turned the cotton black. Then Gallo Winery, exercising its monopoly, squeezed Blackwell on its grape contract. Then the market for almonds, which cost $1.30 a pound to grow, sank to 65¢ a pound.

"My brother Ron was running the whole show for Blackwell," Luther Khachigian, a legendary nurseryman in the valley, recalls. "I sold them a lot of the vines. Everything was done first-class. They built houses for their workers and an airstrip for their executives. They had a brand-new dehydrator and almond- and pistachio-processing plants. And then bad luck shook the hand of bad luck, and it all went to hell. They lost six million dollars in one year alone."

Then the drought of 1987–92 struck. The worst of that dry, the year 1991, found the State Water Project, for the first time, delivering only a trickle of water to Kern County. With no groundwater as backup, Blackwell's trees and vines and row crops went thirsty. That was the year the House of Lazard decided that the parched conditions of western Kern had vexed it for the last time. The company sold its pistachio orchards to Resnick for next to nothing. The almond orchards ended up in the hands of a Silicon Valley investor named John Vidovich. The grapes withered on the vines. All that was left to unload was Blackwell's draw of state water. The men in New York had no compunction about selling their permanent water supply to real estate developers. The state of California approved the multimillion-dollar sale without a prick of guilt.

Luther is still irked by the water sale. He knows that western Kern is a gamble. With no water in the ground, drought comes and the farmer has nowhere to turn. But using the state's vast network of plumbing to trade crops in Lost Hills for golf courses in Palm Springs is what Luther, a grape farmer's son, considers a mortal sin. "That water didn't belong to Blackwell. The right to use it had been given to them by the people of California so that crops could be grown in the valley. It should have gone to other farmers."

I tell Luther that the Blackwell water sale was only the first of many transfers out of western Kern. I have a buddy named Roger Sanders who grew cotton in the Wheeler Ridge–Maricopa water district for thirty years. His father and grandfather had been cotton growers on the same slope. The yo-yo price of cotton each year was Roger's Las Vegas. Up or down, he felt he was alive. Then one day his wife told him she couldn't live that way anymore. To save his marriage, Roger sold his draw from the State Water Project for a couple million dollars to the developers of Newhall Ranch. Roger's water is one of the reasons Newhall got a green light to build the largest subdivision in L.A. County history. Roger bought a vacation house in Santa Barbara and is looking for another one in Bangor, Maine. He couldn't be more happy and more miserable—that's how much he misses his cotton.

"Resnick himself has sold a lot of his state water to cities," I tell Luther. "Tejon Ranch, for one, is drawing up plans for houses, shopping malls and golf courses based on water he's sold them. Tens of thousands of acre-feet for tens of millions of dollars."

"That's right," Luther says. "And it's those water sales that are now biting Resnick in the ass. He got cocky. Now it's drought. How's he going to water his trees?"

I'm standing inside Luigi's restaurant in Bakersfield staring at decades of framed black-and-white photos of the town's high school football stars, including Hall of Famer Frank Gifford, an Okie kid like the rest whose jaw was just a bit squarer and hips a little shiftier. The Drillers (this is an oil town as much as a farm town) have won more section championships on the gridiron than any other high school in the state, not to mention graduating a clarinet player from the marching band named Earl Warren who went on to become governor of California before he served as chief justice of the U.S. Supreme Court. Luigi's lunch crowd, far more beautiful than what I'm accustomed to seeing in other valley towns, is lined up out the door waiting for tables. Because I'm here with Gary Bucher, who made some of the men in this room wealthy during his years as Tom Clark's right hand at the Kern County Water Agency, we're seated in no time. Over bowls of minestrone and a half loaf of Basque sourdough, he recalls in a raspy smoker's voice the delirious days of the 1970s, when agriculture grew to be even bigger than oil—and stayed that way.

"The early deliveries from the State Water Project were way beyond what we expected. Because L.A. didn't need it, we were taking as much surplus water as our contract water," he tells me. "The beautiful thing about the surplus water was it didn't come all at once, like floodwater. We could schedule its delivery to the day, even in the summer months when our farmers needed it the most. And it was essentially free water."

By 1975, hooked on that extra water, the farmers of western Kern had planted 130,000 acres of cotton and grain on land that had been desert only five years before. No one from the state of California, and surely no one in Bakersfield, bothered with the complication that agriculture was expanding in a way that could not be sustained. Much of the farmland in western Kern was on salty soil with no underlying groundwater. And Los Angeles would eventually be taking its full share of the water to turn its own desert into more houses. But the early availability of state water established a pattern in western Kern that has held to this day. The farmers don't plant to the real. They plant to the ideal. They don't plant to the constraints of weather, water and soil. They plant to a fancy.

It pains Bucher, who's retired to a life of golf and toy train sets, to admit that farmers in western Kern got too big for their britches because of the inducement of surplus water. Tens of thousands of acres had to be fallowed when that extra water was finally sent over the mountain to its rightful owner. As the historic drought of 1976–77 struck—and Kern County saw its one million acre-feet of state water cut by more than half—the farmers were forced to idle tens of thousands of additional acres.

Had western Kern been flush with groundwater, you can bet that not a single acre would have been fallowed. Consider how farmers in the parts of Kern County that are flush with groundwater kept digging deeper wells and installing more powerful pumps to pull themselves through drought. In 1976 and 1977, they pumped an astonishing 3.4 million acre-feet out of the ground. Over the past half century, even with the generally steady flows of the Central Valley Project and State Water Project, Kern farmers have mined 60 million acre-feet from the aquifer to outrun drought and fuel their boom. This is enough water to slake the thirst of Los Angeles for one hundred years.

"The locals would like to believe that all that pumping is a consequence of drought," Bucher says. "But it's growth."

In a big wet year, Kern County is able to call on 3.1 million acre-feet from its three sources: the Kern River, the Central Valley Project and the State Water Project. Yet the water needed each year by the farms and cities of Kern County amounts to some 3.5 million acre-feet. So even in a wet year, agriculture in Kern has to suck nearly a half million acre-feet out of the ground to grow its crops. All that pumping requires deep pockets. The smaller farmer who can't afford to keep chasing groundwater falls by the wayside. The big guy who can chase his groundwater all the way to hell keeps getting bigger. Water isn't the equalizer that the state and federal projects promised. Water is the means by which the valley has become one of the most unequal places on earth.

Like the paradox of drip, I tell Bucher, there's the paradox of the System. Each irrigation project was designed to reduce reliance on groundwater and keep the best farmland in production through cycles of drought and flood. But both projects have unleashed a tail-chasing growth in Kern County that has subverted their original purpose. Never have Kern farmers been more reliant on groundwater than they are today. And never have they more drunkenly flouted the swings between drought and flood to intensify their use of the land. This intensification of cropland requires that ever more water be put to earth to perpetuate production. It also means that when trees and vines are expanding onto inferior ground, water is being taken from the best soils to feed the poorest ones.

From the mid-1970s to the early 1990s, from one epic drought to another, farmers in Kern County increased their plantings of almonds by 50 percent, their plantings of pistachios by 100 percent and their plantings of citrus by 70 percent. They grew so many carrots that they invented a baby carrot—not a real miniature but a regular carrot cut into bite-sized pieces—to get rid of their excess crop. Who knew the baby carrot would turn vegetables into a snack? Kern farmers then planted thousands of acres of cherry trees, even though cherries had no business growing in ground this far south. When the trees couldn't grab enough chilling hours to produce a big enough crop, the farmers started pouring on a harsh agent, hydrogen cyanamide, which made the trees believe they had been dormant all winter. They tricked the trees into throwing off cherries that ripened before all the other cherries on the West Coast. With those prices, what did it matter that trees doused in hydrogen cyanamide lived only half a life? As for water, Kern farmers learned not a whit from those earlier droughts, unless you count the lesson of planting more fruits and nuts that need more water until the next drought comes soon enough. The farmers saw no reason to pause, even in the wake of federal court decisions that gave more water to delta fish and effectively cut agriculture's supply, in the best years, by a fifth. So it's no surprise that they're responding to this drought of droughts with the same donkey logic.

Since the latest hot and dry arrived in 2012, farmers in Kern—and the investment groups, hedge funds, insurance companies and teacher pension portfolios right behind them—have turned more bullish. They've added two hundred thousand acres of almonds, pistachios, mandarins and grapes. The water deficit in Kern is so alarming that the

Pistachio orchard charging up the hills of western Kern

outgoing director of the Kern County Water Agency had made a rare admission to me weeks earlier: farmers were overdrafting the aquifer to the tune of seven hundred thousand acre-feet in a dry year. When the state's new groundwater sustainability regulations go into full effect in the next few decades, he confided, at least three hundred thousand acres of local farmland will have to go out of production. That's more than one-third of all the farmland in Kern.

This doesn't startle Bucher. "We're looking at a world of hurt when that law clamps down," he says. Then he smiles. "That's *if* it clamps down."

There's the drought that nature imposes on the growers, I tell him, and there's the drought that the growers impose on themselves. Since 1997, the four irrigation districts of western Kern have sold their rights to 140,000 acre-feet of state water. "Farm to urban" the program is called. The deals are lucrative in the short term but make no sense if you're growing a tree with a life span of twenty years. Once sold, the water never comes back. So why would a grower planting orchards in desert ground let go of any water in California?

Bucher knows the answer. At the time, Resnick believed he had all the water in the world because his right-hand man had gone out and snatched a water bank for Kern. It allowed Resnick and his soon-to-be-branded Wonderful Company to outmaneuver drought and flood. With water in the bank, it no longer mattered that nature had gypped western Kern out of an aquifer.

As Resnick began withdrawing from his surplus supply, the trees in western Kern started marching outward. Two million acre-feet of water have moved in and out of the bank since the first deliveries. Resnick has helped himself to more than half of this water. By combining banked water with state aqueduct flows, he's been able to fuel a nut rush that has transformed not only the Kern mesa but farmland throughout California. Taking their cue from Resnick, farmers up and down the state have more than doubled the plantings of almonds from 500,000 acres in 1995 to 1.3 million acres today. The acres of pistachios have jumped from 90,000 to 275,000.

"That incredible turn to trees would not have happened without the water bank," Bucher says. "As soon as we got the bank, the flood years started piling up. We got lucky twice. We were able to put a lot of water in the bank, and Resnick and other farmers were able to pull a lot of water out. But it wasn't just water that turned the ground from cotton to nuts. It was the cost of electricity. It kept going up and up. That gave our farmers all the more reason to plant high-dollar crops like almonds and pistachios."

In the wet years of 2005 and 2006, Resnick had more water than even his trees could drink. So much water came down the aqueduct that he could afford to sell some of the surplus from the water bank. These weren't farm-to-city transfers. This was public water he was selling back to the state through a program called the Environmental Water Account. Its purpose on paper struck a noble note. With water marketing now in vogue, farmers were encouraged to sell surplus water back to the state to help endangered fish in the delta. Never mind that these same fish were being imperiled by state pumps working overtime to satisfy the demands of farmers. The program allowed Resnick to masquerade as an environmentalist while raiding California's ecological kitty. He was paying the state anywhere from $28 to $86 an acre-foot for the water he deposited in the bank. He was then selling this water back to the state—and the fish—for $200 an acre-foot. The trade not only generated $38 million in profits for Resnick; he was also able to offer some of the cheap surplus water to independent nut growers as an inducement to process their almonds and pistachios with him. The water bank had become an instrument to further his monopoly.

What to now make of the Kern Water Bank going dry? Or a desperate Resnick wishing he hadn't sold some of his state water allotments to housing developers? Or the rumors of his newest scheme to siphon groundwater from one basin and haul it across the dry Tulare lakebed to keep alive his nuts in another basin?

Before I head to Beverly Hills and knock on Resnick's door, I need to find out more. On the chuckholed back roads of Kern County, I look for the signs of such a plot. I drive for days but all that stares back at me is farmland. Not a single acre sits idle. I've lived in this valley long enough that I can recite the lineage of the land—and I trace these sections back to the Kern County Land Company and the empire of James Ben Ali Haggin, a.k.a. "the grand khan of the Kern," the third-wealthiest man in America in the 1870s.

A century later, Tenneco, one of the oil giants tapping into the dirty crude of Kern, purchased Haggin's old land company and planted some of the first orchards on the plain. The oil boys knew almost nothing about farming. They hired a kid named Howard Marguleas to run their agricultural division. He knew almost nothing about farming, either. Marguleas had grown up in the business of buying and selling fruit. His father, Joe, and Joe's partner, Frank Heggblade, sold themselves as "the hardest-working fruit brokers in the West." H&M, they called their enterprise, which stood for Heggblade and Marguleas, one a Christian Scientist and the other a Jew who had converted to Christian Science. Heggblade would die before his time when a speck of melanoma, untreated because he believed in the science of God's healing, ate away half his face. Marguleas would be luckier. He'd end up with only a hernia, albeit one that got so big it turned into a loaf of bread beneath his pants.

Howard, the son, would go on to invent SunWorld and introduce Hawaiian pineapples to the U.S. mainland and revolutionize the breeding of new varieties of table grapes, bell peppers and tomatoes. First, though, Tenneco needed him to unload thirty thousand acres of its Kern County holdings on both sides of Highway 99—land that now engulfs my car in almonds. Marguleas's bosses gave him one week to find a buyer and close a deal. It was the early 1970s, and the kid knew only one farmer in Kern who could dream that big: Hollis Roberts, a six-foot-three, 325-pound Texan who dressed in a three-piece suit, felt Stetson and breakfast-stained tie. Marguleas found Hollis driving his black Cadillac Fleetwood down an orchard row, chewing on an unlit cigar. He had spit out so many specks of tobacco that he could hardly see out the windshield. Marguleas persuaded Hollis that Tenneco's thirty thousand acres was a steal, and indeed it was. Hollis got the land for dirt cheap with Tenneco carrying most of the financing on its books.

Three harvests later, Hollis owned the land outright and planted more almonds and citrus. Backed with all the cash he needed from the United States National Bank in San Diego—owned by C. Arnholt Smith, a close pal of President Nixon's—Hollis kept on growing until he possessed 140,000 acres. This was more land than any other farmer in California. Then Smith's bank came crashing down in a mudslide of debt and fraud, taking with it a dozen dummy corporations that he and Hollis had set up to farm the land and seize new surface water coming down the aqueduct. Hollis was the first man, but not the last, to turn the federal and state water projects into a Ponzi scheme. He wound up flat broke.

Hollis had built his main ranch house just east of McFarland and added a small chapel to the back of his living quarters, and that's where I am sitting now, in one of his pews. Hollis invited Cesar Chavez inside this chapel forty-five years ago when he became one of the first farmers to sign a contract with the United Farm Workers. "I learned to like Chavez, and I found that a lot of things we had been told about these people were not true," Hollis explained at the time. "I had been told they were Communists, and I had been advised never to talk to them in person. Now I don't think we could have been any more wrong."

The present owner of the ranch, a beekeeper from North Dakota named Will Nissen, is standing next to the pulpit. A sign on the wall says, "PRAYER CHANGES THINGS." What little the sturdy and straightforward German beekeeper knows about the life of Hollis Roberts intrigues him. "I'm told there wasn't a religious bone in him," Nissen relates. "But he and his men would come in this chapel before work and say a little prayer about the water and soil." Nissen runs Five Star Honey Farms with his wife and three sons. They employ ten Nicaraguans who are here on special work visas—"There are no better beekeepers in the world," he tells me—to help run his California production. It's a show, all right, transporting 12,000 colonies, 360 million bees, aboard twenty-five big rigs that leave North Dakota in mid-October and arrive in Kern County three days later.

It used to be that the bees would sit in their boxes for most of California's winter and start foraging in early February. That's when the almond trees began to flower and the bees could begin their pollinating. But because of global warming—a term that doesn't exactly roll off Nissen's tongue—December now feels like March. The bees are out foraging more than a month early. The extra miles, and the extra pesticides, herbicides and fungicides they pick up in their flights, are taking a toll. Last year, more than 40 percent of his bees perished without replenishing themselves, a tripling of the die-off from the late 1970s, when he first got into the apiary business. "The California winters have been getting hotter and hotter. The bees are confused as hell," he says. "There used to be no reason to go flying in December. Now it's so warm, they think it's spring. We have a saying for our bees: 'Stay home, stay strong.' But they're not staying home, and they're picking up all sorts of nasty things out there."

The life span of a worker bee is six weeks. The life span of the queen is four years, or at least it used to be. Now Nissen is lucky if he can squeeze a year of maximum egg production out of her. The industrialization of beekeeping, which must keep pace with the industrialization of almond growing, is surely to blame. So are the abbreviated winters and the refusal by county agriculture officials to stop fruit farmers from spraying toxic chemicals on their trees and vines during bee-flying hours. More and more, Nissen says, he has to cull out queens only a year old to make room for fresher models. "When the queen is going well, she'll make thirteen hundred eggs a day. When she breaks down and starts producing only four or five hundred eggs a day, we go in and kill her ourselves. A new queen emerges."

Allergic to bee stings, I tiptoe in and out of the columns of hives, trying not to rile the insects up. Like the owner of a pit bull, Nissen assures me there is no reason for fear. The bees have mainlined so much sugar, corn syrup and amino acids (the goo is stored in a six-thousand-gallon tank a few feet away) that they couldn't be more docile. Most of these colonies will be sent into the orchards of one grower: Stewart Resnick. The Nissens rent out each colony for $200. At the end of the bloom, they'll be paid $2 million for the duty of pollination. "I've got no complaints with the Resnicks," he says. "We bill them on Mondays and get the check on Fridays."

I steer through the dizzy of trees and manage to stumble upon Highway 99. If I turn left, the two lanes will take me south to the other side of the Tehachapi Mountains, to Los Angeles 130 miles away. I used to drive the Grapevine, the last twisted descent of that road, at two in the morning to get from my newspaper job in L.A. to my mother in Fresno. It was the winter of 1984, and she was dying of lung cancer, and I propped her up in the family room where she could see the citrus ripening in her backyard. Little did I know she would ask me for one sweet mandarin, and I would have to say no, and then she would ask me for one slice of one sweet mandarin, and I would have to say no. We had put her on a cancer-fighting macrobiotic diet that balanced yin foods with yang foods, and citrus was too yin. "No mandarin," I told her. She died a week later at the age of fifty-one, in the same tule fog that had swept in twelve years earlier on the night my father was murdered. I wrote her eulogy driving down the mountain and said good-bye to Fresno on the way back up. I was sure I was never coming back.

Then the search to find my father's killers—what a friend called my "Moby Dick"—brought me home. When I had finished with all the questions, my wife, a Fresno girl, wanted to stay. We raised a daughter and two sons, and one Moby Dick turned into another until our marriage ended after twenty-five years. The boys and I moved a few miles away to a 1950s ranch house with enough open ground to let me pretend I was a farmer. I planted a fig tree, an Elberta peach, an O'Henry peach, a Santa Rosa plum, a Page mandarin, a clementine, a grapefruit and the three apricot trees that convulsed one night in the middle of drought and have given no good fruit since.

I turn right and find my way back to Fresno. Thirty miles out, I pass a sign on 99 that reads "TRAVER," but the town no longer exists. It shot up overnight in the late 1800s, a rollicking hamlet with sixteen saloonkeepers, eleven blacksmiths, one preacher, one teacher, two physicians, one undertaker, two whorehouses, one Chinese gambling den, two Chinese laundrymen and a Mexican tamale maker named Jesus. Traver held the world record for the greatest amount of wheat shipped from a producing point during a single season. But as fast as it sprouted from the plain, the town vanished in a cloud of alkali dust, its soil poisoned by salts bubbling up from the waters of irrigation.

The farmers along this stretch of road have found a new trick for the rickety trailers that used to transport their cotton from field to gin. They've turned them into highway billboards draped with banners that blame the water crisis on everything but drought. The culprits lurk near and far: Democratic politicians refusing to fund the next dam; liberal federal judges siding with the tiny delta smelt over humans and cutting exports of northern water; the American people, who have forgotten that it's the farmer who feeds them and there's no food without water. The word "drought" never shows up on any of the signs unless it's preceded by "man-made." The negation of nature is ingrained in the fiber of a California farmer. For one thing, nature is far kinder here than it is in Iowa. And he's been using scraper, plow, tractor, shears, canal, pump and chemical for so many generations that the only imprints he sees on the land are the imprints of his hands, and of those hands that seek to take from him. In California, drought isn't nature. Drought is man.

Part Two

FATHERS OF EXTRACTION (1769–1901)

1860s gold miners tearing away at a mountainside
with their hydraulic jets of water

Six

STAKING EDEN

As much as we tried to believe it, the tinkering didn't begin with us. In one degree and another, it had been going on for at least ten thousand years. As a student of California public schools, I learned in the fourth grade that our Indians were different from the Iroquois, Cheyenne, Cherokee, Sioux and Seminole. Our Indians didn't come with war whoops or ponies gaily decked in feathers and scalp locks. Our Indians weren't butchers who sliced men and buffalo open from breast to groin. They didn't have chiefs named Sitting Bull or Crazy Horse or warriors of "prodigious psychic and physical energy," like the massive and haughty Gall, who writer Evan Connell so memorably captured in his book on General George Armstrong Custer, *Son of the Morning Star*. We had no Little Bighorn battle sites to visit on our field trips, though we did tour Mission San Juan Bautista, the restored Franciscan outpost closest to us, on the way to the fields of Salinas, the lettuce capital of the world. I remember my mother looking over my shoulder as I put the finishing touches on a replica of the mission as my end-of-the-semester project. I painted the padre's robe in drab gray, but I don't recall making a clay figure of the California Indian. I had never seen a California Indian, though one kid at school called me a "Fresno Indian," which apparently was the way his family and other white families in town referred to the dark-haired, dark-skinned Armenians. I had reddish hair and a face that burned in the sun. My tormentor danced in a circle and kept striking his mouth with his palm in a "Woo, woo, woo, woo, woo, woo, woo, woo" chant. This was the war dance, poor kid, of a Plains Indian.

That semester, we were shown a handful of photos of the Tachi and Mono tribes weaving their traditional baskets long after they'd been transplanted onto some nearby rancheria, California's version of a reservation. The pictures seemed to confirm the idea that our natives were placid and lived light and easy on the land. They erected small dams, slowed down rivers and made the salmon sit still long enough to spear them. They were peaceful people, by and large, because California had no shortages of food or struggles over land to turn them against one another. By the time my own children reached the fourth grade and built their own versions of Mission San Juan Bautista, the lesson had evolved slightly. Yes, their teachers conceded, a disservice had been committed against the California Indians by the well-meaning fathers of the Catholic Church, who had used some unkind means to tame them. But that was all a very long time ago and thank God the Indians were building casinos up and down California, not always on tribal lands, to get back a little of what had been taken from them.

Like most everything else about California, its natives were of a singular kind: the greatest concentration of indigenous people in North America. Some 250 distinct tribes of natives, perhaps three hundred thousand people, had remade the land in their own way. They tapped the pines for sugar and set fire to hillsides to catch grasshoppers and game. Those same fires singed the redbud shrub just enough so that it would send out tender shoots for their basketry. They cultivated the soil to increase production of clover and built small canals to move water and make the wild rye grow more profusely. In pools of rivers, they threw down brush to catch the steelhead trout and salmon with ease. In times of drought and flood, they migrated to places that better sustained them. They moved as California moved.

The Chumash, Yokut, Tachi, Chukchansi, Miwok, Mono, Paiute, Washoe and Kumeyaay—to name a few—weren't fierce tribes who fought over a scarcity of resources but fat tribes who knew mostly abundance and peace. Unlike the indigenous cultivators of the desert Southwest who'd been practicing irrigation for two millennia, California natives didn't need to move the water to survive. Only the Paiute of the Owens Valley and the Cahuilla of Palm Springs erected water-conveyance systems that sought to even out the extremes of mountain and desert climes. In their little valley four thousand feet high in the Sierra, the Paiute dammed the Owens River with boulders, sticks and mud and dug a latticework of canals and ditches to send the flow to plots of yellow nut grass and hyacinth corms. Each year, the tribe elected a head irrigator, the *tuvaiju,* who kept the water moving with his wooden pole, called a *pavado.* Once the crops were harvested, he made sure to destroy the diversion dam so the flow would return to the river.

The European mapmakers of the fifteenth and sixteenth centuries, taking the word of the earliest explorers from Spain, drew California as one big island standing near but still apart from the rest of North America. They imagined it as myth, a paradise filled with gold where a giant black queen named Calafia and her tribe of warrior women ruled earth, water and beast. Over the next two centuries, the deeper forays of Cortés, Cabrillo, Vizcaíno, Fages and Moraga found it to be a land connected to a continent but an island in every other way. The explorers did not tread on its myth. The river running north and south struck Moraga as a holy sacrament, and he christened it the Sacramento. The river that ran in the opposite direction, no less holy, became the San Joaquin, in honor of the father of the Virgin Mary.

For all its poking around, Spain was a fickle suitor. The Crown went back and forth on whether to extend its empire beyond Mexico and turn California into a settlement. Then, in 1768, Spain's ambassador to Moscow heard that the Russians were eyeing the fabled port of Monterey. The Spaniards naturally took this as an insult. A century and a half before, Vizcaíno had given Monterey its name. To outrace the Russians, King Carlos III turned not to his soldiers but to his Franciscans. The padres in their earnest gray robes had accomplished in Mexico what the military men could not: the submission of its native peoples. The Franciscans, the blunt tip of the Spanish sword, had been advancing north toward San Diego, erecting a series of missions up and down the Baja Peninsula—a "ladder with conveniently placed rungs," in the words of Father Junípero Serra.

Friar Serra was the master builder who'd been chosen to carry providence forth. He had joined the Franciscan order as a fifteen-year-old boy in his native Majorca. A brilliant theologian, he was teaching philosophy at a local university when church superiors recruited him for the "long journey" to Mexico. Once there, he began walking the rugged countryside of Mexico's indigenous people, one village to the next, until an infected foot wouldn't let him walk any farther. "I have never seen a priest more zealous for founding missions than this Father President," a

The vandalized statue of Father Junipero Serra
looking out to Monterey Bay

Spanish military commander wrote snidely of Father Serra. "He thinks of nothing but founding missions, no matter how or at what expense." The padre's sojourns had turned thousands of "barbarous" Indians into Christ-fearing farmers growing corn, beans and pumpkins for the good of Mexico. California, up the road, was simply the next geographical rung on the imperial ladder.

What next took place along the California coast under Father Serra's watch is a history that has never quite resolved itself, a chronicle told in nonfiction books and scholarly studies that centers on the motivations and acts of the "Father of California" and what precise role he played in the plunder of California natives and whether or not, two centuries later, he deserved to be crowned a Catholic saint or branded the father of a genocide. The books and journals I haul from my office and take with me on the road—an exploration of California literature that runs along a parallel road—were written in three distinct periods, each one colored by different sensibilities that allow for varying degrees of examination.

The histories written from the late 1800s to the mid-1900s, influenced by the selling and reselling of the "Golden State" myth and a deference to the Catholic Church, shy away from declaring any harsh judgment about Father Serra and the building of the twenty-one missions that formed El Camino Real, the King's Road, connecting one end of California to the other. John Sutter and the other fathers of extraction who follow in Serra's path are treated much the same, which is to say delicately and gingerly. The histories written in the mid- to late 1900s, while still treading lightly on the hallowed ground of California conception, begin to reckon with the wiping clean of native culture that accompanied the taking of land and rivers. They attribute not so much malice or design to the act but, rather, a benign culpability, more accidental than intentional. The histories written in the 1980s, 1990s and early 2000s, revisiting and revising this past, focus on the cruelest episodes of Spanish, Mexican and early American occupations of California, reading not only malice into the acts of each occupier but a genocide planned, paid for and executed. Finally, there is the immersive *Journey to the Sun,* written by Gregory Orfalea, which depicts Father Serra as an honorable, conflicted and at times naïve padre who wasn't seeking the conquest of the natives or their land, and certainly was not intent on genocide.

That California's colonial history remains alive, contested and bitterly unresolved today may or may not be fully appreciated by Pope Francis as he decides, in the fall of 2015, to visit the United States for the purpose of canonizing Father Serra. The first Latino pope is coming to America to present to his flock the first Latino saint. It is interesting to note that the canonization Mass takes place not on mission grounds in California but in the nation's capital at Catholic University. Pope Francis praises the friar's ferocious devotion to Christ and his willingness to travel the last mile to evangelize every native in his path, while seeking "to defend the dignity of the native community, to protect it from those who had mistreated and abused it." Who these abusers of the Indians were, the pope does not make clear. Perhaps he is speaking of the Spanish military men charged with defending the missions who did quite the opposite in some cases. Not counting the padres, the soldiers were the only nonnative people in California at the time. Or maybe he is pointing a finger at some of the padres who toiled under Serra and got carried away with their chore. "Mistreatment and wrongs which today still trouble us," the pope says, "especially because of the hurt which they cause in the lives of many people."

If this is an attempt at confession on behalf of the church, it turns out to be an evasive one. In the end, perhaps for the wiser, the pope leaves the question of genocide to the historians to decipher. Father Serra, by an edict of the Vatican, is declared an official saint of the Catholic Church. The leaders of fifty native California tribes are left to condemn the ceremony from afar. "We believe saints are supposed to be people who followed in the life of Jesus Christ," Valentin Lopez, chairman of the Amah Mutsun tribe in Monterey, tells CNN news. "There was no Jesus Christ lifestyle at the missions." Three days later, vandals strike the Carmel Mission, where Saint Serra is buried. They topple his statue, splash paint on the mission walls and leave behind a message scrawled in graffiti: "SAINT OF GENOCIDE."

In the company of his personal servant, two fellow priests, eight soldiers, a blacksmith, a carpenter and eleven Baja Indians (thirty others had deserted along the way), Father Serra crossed by mule into San Diego on July 1, 1769. He was fifty-five years old, described as diminutive in height, "dark eyes, scant beard, swarthy." He praised the Lord and kissed the earth and gave thanks to the Divine Majesty for "granting me the favor of being among the pagans in their own land." This land, he noted, was "very good land with plenty of water." The valleys and banks of rivulets were full of vines of a large size and "quite loaded with grapes." The ground was neither rocky nor overrun with brushwood but, rather, a clean, strong-smelling earth filled with a multitude of hares, deer and wild goats.

Father Serra and his brother friars were remarkably gifted men who served as teachers, musicians, weavers, carpenters, masons, architects and "physicians of the soul and body." They were not men who wished to see themselves as the first protagonists in an act of genocide. So when the natives did not immediately flee or grab their bows and arrows, the padres saw this as an expression of consent. They were encouraged by the fact that the natives were completely open to the gesture of a gift, all the better if that gift was a piece of cloth. For the feel of cotton on their skin, it was said, the Indians would trade almost anything, and if enough pieces of colorful cotton were thrown their way, they'd even hand over their children. Thus began the caricature of California natives that would prove a first step in their erasure. The offer and acceptance of gifts allowed the invader to perceive his invasion not as a taking but as a giving. The friars were delivering not only eternal life to the Indian but they were delivering, in this life, the warmth of an adobe dwelling, cooked meals, a daily job and the comfort of cloth.

Had the padres understood the language of the natives, they might have appreciated how preposterous their invasion looked from the other side. The Indians did not know what to make of the strange men and their caravan. Were these Indian ancestors who had returned to life in a different form? Were these avenging gods? Father Serra had been granted ten years by the Crown to build his missions and convert as many Indians as he could. After that, the king of Spain insisted, the natives were to receive all the farmland, waterworks and wealth their labor had created. By the time this promise was officially broken, Father Serra was many years in the grave. What history's own inventions and reinventions seem to agree on is the padre was a man guided almost entirely by religious fervor. He fought endlessly with the Crown, a cheapskate when it came to California, and shamed the administrators of colonial Spain into giving him more resources for his missions. He relished taking on the military commanders—the leather jackets, he called them—about the feckless way they oversaw their soldiers. His challenge to authority eventually turned into an all-out feud when soldiers on duty and deserters began trespassing onto tribal lands and the missions' barracks to steal food and fish. They were stealing more, too: the rape of indigenous women visited the scourge of syphilis on California.

The feud between the Franciscans and the military men dwelled on a central question of mission life: Who owned the body of the Indian? For such spiritual men, the friars approached the question as pragmatists. California's rivers and soils, they believed, were divine gifts to be exploited in the name of God and king. To capture water and earth, they first needed to capture the sweat of the Indian. More often than not, the taking of the California Indian—his physical form first and then his spiritual and cultural forms—happened by way of inducement, a wheedling that grew out of the Christian notion that a heavenly "calling" had to occur first. There were the gifts of cloth and trinkets. There was the lure of a new civilization rising in their midst. When drought appeared, the missions had food. When the shaman could not heal a child, the missions had medicine that could. Finally, there was the pride that came when one crossed over from heathen to neophyte, the satisfaction in seeing what their bodies had wrought on behalf of a mission: streams that flowed into irrigation canals; canals that watered fields of wheat, apples, oranges, lemons, figs, dates, olives and grapes; pastures that fed cattle; hides that became leather; granaries filled with acorns; tallow turned into soap to cleanse the body.

Father Serra and his friars sweated alongside their neophytes. Male natives stooped, squatted and crawled in the first vineyards. The women, who weren't allowed in the fields, had their own quotas to meet. They milled grain, ground corn, fermented grapes, pressed oil, flailed hemp and turned the fat of cows into candles. Together, the natives and padres at Mission San Buenaventura constructed the first aqueduct in California, a five-mile-long canal of dirt and intricate brickwork. The seeds they planted in 1774 at the three earliest missions yielded a first harvest of wheat and corn. By 1805, nineteen missions were harvesting a total of ninety-six thousand bushels of wheat, corn, barley and beans, a thirty-fold increase. At their agricultural peak, the missions and the adjacent pueblos were farming ten thousand acres of vineyards, orchards and fields.

To get past drought, the friars harnessed Indian power to erect more than a dozen dams and dig scores of ditches and wells that diverted the streams and altered the hydrology of California far beyond what the natives had ever done on their own. At Mission San Diego, a dam standing 12 feet high and 250 feet across was built out of stone. At Mission San Antonio de Padua, the dam caught the flow of the San Antonio River and sent it into a main canal carved out of limestone. The catch of water allowed the mission to experiment with different grains, vegetables and exotic fruits, including the first pear tree planted in California. At the Mission San Gabriel, natives planted the 170-acre La Vina Madre, "the mother vineyard." A visitor in the early 1800s described the mission's "rich profusion of fruits from every clime" growing under the Southern California sun. Herds of cattle and sheep driven overland from Baja had multiplied so many times that livestock foraged far beyond mission grounds, mowing down native plants and dropping the seeds of foreign ones. This is how California bunchgrass was pushed aside by European filaree.

Charting the population of California Indians from various accounts is not unlike tracking the rate of subsidence. The numbers tell a far different story than a land discovering its fertility. Something in the range of 60,000 natives lived along the California coast alone in 1770. The population then drops to 57,000 in 1780; 44,000 in 1790; 36,000 in 1800; 26,000 in 1810; 22,000 in 1820. Desperate neophytes fleeing coastal mission life and heading into the tules of California's middle—"fugitives" in the estimation of the padres—explained some of the bodies vacating. Most of the loss, though, took place inside the missions themselves from diseases the padres knew well: pneumonia, diphtheria, smallpox and measles. In the matter of a single decade, tens of thousands of natives from San Francisco to Santa Barbara died from foreign germs. "There had come upon the people a great epidemic," Father Francisco Palóu wrote in 1777, documenting the deaths but not the most devastating of the scourges. "The Fathers were able to perform a great many baptisms by simply going through the villages. In this way, they succeeded in sending a great many children, which died almost as soon as they were baptized, to Heaven."

In his report to the Crown, Governor Diego de Borica did not pretend that baptism in the hour of death made for less of a tragedy. The Indian children, he reported, were dying of syphilis, a disease of rape. "They are permeated to the marrow of their bones with venereal disease, such that many of the newly born show immediately this," he wrote. "This is the only patrimony they receive from their parents, and for which three-quarters of the infants die in their first or second year."

In the shadow of the epidemics, Father Serra could sense his own death growing near. In August 1784, he wrote Father Palóu, his old friend, and invited him for a visit. He did not mention that he needed him for the occasion of his last confession. Father Palóu greeted the "Venerable Father" in the manner of a student greeting his mentor, for their relationship had been such all the way back to Majorca. Palóu fed Serra a cup of broth and placed a foot-long crucifix on his chest. This was the same cross Serra had borne on all his journeys across Mexico and California.

"Great fear has come upon me," Serra confided. "I have a great fear. Read me the Commendation for a Departing Soul."

This Father Palóu did.

"Thanks be to God, thanks be to God," Serra sang in joy. "All the fear has now left me."

Father Palóu stepped out of the room for a moment, only to return to a find a body that held no trace of agony, showed no hint of death other than the cessation of breath. He wrote: "We piously believe that he went to sleep in the Lord a little before two in the afternoon on the feast of St. Augustine in the year 1784, and that he went to receive in heaven the reward of his apostolic labors."

And what became of those labors? Piece by piece, as is the case with even would-be saints, they were dismantled in the years after Serra's death. Spain, too busy with Napoleon, lost interest in the missions and then in California itself. By 1821, the flag of the Mexican Republic, freed from Spanish yoke, flew over California. In the name of secularization, Serra's missions fell into disrepair and then squalor. Mexico's new liberal government promised the Indians the equivalent of forty acres and a mule. With land, it was reasoned, the Indian would shake off his sloth and free himself from the curses of liquor and gambling. He would produce food for market and become a tax-paying Mexican citizen. Even the Californios, the Spanish-Mexican gentry living an aristocratic life on their ranchos, thought it wise to do right by the Indian. In the initial flowering of the Mexican Republic, the dons talked endlessly about the reforms that would give Indians full rights, if not outright citizenship. They would even seek to name their new state Montezuma and emblazon its coat of arms with a feathered Indian carrying bow and quiver. For the Californios who had taken the prettiest native girls as mistresses and wives, it wasn't such a leap.

Like so much else in the Mexican experiment, Montezuma would never come to be. Even as the Indians left the missions shouting, *"Soy libre!"*—I am free!—the life of a yeoman farmer was not in the cards. That many turned into gamblers and drunks of the most dissolute kind should not have surprised anyone. Ten thousand years of culture had been ripped away from them, and a new culture of servitude imposed and then ripped away, too. The first pueblo councils of Los Angeles passed a law making it a crime to be drunk and filthy in public. No one in the pueblo pretended that the Indians weren't the targets of the decrees, and the jails soon filled with them. The Californios, guilt-free, went about accumulating vast tracts of land deeded to them by their friends in the new Mexican government. Hundreds of thousands of acres from coast to interior, the first great California land grab, were snatched from the Indians and converted into baronial estates, or ranchos. The short, stubby dons of the Pico clan owned seven hundred thousand acres—more than one thousand square miles—in what is now Los Angeles County.

The Californios grew fat on the land. They slaughtered a calf a day to feed their relatives and friends, drank vast quantities of wine and brandy and threw Fiesta Day parties and fantastic weddings in which daughters who'd been locked away in finishing rooms all their lives finally came out into the sun. The Indians who became their labor did not insist under the law that Mexico honor its pledge to them. They were the lucky ones. One hundred thousand of their brethren had perished of disease and violent death during the mission years. The continent's largest concentration of indigenous peoples had been reduced by a third. Thousands of survivors wandering the land in fugue fled their mission plots and headed into California's middle to resurrect their culture. They had no idea that their liberated bodies vectored the germs of Europe into the villages of the inland tribes. A new epidemic erupted, wiping out tens of thousands more. What was left of them in the year 1839, perhaps 150,000 natives, now hid in the sticks, waiting for the white man's massacre.

Here comes Johann August Sutter, first planter of wheat and the white man's flag, an immigrant so rich in reinvention that no one can pin him down. Not the wife or four children he leaves behind in Switzerland. Not the motley crew he picks up along the western trail to civilize California's interior. Not the natives ripped from their ancient ways who submit to life and death by his hand. Not the settlers who stumble out of the Sierra snowdrifts and onto the plain of the Central Valley looking for provisions at Sutter's Fort. When they find it, the place he calls New Helvetia, they encounter a man who seems to hold within his hands the destiny of California.

He had left Burgdorf on a May night in 1834, a thirty-one-year-old fugitive fleeing debt and carrying a new wardrobe and the complete works of Sir Walter Scott. By the time he showed up in Missouri that summer, he was Captain John A. Sutter, a slim, dapper man of dignified bearing. He had a balding head, full side whiskers and a curled-up mustache set off by clear blue eyes and a clean-shaven chin. He wore a long black silk velvet coat lined in satin, a silk vest, a gold fob, knee britches and high-topped boots, and the story he told in broken English was not unlike the stories the other men told. He was a veteran of the Swiss Guard under the command of the king of France—his uniform still fit perfectly—and he was looking for the new Nile River valley he had read about in a book. How he made his way to such a valley has to be one of the strangest roundabouts in the annals of the California invasion. He crossed the Great Plains, followed the interminable twists of the Snake River, landed in Fort Vancouver, the capital of Britain's Hudson's Bay Company, king of the world's fur trade, and sailed on to Hawaii, which was under a native king's rule, and then Sitka, Alaska, an outpost of the Russian monarchy. The U.S. consul in Honolulu and the Russian governor in Sitka were so charmed by his courtliness that each agreed to write him a letter of reference attesting to his strong character and honorable intentions. This was no small favor. In a place as confused as California, a man needed the right letters to help open the right doors.

Almost five years to the day after he had left home, Sutter boarded the *Clementine* with his sidekick Pablo Gutiérrez, one Indian boy he had purchased as chattel and a crew of eight Hawaiian Kanakas and two Germans who had pledged their service to him. The eighty-eight-ton brig with its two masts crossed the gale-rough seas and crept past the fog of the Golden Gate and set anchor in the mud of Yerba Buena, "the land of good herb," on July 1, 1839. Sutter could see the bare sand hills of the future San Francisco where a shanty or two clung to earth gullied by rains. Up the slope, a forest of trees and wild mint stood over the bay. There was no lighthouse, no marker, no earshot of civilization. The Mormons had not yet sailed around Cape Horn to reach California, and perhaps fifty souls at best lived there. Three or four miles in the distance lay the ruins of a Spanish presidio and mission where a few natives still scratched out a pitiful living. Startled by the sight of the brig, fifteen soldiers and an officer of the Mexican government rushed aboard the *Clementine*. No vessel, they informed Sutter, was allowed to enter Yerba Buena. He would have to turn around and head farther down the coast and enter through Monterey Bay. Two days later, clutching his sheaf of letters, Sutter set ashore in Monterey and knocked on the door of the governor of California.

John A. Sutter, counterfeit captain, planter of the white man's flag in California

He was walking into a void. The almost nonexistent rule of Spain for fifty years had yielded to the almost nonexistent rule of Mexico. Neither nation was tuned up for the hard work of empire building. Both nations had heard about gold and diamonds and silver, too, but had sent none of their citizens to mine any of the riches. Even a blinkered man could see that California, the idea of the place, the dimensions of the place, was a gigantic proposition. Who could blame the Mexicans, or the Spanish before them, for deciding to rule it with hands off and attentions fixed only on their own little fiefdoms? Here was the governor and his military men in the north, headquartered in Monterey, and a rival Mexican leader and his military men in the south, headquartered in Los Angeles. Their bickering, more or less constant, had the feel of a family feud, and for good reason. The rivals, prone to marrying multiple times and fathering multiple sets of children, were, in fact, members of the same extended clan.

White man's invasion began with Sutter kissing the ring of Governor Juan Bautista Alvarado, who considered himself neither Mexican nor Spaniard, although both strains ran in his blood. Neither was the governor quite sure what Mexico was attempting to accomplish in the Far West. California belonged to no one and everyone. The son of a Spanish military officer, Governor Alvarado had been born in Monterey and saw himself as the spiritual graft of Spain, Mexico and California—a member of the tribe of Californio. He was protected, at least in theory, by a military unit under the command of General Mariano Vallejo. Not only was Vallejo his chief nemesis; he was also his uncle. Vallejo had been born in Monterey to Spanish parents, as well, and though he was an elder to the governor, the two men were only a year and a half apart in age. An aristocrat who groomed his sideburns into grand muttonchops, Vallejo had married one of the most beautiful women in all of California, Francisca Benicia Carrillo. The Vallejos lived up the coast in Sonoma on a cattle barony that took in two hundred thousand acres. The general, an avowed admirer of democracy and the United States, boasted the finest library in California; he so delighted in literature that he gave each of his eighteen children, including the two bastards, the names of authors and famous historical figures.

Vallejo's empire sat far enough removed from the capital in Monterey to be its own regional power. This suzerainty, it was said, vexed his nephew. Governor Alvarado had only so many eyes to give to the threats, real and imagined, that surrounded him. Farther up the redwood coast, in Bodega Bay, the Russians had grabbed a piece of California to hunt sea otters and sell the prized fur to the world. At their Fort Ross, the Russians were farming wheat and fruit and breeding their own type of cattle. Then there was the matter, ever more pressing, of the American fur trappers and mountain men arriving by way of rugged trails. Borders meant nothing to them. The uncouth Americans, ingrates to a man, came and went without ever giving Mexico notice. The question on Governor Alvarado's mind—the question that would soon occupy Sutter—was whether these overland invasions were the ambitions of solitary men or the designs of a U.S. government eyeing California for its own.

A jaunty Sutter wasted not a moment in sharing his vision with Governor Alvarado. The governor immediately sensed an opportunity. California was a place up for grabs, that was true. But Captain Sutter, strangely, wasn't like all the others. He had no desire to settle on the precious coast. He wanted to go inland, to the delta, to build a colony, of all things, amid the tules. If he succeeded, he might help check the empire building of Vallejo and the Russians and perhaps co-opt the renegade Indians and the overland settlers, too. It was a tall order, folly by most estimation, but the captain seemed to believe in nothing more than himself. The two gentlemen shook hands on the deal: Sutter would establish a colony where the two rivers met in the delta and a tribe of natives still roamed. Once he had done so, the governor would grant him forty-eight thousand acres—seventy-five square miles—of interior lands. With this, Sutter boarded a twenty-two-foot schooner, the *Isabella,* and headed into the sticks.

Sutter's first turn in the interior was a wrong one. He got lost in the tules, California's boondocks. On the other side of the Montezuma Hills, in the maze of delta islands and peninsulas, he thought he'd found the Sacramento River. But this river twisting southward was the smaller San Joaquin. His seventeen-year-old pilot, William Heath Davis, a.k.a. "Kanaka Bill," half Polynesian and half white, steered the *Isabella* for eight more days before he located the Sacramento's mouth. By then, it was the midsummer of 1839 and several hundred Indians, tricked out for war, were eyeing their every move. Two vessels carrying supplies and a half dozen white men sailed behind Sutter. These were the vagabonds who had been eager to join the excursion when Sutter had hired them back in Yerba Buena. But the tules proved a miserable slog. Reeds fell and rotted in the marshes, and the water belched a foul gas that carried onward toward the menace of Indians. The men began to plot an exit back to Yerba Buena. "I saw plain that it was a mutiny," Sutter wrote in his diary.

He slept on their threat, rose up the next morning and instructed Davis to sail to the spot where the American and Sacramento Rivers met. As they drew near, he began to shout, "Here, here!" The rivers, tame in August, gave way to a sandbar, and from the clearing he could see the valley rolling out lush and level, an amphitheater of nature with no end. Beyond the tules, herds of deer and elk grazed on thick grass that extended in a giant wave to the oddest set of mountains, three little buttes in a perfect row. Halfway around the world, Sutter had found his valley. In a decade's time, the sandbar and buttes would take his name, but it would be the city of Sacramento, not Sutterville, that would rise at the confluence of the two rivers, the most hazardous flood zone in all of California. Sacramento would become the capital of the thirty-first state in the Union. Of course, no man standing in that spot at that point in time, not even the most fevered dreamer, could have imagined such a hurtle forward. As Sutter surveyed the land, he noticed a pleasant knoll in the distance. There he would build his fort and plant the flag of New Helvetia, New Switzerland, and alter the course of the river and change the path of the state-to-be.

Not long before, near this same spot, a party of Spaniards led by Gabriel Moraga had come upon the river and a tribe of Indians who saw their presence as a violation. Moraga would name the river the Rio de las Llagas, the River of Sorrow, in honor of the men he lost there. The Indians would change its name to the Rio de los Americanos, the American River, to mark the white trappers and mountain men who were hard at work obliterating the beaver, mink and grizzly bear. Now came this German-Swiss captain, short, stout and broad-shouldered, in his high military dress, flanked by his Indian boy guide, a young Polynesian woman, his Mexican sidekick, three white roustabouts and one Hawaiian bulldog. Six burly Kanakas, their cheeks tattooed in red and blue ink, their long black hair oiled with coconut butter, were dressed in their own native gowns. The mutinous men who did not have the stomach for empire building were sailing back to Yerba Buena aboard a second vessel. Sutter had given them his blessing, pitied them for not understanding destiny.

Sutter stood on the deck of his ship with two brass cannons pointed outward. In that moment, young Kanaka Bill, drifting down the river, looked back at the captain and wondered how he'd ever survive. Then came the sound that would stay with Kanaka Bill for the rest of his life. Sutter began to fire the two cannons into a clearing. He fired nine times in all, each shot breaking the sound barrier. The cannons were signal guns that carried no ammunition, but the Indians didn't know that. "As the heavy report of the guns died away, the camp of the little party was surrounded by hundreds of Indians, who were excited and astonished at the unusual sound," Kanaka Bill recalled years later. "A large number of deer, elk and other animals on the plains were startled, running to and fro, . . . while from the interior of the adjacent wood the howl of wolves and coyotes filled the air, and immense flocks of water fowl flew wildly about. Standing on the deck of [our ship], I witnessed this remarkable sight, which filled me with astonishment and admiration. . . . This salute was the first echo of civilization in the primitive wilderness so soon to become populated, and developed into a great agricultural and commercial centre."

The Indians spoke a little Spanish, and Sutter reached for the most precious gift he had—bags of Hawaiian sugar—and handed them to a chief named Anashe. The old warrior of the Maidu tribe nodded his head and spoke enough words, fleshed out by sign language, to state that a great tragedy committed by the Spaniards and Mexicans had befallen his people. With the chief's consent, Sutter instructed his party to unload the provisions. The best shooters went off to hunt elk while the Kanakas, boatmen and builders of great skill, erected a series of Hawaiian-style grass huts. Sutter had agreed to pay the Kanakas ten dollars a month for a period of three years. If they desired to return to their islands after the term was up, he'd bankroll the trip. A young Polynesian named Manuiki likely wouldn't be going home. She and Sutter had begun a romance. As much labor as the Kanakas could take on, Sutter found himself in immediate need of more hands to clear trees and build a blacksmith shop, kitchen and living quarters. The main dwelling, made of sun-dried mud brick, was the first phase of a five-hundred-foot-long fort he had designed on paper. Beyond its white-washed walls and bastions, he drew plots of land where wheat and fruit would grow and cattle and sheep would graze. It would be an outpost as vital to the westward movement as Fort Vancouver, a plantation finer than any of the ranchos belonging to the Californios.

To make this happen, he would have to steal a page from Father Serra. He would have to find a way to control the body of the Indian. Slavery in its cotton-plantation form did not appeal to the gentleman he saw himself to be. Instead, Sutter devised an economic system entirely unique to California. He fed, clothed and housed native Californians and paid for their labors with a currency all his own: money made of tin and stamped with a star. Each hole punched in the star counted as a full day's work. With the tin, the Indians could buy any beads, red bandannas or blankets they desired from his general store. As Sutter saw it, he was offering a new kind of religion, one that promised its own salvation: a piece of paradise that only his conquest of the last American frontier could deliver.

Hundreds of natives signed up for a life inside the fort. Some were runaways from the missions, but many others came straight from their tribal lands. It was true that most of the stuffing had been removed from them already. In the eyes of the Americans, they were half tame. Sutter, brilliant in his wielding of pardon and punishment, tamed the other half. As master, Sutter was protean. He could be anything a situation called for. One night, two Indians sneaked up on his quarters, intending to do him harm. His bulldog leaped from the room and subdued them. Sutter shooed the animal off, sewed up their wounds with silk and said that if they ever tried such a stunt again, he would kill them.

He drew a harder line at theft. After stealing from his general store, a group of Indians took off into the night. Sutter mustered a small force of white men and hunted them down. Along a river named for the Cosumnes tribe, Sutter and his men killed six of the warriors. The tribe's leaders begged for mercy. "If you come back and attend to your work as before, all will be forgiven," Sutter said. They walked back as shriven men and passed through the fort's massive oak gates topped by sharpened spikes. That was the last of Sutter's problems with the Cosumnes.

In a year's time, the captain had managed to subdue or co-opt almost every tribe in the Sacramento Valley. One old frontiersman who found respite at the fort watched the process in fascination. "He was probably the best Indian tamer and civilizer that I know of or ever heard of," he said. Sutter boasted that the California natives had grown as fiercely protective of him as his Kanakas. "Whenever strangers came into the valley, my Indians give me notice of their approach," he wrote. Sutter had come to see himself in the reflection of their loyalty. If his buying and selling of their services bordered on slavery, if some of the younger female Indians tended to his nighttime comfort, he had been called upon by time and place to be their lord. "I had no clergy, no church. At burials, at marriages, I officiated myself. I was everything: patriarch, priest, father and judge. . . . I, Sutter, am the law."

Sutter's Fort, 1848, before the U.S. takeover of California

The captain looked proudly upon wheat fields that had doubled in size from his first year. Another good crop, he told himself, and he would turn a profit. It did not occur to him that his spot at the juncture of two great streams could will itself dry in a season. In 1841, no decent rain fell on the valley and no deep snow blanketed the mountaintops, and he watched his crops wither. Sutter found himself short of cowhides and beaver pelts—what passed as tender in a cashless California. His creditors along the coast began comparing notes. One don was threatening to show up at the fort in person to seize several hundred cattle in lieu of payment. Sutter grew more surly and despondent, besmirching one creditor as an "infamous liar." He wasn't sure how much longer he could hold on. To buy some time, he sold several native girls to a few of his creditors.

A schoolteacher from Ohio seemed an unlikely savior. John Bidwell was only twenty-two years old when he arrived at the fort in the autumn of 1841, after leading the first group of immigrants to trek overland to California. Their provisions had run out on the western side of the Sierra, and he and the others had crossed the mountains on foot with little but mule meat to hold them over. When they finally made it down into the valley, sunbaked by drought, they wondered whose cruel joke this was. Bidwell could see up close what the singed earth had done to Sutter's wheat and to Sutter himself, who was "immensely and almost hopelessly involved in debt."

In those first weeks, the young man showed himself to be dependable and honest and possessed of a sharp mind. Observing his talents, Sutter made Bidwell his business manager, in charge of everything from cattle to brandy. Unlike Sutter, Bidwell knew how to soothe the hurt feelings of their creditors on the coast and guide New Helvetia through drought and crop failure. No matter what the books might look like, he made certain that every morning the fort's Russian bells pealed the arrival of a new day. Three hundred Indian workers were summoned from their barn houses to a hardy breakfast of beef, bread and cornmeal gruel that they slurped from a cattle trough. Stomachs filled, they headed to the fields and orchards, the tannery, slaughterhouse and loom to work for a day's tin coins.

Drought got Sutter thinking along a new line. There was no need to rely on rain when he had two rivers in his own backyard to call upon. He dispatched one of his crews to the American River, and, with shovels and crude scrapers, they excavated a canal that connected snowmelt to wheat. Irrigation was nothing short of a miracle, Sutter calculated, the sure means to bumper crops that would lift him out of debt. With fresh canal water flowing at a steady volume, he sowed enough wheat for a harvest of thirty-five thousand bushels. "Employing all the experience which I now have with the soil and climate, a very large and good crop must be raised," he wrote in his diary. "Nothing shall, this time, be neglected, that I am once liberated from all my troubles."

His biggest trouble was the debt he owed to the Russians. In one trip to the high coast, he had bought Fort Ross lock, stock and barrel for the price of $32,000 in future wheat. He hauled back nearly the entire contents of their colony: 4,000 cows, sheep and oxen; 1,000 horses and mules; a dairy; a cannon Napoleon had left behind in Moscow while in retreat and a giant millstone to grind his wheat.

To make flour, Sutter now needed to quiet the flow of the American River. Ten miles upstream from his fort, at a landing called Brighton, Sutter's men dammed the river. Piling rocks, brush and earth, they slowed down the flow and diverted water into a five-mile-long ditch. This was the canal that would irrigate the wheat fields. By pacing the flow, the canal sent a steady volume of water to the wooden wheel. The churn of the wheel rotated the five grinding stones of the flour mill. With waterpower, Sutter's wheat became loaves of Prussian bread, and the bread drew the emigrants from overland and by ship. Into the gates of his fort came the world: Americans from the two dozen eastern states and from territories not yet states; Mormons waiting on Brigham Young to locate Zion and whistle them home; the tattered remnants of the fabled Donner Party, who'd survived twenty-foot snowdrifts in the Sierra by resorting to cannibalism; Europeans from Britain, France and Germany, and the Russians, too.

With land, labor and water, Sutter found he could be anything. He became the biggest farmer, storekeeper, innkeeper, distiller, miller, tanner, manufacturer, enslaver and liberator in California. None of this making was lost on colonial Mexico. When Sutter returned to Monterey, Governor Alvarado greeted him heartily as a treasured citizen of Mexico. In regard to his land grant, no further case had to be made. Alvarado noted that Sutter had proved "his assiduity, good behavior and patriotic zeal" by subduing a great many savage Indians born in the interior. He was pleased to make good on his pledge, handing over the title to forty-eight thousand acres along four rivers, the whole of New Helvetia, to the captain.

Already, Sutter was looking to extend his empire 150 miles beyond the fort. The new grant he desired took in ninety-seven thousand acres north of New Helvetia. This decision, however, rested in the hands of Alvarado's successor, Manuel Micheltorena, a handsome general who brought a regal bearing to the governor's office. Micheltorena assured Sutter that this second grant was his already, but the gift came with one small favor in return. Micheltorena was feuding with José Castro, a former general and governor who had moved to Southern California for the sole purpose of instigating a revolt against the north. Castro now boasted a powerful ally in Alvarado. Sutter would have to pick between his old allegiance to Alvarado and his new allegiance to Micheltorena. In a decision that had little to do with loyalty, Sutter chose the latter.

In the late winter and early spring of 1845, Mexican leaders from the north and south had grown tired of egging each other on. The time had come for a civil war. The accounts of the hostilities paint an episode far more civil than war. One can imagine, without too much invention, a comic opera that features ragtag soldiers who can't shoot straight, or shoot at all. The Battle of Cahuenga took place outside the pueblo of Los Angeles. Sutter's band of Indian soldiers had journeyed half the length of the state to get there. Dressed in the hand-me-down uniforms of czarist Russia, they were prepared to die to see Micheltorena remain the governor of a united California. So, apparently, was Sutter. He was wearing the purfled uniform of a high-ranking officer of the Mexican military. The accounts describe him as forty-two years old, fleshy but not yet corpulent. For all his concocted legend, he'd never been a soldier in an actual battle. He didn't know that Governor Micheltorena had already cut a deal with the enemy. Even before the firing of a musket shot, the governor had conceded defeat to General Castro, his rival from the south.

At an arroyo beside the Los Angeles River, Sutter and his Indians closed in on the enemy. The sky was pouring rain. His fifer and bass and snare drummers signaled the assault. One hundred rounds of grapeshot were fired at the soldiers from the south. General Castro ordered a return volley. Whether by design or pure incompetence, both sides kept firing over the heads of their opponents. The Battle of Cahuenga lasted only five minutes. When it was over, the casualties numbered one: a rebel mule whose head had been blown off by a cannonball.

Sutter and his woebegone army straggled back into the fort on April Fool's Day 1845, and the captain promptly fell into despair. He had to dismiss his cook for tampering with the affections of Manuiki. His Mexican sidekick, Pablo Gutiérrez, had been taken hostage while delivering the fort's mail and hanged from a tree in Gilroy. Because the south had won, a new governor, one of the dons of the land-grabbing Pico clan, was sworn in at Los Angeles.

The shift of power would be short-lived, though. The following summer, as the Mexicans were still sorting out the spoils of their war, U.S. Army Major John C. Frémont and a band of American settlers staged a coup under the flag of a grizzly bear. The banner was the crude construction of insurrectionist William Todd, a nephew of Abraham Lincoln's. Todd had taken an unbleached cotton strip from one of the men's wives and red flannel from the petticoat of another and painted it with pokeberry juice. He either couldn't paint or had an ironic eye because the bear looked like a pig. The whole affair, sordid even by frontier standards, would have gone down as the last of California's political spasms on its way to American statehood were it not for the murderous role of Major Frémont and his guide Kit Carson.

Earlier that summer, the two explorers had crossed the Oregon border into California with their team of U.S. topographical engineers. It might have been asked what their surveying of the West was meant to accomplish if not the theft of California from Mexico. But for two decades, both the "live and let live" Mexicans and the implacable Americans had dodged the question of whose rule controlled California. Mexican leaders had almost pathologically refused to root out the presence of Americans from their land.

This time, however, the new governor, Pío Pico, and his military commander took a stand that sounded resolute. They declared that Frémont and his men weren't surveyors on a harmless mission but a band of highwaymen bent on plunder. This decree, not surprisingly, did not comport with Frémont's image of himself. He was a lover of literature who had taken the hand of the beautiful daughter of a powerful U.S. senator and journeyed west to find himself and the future of America. Though Frémont had ridden all over California and wrote passionately of his travels, truth is the man nicknamed the Pathfinder had not found a single trail on his own.

For this reason, the slander of "highwaymen" from the lips of Governor Pico struck Frémont straight in the gut. The arrival of the Bear Flag rowdies nursing their own virulent grudge against Mexican rule must have seemed an opportunity too perfect to pass up. Like the discontents, Frémont regarded the Mexicans as slothful. He could see from their two decades of indolent rule that they had no idea what to do with the glorious possibility that was California. Frémont and Carson met up with the Bear Flag rebels under the Marysville Buttes, and two hundred men rode off together with a crackpot's plan to snatch California from the Mexicans.

Frémont confronted poor old Sutter at his fort. The two rivals hadn't seen each other in several years. On the last visit, Frémont and his guide Kit Carson had arrived at Sutter's Fort looking wayworn after a Sierra crossing. Sutter had treated them like royalty back then. He had fired his cannon in salute and served a lavish meal of beef, ham, venison and bear meat, salmon fresh from the river, vegetables from his garden and bottles of Rhine wine. This time, Frémont, sour and aloof, had come on official orders. This was now the republic of California, he informed Sutter, and the fort at New Helvetia was Fort Sacramento. Frémont grabbed the keys from his host, who had never before relinquished them. Anyone who disobeyed his command would be locked up, Frémont barked. Where his orders came from, he did not say.

Meanwhile, the Bear Flag boys were heading to the coast without Frémont to confront the Mexicans. Just which soldiers they were seeking to engage in battle was not clear. Mexico had almost no military presence north of San Francisco. A trio of insomniacs led the marauders: a firebrand Yankee schoolteacher, an ex-sailor wanted for murder and a Rocky Mountain trapper named Ezekiel Merritt. Big Zeke was a huge and brutal man with bloodshot eyes and a terrible stutter that disabled his paranoiac rants just enough that they sounded almost plausible. The Americans regarded themselves not as robbers but as liberators, and to prove their highest intentions, they scribbled down a solemn proclamation. All these years later, the reader of history can see that their proclamation does not stand up to scrutiny. The stated provocation—that the Mexican government was threatening to seize their guns and beasts of burden and run them into the desert to be massacred by Indians—was a canard at best. And their pledge to the residents of California—to right the wrongs of the Catholic missions and build a "Republican Government" that would protect liberty, industry, virtue and literature—was simply not theirs to offer.

They rode to Mariano Vallejo's headquarters in Sonoma looking to surprise the general and his men. They pounded on the door of his hacienda. They could see herds of somnolent cattle but no fighting men. As for the general, he was enjoying a siesta. He invited them in, poured drinks from his best bottle of pisco brandy and explained that he was a liberal man with an incomparable library of great Western works who desired nothing more than the U.S. annexation of California. The Americans were pleased to hear of his democratic affection, but it was too late to change their course of action. Their host was now a prisoner of war. Vallejo could not help but catch a glimpse of their comical flag as they rode him off to Sutter's Fort, where he would remain under lock and key until the fighting was finished.

Governor Pico, ensconced in Los Angeles, did his oratorical best to rouse his people in defense. "Fly, Mexicans, in all haste in pursuit of the treacherous foe; follow him to the farthest wilderness; punish his audacity; and in case we fail let us form a cemetery where posterity may remember to the glory of Mexican history the heroism of her sons." No such glory awaited the fifty or so Mexican irregulars and soldiers who rode north to Sonoma to punish the Americans for their audacity. In a skirmish or two, the Mexicans managed to kill a pair of Bear Flag rebels and sacrifice one of their own. The twenty-four-day California Republic might have ended there, but Major Frémont, riding with his own band of pirates near San Rafael, came upon a small boat in which four Californios were rowing across the water. Twin brothers, Francisco and Ramón de Haro, and their uncle, José de la Reyes Berryessa, were trying to reach the grounds of the old mission. As they made their way ashore, Frémont could plainly see that they brandished no weapons. All his letters of explanation and paragraphs of memoir to follow would never give a reason for what took place next, except to say that this was war, and any Mexicans crossing the water (they were actually Basque) were the enemy. Under the Pathfinder's eye, Kit Carson and his corporal's guard killed the men in cold blood.

Ten days later, on July 7, 1846, U.S. naval commodore John Drake Sloat, citing an old fear that the British were about to seize California, raised the Stars and Stripes over Monterey. Without firing a shot, the United States had taken California from Mexico only a year after it had seized Texas and a year before American troops would invade Mexico City and force the Mexicans to sign the Treaty of Guadalupe Hidalgo and relinquish the territory of New Mexico, too. Back at the fort, Sutter now flew the U.S. flag with the pride of a conqueror. His New Helvetia had become an outpost of the American empire, though his hold on it was about to give way.

Seven

EUREKA

What is gold but a vein. What is water but the blood that runs inside a vein. The mining of gold is the mining of water first. The second taking of California begins in the same water that Sutter turned into wheat. A man in Sutter's employ is standing in a ditch alongside the American River fifty miles upstream from the fort. This is where foothills meet Sierra. The man is building a lumber mill for New Helvetia that utilizes the same mechanics of river diversion and flow as the flour mill. He has been working on the project for seven months, and the structure is nearly done. It is the next piece in Sutter's empire, the one that will guarantee him a decade of building to come. The man, James Marshall, a New Jersey boy who's had his flirtation with the Bear Flag gang, is trying to start over. He gets through winter with his rifle, blanket, crackers and venison. He oversees forty Indians who have put up a brush dam in the river and cut a ditch through a sandbar at the rear of the mill. At night, he raises a gate and lets the water run strong to flush out sand and gravel. And now it's the clear, cold morning of January 24, 1848, and his men are eating breakfast, and he shuts off the flow and lets the water sink back into sand. He ventures a few steps into the ditch, and his eye catches a glimpse of something shining in the shallow water. He reaches down and picks it up. It is half the size of a pea. He can feel his heart thump. A few yards away, he sees the glint of another half pea. Could it be? Could it be? No, the gold he knows, the gold of a coin, has a reddish tinge. This is more like brass. He sets the pieces on a hard rock and anvils down on them. The metal bends the way he's heard gold bends. He suddenly thinks the whole world might be watching. So he lodges the pieces inside a rag and stuffs the rag in his pocket and lets a week pass in which another phase of Sutter's lumber mill is completed. Then he leaps on his horse in a flood rain and rides back to the fort to show the captain.

It is not enough that Sutter invites him, dripping wet, into his private quarters and shuts the door. Marshall wants him to lock the door. He removes the rag from his pocket and opens its corner to display the metal. It is gold, Sutter says. Or maybe it isn't. He dashes into his apothecary shop and applies nitric acid to the metal. The liquid fails to disturb the metal in the least. Gold. He grabs a volume of his *Encyclopedia Americana* and flips through the pages until he reaches "Gold." He reads about its properties and hustles a scale and three and a half dollars in silver from some of his men. Sutter and Marshall perform a simple gravity test. Gold, but not just any. Twenty-three-carat gold. The two men, who agree to be partners in gold's first dibs, seem almost frightened by its implications. They swear themselves to silence.

What Sutter and Marshall didn't know was that two men were eavesdropping through a crack in the door that rainy night. They were among a group of Mormons who had marched across the prairie in 1847 in search of their own Eureka. Their prophet Joseph Smith had been killed by a mob in Illinois for founding a religion that he claimed was written on buried gold plates and allowed him to take as many wives as he wished. The new prophet, Brigham Young, a carpenter by trade, didn't know where to steer the flock. Then one night Joseph Smith, like the angel who had gifted the gold plates, came to Young in a dream. The old prophet spoke in the manner of a commandment: A new Zion, where a new River Jordan flowed into a new Dead Sea, could be found in the American West. Take our Latter-day Saints and build another Israel there. As the Mormons departed the Midwest, their exodus did not have an exact destination in mind. Young would know the land of Canaan when he found it. Guided by signs from up on high, they kept their white canvas wagons moving westward in the path of the vision.

At the same time, another Mormon leader, Samuel Brannan, a womanizer, drinker and brawler, had sailed from New York to California with his own flock of Latter-day Saints. His Mormon battalion landed in Yerba Buena, where Brannan began publishing the *California Star*, San Francisco's original newspaper. He believed he had found Canaan right there on the edge of the Pacific. He hopped on his steed and galloped eastward to guide Prophet Young and the rest of the tribe to California. The prophet already had set eyes on "the valley where the broad waters of the Great Salt Lake glistened in the sunbeams." The Salt Lake Desert was not an easy land; nor did Young think it should be. Only a people deserving of the crown of Latter-day Saints could make a community thrive in such a place. The suffering they'd endure and the land they'd reclaim would sow in future generations a fellowship not to be broken.

Brannan thought the prophet had gone mad. Upon hearing Young's choice, he mounted his horse and rode back to San Francisco, stopping on the way at Sutter's Fort and cutting a deal with the captain to open a general store. That was how dozens of skilled Mormons came to work at New Helvetia and how Brannan, their chief elder, was entrusted with collecting the "Lord's tithes" from them. In the spring of 1849, these tithes began to show up as flakes of gold. The Mormons, aware of Sutter's secret, were digging gold from a spot called Mormon Bar. Word of the riches got back to Prophet Young in Salt Lake, and he sent an apostle to the general store to collect the tithing. Brannan, still bent out of shape by Young's rejection of San Francisco, ran the man out, shouting, "You go back and tell Brigham that I'll give up the Lord's money when he gives me a receipt signed by the Lord!"

Brannan was too shrewd in business to remain a newspaperman for long. The route from the Golden Gate to the gold fields ran straight through his general store at Sutter's Fort. He stocked the shelves with pans, pickaxes, shovels, wood and tack, just to start. As for drumming up customers, the old headline writer knew exactly what to do. On May 12, 1848, Brannan set his plan into motion. Did he feel like an insurrectionist as he boarded the ferry on the Sacramento River and paid his fare? He was only looking to incite what was about to happen on its own anyway. But what a match he held in his pocket. He got off the ferry in San Francisco and bounded down the straw and mud of Montgomery Street, where drunks often fell and suffocated in the mire. He had not a drop of whiskey in him as he started to showboat in front of a puzzled crowd. It was one of the great carnival acts in a city that would become famous for them. Whooping it up with his hat in one hand and a quinine bottle filled with gold flakes in the other—the Lord's tithing—he began to shout, "Gold! Gold! Gold from the American River!" It made for the perfect banner headline. His shout reached all the way to the *New York Herald,* and then it reached the world.

Another place gets the luxury of finding itself. Another place is made of many movements. It lurches forward and then backward, depending on how the forward has gone. It invents, exploits, extracts, destroys. Between boom and bust, it catches its breath. Manifest Destiny, as it moved across the plains, would have had its way with California eventually. In fits and starts, it would have done its reshaping and reconstituting. Riches would have been found and possessed by the few, mountains blasted, rivers dammed, rivers dispatched to places rivers never go. Wheat and then peaches and plums and grapes would have been planted. Nuts and houses, too. But here was a force of a different magnitude come down on the young history of a land. Gold's cataclysm hit the ground with suddenness, infused change with a warped speed, and in that blast of reinvention, no one had the time to stop and ponder poor old John Sutter. He had hatched the dream of farm and city together, paid men in tin coins to build it high, and now he would watch it brought down by gold. California starts off jury-rigged and explosive, and it never settles down. It skips over normal, careens between extremes. It does not rest on the steady of farming. It does not rest on the steady of city building. The volatility of its nature rubs off on the people from wherever they come. They must conquer a place of too much. Is it any wonder they employ the implements of too much?

Eighty thousand gold seekers arrived by ship, wagon and foot in 1849 alone. Overnight they came. They were all mad. The Frenchman, the Chinaman, the Chilean, the Hindu, the Mexican, the German, the Russian, the Italian, the Greek, the Irishman, the Welshman, and the "Digger Indian," maddest of them all. They came with no plan. Only the Chilean who had mined back home knew what he was doing. The rest had no idea where they were going or what they were digging into with the tools they bought at wildly inflated prices at Samuel Brannan's general store. They were preachers, lawyers, doctors, cooks, millwrights, blacksmiths, cobblers, soldiers, philosophers, poets, killers, dancers, whores and schoolteachers. A few of them were chroniclers who put down what they saw in letters back home.

The missives of Louise Amelia Knapp Smith Clappe, who came from

Elizabeth, New Jersey, were among those collected in a book titled *Gold Rush: A Literary Exploration*. Clappe and her husband and their horses couldn't get away from the "abominable odors and intolerable fleas" of San Francisco fast enough. Over the middle of California they galloped. No roads, houses, hedges or ditches confronted them, only a vast plain as smooth as a calm sea. "We might have been steering by compass for we emerged from a land-locked harbor and followed our own course over the wide wide world," a gold seeker in their company recalled. "Here we were upon an ocean of grass-covered earth dotted with trees and sparkling with the gorgeous hues of wild flowers. At last, indenting sky, came the snowy peaks of the Sierra." Inside the mountain, men like gravediggers shoveled at the hard earth. Log cabins and clapboard shanties hugged the sugar pines. Where enough dwellings had been grouped together, the naming of a town dignified the scene.

The Clappes arrived in Rich Bar, on the North Fork of the Feather River, in the late summer of 1851. A single lane was thickly planted with forty residences that varied in elegance from the palatial splendor of "the Empire" to an abode made of pine boughs and covered with old calico shirts. Over the next year, Louise Clappe would write twenty-three near perfect letters to her sister back home, each one set down in the whimsical voice of an alter ego she called Dame Shirley. "How would you like to winter in such an abode? In a place where there are no newspapers, no churches, lectures, concerts, or theaters; no fresh books, no picnics, no tableaux, no charades, no latest fashions, no daily mail (we have an express once a month), no promenades, no rides nor drives; no vegetables but potatoes and onions, no milk, no eggs, no nothing? Now I expect to be very happy here. This strange, odd life fascinates me."

Rivers coursing down the mountainside dislodged the easy stuff first. It glinted in the streambeds like baby salmon. The "Mother Lode" was how the forty-niners described it in the aggregate—$400 million in those first six years alone. It worked out to be something more routine when measured pan to pan. The average miner came and went with about $1,000 in his pocket. James Marshall, who had a head start on everyone else, died a drunkard with $218 to his name. The banks and gold reserves made out. The cattlemen, slaughterhouses, butchers and wheat growers made out. So did the fabulous palaces of chance and the barkeeps and madams in the distant city. Young men coming down the mountain with their gold flakes, lusty the other way, scampered straight to the ladies working "the cribs." Cracks between the wooden planks gave the passerby plenty to see. For the more fastidious, "the Countess," San Francisco's leading courtesan, sent out cards inviting the town's bigwigs, clergy included, to her resplendent parlor where six ounces of gold dust, worth $96, bought you a night with the best. The ideal age for a much-prized Chinese prostitute was said to be fourteen, and men swarmed to get a peek at the fascinating creature known as Ah Toy. She charged each man one ounce of gold simply to gaze upon her "countenance," though she had a rather elastic way of defining the word.

The first Chinese immigrants, two men and a woman from Hong Kong, sailed through the Golden Gate in February 1848. Three thousand more arrived the next year. By 1852, the Chinese population of San Francisco had shot past 12,000—and 11,993 of them were male. "The man who can run for a few minutes in a short race, and make very fast time, is not the equal of him who can run all day. The Chinese are all-day runners, and those who compete with them will need to rise early and sit up late," the *Daily Alta California* observed. San Francisco was the most polyglot place on earth, and one of the most deadly, notching a staggering 150 murders a year. How to begin to count the thefts? One apple cost five dollars. A dozen eggs sold for fifty dollars. A loaf of bread, four cents in New York City, cost seventy-five cents. A canvas tent measuring fifteen by twenty feet, if situated in the right part of downtown—that is next door to the gambling dens and whorehouses—rented for forty thousand dollars a year.

There were no cops or firemen or inspectors to speak of. Public safety had given way to public intoxication. Rudimentary systems for water and waste could not keep up. The city, first as canvas and then as wood, went down in flames six times. Inasmuch as the streets were made of mud, there was no way to grade them. One side rose fifteen feet higher than the other side. In the deluge of 1849–50, scores of animals drowned in the muck. Hide and hoof became part of the street. "This street is impassable; not even jackassable," became the utterance of the San Franciscan.

Sam Brannan, the Mormon newspaperman who had shouted "Gold!" and incarnated this mess, took it upon himself to form a vigilance committee. His crackdown on a group of Australian outlaws known as the Sydney Ducks was swift and brutal: four lynched and twenty-eight deported. Ward heelers stuffing ballot boxes passed civic measures aimed at cleaning up the more official corruption. Plank sidewalks, manifest of civilization, were laid down. This enabled "tall, finely proportioned women with bold, flashing eyes and dazzling white skin" to be escorted without splatter by tall men with great chins to the St. Francis Hotel, the Dramatic Museum and the opera house. The latter is where impresario Tom Maguire, second only to P. T. Barnum, brought sleight-of-hand artists, jugglers, opera singers, minstrels, leg shows and Shakespeare's plays. If San Franciscans desired a form of entertainment truly peculiar to the West, they could do no better than the sideshow of Oofty Goofty, the "Wild Man of Borneo," who menaced the plank sidewalks of the Barbary Coast, the city's red-light district, in a "garb of fur and feathers," emitting weird animal sounds. For ten cents, he'd let you kick him anywhere; for twenty cents you could hit him with a cane or a billiard ball; for a half dollar you could step up to the plate with a baseball bat. When heavyweight champion John L. Sullivan tried his luck, Oofty Goofty had to be hauled to the hospital with a fractured spine. Upon recuperation, he became the city's leading "freak show."

The emergence of San Francisco as a world-class city came at a time when its biggest newspaper was calling for the massacre of Indians who refused to be herded onto rancherias. The state legislature was paying a bounty, four dollars a day, for any killer of Indians who acted under the cover of a militia. The most ingenious of these killers was a lapsed Quaker named Ben Wright who affected the garb of the northern tribes and killed scores of Modocs with stealth and knife. He collected as trophy pieces the scalps, noses, fingers and ears of women and children. For his tidy work, the legislature paid him $744. In the record of current events that ran in a popular California magazine, the following event was put down for January 1859: "Three white men attacked a rancheria of Digger Indians near the Russian River Valley and killed fourteen of them on the supposition that the Indians had been stealing their cattle." The next item in the same column of ink noted this: "The passenger arrivals at San Francisco for 1858 were 37,167 men, 4,752 women and

1,360 children; total 43,279. The number of departures were 35,875 men, 1,562 women and 714 children; total, 38,151. Total gain: 5,128."

The erasing of California's natives might yet take its place alongside humankind's other crimes of genocide. This is certainly what UCLA scholar Benjamin Madley argues for in his monumental work *An American Genocide: The United States and the California Indian Catastrophe, 1846–1873*. To debate such a crime a century and a half after its fact is to quarrel over numbers of victims and intentions of governments and the methods and means that killers of vastly different eras employed. Scholars committed to the "oneness" of the Holocaust, for instance, argue that paying settlers and gold miners for time spent in the killing fields does not amount to a government "planning and executing" mass murder. Besides, the militias and bands of irregulars, sanctioned by the state or not, took only 10,000 to 15,000 Indian lives. Fair enough. The extermination of the Indian culture, both its unwitting and witting parts, played out over eighty haphazard years. If the methods of extermination do not neatly fit the modern and legal definition of genocide, it surely was genocide in what it accomplished. In a fight over who owned the natural resources of California, one culture supplanted another. The job of that taking may not have been elegant, but it was done well. There were 300,000 California natives when Father Serra arrived and 150,000 when Sutter headed into the tules. There were 16,277 at the time of the 1880 census.

Beneath the sheer granite domes and towering falls of Yosemite, no white man had ever trod in the deep grass valley. The Merced River shot through a forest of giant sequoias and ponderosa pines watched over by the Wawona, a white horned owl. The Ahwahnechee were scarcely a tribe, much less a warrior nation prepared to do battle. They numbered maybe seventy-five, most of them belonging to the family of Chief Tenaya, when the Mariposa Battalion rode over the mountains and into their sequestered valley. The soldiers arrived in two excursions, in the early and late spring of 1851. The first was led by Major Jim Savage, the "king of the tules," a sorcerer in the eyes of California natives who believed he could catch any bullet fired at him with his bare hands. Savage had five Indian wives and spoke five Indian tongues in addition to German, French, Spanish and English. He was said to be a breed of man and wolf that required not a moment of sleep and could smell the smoke of an Indian fire miles away. Savage tracked down Ahwahnechee huts, caches of acorns and one squaw so ancient she looked like a "vivified Egyptian mummy." As for Chief Tenaya and the rest of the tribe, they had taken to hiding inside a rocky gorge covered with snow, beyond the detection of even a wizard. Savage, perhaps the only member of the Mariposa Battalion not dazzled by Yosemite's magnificence, gave orders to burn the village down and then guided his men back home.

The second excursion a few months later, led by Capt. John Boling, wasted no time capturing two of Tenaya's sons. When the chief finally came down from his hiding place, the body of his youngest and most beloved son lay in the meadow next to the swollen Merced River. The boy had been shot in the back by a young guard who had come under the sway of an Indian-hating mentor described as an "old Texan sinner." Captain Boling was said to be furious, though not mad enough to actually report the murder to higher-ups. He could now see that poor old Tenaya, his gaze riveted on his dead son, was stricken with the worst grief. If what the captain felt for the Indian in that moment was close to pity for another human being, this did not alter the fact that the chief still needed to surrender and march his raggedy people out of Yosemite and down into the dirt valley where a rancheria life awaited them. The chief turned around and faced the captain. One eyewitness described how Tenaya drew up to his full height and, with his chest heaving and his eyes flashing, cried out a curse in mostly Spanish. How much of the curse is white man's guilty invention is hard to say, but as curses go, it doesn't get much better:

"White men, you are a bad people. You have invaded my country. You have killed my people simply because we have stolen a few horses—a privilege granted to us by the Great Spirit. We steal that we may live. I know very well that you steal. You steal among yourselves that you may be rich; we steal something to eat. You come and steal my country. You steal me and my people from my hunting grounds. They were given to me and to my people exclusively by the Great Spirit. Yes, when these mountains, now so high, were but little hills, this was our country. Now you come and take us away. I would rather leave my ashes here than to be a slave to the white man. Kill me, sir Captain. Yes, kill me as you killed my son, the child of my heart. Shoot me! Murder me! And the echo of my voice shall be heard resounding among these mountains of my native home for many years afterward, and my spirit, which you cannot tame, shall linger around these old gray granite hills and haunt you and your posterity, as long as there is one of you or your tribe remaining."

Totuya, "Foaming Water," granddaughter of Chief Tenaya and the last survivor of the Ahwahnechee

The Ahwahnechee were marched to a rancheria along the Fresno River in the hot valley below, where the canker worm of grief bored its way into the old man's heart. Government overseers took pity and allowed him to leave. Chief Tenaya found his way back to Yosemite, where he was stoned to death during a feud with a rival Mono tribe. Because he had refused to sign a peace treaty with the United States, his people were never declared a sovereign nation. They would never get the chance to open a casino. We Americans did, however, find a way to honor them. The junior high I attended was named Tenaya. We were the Braves, our color was maroon and we played against kids who went to junior highs named Ahwahnee, Yosemite, Wawona, Tioga and Sequoia. The names meant nothing to us. We were never told the story.

From her log cabin, Dame Shirley watched the mining of gold, the mining of water, take its industrial turn. On a Sunday in the summer of 1852, she and a group of friends walked three miles to see the "Ditch" the local miners had dug. "I do not believe that Nature herself ever made anything so lovely as this artificial brooklet," she wrote. "It glides like a living thing through the very heart of the forest." Dame Shirley was now living in Indian Bar, a mining camp perched along the Feather River. It sat in a long, broad, slow rise of mountain neither foothill nor alpine, about two thousand feet in elevation. From Indian Bar in the north to Mariposa in the south, the gold country extended several hundred miles over eight rivers, scores of streams and now the first of three hundred lovely ditches. Why ditches? A miner couldn't prospect without water. Water was how gold moved down the mountain and came to rest in the silt of a river. Water was how a miner, with a swish of his pan, separated gold from dirt and pebble. Water was how he came to invent the rocker and the long tom, the wooden box and wooden sluice that washed more gravel and snagged more gold. Water was how he dug a hole deep into the mountain to reach the richer vein. Water is how he (or was it she?) came to write the "Miner's Water Song":

There is joy in the miner's camp to-night
There is joy, and the miner's heart is light;
There is mirth and revelry, shouting and song,
For the rain has been falling all the day long.

We'll have water plenty, and water to spare
Enough for each miner to have his full share;
The sluice will be full, and the ditch overrun,
And the goal of our hopes will be speedily won.

—Carrie D.

In the beginning, mining was a solitary pursuit. This suited the miner fine because gold had put suspicion in his eyes. By himself, he bagged the stupid nuggets that nature left along creeks. As early as 1851, word out of Indian Bar, Dutch Flat, Yankee Jim's, Iowa Flat and Timbuctoo told of the easy gold all fished out. There was plenty of lucre left, but it was buried at the bottom of the ancient streambeds, ten feet above bedrock, and had to be ripped out of the river canyons. Gold's extraction now required the muscle of water moved by the muscle of men. To bring the river to pay dirt, miners put aside their wariness and began working as teams. Water and shovel came together as miners, shoulder to shoulder, dug ditches, felled pine trees and erected flumes to guide the river's flow onto distant gravel. Who knew anything about civil engineering? The early ditches were three feet wide and three feet deep with just enough grade, three feet each mile, that water kept moving. In those places where the terrain didn't allow for ditches, miners constructed elaborate wooden flumes that clung to cliffs and wended through canyons.

The greatest flumes might well have been aqueducts the way they carried such enormous volumes of water over great hikes. On even ground, the flumes traveled on the shoulders of big wooden trestles. When a gorge had to be spanned and the tall stilts of a trestle would not do, the miners were lowered by rope hundreds of feet down the canyon wall. Into the granite, they drilled holes to fasten the flumes to metal brackets capable of bearing fifteen tons of weight. Across one ravine in Butte County, a flume built four feet wide and three feet deep hung 118 feet in the air. When the water shot across, the planks shivered. On the flume's piggyback, the river was carried from one side of the ravine to the other, a span of 162 yards.

With working water, the miners tore at hillsides and loosened dirt and rock, a muddy gruel that flowed down and down into the maw of long wooden sluice boxes. Because gold was heavier than earth, the shiny flakes settled behind riffles set crosswise in the box. A social order, and maybe even trust and loyalty, too, grew out of the communal toil. Song and verse came to the camps. Teamwork civilized not only

Flume erected in Yuba County to move water from river to gold diggings

the mountainside but the faraway city, too. At least until one team's claim to earth and water conflicted with another team's claim and the California Legislature, in its first official acts, decided to tax and then exclude miners along racial and ethnic lines.

Even linked as teams, the miners could ill afford the cost to dig enough ditches and hang enough flumes. They lacked the capital to build canals capable of moving greater volumes of water, much less to erect dams to capture and hold snowmelt. Without dams and reservoirs, miners had no way to portion out a river's flow throughout the year. Their ditches ran dry in July, and their diggings fell quiet for months. The economy sputtered during the summer, and California slowed to a lull. As to the question of who would invest in the conveyance systems to bring full-time water to the miners, the cries of one promoter of river diversion could be heard in a popular magazine of the day: "Is there no water in our mountain stream? Plenty. Cannot that water be taken out from thence and conveyed to the mining districts? Easily. Then why in the name of our prosperity is it not done? Instead, the capital that should have built canals is almost exclusively invested in real estate. Where one man is now prosperous, twenty would be if they had plenty of water. Water we want, and water we must have!"

Edward Matteson, a forty-niner from Connecticut, had been scheming of ways he could bring greater digging power, more head, to his water. Conveying water long distances to a miner's claim was one miracle; making that water strike pay dirt with extra force was another. First, Matteson built a flume a good height above his claim to mimic a waterfall. This by itself gave the water significantly more force. Next he attached a rawhide hose to the end of his flume and pressurized the water. This was a manifold improvement. Finally, in 1853, he stuck a three-quarter-inch nozzle made of sheet brass onto the spray end of a canvas hose and created a hiss, a jet, a roar. Hydraulic mining, the industrialization of the gold fields, had been born.

Up until that moment, digging for gold had been an enterprise apart from the city. Miners went to town to buy their supplies. Miners returned to town to spend their lucre. But now, with nozzle fastened to hose, the capitalists of San Francisco and Sacramento wanted in. They formed their own companies that specialized in building water systems—earthen dams, reservoirs, canals, ditches, flumes, pipes and hoses—and then engaged investors from New York and Europe to finance the enterprises. California's gold fields went global. At first, the miners welcomed outside money taking on the burden of water's conveyance. It let them do what they did best: dig for gold. They found out soon enough, however, that industrialization didn't work that way.

Thirty San Francisco capitalists, led by railroad baron Lester Robinson and Bank of California founder Billy Ralston, had launched the North Bloomfield Mining and Gravel Company. Capital wasn't a problem. They hired eight hundred Chinese miners and paid them thirty-five dollars a month to shovel out ditches and reservoirs and build the first dams of a sprawling water system. Now five miners could extract in a day what it had once taken fifty miners to yield. And what did this mean for the forty-niner as an individual? It meant his gig was up. His water systems could not compete with the deeper and broader systems built by the mining giants. As long as water was plenty, he could get by. But as soon as drought struck again—and it struck hard in the 1860s—his ditches and flumes dried up. The forty-niner suddenly found himself obsolete.

With water now weaponized and held in the hands of a coterie of industrialists, a new hierarchy emerged. The miners who stayed on became paid-by-the-hour men. In the town of Humbug, in Nevada County, crews dressed in North Bloomfield blue. In the town of Cherokee, in Butte County, they wore the green of the Spring Valley Canal and Mining Company. They wheeled in "hydraulic behemoths" that looked like cannons and fired out water at such a velocity—800 feet in distance, 150 pounds of pressure—that one observer marveled that it "could cut a man in two if it should hit him." They blew the sides off the mountains with the will of the ice age. One famous photo snapped by Carleton E. Watkins shows the monsters of North Bloomfield at work shooting water across what was once a mountain but is now a massive void. The long arcing streams are operated by men who, hardly miners anymore, appear as ants on the scene. They are aiming at what little is left of the mountain, and the convergence of their streams creates a cataract of mud and water than runs back down into the abyss.

This was the immense crater of North Bloomfield's notorious Malakoff Diggins, where a 7,800-foot-long tunnel had to be carved through solid bedrock to drain the runoff. The more mud the miners produced and ran through boxes and screens, the more gold they captured. The big cannons—one variety was called "the Little Giant," another "the

Monitor"—cut the cost of gold extraction from five dollars a cubic yard to less than a penny. Their unrelenting streams of river brought down cascades of brown water, boulders, cobblestones, pebbles, sand, clay and gold. "There is a real pleasure about this gigantic force," one reporter wrote. "Not merely the force of much gravity, but also a wicked, vicious, unutterable indignation. Rocks two feet in diameter fly like chaff when struck by the stream." The whole mess was then sent streaming back into the canyon, and what didn't clog up the river moved far enough downstream to clog up the delta and the San Francisco Bay.

From one end of gold country to the other, crews of Chinese, Irish, French, Italian and Portuguese built six thousand miles of ditches. Of the three hundred ditches that crisscrossed the Mother Lode, sixteen extended fifty miles or more in length. These weren't the crude models carved out by weary miners who could only watch in frustration as the flow backed up with silt. These ditches, eight feet wide and five feet deep, were surveyed by one engineer and designed by another engineer so that the gradient dropped precisely ten feet every mile. The water never froze as it flowed out at 7,500 miner's inches—84,375 gallons each minute.

The era of hydraulics saw the demand for water shoot up fifty-fold. The large water and mining companies swallowed up smaller ones, and entire watersheds suddenly belonged to single entities. In the call to build reservoirs that would extend mining year-round, more money poured in from abroad. English capitalists alone invested $1 million in 1871. The North Bloomfield Mining and Gravel Company erected a dam nearly one hundred feet high and more than two hundred feet in length. The company then went about adding to its network of dams, reservoirs, canals and ditches until it was capable of storing 23,000 acre-feet of water. The Spring Valley Canal and Mining Company built a dam nearly as high, with a main canal that ran fifty-two miles. The flows of the Feather, Yuba, Bear, American, Mokelumne, Stanislaus and Tuolumne Rivers were now dictated by a handful of men.

The taking of the rivers to mine California evolved along three basic principles of law and practice. Right from the start, these concepts butted heads in the gold rush, and they would continue to butt heads during the rushes of wheat, fruit and nuts to come.

One concept held that the first person to lay claim to a river's flows got to keep these first rights even in times of drought. He needed only to pursue his mining and farming in earnest. "First in time, first in right" became the prevailing principle of a system largely ad hoc and self-governing, a "finders keepers" way of assigning water rights. Conversely, the last person to show up on the scene had a diminished right, or sometimes no right at all. And whether a taker stood first in line or last in line, he did not own the water. The water belonged now and forever to the public. However it was measured—by miner's inches, cubic feet per second, acre-feet—he owned only the right to use it. At the end of the day, though, the right to "appropriate" but not to own the water became a meaningless distinction. The *right* was the *water*. A man and his company could be irrigating one acre or one million acres—the law of appropriation cared not as long as the flow was going toward "beneficial use." The parceling out of water had proceeded differently under Spanish law. The Mexican governors, for one, had weighed the equity and justice of who got the water and how much. No such heart found its way into the California state constitution.

A second concept ordained that if a man bought land along a river, he owned "riparian rights" to as much of the river's flow as he wanted. The riparian owner needed merely to put the flow to beneficial use and not unduly interfere with the draw of other riparian owners. In the midst of drought, this meant that a man who had purchased land along both sides of the river could deny flow to another man whose land was beyond the riverine. California's legislature and courts adopted riparian rights as a legal concept even though it made little sense in a place where aridity ruled. Riparian rights grew out of common law in England, where rivers never went dry and, in fact, routinely flooded. In the British swamps, a riparian owner would hardly think to call into question someone else's use of his river water. "Have at it! The more straws the merrier! Please, by all means, drain my swamp!" In California, by contrast, a riparian irrigator might have every reason to hog a river's flow.

The third concept was an uneasy blend of the first two, one part riparian and one part appropriative. It would take endless court battles to smooth out and would remain contentious enough that it was still evolving a century later.

By the mid-1870s, California's first industry counted twenty thousand employees and fifty-three million gallons of water stored in reservoirs. For the $100 million it cost to erect the water conveyance systems, companies like North Bloomfield and Spring Valley had extracted $300 million in gold. The high returns begged a question: Why not operate the mines as twenty-four-hour-a-day extractions? Man and machine weren't a problem. North Bloomfield had plenty of both.

To mine by night, the company first lit bonfires and torches. Nighttime's glow inside the Malakoff crater was hellish. Locomotive engines were then brought in, but the miners did no better by headlight. Finally, North Bloomfield pioneered a 12,000-candle electrical light system, a grid that harnessed water's power in another way. One old forty-niner who toured the mine during the late-hour shift was transfixed by its otherworldliness. "A night scene of this kind is the highest degree weird and startling, and it cannot fail to strike the stranger with wonder and admiration." In an effort to match North Bloomfield's audacity, one massive mine in Butte County never ceased running. In a twelve-year span, its operation halted only once, for the funeral of President James Garfield.

The men who industrialized water to find gold became fabulously wealthy. They built mansions on San Francisco's Nob Hill and took care to diversify their fortunes as a hedge against the next drought. Mining towns and their mountain people didn't have that luxury. It was all or nothing. They survived, and even prospered, as long as the rain fell and the snow piled up. When drought struck, it always came "out of nowhere."

In the hills of Butte County, the little mining community of Cherokee recorded its stunted history thusly:

In 1853, a schoolteacher named Sol Potter from the Cherokee lands of Oklahoma discovers gold along a creek called Concow. A year later, a Chinese miner unearths a two-pound specimen in the same spot. Word spreads, and people come. A post office is established, a school is built, a daily stagecoach directs its route through town. The citizens of Cherokee hold their first cotillion ball on December 31, 1862. A severe drought hits the next year, and people leave. Two men argue over the merits of Abraham Lincoln, and one man stabs the other. Two mine owners feud over the scarcity of water. It's 1870, and wet times are bound to return, or at least that's the calculation of one George Perkins, soon to be governor of California, who starts the Spring Valley Canal and Mining Company with $800,000 in capital.

It rains and snows again; the company hires two hundred Chinese. The "Celestials" lay eighty-seven thousand feet of iron pipe to convey water down a new flume to a reservoir behind an eighty-foot-tall earthen dam. The nozzles of the hydraulic giants spew out forty million gallons of water a day, three times more than the city of San Francisco consumes. The Reservoir School is established. Two hotels, a brewery, a bakery, an Independent Order of Odd Fellows hall, a church, five saloons and a cemetery open. The Spring Valley enterprise builds an assay office and a company store. The mine is sold for $1.2 million to an English concern. In 1875, the company recapitalizes and is valued at $5 million. The mine produces so many cubic yards of runoff—mud, pebbles and silt—that the tailings clog up Concow Creek and then the Feather River itself.

The river stops flowing, fish die, drought returns and a cloud of dust descends on Cherokee while President Rutherford B. Hayes and his wife visit the mine. A stagecoach driver sets out to deliver them a fine lunch, but he loses his bearings in the dust cloud. The president and his wife leave town hungry and so thoroughly covered in dirt that they are unrecognizable. Wet times return, and the farmers sue the mining company for dumping tons of silty runoff onto their fields and smothering the crops. The company buys a dredger and builds forty miles of canals in a doomed effort to divert the silt and clean up an environmental disaster. In 1877, the mine closes and the hamlet of Cherokee shutters. It breathes anew today as a ghost town for tourists who love to pan for a flake of gold. Meanwhile, all around it, enterprising farmers have planted tens of thousands of acres of almonds, a $250-million-a-year gold mine of a crop.

Eight

TAILINGS

Water! Water! Water!

We would, if we could, write those words in characters of fire. For in them is the gospel of California's pecuniary salvation. Nearly every capitalist has the words upon his lips: "We want population. Nothing can improve California until we get more population. The value of property would double if we had population."

Oh, yes, gentlemen, that is all very fine, but there is something we want much more, immeasurably more than population—now, immediately—and that is Water! Water! Water! Not water to drink, for that can be found bubbling up on every mountaintop, but water to work with; that is what we want and what California wants more than anything else.

No thirsty traveler upon a weary desert, no bedridden patient with burning brow and fevered pulse ever needed water more. Water enables men to work. Working men dig gold. Gold, thus dug, would be put in circulation. That circulation would give prosperity, and all would be content. We will therefore, with the same language as the horseleech, cry, "Give, Give," but let the gift be Water! Water! Water!

This was the cry of James Mason Hutchings, an Englishman who came west in 1848, made a fortune in gold, lost a fortune in bank failure and then founded a journal of unparalleled excellence in the West, *Hutchings' Illustrated California Magazine*. How it must have struck all those new Californians who had little to explain their world to them, and then suddenly *Hutchings* rolls off the press in July 1856, a periodical stuffed with verse and memoir, first-rate reportage and feature writing, narratives of trips to undiscovered landscapes, editorial commentary, slick promotion and beautifully engraved illustrations of California's wonders: the giant condor and grizzly bear, the tarantula and lizard, the pear and sunflower, the alabaster caves of El Dorado and the mountain valley the Indians called Yo-Ham-i-te. In his passion to render a country brand-new, Hutchings invited his readers to become his writers. "Send us some soul thrilling sketch of California, that is the kind we want; something that enters into the soul-experience of the man."

The magazine had a short run, or maybe it was a long run, considering how fast California was burning through everything. In its life span from 1856 to 1861, *Hutchings' Illustrated* accomplished something that few publications ever do: it captured a place as it was being made and in that capture made the place different. From the opening paragraphs of the first edition, the magazine did not apologize for its belief that California was the greatest story ever told. The lengthy features never carried the writer's byline, but it didn't take much detective work to figure out that Hutchings traveled the state in wide-eyed wonder and wrote most of the dispatches himself. He wrote in the true conviction that nothing could stop California from becoming man's finest expression, if man could only allow himself to seize it. Every rough patch was a birth pang. The 1858 earthquake wasn't an earthquake but an electrical phenomenon. "We frequently have little shakes—often barely perceptible," he noted, "but no person nor any substantial building has been injured by an earthquake in San Francisco since the American conquest." (He would die before the earthquake of 1906 ravaged San Francisco.) Issue to issue the voice is familiar, and always emphatic, no more so than when the subject turns to water. Hutchings fairly shouts his judgment that nothing can move forward in California—not gold, not grain, not city—without the forward movement of water.

In the summer of 1857, pleased by what he beheld on one of his journeys, he wrote a piece titled "River Mining." "It becomes desirable to chain the mountain torrent, which is heedlessly rushing past, and turn it out of its natural channel so that the glittering gold lying in the river's bed may be transferred from thence to the buckskin purse of the miner. A ditch has to be dug, a flume has to be built. This being done, a dam has to be constructed across the river. Pumps are attached by which the water still remaining in the river's bed is piped out. Now, river mining is commenced in real earnest."

By the time the winter of 1861–62 showed up, *Hutchings' Illustrated* was no more. The story of the greatest flood in California history fell to others to tell. On Christmas Eve, the rain started pelting and didn't stop for the next thirty days. The downpour was so unremitting that the sun's brief appearance wrote headlines. "The phenomenon lasted several minutes and was witnessed by a great number of persons," one journalist joked. No mail could be delivered for three weeks. One village in a small valley nestled along the west bank of the Santa Ana River was sleeping when the roar sounded. The farmers of Agua Mansa—the name translates to "Calm Water"—had been praying for rain for months. In the first hours of downpour, their adobe houses melted in the churning brown water. The river swept away vineyards and orchards and a forest of sycamores, willows and cottonwoods. All that was left of the church were two marble pillars. By week's end, the little town had been wiped off the map. The Santa Ana River was running at an incredible three hundred thousand cubic feet per second. The poor cattle couldn't get out of the way. All across Southern California, lakes materialized on the plain. In a single month, thirty-five inches of rain fell on Los Angeles. Never since has this happened. To the north, on the Yuba River, a camp of Chinese miners did not see the water coming. En masse, they were washed off Long Bar and swept away. Hundreds, if not a thousand, drowned.

The town of Sacramento had outlasted the deluges of 1846, 1849, 1850, 1852 and 1853 and grew to fifteen thousand residents. But not one thing had changed about the Sacramento River. Narrow in channel, quick in drop, the river had far too much water and not nearly enough plain to absorb any flooding. Its ratio of water to plain measured 22 to 1. The mighty Mississippi, by comparison, had a ratio of water to plain that was nearly equal. Residents brought in earth to elevate their houses and storefronts. They built a levee five miles long and twenty feet at the crown. Their community-wide effort subscribed to the notion that the more earth you applied to the equation, the more chance you stood of keeping your city dry. But engineers advised that even the most formidable levee could not do the trick by itself. What was needed was a parallel system of sloughs, bypasses and old river channels that were off-limits to houses and farms and allowed the river to find its range. Only then would the levee, relieved of enough pressure, stand its ground during a flood.

As the waters of 1862 rose around them, Sacramento citizens could now see that blocking the river from its plain gave the torrent no place to go but straight at them. The river was climbing at a rate of one foot an hour and would soon rise to an incredible sixty feet. Because people, and their memory of flood, had built the levees with such extraordinary staying power, the water hewed to the earthen contours without rupture. The wave kept climbing until it carried off men, women and children, two-story houses, horses and cows, hogs and chickens, dogs, cats and rats. Only the knoll where Sutter had dreamed of building his city could be seen holding its head above water. All the rest of Sacramento was drowned.

Newspaperman Alfred Doten, a colleague of Twain's, kept a daily journal that chronicled the birthing pangs of the Old West. His vivid account of the great flood appears from the vantage point of a raven, drunk on irony, swooping down on Sacramento. "The raging floods of the American and Sacramento attacked the devoted city both in the rear and in the front," he wrote. "Over the levee came the leaping waters, scornfully laughing at the puny obstructions that the presumptuous hand of man had placed in its way. The alarm bells sounded, and people rushed hither and thither to save what they could. Along the street levels, and over the sidewalks, rushed the gliding demon of destruction, submerging street after street, until at last it had complete possession of the doomed city. Still and steady rose the water over the curbstones, over the doorsteps, and into the houses, stores and hotels it rushed. Many small wooden buildings floated off down stream. Boats were out everywhere, rescuing those in danger."

California's new governor, railroad magnate Leland Stanford, was preparing for his inauguration that January day. The water had flooded the entire first floor of his mansion, which stood across the street from the state capitol. Stanford rescued several women and children by boat and sheltered them on his second floor. The inauguration, it was decided, would go on as planned. He rowed from the top of his house to the swearing-in. The speech he carried in his pocket mentioned not a word of the people or their fight to hold back the water. Instead, he spoke about the rupture of the nation's Civil War and the need for Californians to support the fabric of the Union for future generations. Those generations, he warned the assembled, must never include immigrants from Asia. "There can be no doubt but that the presence among us of

Flood-ravaged Sacramento, the deluge of 1862

a degraded and distinct people must exercise a deleterious influence upon the superior race," he said. "It will afford me great pleasure to concur with the Legislature in any constitutional action, having for its object the repression of the immigration of the Asiatic races." Plenty of exclusion would happen, of course, but not before Stanford and his partners transported eight thousand Chinese "coolies" to the high cliffs of the Sierra to do the impossible: bore a mammoth hole through the solid granite to connect the Central Pacific tracks to the Union Pacific tracks and open California to the transcontinental railroad.

The floodwaters took months to drain. The state legislature was forced to convene in San Francisco. Sacramento's dead had to be buried there, too. Across the length and breadth of the Central Valley, a great inland sea carried over the land. Carcasses of tens of thousands of cows and an unknown number of people lay rotting. William Brewer, who studied agriculture at Yale before coming west to help survey California's natural resources, chronicled the flood, and so much else, in his classic work *Up and Down California in 1860–1864*. "Nearly every house and farm over this immense region is gone," he reported. "America has never before seen such desolation by flood. Not a road leading from the city is passable. Everything looks forlorn and wretched." Yet Brewer had come to recognize a peculiar fortitude in the Californian that could outlast everything, even this. "No people can so stand calamity as this people. They are used to it. Everyone is familiar with the history of fortunes quickly made and as quickly lost. It seems here, more than elsewhere, the natural order of things."

Even before the floodwaters had receded, the *Sacramento Daily Union* was urging citizens not to relocate their bankrupt city to higher ground. Instead, the people needed to raise eighty thousand dollars to erect a new levee, this one with a base wide enough "to ensure strength and permanency" and an elevation sufficient to "bid defiance to the highest flood."

As the work proceeded, the dry times—three straight years of wicked drought—returned across the state. Herds of gaunt cattle wandered off the ranchos in search of food and water. In Anaheim, a group of colonists had planted a vineyard behind a fence and kept it irrigated. Starving cattle, excited by the rare sight of succulence, swarmed about the barricade and made a desperate charge. A mounted guard, patrolling day and night without pity, kept the cows at bay until they melted in the heat. By the time the drought let go, hundreds of thousands of cattle wearing hacienda brands had perished, their bleached bones littering Southern California landscapes. The ranchero life vanished from the scene.

A pattern took hold in those wild swings between drought and flood. California moved only when nature moved. When the rivers were content, the people were content. They didn't want to be bothered with proposals to fund swampland commissions that would divide the region into districts and tax the people for reclamation. They had no interest in hiring engineers who could tell them at what cubic feet their rivers flowed, a science that might allow them to better prepare for the next fit of weather. In times of good nature, they cared not to be reminded of ill nature. In the desire to forget, their memories were able to play such tricks that when flood and drought returned, they were genuinely perplexed.

The need to forget was surely one reason why farmers and city folk alike abided the era of hydraulic mining, even looked the other way as 1.5 billion cubic yards of debris washed down from the mines. But what were the farmers of Marysville and Yuba City now to do? More than thirty thousand acres of their most productive farmland, rich alluvial soils along the Yuba, Bear and Feather Rivers, were choking on sediment from the gold mines. Entire stretches of the Yuba were so densely charged with detritus that no human or cow could drink from it. By 1860, mining debris had displaced enough of the river's flow that even modest floods were turning into catastrophic ones. The farmers reached for the nearest solution they could find: the soil. They built new embankments that were taller and stouter—and no less doomed. Straitjacketing a river only made it madder.

Some of the Yuba bottom farmers began to discuss the unthinkable: Why not instigate for a court injunction to shut down the mines? Their neighbors told them to hush. The miners were loyal customers, buying fruits, vegetables and grains grown on the same bottomlands. The hydraulic cannons were fabricated in local foundries. The mayor of Marysville wanted nothing to do with such crazy talk. The clotted-up river, he insisted, was proof that the mines were creating prosperity for all. The editor of the *Marysville Herald* hiked up the mountain to see if a compromise might be struck. The network of ditches and flumes was an impressive body of work, he told the activists. We should rejoice that the miner has conjured such a system to conquer his water problems. As for the bellyaching farmer, he would best be advised to abandon the bottomlands and move his crops to higher ground.

George Ohleyer, the editor of the *Sutter County Farmer*, wasn't going to be cowed. Mine tailings had raised the Yuba River sixty feet higher than it had been in Sutter's time. Sixty feet higher! It was folly investing in ever-bigger levees while the mines kept pushing so much sediment downriver that fifteen thousand more acres of farmland had turned to sand. What would it take to rouse the people? he wondered. Part of their inaction stemmed from fear. Part of it stemmed from defiance rooted in the liberty-loving, government-hating politics that many had carried with them from the South. A farmer himself, Ohleyer understood enough about Californians to bide his time. He would wait for the next flood or drought, whichever came first, to agitate his neighbors and make them see the mines for what they were: the enemy.

The drought that arrived in 1868 kept up for seven years. Was it an extension of the drought that had ended in 1865 or an entirely new episode? Before Marysville's citizens could settle on an answer, the flood of 1875 struck. Engineers assured the residents that all would be fine. A few years before, they had put aside their distrust of public works and passed a tax to build a new levee. It was seven miles long and encircled the city, protecting it from both the Feather and the Yuba Rivers. What they didn't count on was that the Yuba River, fed by a week of rain and snowmelt, would be packing the extra punch of debris washed down from ever-bigger mines. The supercharged river found a weak spot near the Marysville cemetery and broke through. What made the break even worse was that the new embankment held fast elsewhere. Water and mud buried the town right up to the lip of the levee. Farmers had done all they could to spare their orchards and pastures. After mine tailings had blotted out their lands in 1861, they moved to higher ground. When they went to inspect the damage from this new flood, they were shocked to see that the damage was exactly the same as before: their rich black earth was hiding beneath a wide, bleak expanse of sand and silt.

In the months it took for Marysville to dig out, something of a consensus emerged among its citizenry. The hydraulic mines had to go. California's future was agriculture. Since the mines and farms counted on the same rivers, politicians and judges had to make a choice. Whose diversion of the river was the highest and best use? Whose diversion did the least damage to the natural resources? The *Sacramento Daily Union* now borrowed from the language of farmer George Ohleyer: "We believe that if no measures are taken to abate this evil, five years from the present time will see a larger proportion of the valley lands desolate, the navigation of the Sacramento and other rivers completely destroyed and an annual destruction of property exceeding the net value of the products of the California mines."

Inside taverns and church basements, farmers and city elders looked one another in the eye: Who among them would pay for an attorney and sign their name to challenge the behemoth that was North Bloomfield? There were no willing takers, only a few who might even consider it if a war chest could be funded. Then someone offered up the name of Edwards Woodruff, who owned an entire city block and one thousand acres of the county's finest farmland. He had bought the farm from

John Sutter himself. It was a good thing that Woodruff lived in New York. This way the lawsuit wouldn't pit neighbor against neighbor.

Woodruff was most certainly an aggrieved party. Mine tailings that plugged the Feather River had destroyed his steamboat landing. The river's once-sparkling waters were no longer navigable or drinkable. His wheat fields, choked by sand and more prone to flooding than ever, were "utterly destroyed for farming purposes." As the facts were gathered up, Woodruff found himself compelled by the case. The Bloomfield company tried to buy favor. It spent $500,000 to build a fifty-foot-high dam to impound waste from its Malakoff mine. But the structure proved "wholly inadequate," filling up with debris and then spilling it into the river. In the Yuba bottoms above Marysville, twenty-five square miles of farmland were now dead. No levee could stand up to the river, which had risen another thirty feet in elevation.

Woodruff's lawsuit to enjoin the North Bloomfield Mining and Gravel Company from mining wended its way to the U.S. Court of Appeals for the Ninth Circuit, where Judge Lorenzo Sawyer, an old forty-niner, presided. The judge sifted through twenty thousand pages of testimony from more than two thousand witnesses and even paid a nighttime visit to North Bloomfield's most notorious mine, finding the glow of lights in the depths of its cavern to evoke Dante's *Inferno*. Sawyer did not intend his decision to represent a landmark in the cause of environmental protection for California, much less for the United States. He saw the case as a businessman might see it: commerce versus commerce. One industry was taking the water that belonged to the people and using it to advance a private enterprise. That enterprise, for all its profits, was polluting rivers, fouling farmland, flooding cities and rendering impossible the enterprise of many others. Because the mining industry had yet to devise an effective solution to its waste, he had no other choice. In granting the injunction, which would shut down North Bloomfield and all the lesser giants of hydraulic mining, Sawyer was practically apologetic.

"It would be difficult to appreciate too highly the importance of the mining interests," he wrote. "The boldness with which capitalists, and especially these defendants, have invested large amounts of capital; the vast enterprises they have undertaken and successfully carried out; the energy, perseverance, great engineering and mining skill displayed in pursuing these enterprises, excite wonder and unbounded admiration. We have therefore sought with painful anxiety some other remedy, but none have been suggested that appears to us to be at all adequate. . . . After an examination of the great questions involved, with a painfully anxious appreciation of the responsibilities resting upon us, and of the disastrous consequences to the defendants, we can come to no other conclusion than that complainant is entitled to a perpetual injunction."

As word of the decision reached Marysville and other farm towns of the Sacramento region, church bells pealed and school bells chimed. Whistles blew, cannons roared and grown men and women cried. That night, the farmers and businessmen lit bonfires in the streets and watched the flames flicker like the old glow of the now-dying mines. George Ohleyer could not be faulted for seeing the court's decision as vindication for himself and those few who had stood beside him against a powerful force that had destroyed so much in such a short time. He was not an editorialist given to metaphor, but the occasion seemed ripe to compare North Bloomfield to a sunken ship finally buried with all the debris of its gold mining. "On last Monday, the 7th of January, 1884," he wrote, "the ship and her crew went to the bottom never to rise again."

New Helvetia, Sutter's empire, had been the instrument by which the suit had been filed and the injunction won. Gold had defeated the old captain and fouled his dream. Now his dream of a California interior dedicated to agriculture had ruined gold. Sadly, he did not live to see his revenge. He had died a few years earlier. He raged, and justly so, right until the end. All that he had built had been taken from him; to his last breath he believed that the government of the United States, the conqueror of his land, owed him payment for that thievery. Old Sutter haunted the halls of Congress, pursuing his legal claim for $120,000. He buttonholed legislators from California and other states and got Mark Twain to petition both the House and Senate on his behalf. "A Bill for the Relief of John A. Sutter" was introduced. It went nowhere.

Sutter was living in exile when historian Hubert Howe Bancroft tracked down "the father of California" at a German retirement village on the East Coast. Blind to his irony, tears in his eyes, he cursed the iron heel of civilization. "I have been robbed and ruined by lawyers and politicians," he lamented. "I had my fortress, my mills, my farm, leagues of land, a thousand tamed natives at my bidding. Where are they now? Stolen. My cattle were driven off by hungry gold seekers. My fort and mills were deserted and left to decay. My lands were squatted on by overland emigrants. All Sacramento was once mine." Suffering from kidney trouble and rheumatism, he wrote a last embittered letter to California declining an invitation to attend a reunion of pioneers. He died on June 18, 1880, and was buried three thousand miles from the tules, in the village of Lititz, Pennsylvania, leaving one to contemplate whose theft of California was the original theft.

Even Hutchings, in the pages of his dying magazine, had come to see that California had gone too far. "There is no disguising the fact that our great prosperity was unreal and made us all reckless," he wrote. "Real estate advanced to enormous prices. Money was plenty and credit still more. Every class of people rode 'fast horses,' gave champagne parties and lived and fared sumptuously. Such a state of things could not last long. It was a fictitious and unreal prosperity." Even so, Hutchings could not help recognizing in the face of every newcomer who entered the gates of San Francisco the promise of new riches beyond. Not in the city, not in the mines, but in the great interior valley, where a man of modest merit and much industry would find amplitude of space, an "emporium of the grandeur," to make the California dream yet come true.

Nine

MINING SOIL

How fast did it happen? How fast did the ethos of the gold mine come down the mountain and transplant itself onto the soil of the valley floor? It happened in California time, which is to say the second rush began before the first one ended. By 1862, eighteen thousand men, as well as a handful of women, were calling themselves farmers in California. It had been God's belief first, and then Thomas Jefferson's, that farming was the most noble of pursuits, a builder of man's soul and community's heart. In the East, a wayward American society had come to embrace the rapacity of commerce and industry as its future. Out West, the virtue of the agrarian ideal could still hold true. Gold may have sold California, but it would be the soil that would settle it.

Or so believed the members of the Order of the Patrons of Husbandry, a kind of rural secret order founded by Oliver Hudson Kelley, an employee of the U.S. Department of Agriculture who toured the South in the 1860s and was shocked at the widespread flouting of sound agricultural practices. In rural communities across the country, fellows of the Patrons of Husbandry gathered in groups known as "Granges" devoted to the principle that agriculture, if practiced correctly, was the only source of legitimate wealth and the foundation of an egalitarian society. In California, 250 local chapters of the Grange sprouted up as fast as the wheat. In the eyes of the Grange, the farmer stood not at the margins of American life but at its very center—the virtuous man behind his horse-driven plow shouting, "I feed you all." Every man had a natural right to his own land, though dominion was best limited to 20 or 40 acres and never more than 160. "The equal right of all men to use the land is as clear as their equal right to breath the air," wrote Henry

George, a social critic and a Grange sympathizer who led the Progressive movement that dominated so much of politics from the 1880s to the 1920s.

The task fell to the state and federal governments to find those worthy yeoman and guide them westward, where they might become an "implement of Providence in completing the task of Creation," as Reverend Thomas Starr King exhorted the San Joaquin Valley Agricultural Society in the late summer of 1862. "The earth is not yet finished. It was not made for nettles nor for the manzanita and chaparral," the preacher told his audience of pioneer farmers. "It was made for grain, for orchards, for the vine, for the comfort and luxuries of thrifty homes." The moral man of soil needed only to look past the "abomination of desolation" that was the Central Valley in its native state and gaze upon two immense horns of plenty, one carved out by the Sacramento River and the other by the San Joaquin, to awaken to the promise of riches greater than gold.

At that same moment, one of the biggest real estate grabs in North American history was under way. It had begun a decade earlier when

Grange Society poster

the Mexican government, on the eve of the U.S. takeover of California, rushed to reward it close friends, both Mexican and American, with lavish gifts of land. More than eight million acres were doled out to eight hundred men. Many of the grantees hadn't even bothered with surveys or filing paperwork; some couldn't even muster a single document to back up their claims. The U.S. Land Commission for California was supposed to determine which Mexican grants were bogus and which ones would carry the new government's imprimatur. Instead, it became a tool to validate land monopoly. The commission approved nearly every single Mexican grant in the form it was conferred. Then it set the stage for even more wild speculation through a system of giveaways stamped "U.S. Government."

First was the handout to the railroad in return for laying down all those miles of tracks. The Southern Pacific was awarded every other 640-acre section along its sprawling route. This added up to twelve million acres, more than a tenth of all the land in California. Each federal mechanism for land distribution that followed—the Military Bounty Act, the Swamp and Overflowed Lands Act, the Desert Land Act, the Morrill Act of 1862—spoke to the notion of thwarting concentrated holdings. Each program had the potential to be an instrument for small farmers to acquire 160 acres and build the rural villages envisioned by the Grange. But from the start, speculators from San Francisco, Sacramento, Stockton and Los Angeles—bankers, merchants, capitalists made rich by the gold rush or the silver from the Comstock Lode—perverted the law's intent. Federal and state officials refused to intervene to curb the abuses.

The buying, selling and trading of government scrip became riddled with fraud and deceit. Issuing scrip was how the federal government dug itself out of debt, if not moral quandary. Each scrip was worth $1.25 or one acre of government land. When soldiers needed to be paid for "quieting" the natives, the United States handed them scrip. When surviving natives sued to recover their stolen lands, the United States handed them scrip. The funding of agricultural colleges across the country was underwritten by scrip. Each scrip came with its own power of attorney and could be used to purchase any public lands in any state. This was how San Francisco's wealthiest men, none more diligent than William S. Chapman and Isaac Friedlander, came to hoard huge blocks of scrip acquired from half-breed Sioux and half-built colleges. The corruption of scrip allowed Chapman and Friedlander to seize one million acres of rich valley soil for as little as fifty cents an acre. Their Nob Hill neighbors were able to pluck millions of acres more through the fleecing of federal programs to reclaim so-called swamplands and desert lands.

The list of San Francisco's leading industrialists who gulled their way to owning huge chunks of the state's middle included Lloyd Tevis, the president of Wells Fargo, and William Ralston, the founder of the Bank of California, and James Ben Ali Haggin, a lawyer and private lender, and Henry Miller, the cattle king. By 1871, after twenty years of statehood, California found itself a more entrenched oligarchy than at any time during Mexico's rule. Nine million acres of its most fertile land were in the firm grasp of 516 men.

The aristocrats in the big city had no desire to farm the plain themselves. They were looking to industrialize the hinterlands the same way gold had allowed them to industrialize the mountain. Planting vines and fruit trees was a doctor's hobby. There was only one crop that answered their need to be distant and untethered from labor or irrigation, one crop that could be planted, harvested and moved to tidewater in fell swoops, one crop that lent itself entirely to late-nineteenth-century mechanization. And so the San Francisco capitalists turned to the glory of wheat. The corporate farmer of California was thus born.

Unlike the Midwest, the grower here could sow his grain in November or December, when the first rains made a dent in the sunbaked soil. Not only was a good stand possible through the mild winter, but if it rained a dozen or more inches—not unusual for the valley—a bumper crop would greet the farmer come May. Because no rain fell in summer, the crop could be piled high and left in the field for several weeks while the wheat barons haggled price and shipping costs. In the broad, flat valley, the yield of wheat was akin to a one-thousand-pound pumpkin. The average harvest produced sixty to eighty bushels an acre. In the Midwest, a farmer was lucky to take home fifteen bushels an acre. In most cases, California wheat was destined for Great Britain aboard clipper ships that sailed around Cape Horn and reached Liverpool in one hundred days. The Englishman greeted each load, which arrived without shrinkage or spoilage, as "California white velvet," the best wheat in the world.

The grain fields naturally caught the attention of the Big Four: Leland Stanford, Charles Crocker, Collis Potter Huntington and Mark Hopkins. To transport wheat to market, the railroad tycoons decided to run the tracks of their Central Pacific down the heart of the valley and rename it the Southern Pacific. North of Sacramento, wheat ranches spread across the counties of Yuba, Colusa, Butte and Tehama. The grain crop was so prodigious in Stanislaus County that a former mayor of Modesto said "the entire country was a wavy wheat field from one extremity to the other." Between Stockton and Merced, six hundred square miles were sown to wheat. Along the alluvial fans of rivers ran tracts of wheat ten miles in length, for the simple reason that ten miles was the distance that a load of sacked grain could be hauled by wagon in a day. It took the culture of grain only a few decades to supplant the culture of gold. In 1862, a million acres were planted to wheat, yielding 14,432,883 bushels. By 1884, California had surpassed Minnesota as the nation's leading producer of wheat, with 3.6 million acres yielding 57,420,188 bushels.

In wheat country, one could ride an entire day without seeing a house, a barn, a farmer, a field hand, a milking cow or a pig. Only at the first blast of hot weather did the men and machines descend. The workers weren't asking for much. Many had lost their jobs on the docks or in the mines and carried all they owned in bindles, now dedicated to the life of a tramp. Riding the rails from Los Angeles to San Francisco, they stopped off in the valley to wash the coal dust off their backs and earn a few bucks from the pull of wheat. Young and old went by a nickname. There was Silver Tip, a boy of nineteen whose hair had gone white from a fever, and Seldom Seen, who suffered a social anxiety, and Flipity Flop, an ex-soldier who had a form of sleeping sickness, and the Grand Duke, who was always drunk and spouting Latin and Greek, and any number of Swedes—Loco Swede, Gunny Sack Swede, One-Eyed Swede. If the grain king bothered to provide them with a bunkhouse, they took the bed. If not, the weather was mild enough that they could sleep easy on their bindles under the stars. No worker ate better. Chuck wagons fed them a breakfast of eggs, pancakes, hash, ham, buttered biscuits and jam before sunrise and a dinner of equal proportions at sundown.

From one end of the Great Central Valley to the other, the land gave itself over to the giant scythes of the combined harvester. A single machine, drawn by thirty-six jackasses and driven by a wily mule skinner, could duplicate the labors of more than a hundred men, harvesting up to thirty acres in a summer's day. Like a military advance, the big growers staggered eight to ten of these monsters across a horizon shimmering of grain. The mass of reaping, threshing, blowing and bagging—one continuous rattle and clang—shook the earth. Three or four men straddled each machine and read the vibrations for something amiss as the big bull wheel sank its teeth into the earth and gave power to the forty-foot sickle. The mule skinner could move his entire team right, left or forward with a simple "gee dock" or "haw dock" and the slightest jerk of his line that laced each bridle.

Along both sides of the Sacramento River for twenty miles, the baronies of Joe Cone and Dr. Hugh Glenn were sown in wheat. Cone had come out from Ohio during the gold rush and grazed more than fifty thousand cattle and sheep in the hills of Lassen County. The drought of 1864 had forced Cone to diversify. He had acquired an old Spanish land grant and planted ten thousand Bartlett pear trees and sixteen thousand acres of wheat. His neighbor to the south, Dr. Glenn, a Virginia native, had finished medical school in St. Louis shortly before gold was discovered in the American River. He arrived in California with $110 in his pocket and staked a claim at Murderer's Bar, near the spot where James Marshall found those pea-sized nuggets. Glenn shifted from gold farming to wheat farming on fifty-five thousand acres along the river. The way he industrialized wheat—he was known as "the monarch of the prairie"—earned him comparisons to Cornelius Vanderbilt and Jay Gould. He hired as many as seven hundred field hands, and his payroll topped thirty grand. He chartered his own fleet of vessels to sail the crop to Liverpool.

Only one man, though, could rightly claim the title of "wheat king," and that was Isaac Friedlander. From field to ship, he built such a perfect operation that he paid no mind to drought or flood. The son of Jewish parents who'd left Germany shortly after his birth in 1823, Friedlander grew up in Charleston, South Carolina, where he learned all the courtliness of a plantation gentleman before making his way to California during the gold rush. He tried mining for a short while, fell sick and returned to the more congenial atmosphere of fast-growing San Francisco. He went into the mercantile trade and soon cornered the market on flour for the mining camps. He and his partner William S. Chapman then piled up blocks of Georgia agricultural scrip and starting buying their one million acres in the valley. From end to end, he planted nothing but wheat and then put together a multinational consortium of warehouses, mills and grain-sack factories that imported their jute from Scotland.

Friedlander stood six feet, seven inches and weighed more than three hundred pounds. He consumed the streets of San Francisco with a stride twice the length of a normal man's and seemed to study every position from a lofty place. When he quizzed a person, peering through his spectacles, his arched eyebrows grew even more arched. Fellow growers respected him as a man of his word who offered a fair price for their crop and stuck to it no matter weather or pests. Since the eastern states were glutted with Great Plains wheat, Friedlander set his sights on Asia and Great Britain. Day and night, his assistants worked the telegraph machines in his San Francisco offices, communicating with railroads, ports, clipper ships and overseas buyers. Friedlander and his agents were soon buying and exporting to Europe and Asia three-quarters of all the wheat grown in the Golden State.

Once the railroad tracks and seeds of wheat were thrown down, the selling of a civilized California to the rest of the world could begin. Gold had been its own huckster. Wheat needed language that framed new myths based on the fecundity of earth, climate, crop. No writer painted a more fetching picture of early California and its infinite possibility than Charles Nordhoff, a seafarer and journalist of Falstaffian proportions who wrote for *Harper's* and three of the New York dailies, the *Post, Tribune* and *Herald,* before signing on as a barker for the Southern Pacific. Nordhoff became the first official mythmaker of California. He knew how to write a captivating sentence and traversed every corner of the state on horseback to report in detail what he saw and whom he met. His dispatches, both as journalist and as promoter, chronicled extraordinary changes wrought to the state by settlers from the East and the Midwest, stories that lured tens of thousands more settlers west.

As a New Yorker, Nordhoff loved poking fun at the New Yorker's scorn for California the Ruffian. In a piece titled "The Agricultural

Men, mule and machine harvest a field of wheat
in the Sacramento Valley

Wealth of California—a General View," he punctures East Coast airs and performs his puffery, too. "It is generally acknowledged," he wrote, "that some very respectable people live in California; but we who live on the Atlantic side of the continent are sorry for them, and do not doubt in our hearts that they would be only too glad to come over to us. Very few suspect that the Californians have the best of us, and that far from living in a kind of rude exile, they enjoy, in fact, the finest climate, most fertile soil, the loveliest sky, the mildest winters, the most healthful region, in the whole United States."

California's first promoter was not above being a scold. He couldn't understand the compulsion of even small farmers to plant only wheat. How could they not see the wisdom of turning their modest acres into everything that could grow under California's splendid sun? "Wheat, wheat, wheat is their only crop. They do not raise even a potato for their families," Nordhoff moaned. "They live on canned fruits and vegetables; all their house supplies are bought in the nearest town. In a good season they sell their wheat for a large sum, and either buy more land or spend the money in high living; when a dry year comes, they fall into debt, with interest at one percent a month. And when the next dry year comes, it brings the sheriff."

In the Alhambra Valley, northeast of San Francisco, Nordhoff found the fits and starts of a Mediterranean fruit culture taking form. A physician named John Strentzel, one of the fathers of California pomology, was planting plum and pear trees and Muscat, Tokay and Malaga grapes. As a young man in Budapest, Strentzel had learned how to ferment and dry grapes, and soon he was producing some of the best wines and the first raisins in the West, winning blue ribbons at the 1861 California State Fair. By the time his son-in-law, John Muir, took over the ranch, Strentzel was growing thirty-six varieties of apples, thirty-five varieties of pears, four varieties of quinces and five varieties of plums, not to mention mulberries, lemons, cherries, pomegranates, figs, pecans and walnuts. Muir, who would become the bearded, beatific prophet of California's mountain wilderness, planted fewer varieties at greater spacing, covered the orchard floor with legumes to draw in nitrogen and complained throughout each growing season that on a clear day, he could see but could not caress his mistress, the Sierra.

As Nordhoff trotted from coast to interior enveloped by the emptiness of wheat, he sounded one of the earliest warnings of the scourge of industrial agriculture: "I advise farmers coming from the East to be content with small farms. The rage for large possessions has been a curse to the farmers of the State. I am certain that an industrious farmer who cultivates one hundred and sixty acres, who plants oranges and almond and olive orchards on twenty of these acres, who keeps a good vegetable garden for his family and attends to his crops with care and thoroughness, will be worth more money at the end of ten years than his neighbor who has ten times as much land and has raised wheat only."

The San Joaquin Valley had fallen into two rival camps that held two starkly different visions of the land. There were the Sandlappers and the Pikes, as I had written in *The King of California*. The Sandlappers despised cattle and grazing. They grabbed fertile dirt a good distance from the rivers and planted wheat and a fruit tree or two. They were content, for the time being at least, to rely on rain. This practice, ironically enough, was called dry farming. The Pikes, on the other hand, laid claim to the rivers and swamps and raised cattle and grain. Not every Pike hailed from Pike County, Missouri. Among the Pikes in the valley were saloonkeepers from Kentucky, miners by way of Tennessee, tobacco farmers from Virginia and North Carolina, and stockmen from Arkansas and Texas. To a man, they were of a decidedly Dixie bent. In fact, their loyalties to the South were so absolute that they stole hundreds of horses from local ranchers and dispatched them to the Confederate army. The federal government, fearing these guerrilla bands, established a fort on the outskirts of Visalia and manned it with pro-Union soldiers.

The Pikes and Sandlappers were knocking heads over a law that allowed cattle to forage anywhere a Pike pleased. When this foraging mowed down an orchard or grain field belonging to a Sandlapper, well, that was just the way of the plain. The Sandlapper couldn't sue for damages unless he had erected a fence around his crop and the cattle had barged through it. Over time, however, as more settlers planted more crops and took their complaints of ravaged fields to lawmakers, the interpretation of trespassing grew less literal. The cattle no longer enjoyed such free roam, and the Sandlapper needn't have a fence. A shift in culture had begun.

"All over the great plain south of Visalia, and in the foothills and even down near the shores of the great Tulare Lake," Nordhoff reported, "you see little boxes of houses standing far apart, the signs of small farmers who have chosen each his one hundred and sixty acres and who will no longer be worried and bullied by the cattle owners." Now that the Southern Pacific had arrived, there was nothing standing in the way of the "Great San Joaquin Valley," as Nordhoff called it, to fulfill its promise. In those first cultivated vines, he could glimpse a future when three million acres of valley plain would be covered in fruits and nuts, none more promising than the almond. The only element missing—and not really missing but simply stuck in the mountains and streams—was water.

Among the Sandlappers was a group of tall and handsome men boasting first-rate educations, though it wasn't always easy to pick them out, hidden as they were under layers of grime. Only at night, after they'd finished another long day of hand-digging holes and connecting those holes in a manner that revealed they were building an irrigation canal, did they give themselves away. Too restless to fall asleep, they huddled inside their barn and broke out in tune. "Tired, aching limbs would not allow their possessors sleep without first an hour of relaxation, and that hour of wakeful rest was devoted to song," William Sanders, their leader, recounted. "Favorite airs from Beethoven, Mozart, Franz

Abt would ring out on the evening air from our improvised choir. Our Sundays were spent reading about and discussing events passing in the world around."

Sanders was a botanist and schoolteacher who had fought in Arizona's Indian wars and, like the rest, had come to California to find gold—at least until he'd stuck his hands into the sandy loam of the San Joaquin Valley. Like Nordhoff, Sanders grew to believe that the alluvial plain was much too fertile to be squandered on grain. He would travel the globe collecting grapevine cuttings and gathering facts on raisin drying, fig tree propagation and grafting. He would plant one hundred thousand vines and an Edenic array of fruit trees on his 320-acre spread in the Tulare basin, a kind of demonstration project for dreamy orchardists. But first he and his gang of Sandlappers needed to tap into the Kings River and sluice water through jackrabbit country. It was 1875, and in the parched dirt outside Fresno, Sanders found Moses James Church, a small, steely, hawk-nosed man already well into his experiment of damming and canaling the Kings River.

Not one thing in Church's early life would have foretold his role as "the father of irrigation" in the valley. He had grown up in rural New York and taught himself to blacksmith. He forged wrought iron in Georgia, Alabama and Chicago and then gave it up to hunt for gold in Hangtown. He collected enough nuggets to purchase two thousand head of sheep dying of thirst in the Napa Valley. In 1868, he drove them past Fresno to the edge of the Kings River, built a cabin and corral and planted wheat. This put him in the vicinity of Centerville, where a band of cattlemen with revolvers and lariats didn't take kindly to wheat growing. They burned his cabin down, kicked over his corral and fed his seeds to feral pigs. Church had encountered enough dead men hanging from trees beside the river to know that the wrath of the cattle lords wasn't lore. He decided the prudent thing to do was to take his sheep to another spot a good distance away.

This was how Church landed in the middle of eighty thousand acres owned by the "German Association" from San Francisco, whose members had seen the great irrigation works in Egypt and India. They were pleased to hear of Church's plan to erect a brush-and-cobblestone dam across a section of the Kings and to build a canal to grow his wheat. Church signed up with the syndicate and enlisted other farmers to join him in the fight against the cattlemen. The deal Church and William Sanders hashed out between the fields of wheat in 1875 called on the botanist and Indian fighter to double the width of Church's original canal. In return, Church would grant Sanders and his twenty-two Mozart-loving ditchdiggers enough water to irrigate their own acres.

The brutal job of deepening and enlarging the canal began that summer. "Weeks passed away, months passed away, each but a repetition of what had preceded," Sanders wrote. "Under the constant wear and strain, horses finally became poor; men became haggard, sunburned, morose and irritable. Still, the daily toil went on, on, on . . . the ditch gradually becoming lower and the hills of earth on either side becoming higher. We saw nothing, realized nothing and cared for nothing, only that long ditch of loam and rock. This was our prison, our whole earth and heaven; we knew nothing beyond it."

They struck with shovels and crude metal scrapers drawn by mules. There was no mortar or brush to adhere to the earth, just earth that they packed and packed only to watch a solid mound run off like molasses when the first rain found a weak spot. When they finally had it up and running, the water rushed too fast, and the canal had to be graded again and checked with wooden weirs to govern the flow. Even then, amid the canal's midnight rush, the water didn't reach their farms but instead tumbled down sinkholes made by gophers. At last, the disappearing water gurgled and hissed, and the dirt sank like sugar until the burrows were no more. This was when the water inside the banks bubbled to the surface and their fields at last filled with the mercy of irrigation. Smaller canals and branch ditches soon joined the main channel and spread water over a plain transformed.

As their wheat fields sprouted, Church headed up to Sacramento to lobby the state legislature to pass a "no-fence law." This would allow an aggrieved farmer to claim crop damages even if he hadn't built a fence to keep out a Pike's cattle. The political battle inside the capitol was an all-night affair that saw Church and the farmers prevail. Nothing would now stop the building of an irrigation system the likes of which the world had never seen. "The wildest, maddest, most enthusiastic enthusiast never dreamed of such a change as has taken place in this region," the *Selma Irrigator* gushed.

Scientists would one day record California's irrigated miracle as the greatest human alteration of a physical environment in history. All but extinguished from the San Joaquin Valley were the grizzly bear, the pronghorn antelope, the condor, the mink. As the last of the tule elk sought refuge in the bulrush thickets, bands of hunters took to rowboats to shoot them down. They were such communal animals that a single shotgun blast could kill three at a time. The extermination of the jackrabbit, on the other hand, wasn't exactly hunting. Notices got passed from farmhouse to farmhouse. The rooting out of the tormentor's latest infestation was going to be staged, say, on the second Saturday of the month at the junction of Country Road and Second Street, four miles beyond the town's limits. People dressed up as if it were a fancy picnic they were attending. Excited men, women and children arrived by the hundreds in carriages, on horseback, on foot. They lined up in two long flanks across the treeless basin and waited in the hot sun for the bugle call. With a whoop-up that could be heard for miles, they began to sweep the prairie in a precise pincers movement, a rumble that shook the brush and roused thousands of jackrabbits from slumber.

No pest bred more offspring or raided gardens more voraciously than the long-eared and lanky jackrabbit. Its existence seemed to mock them. As the coordinated flanks of the settlers squeezed tighter, terror struck the faces of the rabbits. So tight was the line of humans that the animals had no choice but to move in the direction they were being herded. The execution was now clear. The rabbits were being driven straight into the waiting snare of a pair of wire fences that extended like a chute for a half mile. At the far end, the fences funneled into a seven-foot-tall pen made of the same wire. As lines met and the shouts of the people turned into a stadium's roar, two men swung open the corral's gates. At this point, one could not distinguish the yelps of the Sandlappers from the almost human cries of the rabbits. The animals rushed against the fence, looking for a way out—there was no way out, so tight was the wire—and knocked themselves silly. Every rabbit might have followed in mutual suicide if the settlers had only shown more patience. But scores of men, women and children now leaped into the thunderous mass inside the pen and proceeded to club and stomp to death thousands of rabbits.

The slaughter lasted but a few minutes. Dead tired, the Sandlappers sank waist-deep into a pile of fur, blood, urine and feces. This is what passed for entertainment in the valley during the era of ditch building and plains fruiting. Twice a year, settlers gathered in the middle of the desert for the West's version of the foxhunt. In time, local and federal governments would underwrite the expense of killing pests as a way to rid the valley of bubonic disease and other communicable ailments. A coyote's scalp fetched five dollars, a squirrel five cents, a gopher two pennies. In the county budget, the line item for eradication absurdly read: "For the destruction of agricultural pests serving no known purpose in nature's economic plan." At the end of their two-hour rabbit hunt, the Sandlappers posed for a photograph beside the carnage, twenty thousand dead animals stacked high or hanging from the rails of the makeshift corral. Then they found shade, broke out their lunch baskets and enjoyed a picnic. The hides were sold to fur makers in San Francisco, the coats marketed to society matrons as fine English hare.

With the earth reasonably wiped clean of critters, the digging of ditches and canals proceeded apace across the San Joaquin Valley. The "first great experiment in irrigation by the Anglo-Saxon race," crowed the official record, *History of Fresno County, California*. It had taken but a single decade for settlers to fully claim the flows of the five local rivers. Sanders and Church and the rest of the Sandlappers told themselves they weren't stealing water so much as taking advantage of California's other great contradiction: the conflict between riparian and appropriative rights.

When it came to adopting a law that would rationally govern California's water, state lawmakers still seemed bewildered. They continued to embrace the English common law of riparian rights. In the British countryside, gentry divvied up the river's flow according to who owned the riverbank. This made sense in a land of steady rain. English farmers who didn't live along a river counted on the sky as their irrigator. In fact, the English farmer who lived a safe distance from the river considered himself rather fortunate. He didn't have to endure the river's routine rages to grow his crops. Likewise, riparian rights made sense in New York or Virginia, where the ample rain also allowed for farming beyond river's reach.

California was a different story. The conditions were almost entirely reversed. Here, the limited rainfall showed up in months when the crops needed it least. Here, winter rain counted twice, once as precipitation and once as spring snowmelt. The practice of appropriation in California and the flouting of English riparian doctrine didn't begin with Moses Church and his band of ditchdiggers. The doctrine was present in the state's very birthing. As the miners siphoned Sierra river flows into ditches and flumes, they were able to use the brute force of appropriation to realize the greatest windfall of the gold rush. Now that gold had become wheat, the lawmakers didn't mind the Sandlappers doing the same.

On paper, at least, riparian rights and appropriative rights were not only antagonistic but irreconcilable. Riparian law existed by virtue of statute; appropriation existed by dint of settler practice and court decisions. Those in favor of river diversion argued, with some merit, that riparian law was a lousy vehicle to develop the arid West. The doctrine did a terrible job of distinguishing between wise and unwise use. It mattered not whether the holder of river rights was a farmer living along the banks and raising communal crops or a cattleman who mostly fouled his section of riverbed. Taken to an extreme, riparian rights in California would "make a dangerous monopoly of the water supply and condemn to perpetual sterility millions of fertile acres which might otherwise make homes for millions of prosperous people," wrote the editor of the *Irrigation Age*.

As lawmakers and judges waffled between riparian and appropriative rights, California existed in a bipolar state. Excited Sandlappers, true appropriators, kept tapping into the upstream flow of the rivers and adding to the reach of their dams and canals. In times of generous spring snowmelt, the riparian Pike downstream scarcely noticed that his river was being robbed. Only when another drought hit and his run of the river went dry did the Pike instruct his lawyers and saboteurs to get to work. In the 1880s, as the courts filled with lawsuits and countersuits, and dynamite began to blow up one dam and another, the fight no longer only pitted Pike against Sandlapper. The entire basin had come to war: farmer against farmer, neighbor against neighbor, appropriator against riparian, riparian against riparian.

In the late 1890s, a federal government inspector on horse and buggy traveled the breadth of California with a team of fellow surveyors. They gathered data on every stream in every corner of the state. When they finished their fieldwork and sat down to add up the proliferation of claims on each river, the totals could not be believed. The water flow claimed by farmers and miners amounted to "enough moisture to submerge the entire North American continent." Citing riparian and appropriative rights, 316 men had filed claims along the San Joaquin River. Their entitlements exceeded 480,000 cubic feet per second of water. The river at its greatest flood flow ran at only 59,800 cubic feet per second. The amount of claimed water thus exceeded the actual average flow of the San Joaquin by 172 times. On the Kings River, 355 men had filed claims that added up to 750,000 cubic feet per second. Only a few times in recorded history had the Kings even hit 40,000 cubic feet per second. California's snowmelt at the turn of the twentieth century wasn't merely oversubscribed, one federal investigator concluded. It was a fountain of madness. "The whole system is wrong," he wrote. "When the right to water is insecure or not defined, the instinct of self-protection makes an Ishmaelite of every water user. His hand must be against every man, as every man's hand is against him."

The investigators from the U.S. Department of Agriculture were led by Elwood Mead, an Indiana boy who had graduated from Purdue and would go on to pioneer irrigation in the arid West and head the U.S. Bureau of Reclamation. His peregrinations up and down the state in 1901 convinced him that California was truly singular. No other commonwealth, arid or humid, was so marvelous in its possibility. The usual limitations of latitude did not hold here. Oranges ripened as early and surely at Oroville, one hundred miles north of San Francisco, as they did in San Diego, five hundred miles south. On the same acre of land, California could harvest all the cultivated products of New England and Florida at once. The future of the state, Mead argued, rested on crops that could grow to their fullest only here: grapes, stone fruits, salad greens, tomatoes, nuts, olives, varieties of citrus and apples. Wheat had no business in the valley. Cattle belonged on hillsides.

The California legislature had passed the Wright Act in 1887, turning irrigation districts into public entities with the power to tax landowners within their boundaries and issue public bonds. The act did little good, however, when violence and legal battles were stifling the "magic of irrigation." Growing fruits, vegetables and nuts demanded a full-scale commitment to irrigation. Yet the valley that confronted Mead, after decades of ditchdigging, was still trapped between cowboy and farmer. "The cowboy on horseback was an aristocrat; the irrigator on foot, working through the hot summer days in the mud of irrigated fields, was a groveling wretch," Mead wrote.

If one needed proof of California's halfhearted embrace of irrigated agriculture, Mead found it in the state's interior. Fewer than twenty people per square mile populated the Central Valley. In the Nile Valley, 543 persons inhabited each square mile. Even as the towns in California's middle sprouted attractive houses embroidered by gardens and orchards, the land just beyond was a "world without turf, a dreary desert." Mead rode from one bonanza wheat field to another, thirty-five miles in distance, and encountered only two schoolhouses, instructing fifteen children. Only one of the children came from a family that owned their land. The rest were offspring of foremen and tenants. "These conditions of alien landlordism, tenant farming, unoccupied homes and scanty population in a country so rich in possibilities show a vital economic defect in methods," he wrote.

Among his crack team of federal investigators was journalist William E. Smythe, who would go on to write the groundbreaking work *The Conquest of Arid America* and establish the Little Landers utopian village, which would get washed away in one of Hatfield the Rainmaker's storms. Smythe was sure that irrigation could reclaim the desert for millions of families farming forty-acre plots. But this required a federal government willing to take on the chore of damming the rivers, dividing the flows and portioning out every drop to man. The vision wasn't Jeffersonian. It was a new "industrial ideal" based on rationality, precision and science.

A few years earlier, at Smythe's instigation, the second International Irrigation Congress had convened in Los Angeles to call for reclamation across the West. Delegates gathered inside the Grand Opera House, festooned in red, white and blue, and exulted to a choir singing odes to ditch water. "O glorious land! O glorious land! Where the fruits purple, crimson and golden roll forth." This was the gathering at which Major John Wesley Powell, admired for his daring exploration of the Colorado River, was famously booed off the stage when he dared to utter, "Gentlemen, there is not sufficient water to supply these lands." Smythe, on the other hand, blamed California's desolate stretches on the government's cowardly refusal to intervene in the water wars. "Everything is left for the irrigators to settle among themselves," Smythe wrote. "Each man manages his own head gate. His object is to get all the water he possibly can. One neighbor shuts down the head gate of another and stands over it with a shotgun. There is no law but force."

By now, the 250 local chapters of the Grange in California were mobilizing a public campaign against Isaac Friedlander. Farming wheat was mining soil, they cried. Wheat yields weren't declining because of a lack of rain; bonanza farming was exhausting the ground. Season after season, the impoverished earth was being sown to the same crop, stealing the same nutrients. Friedlander didn't need the Grange to tell him his land was tired and the world market for wheat glutted. If he could keep growing bigger, he believed, he might outrun the drops in yield and price. Then the drought of 1876–77 hit at the same time that Friedlander's main financier, William C. Ralston's Bank of California, went belly-up. Ralston's undoing had been his dream to erect the swankiest hotel in San Francisco. At the corner of New Montgomery and Market, he had built the Palace Hotel, with first-of-a-kind elevators ("rising rooms") and electronic call buttons in each room. The $5 million price tag worked out to be more than even Ralston could absorb. He no longer had the means to bankroll the wheat king or anyone else, and on August 27, 1875, he swam out into the choppy waters of the San Francisco Bay and drowned himself.

Three years later, his empire crumbling, Friedlander was felled by a heart attack. "The California Grain King" is dead, noted the *New York Times*. Dr. Glenn, "the monarch of the prairie," passed from the scene a few years later in a most uncivilized manner. He had confronted his drunken bookkeeper at his Jacinto ranch and slapped the man down. After brooding for several days, the bookkeeper set up an ambush of Dr. Glenn and filled his brain with buckshot. In his honor, the citizens of the Sacramento Valley named the county where he grew his wheat Glenn County.

As fast as grain had gripped the land, it let go even faster. At century's turn, a mere six million bushels of wheat were harvested. A traveler along the Kings River found a plain once shimmering with golden fields now given up to desolation. "Not a spear of anything green grows. The houses of former inhabitants are empty, the doors swing open or shut with the wind. Drifting sand is piled to the top of many fences. The windmills, with their broken arms, swing idly in the breeze. Like a veritable city of the dead."

With bonanza wheat vanquished, the barbarism of the frontier could now give place to a real civilization. The California colony, poor man's paradise, would finally have its chance in the sun. "The opening years of the Twentieth Century will witness a new era of homemaking in the West," Mead predicted. One man, however, still stood in the way.

Ten

POOR HENRY

It's been 150 years at least since Henry Miller first rode over the mountain from San Francisco to inspect his cattle, tens of thousands of head, grazing on the natural and unnatural grasses of the San Joaquin Valley. His ranch house still sits under the same eucalyptus tree en route to Los Banos, his old company town. If you walk inside the ranch office, a secretary can retrieve from her desk drawer the deed by which Miller, who arrived in California with six dollars in his pocket, bought this piece of the forty-eight-thousand-acre Rancho Sanjon de Santa Rita in the spring of 1863. She can guide you to the shed out back, lift a dusty plastic cover and unveil the old buggy Miller used to ride in local parades. "It still works perfectly fine," she says. To show you the reach of the old German, she takes you beyond the shed and points across the wide-open territory that finds the Coast Ranges. For all the dignified erasing done by modern agriculture, the cattle king still engraves this land: his clutching of river, his raising of dam, his carving of fields, his notching into earth the canals that funnel snowmelt from river to crop. That one man's grasp can still hold a century after his death—in California, of all places—says something about Henry Miller.

He had killed too many pigs, sheep and cattle with his own hands to enjoy a sound sleep. He counted the number of rats his cats caught in each of his granaries. He checked the hooves of his horses to make sure they were shod in copper and not steel, because steel sparked when it hit a rock and could cause a grass fire. He surveyed hundreds of miles of irrigation ditches and canal banks for the holes gophers dug. He used water to drown them, wheat laced with strychnine to poison them and finally paid his best hunter thirty-five dollars a month, a princely sum, to shoot them. He knew which of his Chinese cooks stewed rancid meat and which stewed meat too prime for his ranch hands. He'd walk into the cookhouses, lift the lids on each of their pots and take a whiff. If the cooks had left any scrap of meat that they were intending to feed to the pigs, he knew that, too. He'd roll up his shirtsleeve, stick his arm three-quarters into the swill barrel and pull out the evidence. "Ah, there is meat on the shank," he'd growl. When he came across the slaughtered remains of one of his cows on the grassy plain, he knew right away if a thief or a hungry man had wielded the blade. The thief left behind lots of good meat, and this was a sin he couldn't abide. The hungry man took everything but the hide, and he learned to forgive him. He made a game of inspecting his seventy miles of wooden fences to recover the unbent nails lying on the ground. After collecting several hundred, he returned them to the equipment shed, only to discover that every variety of nail was mixed up together in the same bin. He calculated the time his workers must have been wasting trying to find the right nail for each job and began to shout until he was practically crying at his foreman. He pulled off his hat, threw it into the dirt and stomped on it—the Henry Miller dance.

He was a strange, lonely man. He regarded fraternity as a waste of time. Rubbing elbows with the Nob Hill boys was just about the last thing he cared to do. Thank goodness he had a partner, Charles Lux, who enjoyed the social hour. It wasn't as if Miller had nothing in com-

Statue of Henry Miller, the cattle king,
in downtown Los Banos

mon with the gentlemen of San Francisco. Many had come from the same Germany he'd fled as a young boy. As financiers and industrialists, they were among the few who had realized gold's fortune. Together, they had willed the city into being. But the way Miller saw the world was fundamentally different from the way they saw it. He was a master butcher, and they were moneymen. He had made his path carving up meat, leaving not a fiddle string to waste and setting aside the bull brains for his customers from France. Truth be told, he thought of the Nob Hill nobles, only a generation removed from their father's workbenches, as mostly crooks and fools. They'd idle all afternoon in their downtown clubs sketching out plans for their capture of California's hinterlands. They saw the San Joaquin Valley as just another resource to conquer, like the gold fields. Their schemes to channel a river or build a grand canal that moved water from one end of the valley to the other always made sense from afar, all the more with brandy and cigar on their tongues.

If he cared for the company of any men, it was his vaqueros in their jingling spurs and buckaroo trousers as they finished another long day branding cattle on one of his ranches. They'd gather about an open fire and stuff enormous wads of tobacco into their checks, spitting out salvos of juice with "accuracy, neatness and precision" and swearing with "great gravity and decorum." The next morning, dressed like a cleric in a black jacket and slacks cut old-style, a spotless white shirt and a string tie, he'd saddle up his horse and ride across the never-ending empire that was Miller & Lux. He knew its sinew, tendon, flesh and blood, how each part made the whole and no part could go overlooked. One year desert, one year lush grass, the valley made a wreck of man's designs and then teased him back for more. To subdue what remained of its wildness, he trusted not even his most skilled superintendents. "There is only one man out of a hundred that gets my confidence, and then only partly," Miller confided once in a rare interview.

Across the sprawling west side, in Los Banos, Firebaugh, Dos Palos, Mendota, Buttonwillow and a handful of other settlements rising from the plains, Henry Miller was a man loved, reviled, feared and respected like no other. The beaky German stood five foot eight with a bald head and a beard that rimmed his plain wide face. The years of butchering had given him the forearms and chest of a man whose menace could be physical, but it was his phenomenal ability to store every detail of his massive operation in his head that left the greater impression. He conducted business without even a pocket notebook and knew to the exact number his herds of cattle and plots of land so widespread that, legend had it, he could ride from the border of Mexico to the border of Canada and never need to camp on ground that wasn't his own.

When he left his home ranch in Gilroy and rode over the Pacheco Pass, which connected the coast to the valley, even the Mexican outlaws left him alone. Only once did he have to endure the thievery of Tiburcio Vásquez, the best-dressed bandit in California, before he calculated that it made more sense to give the Mexican several hundred dollars and a horse. The thefts of Miller & Lux cattle became a rarity after that. When Vásquez was later caught in Salinas, then hanged in front of ten thousand people in San Jose (his last word as he walked to the gallows was "Pronto"), it was Henry Miller who bought him a coffin.

Miller dealt with tramps and winos the same way. Though he abhorred their drinking, he couldn't stand to see any man go hungry. He instructed his chow houses to feed a meal to every wanderer passing through. As word got out, some of his ranches were serving twelve hundred free meals a month. Of course, the hungry had to be willing to wait until Miller's employees had finished eating first and then eat from the same dirty plates. This way, the dishes had to be washed only once. The Dirty Plate Route—the "DPR," as the tramps fondly called it—turned out to be not only good charity but good business. Hoboes on the road, their bellies full, stopped setting fire to Miller's haystacks and rustling his cattle.

Miller's fastidious manner was thought to be Teutonic in nature, but he explained it as good old-fashioned Christian thrift: "I would rather have a dollar saved than five dollars made," he said in broken English. "When a man can save a dollar, it learns him to save on a large scale." Large was the only scale that made sense to him. No man, not Stanford or Huntington or Crocker or Friedlander, had seized a bigger slice of California than Miller. Whenever the lawyers called him to the witness stand, it was the first question they asked: How big are you? He was a stern man, not prone to even the hint of a smile in photographs, but he had a capacity for self-deprecation and occasional humor. He joked that he had made three fortunes in his life: one for his partner, Charles

Lux; one for himself, his wife and three children; and one for the attorneys who both defended and opposed him. As to the question of size, he saw no reason to tell them the truth. He doubled the acres he owned in one trial and halved the acres in another trial.

The title "cattle king" scarcely did justice to Miller's say-so over the West. He governed more land and riparian water rights than any other man in the United States. He owned 1.25 million acres outright and controlled maybe 10 million more through lease or squat. In his accumulation of real estate, he came to conclude that if he was going to assemble an arid expanse across California, Nevada and Oregon, it was probably wise to acquire a few of its rivers, too. The San Joaquin, for a one-hundred-mile run on both sides, was his. So was the Kern as it flowed beyond Bakersfield into the salt flats of Tulare Lake. These were the acres he truly counted, for they came with water, and the water grew the alfalfa he planted and the grasses that sprouted up on their own; each one made excellent feed for his one hundred thousand cows, eighty-five thousand sheep, tens of thousands of hogs and who knew how many chickens.

For more than a half century, from his first purchase of land in the mid-1800s to his last purchase in the early 1900s, no one played a more consequential role than Henry Miller in reshaping the valley. He arrived to glimpse the last remaining herds of elk bolt from the tules and gallop across the plain, and he was so taken by their majesty that he ordered his vaqueros to round up the survivors and set aside enough protected land for their preservation. Of the domesticated herds that replaced the indigenous ones, none dominated the plain more than Miller's Shorthorn and Devon-mixed cattle. What they didn't trample with their hooves they devoured.

The native grasses and wildflowers that survived the Spanish and Mexican presence did not survive this great bovine mowing machine. Using horse and scraper, Miller turned the rivers into waterways and the rolling savanna between the rivers into flat irrigated fields. He had wrested enough predictability from a drought-and-flood geography to dominate the supply of livestock and monopolize the wholesale market for meat in California. His was a model of both horizontal and backward integration, historian David Igler noted in his *Industrial Cowboys:*

Miller & Lux and the Transformation of the Far West. Miller wedded city to hinterland, linking his slaughterhouses in San Francisco to his cattle that grazed on land he owned beside rivers he controlled. "I devote my whole time and thought to the business, studying how I can advance it and how I can make those men do all possible economizing and getting work out of the men and making a dollar go as far as possible," Miller explained. "We have men that we talk to freely in a social manner and in our business, but ordinary sociability has not room to get in. It is business and nothing else. And I superintend all the business myself."

He once told his buggy driver, a man he regarded with fondness, that a vision of his life in California, right down to the smallest detail, had visited him when he was a boy of nine in Brackenheim, Germany. His name was Heinrich Alfred Kreiser back then, and he was learning everything he needed to know about cattle from his father, Christian, a master butcher with a cruel streak. It was his task as a young boy to move his father's cattle from auction yard to feedlot. During one hot trip, he stopped to take a rest under a tree and fell asleep. He dreamed of a green valley cut by rivers and surrounded by blue mountains covered with snow. The strangest herd of cattle, red-bodied with white faces, grazed on the plain. Each cow wore the brand of a Double H. At home that evening, he described this dreamt land to his parents and three older sisters.

Who ever heard of a red cow with a white face in Germany? The only cows they'd ever seen were black ones. And what kind of brand was HH? His apprenticeship under his father grew more heavy-handed after the death of his mother when he was fourteen. He had learned to never question his father's orders, but now he was being asked to herd flocks of geese from one hamlet to the next. Geese weren't cows. They minded no one. He believed that his father had designed the task as a way to humiliate him. That night, he packed a bundle of clothes and decided to leave Germany for good. "It was not a pleasant country for me to live in," he recounted. "Home had no charms."

He spent time in Holland and England as a journeyman butcher and then arrived in New York City in 1847. He slept in the same Washington Market shop where he slaughtered pigs, earning eight dollars a month and an extra dollar a day if he turned enough intestines into sausage casings. He befriended a shoe salesman named Henry Miller, and they both caught gold fever in the worst way. On the eve of their departure to California, his friend got cold feet and sold his ticket, embossed with his name, to the young butcher. This was how Heinrich Kreiser became Henry Miller as he stepped aboard the steamer *Georgia* and set sail for the Pacific Coast at age twenty-three. He nearly died of a fever crossing the Panamanian isthmus on a mule, and when he landed in San Francisco on September 24, 1850, he had six dollars left in his pocket. His idea, hardly novel, was to mine the miners. He'd sell them fresh meat at a quality and price no competitor could match.

Miller's skill with a knife soon became the talk of San Francisco's Butchertown. Most butchers had trouble killing eight hogs a day. He killed sixty Sandwich Island hogs in half a day and then dressed them. Within three years he had peddled enough pork sausage to become the second-largest meat dealer in San Francisco. This naturally attracted the attention of the city's largest meat-packer, an immigrant named Charles Lux from the same region of Germany. The two men not only shook hands on a partnership but married sisters from the Sheldon clan, blue-blood gentry out of Rhode Island. When Miller's wife died a short while later in childbirth, he kept his relations in the family by proposing to her twenty-year-old niece, Sarah. He gave her a single afternoon to decide. A plain, down-to-earth girl, she said yes.

Miller observed that he and Lux as individuals shared "no similarity" in temperament. Their differences, it turned out, served their partnership well. He carried cigars but didn't smoke them. He went into bars but didn't drink. Lux, by contrast, had twinkling eyes and a warm smile that made for easy social graces. As a lonesome Miller scoured the range, looking for the best deals in cattle and sheep, Lux dressed in his most elegant suits and cultivated friendships with San Francisco's aristocrats. Lux's genial nature secured the capital and connections that allowed Miller to buy the land and livestock he needed to corner the market on meat.

Miller had no patience for building an empire 160 acres at a time. He was looking for big pieces he could purchase in single deeds. In the spring of 1863, he followed the trail of the Spanish land grants. Crossing the Pacheco Pass, he headed down into the treeless, manless, grassy valley and kept riding in the direction of the snowcapped Sierra. A solitary clump of willows stood beside a creek called the Los Banos. To the southeast, he could see the rising of a bigger woodland and followed it to the swollen banks of a river, the San Joaquin. There, he encountered a large herd of grazing cattle, red-bodied and white-faced, the hair of their left hips branded with the two letters: HH. This was the southern end of a forty-eight-thousand-acre Spanish land grant known as the Rancho Sanjon de Santa Rita. Thomas Hildreth and his partner, who had fallen on hard times, owned close to nine thousand acres of grassland and seventy-five hundred head of cattle that were nothing like the small, thin, deerlike cattle the Spanish had brought over. Miller rode up to the ranch house and got to talking with Hildreth, a large man with a roaring voice. When they finished haggling, a few days later, Miller had bought the ranch dog cheap: $10,000 for the land and $5 a head for the cattle.

Miller soon found out that the true value of the Santa Rita Ranch wasn't the acres it encompassed so much as the river it skirted. Within months, the drought of 1864 struck, leaving almost every acre of California parched. Up and down the state, stockmen had no feed or water to keep their cattle and sheep alive. From bird's-eye, the entire southern end of the valley, except for thin green strips alongside the San Joaquin, Kings and Kern Rivers, became a sere landscape scattered with the bones of livestock. Miller hadn't yet erected a system of ditches and canals to carry the water to distant parts of his land. He had too little grass to maintain a herd of seventy-five hundred cows, and two-thirds of his animals ended up dying. Even so, by tapping into what meager flow was left of the San Joaquin, he was able to save enough cattle to sell their meat at premium prices. So many bankrupt cattlemen were ridding themselves of their last remaining herds that Miller was able to replenish his stock, and then some, at $5 a head.

By the time the rain fell again, no agricultural operation had prospered more from the drought than Miller & Lux. Dry times had taught Miller the golden rule of riparian rights: he who owned the most land along a river owned the water in that river, too. Dam, dike, ditch, levee, canal—he could employ whatever means he wished to direct the flow in drought years and divert the flow in flood years.

Thus began a magnitude of land acquisition by a single enterprise never previously witnessed in California. Miller & Lux took over the

Old pump house at Miller's Santa Rita Ranch

offices of every county recorder from Merced to Bakersfield. The real estate transactions filled page after page of large ledger books. The capture of public lands was documented in a handwriting that could not have been more meticulous. Each county recorder kept a different ledger for each government program—one for military scrip, one for agricultural college scrip, one for swampland reclamation and so on. The names of the men seizing the land never varied. The first seven pages went to Chapman, the next forty pages to Friedlander, the next one hundred pages to Miller & Lux. In a single day in Visalia, Miller made entry upon 140,000 acres of land. In Merced County, he snatched up the rest of the Santa Rita Ranch, the 40,000 acres on the north end, and then added thousands more acres on both sides of the river, until he owned a total of 201,307 acres. In Fresno County, he purchased 186,150 acres between 1863 and 1879. In Kern County, the acquisitions came a little later but quickly added up to 120,587 acres.

To make it appear less rapacious, Miller used a "dummy system" that relied on scores of employees and winos he had picked up along the way. He had each man walk into the appropriate county recorder's office and present enough scrip to buy a 160-acre chunk, only to hand it over to Miller & Lux in a later transaction. Keeping one step ahead of the government fraud inspectors, Miller traded in military scrip and Sioux Indian scrip and, finally, agricultural college scrip. "Lux and I were very different," he explained. "He wanted to invest in gas stock and collaterals, government bonds and the like, but I told him we were not calculated for that business. We were calculated to put our money where we could not take it back again, where it had to stay. So we invested in country lands. They never rot on your hands or waste away."

When he was finished investing in country lands, Miller & Lux owned 900,000 acres in the San Joaquin Valley and another 200,000 in the Santa Clara Valley. The company employed 1,200 workers, one of the largest labor forces in the country, and organized them in assembly-line fashion from corporate headquarters to butcher shop to slaughterhouse to grazing land and watering hole. Miller had established the valley's first company town in Los Banos, where he built a hotel and a park and sponsored an annual May Day festival, for which he provided all the food and even got out his knife and carved plates of meat for each resident. He could be something of an uncle, forgiving their debts when misfortune visited and digging ditches to irrigate their crops if they'd had the good sense to buy their farms from him. But they all understood one thing: Don't think of crossing him ever—because he'll crush you.

Just ask Jefferson Gilbert James, who hailed from Pike County, Missouri, and mined gold in Hangtown before buying a ranch right next to one of Miller's on the far side of the San Joaquin River. James covered the plain with thousands of livestock, opened a wholesale meat company in San Francisco and sat on the county board of supervisors. This was too much for Miller not to see as a poke in the eye. He let James dig his big canal and erect a headgate in an effort to increase his flow from the river they shared. When James was done digging and packing down the earth, Miller ordered two plow teams and fourteen scraper teams to meet him on the canal's bank at midnight. By dawn, Miller's crews had built a dam six hundred feet wide that buried James's canal and any water he had in it.

Miller, after all, was Pike and Sandlapper at once. Inasmuch as he owned two rivers and a great deal of the land in between, he was both a riparian water user and a long-distance appropriator of water, wearing the hats of cattleman, grain grower, fruit grower and colony developer, too. Philosophically, Miller wasn't wedded to one or the other. He believed that the land's cycle fell into distinct phases. He had happened to arrive in one phase and would stay long enough to see the possibility of another phase. Politicians could argue all they wanted about "the highest and best use of the land." It was Miller and a handful of men like him who would decide the answer. Gold gave way to cattle, and cattle to wheat, and wheat to fruits and vegetables, and fruits and vegetables to houses and cities. Each model of extraction had its life span, and it was best not to romanticize one over the other, lest you not see when the time for change had come. The rich man who waxed sentimental wasn't a rich man for very long.

"Booms are only beneficial in one sense," Miller said. "They have developed a certain portion of the state and the people that went in will be compelled to stay and improve the land in order to pay for it. Our resources are unlimited. Our population will be unlimited. I think there is no doubt but that California will be the most densely populated of any portion of the United States. I see nothing to hinder it."

For Miller & Lux, the future lay not in fighting over the drought-and-flood flows of the rivers but in capturing a much larger share of California's snowmelt, whether the year turned out wet or dry. Miller understood that only a fool would seek to defeat drought and flood. What was needed was a way to soften nature's twin blows when they struck. To make that happen, Miller and a handful of other San Francisco industrialists—Tevis, Friedlander, Ralston and Chapman among them—lent their names and pocketbooks to a colossal irrigation and navigation project that would rise along the valley's west side.

The plan called for a grand canal running from Tulare Lake to the Sacramento–San Joaquin Delta, a 230-mile-long artery through the state's midsection. The name of the enterprise—the San Joaquin and Kings River Canal and Irrigation Company—spoke to its sprawling ambition. It would tap into the valley's three biggest rivers, carry grain aboard barges to compete with the railroads and shunt water to three million acres of prairie land. Nothing like it had ever been attempted in the West, a vision lifted from India, where the British had built six thousand miles of irrigation canals to claim ten million acres from the desert. Indeed, the British engineer who had surveyed colonial India's hydraulic miracle, Robert Brereton, was lured to California in 1871 to guide the canal's completion at a salary of $1,000 a month in gold.

Four hundred Mexicans, native Indians, Italians and Irish—Miller's immigrant crew—had already excavated a forty-mile-long stretch of the canal, a first phase that Brereton regarded as rather shoddy. The new and expanded version, known as the "People's Canal," would extend the gift of controlled water across six county lines. Irrigation, Brereton promised, would explode the land. "I saw in Bakersfield and its environs magnificent crops of Indian corn growing," he said. "In one field, the corn averaged from 16 to 18 feet in height; the cobs were of immense size. This was the result of irrigation."

From the seat of his horse, Miller watched over construction of the grand canal, this time directing one thousand Chinese ditchdiggers whose immigration he regarded as a "necessary evil" because no people worked harder or complained less. Of his fifty cooks, forty-nine were Chinese. By year's end, a fifty-eight-mile rut had been carved into the earth and a 350-foot-long dam erected across the San Joaquin River at Mendota. Miller hadn't greeted the idea of the canal with full ardor. More than once, he had vowed that he would never become a farmer. Now hundreds of miles of lateral ditches were diverting riparian flow from the canal onto his wheat and alfalfa fields. "Taking wild land and putting it under systematic cultivation" was how Miller the farmer now described it. "Some of the land that this waters is sandy loam, some of it is alkali bog," he said. "We have around the canal something like 150,000 acres, raising grain, cutting our own hay and improving the land. We are fattening between six and eight thousand cows by artificial means. Making a steer weigh a third more than he would otherwise by feeding him hay and grain."

As the digging wore on, Miller grew irritated with Brereton's gassy talk of a canal system running down both sides of the valley, carrying barges and irrigation water. The canal's cause wasn't helped by the fact that Tulare Lake, the plan's centerpiece, had begun to dry out from all the upstream farm diversions and a succession of parched years. For Miller, the seventy-five miles of canal already built, already coursing water through the heart of his empire, was plenty enough. The grand canal ended up dying on Miller's plain, though its vision would keep surfacing, in one form or another, for the next century.

Miller began to suffer from a series of physical ailments in the mid-1870s that linked up with mental ones. He built a nineteen-bedroom mansion at his Bloomfield Ranch in Gilroy and a summer cottage near the coast on Mount Madonna, but neither gave him much joy. He could no longer find sleep, and food had no more taste for him. He ached for a friend. "My social side has never been developed," he confided to an employee. "I guess I've been too busy." He scarcely kept a relationship with his own son, Henry Jr., a frail child who had attended private school in San Francisco and now, syphilis-ridden, was drinking his life away. Miller was about to disown him. Then came the death of Sarah Alice, the eight-year-old he affectionately called Gussie. Strong-willed and lively, she was said to resemble him the most in character, "the apple of her father's eye." Gussie had been riding her horse at the Bloomfield Ranch when it fell and crushed her.

Miller tried to throw himself ever more deeply into work, but the grief never let go. He wrote letter after letter during his fitful nights, instructing everyone from his partner, Lux, to the man who skinned his dead cows, elaborating on every last detail. "You should have some cats to destroy the mice in the granary," he wrote to one employee. The next day, he added, "I have directed that two cats be sent to you for the granary." The following day, he inquired, "Have the cats arrived for the granary?" The day after, he instructed, "Do not let the cats get food around the kitchen or they will catch no mice."

He traveled to Europe in 1875 and visited Germany for the first time since he'd left as a teenager. He believed that doctors there might find a cure for him. He stayed for seven months and returned to Los Banos in better shape only to find flood and then drought gripping the valley again. Twenty thousand sheep were dying on the Big Panoche Plains from a lack of water. The canal's flow was shut off, and tens of thousands of Miller's acres had begun to burn in the sun. He flew into a tirade, something worse than the Henry Miller dance, grabbed an ax and marched along the canal bank. Wielding ax the way he wielded a butcher's knife, he chopped open every canal gate and watched cold blue water pour onto his withered grains. The canal superintendent swore out a warrant for his arrest, but it was never acted upon. Miller had bought out enough shares of the San Joaquin and Kings River Canal and Irrigation Company to control the flow. He would keep checking its banks for gophers until his old age. "See that critter," he'd shout at his deadeye. "Shoot 'em."

On history's page, it's plain to see the orbit of James Ben Ali Haggin about to intrude on the orbit of Henry Miller. The two men, their empires separated by only a degree, had been circling each other for years. Now their designs finally collided in the Kern River basin. As a sustained flow of water, the river wasn't nearly big enough for the two of them. It ran cold one year, hot the next. The average runoff, 700,000 acre-feet, might have covered their ambitions, but since when did the Kern hit average? The two men went about buying their separate ends of the river in the 1870s, each one ignoring the other's reach. Haggin set up his canals upstream to develop his agricultural colonies while Miller took the sloughs downstream to water his cattle and wheat. As long as the rain fell generously and the snow melted, there was ample flow for the both of them.

When the next drought arrived, as if on schedule, lawyers for both men were well prepared. The epic courtroom battle over land and water, drought and flood and riparian versus appropriative rights pitted against each other two titans of such contrasting styles that maybe only Mark Twain could have done justice to the proceedings. That's assuming he would have had the patience to wade through the arguments, motions, pleadings, evidence and testimonies, as well as the various and conflicting maps of the Kern River, its forks and swamps, that piled up in lower court and then again in higher court. Twain would have likely concluded that Haggin, in particular, was a man whose story merited more than fact could furnish. Half Turk by blood, full Kentuckian by upbringing, the third-richest man in America behind Rockefeller and Carnegie, Haggin stepped foot into the Kern County courthouse already a tall tale.

The Haggins had migrated to Harrodsburg, Kentucky, about the time of Daniel Boone. They were Indian fighters and breeders of champion racehorses. To honor his family's past, Haggin purchased a spread of land on the outskirts of Sacramento and assembled the largest thoroughbred stable and breeding farm in the world. The most magnificent of his racehorses, Ben Ali, won the twelfth Kentucky Derby. For his wife and five children, he bought an entire block of San Francisco and built the first mansion on Nob Hill, a three-story brick-and-stone palace with mansard tile roof and an eighty-six-foot cupola. The thirty-two-thousand-square-foot interior was divided into sixty-one rooms, eleven baths and a basement, where he played billiards and collected wine. The stable, which fronted Mason Street and held forty horses and eighteen carriages, lacked little splendor itself. This was where the Haggins hosted the city's most elegant balls and midnight supper parties, including one lavish dinner on April 17, 1906, for Enrico Caruso, the world's foremost tenor, who had performed earlier that evening at the San Francisco Opera House. Before going to bed, Haggin noticed his horses acting strange and chalked it up to the late-night merriment. The next morning, the great San Francisco earthquake struck, and the mansion, like so much else of the city by the bay, was brought down by tremor and fire.

Haggin was said to be a man of "reserved dignity" and "wonderful shrewdness" whose powers of mental absorption had few rivals. He'd stride from work to home with his eyes fixed on the sidewalk, seeing no one, hearing nothing, turning over in his mind some knotty problem. When he got stuck one way, he would explore the issue the other way. The other way, friends said, was the "Oriental" way passed down from his maternal side. His mother's father, Ibrahim Ben Ali, had been an officer in the Turkish army who converted to Christianity in the late 1700s and fled the Ottoman Empire. The grandfather found a bride in England and moved to Kentucky, where he mastered the cultured taste of the American South, all the way down to its slave owning. Haggin's mother, Adeline Ben Ali, was a woman of refinement who owned the first piano in Harrodsburg. On courting day, the local paper wrote, "men would assemble in front of her house to catch the music that tinkled from her fingers." Haggin's father, Terah Haggin, the son of Kentucky pioneers, was the young lawyer who eventually caught Adeline's fancy.

The eldest of eight children, James Ben Ali Haggin graduated from a private college near Harrodsburg and then studied for the law at his father's office. After passing the bar, he moved to Natchez, Mississippi, one of the main cotton ports on the big river. There, he became partners with Colonel Lewis Sanders, a leading member of the bar, who had a lovely daughter named Eliza Jane. Haggin and Eliza Jane Sanders married in 1846, and four years later, burning with gold fever, James Ben Ali boarded the same steamer, *Georgia,* that was transporting Henry Miller westward. "We entered the Golden Gate a glorious Sunday morning," he recalled.

Haggin traced Sutter's path through the tules and opened a law office in Sacramento. The lawyer next door, Lloyd Tevis, happened to be an acquaintance from the South. The two men became brothers-in-law (Tevis married Eliza Jane's sister) and formed a partnership that lasted for the next fifty years. Unlike the robber barons of the East, who dominated a single industry, Haggin and Tevis chased after one natural resource, then another. They invested in mines in California, Utah, Montana and South Dakota and struck mother lodes three times: first gold, then silver, then copper. As the riches flowed in, they started the first gas, water and ice companies in San Francisco. Then they turned their attention to real estate, accumulating nearly five hundred thousand acres in California and another million acres in Arizona, New Mexico and Mexico.

James Ben Ali Haggin, "Grand Khan of the Kern"

Through various land agents, none more mercurial than Billy "Boss" Carr, a fixer for the Southern Pacific, they began acquiring large chunks of Kern County in 1873. Carr had been a master builder of levees and ditches, first for the mining companies and then for the city of Sacramento. He impressed Haggin with his knowledge of river diversion, not to mention his loyal ring of mercenaries, who, as one newspaper put it, "steal to get into office, and get into office to steal." U.S. Senator Aaron A. Sargent "belonged body, mind and soul to Billy Carr," the *San Francisco Chronicle* charged. Their "atrocious villainy" in the year 1877 had given the nation another dubious mechanism for land distribution, this one called the Desert Land Act. At Carr's orchestration, Senator Sargent tailored the act to fit the precise description of almost every dry acre in Kern County. Carr, a corpulent backslapper customarily dressed in a gentleman's white suit and chomping on a sweated cigar, then paid hundreds of San Franciscans to pretend they were farmers and file dummy claims for these acres. The dummies were nothing if not methodical. On behalf of James Ben Ali Haggin, they amassed more than one hundred thousand acres north and south of Bakersfield for twenty-five cents an acre.

This wasn't the swampland downriver that belonged to Henry Miller. Haggin needed to go out and divert water to make the desert bloom. He sent Carr back to Kern County to sweet-talk more settlers, buying out their land and ditches. Before he was through, Haggin had grabbed three hundred thousand additional acres—and the canal companies that came with them. He now controlled the Kern River's entire upstream flow. Whenever any Sandlapper in the county wanted to irrigate his crops, he had to pay homage, and a fee, to "the grand khan of the Kern." Some settlers in the juggernaut's path refused to bow. Miss Conway, a schoolteacher who owned a small farm, vowed not to be "bought out, fenced out or duped out." Boss Carr dispatched a crew to build a fence that blocked Miss Conway from using the local canal. When she grabbed an ax and chopped down the fence in front of Carr's men, they decided not to risk a confrontation. The next time the schoolteacher went to draw water, however, she discovered several dead hogs fouling the bottom of her well.

The local rag, the *Californian,* rarely found occasion to criticize any business practices of Haggin and Carr, a hands-off policy that extended to their henchmen in the field. The last thing the newspaper wanted to be accused of was playing the role of "knocker." Reporters and editors in Bakersfield and Tulare generally stuck to the belief that Haggin's Kern County Land Company, as its name implied, was gathering the natural resources of the region under one development roof and making the necessary improvements the citizens couldn't undertake for themselves. "My object has not been to monopolize large bodies of land," Haggin insisted. He was only aggregating the land in an effort to build a large enough system of levees, ditches and canals to then sell everything back to the people in "small tracts with the water rights necessary for irrigation."

Already, the Kern was a river with too many siphons. When the drought of 1877 descended, Henry Miller could no longer pretend that Haggin's upstream diversion was causing him no harm. Miller's eighty thousand acres of swampland, where the Kern River became Buena Vista Slough and then sank into Tulare Lake, were reverting to desert. His vast canal system was parched. Miller no longer had enough water or grass to feed his cattle in western Kern. The time had come to file a lawsuit against Haggin. It did little good to own all that riverfront land if the grand khan of the Kern was planting his intakes upstream and diverting the flow onto his faraway farms.

As the two giants prepared for legal war, Californians took up sides. It was Sandlapper versus Pike all over again. Those who owned land along a river and counted on riparian law for their water took Miller as their champion. Those who lived at a distance and needed to move water through ditches to grow their civilized crops lined up behind Haggin. Though neither man was much loved, Haggin's interests aligned with the clear majority of valley people. For every riparian landowner, there were scores of dryland settlers who desired access to river water. Robber baron or not, Haggin had demonstrated that the right of "prior appropriation" was the most democratic approach to portioning out snowmelt in the arid West.

On the eve of the courtroom battle, a state convention of irrigators met in Fresno for an emergency session and posed the question as only irrigators could: "Which is best? The desert with a few herds and their scattering attendants? Or the green fields, orchards, the vine, the olive, the orange, the ripening grain and the happiness and prosperity which attends safe and certain husbandry?" Their answer surprised no one. "The consequences of depriving all, or all but riparian owners, from irrigating are simply too frightful to contemplate."

In the spring of 1881, the cattle king and the grand khan walked into the Kern County Superior Court in Bakersfield, a town built not alongside the river's plain but in its very path, and laid out their respective cases before Judge Benjamin Brundage. The parade of witnesses lasted forty-nine days. Haggin's legal team was led by his eldest son, Louis, who had grown up in the manner of a royal heir and married the brilliant and talented San Francisco socialite Blanche Butterworth. Louis advised his father that it was futile to challenge the law of riparian rights since the California Supreme Court, more than once, had shown its sympathy for the doctrine. Instead, he put forward the argument that the Buena Vista Slough, where Miller had built his waterworks and ran his cattle, wasn't riparian land. The slough had no defined banks and changed its course from year to year. The ground was so porous and evaporation so harsh that the slough commonly disappeared in dry years—with or without any upstream diversions. The slough wasn't a river but a phantom. It came alive only in wet years, and then for only a few months.

Miller's lawyers dismissed such contentions as preposterous. They countered that the Kern's entire run, from mountain to slough, was subject to frequent changes. Indeed, variability was the very nature of the river. In flood years, its banks washed out and its forks rushed off in many directions. In dry years, it quieted into its more defined channels. Buena Vista Slough wasn't Henry Miller's invention. It had existed for ages as part of the same river system that shot down from mountain gorge. Haggin's greed, they argued, was moving the flow of the Kern River thirty miles from its natural channel. This was ground God intended as desert. Why should the rights of dry earth supersede the rights of a natural slough? Here, of course, Miller's lawyers were playing a risky game. They were accusing Haggin of the same evil of appropriation that Miller himself had been carrying out for decades along the larger San Joaquin River.

On November 3, 1881, after entertaining final arguments in San Francisco, Judge Brundage sided with Haggin and the rights of all appropriators. He ruled that the Buena Vista Slough did not constitute a "continuous or defined channel." While he did not reject the riparian doctrine outright, he found that its extreme application would "condemn to perpetual bareness" nearly the whole of California's great interior valleys and would "carry widespread disaster and ruin to many prosperous communities." Irrigation by way of the liberating arm of appropriation, he concluded, was "a natural necessity."

Three years later, to the delight of riparians, the California Supreme Court agreed to hear Miller's appeal. Though the arguments had not changed, the justices ruled that Miller's slough was indeed a natural watercourse. Its flow was as valid as the flow inside the Kern's more defined banks. This made Miller's slough an extension of the river and gave the cattle king first rights to its draw. At the same time, the supreme court ruled, riparian law did not mean that one land baron had the right to lord over a river's beneficence. Because the tradition of appropriation exercised by Haggin and countless settlers was so embedded in California, the busy work of diverting rivers and digging canals should carry forth.

Over the next four decades, through legislative act and constitutional amendment, California found a way, often tortuous, to combine riparian and appropriative rights under a formula of "beneficial and reasonable" use. What this meant on the ground was that water generally ran to the men able to afford the most creative lawyers and engineers. While lawsuits over the taking of California's other rivers would continue for years, the war on the Kern River more or less came to a resolution when Miller and Haggin, big men who aimed to get bigger, shook hands and became partners in an upstream reservoir that put even more control in the grasp of a few. Whether riparian or appropriative, it no longer mattered. The two laws, by dint of a shotgun marriage, had become one couple. Under the California Doctrine of water, the rivers flowed into the same deep pockets.

Part Three

SYSTEM TO THE RESCUE
(1901–1967)

The California Aqueduct carrying snowmelt down
the San Joaquin Valley

Eleven

FRUITING THE PLAIN

The letters traveled from Fresno to Constantinople as the First World War was coming to an end. They were written with the purpose of selling a man without a country—my grandfather in this instance—on the idea of California. While the letters did not survive the years, whole passages remained alive in his mind when he began sharing his story with me in the late 1970s. Even as senility took over, he would recite the lines in his broken English, his square hands making gestures out of each California exaggeration—the "big talk," he called it. The letters postmarked "Fresno" had been written to him by his mother's brother, Yervant Demirjian, who had survived the 1915 Armenian Genocide and was the last patriarch left in the family. On his trek to America, Uncle Yervant had sojourned in Bulgaria, the first stop in a shattered new life. There, engaged in some menial labor, he raged over an offense committed by two Turkish coworkers. After their shift was completed, he followed the pair back to their flat. With his bare hands, he murdered both men and fled to California with a different last name: Janigian.

The story—what parts were true, what parts were myth?—was passed down to me as a family's act of vengeance. Among the 1.5 million Armenians massacred or starved to death by Ottoman Turkey between 1915 and 1918 were Uncle Yervant's wife, son and daughter. They lived on the shores of Lake Nicea in a village that had been our home for generations, a place my grandfather called Medz Nor Keugh, or "Great New Town." The mulberry and olive orchards rolled out beneath the Duman Dagh, the "mountain of mist," he told me. Uncle Yervant's letters from Fresno to Constantinople were written in the melancholy of a man who had lost everything, and yet he had begun to believe, out of some obstinacy deep inside, that a new start was possible in a valley at the edge of the Sierra. Here, he wrote, in vineyards and orchards fed by mountain streams, a "new Armenia" was being created. He had no one else in the world and wanted my grandfather, the eldest of his nephews, to join him.

My grandfather, Jonig Housepian, who had lost his father to typhoid fever when he was fifteen, had his heart set on another road. He and his widowed mother, sister and brother had been spared the fate of his uncle's family only because they had left the village to find work in Constantinople. As the Turkish military began rounding up Armenian males in the city, my grandfather climbed into the attic with his books—Maupassant, Verlaine and Baudelaire—and waited for genocide's fever to pass. When the Ottoman Empire finally crumbled, he came down from his nest and went to work at a nearby Armenian bookstore. There, among the tormented survivors, several Armenian writers met each day to drink tea, play backgammon and figure out what words were left. The group included Yervant Odian, the fine satirist, and Hagop Oshagan, my grandfather's mentor who was writing a monumental work of memory called *The Remnants*. They took seventeen-year-old Jonig under their wings, read his earliest poems and sketches, critiqued his flowery ardor and bandied about a pen name that might enhance the appeal of a young writer with a naïve yet subversive bent. It was Odian, perhaps in a mood of satire, who fit him with the nom de guerre "Aram Arax." Arax was the river, the mother river, that flowed down from Mount Ararat across a nation that hadn't existed for more than a thousand years.

Soon after, the letters from Uncle Yervant in Fresno began to arrive. "Here find an Eden of pomegranate and peach," he wrote. "Grapes that hang like jade eggs. Watermelons so capacious that when you finish eating their delicious meat, you can float inside their shells in the cool waters of irrigation canals. Armenians by the thousands have come. We are farming raisins. We have started two newspapers, a theater group, a literary group and two coffee houses. You must see it with your own eyes to believe it!"

My grandfather's first writings had caught the attention of an Armenian railroad magnate who had no children and offered to fund his education at the Sorbonne. His plan was to go to Paris, study the French symbolic poets and become a writer. But his uncle's letters kept arriving, each one more blood red than the one before. There was a fine university in California at Berkeley, his uncle wrote. Perhaps after earning enough money in Fresno, he could attend classes there and become a journalist. His mother, sister and brother would be able to join him in a year. Paris or Fresno, which to choose? I have often told his dilemma as a joke that gets laughs. But my grandfather's failure to take up the railroad man on his offer became one of the real regrets of his life. Only years later, in the hold of senility, would he make the choice right. He would imagine he had chosen Paris and its thousand-year-old university, where legs of lamb hung from trees and coeds greeted him with their bosoms bared.

The Armenian Boy Scout band of Constantinople, tattered and full of orphans, played a rousing send-off. It was May 1920. He was nineteen years old and sitting in steerage with an Armenian boy named Jeskalian and two pretty Syrian girls. "We slept on the bottom of the boat. Just like catfish. On the Sea of Marmara it was moonlight. Family, good friends, all behind me. A sadness you could never describe."

My grandfather would find out soon enough that he had been played for a sucker. His uncle could hardly be blamed. Like so many Fresno newcomers, Yervant had been caught up in the hype, unwittingly enlisted in the legion of promoters. Not since gold rush times had such spectacular tales been told about California. In slick pamphlets, each city and county, like pros in an Old West brothel, lined up to show what God had given them best. As a matter of fact, the stories of nature producing wonderful monstrosities in one blessed ground or another were true. The impression they left—that gold could now be plucked from trees—was another matter. The stories crossed over into agricultural lore. In the little town of Parlier, outside Fresno, founder I. N. Parlier had grown in his front yard a Calimyrna fig tree (half California, half Turkish Smyrna) so magnificent that its wingspan measured eighty-eight feet wide and its trunk nine feet around. It became so laden with crop that the Parliers had to move their house three times to get out of its way. In Santa Barbara, a single vine bore in one season not pounds of grapes but tons. In San Jose, a giant pear weighing two pounds, twelve ounces astonished visitors to the state fair. In Chico, one of the several towns claiming title to the "City of Roses," John Bidwell, Sutter's old right hand, was now a gentleman farmer whose cherry trees included a freak that produced seventeen hundred pounds of fruit one season. Outside Visalia, a French plum tree belonging to a farmer named Briggs yielded one thousand pounds of dried plums, otherwise known as prunes. This was considered a farmer's fish story until Briggs summoned bankers and agricultural tradesmen to his orchard to document for themselves the tree's exuberance. In Los Angeles, one pumpkin grew to such proportions, a reported twelve hundred pounds, that the farmer had to chop it off the vine with an ax.

As my grandfather undertook his seven-thousand-mile journey by boat and train, a folklore of California climatology was published to explain such aberrations. The California State Agricultural Society, Department of Meteorology, had chosen a booster from each county to sing that county's glories. "The climate of Solano is a benediction," one pitchman began. "We have but little fog, no thunderstorms, lightning or tornadoes, no cyclones, no earthquakes, no blizzards, no sleets, no snow-drifting snows, no storms, not scalding heat in summer or freezing weather in winter. The wet and dry periods come with such regularity that the farmer knows just how to provide for them. He sows his seeds and cultivates his land with the positive assurance that the rain will come to sprout it and the sun will shine to warm it into life and cause it to grow luxuriantly. When winter comes, it is only so in name and called such in order to distinguish different periods of the year. We have a rarity, crispness and tone of the atmosphere, freedom from malaria-breeding swamps, a perfect system of drainage so that epidemic disease, either among men or animals, is rarely known."

The curative powers of sun and air had made Southern California the first tropical land that "our race has mastered and made itself at home in," Nordhoff wrote. Even Carey McWilliams, California's designated deflater, couldn't contain himself when describing how the harsh desert light turned into a thing of beauty the moment ocean mist rolled in. "This is not a desert light nor is it tropical for it has neutral tones," he wrote. "It is Southern California light, and it has no counterpart in the world."

Trainloads of the pallid from New York, Ohio, Illinois, Missouri and Iowa were shipped to bathe in this light. Carrying a doctor's diagnosis of jaundice, cirrhosis of the liver, tuberculosis, chronic bronchitis, pneumonia, fatty liver, weak kidneys, scarlet fever they gave themselves to the sunshine and liquid air. Thanks to Nordhoff, whose dispatches extolling the state had been collected in *California for Travellers and Settlers,* sanitariums across the San Gabriel Valley kept filling with consumptives. He related the story of an old friend who'd been battling tuberculosis for years, traveling a circuit of European and American resorts in search of a climate that might calm his symptoms. The man nonetheless was "losing ground," his body racked by coughing, night sweats and sleeplessness. Nordhoff consigned his friend to the list of the dying and waited for the news to arrive.

Then one day a few months later, he was standing in the doorway of a Los Angeles hotel when a wagon drove up and out leaped a traveler who sang in a hearty voice, "How do you do?" It was his consumptive friend, now a restored man. They took a walk of several miles that evening. His friend told Nordhoff that he ate heartily, slept well, enjoyed life and coughed hardly at all. What an amazing change three months in California had brought! "I shall never be a sound man, of course," the friend confided. "But this climate has added ten years to my life."

My grandfather never talked about the Statue of Liberty, the first skyscrapers rising out of the prairie or the great expanse of salt desert that had called the Mormons west. From the straits of the Bosporus to the edge of California, it was as if America didn't register with him. Then his train found the mountain where the Donner Party got trapped in a bad winter's storm, the same mountain the Chinese railroad workers had dug through. As the engine chugged down the mountain and descended into a valley knifed by two rivers and a webwork of ditches, Aram Arax finally gazed upon the country his uncle had written about. Outside his window, beneath the snowy caps of the Sierra, the big valley shimmered. Vineyards and orchards and vegetable fields, row after perfect row. He'd made a fool of himself a few days earlier when he'd put down a dollar bill at the train station counter and pointed to a chocolate bar. He spoke Armenian, Turkish, French, Greek and some Arabic, but not a word of English. "You want a whole dollar's worth?" the clerk asked. Yes, he nodded. He took his train seat with an empty wallet and a bag full of chocolates, and that's what he ate on the way over. If he now wanted to jump for joy at the unfolding of such a garden, he didn't dare. As he stared out the window, he kept muttering the same words in Armenian: "Just like the old land."

He would soon figure out that it was nothing like the old land. This was fertility supercharged by irrigation and the science of the Agricultural College at the University of California. This was the most extensive and intensive farming experiment in the world. The pear orchards he was passing through contained not one variety but a dozen. Bosc, Madeline, Bloodgood, Dearborn, Le Conte, Beurre Hardy and the Bartlett, already renowned in San Francisco and New York. Men were still fighting over the water and would continue fighting into the next century, but the lawsuits and countersuits over the previous decades had beaten both riparian and appropriative water users into a kind of submission. This was the truce that Nordhoff and Mead had thought possible in California if reclamation could be freed of the oligarchs and common settlers could accept a system of irrigation that involved a degree of subordination, if not absolute obedience, to the river master, canal operator, ditch tender. In the name of such peace, farmers had assigned their respective rights to the public canal company.

From 1900 to 1920, as people softened in their repugnancy to government, the irrigated crops in California tripled to 4.2 million acres, half of agriculture's eventual reach. Nearly 60 percent of the farms, those along the rivers and those a good ways beyond, were now irrigated. The U.S. government had spent $200 million making reclamation and settlement happen in California. In spite of the widespread corruption along the way, who could argue that it wasn't now a wise investment?

In 1920, the year of my grandfather's landing, banks across the state swelled with $400 million in deposits—the greatest annual increase in California history. The value of the harvest had doubled over the decade, to $588 million. More than 153 million grapevines—Malagas, Emperors, Cornichons, Tokays, Muscats, Sultanas, Thompson Seedless—had been planted. The raisin crop now weighed 185,000 tons. Ten thousand citrus ranchers, the fabled gentlemen of agriculture, were growing 200,000 acres of oranges, lemons and grapefruits. The Washington navel that birthed the myth of Los Angeles as the sun-kissed capital of America had traveled up and over the mountain to a new citrus belt in the foothills of eastern Tulare County. Vegetables were being raised on 146,000 acres. In the black adobe soil of the upper Sacramento Valley, farmers were growing more than 50,000 acres of rice. Even in the midst of this greening, livestock and grain had not vanished. Two million head of cattle—two-thirds beef cows, one-third dairy—were now consuming an alfalfa crop that stood on more than 1 million acres. There were 2.4 million sheep, 1 million swine, 10.5 million chickens and 148 ostriches. Four decades after the death of Friedlander, wheat and barley still covered a quarter of the farmland. Vast tracts of the best soil and the most reliable water continued to be held by the king of one crop or another. Even so, the proportion of farms 1,000 acres or larger had fallen slightly from 1910 to 1920, reflecting the arrival of more small farmers. Likewise, the average farm size shrunk from 400 acres to 246 acres.

As for the farmers themselves, they now numbered 117,000. Two-thirds were white men born in the United States. Most of the rest were like my grandfather, immigrants from Turkey, Germany, Italy, Portugal, Sweden, Norway and Denmark. Among the six thousand farmers of "color" were 200 blacks, 406 Chinese and 5,000 Japanese, who, much to the public's dismay, were farming 430,000 acres and operating a growing line of canneries. The United States had excluded the Chinese by official act in 1882. The so-called Gentlemen's Agreement that allowed Japanese to settle in California had envisioned them as field hands, not as agriculturalists intent on controlling their own realm. What to do now? "Under present conditions, we virtually are at the mercy of the Japanese," the *Los Angeles Times* groused in 1920. "Los Angeles must have vegetables in order to live, and the Japanese have taken advantage of this fact to corral the vegetable gardens about the city."

In the delta lands of Sacramento, by contrast, landowners were more than happy to lease out their rich peat to Japanese farmers and their "picture bride" wives. "No anti-Japanese agitation in the delta region," the leading Japanese newspaper in San Francisco reported. "Plan canneries." The Italian and Chinese fishermen who caught and canned the native species had retreated from the delta after the herring and anchovy retreated first. Three olive-brining plants and a dozen other canneries processing the fruit and asparagus crops arose in their place. The canneries in the delta town of Rio Vista would later summon my grandfather Aram and his mother, Azniv, and his sister, Mariam, and his little brother, Harutoun. But that was two years in the future, after he had settled in Fresno and they had joined him in the army of fruit tramps.

The 1920 California State Fair drew a record crowd to celebrate a record harvest. Los Angeles and San Francisco had become rival cities with populations that had each shot past the half-million mark. Two-thirds of Californians counted themselves as city folk. When it came to the dominance of water, however, California could not have been a more enthusiastic farm state. More than 95 percent of the snowpack captured in the rivers and shunted by man flowed to the crops. The Golden State produced 57 percent of the nation's oranges, 70 percent of its prunes and plums, more than 80 percent of its grapes and figs and virtually all of its raisins, apricots, almonds, walnuts, olives and lemons.

Like my grandfather, the budwood and cuttings had traveled to California by ship and train: oranges from Brazil; plums from Japan and France; grapevines from Italy, Spain, France and Serbia; figs from Turkey and Greece. In the dirt pockets of immigrants came the seeds of the Persian melon, Casaba melon, Crenshaw melon, Japanese cucumber, Japanese eggplant and the Armenian cucumber, *gootah,* ridged and nutty-flavored. The immigrant farmers planted the exotic and waited for the taste buds of city folk to catch up. If city folk made a sudden shift in their produce buying, the farmer wasted no time in pulling out the old and planting the new. When the First World War dried up imports of raisins and figs from Asia Minor, the California farmer jumped right in. Across Fresno County, ten thousand acres of raisin grapes and fig trees were rushed into the ground the year the Ottoman Empire fell.

My grandfather had come in a dry year when the Sacramento River was running at half its better flow. Still, it was spring, and the delta sloshed with fresh water gliding down the mountain and seawater pushing in from the Pacific. The scene outside his window was common and strange at once. He had lived all his life on the seashore. Village elders had tied hashish to his body when he was twelve and sent him on a boat ride across the Sea of Marmara. His father's sudden death had come after a sea trip to trade olive oil. So the delta, at first glance, seemed like a thing familiar. Yet what place other than Holland had reclaimed farm from sea? It looked to be a funny business. The Sacramento and San Joaquin Rivers coursed through the maze of islands at a water level more than twenty feet above the fields of wheat, alfalfa and vegetables. On the contoured banks of the river, two trucks could pass each other. The vineyards and blossoming pear, peach and plum orchards relied on a levee one hundred feet wide and thirty feet tall to keep dry.

This was how all the virgin swampland, more than four hundred thousand acres, had been reclaimed. This is how the jacked-up city of Sacramento, its streets raised a dozen feet from their natural level and a new downtown built upon a bed of borrowed earth, had been reclaimed. *Reclaimed.* What an odd word. It implied that humans once had domain here, lost it to nature and then returned to take back what was rightfully theirs. There existed no such word in the Armenian language. The concept itself was foreign. We were a people accustomed to being conquered, not conquering. It took at least a sentence, *Hogh ee agha zedum,* to get close to *reclamation,* and even then it meant only "to purify the land of salts." The word in French depended on what kind of reclamation—reputation, title, taxes—one was talking about. The reclaiming of land from sea was *assèchement*. The reclamation that greeted my grandfather as his train rumbled down the core of the state was a crazy, fertile patchwork that extended from the Sacramento Valley, "the heart of California," to the booming town of Fresno, "ash tree" in Spanish, though since the turn of the century known in the promotional literature as "Fresno County: A Wonderfully Prosperous District in California. The Land of Sunshine, Fruits and Flowers. No Ice. No Snow. No Blizzards. No Cyclones."

Uncle Yervant, a small man with an enormous capacity for preening, wasn't finished selling the move to his nephew. He drove up to the depot that spring day in a gleaming Model T Ford. With a fresh haircut framing his square head, he wore a suit and tie and pair of two-toned polished shoes that laced up to his ankles. He was not yet forty years old, his jaw, cheekbones and brow still dominant. He was about to embark on a new family life with an Armenian widow who had five children and would bear him a daughter and son that would replace the daughter and son he had lost to the Turks. My grandfather knew his uncle to be a man who wounded easily and relished his flattery. After those initial hugs and kisses, as he was being shown around town, young Aram Arax surely suppressed what he felt as his eyes took in the

Aram Arax and his uncle Yervant Janigian,
Fresno, 1921

irrigated desert and its supposed mecca, a city of 45,086 residents where even the undertaker and the master violinist doubled as raisin farmers. Where was the sea and its gentle breezes? Where were the bookstores and museums? The college wasn't a university but a "normal" school, a place to train high school graduates to become teachers.

Fresno was a creature only a half century in the making. It was situated on the blazing hot ground because that's where Leland Stanford and his railroad had put it. Had those early exiles from the Dixie South gotten their way, the county seat would have remained up in the hills next to the river, in the gold-mining town of Millerton. Henry Burroughs brought his slave, Negro Jane, to Millerton in the 1860s and freed her. All of his farm animals were named Jefferson Davis. The southerners built the Oak Hotel, the county courthouse, the jail, the Odd Fellows Lodge and the Mississippi School. But by February 1874, the county seat had fled Millerton and slid down the hill to Fresno. The splendid courthouse became a refuge for bats and owls. What was left of Millerton was sold at a public auction. Negro Jane's house fetched thirteen dollars.

The valley had been growing in a different pattern ever since Leland Stanford had come through in 1871. As the story goes, he was traveling to the growing burg of Visalia to see where he might extend his railroad next and happened upon a two-thousand-acre wheat field near the Fresno townsite. This was the wheat that belonged to Moses J. Church, the wheat fed by the original canal that tapped into the Kings River. Stanford hadn't seen a spot of green since leaving Stockton the day before. "Gentlemen," he told the dreamers of Fresno, standing on the hot earth between the San Joaquin and Kings Rivers, "this place can never go bankrupt with resources like this to draw on. Here's where we must locate the town." Stanford's railroad put its tracks through the nowhere of Fresno in return for the dreamers selling the 4,480-acre townsite, on easy terms, to the railroad.

It was the railroad's custom to hold a public auction along its roadbed to sell a town's best lots. But there were no bidders for Fresno. It began life as a squatters' village. No one besides a man named Massen was willing to live on ground this parched. The squatter "put up a diminutive, shaky shanty" and hung out a shingle that offered a drink of water from his own well to any man or horse who happened by. The railroad figured that Massen was at least a start and allowed him and other squatters to stay. Within three years, they were joined by twenty-five residents and twenty-nine businesses, including the French Hotel and Russell Fleming's livery stable. It took another dozen years for the town to import enough water and feel sufficiently worthy to incorporate as an actual city. What to call themselves? its people wondered. For a time, the word "Fresnoite" appeared in the local *Republican*. At some point, townsfolk began to refer to themselves as "Fresnans." It stuck.

The culture of the small farm hadn't incubated all on its own. It had been ginned up by the old wheat barons and exalted by their real estate men. They were looking to salvage the value of hundreds of thousands of acres robbed of fertility by wheat and now given a second chance by the canals and ditches bringing snowmelt to the fruit plains. Between 1875 and 1890, Isaac Friedlander, William Chapman, Dr. E. B. Perrin, L. A. Nares, Moses J. Church and others laid out more that twenty-five agricultural colonies in and around Fresno. This was farming on a communal model. The promotional literature they cranked out found its way to Germany, France, England, Norway, Denmark, Sweden, Holland and Australia, plus every state in the Union. The marketing of the settlements did not emphasize their ideological missions, even though many of the colonies were being formed along ethnic and political lines. Rather, what they promoted was the realization of man's entrepreneurial destiny. The colonies would create "a system of ideal rural homes and communities, where the science of tillage is carried to its greatest perfection, and where comfort, good taste and an admirable spirit of helpfulness and neighborliness abound," in the words of the *Fresno Morning Republican.*

The first of the settlements on the Fresno plains, the Alabama Colony, took root on land that Chapman and Friedlander had sold at twice the government price of $1.25 an acre and more than four times what they had paid for it. The idea seemed an honorable one: to peddle twenty-acre lots to Confederates aiming for a fresh start after the Civil War. The first group of southerners included a judge and a major who were sent as *avant-couriers* to report back the conditions of middle California to family and friends. Their letters home described a land of such glories that one had to wonder if they had never ventured beyond the California coastline or had secretly signed on as paid agents for Chapman and Friedlander. The settlers arrived in droves from Alabama, Mississippi and Tennessee only to discover "no green fields of alfalfa, no prolific orchards and gardens, and scarcely a windmill to break up the wearisome monotony," the same *Republican* reported.

It got to be a joke. One sheepman passing by pronounced the settlers mad and began listing all the reasons why they should go back. "Don't you know that the climate here is the worst in the world? Birds drop down dead from the heat of the sun. Fruit bakes into sauce before it ripens. The potato crop fails five out of every six years. The year the potatoes don't fail, they rot as soon as they are dug from the earth. The little grain you manage to raise will have to be guarded day and night from the depredations of cattle and wild horses." The sheepman kept talking, but the settlers were sure that irrigation water would be arriving soon to change all that. The drought of 1869 rolled into the drought of 1870. At some point between the dry years of 1871 to 1875, the settlers grew tired of gazing out on a crisped plain where the heat waves "wimpled and quivered like a wounded servant." Even as the waters of irrigation arrived, they turned their backs on their meager grain fields and fled "Hell's Half Acres."

The Alabama Colony died soon after. The Nob Hill capitalists and their real estate promoters were hardly discouraged. By 1880, land syndicates belonging to Chapman, Friedlander and Church had connected their private canal companies to more than three hundred thousand acres of virgin territory. The syndicates decided to market the colonies not as agricultural utopias to mend the spirit but as real estate schemes to wheel and deal. They platted each colony, subdivided the 640-acre sections into twenty-, forty- and eighty-acre parcels, carved out roads named for trees, and then they lined those roads with the same trees, so that two miles of White Adriatic figs became Fig Avenue, nine varieties of cherries became Cherry Avenue, a perfect line of English walnuts became Walnut Avenue and the pink-and-white blossoms of peach, nectarine and plum became Fruit Avenue. When they exhausted the inspiration of horticulture, they named the streets Vanderbilt, Astor and Huntington.

Their slick brochures showed not gopher country but fertile valley stretching idyllically to meet the Sierra. The illustration on the cover was laden: the mountain with snow; the river and canals with water; the trees with fruit. The terms of the purchase price were designed not to overly burden: fifty to sixty dollars an acre, paid on installments with no interest. The syndicates even agreed to plant two acres of raisin grapes on every twenty-acre lot and cultivate the vines as a favor to the settler, at least until he or she learned how to make a raisin. On sales day, real estate agents in San Francisco herded prospective investors and settlers onto trains for the nine-hour journey to rural paradise. Bands played on both ends, and a fancy picnic lunch was served on the grounds of each unveiled colony. Only then was the pressure applied. Curbstone brokers turned some of the lots two and three times in a matter of hours, each turn doubling or tripling the price a settler would have to pay.

No colony was planned more painstakingly than the Central California Colony, a partnership between Chapman and Bernhard Marks that developed twenty-one square miles of superior valley loam. Chapman was quite certain that the colony system would never succeed, and more than once, he tried to talk Marks into abandoning the 13,500-acre project. But Marks, a native of Poland who'd been a rare Jewish gold miner and then a San Francisco grammar school principal and finally a delta farmer, would not be dissuaded. Under his exacting eye, surveyors laid out twenty-three miles of avenues, along with a ditch that linked to the Fresno Canal and Irrigation Company. Nurserymen planted thirty-six miles of trees, not common species but Monterey cypress, cork elm and red gum. In keeping with the promise to plant two acres of raisins as a favor to each buyer, Chapman imported thousands of Muscat vines from Spain. Marks offered liberal terms. A lot of twenty acres was priced at $1,000. The settler needed only to put down $100 and pay $12.50 a month, interest-free. The two partners then handed over matters to their sales agent in San Francisco, whose advertising campaign went like this: "Sit back and watch your money grow on vines and trees! Only nine hours from San Francisco by rail. The perfection of California climate! No fever and ague! The natural home of the fig, citron, raisin, prune, olive, walnut, orange and lemon!"

If the eyebrows of the immigrants began to raise as the train moved from coast to dry interior, the sales agent had a trick up his sleeve. As soon as they hit Fresno, his team was ready with horse and buggy to take them on a tour of the estate of Francis T. Eisen, one of the aristocrats of San Francisco who was now making a splendid life here. The 640-acre Eisen farm could not have been more compelling. Its entrance was lined with the first of the pink and white oleanders that would become the unofficial bush of the valley, dividing highway lanes and fortressing houses. A giant grape arbor arched overhead. More than three hundred varieties of vines and fruit trees were laid out in beautiful rows. A fine-looking winery took in the haul of a dozen varieties of grapes and churned out three hundred thousand gallons of vino each harvest—Muscatel, Angelica, Tokay, Claret, Riesling and Sauterne. The Victorian mansion with its wraparound porch looked out to 250 varieties of roses that flourished in the heat. The whole wonder had been made possible by the same main ditch of the Fresno Canal and Irrigation Company, whose eight-foot fall furnished all the windmill power Baron Eisen desired. "Give me one of those!" the settlers shouted as their buggies headed back to the Central California Colony.

By the summer of 1877, nearly two hundred settlers had joined the colony. Among them were four schoolteachers from San Francisco—Misses M. F. Austin, Lucy H. Hatch, E. A. Cleveland and J. B. Short—

who had pooled their resources to buy one hundred acres along Elm Avenue. With whatever money they had left, the teachers splurged on experimental varieties of fruit trees. They planted the saplings and waited for a crop, visiting the site periodically to check on its progress. When the crop didn't come, they pulled out the trees and taught themselves viticulture. Miss Austin was the first of the teachers to relocate permanently to the colony. Her first raisin pack, in 1878, amounted to thirty boxes sold under the Austin brand. The following year, she and Miss Hatch put up three hundred boxes. By 1886, they were farming seventy-four acres of vines and nineteen acres of orchards and producing twenty thousand pounds of raisins at their Hedgerow Vineyard. The colony was now a community. Its men had built the two-story wooden Grange Hall for social functions and the Orange Center School to educate the children. The Histrionic and Literary Society convened monthly for theater productions, and each Sunday a different minister from the city came to deliver a sermon.

On the Southern Pacific line, the little chicken coop of Fowler spawned four colonies. Along the Kings River, Swedish immigrants founded Kingsburg. In the Barstow Colony, Frank Silva, one of the first sheepherders to emigrate from the Azores, was producing A1 alfalfa. All by himself, real estate agent Charles Teague colonized sixty thousand acres, including a full section set aside for Belgians, guaranteeing their grocery bills until the land had given them a crop. In the summer of 1887, the first group of German wheat farmers from Russia's Volga River valley stepped off the train at Fresno Station in full peasant dress. That same year, Andrew Mattei, an Italian from Switzerland, made his first purchase of vines; his operation kept getting bigger until he became the largest grape grower and winemaker in the United States. Giuseppe "Joseph" Gallo bought a run-down grape ranch in Fresno and started his own wine-distribution business, only to fall on times so desperate that one morning, while his wife, Susie, was feeding the pigs, he picked up his gun and shot her to death and then killed himself. The couple's three sons, Ernest, Julio and Joseph, young ranchers in Modesto, were determined to redeem the family name.

I don't imagine my grandfather turning up his nose as his uncle Yervant drove him from town to country in his new Model T. He'd come too far, and there was no going back. Besides, something singular was taking place here. One-third of Fresno County, two thousand square miles, was now farmed. Almost half this farmland, 518,000 acres, was irrigated. Fresno led the state in the number and reach of its canals and ditches, with more than double the irrigated acres of any other county. Without a single dam yet built, diverters of valley water were capturing 85 percent of the flows of the San Joaquin, Kings and Kern Rivers. So much river water was being shunted across Fresno County that the aquifer had reached its brim. It couldn't handle any more percolation. Dry land was turning to bog. For thousands of years, the aquifer had never been tapped. Five or six feet below the ground, the water sat in pressurized chambers. When a farmer breached the membrane between earth and aquifer, the artesian water shot up as if through a whale's blowhole. This same aquifer was now absorbing the seepage of rivers as their flow was moved onto Fresno farms. The aquifer had become so swollen with excess water that the foundations of houses could only be dug six feet deep. Any deeper and basements would hit the artesian zone. So full was the aquifer that ancient salts bubbled to the surface and poisoned good farm soil. Where the water table was perched, only salt grass thrived. Thousands of Fresno acres were salting white as snow.

As chance would have it, 1920 happened to be a milestone year for irrigated agriculture. The first turbine pumps capable of reaching hundreds of feet into the earth and pulling out easy water became available. Vineyardists and orchardists who'd been locked out of farming because the nearby canals and ditches were overbooked now had a plentiful source of water. Depending on the local aquifer, they drilled wells fifty feet down or five hundred feet down. With a flick of an electrical switch, they began pumping a dam's worth of water out of the earth.

A race to plant more grapes, peaches, figs and cotton fast lowered the water table and un-bogged the land. The pumping of groundwater, at least for the time being, was an act of community restoration. Twenty thousand acres a year in Fresno County were moving from desert to crop. More than 200,000 tons of raisins came off the vine in 1920—a new world record. Fresno was now the second-richest agricultural producer in the state, behind Los Angeles County. Not only did its 2.5 million peach trees make fresh and dried fruit shipped across the country, but the pits were turned into an extraordinary grade of charcoal through a process kept top secret by the government. The char-

Downtown Fresno circa 1920s

coaled pits were used in the manufacture of gas masks that protected U.S. soldiers in the trenches of World War I. The old masks might keep deadly gasses at bay for three hours; the peach pit masks kept a soldier alive for eighteen hours in the most perilous situations.

Fresno could now brag that it was among only a handful of counties in California that carried no public debt. The raisin had done good. Over the previous decade, the number of farms had shot up from 6,243 to 8,917. Remarkably, four years after his death, Henry Miller still ranked as the No. 1 contributor to Fresno County's tax rolls. Even as his son-in-law, James Leroy Nickel, was running the empire into the ground, the company still owned 300,000 acres, the domain extending from the railroad tracks outside Fresno to the Coast Ranges. By 1920, the cattle were nearly gone, and Miller's heirs were engaged in another lawsuit pitting one side of the family against the other. Nickel had taken a company that owed not a penny at the time of Miller's passing and piled on $15 million in debt. Miller's grandchildren and great-grandchildren, the Nickels and the Bowleses, kept feuding for the better part of the next half century, trust-fund baby versus trust-fund baby.

Across the county, barons still commanded their spreads. J. G. Stitt had sixty-eight thousand acres along the Fresno River. Gustavus Herminghaus ran twenty thousand acres along the south side of the San Joaquin River. Llewelyn Arthur Nares, better known as L. A. Nares, a British banker who'd come to California on behalf of English capitalists, controlled 95 percent of the irrigation canals along the Kings River. Yet the realization had now set in that the valley's economic future rested not on the shoulders of immense agricultural operations but on small irrigated orchards and vineyard farms. If you had good water, the local saying went, all you needed was twenty acres of good fruit to live the good life.

Marks, Teague, Temperance, Church. They didn't exist to me as history's characters. These were the names of the roads where I grew up, rode my gas-engine minibike, hunted for jackrabbits, drowned gophers, threw dirt clods at turkey vultures, floated down Fancher Creek Canal in a Goodyear tube and lived to tell Grandma Arax about it. These were the fields where the earth was freshly plowed but never planted, a spot between suburbia and the farm. If the Japanese lived on the east side, and the Italians and "German-Rooshians" lived on the west side, and the Swedes stayed in Kingsburg, and the Mexicans in Malaga and we Armenians couldn't buy houses on the fancy north end because of real estate covenants that barred us, who knew we had the old colony system to thank and blame? When it came to the polyglot, New York City had nothing on us. Fresno was one of the most diverse cities in the country, and also one of the most racially partitioned. The long practice of redlining traces back to our colony past, too.

The colonies served their purpose, no doubt. They pulled migrants across a great landmass and immigrants across an ocean, and when the settlers sent word back home, their hundreds became thousands. In the months preceding my grandfather's arrival in Fresno, local historian Paul Vandor had observed with more than a hint of ugly boast: "Unlike other California towns, the Chinese quarter is not located in the white portion of town but is located to itself on the west side of the railroad track and fully one-fourth of a mile from the town proper." At that moment, the census counted the local Indian population at 347. "The Fresno Indians of today court the seclusions of their foothill or mountain rancherias," Vandor wrote. "In the fruit season, they mingle with the whites on the plains to seek employment in the orchard or vineyard. Otherwise, they are not seen save on the days of the visiting circus or for the Fourth of July parades."

There was never any colony set down on Fresno's hot ground to court the Armenians. Had the city fathers tried, I don't imagine the enterprise would have met with a financial windfall. We were a feuding people. Already small, we made ourselves smaller. "Are you from Bitlis or Moosh?" the Armenians of Fresno inquired of my grandfather during his first week in town. "Van or Erzurum? Village or city? Mountain or valley? Peasant or pasha? Tashnak or Ramgavar?" In Fresno, he quickly learned that the white people referred to his people as "Fresno Indians." Perhaps they meant it as a compliment because the Armenians were a tribe of the land. Or maybe they wanted us to scram like the Indians had been made to. Either way, without a colony to call their own, the Armenians came and stayed. The first Armenian family to settle in Fresno had renamed themselves Normart, which meant "New Man." The first Armenian newspaper in town was named *Nor Giank*, "New Life." My grandfather would name his first son Navasart, Navo, "New Beginning." These were the hopes they pinned on Fresno.

I don't know where Uncle Yervant took my grandfather to stay, but it was close enough to the north end of town that he was awakened each morning by the blasts of dynamite. A new colony was being dug in the hog wallows near the San Joaquin River, a settlement called Fig Garden. The ground was out-and-out hardpan. "The whole town was booming," my grandfather recalled. "I thought it was an earthquake. And then I thought, 'I'm in the middle of war again.' *Boom. Boom.* The ground shook. It was dynamite. Blast after blast. They were bombing the earth. The hardpan would shoot up in the sky. They were planting figs. The Kadota. Luscious and golden yellow. And the new variety, the Calimyrna."

Jesse Clayton Forkner, the developer of Fig Garden, believed the hardpan only needed to be broken up to reveal its special fertility. No one in the six-thousand-year history of fig culture had ever tried to plant five thousand acres at once. In Smyrna, the ancient home of the fig, only twenty thousand acres of the fruit even existed. The job before Forkner was an industrial one. He had to level the mounds and depressions that came with so many miles of hog wallow—the enduring work of pocket gophers. He called up Henry Ford and ordered eighty Fordson tractors fresh off the assembly line. He bought six hundred thousand pounds of dynamite to blast holes for six hundred thousand fig trees, a pound for each hole. As to the question of where he would find more than a half million fig tree cuttings, Forkner turned to the Armenian fig king himself, Henry Markarian.

By 1922, the figs were planted and some of the mansions, too. The irrigation system was a marvel. The first rights of the Kings River were shipped in through the Enterprise and Herndon Canals under the direction of master colony developer Dr. E. B. Perrin. More than 25 miles of ditches and 135 miles of laterals ran through the development. The colony's twenty-four-page brochure touted Fig Garden as a place for everyone: "People of all walks of life live here. Farmers, bankers, lawyers, doctors, laborers, school teachers and businessmen have all joined hand in making these Fig Gardens a prosperous community and an ideal home place."

The welcome mat didn't extend to my grandfather and his fellow Armenians. Their fig cuttings were allowed in by the half million. Their flesh and blood were not. The exclusion didn't sting at the time, my grandfather told me. He was a fruit tramp, lowest of the low. He was headed south to Weedpatch to pick American Wonder potatoes and Sultana grapes for Villa Kerkorian, one of the raisin kings who were pumping water out of the ground day and night to add more crop. It was the early summer of 1920, and my grandfather, like the farmers of fruits and nuts, vegetables and alfalfa, thought the great harvest would keep on rolling. He didn't have a clue that the well was about to run dry, and the raisin was about to go bust, and the hardest of droughts was already in the air. So was the talk of stealing a river from way up north and building a system capable of forcing the nature of California to finally conform. The young poet in Constantinople might have had an opinion about that. The hungry picker headed down the Golden State Highway did not.

Twelve

STEAL US A RIVER

Eight months out of the year, Professor Sidney T. Harding taught irrigation classes at UC Berkeley and wrote books that became standard texts on the siphoning of rivers to grow crops. His meticulous grasp of his subject, his fine education as a civil engineer, his upbringing by New Englanders with roots back to the Revolutionary War might have made him a fussy man. But Harding had grown up in the rough-and-rowdy of Wichita, Kansas, the wildest of midwestern boomtowns, and became fascinated with the struggle between man's nature and nature's nature. The interplay between those two hostile forces turned into a life's study that he shared with his children and grandchildren as he roamed the West from 1911 to 1966. Four months out of the year, during summer and winter breaks, he offered his services as a consultant, sometimes working for a government agency and other times working for farmers. A tall, friendly man, he managed to convey his remarkable grasp of science without intellectual airs, and his opinions were hard-earned. No outsider would come to know the soil of the San Joaquin Valley, its feel in the fingers, its smell in the nostril, better than Harding.

By 1920, the hunt to find more water to grow more crops had brought out the worst impulses of the appropriators. The age-old question of whose draw of the river was more righteous now had a corollary: Whose pumping of the groundwater was doing less damage to the aquifer? How much of that pumping could be sustained before the water table plummeted beyond the reach of most wells, beyond the wallets of farmers? In the counties of Fresno, Tulare and Kern, 1.4 million acres were now being farmed thanks to the flows of irrigation, a doubling of acres since 1910. As a producer of crops, Tulare County had ranked ninety-fourth in the nation in 1910. A decade later, it stood in fourth place. The farmers were gritty and brave, but it was one resource, above the rest, that accounted for this meteoric rise: groundwater. In 1909, Tulare counted 739 pumps in the ground. By 1919, the pumps numbered 3,758. In the watershed of the Kaweah, St. John's and Tule Rivers, farmers were irrigating 239,000 acres. More than 80,000 of these acres extended beyond the rivers and were completely dependent on the pumping of groundwater. The farmers in the Fresno Irrigation District were pumping three times more water out of the aquifer than their previous high. From the banks of the San Joaquin to the banks of the Kern, the water table was plummeting ten feet a year in many spots. Strangely, the land itself was sinking.

Wells drilled several hundred feet deep had become a farmer's last line of protection against drought. If the canal was short on river water because the winter sky had turned miserly, a farmer could see no other choice than to stick his straw into the earth to suck out what he needed. But groundwater wasn't only being used by farmers seeking to maintain their cropland in parched times. It had become the means by which the San Joaquin Valley harvested a record crop of alfalfa, cotton, grapes and stone fruit each year. For all those new farmers and old farmers expanding onto virgin acres—land beyond river and canal flow—the aquifer wasn't merely an insurance policy. It was what you drew upon night after night. This was what explained the strange phenomenon that greeted Professor Harding during his investigations of Fresno, Tulare and Kern Counties in the 1920s. Even in the midst of one of the worst droughts California would ever know, farmland was marching farther out into the desert.

As a matter of modeling, Harding knew such growth couldn't be sustained. Lowering the bowls on your pump to catch the aquifer as it receded wasn't a sound way to build a farm economy. Before he arrived, a small number of farmers already had decided that they wouldn't be chasing groundwater any lower. Their electricity bill, for one, was skyrocketing. And because so many new acres had joined the crowd, prices paid for their crops were dropping. The dry weather, in other words, was only half their desperation. A glut of fruits was the other half. Prohibition, all those grapes no longer going to the wineries, was only adding to the surplus of raisins. If it didn't rain soon, if snowmelt didn't recharge the aquifer and bring down pumping costs, Tulare and Kern Counties feared that whole swaths of agriculture would revert to desert. By the early 1920s, a new shout from the rural lands could be heard in cities and the state capitol: "You need to save us!" Since water in the rivers and the ground was finite, the first question for the state became what land deserved to be saved.

State Engineer Wilbur F. McClure had been warned about farmers in rival irrigation districts threatening violence against one another. If the government was going to play intermediary, or even savior, he needed to figure out which lands would be a poor investment for a government irrigation project. He searched among his staff for an engineer who could evaluate the different soil types in the valley and also determine to what extent the farm boom depended on river water, groundwater or a combination of the two. To quiet local fears about a government take-over of water supplies, he knew he had to find someone who could earn the trust of the farmers but also make it clear that his research wasn't bendable. He reached out to Professor Harding, who had a young wife and a baby son in Berkeley; Harding jumped at the chance to earn some side money and put his theories about irrigation into practice.

Harding headed out in a Buick roadster in the spring of 1920. No sooner did he arrive in Tulare than he found himself in the midst of a backyard broil. Alfalfa, cotton and grape growers in the bottomlands were warring with citrus ranchers on the hill over the flows of two local rivers. The men on the flatland had gotten to the water in 1891, buying shares in the first ditch companies that tapped into the Kaweah and St. John's Rivers. From those ditch companies, they formed the Tulare Irrigation District, one of the earliest such districts in California. The two rivers they drew upon actually shot out of the Sierra as one. The river cleaved itself into separate forks as it hit the valley floor at McKay Point, creating what the locals called "the Great Swamp." Was the Great Swamp part of the flow that the Tulare Irrigation District had been tapping for decades? Or was it a separate aquifer open to extraction by the citrus boys on the hill?

It only inflamed matters more that the citrus intruders were tall and blond and the sons of well-to-do orange and lemon ranchers from Pasadena and Sierra Madre. Their fathers, who would soon be selling their Southern California groves to housing developers, were looking

Sidney T. Harding,
UC Berkeley soil scientist

to continue the blessed life of the citrus gentry in a new valley. Their sons began arriving at the turn of the century and quickly figured out that the aquifer beneath the hills was too meager to grow citrus. They formed the Lindsay-Strathmore Irrigation District and bought fifteen hundred acres of the Great Swamp in 1915. With the Tulare irrigators looking on, they proceeded to dig thirty-seven wells and build a redwood-pipe irrigation system that boasted enough power to siphon groundwater from under the swamp and push it twenty-five miles up the hill to their orange trees.

Harding could see that the citrus growers were pumping so much water from the ground beside the river that they were altering the river's flow. This was causing clear harm to the flatland farmers in the Tulare Irrigation District, whose river siphoning had preceded theirs by twenty-five years. Tulare growers, pointing to the lower runoff, filed a lawsuit against the citrus ranchers. "First in line, first in right," after all. No impartial judge could be found in the county, and the case languished. Then the drought of 1924 brought its heat.

Professor Harding drove from orchard to vineyard to field, gathering details on soil and water, talking to farmers in both districts who weren't kindly disposed to the state of California's meddling but grew to trust him. Water levels in some of the Lindsay and Strathmore wells had dropped eighty feet in five years. Citrus ranchers uniformly blamed the dry skies, but Harding knew that a line had been crossed: Agriculture in Tulare County had grown too big to withstand even a few dry years, much less an extended drought. First, the farmland had taken all the flows of the rivers. Now the water table was dropping beyond the powerful suction of the new turbine pumps. Even so, on each trip Harding made to Tulare County, putt-putting alongside the foothills beneath the Sierra crags, he counted ever more orchards and vineyards going in. The professor had heard all about the madness of frontier booms from his father, a water engineer in the wild days of Kansas and Texas. But to see it playing out before his own eyes in California, as a consequence of the irrigation systems he'd written about in his textbooks, only proved that the miner mentality had not died with the gold rush.

The district known as Terra Bella, shot full of third-rate ground and piss-poor groundwater, was a case in point. A strong argument could be made that it should have never been developed into citrus land. But the land syndicates in Southern California had discovered that Terra Bella's microclimate produced a ripe orange that caught the red-hot early Christmas market. Ranchers were planting a thousand new acres and pumping the aquifer at twice the runoff of its local creek. Only farmers with deep pockets could keep digging wells deeper to chase that kind of depletion. "Such a process will eventually result in the survival of the fittest," Harding wrote in a state report known as Bulletin 11. "The path [will be] strewn with the wreckage of the farms and homes of those who attempted development and could not survive."

Over time, farmers in Lindsay and Strathmore had grown more reliant on the aquifer of the Great Swamp. To mine twenty-five thousand acre-feet of water for their orchards, they planted more wooden derricks with small pump houses that studded the wetlands in the fashion of an oil field. Irrigation boss George Trauger knew how each of these new wells grated on the rival Tulare Irrigation District, and he started packing a pistol. It did him no good when the main pipe serving Lindsay and Strathmore was blown to smithereens on the night of June 2, 1926. Trauger sent his attorney south to Los Angeles to haul back enough detectives from the Pinkerton agency to hunt down the men responsible. The Pinkertons were a diligent bunch. They turned up plenty of bootleggers making a mockery of Prohibition and no shortage of prominent citizens who belonged to the Ku Klux Klan. The saboteurs, however, were harder to find.

At a local print shop, one Pinkerton chatted up a Klansman who was ordering a thousand membership cards for the Visalia Klan No. 1. Lindsay-Strathmore was stealing water, the Klansman declared. Without those pumps in the Great Swamp, the orange and lemon groves would look "like the Arizona desert." The citrus boys were using their wealth to buy off judges, lawyers and politicians, he told the private eye. Make no mistake, that little blast, courtesy of the Tulare boys, was only the beginning. "A larger hole," he added, "can be blown at any time." The Pinkertons eventually figured out who was behind the dynamiting.

The culprit, though, was deemed too prominent a citizen to take on. In court, the lawsuit between the two districts kept going. It lasted twenty-five years and took up 26,936 pages of testimony. By the time it ended, in an inglorious compromise, the Great Swamp had been bled dry.

For all that divided them, the two warring factions on the valley's east side shared a basic conviction. The farmland already developed, the farmland yet to be developed—both were too valuable a resource for the state of California to allow the parched conditions to prevail. What we're doing here might not be so pretty, they conceded, but we've clearly moved beyond the capacity of local rivers and canals to serve us. And now we're doing the same with the groundwater. Only one path forward makes sense, and that is to bring in water from the outside. It comes down to this: We need to steal us a river.

Charles W. Cleary, a citrus grower from Lindsay who moonlighted as a state assemblyman, could see where that river ran. As chairman of the Assembly Irrigation Committee and a close pal of Governor W. D. Stephens, he knew which levers to pull. Cleary holed up in his capitol office and began drafting a bill that would give the state engineer $500,000 in funds to develop a complete and coordinated plan for the "maximum utilization of all the waters of California." The bill's preamble spoke to the inequity of the situation: three-fourths of the water supply lies within the northern one-third of the state; three-fourths of the water demand rests in the southern two-thirds. The time to address the wrong was long past, he declared. The solution to California's misfit was the flow of the Sacramento River.

Sitting behind a desk in Cleary's office, typing up the bill as fast as the assemblyman spat out its language, was a young aide named Ford Chatters. He'd landed the job of main clerk of the irrigation committee for the 1921 legislative session. A budding journalist from the citrus belt whose family ran the *Lindsay Gazette*, Chatters didn't need any assemblyman to explain the sense of urgency. "We were drying up in Tulare County," Chatters would recall in an oral history interview a half century later. "The water levels in our wells were dropping at a rate of five feet a year, steadily depleting an underground reservoir that had built up over many centuries. Our orange and olive groves were dying. In the meantime, water was rushing wastefully down the Sacramento River into the ocean." Taking a fair portion of the flow of the Sacramento River and sending it to the singed fields of the San Joaquin Valley wasn't really stealing. What could be a more elegant solution than a system that saved one valley in the north from flood at the same time that it saved another valley in the middle from drought? Governor Stephens signed Cleary's bill and located $250,000 in his budget to help develop the water plan. What this meant on the ground was that two dozen field engineers, geologists and topographers from the state would soon be joining Harding.

Sixty miles south along the Golden State Highway, in the fields of Kern County, the professor had come upon another extreme scene. Cropland served by groundwater pumping had doubled over five years to one-hundred thousand acres. Groundwater was now the sole source of irrigation for fully half the farmland in the county. In one year alone, a drought year at that, the footprint of irrigated agriculture had expanded by 25 percent. The farmers were going crazy planting thousands of acres of Egyptian long-staple cotton. The U.S. Department of Agriculture had just opened a cotton research station in the town of Shafter. The fiber was being used to make car tires and airplane wings. To catch the boom, farmers were drilling so many new wells that county officials couldn't tell Harding their numbers or locations. They tried to assure the professor that river water carried by the canals was seeping back into the aquifer. But Harding knew that this sort of recharge was nowhere near enough to offset the day-and-night pumping. On the northern end of Kern County, the water table had fallen thirty feet in four years. "If such lowering continues, the increase in the pumping lift will eventually become so large that there is no longer a profit from pumping," Harding wrote. Tens of thousands of acres of farmland had sprung up out of nowhere because of those pumps. The crops could just as easily disappear into sand.

In the far southeastern corner of Kern, beyond the reach of any river or canal, a huge dust cloud hung in the pale blue sky. A newcomer named Joseph A. Di Giorgio was leveling six thousand acres of absolute desert outside Arvin. He wasn't using Ford's new tractors. They weren't powerful enough for the job. He had gone in with twenty-mule teams that were dragging massive plows through cactus, sagebrush and salt grass. Di Giorgio was a fruit merchant from Sicily who had accumulated a fortune selling lemons and bananas to grocers on the East Coast. He'd come to Arvin believing that enough water lay hidden below the ground to grow thousands of acres of raisin and wine grapes. He wasn't the least bit concerned that it was the height of Prohibition. He would sell his Alicante Bouchets to thousands of Italian and French immigrants who were making wine in their basements back east. He drilled his first wells twelve hundred feet deep. Half the pumps coughed up salt water. In the event the experiment failed, he had a fallback. He had purchased two thousand acres of fine vineyard ground in Delano, some fifty miles north, where farmers were expanding their plantings of grapes, cotton and alfalfa. The aquifer in Delano was certainly falling a couple feet each year, but unlike many of his neighbors, Di Giorgio could afford to pay his electricity bills. He would chase water all the way to China, if need be.

The closer Harding got to Bakersfield, the more the aquifer was being recharged by flood-year runoff from the Kern River. This more balanced realm still belonged to the Kern County Land Company even though its boss, James Ben Ali Haggin, had been dead for a decade. The company—and the county—was now in the firm hold of Henry Jastro, who had come to California in 1863 to drive cattle and sheep. He drove a herd from Los Angeles to Bakersfield in the early 1870s and decided to stay put. He then went into the beer brewing business with Colonel Thomas A. Baker, Bakersfield's namesake, and married his seventeen-year-old stepdaughter. By 1883, the five-foot-seven Jastro, a cigar stuck between his teeth, was managing Haggin's ranches, overseeing the dairies, cattle and sheep. In 1892, he ran for a seat on the Kern County Board of Supervisors and won by a single vote. Jastro needed only a term in office to take control. No project in the county went forward without his blessing. When he was out of town on Kern County Land Company business, his fellow board members tabled every important item until his return. They referred to Jastro as the "commodore of Kern," and the moniker spoke not only to his vision and guile but to his success at disguising the fact that he was Jewish. Bakersfield was a hidebound, racist town still clutching to the notion that it represented some western rising of the Confederacy. Jastro had married a Gentile, gave generously to the Catholic Church and sat high in the Masonic temple.

Professor Harding found Jastro to be a man of his word who could even put aside company gain if the county's future called for it. Jastro was so keen on supporting Harding's work that he wrote a check to the state engineer for $5,000 and offered Harding access to the well records of the Kern County Land Company. The readings documented such a dramatic drop in water that Jastro stopped all sales of new farmland in the Shafter-Wasco area.

When it came time to write his report to the state engineer, Harding made sure that Bulletin 11 did not read as if an engineer had written it. The present situation was no longer tenable. Of the 1.4 million acres of irrigated farmland in the three counties he'd studied, 800,000 acres were either partially or wholly reliant on groundwater pumped from ever-deeper depths. Nearly 200,000 of these acres existed in a state of serious overdraft. "If the present extent of use is continued," Harding wrote, "the records now available indicate that an area now developed of about 100,000 acres will eventually revert to wasteland. The time when this condition will be reached cannot be predicted with any definiteness."

The professor's call for the state to regulate groundwater would go unheeded for another century. For the first fifty of these years, California at least had a passable defense. Conservation didn't mean then what it would come to mean in the wake of Rachel Carson's *Silent Spring*. Dams were conservation. Canals were conservation. Not letting a drop of water go unused by farms and cities was conservation. The last fifty of these years, which took place amid an era of heightened concern about the environment, make for a sorrier tale.

There was one big specter that Harding failed to mention in his final report, though it shadowed his investigation every step of the way. In the months before the professor set out for California's interior, a former colonel of the United States Geological Survey had published a far-reaching plan to solve California's water woes once and for all. Colonel Robert Bradford Marshall had driven with mule teams and buckboard all over the state in the 1890s, surveying mountains, rivers and valleys. Few men knew California more intimately, it was said. For twenty-five years, even as he performed the duties of the nation's chief geographer in the charge of the Topographic Branch, Marshall worked to perfect every detail of his plan. After he retired to his ranch in Patterson, the northern valley town that called itself the "apricot capital of the world," he published the paper in 1919 under the imprimatur of the California State Irrigation Association. The front cover shouted:

Irrigation of Twelve Million Acres in the Valley of California
California's Great Opportunity
Reclaiming an Empire—The Valley of California
Making Homes for 3,000,000 People
Increasing the Present Value More Than $6,000,000,000

By Col. R. B. Marshall

"The people of California, indifferent to the bountiful gifts that Nature has given them, sit idly by waiting for rain, indefinitely postponing irrigation, and allowing every year millions and millions of dollars in water to pour unused into the sea," the colonel wrote. "In the Valley of California—in the Sacramento and San Joaquin valleys combined—lies the largest, richest and most fertile body of indifferently used or unused land in the United States, perhaps in the world."

Marshall's call for a gargantuan system that would divide the waters of the state, moving rain from flood land to drought land, north to south, and stopping the outflow to the ocean, was about to find its moment in the California sun. For all its audacity, it was a simple idea. By dint of three dams and four canals, reclamation could tap into the great overflow of the Sacramento River and shoot water to all the unrealized dirt in the state's middle.

A dam on the Sacramento would feed two grand canals moving water south by gravity down through California. The west side canal would serve San Francisco and San Jose and extend to the San Joaquin Valley town of Dos Palos, Henry Miller's old haunt. The east side canal would serve Sacramento and Stockton, Modesto and Merced, and end up, of all places, dumping into the main stem of the San Joaquin River. But how could that be possible? The flow of two rivers in one channel? Surely, the San Joaquin did not have the capacity to take on the excess flows of the Sacramento River?

A closer look at the colonel's map answered the question. A dam would be built on the San Joaquin River and divert its flows. The San

Joaquin would no longer be the San Joaquin. Instead, its waters would be shipped south by a third grand canal to the Kern River. This canal, carrying San Joaquin River flows, would then circle around Bakersfield like a beltway and move back up the state, where it would deliver water to the desert of western Kern and western Fresno. But what would this canal mean for the flows of the Kern River? the reader asked. Well, the Kern would no longer be the Kern, either. Its flows would be pumped up and over the Tehachapi Mountains to a Los Angeles hell-bent on sprawling. Each river in the chain would swap places with the river below it, a cascade of waters from the top to the bottom of the state. The plan was simple but mind-boggling. "It is a large undertaking, but this is a day of large undertakings," the colonel wrote. "Although it is a comprehensive statewide job, its immediate practicability and success depend only upon the successive building of its various parts to form a consistent whole." The Big Job, as he called it, would employ brave soldiers back from war, generate hydroelectricity that would light up cities and blossom twelve million acres of a valley "bristling with invitations." The devastating floods of the north would be no more. The parched land of the middle would be forever quenched.

Marshall was scarcely the first, or even the most eloquent, of the dreamers who had looked at the valley and imagined the riches of agriculture that would sprout from its soil if the rivers could just be dammed and snowmelt portioned out in engineered doses. In the 1870s, John Muir himself came bounding down the magnificent Kings River canyon and encountered a new kind of farmer on the valley floor, one who was thumbing his nose at the wheat culture and building ditches and planting crops from corn to figs. "Most California farmers are afflicted with dry rot," Muir wrote in his *Letter from Grangerville*. "Out here in the smooth Tulare levels, I found a group of gentle grangers that are the most radiant and joyful set of farmers I have yet met in California. Every specimen is bright with smiles like housebound prospectors who have 'struck it rich.' It is now autumn, but their fields are yet full of spring. The generous soil seems unwilling to rest. 'Look,' say these jubilant fellows, as they triumphantly showed me their wealth. 'Look at that Indian corn with ears so high you cannot reach them; and at these level sheets of alfalfa mowed, heaven knows how often. I tell you, sir, we have found it out; we want no better thing, no bigger bonanza.'" Muir, the father of conservation, ended his dispatch with a boomer's riff on how the grangers needed only to preserve the forests above them and build the proper dams in the canyons for all the bounty of the mountain to be put to glory down below. "Then will theirs be the most foodful and beautiful of all the lowland valleys of like extent in the world."

The theft of a distant river. What Marshall was proposing in the Big Job didn't strike Californians as inconceivable in the least. The drying out of one region to enable the blossoming of another had already been consummated in the Far West. The swindle, all the more a crime because it managed not to break a single law, was a story I gleaned from books and a much-acclaimed movie and my own reporting during the years I worked for the *Los Angeles Times,* a newspaper owned by the Chandler family. It was their kin who had set the whole thing in motion, a caper that would come to define the metamorphosis of the Pueblo de Los Angeles from a "vile little dump" cut off from gold's riches into one of the great thriving cities of the world. The word "Chinatown," invoking the title of the movie, would come to represent for many the injustice of water taken by the big guy from the little guy. If it didn't make for an easy metaphor, what did in a basin surrounded by desert on three sides and an ocean on the fourth, where the weather was both semitropical and dry and the mango grew as profusely as the date, and the water was brought down from the top of Mount Whitney, 250 miles away, to grow oranges and then houses until Eden was no more? Chinatown was just one of its convolutions.

The theft had been hatched by many men, but its engineering—dams, tunnels and aqueduct—belonged to only one. William Mulholland, a lover of literature who left Ireland and came to California on the written words of Charles Nordhoff, had taken a job with a well-drilling crew in 1877. He was twenty-two years old and not sure where he was headed when the crew trekked from the San Joaquin Valley to San Pedro to poke another hole in the ground. This hole, the way he told it, changed the rest of his life: "When we were down about six hundred feet we struck a tree. A little further we got fossil remains, and these things fired my curiosity. Right there I decided to become an engineer." He dug ditches for the privately owned Los Angeles Water Company and came to know every oddity of the Los Angeles River. It ran quietly and might have been considered a creek if not for the now-and-again tropical storms that didn't stop until the river had swept crops and houses into the sea.

The river, in Mulholland's eyes, was a "beautiful, limpid little stream with willows on its banks. It at once became something about which my whole scheme of life was woven. I loved it so much." A large open ditch delivered water from the river to the old pueblo. As the *zanjero,* the public ditch tender, Mulholland understood that building a city on the river's puny flow—forty thousand acre-feet in an average year—couldn't be done. The Colorado River, by comparison, produced fourteen million acre-feet. What the Los Angeles River had going for it wasn't the water in its bed but the vast underground lake that it fed and drew from, almost one million acre-feet beneath the San Fernando Valley. By force of a California Supreme Court ruling in 1885, the city no longer had to abide by the old Spanish law that balanced the rights of the pueblo and its people and portioned out water in a communal way. Los Angeles now had first rights to the river and its aquifer.

Mulholland's rise through the ranks of the Los Angeles Water Company in the 1890s was swift and well timed. The city was poised to take over the company's operation and turn water into a municipal utility. A distribution system complete with three hundred miles of pipes and pumping plants and six reservoirs served a population of one hundred thousand, a near doubling of people in only a decade's time. Mulholland had been groomed to run the system by his predecessor, Frederick Eaton. The two young men, just a year apart, were opposites who'd formed a strong bond. Mulholland was an Irish immigrant who'd signed on as an apprentice seaman aboard a Glasgow-bound merchant ship at the age of fifteen. Eaton was the son of a Harvard-trained lawyer who had founded the Pasadena Colony and developed its orange groves. Among the first generation of Americans in Los Angeles, the Eatons were akin to western patricians, though the son would chafe at any such characterization.

Eaton had gone to work for the water company when he was fifteen and within a span of five years had taken over as superintending engineer. He liked to believe that his success was the product of tireless endeavor. At the same time, he was strikingly handsome, smooth in manner and blessed with his father's brilliance, and he would use all

The visage that was William Mulholland

those gifts to become the city's first mayor of the twentieth century. One of his first acts was to create the Los Angeles Department of Water and Power and put its operation in the hands of his buddy Mulholland. In their official portraits, both men are half-turned toward the camera and dressed in dark, elegant suits with silk neckties looped around tall, starched white collars. Eaton is broad-shouldered and clean-shaven, with a full head of hair. His left hand rests on his left knee, and between his index and middle fingers he gracefully holds a lit cigar. Mulholland, balding, wears a mustache as bushy as Teddy Roosevelt's and a narrow-brimmed fedora low over his scowling eyes. There is nothing gentle about his lit cigar. It juts right out of his "don't mess with me" clenched mouth.

Initially, the two men didn't agree on how much water the city needed for growth. "We have enough water here to supply the city for the next fifty years," Mulholland had told Eaton in 1893. "You are wrong," Eaton had replied. "You have not lived in this country as long as I have. I was born here and have seen dry years, years that you know nothing about. Wait and see." It had been Eaton's judgment, as far back as a decade, that the Los Angeles River and its aquifer would never do. The city needed to import a river. The flow of that river had to be close enough, and reliable enough, to justify the expense of its taking. He believed that the perfect river for the job traced it headwaters up and over the mountain range to the snowcapped peak of Mount Whitney. There ran the river Owens. The modest plain it fed, the Owens Valley, had been described by John Muir as "a land of pure desolation covered with beautiful light."

Did it now matter that 424 farms encompassed 141,059 acres of fertile soil? Or that nearly all of these farms were cultivated by settler families who lived and worked on plots that measured 175 acres or less and were growing alfalfa and wheat and harvesting fruit? Eaton had observed for himself the proximity and ease of the taking. The terrain between Los Angeles and the Owens Valley was rugged and extended

230 miles as the crow flies, but it had the virtue of being straight uphill, which meant that any aqueduct covering such distance would be running straight downhill. The flow would be powered by gravity, an engineer's sure thing.

Mulholland watched the trains from the Midwest deposit invalids headed for the sanitarium hills as well as their healthy families looking to plant oranges. In a period of four years, the population of Los Angeles had nearly doubled to two hundred thousand. The city was growing not only from the migrants who poured in each week but from its own annexations that kept gobbling up towns and farms on its fringes. Soon enough, it would devour the entire 169 square miles of the San Fernando Valley. "The time has come when we will have to supplement [the river's] flow from some other source," Mulholland now urged. Already, Eaton had taken him by buckboard and mule to spy the Owens Valley, where both had agreed that here ran the water to support the next two million Angelenos.

No man of honor would execute a fraud to acquire lands from a stranger, lands that would give him rights to the stranger's water. Mulholland and Eaton both considered themselves men of honor. But what if that man was simply a neighbor looking to buy the land of another neighbor? What if he was a local cattle rancher interested in acquiring the lands of other local ranchers and was willing to pay a remarkably high price for the privilege? What if those purchases then allowed the water associated with that land to be transferred to another basin?

Such was the masquerade that Eaton cooked up in the spring of 1905. He would assume the role of an Owens Valley cattle rancher and a good neighbor, at that. First, though, he needed to pose as an agent of the new U.S. Reclamation Service on assignment to turn the Owens Valley into a federal irrigation project. In this guise, he didn't labor alone. His co-conspirator was a real-life Reclamation Service engineer named Joseph Lippincott, a backslider who would go down as the slyest of the men involved in L.A.'s plunder of the Owens Valley. In the 1880s, Lippincott had served as one of the brash young engineers under Colonel Marshall at the U.S. Geological Survey before heading to Los Angeles to work as a consultant for cities and water companies. His job put him in close contact with Eaton and Mulholland, who hired him more than once to assist L.A.'s water department. In fact, his private practice was so lucrative that he refused to give it up after joining the Reclamation Service in 1902 as its supervising engineer for California. Wearing two hats, Lippincott was able to set in motion the theft of a river on Los Angeles' behalf.

First, he hired Eaton and provided him with the cover of a Reclamation Service agent. Eaton then used this cover to walk into the government land office in Independence, the Inyo County seat, and pore over land deeds that revealed who owned the Owens Valley. The clerks naturally assumed that the handsome man who exuded charm was there to aid the Reclamation Service in its planned irrigation project for their valley. Eaton's actual purpose was to advance the river heist to its next phase. This involved the city of Los Angeles, at Mulholland's behest, hiring Lippincott as an outside consultant. Lippincott's task was to advise the city on where it might locate a suitable supply of water. He knew exactly what Los Angeles wanted. It wanted him to finger the Owens Valley as the source. The city would pay him the going rate of a bribe, $2,500, to put his scrupulous stamp on such a recommendation. This amounted to half his annual federal salary.

In a matter of months, Lippincott was advising his superiors at the U.S. Reclamation Service that the waters of the Owens Valley would be best utilized by the city of Los Angeles. "The greatest public necessity is certainly the use of the water in Southern California," Lippincott told his bosses in Washington. "So far as I am concerned, I certainly favor aiding them in their efforts." Lippincott's dual loyalties maddened Frederick Newell, the first chief of the Reclamation Service, who saw his mission as converting deserts into farms and establishing a western beachhead for civilization. This mission was hardly served by the stance Lippincott was now advocating on the Owens Valley. But Newell lacked the fortitude to make Lippincott choose between his private and public duties. Instead, the Reclamation Service agreed to lay aside its own designs to develop the valley and get out of L.A.'s way. The future of Owens was Eaton's and Mulholland's to decide.

The time had come for Eaton to get neighborly. He dropped in at the ranch of Thomas Rickey, one of the biggest landowners in Owens Valley whose property line extended to the shallow gorge of the upper river. For Los Angeles to acquire the land and water rights it needed in the valley, it was best to start high up, and there was no place higher than Rickey's place. Eaton sat down with Rickey, and the two men negotiated for hours. Each time Eaton thought he had reeled Rickey in, the cattle rancher found another reason to say no. Eaton got so frustrated that he stomped out the door. He was waiting at the railroad depot for the train to take him back to Los Angeles when Rickey rode up in his carriage. If Eaton would sweeten the offer just a bit, to $450,000, he would sell him the ranch on the spot. The two men shook hands on the deal, and Eaton ran down to the telegraph office and dashed off a wire to Mulholland. The deed was done.

With the upper river in his hip pocket, Eaton went lower on the river, where Mulholland was looking to build his reservoir, and made deals with other ranchers. Because each rancher dared not speak to his neighbors about "selling out," Eaton could operate in relative stealth. Deal after deal landed in the lap of Los Angeles by way of this same psychology of reward and shame. No one in the Owens Valley wanted to be known as a traitor. But what was so treasonous about selling the hard work of your land to a cattle-ranching neighbor paying a generous sum?

Wilfred and Mark Watterson, two handsome brothers who ran the Inyo County Bank, wrote Fred Eaton off as a phony. His cover story—a former Los Angeles mayor wanting to retire to a life of cattle and be their neighbor—never rang true to them. In the early summer of 1905, Wilfred watched a young man stride with odd purpose into his bank. What happened next is recounted with perfection in Reisner's *Cadillac Desert*. The young man was carrying a written order from Eaton to pick up a parcel from a safety-deposit box. Parcel in hand, he rushed out of the bank. "Who was that?" Wilfred asked his teller. That was Harry Lelande, the city clerk of Los Angeles, who handled all transactions involving land and water. Wilfred dashed out the door and ran down the street. He found Lelande standing near the post office and requested that he return to the bank, using the ruse of uncompleted business. Once Lelande was in his office, Wilfred demanded that he hand over the parcel, which he suspected contained a deed of land.

"What deed do you mean?" Lelande asked.

"The deed by which your city is going to try to rape this valley," Wilfred snarled.

"I haven't any idea what you're talking about."

Wilfred bolted his office door and pulled out a gun. He ordered Lelande to strip off his coat and trousers. He turned the man's pockets inside out. No deed could be found. Lelande must have given it to the postman before Wilfred found him on the street.

"You've paid high prices not because you're dumb but because you're smart," Wilfred said. "You're masquerading as investors and all you're going to invest in is our ruin."

The denizens of Los Angeles kept up their excellent performance as if it were a piece of theater. Mulholland organized a group of wealthy and powerful citizens, led by Mayor Owen McAleer, to visit the Owens Valley on the pretext that they were investors looking to develop a resort. They arrived as the early snowmelt was filling up the river's feeders. Any doubts they may have had about the bounty of these waters, and the fortunes they might furnish, were put to rest right there. With the group's money behind them, Mulholland and Eaton now had what they needed to grab their high-reaching city a river. After a week of underhanded buying, the two men stood before the water commissioners of Los Angeles and declared, "The last spike has been driven. The options are all secured."

Harrison Gray Otis, the publisher of the *Los Angeles Times,* had been keeping the deal secret for three months. For the former general, who looked and bellowed like a walrus, it had been one herculean feat of restraint. His every fiber had been coiled. He'd been counting down the days to when he could finally reveal what the good citizens of Los Angeles had foisted upon the hayseeds of Owens Valley.

Otis's heart had been diagnosed as gangrenous by more than one observer. He breathed to destroy his foes and doubters, whom he imagined were legion and forever conniving to bring down all that he was building in the city of his second act. Another man of his stature might have dismissed lesser detractors as unworthy of his attention, but Otis took gleeful aim at skewering all. His bawl was described as "majestic," and it helped that he could vent bile and pursue a grudge to the ends of the earth, and all for free, on the pages of his own newspaper. He had come west after the Civil War brandishing the title of captain. Unlike the many military posers, he had actually fought with distinction on the side of the Union Army and then in the Spanish-American War. He took pride in his battle wounds. Problem was, his war never ended. The front had simply moved from the swamps of the Philippines to the orange-blossom-scented air of Los Angeles. He now referred to himself as the General. Fighting to keep the city free from the "corpse defacers" who ran the unions, he united merchants and business leaders under one anti-labor umbrella. He took to the streets in a car mounted with a cannon. He referred to his mansion as the "bivouac" and his newspaper headquarters as "the fortress." His reporters became the "phalanx."

Otis kept the Owens Valley heist a secret until the evening of July 28, 1905, when he put his paper to bed with the headline "Titanic Project to Give the City a River." Eaton, Mulholland and Lippincott must have winced that Saturday morning as they read the columns of praise the General heaped upon them. Any fool could see that the glee amounted to high insult to the snookered citizens of Owens Valley, and it would only complicate the grab of land and water that still needed to be done. Otis didn't a give damn. He was having too much fun snorting. "A number of the unsuspecting ranchers have regarded the appearance of Mr. Eaton in the valley as a visitation of Providence," the *Times* story read. "In the eyes of the ranchers, he was land mad. When they advanced the price of their holdings a few thousand dollars, their cup of joy overflowed. The price paid for many of the ranches is three or four times what the owners ever expected to sell them for. Everyone in the valley has money, and everyone is happy."

There was no reason for the citizens of Los Angeles to feel guilty, the newspaper asserted, no reason to pity the people of Independence. If you traced the Owens River back to a time when the mountain range wasn't even a mountain range, its flood flows had actually emptied into the Los Angeles River. This was no theft. This was simply a reversal of millions of years of geology. The *Times* story saved its most effusive praise for the turncoat labors of Lippincott, the federal bureaucrat: "Without Mr. Lippincott's interest and cooperation, it is declared that the plan never would have gone through." With praise like that, who needed a public damning? Lippincott's bosses at the Reclamation Service weren't pleased. The story raised one question: Had Otis written it himself? The fustian lead sentence was classic General: "The cable that has held the San Fernando Valley vassal for ten centuries to the arid demon is about to be severed by the magic scimitar of modern engineering skill." It was a sentence only an insider to the deal could have written. For who else knew that the water was destined not so much for the city of Los Angeles but for the desolate plain of the San Fernando, so that it could blossom first into oranges and vegetable fields and then into houses?

Sitting in the editor's chair at the rival *Los Angeles Examiner* was fifty-year-old Henry Loewenthal, a New Yorker with a law degree from Columbia College. He had thought he would practice a little journalism on his way to lawyering, but after covering the courts for the *New York Times,* he found himself hooked. He had risen to the position of managing editor at the *Times* when William Randolph Hearst lured him west to run the seventh newspaper in his growing chain. The *Examiner* wasn't a booster rag. It had been started with funds from the local typographers' union and attracted readers with its bent for muckraking. As a newcomer to Los Angeles, Loewenthal was enthralled by its tantrums. The city truly harbored a deep need to be loved. Any little pinprick teased out its insecurities. And no one reacted with more overwrought wounding than the General himself.

Loewenthal believed that the city's lust for growth would prove its undoing. He had encountered "a spirit of lawlessness that prevails here that I have never seen anywhere else," which was saying a lot for a journalist who knew the Irish Catholic bosses of Tammany Hall. When Loewenthal read the "scoop" on Otis's front pages, he caught the odd reference to the San Fernando Valley. He dispatched a couple of his best reporters to the courthouse in San Fernando to see if his hunch was right. Sure enough, the General and his group of wealthy Los Angelenos had left in the open evidence of their plot. Maybe they believed themselves immune to discovery. Or maybe they didn't care if the world found out.

The timeline was damning. Six days after Los Angeles had paid Joseph Lippincott $2,500 to act not in favor of the Reclamation Service but in the city's favor, a syndicate of downtown investors showed up at the offices of the Porter Land and Water Company with a $50,000 check. It was for an option to buy sixteen thousand acres the company owned in the San Fernando Valley. The syndicate closed the $500,000 land deal exactly four months later—on the same day Fred Eaton shook hands with rancher Thomas Rickey, and on the same day William Mulholland was assured that 250,000 acre-feet of Owens River water was coming his way. The land in the San Fernando Valley was a steal because no one but the syndicate members knew that the water was guaranteed. Reading their names on the documents before him had to be one of the great satisfactions in Loewenthal's ink-stained career. Oh, what a lineup it was. The amnesiacs of greater Los Angeles would one day name towns, streets, hospitals, schools and libraries after these men. But on the front pages of the *Examiner,* in the year 1905, each one joined the others in a company of scoundrels. These were gladiators of capital who in their previous ventures had regularly despised one another. There was nothing like a great real estate swindle traded on insider information to turn enemies into confederates.

There was L. C. Brand of the Title Guarantee and Trust Company and Joseph Sartori of the Security Trust and Savings Bank; there was Moses Sherman, the heartless trolley magnate, and Henry Huntington, owner of the Pacific Electric Railway; there was Edward Harriman, chairman of the Union Pacific, and William Kerckhoff, the electrical power tycoon; there was Harry Chandler, who had shared with Otis his newspaper circulation routes and then took the hand of Otis's daughter, and there was the General himself, who had kept from his readers his role in the syndicate and had signed the check to secure the option on the San Fernando lands.

The *Times* could not be bothered by the revelations in the pages of the *Examiner*. "The San Fernando Valley can be converted into a veritable Garden of Eden," it gushed. "Vast areas of land, devoted now to grazing and grain, will be converted into orchards and gardens, the peer of any in the world." Already, land values were skyrocketing. Agriculture would be merely a pause on the way to houses, "the highest and best use" of the land. "With the great increase in population that will follow," declared the *Times,* "there will be ample demand for every acre of land."

Eaton and Mulholland found enough decency to personally steer clear of the deal. Mulholland, for one, had done what he'd done for reasons other than money. His was a different greed. When it came time for the citizens of Los Angeles to approve bonds to underwrite different phases of the aqueduct that he would proudly build, Mulholland lied the same way Otis had lied. He fabricated numbers from inside the water department and ginned up a "water famine" to make it appear as if the city were one drought away from being parched. He used his position to sow fear among the people, and that fear rallied voter support for his project.

It took Mulholland six years and $23 million to construct his aqueduct and make good on his prophesy that "whoever brings the water will bring the people." His five thousand rugged men—Serbs, Greeks, Italians, Bulgarians, Swiss, Mexicans and Native Americans—took one million barrels of cement and six million pounds of dynamite and fabricated 280 miles of pipeline and 142 tunnels. This aqueduct began in the rocky canyon above the Alabama Hills and wended through Independence and Lone Pine and past the Owens Lake, which it would turn into dust, and along a flank of the Mojave Desert and down through the San Gabriel Mountains until it busted through the last rock above Sylmar, where five men were standing in the sunshine of November 5, 1913, to the turn the wheel that would shoot the first gushing water, 430 million gallons a day, down the stone stair steps into the waiting San Fernando Reservoir. Nearly fifty men had lost their lives building the project. That more did not die, and that it was completed on time and below budget, was a testament to Mulholland, who was alongside his workers in the high desert nearly every step of the way. He was right, of course, that the more water you brought to California, the more people would come and the more water you would need to bring.

Over the next ten years, growing at a pace ten times faster than New York, the population of Los Angeles would blow past the one million mark. The irrigated lands of the San Fernando Valley would blossom from three thousand acres to eighty thousand acres. The size of the city would more than triple, from 107 square miles to 364 square miles. Otis, Chandler and Sherman would grow rich beyond compare. Even before the water came down the pike, they had bought another 47,500 acres nearby and were planning the largest subdivision in the world. Up the road, where the Tehachapi Mountains gave way to the other valley, the San Joaquin, they acquired the 270,000-acre Tejon Ranch. Harry Chandler—real estate mogul, newspaper publisher—was well on his way to becoming one of the richest men in the world. His daughter

Ruth would marry the cotton king, Colonel J. G. Boswell, who was fixing to drain Tulare Lake dry.

As for the citizens of Owens Valley, they passed through all the psychic phases of loss. They did not believe, even as the deeds of sale stacked up in the courthouse, that it would really happen. When it was happening before their eyes, they erupted first in recrimination against their neighbors who had connived with Eaton and been paid handsomely for it, and then in explosion against Los Angeles. More than a dozen times, from 1927 to 1976, they pulled out boxes of dynamite and blew up one section or another of the aqueduct. Out of his cigar-stained lips, Mulholland had assured them that Los Angeles would never dry up the lower Owens River. Then he went about sinking hundreds of pumps into its alluvial plain. Mary Austin, who had written the acclaimed *Land of Little Rain,* a volume of essays about the Owens Valley that reached back to its native Paiutes, went to confront the gruff Irishman about his lie. He gave her no confession. When she sat down to write her autobiography, she told it in the third person. "She knew

The day the Owens River was delivered to Los Angeles

that the land of Inyo would be desolated, and the cruelty and deception smote her beyond belief. She sold her house in Inyo; she meant not to go there again."

Los Angeles would complete its purchase of the Owens Valley—nearly every plot of farmland, nearly every parcel of city—in 1935. This was the same year the City of Angels—or, more precisely, its Hydra called the Metropolitan Water District—would finish its new aqueduct project, "one of the seven wonders of American engineering," hauling Colorado River water to subdivisions that stretched from Ventura to Riverside. Chandler's newspaper would insist on bestowing on this region a new name to match the sweep of its waterworks. It was this system, if nothing else, that knit the distinct landscapes into one unified place. It was now presented to the world as "the Southland."

Colonel Robert Marshall wasn't content to simply publish his plan to manhandle the rivers of Northern and middle California and build a massive Central Valley irrigation project. He traveled up and down the state in the 1920s to sell his vision to voters, who would need to pass the bond measures to fund the project. Outwitting aridity didn't come cheap. The scale and costs were enormous. No state in the country, no country in the world, had ever erected such a colossal system of hydraulics. The people of Sacramento, whose river would be called upon to sacrifice as much as 20 percent of its flow, had to be persuaded of the benefits. The price tag for the dam on the Sacramento River alone was $70 million. But Marshall was an irrepressible force even into his later years. The money, he argued, was a pittance compared to the gain. The great fury of levee building that had occurred in Sacramento over the previous half century did not mean the river was beaten, he warned. Civic leaders who promised otherwise were fools. Only a gargantuan plug in its canyon would prevent the Sacramento from flooding again.

Flood control wasn't the only benefit offered to the people of the north. Saltwater intrusion menaced farms and industries in the delta and along the narrow strait that led out to the Pacific Ocean. In dry years, the river lacked sufficient flow to push back on the brackish water that sloshed in with each day's high tide. Salinity's creep in summer and fall migrated so far inland that sugar refineries in the East Bay town of Crockett had to go searching for fresh water. Damming the river and subjecting it to rational management was the only sure way to fight ocean intrusion, Marshall argued. The water master would be able to portion out enough flow in summer and fall to keep the tides from migrating too far inland. But the delta folk were fickle. When you caught them in a flood year or a drought year, they were inclined to get behind the Big Job. When everything was flowing as it should, their support for the project dimmed.

The north's desire to keep the Sacramento River at home wasn't the only pushback to Marshall's plan. Pacific Gas & Electric, the utility organized in the 1890s as a merger of small independent providers of gas and electricity, had grown into a cartoon caricature of the diabolical beast that sucked the blood out of its customers. The utility had benefited time and again from the government's largess and blind eye. Even so, it would not sit on the sidelines watching the state or the feds dam rivers for irrigation and offer hydroelectric power to a rival. Colonel Marshall understood that PG&E would pull whatever stunts necessary to kill his project and preserve its monopoly, and this made him hunker down even harder.

As the colonel sought to rally statewide support for a California water fix, he found himself bolstered by two new realties on the ground. First was the drought of 1924, one of the worst dry years ever recorded in the West. Drought was the only time Californians ever solved anything. Second was the fact that San Francisco, overcoming similar opposition, had gone out and stolen a river, too. Its theft of the Tuolumne and the building of a reservoir in the Hetch Hetchy Valley in Yosemite National Park was nowhere near as duplicitous as L.A.'s theft of Owens. But it did feature a city-leveling earthquake, a 155-mile-long aqueduct, a 25-mile-long tunnel and no shortage of conniving men, including an Irish mayor named James Phelan, an Irish engineer named Michael O'Shaughnessy and a familiar double agent, Joseph Lippincott. When the city's secret filing of claim on the Tuolumne River was discovered in 1906, it led to an eight-year battle that pitted the three men against old graybeard John Muir, the Scot with bog juices "oozing through all my veins." Muir considered the Hetch Hetchy Valley to be "one of the most sublime and beautiful" places on Earth. To preserve it, he used his powers as president of the Sierra Club, only to discover that some of its most prominent members had betrayed him. They sided with Mayor

Phelan, who did not hide his scorn about preserving it. "There are a thousand places in the Sierra equally as beautiful as Hetch Hetchy," Phelan argued. "It is inaccessible nine months of the year and is an unlivable place the other three months because of mosquitos." The same had been said of early San Francisco, and its fog and fleas, but who remembered?

Already, Colonel Marshall had the state of California on his side. The state engineer had made no secret of his desire to save the "imperiled" lands of Tulare and Kern Counties. He had joined hands with local farmers and real estate developers to push for a Central Valley irrigation project that was less ambitious than Marshall's plan but still a job of immense enterprise. At the direction of Governor Stephens, the Department of Public Works had conducted a remarkable series of studies on why the project should be built. Among the citizens appointed by the governor to help guide the state's planning were William Mulholland and Colonel Marshall. The studies, funded by the two biggest branches of the chamber of commerce in response to pressure from Tulare County, were published from 1923 to 1925 and became known as Bulletins 4, 9 and 12. Their call to dam the Sacramento River and send its "excess" flows to San Joaquin Valley was emphatic. "The valley as a whole had little more than half enough water for its future needs," Bulletin 12 read. "The exhaustion of the water supply is of statewide concern for there is no simple means of relief." The need to outlast drought and weaken flood was only part of what motivated state water bureaucrats. Just as powerful a driver was the dream to scale up farming's reach, to move well beyond what the local rivers and aquifer could furnish and employ imported water to expand agriculture from one end of the Central Valley to the other. Aridity, they believed, could be conquered a third time. The first by river, the second by aquifer, and now the third by dam.

In their ardor to sell the project, state water engineers snubbed the findings of Professor Harding. He had identified one hundred thousand acres of farmland in the southern San Joaquin Valley that were in danger of returning to dust because of groundwater depletion. This land, and no more, needed to be rescued with imported water. But now state water engineers were pointing to five hundred thousand acres that they considered threatened and in need of salvation. Bulletin 9 plainly threw science out the window. Yes, agricultural lands in Tulare and Kern Counties were expanding at too fast a clip. Yes, farmers were growing crops beyond the capacity of the local water supplies and also beyond their own expertise. But in the final calculation, this did not alter California's imperative. "To defer action is to invite future disaster," the engineers wrote. The state, driven by growth's logic, was obligated to capture surface water from Northern California and ship it to the valley, even if these supplies induced farmers in Fresno, Tulare and Kern Counties to raise new crops on new land. A glut of peaches or raisins or milk wasn't the concern of state water bureaucrats. Surplus food was a function of the market. Surplus water was the charge of the irrigation engineer.

The seeds of agriculture's overreach in the coming decades—a scale of extraction and subsidence unseen in the world—were thus written: "The lands in the southern San Joaquin Valley that are now overdrawing their local supplies, together with those approaching a similar situation, approximate a half million acres as fertile as any in the state," the report stated. "Adjacent to these lands are several million more acres of rich agricultural soil, unproductive without water, that will forever remain so unless an outside source of supply is obtained. Therefore, a very large quantity of imported water will eventually be needed."

Bulletin 9 called for a system of "maximum productivity" to be unleashed on California. In an industrial setting where the inputs were less finite, this might have meant pushing men and machine to their limits to create more and more output. Applying maximum productivity to the workings of land and water, however, had the potential for a completely paradoxical result: Let's provide enough water to not only save five hundred thousand acres of farms but add hundreds of thousands of acres of new farms that will then compete for resources with the farms we just saved.

Likewise, state engineers jettisoned Harding's formula that only the best soils deserved imports of subsidized water. They replaced it with a model of what might be considered "bureaucratic egalitarianism." It held that each plot of land and each community of farmers deserved an equal place in the water conveyance line. Only then would the system deliver water aplenty to maximize the productivity of each unit of land. The resource, in other words, would find its way to a logic rather than a logic finding its way to the resource. If this sounded ass-backward, well it was. Had a critic been allowed onto the pages of Bulletin 9, he might have pointed out that such an approach, played out within the extremes of California weather, promised more backyard water wars, more hard times for the small guy, more concentration of natural resources into the hands of an entitled few.

The state water engineers saw no reason, at least at the project's outset, for constraints. When asked to add up the agricultural lands in California—those irrigated, those that deserved to be irrigated—they arrived at an incredible figure of 22.5 million acres. By any calculation, this was an absurd number. In the years ahead, California agriculture, at its very peak, would never expand to even half that size. But the "duty of water," as they saw it in that last roar of the 1920s, before the Great Depression, extended to the Mojave Desert and the foothills of the Sierra. Salt brush, sagebrush, tumbleweeds, rock, loam were judged equal in their capacity to be transformed by the magic of irrigation. At least four-fifths of the 22.5 million acres, the engineers concluded, could be reclaimed through a "scientifically coordinated plan to equalize the erratic flow in California's streams and largely overcome the unequal geographic distribution of the state's waters."

This was the gung ho spirit by which the engineers of California came to hatch the killing of the San Joaquin River. Its location in the middle of the state made it the perfect candidate. Pumping the flows of the Sacramento River all the way south to Tulare and Kern Counties wasn't a good option. Such a canal would need to traverse three hundred miles of altering terrain and climb three hundred feet in elevation to reach the citrus groves of Exeter and Lindsay before it continued south to the vineyards of Delano and the cotton fields outside Bakersfield. It would consume no small amount of electrical power. The San Joaquin River, by comparison, was cheap and easy, a downhill flow propelled by gravity instead of pumping. The idea was to build a dam on the San Joaquin River as it moved west through Fresno County and render it streamless. Snowmelt plugging its canyon would be shipped south via a 155-mile concrete canal to the thirsty growers of Tulare and Kern. Farmers in Fresno who had long relied on downstream flows from the San Joaquin River would have to be compensated, of course. This would be done by way of a second canal that would run between the delta and their farms. This canal, 117 miles north to south, would carry a guaranteed flow from the Sacramento River to their crops to make up for the loss of the San Joaquin.

The Great Exchange, it was called. Few people in Fresno or Madera, the two counties that shared the San Joaquin, saw it as the vanishing of their river. The San Joaquin, after all, had been taken a long time ago, first by Henry Miller and then by all the men trying to be Miller. No sense of communal ownership of the river had ever taken root. Indeed, the confiscation of the river had happened before the people even landed here. Those who weren't farmers had gotten used to the flows of the San Joaquin disappearing before their eyes as soon as the irrigation season began. In the valley, water wasn't something that ran unleashed down the river. Water was a block, a chunk, a lot, a unit that was divided and delivered to all the siphons along the way.

So when the state of California told the people of Fresno and Madera that their river would be bled out and then refilled partway by a transfusion of liquid from the great river to the north, they had no pride in the matter. As long as the farms that relied on the flow of the San Joaquin could now rely on the flow of the Sacramento, what difference did it make? There were no John Muirs, no Mary Austins, no Fresno chapter of the Sierra Club to make a peep about the miles and miles of San Joaquin River that would soon turn to sand or the salmon that would never come home again. Only when it was too late would the farming families along the San Joaquin file a lawsuit to stop the construction of the dam. It would have little to do with preserving the river, however. They were concerned instead about keeping enough flow past their pumps to water their crops.

The Central Valley Project—the damming of the Sacramento and San Joaquin Rivers, the shunting of their flows to distant lands in the name of conquering flood on one plain and drought on another—would confront its share of challenges over the next quarter century. There would be the Great Depression, the Second World War, a fight between the state and the feds over who would control the project, a fight between feds and farmers over limiting the size of farms that could receive subsidized water. Answering to the crime of killing one of the great western rivers that flowed from mountain to sea, however, would not be one of them.

Thirteen

MOVING THE RAIN

In the lineup of mayors who have brought water to San Francisco and kept it flowing for the past 168 years (forty-three men and two women) I look for clues in the framed portrait of James Rolph Jr., a.k.a. "Sunny Jim." His sunniness was said to be a natural state. He'd been born in 1869 to two cheerful parents who had met on the ship ride over from London. The good fortune of being a child of San Francisco's Mission District—the sunniest neighborhood in an often fog-shrouded city—only added to his lightness. He hitched up with a pack of neighborhood kids who roamed San Francisco from wharf to hilltop, all through the night. "We wanted fun and we were willing to meet the dawn to get it," he said. At a young age, he became enchanted with the docks and its sea dogs and took a job as a clerk for a shipping company. The boss put him out front to see how the customers would take to him. The kid had a magnetic personality and the looks to match. His hair was the color of charcoal, and he had clear blue eyes and a ruddy complexion. He grew a thick mustache that he turned up at the ends and dressed in a black derby hat and a black suit that gave him the air of dapper. He rose up the company's ranks and was about to launch his own shipping company when his mother died. He put his career on hold to raise his two youngest siblings and then married and fathered a child of his own. By his mid-thirties, he had become a shipping magnate with a mansion in the Mission District and a 160-acre farm down the peninsula near Stanford University.

This might have been his life, but Sunny Jim listened to the entreaties of San Franciscans and decided to run for mayor. His theme song, "Smiles," began with the line "There are smiles that make you happy," and despite a campaign that featured egg throwing, fistfights and police riots, he won handily. He had no patience for the day-to-day of governance. He paraded about town with a smile on his face and a carnation in his buttonhole. Nob Hill industrialists adored him. So did the Communists. He was loved in Chinatown, loved in North Beach, loved in the gambling dens and in the red-light district where he owned his own whorehouse, the Pleasure Palace. No mayor in America more openly flouted the laws of Prohibition than Rolph. He saw no reason to hide a thing from the people—not his public drunkenness, not his carrying on with movie star Anita Page. Fatty Arbuckle put him in one of his films, and the voters kept putting him back into office. He served from 1912 to 1931, the longest reign of any mayor in San Francisco history. Then, as the Great Depression crippled the country, and the state planned for a water-delivery system that would whip nature for good and put people back to work, Rolph threw his hat into the race for the governor of California and won.

He wasn't the same Sunny Jim. His clear eyes had grown cloudy. The little hair he had left on his head was gray. His chin and belly had gone south. He kept fiddling with his famous mustache until the only thing visible was a nub. The state of California was nearly broke. The grip of a six-year drought wouldn't let loose. The farmers were screaming for the Central Valley Project to save them. Their fields were not only parched but convulsed by labor strikes. In the valley town of Pixley, growers murdered two cotton pickers who were protesting for higher wages. The utilities, led by Pacific Gas & Electric, feared any water project that would create public hydropower and weaken their monopoly. The governor, in other words, was feeling punched and slapped. Then came a crime of cold blood in San Jose that would captivate newspaper readers nationwide and turn James Rolph Jr. from "Sunny Jim" to "Governor Lynch."

On the evening of November 9, 1933, Brooke Leopold Hart, a twenty-two-year-old heir to a department store fortune, left work in his green Studebaker Roadster, a gift from his parents for graduating from Santa Clara University. He had no idea that two men had been tracking his movements to and from the department store for weeks. Waiting along the street in downtown San Jose were Thomas Thurmond, a jobless oil worker whose sweetheart had married another man, and John Holmes, an out-of-work salesman who had separated from his wife and two children. Both were lean and rawboned with faces that made them look like the villians in a Dick Tracy cartoon. One of them flagged Hart down, pulled out a gun and jumped into his roadster. The other trailed in a dark sedan.

Hart was a gorgeous kid with wavy blond hair and blue eyes. The girls, it was said, used to shop at the department store on the corner of Market and Santa Clara Streets just to get a stare at him. Now he took every turn the gunman instructed him to take, driving ten miles to a rural road outside of Milpitas. There, he abandoned his car and got into their sedan. Thurmond and Holmes put a hood over his head and took him to the San Mateo Bridge. They nearly crushed his skull with a brick and then bound his hands and feet with baling wire. He was still conscious as they weighed him down with concrete blocks and dumped him into the San Francisco Bay. It was low tide, and Hart managed to free himself in the water. He was struggling to get ashore when Holmes grabbed a pistol and shot him to death.

Governor Rolph knew the Hart family well and followed every detail of the case as local and federal authorities tried to determine Brooke's whereabouts. The two kidnappers telephoned the Hart family and demanded a $40,000 ransom to free their son. The line was tapped and traced to a garage in downtown San Jose. Both men were arrested and confessed. As details of the murder leaked out, citizens gathered outside the jail and shouted their outrage. The governor could see that it was personal. Just about everyone in San Jose shopped at Hart's. The local paper ran a front-page editorial that branded Holmes and Thurmond, two San Jose boys who'd never finished high school, as "human devils" who deserved the sort of justice that only "mob violence" could inflict. As police kept searching for Brooke's body, Governor Rolph told the press that if the people's anger turned to violence, he would not send in the National Guard. Three days later, on November 26, the body of Brooke Hart, his features eaten away by crabs, was found floating in the bay a half mile from the San Mateo Bridge. Radio stations across Northern California blared the news that a lynching was going to take place that evening, at eleven p.m. sharp. Governor Rolph canceled an out-of-town trip to prevent the lieutenant governor, his rival, from calling in the guard.

What occurred next in San Jose's midnight chill was an American lynching in the full glare of the media spotlight. A radio station in Los Angeles broadcast it live. Five to ten thousand men, women and children stormed the jailhouse. Deputies tried to stop them with tear gas, but it only enraged them more. They dragged the two whimpering killers out of their cells and across the street to the stately grounds of St. James Park. They stripped off the men's pants and underwear and hung one of them from a cork elm and the other from a mulberry. "Thurmond and Holmes were yanked to their doom in less time than it takes to tell it," the newsreel narrator said in his staccato. The mass of people lingered for hours gawking at the two dead men, their crooked necks, their exposed penises. Then they roused up one more time and went after the two trees, tearing off twigs, branches and bark to take home as souvenirs. When it came time for Governor Rolph to issue an official statement, he looked into the cameras and said, "The people were determined to give notice to the world that [such a crime] would not be tolerated in this state," he said. "If anyone is arrested for the good job, I'll pardon them all."

Twenty-four black men had been lynched that same year in America. But no governor of a state, not even one in the Deep South, had so proudly egged on a mob holding a rope in its hands. In the days that followed, Rolph was venerated by some and vilified by many more. The timing of the lynching made for a perfect paradox. Here was the governor appealing to the primitive instincts of man at the same time as he was calling on Californians to seize a future of engineering and hydraulics to push man into an entirely modern age. Just weeks earlier he had signed the Central Valley Project into law with these words: "I will not stand for any sideshows on this serious matter. If any special interests try to block this measure or delay it in any way, I am prepared to fight them to the last ditch of my executive authority."

He knew a fight was coming. Already, PG&E was making noise that the project would throw open the energy market by adding new sources of hydroelectric power for Northern and middle California. To preserve its monopoly, the utility had gathered enough signatures to challenge the governor's law with a vote of the people. The way Rolph saw it, PG&E couldn't give a damn about its customers, none less than the farmers paying more and more to pump water from an ever-plunging aquifer. By opposing the project and its relief of supplemental electricity and water, the utility was only looking to strengthen its stranglehold on the farm communities.

The governor calculated that his selling of the Central Valley Project would provide a way to distance himself from the lynchings. It would appease his critics by offering the most effective of California elixirs: water. This is not to say that his embrace of the most ambitious reclamation effort in U.S. history wasn't genuine. He believed that the arguments in favor of the project had only gained strength in a time of economic devastation. The construction work would provide twenty-five thousand jobs for no less than three years. Not a single dollar of the $170 million price tag would be borne by the California taxpayer. The project, part of FDR's national recovery program, would be financed through state revenue bonds purchased by the federal government. The future of California, Rolph argued, depended on changing its nature. The Sacramento River, dammed in its final canyon, would no longer pack the threat of flood. Flows would be portioned out to exploit the resource of water to its fullest. Cities and farms in the delta would have enough year-round flow to beat back salty tides. The power generated by the Shasta Dam on the Sacramento and the Friant Dam on the San Joaquin would assure cheap electricity for millions of customers. The project would save California agriculture, or at least the two hundred thousand acres (the number kept changing) in the San Joaquin Valley that were about to revert to desert.

As the referendum vote drew near, farm belt folk did their best to tug on the heartstrings of city folk. It was 1933, after all, and the Dust Bowl exodus from Oklahoma, Texas and Arkansas had hurtled into full motion. Hundreds of thousands of Okies and Arkies, human tumbleweeds, rolled across the American prairie and came to rest in the valley. Drought's oppression had followed the people out. "Save the Back Country," urged one pamphlet published by the Tulare County Unit of the California State Irrigation Association. "Only Immediate State Action Can Prevent a Great Tragedy." The illustration on the cover pictured a goddess of the valley in a wide-brimmed hat holding a basket of fruit in one hand and pointing to the sere middle of California with her other hand. "Hundreds of producers will be forced to abandon their homes unless surplus Sacramento waters are turned into the South San Joaquin Valley," she declared.

Governor James Rolph

Governor Rolph wanted voters to know that valley growers would not be using the imported water to add new farmland. The project would be furnishing supplemental water to only those farms that already existed. This had the sound of a concession. The governor was backing away from the bulletins of the state engineers, who only a few years earlier had identified five hundred thousand acres in Kern and Tulare Counties alone that needed to be saved and millions of acres more that needed to be developed.

The opponents of the project, led by PG&E, sounded like conservationists as they laid out their case. The federal government had never explicitly pledged to underwrite the $170 million project, they said. The taxpayers of California needed to be prepared to foot the entire bill. The dams, canals and pumps would likely end up costing double the projected amount. Taming California was a fantastical idea. In those years of Hatfield-caliber storms, it would take a great deal more than one dam to prevent Northern California from flooding again. In the depths of drought, opponents argued, there would never be enough water released from the dam to keep the tides from salting the delta. And what would the water imports truly bring to the farm belt? A surplus of crops already existed. How many times had the California raisin gone from boom to bust in its short life? How many millions of dollars was the federal government spending to pay cotton and wheat farmers *not* to plant their fields? The history of agricultural development in California was already one of no restraint. There was every reason to believe that the delivery of two or three million acre-feet of supplemental water to the valley would only wind up fueling more glut.

What had taken place on the ground in the grips of another drought bolstered the cynic. In the summer of 1930, the U.S. Bureau of Reclamation had dispatched two investigators to the valley to document the devastation in Tulare and Kern Counties. The locals happily showed them patches of farmland where the soil had dried up and blown away. The investigators snapped photo after photo of fruit orchards, vineyards and cotton fields that looked as if a plague of locusts had visited. They wrote a lengthy report that concluded that the water-starved southern San Joaquin Valley needed immediate relief. The region didn't have enough river flow or aquifer supply to meet the present needs of agriculture, much less answer the desire for more cropland. But for every orchard ravaged, the same study found ten orchards that remained lush. Even as their report came down on the side of the Central Valley Project, the investigators talked to bankers, businessmen and farmers who told a far more nuanced story about the land. Many of the farmers who had yanked out orchards or fallowed fields to get through the 1924 drought had only grown bigger in the decade since. The lesson of dry times was the opposite of what a rational observer might expect. Rather than keep their acreage within a comfortable range of their water, farmers were planting to the absolute extreme of what the water could serve. Time and again, their calculations had forgotten that drought was a reality of the land. Indeed, their calculations had wished drought away.

In the mid- to late 1920s, one of the driest periods on record, the farmers of California had pumped enough groundwater to add almost one million acres of new crops. From 1929 to 1939, a period punctuated by several more drought years, the harvested farmland in Madera, Fresno, Tulare, Kings and Kern Counties did not diminish but grew. The "Dust Bowl" of the valley was mostly a fabrication of the farm bureaus and chambers of commerce to amplify their shout for a hydraulic system to rescue them. In the bustle of boom, the federal investigators found, the distinction between poor ground and fertile ground had mattered little. The banks had loaned money to any white man who showed up in a pair of boots and blue jeans with an aching to plant. Whether in Orange Cove or Terra Bella or Lindsay or Tulare, nearly every farmer who defaulted on his loan had fallen victim to the same two forces: poor soil and surplus crops. Building a project that would deliver more water to such a place wouldn't solve a thing, opponents warned. The farmers would only use imported water to plant more acres and then punch deeper holes in the ground to plant even more. Without a law in California to regulate groundwater pumping, it was folly to expect agriculture to keep to a boundary line. In a race to the bottom of the well, only the big farmers would win.

It was anyone's guess how the vote on the Central Valley Project would tally. Southern Californians had no straw in the game and were expected to vote no. Residents of the San Joaquin Valley would surely vote yes. Even in Fresno, where the dam would steal a river, support for the project was strong. Northern Californians, both in Sacramento and in San Francisco, were more divided. It was true that the project would provide a more dependable supply of water to rice farmers in the upper counties. And many residents saw the benefit of protecting their houses and delta farms against floods and seawater intrusion. But hijacking even 15 percent of their river for the benefit of faraway farmers didn't sit well with many others. Unlike the San Joaquin, the Sacramento threaded its way from community to community. The river belonged to everyone. The delta wasn't simply a place to farm. People lived there, fished there, boated there, took Sunday picnics and vacations there. As for San Franciscans, they likely would have supported the project on the word of Mayor Sunny Jim alone, but many had grown weary of his antics as governor. The real wild card was how the 202,000 stockholders of PG&E who resided in California would vote. Would they line up with the utility or see the issue through the eyes of their own local communities?

In the days leading up to the December 19, 1933, vote, PG&E's president sent a letter to each stock- and bondholder, asking for his or her "immediate help in defeating the act." The utility doled out great wads of cash to local social and athletic clubs, chambers of commerce and charitable organizations to persuade people to vote its way. "PG&E has spent hundreds of thousands of dollars in a vicious campaign of falsehood and humbuggery," state senator J. M. Inman of Sacramento bristled. "The money, of course, has been gouged from the people of the state in high electric costs."

On Election Day, just a week before Christmas, most people chose to stay home. Barely a third of the electorate bothered to vote. The project passed by a slim margin: 459,712 in favor and 426,109 opposed. Los Angeles and San Francisco managed to cancel each other out. Los Angeles voted two to one against the act, while San Francisco, which would one day sprout an environmental movement declaring holy war against the project, voted two to one in its favor. In the Sacramento Valley, two-thirds of the electorate supported the act. In the San Joaquin Valley, 90 percent voted yes. In Tulare County, the act passed by such an overwhelming margin that residents wondered who the six traitors were. Governor Rolph rejoiced in victory, but he wouldn't live to see the project funded. Six months later, during his third year in office, he suffered one heart attack, then another, and died on his ranch. He had done his part to move the rain.

In the winter of 1935, Edward Hyatt, the state engineer who had authored a report titled "Water Is the Life Blood of California," sat in front of Congress for the first of many hearings on funding the Central Valley Project. California had tried and failed to sell the $170 million in construction bonds on its own. If the project was going to get built, the federal government would have to cover the entire cost. Congress and the White House seemed inclined to do so, but first the legislative committees needed to hear from Hyatt that it would be a federal project and not a state project. Would the citizens of California defer to either the U.S. Bureau of Reclamation or the Army Corps of Engineers, the two federal builders of dams, to design, construct and operate the project? Hyatt squirmed in his chair. He knew that pleading for federal dollars while insisting on state control was not good form, but a lot of important people in California didn't want Washington to have any say on how they used their water.

"The state wants this project before the country dries up and blows away," Hyatt testified. "My personal view is it would be handled better under state authority than it would under federal authority."

Congressman Riley J. Wilson from Louisiana pressed him on this:

"It is your view that this project should be undertaken as a federal project with state assistance or as a state project with the assistance of the federal government?"

"This is a matter of secondary interest in California," Hyatt replied. "California wants the project constructed, and if the federal government desires to take charge of it, I am sure the people of California will say well and good. They are desperate."

Over the next several years, Hyatt testified multiple times before Congress to push the project forward, first through the weary of the Depression and then through the anxiety of the Second World War. He was joined by California's political leaders and big farmers who grudgingly accepted federal control, too. But with each round of questions and retorts, the project's ambition—how many acres of farmland it might save—seemed to grow. These changes were subtle enough that no congressman called out California's delegation for supplanting one bold vision with an even more far-reaching one. Hyatt was no longer pledging that the project would save only two hundred thousand acres from the ravages of a Dust Bowl come west. "It will save one-half million irrigated acres from returning to desert and prevent the extinction of a high-type of civilization on this vast area," he testified. "It will save fifty thousand American citizens from abandoning their homes."

To the skeptical committee member, this last figure seemed to be pulled right out of his backside. "If this irrigation project goes through, it will put more acreage into production, will it not?" asked James Fitzpatrick, a congressman from New York.

Hyatt's equivocation was engineer-like: "No sir, it is not so designed. The canal capacities and the amount of water are all designed to serve only the land that is now under irrigation. It is not designed for new land. Of course, one cannot say that there will not be some acres here and there coming in, but the increase will be slight and slow, if any at all."

As the Bureau of Reclamation took control of the project, federal and state bureaucrats boasted not only of the half million acres of farmland it would save. They began to sell the idea that the project would add 100,000 to 225,000 new acres of farmland. Those who had fought against the project either didn't notice or didn't care to protest this embrace of growth. Even PG&E, after finagling a deal to acquire and profit from the hydropower, was now on board. More than $193 million in federal funds had been appropriated through the U.S. Department of the Interior. While this was no small amount, consider the floods of 1937 and 1938. Together, they had cost California and the nation more than $150 million in property damage and disaster protection.

The time had come for the writers and photographers of the Work Projects Administration to take their notebooks and cameras into the river canyons and document the raising of Shasta and Friant Dams. They'd been tasked with telling the story to the schoolchildren of California, which probably helps explain the purplish prose they used to capture the bigness of the Central Valley Project and the theme of a country embarking on the new frontier. To be fair, the writers had many masters to make happy: the U.S. Department of the Interior and its Reclamation Bureau, the Works Projects Administration, and the California State Department of Education, which published their volume in 1942 under the title *Central Valley Project*. This was the little green-covered book my father lifted from Pasadena City College in 1952 and carried home to our last ranch along the San Joaquin River, where the ditch water that fed our vineyards and orchards came out of Friant Dam.

The book opens with a picture of Mount Shasta's magnificent snow-covered peak and the manifesto that California's impossible vastness, its too many temperate zones, needs surgical correction. The operation will start at the foot of the volcanic mountain. "There is enough water to keep the fields green and the orchards blooming, but it is distributed in a topsy-turvy manner," they wrote. "The farmer in the northern portion of this 500-mile-long valley is deluged with water while his brother in the south watches his crops dry and die for lack of it. The situation has been described by a leading engineer of the United States Bureau of Reclamation as demanding the greatest water-conservation plan since time began."

Five thousand men (not twenty-five thousand, as the promoters had promised) were working in the two canyons above Redding and Fresno. They were blacksmiths, bricklayers, carpenters, electricians, firemen and locomotive engineers. They were machinists, mechanics, miners, ironworkers, pile drivers and riggers. They were riveters, welders, steamfitters, plasterers and plumbers. They were raising Shasta

Dam to a height of 602 feet. Only the Boulder Dam on the Colorado, stood taller. Friant Dam, the project's other keystone, would be half that size. The canals they were digging were the longest ever dug. The materials and sweat to pull off such a stunt were documented, as well: 40 million bags of cement weighing 94 pounds each; 170 million tons of steel; 70 million board feet of lumber (the clear-cutting of 2,500 acres of forest); 3,500 tons of dynamite and 80 million man-hours.

Somewhere in the middle of this chore, California took a change of heart. It appreciated everything the federal government was doing, but once the last bag of cement had been poured, the state would need to take over the project. Whatever pledge California leaders might have made to the federal government could not be kept in light of a rule that each farmer served by the project could use the water on 160 acres and no more. If the farmer had a wife, the two of them could use the water on 320 acres and no more. The farmers and their politicians believed the valley had righteous cause to be excluded from the law and took their case to Harold L. Ickes, secretary of the Interior. The middle of California wasn't like other reclamation projects around the country, they argued. Indeed, it wasn't even reclamation. The valley was desert only by measure of rainfall. The snowmelt that ran down its rivers had already intensified agriculture to a degree not seen in the world. The farmers didn't need the federal government's intervention to remake the valley's nature. For almost a half century, they had done that and more.

Instead of sticking to the merits of why the 160-acre rule fell unjustly upon California, the farmers and their legislators let the red-baiters among them argue their cause. "Secretary Ickes not only wants to set up a Communistic Socialistic agricultural program in areas to be irrigated by the Central Valley Project but in the whole Central Valley," state senator Bradford S. Crittenden of Stockton said. "The 160-acre rule would make California the testing ground for a Communistic scheme of splitting up long-established farm holdings and parcel them out to small owners."

On March 7, 1945, Secretary Ickes sat down in his Washington, D.C., office and wrote a letter to California Governor Earl Warren, a Bakersfield boy who wasn't stoking the call for state takeover of the project but wasn't exactly putting out its fires, either. Ickes had first dismissed the talk of a California rebellion as the noise from a handful of rabble-rousers. Now the farmers in Kern and Tulare were pushing their lawmakers to draft legislation that would fund two lobbyists and a publicity agent to louden the decibels. Ickes saw California as an insatiable child. While he was too consummate a politician to say, "How dare you renege on our deal?," he was irked to have to remind Governor Warren of all the handshakes they had shared up to that point. "If the state has arrived at a financial position where it is ready to reimburse the United States Treasury for expenditures already made on behalf of the people of California, and is further prepared to guarantee the additional financing necessary to complete the project within a reasonable number of years, the Department of the Interior is prepared to withdraw from the project," Ickes wrote. "Do you think the State is now prepared to resume full responsibility for the project?"

Ickes was calling the governor's bluff. He knew full well that California was not in a position to do any such thing. As the Central Valley Project neared completion, more and more farmers reconciled themselves to the reality of federal control. Yet this did not stop them from taking their 160-acre fight beyond Ickes—to the halls of Congress. The attempt to gut the rule made for odd alliances, none odder than that of Sheridan Downey, a liberal water attorney who was California's newest U.S. senator, and Joseph Di Giorgio, the Sicilian who had willed the desert of Arvin into an agricultural wonder. Downey had grown up in Wyoming, earned his law degree from the University of Michigan and moved to Sacramento to join his brother's law firm. A champion of progressive reform, he had decided to run for California governor in 1933 only to learn that Upton Sinclair, the muckraking novelist, was running, too. They joined hands—Sinclair for governor and Downey for lieutenant governor, the "Uppie and Downey" ticket. Downey came closer to winning his race than Sinclair did, close enough that supporters urged him to run for the U.S. Senate. And so began his metamorphosis from a staunch liberal who had stumped the state touting an End Poverty in California (EPIC) plan to a pliable conservative advancing the agendas of big oil and agribusiness.

In his travels to Kern County to build support for his Senate race, Downey had caught the notice of old man Di Giorgio. The grower, the biggest producer of fresh fruit in America, wasn't easily impressed by politicians. Downey, though, was not only an excellent lawyer and a first-rate orator but a handsome man full of charisma who would win the Senate seat going away. Halfway through his first term, as debate on the 160-acre limit heated up, Downey drove down to Arvin to see Di Giorgio. The purpose of his visit may have been nothing more than to kiss the ring of the old man dubbed "the fruit king" by *Time* magazine. Plenty of politicians had made the same pilgrimage to Casa Di Giorgio, leaving with either a lecture in broken English or a signature on a big check from the grower, who lolled about all afternoon in his pajamas and bathrobe. Downey, by contrast, made the visit again and again.

Di Giorgio had quite a story. He had come from Cefalù, a town along the north coast of Sicily that grew lemons consumed in New York, Philadelphia and Baltimore. His father couldn't understand how Americans were paying so little for seasonal lemons they couldn't get from anywhere else. He suspected that fruit brokers were stealing profits from him and his fellow growers. In the late 1880s, he packed a cargo of lemons and fourteen-year-old Joseph and shipped them off to America to figure out how much the middlemen were skimming. It turned out to be plenty. Di Giorgio set up shop in Baltimore amid a sizable community of immigrants from Cefalù and began selling the lemons from his village. At sixteen, he became the most important lemon receiver and distributor in the Mid-Atlantic States and then used his connections to corner the trade on bananas from Jamaica and Cuba.

For Di Giorgio, it wasn't enough that he was a millionaire merchant at twenty-one. He wanted to grow the fruit, too. This was how, in 1919, he came to the scorched earth of Arvin, where water sat deep beneath the ground and the soil in its best stretches proved fertile and early-producing. Fruits and vegetables ripened there before they ripened almost anywhere else, turning routine crops into big-dollar harvests. Arvin wasn't a speck on anyone's map before Di Giorgio made it one. The Arvin that greeted Senator Downey in the early 1940s still wasn't much of a place, a shantytown stuffed with Dust Bowl migrants whose faces would be made famous in the photos of Dorothea Lange. Arvin had no sidewalks or paved streets. A single school, Di Giorgio Elementary, educated the children. A knot of bars on main street liquored up the adults. Tent churches furnished redemption. If Arvin was squalid—

one visiting pastor called it "the worst town I ever saw"—it was only too easy to blame the old man whose eight thousand acres of fruits, vegetables and cotton made the whole place hum.

By Downey's reckoning, Di Giorgio was no villain. The Sicilian with the "nut brown face and chestnut eyes," as the senator described him, had taken the desert and created a garden that gave immigrant families a chance at a new life. No river ran through his land. The only water to keep alive the Santa Rosa and Wickson plums was water he pumped from the ground. Di Giorgio was genuinely perplexed at the intent of reclamation law. If the purpose of the Central Valley Project was to import water north to south to save farmland, why was the federal government insisting on limiting the supply to farms no bigger than 160 acres? He was the original homesteader of Arvin. Why should he be punished for having gotten there first? He didn't need the Bureau of Reclamation and its waterworks to push him to reclaim even an acre of land. He had reclaimed ten thousand acres with his own hands. If he was big, it was for good reason. The costs to pump groundwater from a plummeting aquifer could not easily be borne by a small farmer. Arvin was ground that had started big and needed to stay big because of the high costs of water, equipment and labor. There were plenty of civilized places in the valley where land could be farmed small, places with a local river or a more generous aquifer. Arvin wasn't one of those places.

Senator Downey was so convinced of this viewpoint that he spent two years researching and writing a book, *They Would Rule the Valley,* financed by cash contributions from Di Giorgio himself. It became his prosecution against the 160-acre rule. He knew that the arguments of big farming versus small farming would only divide his fellow senators into the same two opposing camps that had existed since reclamation became law in 1902. So he spent a good many pages of the book arguing what he regarded as the most fundamentally flawed premise of the Central Valley Project: Water didn't stay put. Even the water delivered by canal would eventually percolate down into the aquifer, where it would be free for the taking. Federal surface water delivered to the small farmer would eventually become local groundwater sucked up by the big farmer. A grower like Di Giorgio, Downey argued, need not sign up for the project to be its beneficiary. There was no law preventing him from tapping into the same aquifer that was being replenished by the federal water. Instead of relieving the tremendous stress on the aquifer, Downey said, the project would only unleash the pumping of more groundwater by the big boys. The federal government had no sane way to keep Di Giorgio from mining groundwater that, a season or two earlier, had been Sacramento River water. Feds or no feds, the flow would follow its own law of movement.

"You cannot repeal the law of hydraulics," Senator Downey wrote. "If you allow a man with 160 acres to have the water, you cannot prevent the owner adjacent to him from using it on a parcel of 640 acres. The acreage limitation clause is a wholly inadequate club with which to coerce the big landowners into dividing their baronies among the serfs."

For all his flourish, Downey could not persuade his fellow senators to abandon the notion that reclamation dollars needed to promote reclamation law—even in a farm belt as developed as California's. The senators weren't about to pretend that the interest-free delivery of subsidized water didn't enhance the value of a farm. In districts where the aquifer was dropping, the flow of cheap federal water could increase a farm's worth by as much as six-fold. The U.S. government couldn't very well allow only rich men to reap such a windfall.

Downey did his best to counter the numbers with calculations of his own. He found himself outmatched, however, by one of the nation's fiercest proponents of acreage limitation, a University of California economics professor named Paul Taylor, the husband of photographer Dorothea Lange. A quiet but tenacious man, Taylor had taught himself the history of reclamation law by scouring archives at the Department of the Interior. In front of the congressional committees determining the contours of the Central Valley Project, Taylor wielded figures and economic models like a Gatling gun. He argued that if big landowners wanted to farm marginal land—ground that was alkali or boggy or sitting atop a plummeting aquifer—they needed to assume that risk without the federal government guaranteeing their overreach. No one was stopping them from farming in the manner they had been farming for decades, ebbing and flowing with drought and flood. But if they wanted to deploy federal water on their ten-thousand-acre republics, they needed to adhere to the "common good" ethos of reclamation law.

They had to restrict those imports to a total of 160 acres or 320 acres, as the case may be.

In the end, the senators rejected the California exception to the 160-acre rule. This did not stop Downey from devising another tactic to win his fight: Wear down the bureaucrats at the Bureau of Reclamation who administered the rule. The boss of the Interior Department, Secretary Ickes, was refusing to budge. But Michael Straus, a government PR man who now served as commissioner of reclamation, seemed to regard the acreage-limit law as negotiable. At a contentious hearing to push along the project, Straus sat before the senators as if he'd rolled out of bed only minutes before. A big bear of a man, he hadn't bothered to comb his hair or iron out the wrinkles in his cigarette-stained clothes. Straus, one of FDR's New Dealers, had come to see his mission as nothing short of bringing the fruits of technology to the nation's small farmers. Strange, then, to be confronted with his backsliding on an acreage rule that was the country's sincerest pledge to small farming.

Senator Zales Ecton, a cattle rancher from Montana, asked Commissioner Straus how he would view a farming operation with sixteen hundred acres and, say, ten stockholders. What if each stockholder owned his own 160 acres within the structure of a corporation? Could all sixteen hundred acres then be eligible for cheap federal water?

"I think he would bring himself into technical compliance with the law as now written," Straus replied. "Whether it would be spiritual compliance or not, I have my doubts"—this remark was greeted with laughter—"but the law goes to technical, legal compliance."

This, naturally, caught the ear of Senator Downey, who had in mind an example from real life. A big grape grower and winemaker in Madera named Krikor Arakelian was prepared to deed 2,500 acres to his children and other relatives but wanted federal water to flow to all of them. If he broke the land up into 160-acre chunks—each chunk "owned" by a different relative—but still operated it as one ranch, would he be in technical compliance? Would the entire 2,500 acres be entitled to subsidized government water?

Straus nodded. "Yes, if each ownership did not exceed 160 acres per individual owner and was, indeed, a beneficial ownership."

The 160-acre rule would one day evolve into the 960-acre rule to reflect a more modern economy of scale in California's farm fields.

The rule as an edict, however, would lose much of its force in the wake of Straus's testimony. His willingness to entertain one loophole and another would become, to the horror of Paul Taylor and his disciples, an invitation to the valley's biggest growers to defy the law.

The time had now come for the U.S. Department of Agriculture to weigh in on a federal project designed to save the skins of California's fancy fruit and vegetable growers. Who would have thought that the agriculture bureaucrats, at the eleventh hour, would decide to take on the very premise of the Central Valley Project? The contrarian at the heart of the challenge was Charles Brannan, a bald and bespectacled lawyer from Denver who had specialized in agriculture, mining and irrigation cases before becoming the assistant secretary at the USDA.

As the dams and canals of the Central Valley Project neared completion, Brannan began to study the economic models put together by the Interior Department. He became convinced that practically every assumption used to sell the project to the American public was false or inflated. In the tens of thousands of pages of government reports and studies that had propelled the project forward, Brannan found himself sounding a solitary voice of caution. Yes, reclamation in California may very well deliver on its promise, but he could also foresee a day when the imports of supplemental water would turn the San Joaquin Valley into a water-guzzling monster. The project would continue to plant more crops and pump more groundwater until the farm economy became so glutted that only the richest men could survive.

Brannan was concerned that the Interior Department had no means—indeed, no intention—of limiting its mission to save farmland. The Bureau of Reclamation was now fixing to grow agriculture in the valley by 650,000 acres, if not more. Instead of insisting that California finally regulate groundwater extraction, the Reclamation Bureau was letting the state off the hook. Without such limits, the federal water would only serve to extend agriculture onto poorer ground that would then induce more pumping. Brannan found that the Department of the Interior, in its cost-benefit analysis, had rigged the calculations to make the project appear more beneficial than it was. The feds were using gross crop values instead of net crop values. They were understating the costs to produce fruits, vegetables and fiber.

Inside the USDA labyrinth sat an obscure office in the city of Berkeley known as the Bureau of Agricultural Economics. Brannan had staffed it with eight smart and tenacious investigators, who he then set loose on the Central Valley Project. The unit was headed by Marion Clawson, who had grown up on a Nevada cattle ranch and earned his doctorate in economics from Harvard. His assistants included Walter Goldschmidt, who was about to publish a groundbreaking study comparing the farm towns of Dinuba and Arvin. Goldschmidt would show that Dinuba's many small farms had created a full-fledged community. Arvin, by contrast, the province of Di Giorgio alone, was a glorified farm labor camp.

To bolster the unit, Clawson put out a call for another researcher. Into his office walked a tall, raven-haired woman named Mary Montgomery who had earned her doctorate in public policy from UC Berkeley. She was a friend of Paul Taylor and Dorothea Lange's and shaded a good bit to the political left of Clawson. He hired Montgomery on the spot, and she proceeded to turn his world upside down. It wasn't only her fierce commitment to a 160-acre rule. The two of them began an affair that saw her befriend Clawson's wife and grow close to his children. The betrayal became so messy that Montgomery moved to Mexico for a time. When she returned, her work on the project resumed, and so did the affair. Clawson would divorce his wife and marry Montgomery in the Berkeley home of Taylor and Lange. First, though, they had to finish their report, which was published in 1945 and bore a rather unwieldy title: *The Effect of the Central Valley Project on the Agricultural and Industrial Economy and on the Social Character of California.*

In a careful, almost quiet way, their study pulled apart the fictions that had shepherded the project through the halls of Sacramento and Washington, D.C. The San Joaquin Valley had not suffered through a series of devastating Dust Bowls that deserved rescue. Quite to the contrary, the footprint of agriculture in the south valley was expanding at a pace of sixty thousand acres a year. Nearly all of this growth was fueled by groundwater overdrafts. Along the east side of Tulare and Kern Counties, farmers had pumped so much water out of the earth that they had created a massive "cone of depression." Since the advent of the turbine pump in 1920, the water table had plummeted from 10 feet below ground to 250 feet down. The costs of pumping had pushed land ownership into fewer hands. Of the 517,000 irrigated acres in Kern, 240,000 acres were in the hands of seven owners. This wasn't the corn and wheat fields of the Midwest. This was a realm of highly specialized crops whose prices moved up and down according to a variety of factors that the farmer could not control: weather, pests, labor and overseas markets. It was a type of agriculture that inherently favored men with deep pockets, a high-stakes roulette table in which a melon crop could break a farmer one year and make him a near millionaire the next year.

The importing of project water, their study found, would likely introduce more speculation and specialization and create the need for more labor imported from afar. It would likely bring about more surplus harvests and strengthen the already profound forces of land monopoly and income inequity. The valley was a highly stratified society in which ethnic communities and races were kept apart and field hands lived in squalor. Since many owners did not reside on the land, they could pretend that such conditions did not exist. Applying water to a place where inequality already shot through life and expecting that water to be distributed in an equal fashion was magical thinking, the report concluded. There was every reason to expect that the delivery of federal water would only further cement the inequality.

The report, too late to make a difference, would mark the last hurrah of the Bureau of Agricultural Economics. Senator Downey went after Clawson personally. "In this alleged economist," he groaned, "we are presented with an instructive instance of intellectual corruption." Fulton Lewis Jr., the "golden voice" of the militant right wing, declared on his national radio show that the study only proved that Communists had taken over the USDA. Political pressure from Di Giorgio and others blocked a follow-up study; the Berkeley office was soon shuttered. Clawson and Montgomery moved to Washington, D.C., where he headed the Interior Department's land management bureau. Goldschmidt found himself tailed by goons hired by the big farmers and then investigated by the FBI. A congressional subcommittee headed by Representative Alfred Elliott, whose district took in both Dinuba and Arvin, trashed his work. "Some silly professor, some dreamer, some man who knows nothing about agriculture, knows nothing about the living conditions of the farmers and the people who work here, is doing this," Elliott proclaimed. Professor Goldschmidt's study on Arvin and Dinuba got buried, but not for long. His 1947 book, *As You Sow,* an expanded version of his research, became a classic of rural sociology.

The criticisms by the USDA team reduced not an acre-foot of the Central Valley Project. In 1950, when it came time for the Interior Department to offer long-term contracts to the twenty irrigation districts served by the project, the farmers could rejoice. The San Joaquin River produced 1.3 million acre-feet of water in years of decent snowfall. Nearly all of this flow would now be captured by the Friant-Kern Canal and the Madera Canal and delivered to farms as far as 160 miles away. In wet years, the growers would have access to another million acre-feet of San Joaquin River floodwater. For the privilege of federal reclamation, they would pay $3.50 an acre-foot. In the event the supply proved insufficient to cover their ambition, they were still free to pump without limit from the aquifer beneath them.

From 1924 to 1949, through two epic droughts and record groundwater depletion, the counties of Madera, Kern and Tulare doubled their harvested farmland to 1.1 million acres. By 1959, a decade after the first waters of the Central Valley Project poured in, growers would plant another 200,000 acres. The lesson of Professor Sidney Harding that only the best soil deserved the gift of government water would not be heeded. Almost every acre of the expansion would take place on soil classified as either marginal or poor. Land passed up by a generation of farmers—some of it barely fit for cattle grazing—would soon come into production because of cheap federal water.

The snowmelt captured by the Central Valley Project began to flow into the sluice at Friant Dam, on the outskirts of Fresno, in the spring of 1949. By the time it ran down the Friant-Kern Canal and reached Orange Cove, the first community in the delivery line, it was a hot July day. Harvey Bailey, a thirteen-year-old kid, knew what that imported water from the San Joaquin River meant. For two years, he'd heard the earth shudder as the boom and bucket of the monster dredger carved out the main canal. Now the whole town was quiet, listening for the sound of snowmelt creeping close. His dad and uncles who farmed citrus on three hundred acres had built a set of pipes over the canal's top to siphon their share of the flow. Orange Cove was entitled to receive almost forty thousand acre-feet of new water, and not a moment too soon. The sky had brought dry times again, and the trees had suffered so much that Bailey could see clear through the citrus groves where the leaves had burned off. There must have been a thousand townsfolk gathered at the east end of Main Street waiting for the water. The Lions Club was holding a sweepstakes in which each participant guessed the exact time the flow would cross a line drawn in chalk. None of them knew to factor in the cracks in the concrete along the way—leaks that the Bureau of Reclamation would end up plugging by throwing tons of manure and straw into the flowing water. Nothing like horseshit to shore up what $61 million could not.

"Someone shouted that the water had been released from Friant

Floodgates opening for the first time at Friant Dam

Dam and was now making its way south to us," Bailey remembered. "There were all sorts of weirs and check stops along the way, so it took its good old time. It didn't arrive as a tidal wave. It showed up in the distance almost like a mirage. The people started cheering. The closer it got, the louder they cheered. *Life* magazine was there. They took a photo of the farmers standing underneath the pipes as the water was flowing out. The headline was something like 'New Canal Gives Water for California Eden.' It was big deal, a big, big deal. For years afterwards, we had an annual parade marking that day."

Walt Shubin, a farmer's son from Kerman who built a wooden canoe in his seventh-grade shop class to paddle down the San Joaquin River, remembered that day as the day the river died in a twenty-mile stretch. When it came alive again in Mendota, it wasn't with its own water. It came alive with Sacramento River water pumped uphill and then downhill from the delta. The water wasn't shipped in for the benefit of the fish or Walt's canoe. It was shipped in for farmers growing cotton and alfalfa on old Henry Miller land. As part of the Central Valley Project, the farmers had demanded and received 840,000 acre-feet of delta flows as compensation for their stretch of river now forever dry. "When I take people down the river today and tell them what it used to be like, they look at me like I have rocks in my head, because now the river seems more like a canal," Shubin said. "Before they built Friant Dam, the San Joaquin was a thing of beauty. I can't even exaggerate how beautiful it was." He and his older brother would camp on the sandbars, where the breeze would stir and keep the mosquitoes away. At night, the Chinook salmon heading upstream would wake them up. "The next morning, when we could finally see them, they were making a wake that looked like a motorboat. I don't have any photographic proof. No one I knew had cameras in those days. It's all just memories now."

Everett "Bud" Rank Jr., who grew up on a ranch in the old river bottom, watched his father's life get consumed by the lawsuit he brought against the Department of the Interior in 1947. It took fifteen years for the case to wind its way to the U.S. Supreme Court, only for the justices to rule that the Bureau of Reclamation had every right to build the dam on the San Joaquin. The ranchers ended up getting a measly five-cubic-feet-per-second flow for their troubles. "I have the whole *Rank v. Krug* file from day one to the end of the trial," Bud Rank said. "The Bureau of Reclamation was hard to work with. There was no environmental protection at all. Nothing. Environmental impact reports didn't exist. I later went to work for the bureau. I worked up there for two years after I graduated from high school, on the survey crew, so I'm not blaming the people that worked for the bureau. It was the people in Washington making the decisions. They sure couldn't get away with it today."

The salmon made one last run in 1947. Bud Rank got into his boat with two friends and paddled down the river. "We speared salmon. We filled the boat up—honest. Oh, what a night we had! That was the last time the salmon ever came up the river. It was dry then from Gravelly Ford on down to Mendota. They put the dam in and that was it."

But that *wasn't* it. The feds had neglected to obtain a state permit to operate Friant Dam. By the time they got around to it, they'd been running the dam illegally for twelve years. In the early summer of 1959, the state Water Rights Board agreed to hear a complaint from the California Department of Fish and Game that the Reclamation Bureau was violating state law. Not only had the feds not bothered with a permit, they were failing to maintain a sufficient flow in the San Joaquin River to keep alive the spring and fall runs of Chinook salmon. Friant Dam hadn't just killed the southernmost run of the salmon in North America. It had dried up virtually every marsh in the central San Joaquin Valley.

Jack Fraser, one of the chiefs of state Fish and Game, had been itching to take on the feds for more than a decade, ever since his men had been made to wade into the San Joaquin and save the last salmon by hand. The run of Chinook on the river dated back eight thousand years and numbered hundreds of thousands of fish in some years. It killed him that the salmon could no longer detect the scent of their birthplace and swim back to the big pools at the base of the dam. They were coded in their deepest memory to find home, but home now lay beyond reach. Fraser understood that challenging the river's diversion ten years into the Central Valley Project was likely an ill-fated mission. He knew how little the federal government cared about the fish. In the Department of the Interior's 431-page book on the Central Valley Project, only four pages, the shortest chapter of them all, dealt with "Recreation, Fish and Wildlife." The only thing the feds could muster about the salmon was this: "On West Coast streams, water-control structures usually impose serious barriers to the migration of anadromous fish. While drastic adverse effects are possible, improvement over existing conditions is also possible." In their green-covered book, the WPA writers were never more credulous than when discussing the fish. "The damage done by past floods to fish, game and livestock has been tremendous," they noted. "But when the Central Valley Project is finished, these creatures, too, both wild and tamed, will be protected."

Where, Jack Fraser wondered, was that protection? In the spring of 1959, he learned that Stanley Mosk, California's new attorney general, had decided not to stand up to the big farmers and represent Fish and Game at the next state Water Rights Board hearing. Fraser, a tall, handsome man with a cleft in his chin, angrily strode across the street to the capitol building and wrangled ten thousand dollars out of state budget keepers to hire legal counsel. Then he strode across the street in the other direction to the law offices of Wilmer Morse, a former deputy attorney general. Morse knew next to nothing about salmon runs or river pulses, but he seemed keen to take on the feds and the big shots of agriculture known as the "water buffaloes." Fraser spent weeks coaching Morse on all the relevant issues. The Reclamation Bureau, without question, was violating Section 5937 of the Fish and Game code: "The owner of any dam shall allow sufficient water at all times to pass . . . over, around or through the dam to keep in good condition any fish that may be planted or exist below the dam." The remedy Fish and Game was seeking would hardly pain the growers. To restore the river's "vital thread" and give the salmon a path to spawn, the Reclamation Bureau needed only to release 77,146 acre-feet of water from Friant Dam at the right time. This was a pittance compared to what the bureau was diverting to distant farms each year.

Fraser held a final strategy session with Morse and then drove down to Fresno to attend the hearing in front of the state Water Rights Board. Morse did a fine job of presenting all the arguments, but there were thirty-two other attorneys in the room, including those representing twenty-five irrigation districts, three canal companies, Miller & Lux, the Di Giorgio Fruit Corporation, the Kern County Land Company and the U.S. Department of the Interior. Fraser could see the deck was stacked against Fish and Game, but he also believed that Section 5937 allowed for no wiggle room. When the three men of the Water Rights Board announced their decision, it didn't sound right. "The Board concludes that to require the United States to bypass water down the channel of the San Joaquin River for the re-establishment of the salmon fishery at this time is not in the public interest."

Fraser walked out of the hearing room beet red with anger. What time, he fumed, would be right? Bill Kier, a young biologist at Fish and Game, saw Fraser pull his state-issued gray Studebaker into the parking garage at Tenth and O Streets in Sacramento late that afternoon. He was still seething. "I've never seen Jack so pissed off," Kier recalled. "He grabbed his briefcase from the car, and his papers flew all over the garage. Then he kicked shut the car door and starting cussing."

Fraser wasn't finished yet. In the name of the public interest, he and Morse decided to challenge the board's decision. They met for two weeks in Morse's office and hammered out an appeal on giant mimeographed sheets of paper. The day they were planning to drive to Fresno to file the action in court, Morse received a call from Governor Pat Brown's secretary. The governor had met with a group of farmers and federal bureaucrats, and now he was going to ask Fraser and Fish and Game to kindly drop the appeal. Morse knew that Brown wasn't likely to change his opinion. In fact, eight years before, when he was attorney general, Brown had blocked the state from upholding Section 5937.

Doomed or not, Morse insisted on a meeting with the governor. As Morse and others would recall, the conversation started out nice enough. Brown let Morse explain all the righteous reasons why the state of California needed to stand up for the fish, and then he spoke:

"I understand all that, Wilmer. But I can handle this. We don't want to litigate this. I can negotiate it."

Morse tried to explain that the lawsuit would only bring the feds and farmers to the negotiating table, but the governor cut him off.

"Here's the way it works, Wilmer. Fish and Game works for me, right? And you've been hired by Fish and Game, right?"

Wilmer nodded.

"Well, that means you work for me. And you're fired."

"Why?"

"Because I say so."

And that was the end of the San Joaquin River.

There was no Hatfield the Rainmaker to blame for the winter of 1955–56. The sky opened up in November, and so much snow accumulated in the Sierra that a warm snap in early December sent the melt pouring

Orange Cove farmers greet the first federal water pouring out of Friant-Kern Canal

down the mountain. And then, like that, California turned cold and rainy again. A mass of warm, moist air had sailed across the Pacific from Hawaii and crashed into a mass of cold air shooting down from Alaska. This was a Pineapple Express with a twist. The meteorologists had to go back to 1862 to find a deluge that was comparable. The Russian and Feather Rivers jumped their banks. The Trinity River bowled over a bridge and cut Highway 96 in two. On the Klamath River's floodplain, only rooftops could be seen peeking above the water. The people ran for the hills. Then the Douglas Memorial Bridge, their escape route, washed out. The levee at Gum Tree Bend, at the junction of the Yuba and Feather Rivers, ruptured and took the lives of thirty-eight people.

From the vantage of the air force rescue helicopters, the folly of living in Marysville suddenly hit home. Over the still-standing bridge that spanned the Feather River, in the dark of morning, ten thousand townsfolk evacuated in an hour and a quarter. A wall of mud along the Marin coast nearly wiped Bolinas off the map. Walnut Creek, the town, became Walnut Creek again. On the St. John's River, near the southern end of the San Joaquin Valley, the main levee ruptured. Three-quarters of Visalia sat underwater. By the time the rain stopped, in late January 1956, sixty-four Californians had perished in the Big Flood, and more than fifty thousand had been left homeless. Property damage topped $200 million. Hundreds of thousands of acres of farmland, bone-dry the year before, had reverted to inland sea.

As California wrung itself out, there was no loud call to clear the floodplains of houses and farms and give the rivers more room to breathe. In assessing the damage, state leaders could only see that Sacramento, as well as every other city that had built a dam on its river, had escaped serious hurt. Shasta Dam had trapped and held back more than one million acre-feet of runoff. The Folsom Dam, completed only months before, had prevented the state capital from drowning. The failure to dam the Feather River, a $400 million project stalled in the state legislature, had cost scores of lives and flooded 156 square miles of farmland. The path ahead seemed clear. Out of drought had risen the Central Valley Project. Out of flood would rise the State Water Project. A giant concrete aqueduct running along the west side of the valley, an idea first sketched on paper by Henry Miller and his gang, would become the state's newest river.

During his campaign for governor, Pat Brown had vowed to break the stalemate on the Feather River dam. He would build the aqueduct and send two million acre-feet of water down to Southern California and provide another million acre-feet to farms along the way. "Development of our water resources is crucial to every segment of our state—the ranchers in our mountain areas, the farmers who make California the nation's leading agricultural producer, and the homeowners in our population which will grow to 20 million by 1970," he said in his inaugural address. This sounded especially sweet to the cotton giants J. G. Boswell and Cockeye Salyer, who together owned practically the entire bottom of Tulare Lake. Salyer's son Fred, a crack pilot, had flown Brown and his bossy wife, Bernice, from farm spread to farm spread collecting campaign money—bags of it. In return, the cotton kings were looking for tens of thousands of acre-feet of state water to ease their pumping of the sinking ground around Corcoran.

Governor Brown cobbled together Democrats and Republicans in a coalition led by state senator Hugh Burns of Fresno and Assemblyman Carley Porter of Compton. They made sure to give every corner of the state a slice of pork from the $1.75 billion bond that would fund his State Water Project. Since the biggest share of water was destined for Southern California, support for the bond in Los Angeles, Orange County and San Diego was solid. The San Joaquin Valley, likewise, saw the new source of imported water as a chance to turn more Kern County desert into farmland. Across Sacramento and the delta, concerns about sending Feather River flows southward were calmed by the dam now being built. The 770-foot-high Oroville Dam, the tallest in America, would keep the Feather from ever flooding Northern California again. The Delta Protection Act of 1959, a pledge by the governor and the legislature to improve water quality in the delta, sweetened the deal. The governor tried to entice San Francisco and the northern coastal counties with $130 million in future water investments, but residents would have none of it. As far as they were concerned, the State Water Project was just another water grab by the southern part of the state.

The Burns-Porter Act showed up as Proposition 1 on the November 1960 ballot. Nearly six million Californians weighed in. By a margin of only 173,944 votes, funding for the State Water Project passed. The giant pumps of the state were built a short distance from the giant pumps of the feds. On the delta's southern edge, the feds and the state became partners and shared in the costs and operation of what was now known as the System. The 444-mile-long California Aqueduct, the "thin blue line" that protected California from its alter egos of drought and flood, carried water for both. In 1968, flows from the Feather River reached the new cotton fields of Kern County, ground that had been nothing but desert. Governor Brown had made certain that the state water came without acreage limits attached. Four years later, the swimming pools of Beverly Hills began to fill with the same water.

California would never be the same.

Part Four

CHILDREN OF THE DESERT (2016–2017)

Stewart Resnick's empire of sprawling orchards

Fourteen

KINGDOM OF WONDERFUL

It's the summer of 2016, eight weeks before the big nut shake, and I'm zigzagging through the almonds and pistachios of Lost Hills, square mile after square mile of immaculate orchards strung with micro-irrigation systems that spit in the face of drought. These are the trees that belong to Stewart Resnick, the richest farmer in America, who lives in Beverly Hills and calls his domain on this side of the mountain the Wonderful Company. I pull into an almond grove in the middle of nowhere and grab at branches heavy with nuts. Of all the wonders of Wonderful, this is the one I find most mystifying. The State Water Project that allowed western Kern County to grow into a farming behemoth has bequeathed no water or very little water over the past three years. If this were any other part of Kern, the farmers would be reaching deep into the earth to make up the difference. But western Kern has no groundwater from which to draw. The aquifer either doesn't exist or is so befouled by salts that the water is poison. As a consequence, the farmland here, nearly one hundred thousand acres planted in permanent crops, is completely reliant on the government's supply of mountain water. This is gambler's ground unlike any other in California, and as I drive from hill to dale, examining each orchard, my head spins. *How can this be? No rain in five years. State water dwindling year after year. No water in the ground to make up for the missing government supply. So why hasn't this place gone to tumbleweeds? How can another record crop be sitting pretty on these trees?*

I do all the calculations from the numbers I am able to gather, and I cannot figure out how these nuts are getting enough water. There is the Kern Water Bank, the underground lake Resnick controls. In years of plentiful rains and heavy snowmelt, it fills up with more than one million acre-feet of stored water. But most of this banked water has been spent by Resnick and other account holders in years two, three and four of the drought. Whatever remains is not nearly enough to make up for the shortfall of imported water from the state.

Then I get lucky. I come upon a Wonderful field man in a white four-by-four truck who listens to my bewilderment and takes pity. As he drives off, he throws a clue out the window. Turn onto Twisselman Road off I-5 and continue west until it intersects with the California Aqueduct. There, he tells me, in the shadow of the state's great concrete artery moving snowmelt north to south, I will find a private, off-the-books pipeline that Stewart Resnick has built to keep his trees from dying. The water is being taken from unsuspecting farmers in an irrigation district in Tulare County, more than forty miles away.

No stranger enters this zone unless it's to get rid of a body or dump waste from cooking meth or drown a hot car. Its vastness makes you feel safe and in jeopardy at the same time. I head straight into the glare of the sun shooting over the Coast Ranges. Through the haze I can see the knoll of the aqueduct come closer. Ever since I was a kid I have felt its pull, a gravitational presence on the land and in my own story. On a fog-drip night in January 1972, two men wearing gloves walked into my father's empty bar and shot him to death. They dumped their stolen car and a thirty-eight-caliber revolver into the canal's black water and got away with murder for the next thirty-two years. In a valley of dead rivers, each one killed on behalf of agriculture, the aqueduct was the one river that was still alive. Its artificiality had achieved a permanence; its permanence had created my California.

I pull over into the dirt of a pomegranate orchard, the ancient fruit the Resnicks have turned into Pom Wonderful, the sweet purple juice inside a swell-upon-swell bottle. The shiny red orbs, a few months shy of harvest, pop out from the bright green leaves like bulbs on a Christmas tree. I study the terrain. This must be the spot the Wonderful field man was describing. Sure enough, cozied up next to the bank of the aqueduct, I catch a glint. I get out of the car and walk down a small embankment. There before me, two aluminum pipes, side by side, twelve inches in diameter each, slither in the sun. Where gravity needs a boost, the pipes run atop wooden crates used to pack boxes of fruit. Where the pipes butt up against Twisselman Road, a more clever bit of engineering is required. Here, a crew of men have dug a culvert beneath the road and hiked the pipeline under the asphalt that divides one field from another. Here, private water from Tulare County and Kings County jumps to Kern County, but government jurisdictions don't count. On one side of the road and the other, for miles in both directions, the dirt belongs to Wonderful. I stand over the pipes and give them a hard slap. They slap back with the cold vibration of water. Where is it coming from? Who is it going to?

In years of plenty, 200 million acre-feet of rain and snowmelt grace California. This blessing is not long-lived. Almost at once, 65 percent of it evaporates or is drunk by natural vegetation. Of the 71 million acre-feet that remain, 40 percent goes to agriculture, 50 percent goes to wild rivers and the sea and 10 percent goes to urban uses. As far as human needs are concerned, in other words, the farm uses 80 percent of California's harvested water while the city uses 20 percent. To understand what this means from the ground where I am standing, consider this: Of the 30 million acre-feet of water siphoned from rivers and aquifers by agriculture each year, almost 60 percent goes to the farmers of the San Joaquin Valley. How they managed to bend the water toward them is one story tolerably told. What they have chosen to do with that water—the miracles and less-than-miracles involving the bending of crop, human, bee, machine and chemical—is where I am headed now.

Like the old barons of wheat, Stewart Resnick isn't of this place. He's never driven a tractor or cranked open an irrigation valve. He's never put his foot on the shoulder of a shovel and dug down into the soil. He wouldn't know one of his Valencia orange groves from one of his Washington navel orange groves. The land to him isn't real. It's an economy of scale on a scale no one's ever tried. He grew up in New Jersey, where his father ran a bar. He came to California in the 1950s to remake himself. Welcome to the club. He remade himself into a graduate of UCLA law school, a cleaner of Los Angeles buildings, a vendor of security alarms, a seller of flowers in a pot, a minter of Elvis plates and Princess Diana dolls, a bottler of Fiji Island water, a farmer of San Joaquin Valley dirt. He purchased his first 640-acre section in the late 1970s and kept adding more sections until he stretched the lines of agriculture like no Californian before him.

At age eighty-one, he's gotten so big he doesn't know how big. He's the single biggest grower of almonds, pistachios, pomegranates and citrus in the world. Last time he checked, he owned 180,000 acres in California. That's 281 square miles, almost the size of the five boroughs that make up New York City. He is irrigating 121,000 of these acres. This doesn't count the 21,000 acres of grapefruits and limes he's growing in Texas and Mexico. He uses more water than any other person in the West. His 15 million trees in the San Joaquin Valley consume more than 400,000 acre-feet of water a year. The city of Los Angeles, by comparison, four million human beings, consumes 587,000 acre-feet.

Resnick's billions rely on his ability to master water, sun, soil and even bees. When he first planted seedless mandarins in the valley in 2000, the bees from the citrus orchards around him were flying into his groves, pollinating his flowers and putting seeds into the flesh of his fruit. He told his neighbors to alter the flight of the bees or he'd sue them for trespassing. The farmers responded that the path of a bee wasn't something they could very well supervise, and they threatened to sue him back. The dispute over the "no-fly zone" was finally resolved by the invention of a netting that sheathes Resnick's mandarins each spring. The plastic furls across the grove like a giant roll of Saran Wrap. No bee can penetrate the shield, and his mandarins remain seedless.

The control Resnick exercises inside his $4.5 billion privately held company does relinquish to one person: his wife, Lynda, vice chairman and co-owner, the "Pomegranate princess," as she calls herself. She is the brander of the empire, the final word on their Super Bowl ads, the creator of product marketing. There's "Cheat Death" for their antioxidant-rich pomegranate juice and "Get Crackin'" for their pistachios and "Untouched by Man" for their Fiji water. A husband and wife sharing the reins is rare for corporate America, rarer still for industrial agriculture. He commands his realm, and she commands hers, and he takes care to mind the line. "If he sticks even a toe onto her turf," says a former business partner, "she gives him a look that sends him right back."

Together, the Resnicks have wedded the valley's hidebound farming culture with L.A.'s celebrity culture. They don't do agribusiness. Rather, they say, they're "harvesting health and happiness around the world through our iconic consumer brands." Their crops aren't crops but heart-healthy snacks and life-extending elixirs. He refers to his

Stewart and Lynda Resnick, California's richest farmers

occasional trek between Beverly Hills and Lost Hills—roughly 140 miles—as a "carpetbagger's distance." It seems even longer, he says, if you add in the psychological distance of being an East Coast Jew in a California farm belt where Jews are few and far between. Lynda is making the trip on the company jet more often these days. She's mostly done giving big gifts to Los Angeles museums and mental health hospitals that name buildings after her and Stewart. The south valley, its people and poverty, its obesity and diabetes, is her latest mission.

In Lost Hills, they call her "Lady Lynda." She shows up in designer fashion and stands in the dust and tells them about another charter school or affordable housing project she is bringing to them. They have no way to grasp the $50 million to $80 million a year that the Resnicks say they are spending on philanthropy. This is a magnitude of intervention that no other agricultural company in California has ever attempted. The giving goes to college scholarships and tutors. It goes to doctors and nurses, trainers and dieticians, who track the fatness of the workers, exhort them to exercise and wean them off soda and tortillas. As she announces the newest gift, the men and women in the back of the crowd smile and applaud politely and try not to show their faces to the publicity crew she has brought with her to film the events. Many are here without documents, after all.

Seventy-five years ago, in his seminal but tendentious *Factories in the*

Field, Carey McWilliams lambasted the "ribboned Dukes" and "belted Barons" of California agriculture. If he were on the scene today, he'd have to add the "sashed Queen" to the list. Empire. Fiefdom. Feudal. Principality. Measuring the reach of the Resnicks, it's tempting to lean on the hyperventilated language of the 1930s, when strikes by farmworkers here were met with murder by farmers, and communism, or at least socialism, had a chance in these fields. Today, most everything in this desolate reach of Kern County, save for the oil wells, belongs to Paramount Farming, which belongs to the Resnicks. But Paramount isn't Paramount anymore. Lynda believed there was a way to capture what they were doing that reached beyond "paramount." No one inside the company, and certainly not Stewart, questioned her genius for branding. This was the same Lynda, after all, who once contemplated a bowl of those juicy little seedless mandarins picked fresh from their fields and on the spot named them Cuties. So she searched and searched until she found it staring right back at her in one of their pomegranate orchards—a variety known as Wonderful. By decree of Lynda, the whole kingdom is now Wonderful.

Water is what took me to Stewart Resnick in the winter of 2003. I had just finished writing *The King of California* only to find out that on the other side of Tulare Lake, without a peep, Resnick had captured the Kern Water Bank and planted millions of nut trees. After my story in the *Times* about his control of the bank, I waited five years before placing another call to his corporate headquarters on the Westside of Los Angeles. It was the early spring of 2008, and this time his secretary didn't hang up on me. I had in mind a magazine profile on Stewart, the nut king. "Why not send an e-mail to him?" she suggested. A few weeks later, I found myself riding up the elevator of a high-rise on Olympic Boulevard.

He sat behind a desk without clutter and stood up to shake my hand. He was a small, trim man, no more than five foot five, in his early seventies with thinning silver hair and brown eyes rimmed in pink. The speech of his parents and grandparents, the Yiddish-inflected New Yorkese, with its humors and cut-to-the-quick impatiences, had not left his own speech in the half century since he'd come to California. He was dressed in Levi 501s, a plain long-sleeved shirt and basic hiking boots. Arrayed before him were small bowls of almonds, pistachios and easy-to-peel mandarins, a plate of ground white turkey meat cooked in olive oil and a glass of pomegranate juice. Everything but the turkey had come from his orchards. He was fighting prostate cancer and had no doubt that the juice was keeping his PSA counts low. Even if he were inclined to wind down, he said, he had no successor in mind. None of his three children had shown the slightest interest in taking over the company. Still, he was starting to think about his legacy, and that was why he had finally agreed to meet with me.

"I've never given an interview to a newspaper or magazine before," he informed me. "I've told them all no. When you're making the kind of money we're making, what's the upside? I'd rather be unknown than known." He had recently read my book about J. G. Boswell and that got him thinking. "I'm not going to live forever, even with the massive amounts of pomegranate juice I'm drinking. It might be nice if my kids and grandkids could turn to a book someday and read about what we've built."

He and Lynda were changing the way food was grown in California and sold to the world. If they were farmers, they were farmers who hung out with Tom Hanks, Steve Martin, David Geffen, Warren Beatty and Joan Didion. They had donated $15 million to found UCLA's Stewart and Lynda Resnick Neuropsychiatric Hospital and more than $25 million to the Los Angeles County Museum of Art to build a pavilion in their name. Unlike many other billionaires, they could poke fun at themselves. During the holiday season, they sent out four thousand gift boxes to their "nearest and dearest friends," and each box was filled with fruits and nuts they had grown, along with a card showing the two of them dressed in skin-colored body stockings, posing as Adam and Eve. "If only Eve had offered Adam a pomegranate instead of an apple," Lynda wrote, "every day could have been a holiday."

The Resnick story certainly deserved a book, but did he really want me to be the one to write it? Boswell had tried to rip apart a copy of *The King of California* put in front of him by a secretary who only wanted his autograph.

"Why don't we start with an interview or two?" I said. "You might enjoy it. You might not."

"How about we meet again in two weeks?"

"Sure. Right back here?"

"No. Let's do it at my house."

The front gates of the twenty-five-thousand-square-foot Beaux Arts mansion on Sunset Boulevard opened magically without a guard having to give a nod. I exited my car and approached the entrance with its fourteen-foot columns and wrought-iron balustrades. Perched up there, a queen might peek out and utter, "Let them eat cake," Lynda once remarked. When the mansion was built, in 1927, it was known to Los Angeles as the Sunset House. I was prepared to knock on the door, but a Chinese housekeeper, flanked by two blow-dried dogs, greeted me on the front steps and led me inside. I tried not to stare at the gold that was everywhere: heavy-legged gold furniture, paintings in thick gold frames, gold-leaf carpet and gold-fringed drapes. From the vaulted ceilings with gold-leaf moldings hung two blown-glass chandeliers. The curtains were made of a fabric woven in Venice and substantial enough that they might finish off a person who happened to be looking out the window in the throes of an earthquake.

It was an awfully big place for two little people. Even the marble statue of Napoleon was seven feet tall. Except for the housekeeper, who guided me to the parlor, the hired help seemed to be missing. The staff included a majordomo of the house, a butler, a chef, a sous-chef, three housekeepers and a trio of assistants who worked in the basement, managing Lynda's calendar and the buying, wrapping and shipping of the gifts she handed out to her Rolodex of "highfalutin people." Stewart had made it clear that Lynda wouldn't be joining us. She had her own book—about her genius as a marketer—going. I imagined her getting ready in one of the upstairs bedrooms, teasing her poodle hair and putting on her stiletto heels, making her burly Israeli driver wait beside the stretch limo. Stewart had spent the morning on his exercise bike reading *Fortune*. Fresh from a shower, a red Kabbalah string tied around one wrist and a pair of multihued socks covering his feet, he welcomed me. If he had his druthers, he said, he'd still be living in a little ranch house in Culver City. "None of this is my idea. This is my wife. This is Lynda."

Where do you begin with a man of great riches if not the distant places you might have in common? And so I began with oppression, dispossession, slaughter and madness and then moved on to bartenders for fathers.

His grandfather Resnick had fled the Ukraine in the wake of another killing of Jews by Cossacks. The bells in the churches pealed, and out came the villagers with their scythes and axes, believing they had found the reason for their poverty. It was the early 1900s, and his grandfather and grandmother decided to secure passage to America. His father was three years old at the time. They settled in Brooklyn among Jews who had fled their own pogroms, and his grandfather went into the needle-and-embroidery trade. His father met his mother, the cantor's daughter, and they married. When the Depression struck, his parents and two other Jewish families left Brooklyn and migrated to Middlebush, New Jersey, where they bought a few trucks and peddled coffee and pots and pans. Stewart was the second of four children, the only son. "I sort of remember growing up on a farm," he said. "But we weren't there long." They moved to Highland Park, a borough along the Raritan River near the home of Johnson & Johnson and close enough to Rutgers University to hear the fans screaming at Neilson Field. Manhattan was thirty minutes in one direction, the Jersey Shore thirty minutes in the other. The borough measured no more than two square miles. It wouldn't even make a couple sections of his almonds.

His father bought a neighborhood bar and ran it with the same iron fist he ran the household. He was short, bull-like, and didn't take crap off anyone. "He was about my size, but he was very tough. He was a big drinker, a big liver who loved the fast life. His bar was a place for guys. Middle-class guys. Damon Runyon–type guys. I never saw an attractive girl in there."

Stewart's childhood pals were all Jewish kids from upper-class families, so it wasn't easy being the poorest one, the one whose father was a gambler and capable at any moment of losing the few comforts they had. He came home from school one day and discovered the family car gone. His father had lost it in a bet. "He was tough on the outside. But inside he had these weaknesses. Compulsive gambler and alcoholic. And then he'd lose his temper and get the strap out."

Like many billionaires, he didn't have a decent explanation for his fortune. Because he hadn't done it with Daddy's money or what he considered a superior brain, he attributed his wealth to luck and a simple lesson he had learned early in life. He was thirteen years old and standing inside the Rutgers Pharmacy on the first day of his first job. The boss showed him a storeroom filled with chemicals tossed here and there and told him to bring order to the mess. He didn't know where to begin. He studied the situation. The stacks of bottles gave him no answer. The boss came back in, saw him doing nothing and said only three words: "Just get started." He began to move, and the job went quickly after that. Digging in was its own wisdom, he discovered. Order finds itself through action. "Just get started" became one of his guiding principles.

At Highland Park High, he excelled in math and struggled in English. Upon graduation, he needed only to look across the river to find his college. The idea was to enroll at Rutgers and study to become a doctor. He was a year into his classes when his uncle Lou Resnick called from California. He had moved out to Long Beach, bought some property and built one of those new strip malls. The money was too easy. His dad had sold the bar and was adrift. Why not California? Once his parents decided to go, he decided to go, too. He left in 1956. "I never liked New Jersey, but I never knew why. California showed me why."

The making of a billionaire over the next half century was a series of dots that connected in the California sunshine. It was linear, logical, fluid and quite nearly destined.

He enrolled at UCLA and joined a Jewish fraternity. One of his frat brothers was a wealthy kid whose father ran a janitorial business. He had an industrial machine, hardly used, that scrubbed and waxed floors. Resnick dipped into his savings from his job at a mental hospital and went in half on the machine. "After school and on weekends, we'd clean and wax floors. It took time for the wax to dry. So in that time, we started cleaning windows, too." They named the business Clean Time Building Maintenance. The slogan on their business cards read, "When it's time to clean, it's Clean Time." His frat brother got bored, as rich boys do, and Resnick bought out his half interest for $300. He started cleaning pizza parlors and drugstores. Business got so brisk that he bought two trucks and hired crews. He changed the name to White Glove. By the time he graduated from UCLA, in 1960, and entered its law school, he was bringing home $40,000 a year—the equivalent of $320,000 today.

At the buildings he was cleaning, he noticed that no one was watching the front and back doors. With that insight, he sold White Glove for $2.5 million and went into the security guard business. He was protecting the same buildings he'd been cleaning only a month before. It then dawned on him that guards were fine but they had to be paid an hourly wage. Burglar alarms, on the other hand, offered round-the-clock vigilance without coffee breaks. He went out and bought a large alarm company. That company led to another company, and he soon owned half the commercial alarm accounts in Los Angeles.

His first wife, the mother of his two sons and a daughter, was quite happy living in their $30,000 condo in Culver City. Month after month, she made ends meet on a $1,600 budget. "She was a very frugal lady. She wanted me to put our five million dollars in an account, draw interest and we could live happily on the fifty grand a year." She didn't understand his drive. He was going to Vegas, hanging out with his own Damon Runyon characters and making plans to get even bigger. He packed his bags and moved out of the house. He was too young for a midlife crisis. He did little, if any, catting around, he said. Then one day after his divorce, he was trying to find a marketing person and got a call from Lynda Sinay, who worked in advertising. She was in her late twenties, seven years younger than he was, and the mother of two children. She had recently divorced and wasn't about to settle for a life in Culver City.

She was the daughter of Jack Harris, a film distributor who had moved the family from Philadelphia to Los Angeles, when Lynda was fifteen, to produce movies. One of his films, *The Blob,* became a cult classic, and they lived in a fancy house on the Westside with two Rolls-Royces in the garage. By age nineteen, Lynda had dropped out of college, married a magazine adman and opened her own advertising agency. She wasn't content to pursue the usual list of wealthy businessmen as clients. She was aiming to surround herself with famous actors and artists and public intellectuals.

The courtship of Stewart and Lynda went fast. They both knew what they wanted. They married in 1972, and he sold the alarm company for $100 million. He then heard from his doctor that the owner of Teleflora, the giant flower-delivery company, was looking to sell. He felt at ease in the customer-service industry, and so did Lynda. He paid a buyer's price, and husband and wife went into the floral business together. It was Lynda who came up with the idea of a "flower in a gift." Roses are short-lived, she reasoned, but the teapot that the flowers arrive in is a keepsake. The concept changed the industry, and she won a gold Effie, advertising's Oscar.

In the late 1970s, he went looking for a hedge against inflation. His accountant suggested that he buy apartments. He could collect the rents while he slept. But he wasn't looking for the monotony of steady. He was in the mood to gamble. Vacationing in the South of France, he heard about a farming company called Paramount that needed a buyer for its orchards in Kern County. "They were selling twenty-five hundred acres of oranges and lemons and a packinghouse for a third of their appraised value," he said. "It was simply a place to park some money and have another opportunity." He drove to Delano, the farm town where Chavez had made so much trouble for growers and history for workers. By the time he drove back, he was a citrus grower. "I think I paid nine million dollars," he recalled. "Look it, I'm from Beverly Hills. I didn't know good land from bad land. But I had some good people helping me."

In 1984, he and Lynda decided to buy the Franklin Mint, hawker of commemorative coins and other kitsch, for $167.5 million. They knew little about the company except that it was peddling keepsakes for five times the profit Teleflora was. Shoving aside the coins, they introduced a Scarlett O'Hara doll that, all by itself, raked in $35 million. They were pushing plates, costume jewelry, perfume and model cars. They issued a commemorative medal of Tiger Woods winning the 1997 Masters that offended the golfer. He called it fake junk, sued and won. Lynda spent $150,000 at an auction to buy the actual beaded gown and matching bolero jacket, "the Elvis dress," that Princess Diana had worn on a visit to Hong Kong. The designers at the Mint crafted a porcelain doll with a tiny replica outfit so precise that it was hand-beaded with two thousand fake pearls. "Just $195," the ad in the back of *Parade* magazine read. "Payable in convenient monthly installments." It was a big hit. Annual sales at the Mint jumped to nearly $1 billion.

Bankers and their fair-weather financing exasperated Stewart. He hired Bert Steir, a Bostonian with a Bronze Star from the Second World War and a degree from Harvard, to come west and work his deals. Oil companies in Kern were looking to unload their farms, Steir learned, chunks of earth that measured twenty thousand and forty thousand acres. Mobil and Texaco were practically willing to give the ground and its orchards away. This was how Stewart became a pistachio and almond grower. In 1987, he paid Prudential Life Insurance $30 million for eighteen thousand acres in Kings County that included a quarter section, or 160 acres, of pomegranates. Sitting in his mansion in 2008, he already owned more than one hundred thousand acres of irrigated orchards across five counties. His trees were drinking from the Central Valley Project and the State Water Project, from rivers and irrigation canals and the Kern Water Bank. "My life is about California. I didn't grow up here, but if it wasn't for California, its openness and opportunities, I wouldn't be sitting where I'm sitting."

No other farmer, not even the winemaking Gallos, had cornered a market the way Resnick had cornered the growing, buying, processing and selling of pistachios. He had his hands on 65 percent of the nation's crop. One of the first things he did with his monopoly was kill the California Pistachio Commission, the industry's cooperative marketing group. He yanked his funding because he and Lynda wanted to create their own ads for their own brand. The independent growers and processors—no surprise—regarded him as a bully eager to employ teams of lawyers and tens of millions of dollars to force his agenda. When a rival grower tried to lure away one of his top men with a better offer, Resnick didn't see it as business. He saw it as a personal challenge. It didn't matter if the rival was a foot taller and a hundred pounds heavier. He'd march right up and tell him to F-off.

One member of the pistachio commission, on the eve of its demise, told me, "Stewart wants to be the benevolent dictator. But if he thinks you're defying him, he'll start with 'Nobody realizes the good I've done for agriculture.' Then he moves on to 'Do you know who I am? Do you know what I am? I'm a billionaire.' He's got an awful temper he's trying to control through Kabbalah. That little red string is supposed to remind him to count to ten. But his ego, there's no controlling that."

Resnick had heard it all before. He was the bad guy in agriculture for no bigger offense than he was big. "Look, these farmers go back two, three and four generations. Me, I'm a carpetbagger from Beverly Hills. But you ask the growers we process, and they'll tell you that year in and year out, no one offers a better price. No one pushes their product harder." It was this persistence and, above all, good timing, that

The Wonderful Company landing strip in the middle of western Kern orchards

explained his bigness. "While I'd like to take all the credit, I'd have to say that fully half of my success has been luck. Now in farming we're in a unique position. The crops we grow can only be grown in a few places in the world. But none of it would have happened without luck."

Luck didn't explain what he and Lynda had done with the wretched pomegranate. They took their original 160 acres and added 640 more acres—half the pomegranates in the country at the time—even though there was zero market. Instead of trying to sell the fruit as a piece of fruit, they squeezed its seeds into Pom Wonderful. Lest anyone doubt the health benefits of the juice, they spent more than $30 million in research to prove that it fought heart disease and prostate woes. Antioxidants that delivered thirty-two grams of sugar in each eight-ounce serving didn't come cheap: eleven dollars a bottle. Lynda mailed the first batches of Pom, week after week, as gifts to David Bowie, Rupert Murdoch and Disney head Michael Eisner. On Oscar night, she handed out free samples to the stars at the *Vanity Fair* party. "Of course I know everyone in the world," she told one reporter. "Every mogul, every movie star. You have no idea the people on my VIP list who drink it.

But that doesn't make people buy a second bottle. They do that because they love it."

A Pom craze followed. Stewart and Lynda planted fifteen thousand more acres and built a new juice plant. "Who would have thought that people would be asking their bartender to fix them a Pomtini?" he said. All of this was Lynda's doing. There she stood in the foreground of the photo that accompanied a *New Yorker* profile titled "Pomegranate Princess." She was wearing a black pants suit with open-toed silver pumps and a single piece of jewelry around her neck. Her short auburn hair was fixed up big, and her thin eyebrows arched high. In the distant background, under the gaze of a ten-foot-tall marble goddess, sat Stewart in a gold-skirted chair, head down. "She wanted to tell the story of the pomegranate," he told me with a touch of sarcasm. "For a long time, she got no credit. Now she's getting lots of credit."

I returned for two more sessions, and then he and Lynda took off to their $15 million vacation house in Aspen, where they were warring with the locals over a housing project for community workers that was blocking their view. By the time they returned to Beverly Hills, he had lost interest in a book about his life, at least one that I might write. I held on to my notes and tapes and waited for another day.

Lost Hills sits on an upslope. This is the closest to hills it comes. Main Street is Highway 46, which slices through the middle of town. At the east end, where the highway meets Interstate 5, the traveler gets a choice: Days Inn or Motel 6. Carl's Jr., Subway, McDonald's, Wendy's, Love's or Arby's. None of the sales taxes go to city hall because Lost Hills isn't a city. It's known as a census-designated place, a fancy way of saying that Kern County has every reason to neglect it. Highway 46 shoots past Resnick almonds and takes you straight into town, population 1,938. The tumbleweeds on open ground give you a peek into what Lost Hills looked like before the aqueduct made a river here.

A sign pokes out of the tumbleweeds. "IS GROWING FOOD A WASTE OF WATER?" it asks. The question is a rejoinder to a budding movement in San Francisco and Los Angeles that seeks to decide which crops deserve water and which crops do not. Almonds, at least for the moment, stand in the bull's-eye of this movement. It takes one gallon of water to grow a single almond, and because half the crop is being exported to other countries, we might conclude that we're exporting a good bit of our water, too. But what about the 106 gallons it takes to produce an ounce of steak or the 72 gallons it takes to grow an ounce of lentils? the almond growers shoot back. If we start treating water like carbon, will the vegan's footprint be any smaller than the carnivore's?

The July sun is a scorcher, and I fuss with the dial on the AC long enough to blow past the town's one stoplight and the aqueduct, too. I'm in another land, an expanse of hard, ugly, cratered-out earth the color of sand. Hundreds of giant praying mantises standing on platforms of concrete are pulling oil from a Chevron field. This is the west end of Lost Hills, the extraction end. The wind kicks up dirt from the reap of oil and almonds, and the dust cloud carries back into town, raining down on the elementary school first.

I park the car and walk in the direction of a scattering of buildings slapped together with stucco and corrugated tin. A meat store, an auto repair, a pool hall and arcade pass for a commercial strip. No one's out and about. They're either working in the heat or hiding from the heat or maybe dodging the white dude who looks like the heat. Three dogs, part pit bull, the menacing part, have given up on the shade and lie on the open road. Their tongues loll to their knees. A half block up, the buildings start to meet code. I walk into the town's one supermarket, El Toro Loco, the Crazy Bull, and ask the clerk for the owner. He directs me to the back office, where a tobacco-chewing Yemeni named Anthony Hussein is sitting beneath a photograph of an uncle in his U.S. Army uniform. The uncle died at age twenty-two fighting in Afghanistan, so he hardly seems like an uncle anymore. "Talk to me," Hussein says, draining a can of Rockstar, caffeine and electrolytes in one slug. "What do you need to know, sir?"

"What's it been like here during the drought?"

"Drought, no drought, makes no difference. The aqueduct was built with tax money, yes? The aqueduct brings the water, yes? So everybody should have it, right? But this is water for Mr. Resnick. Not the people. When it doesn't come, he finds a way to make it come." He spits tobacco juice into the empty can of Rockstar. "The checks the workers bring in here from Mr. Resnick are the same checks they bring in for years. I cash them the same. Nothing changes. Big fish eat the small fish here. . . . Anything else I can help you with?"

Hussein seems in a hurry. He guides me back into the main store, with its fine displays of fresh fruit and vegetables, meats, cold cuts and baked goods. The shelves spill piñatas, gloves, hats, pruning shears and loaves of white Bimbo bread. The wall of Pacifico and sixteen-ounce cans of Bud is rebuilt daily. Vicente Fernández, the legend of ranchera music, croons to no one, but it won't be this way in thirty minutes, Hussein tells me. Today is *quincena* day, the twice-a-month payday, and he needs me to scram because the workers coming in to cash their checks and wire 25 percent back across the border to their families in Guanajuato and Guerrero will wonder if I'm with Immigration and Customs Enforcement. If that happens, they'll go down the highway and he'll lose the $1 he takes for every $100 worth of their checks. "It's a bad day," he says, shooing me out. "You look like border patrol undercover."

I stand in a corner of the parking lot, out of view, and wait for the workday to end. At three o'clock, the Chevy trucks and Dodge vans pull up and out spill groups of four or five men under the sweat-stained hats of the 49ers, Penn State and the Yankees. Each face wears its own weary. The twenty-year-olds look like twenty-year-olds, the thirty-year-olds like forty-year-olds, the forty-year-olds like sixty-year-olds. Summer or not, they're dressed in shirt layered upon shirt and the same no-name dusty blue jeans. Or at least this is what I can see from afar.

To hell with Hussein. I pull out my notebook and pen and walk up to one of the vans. Inside sits a young man named Pablo. The oldest of five children, he tells me he came from Mexico when he was eighteen. He had no papers like the rest of them, just an image of what this side of the border looked like. He had heard there were fields upon fields, but he did not believe there could be this many fields. That was eight or nine years ago. He lives down the road in Wasco, the "rose capital of the nation," though the roses, too, have turned to nuts. He works year-round for Wonderful. This means he can avoid the thievery of a labor contractor who acts as a middleman between farmer and farmworker and charges for rides and drinks and doesn't always pay minimum wage. He prunes and irrigates the almond and pistachio trees and applies the chemicals that cannot be applied by helicopter. He makes $10.50 an hour, and the company provides him with a 401(k) plan and medical insurance.

It's a far cry from his village, and he's thankful to the Resnicks, especially Lady Lynda, for that. "I saw her a few months ago. She is here and there, but I have never seen her up close. She owns this place." He goes on to explain what he means by "owns." Most everything that can be touched in this corner of California belongs to Wonderful. Four thousand people—more than double the number on the highway sign—live in town, and three out of every four rely on a payday from Wonderful. All but a handful come from Mexico. In the Wonderful fields, at least 80 percent of the workers carry no documents or documents that are not real. U.S. immigration has little say-so here. Rather, it is the authority vested in Wonderful that counts. It was Lynda who teamed up with the USDA to develop twenty-one new single-family homes and sixty new townhouses on a few acres where Wonderful tore out some of its almond trees. The neighborhoods didn't have sidewalks; when it rained the kids had to walk to school in the mud. Lynda built sidewalks and storm drains, the new park and community center and repaved the roads. So the way Pablo uses "owns" isn't necessarily a pejorative. "When I crossed the border and found Lost Hills, there was nothing here," he says. "Now there's something here. We had gangs and murders, but that's better, too."

He has come to the Crazy Bull to cash his check and buy some beer. I follow him inside to a long line of workers that ends at a plastic window where Hussein sits on the other side, working the cash register like a teller at Pimlico. When it's Pablo's turn, he hands Hussein a check for $437 and Hussein counts out $433 back to him in cash. On the way out of the market, Pablo buys a case of Pacifico. Tonight, feeling no pain, he'll sit in one of the strip clubs in Bakersfield and maybe buy himself a fancy lap dance.

Across the street, the Soto family has built a new Mexican restaurant named Gabby's that dwarfs every other business in town with its Spanish mission facade. The Sotos made a name for themselves in Lost Hills by rolling their taco trucks into the agricultural fields. Angelica, one of four sisters, runs the restaurant. She tells me that her not-so-silent partner is Lady Lynda, who was so bothered that Lost Hills didn't have a sit-down restaurant of its own that she sought out Angelica. Lynda assisted her with the design and color scheme but otherwise remains hands-off: "She'll check in every so often to see how business is going. But she doesn't dictate this or that." Angelica would prefer not to divulge the details of their financial arrangement. It's been more than a year since the grand opening, and they're still operating in the red. So far,

Lynda has shown only patience. A restaurant built by Wonderful for the purpose of making the company town look better from curbside may enjoy a more forgiving bottom line than, say, the Subway up the road. But that doesn't mean that most people in town can afford to eat here. "We're still trying to figure out who our typical customer is going to be," Angelica says. For now, she's playing country-and-western music on the sound system and trying to lure a combination of local oil field and government workers, supervisors at Wonderful and motorists retracing James Dean's last miles.

I leave Gabby's and follow a winding concrete path through the new Wonderful Park. The grass is green on the verge of blue, and the cutouts for trees are razor-etched, and the mulch is so fresh it smells of microbial lust. A park, by most designs, is an estrangement from place, but these five acres are so flawless and at odds with the town that the whole thing feels like a movie set. Even the community water tank is painted baby blue with a big sunflower. "YOU HAVE FOUND LOST HILLS!!" it says. On the north end sits the Wonderful Soccer Field, with its all-weather track, stadium lights, artificial turf and giant yellow sunburst embossed at midfield. On the south end stands the Wonderful Community Center, where residents are urged to attend thrice-weekly Zumba and core-training sessions, healthy cooking classes taught by the Wonderful chef and weekend cultural outings featuring the likes of "America's Premier Latino Dance Company."

This is a lot of gestures to unpack, and as I exit the grounds, I keep turning around to get one last look that's true. I don't know how Milton Hershey did his Hershey, Pennsylvania, but Lynda is present in every painted sunburst, every planted flower, every blade of grass. The believer and the skeptic do their usual tussle inside my head. This is a park for the people, to give them a break from their hard lives. Lost Hills finally has something to be proud about. This is an offering of cake handed down from king and queen to serfs. It is one more way to extend the brand. Even Wonderful Park is lettered with the same heart-shaped "O" that stamps a bottle of Pom.

The compass in my car says I'm headed east, but that means almost nothing inside a province of fifteen million trees. Each square-mile section is divided into blocks, and each block counts a precise number of rows. When a farmer's orchards encompass 186 square miles, as they do in Wonderful, finding the field man can be a challenge. Section, block and row don't compute; he has to direct me to his location by cell phone and guideposts. My dust cloud tells him I'm getting close.

He turns out to be a kindly, religious man whose hair is shorn tight and dyed shoe-polish black. I ask him about his delivery of services—pruning, pesticides, herbicides, fertilizer, water—that are calibrated and timed to enable the smallest unit, each single almond tree, to achieve maximum yield. Surely, I imagine, no one does this better than Wonderful? He explains that Wonderful has grown too big to hassle such precision. Let the smaller grower walk among his trees and farm by the row. Fussing with one input or another, such a farmer can produce four thousand pounds of nuts an acre. Wonderful, by contrast, shoots for the middle. The scale of production—and the ability to process, market and sell its own crops—allows Wonderful to be mostly mediocre in the fields and still highly profitable. No one's going to get fired for bringing home twenty-five hundred pounds of nuts an acre. "These almond and pistachio trees are pruned by a machine that hedges one side and then the other," he says. "But the smaller farmer still uses a pruning shears on his pistachio trees to make his most important cuts. If he knows what he's doing, the shears can make a thousand more pounds an acre."

It's the beginning of September, and battalions of heavy machinery dispatched from the Wonderful equipment yards pound the ground and rattle the trees. No picking of crop agitates the earth like the picking of nuts. A plume of dust joins up with other plumes of dust until the sky over the valley turns sickly. By the eighth day of harvest, the sun is gone. Not so long ago, we timed our sinus infections by the immense cloud of defoliants sprayed over the cotton fields at the end of Indian summer. Now it's the seven-week nut harvest that brings out the inhalers. All this stirring up, a consequence of mechanization, makes one wonder about the merry road of robots ahead. Because a human picker isn't needed in the almond and pistachio groves, the nut harvest doesn't spread around money the way it spreads around dust. Wages that once went to pickers now stay in the pockets of nut growers. Maybe not since the wheat barons has the income disparity between farmer and farmworker been greater. Growers a tenth of the size of Resnick flee the dust in their Ferraris to their second homes in Carmel.

I follow one of the engines of harvest as it rolls into an orchard like a tank. Giant pincers manned by a single worker grab the tree by the throat and start shaking. For the next two or three seconds, the almonds pour down like hail. The vibration is a stunning piece of violence to behold. It moves in a wave from trunk to limb to nut and back down to earth. The jolt and shudder would tear at the roots of lesser species. When the rubber clamps let go of the trunk, eight thousand almonds—their green outer shells wilted and partly opened, the meat inside a wooden womb—lie scattered over the flat, dry earth. Somehow, thirty or forty nuts aren't compelled to drop. The man and his pincers can't be bothered. The rain of almonds moves on to the next tree. Once each tree has been shaken, the nuts are left on the ground for a few days to dry. They are then swept into piles by one machine and vacuumed up by another, each operation raising an even bigger cloud of dust. All told, nine men operating five machines will pick this orchard clean over the next four weeks. They'll take home $11 an hour for their labors. And how will the Resnicks fare? Each tree produces twenty-two pounds of nuts. Each pound sells wholesale for $3.75. That's $83 a tree. By harvest's end, the Resnicks will have fixed their clamps on 4.5 million almond trees. Nearly $370 million worth of Wonderful almonds will have dropped down from the dry sky.

In the city of trees, I find a paved road with speed bumps that takes me to the harvest of pistachios. The bunches of chartreuse-tipped nuts

The big almond shake, a harvest of nuts and dust

hanging from antler branches never touch ground. Two men sit inside separate cabins of a small tractor with pincers on one side and a catcher on the other. One man drives and shakes the tree while the other makes sure the clusters fall into the butterfly opening of the receiver. The vibration here isn't quite as vehement. As the nuts pour down onto the roof of the catcher, the operator shifts the trough so that it becomes a conveyer belt. The continuous rattle feeds the nuts into a series of bins on the back end of the tractor. There's no waiting around. Unlike the almond, the pistachio is moist and combustible. The nut must be hurried from bin to truck to processing plant to keep it from discoloring. "This is a big crop," the field man tells me. "Last year, we didn't get enough chilling hours in winter. We had so many blank nuts on the trees that some orchards weren't even worth picking. There was a shell but no meat inside. This year, plenty of meat."

All told, thirty-six men operating six machines will harvest the orchard in six days. Each tree produces thirty-eight pounds of nuts. Each pound sells wholesale for $4.25. The math works out to $162 a tree. The pistachio trees in Wonderful number six million plus. That's a billion-dollar crop.

The truck driver hits the wide open of Highway 33 and traces the serpentine of the aqueduct. He's headed to the Wonderful plant thirteen miles north of Lost Hills to drop off his load. He's carrying 55,000 pounds of crop in two swaggering trailers open to the sun. The load will translate into 18,000 pounds of finished kernels in a matter of days. Whether he realizes it or not, he's part of the biggest pistachio harvest in history. California growers, in the grip of this drought, have produced 900 million pounds of the green nut. That's more than double the crop Resnick boasted about when I visited him in his mansion eight years ago. Nearly a third of the harvest—nuts grown by Wonderful, nuts grown by hundreds of farmers who belong to the Wonderful brand—will pass through these gates.

The new plant, the size of seven Super Walmarts and built at a cost of $300 million, rises out of a clearing like some apparition. The eye numbed by the tedium of orchards isn't prepared for the 1.3 million square feet of industrial assault, though the palm trees and red, pink and white roses that line the perimeter try for a transition. This is where the pistachios, four hundred truckloads a day, fifty days of harvest, come to be weighed, washed, peeled, dried, gassed, sorted, salted, roasted, packaged and shipped out to the world.

No whistle shouts mealtime in the modern-day company town. The graders, sorters and beeping forklift drivers head to an immaculate café where the Wonderful Salad—roasted chicken, mixed greens, cilantro, pistachios and slices of mandarin dressed in a blue cheese vinaigrette—sells for three dollars. Lynda believes that if they're enticed in the right direction, the thirteen hundred workers at the plant might choose to prepare the same healthy fare at home. Sugar kills, she tells them. It takes a life every six seconds. And what spikes the blood with more sugar than a can of Coke? A flour tortilla. Eat a corn tortilla instead, she urges. She's built a grocery section in the back of the café stocked with grapeseed oil and "Whole Foods–quality vegetables and fruits that sell at Walmart prices," as Lynda likes to boast. Why grapeseed oil, I ask Andy Anzaldo, head of grower relations and a fitness buff, who's taken on the added duties of what might be called Wonderful's minister of health. "Research is showing that grapeseed oil is healthier than corn oil and canola oil, and may be better for you than olive oil," he says.

Five years ago, prodded by the Resnicks, Anzaldo and the company chef trashed the nacho chips, french fries and soft drinks. The workers didn't react well. That was when the Resnicks decided to sell the concept of wellness to their forty-three hundred employees throughout the valley the same way they had sold workplace safety. "We changed the culture of safety, and we think we can do the same with health," Anzaldo says. The Spanish rice isn't rice but cauliflower made to look like rice. The pizza dough is cauliflower, too. A worker can still order a hamburger, but it's half the size of the old hamburger and costs six dollars—twice what the wild salmon served with creamed leeks and raw asparagus salad costs. Whichever dish they choose, workers are asked not to take a bite until they have considered Lynda's latest concoction: an ounce of apple cider vinegar cut with ginger, mandarin juice and turmeric served in a small plastic cup like the wine of Mass.

Everything about our physical selves, Lynda believes, begins in our guts. To change the microbial life in our digestive tracts and reduce the inflammation that leads to disease, we have to reintroduce fermented foods into our diet. If the workers doubt the benefit of enzymes from apple cider vinegar, it won't be for long. The flat screens in the restaurant aren't tuned to the Mexican soccer leagues. Instead, video banners stream a continuous message of bad food habits to be broken and body mass indexes to be measured and met. "Rethink your drink" isn't just the latest slogan. It's a program with goals. Coke, Gatorade and Monster Energy are sky-high in sweeteners, but don't be fooled by that SunnyD, either. It's no better. Read the labels. "More than half our employees are obese or near obese," Anzaldo explains. "One out of eight has diabetes. You can't reverse diabetes, but you can control it with a blood sugar level between 6.5 and 8. That's our goal. To manage the disease. When we don't manage it, they end up with severe chronic health issues and amputated limbs."

Anzaldo is wired for solemn, though he does manage to smile once during lunch, when talking about the 1,150 workers who've earned bonuses of up to $500 for losing a collective 14,000 pounds in two years. That still leaves the majority of the workforce beyond his cajole. "You and I look at this meal—wild salmon and all these sides made from scratch: goat cheese, lavender, roasted beet, red onions, pistachios and lemon—and say, 'Wow. This is only three dollars? You can't get a meal like this anywhere for that cost.' But for a lot of workers, bringing that big fat burrito from home still makes sense."

I swallow the last morsel and put down my fork. I had seen what J. G. Boswell had done for the town of Corcoran to offset the ills of Big Ag. The hospital, senior citizens' center and football stadium all bore the signature of his giving. What the Resnicks were doing for Lost Hills, though, was a level of philanthropy I had never witnessed from an agricultural company in California. They were hardly the first rich people to use patronage to try to wheedle a citizenry toward their version of a better life. But this wasn't the Resnick Pavilion at the Los Angeles County Museum of Art. This was Lost Hills, where people were captive to the Resnicks, cradle to grave. "There's a lot to commend here," I tell Anzaldo and the PR duo that flanks him. "But is there a limit to social engineering for the common good? Where does persuasion end and coercion begin?"

As a second-generation Mexican-American, Anzaldo says he knows the powerful clench of fast food and soft drinks on his own family. At Wonderful, he says, "We are sensitive to that. We can't insist on wellness the way we can insist on plant safety. Being healthy is a choice. Have we gone too far? The feedback we're hearing is 'No.' In fact, some of the workers think that we haven't gone far enough."

In the maroon of sundown, I follow the workers back to Lost Hills. Their houses made from railroad boxcars have been painted purple, blue, yellow and gold. The colors turn brilliant in the light made spectacular by the particles of dust. Down a crumbled road, one hundred trailers with foundations dressed in plywood back up against an orchard. Even if they had wheels, they aren't going anywhere. The people here have traveled too far. Some of them have paid $12,000 to buy their trailers and spent thousands more to fix them up. The brick-hard ground can't be bought. They're paying $340 a month for its privilege. As farmworker colonies go, this one isn't too grim. There's no garbage piled high and smoldering, no chickens picking at scratch. The Sureños gang tagged the front entrance with spray paint but otherwise left the place unmarked. The junk scattered about could be a lot worse. It's the ditch up the road, the one that carries no water, that is filled with old mattresses and spent appliances. On dirt reserved for a playground, the swing set has no swings. Twine strung trailer to trailer hangs with the laundry of fathers, mothers and children. The space for secrets is only a few feet. Here and there a mulberry tree, its canopy pruned back, for it grows like a weed, breaks up the red-smeared sky.

A woman named Lupe stands above me on the wooden stairway that climbs to the front door of her trailer. She is small, with lively brown eyes and a sweet but confident voice. Her husband, Manuel, will awaken in thirty minutes to prepare for his night shift. Under lights, he sprays and irrigates the almonds. None of the adults, no matter how long they've lived here, speaks English. From the clerks at their markets to the *novelas* on their big screens, the world remains a Spanish-language one, and I must bring a translator with me. Lupe and Manuel, like many of the residents, grew up next to each other in a pueblo called San Antonio deep in the state of Guerrero, a mountainous region of dramatic beauty. They were married for only a short time when Manuel decided to cross the border almost twenty years ago. He worked as a gardener in Los Angeles and then heard about the almond trees on the other side of the mountain where the living was so much cheaper.

Farmworker dwelling in Lost Hills

He landed a steady job with a big grower and a year later paid a coyote $5,000 to bring Lupe and their baby son to Lost Hills.

She remembers handing the boy to her sister-in-law, who carried phony papers, and watching them cross by bridge into California. Because Lupe had no papers, she followed the coyote on foot for many more miles, until they reached a steep pass. Lucky for her that the young man was kind. Before he left her to cross alone, he gave her soda, water, chips and Cheetos. The baby is now a twenty-year-old student at Bakersfield College. Lupe also has two daughters, U.S. citizens, who are now eleven and six and will follow in the footsteps of their brother if she has her way. "We tell the children about the fields when they are young so they don't know the fields when they are old," she says.

More than a dozen family members have followed Lupe and Manuel to Lost Hills. One cousin who arrived a few years ago works in the nut harvest. So does another cousin who arrived only last week. Relatives arranged his passage, paying the coyote the new inflated rate of $12,000. A portion of his wages will be set aside each month to pay down the debt. "We send money home each month to our families left behind," Lupe says. "And then some of the money we save goes to pay the coyote. It takes a lot of work to get ahead."

She excuses herself to prepare dinner. The bowls on her kitchen table are filled with grapes, berries, bananas and red and green bell peppers. She washes two kinds of lettuce and cuts up fresh papaya to mix into a salad. I notice that she keeps the water running for a long time. I ask her if she is concerned about wasting water, given the drought and the distance the water has traveled—twenty miles from a well in Wasco—and that the cost goes up the more they use. Already, they are paying $69 a month to the local utility district. She tells me the water comes out of the tap yellow and foul-smelling, and she doesn't trust it. The family takes showers in it and she washes their laundry in it, and if she runs the water long enough, she will use it to wash her vegetables and cook her rice and potatoes. But she cannot remember the last time she or Manuel or their children drank it.

"It comes out like pee," says her eleven-year-old daughter.

"It tastes like blood," her friend chimes in.

The water is filtered for arsenic, boron and other salts, and the monthly tests show no violation of state or federal standards. "It may not be Fiji," I say, "but it won't kill you." She doesn't get the joke, and why should she? She's never heard of Wonderful Fiji, the water untouched by human hands. What she does know is that no one in her family, and none of her friends living in the trailer park or on the other side of town, drinks the local water that comes out of the pipe, either.

In the kitchen corner, cases of bottled water are stacked halfway up the wall. Crystal Geyser, Dasani, Springfield, six-packs, twelve-packs, twenty-four-packs. These are donations from other farmworker families, but they're not for her and Manuel and the kids. Her brother-in-law was killed recently in a car crash along Highway 46. He was headed to the fields at the same time that another farmworker, drunk on beer, was coming home from the fields. The sober man died. What to give a grieving widow and her five children in Lost Hills but drinking water?

In the trailer next door, Lupe's cousin Margarita lives with her husband, Selfo, and their three young children. They were farmers back in San Antonio, growing lettuce, cilantro and radishes on a small plot of land. Then the drug cartels took over the countryside and planted poppies. San Antonio became a place of heroin and terror. One day, gunmen mowed down residents with AK-47s and threw grenades at the church when it was filled with parishioners. "I saw horrible things," Margarita says. "My husband would have been shot dead like the others, but he was lucky. He had left for the cornfields a few minutes before the killings."

That was four years ago. They are still paying off the $27,000 debt to relatives who hired the coyote that brought them over. The relatives try not to press them, but the arrangement still feels to Selfo like a form of indentured servitude. He is short, stout and dark-skinned like Margarita, and his eyes are bloodshot. He works fifty hours a week as an irrigator and makes $10.75 an hour. This comes out to about $2,000 a month. The rent is $540. The food is more. The gas to and from the orchards costs him $80 a week. They spend $50 a month on bottled water. "There's not much left over," he says. "Our relatives have been patient." He worries because there isn't enough water now to properly irrigate the almonds, pistachios and pomegranates. He wonders what agriculture will look like in western Kern County in ten years.

"A bunch of trees are going dry," he says. "The land is turning to salt. In one orchard, half the trees are dying."

I had traveled the fields of Wonderful from one end of western Kern County to the other, looking for dying trees. But I hadn't seen any. "Because of a lack of water?" I ask. "The drought?"

"Yes. It's happening." The bosses won't speak of it, he says. If I want to know more, I need to talk to Lupe's brother, Gustavo, who has worked as an irrigator at Wonderful for five years and knows what the company is planning for the future.

Lupe and I walk to the far side of the trailer park to find Gustavo. A single man, he rents a bedroom from other family members for $150 a month. Lupe knocks on his door, and he invites us in. The room smells of Vicks VapoRub. A cross of Jesus hangs from the bedpost. "Welcome to San Antonio del Norte," he says warmly. "San Antonio South doesn't exist anymore." He's a small, good-looking man with a patch of black hair under his lip. I ask him how the drought has affected Wonderful. He says his bosses have been instructing him to reduce the water each irrigation. He used to apply three inches to the almonds. Now he is applying an inch and a half. There are plans, crazy as it sounds, to take out ten thousand acres of almonds. When the rain returns, some of the ground will be replanted in pistachios, a tree that can better withstand the next drought, but much of the land will remain fallow. "Wonderful is getting smaller," he says.

The next day, I drive to a spot a few miles beyond the trailer park where a county road dead-ends in a pomegranate orchard, or what used to be a pomegranate orchard before the claws of a Caterpillar came crashing through. Every last tree has been torn out of the ground. Thousands of Wonderful acres now lie bare. The juice isn't selling like it used to. The Pom tanks, I am told, are backed up with a three-year supply. The Federal Trade Commission found Wonderful guilty of false advertising and told the Resnicks to stop claiming that Pom cured heart disease and erectile dysfunction. A balancing of books back at headquarters has decided that too little water covers this orchard and it needs to go. All told, Wonderful has bulldozed eight to ten thousand acres of pomegranate trees over the past several years to shunt more water to its nuts. Across the field, one heavy machine is stacking what's left of the trees into giant mounds and another is pulverizing the trunks and branches into chips and sawdust. I park the car and walk across the barren rows. Here and there my boots crunch down on the dried remains of pomegranates that look like pieces of scat dropped by a coyote. Plastic drip irrigation lines protrude from the ground at crazy angles. Tender sprouts poke out of the dry soil. I bend down to feel their prickle, smell their resin. They're baby tumbleweeds come home.

A giant pistachio nut flashes across the big screen. It cracks open, and out pops a head shot of Stewart Resnick in a pistachio-green tie. When he materializes onstage, he's wearing narrow black jeans, a black mock turtle and a dark jacket. Damn if he doesn't look younger, more fit and hip, than when I saw him eight years earlier. Welcome to the Ninth Annual Wonderful Pistachio Conference at the Visalia Convention Center. Although it's an invitation-only affair, I was able to grab one of the company's annual reports—the pistachio-green cover was hard to miss—and walk in.

He's getting ready to introduce Lynda, the main speaker, but first he launches into a CEO's riff on the pistachio market. Domestic sales are up 42 percent over the past eight years; foreign sales, however, have stalled. He blames Iran. Since international sanctions were lifted, Iran has been crowding the market with its more buttery-tasting pistachios. The rich flavor is a consequence of water. The Iranians don't overirrigate their trees for production but underirrigate them for taste. They rely mostly on rain, which concentrates the flavorful oils. China, for one, prefers the Iranian pistachio. So do the Israelis, who go to the trouble of repackaging the nuts so it doesn't appear that they're consuming the product of a sworn enemy. Iranian pistachios show up in Tel Aviv as nuts from Turkey.

To make up for the market share lost in Asia and the Middle East, the company is pushing its spicy Latin line of nuts into Mexico. Thanks to Wonderful's $15 million "Get Crackin'" campaign—the largest media buy in the history of snack nuts—pistachios now rank among the top ten best-selling salty snack items in the United States. "We are no longer processing nuts," Resnick says. "We are creating foods." Nothing keeps prices high like a monopoly. In case the growers are worrying about the antitrust cops from the Department of Justice, they needn't. For years, agriculture has been given a wide berth when it comes to monopolistic practices. The net return on the pistachio, he says, proves that Wonderful's dominance in the market has benefited every grower in the room. The price for pistachios has climbed from a record $4.50 a pound to an unbelievable $5.25 a pound. It isn't going down because he won't let it go down.

Then he motions to Lynda, who's standing off to the side of the light-dimmed stage. I've never seen her up close, never watched her in action. She seems a little nervous waiting in the wings. Six hundred pistachio growers in blue jeans isn't her usual crowd. "We saved the best for last," he says. "As you know, our philosophy at Wonderful is doing well by doing good. About five years ago, Lynda started our community development organization in Lost Hills, and the journey has been an amazing one. We produced a short documentary film. Every time I see it, I'm inspired and proud of what we've been able to accomplish in such a short amount of time. We hope you enjoy *Finding Lost Hills*."

The eleven-minute film opens with a shot of swirling dust. That was Lost Hills before Lynda. "I had no idea what I wanted to do," she tells the camera. "But I had reached a moment in my life where I had to give back in a meaningful way. When I started to realize the socioeconomic issues of the Central Valley, I decided to stop writing checks to other charities and bring my business acumen into the project. It took time to gain the respect of the people, and I was afraid. What if I failed? If you're messing with people's lives and it doesn't work, that's serious.... It had to work." Dirt and mud paths became paved streets. An almond orchard turned into affordable housing. A gathering spot for drunks and addicts rose anew as the Wonderful Park and Community Center. Tens of millions of dollars spent on philanthropy in Lost Hills isn't just good for the people, Lynda discovered. It's good for the bottom line. Because the more you invest in your employees and their communities, the more productive they become at work. The film ends with the laughter of children playing inside the giant sunburst at the center of the soccer field. "I did not name the town," Lynda says. "But I couldn't have picked a more cinematic name than Lost Hills. Because it's so much fun to say that Lost Hills has been found."

The room full of growers applauds. I applaud, too. Since it is also true that Lost Hills has belonged to the Resnicks for more than thirty years, one of us might have blurted out, "What took you so long to find it?" As the film runs to credits, I can see that one credit is missing. My buddy John Gibler, the freelance journalist, had found Lost Hills a year before Lynda. In the summer of 2010, he'd spent several days documenting the deplorable conditions of the modern-day company town. His account appeared in the *Earth Island Journal,* a small environmental quarterly out of Berkeley. Somehow, it made its way to Lynda. "There is nothing here," one of the townsfolk told Gibler. "This is a forgotten community. And you know why? Because it is a community of all Hispanics."

The piece had left Lynda embarrassed and fuming. It must have wounded all the more because she and Stewart thought of themselves as progressive Democrats. Over the years, they had donated large sums of money to political campaigns, and some of it had gone to Republicans who'd pledged to prop up California agriculture. This is how billionaires in the arid West on the hunt for more water did politics. At the core, though, the Resnicks were still moved by the duty of social justice, not just as traditional liberals but as secular Jews. Stewart would deny that Gibler's reporting played a part in their philanthropy. "Look, I have no guilt. I've done no big wrong in my life that would cause me to have any. Well, maybe just a little guilt, but that's Jewish." The way he told it, the goad for all their giving in the valley happened not in the orchards of Lost Hills but in the mountains of Aspen. In the summer of 2009, he and Lynda had attended a dinner lecture at the house of wealthy friends that featured Harvard professor Michael Sandel speaking about the moral obligations of wealth. "At the time, we were handing out college scholarships in the valley, but we both realized it wasn't nearly enough," he said. A year and a half after hearing Sandel—and in the wake of Gibler's story—Lynda launched their mission to save Lost Hills and several other farmworker towns where Wonderful operated its orchards and processing plants.

She's building an $80 million charter school complex in Delano, just down the road from Cesar Chavez High. It looks like no other campus in California's middle, a modern, minimalist two-story design that uses paneled wood and fabricated metal, wild colors and terraced landscaping to create the feel of a high-tech mountain retreat. When all three phases are done, eighteen hundred students will be attending the high school, middle school, elementary school and preschool. What she has in mind is a utopian village set amid the orchards and vineyards, not unlike the utopias that were tried by the early dreamers of Southern California. She's not only writing the checks, she's designing the school, mapping out a curriculum and devising a farm-to-food program where students will grow fruits, vegetables and grains on a plot of village land. Inside a fully equipped "teaching" kitchen, they'll turn harvests into school lunches.

Already, the high school is filled with hundreds of students bused in from farmworker towns among the poorest in the West. Graduates are headed to Stanford, UC Berkeley, UCLA, Dartmouth and the state and community college systems. When Lynda learned that half the students receiving thousands of dollars in company scholarships were dropping out of college, she threw more resources at them. She's now providing tutors and counselors in every region of California to boost the grad rate. For the bright kids who have no interest in a bachelor's degree, she has designed the Wonderful Agriculture Career Prep program to serve an additional one thousand students. Selling the farm to migrant families means rebranding agriculture. No longer is ag a career that brings Mexicans to their knees. Under her Rethink Agriculture program, the kids will be trained in plant science and irrigation technology, marketing and sales.

Now the lady stands before us, a single light over her head. She is twinkling from earlobe and finger. Whether it's the glint of a fifteen-carat canary-yellow diamond ring, a gift from Stewart on their twenty-fifth wedding anniversay, or one of the pomegranate-colored rubies she says are a girl's best friend, it's hard to tell from the back row. "Stewart bikes forty miles a day when we're on vacation. He's in great shape," she confides. "But I hope you don't think I'm nearly that old. He stole me out of a baby basket." She gestures to the young students in the front row, the ones enrolled in the ag-prep classes, and asks them to stand up and take a bow. "They're our future," she declares. She is determined that their lives will play out differently than the lives of their parents, but she means no disrespect by this. The truth is right there in the numbers. "It's not easy to hear, but I'm not going to sugarcoat this. In Kern County, one in two adults and almost one in five children are obese. And it's even worse for the children in Kings County. Fifty-three percent of our employees are obese. And twelve percent of them have diabetes."

The growers start to fidget. It's not the fidget of boredom. There's an unease about the room. This isn't the Lynda posing for photos with Barbra Streisand. This is the Lynda who endeavors to see farmhands as something more than workers, who pays them decent wages and provides them with a full-time doctor, a physician's assistant, a registered dietician and a marriage and family therapist, who keeps them fit with a gym at work and fruits and vegetables to snack on after they do their fifteen minutes of Zumba and take a walk along a designated path. To the growers, it must feel like a jab in the stomach. They're listening with their heads bent down. Do they sense the shaming about to come? She delivers it in classic Lynda style: "At Wonderful Health and Wellness, we're educating our employees about this health crisis. At the plant, we built our gyms and we have stretching and walking activities. Being Wonderful means more than growing, harvesting and distributing the best of the best. It also means giving back."

She walks off the stage with Stewart. He lingers in the crowd long enough to shake hands with an Iranian Jewish friend from Bel Air who's planting thousands of acres of pistachios in Tulare Lake's worst alkali flats. I walk up and reintroduce myself. His face is blank. I remind him of the time we spent together eight years earlier in his Sunset House. His face is still blank. His partner in the mandarins once told me that when Stewart is done with you, he's done with you. He and the Resnicks had fought an ugly legal battle that tore their Cuties brand in two. The partner kept the Cuties name, and Stewart and Lynda created a new brand, the Halo, from the same varieties of mandarin. The Cuties and the Halos are now warring in the fields outside the Visalia Convention Center. Inside, a Wonderful media specialist sees that Resnick needs to be rescued. She works her way through the crowd and deftly places her body between him and me. When I tell her my name, she whispers into his ear. "Ah," he says, "so you're the one who's been snooping around." She grabs him by the wrist, and they make a beeline for the convention hall door.

I catch Highway 99 in rare somnolence. The miles clock by not as road but as story. This is the route my grandfather took as he hopped from farm to farm in the early 1920s, picking crops. He saved up a down payment for a raisin ranch west of Fresno and harvested five crops in the worst of the Great Depression. He ended up losing the farm to vine hopper bugs is the story he told. My grandmother said it was his leftist politics that ate up that first vineyard and all the ones that followed. One way or the other, we landed in the suburbs, where our last ranch, ten miles to the north of us, wasn't a place in the palpable sense. This is the same road that took me to Selma after my father's murder to pack fruit for his friend Mel Girazian. I was sixteen, and the packinghouse was my first job, a baptism into the "money, money, money" world of the men who grew the fruit and the men who sold it. Girazian was the darkest Armenian I ever laid eyes on, a small, wiry man with a prizefighter's nose who showed up to work wearing purple bell-bottoms and puffing on a Kool cigarette. The growers called him "Sammy Davis Jr."—out loud. The whispers were that his mother, who looked like Zsa Zsa Gabor and would sashay up to the second-floor offices in a fur coat, had once had an affair with an Arab or a Negro and this produced Mel. He put me at the end of the line, where the peaches, plums and nectarines arrived on rollers after they had been washed, sized, graded, packed and boxed. The growers never stopped moaning about how much of their beautiful fruit, tossed in the cull bins, never made it into the box. I learned back then that our farmers thought the whole world was out to screw them.

Maybe this explains why the United Way could declare the valley one of the nation's skinflints, a place where the wealthy farmers donated to the children's hospital or Fresno State athletics but almost never to the communities filled with Mexicans where their crops grew. As a class of people, the farmers and real estate developers raised in Fresno, Tulare and Bakersfield harbor a deep down contempt for what they have built. They hide from the fact that it relies on the subjugation of peasants from Mexico who they themselves have brought here. It exists as one thing that they can almost rationalize out in the fields. It becomes something else as soon as they encounter their workers in another guise—say, as a fellow shopper at Costco or as the parents of the kid who goes to school with their kid.

I cross the Tulare County line, heading south into Bakersfield, and there in front of me, for no eye to miss, stands the Wonderful Citrus complex, with its four-story storage building designed in the shape of an almighty box of Halo mandarins. Conceived by Lynda, it cost one fortune to build and a second fortune to light up at night. I doubt the Resnicks have any idea of the fester that eats at the shadows of this place, the shame piled on shame that makes their philanthropy such a shock to the system. On this stretch of Highway 99, I once wrote a story about farmworkers who moonlighted as meth cookers to make ends meet. Bruce Springsteen turned it into a song on his *Ghost of Tom Joad* album. More than one ballad was about the valley, and so he came to Fresno. The William Saroyan Theatre was packed that October night in 1996. Halfway through his solo performance, he interrupted his set to tell us that a piggy bank had been set up at the exit to donate money to "the hardworking men and women in the fields" whose hands feed us as surely as the soil, sun and water.

When the concert was over, I took my wife and children backstage to meet him. As we sat down to chat, one of his assistants leaned over and whispered into his jewel-studded ear. Springsteen shook his head and smiled a thin, ironic smile. Then he turned and faced me. "Tell me," he asked, though it wasn't entirely a question. "What kind of place is this? Not a single penny was put in that piggy bank."

I cut across Twisselman Road to the pipeline gliding alongside the aqueduct like a silver snake. I get out and thwack both lines. They thwack back. Yes, they're still delivering water from some distant place. If I follow them north through Resnick pomegranates, I can find out where the water is coming from. If I follow them south into Resnick almonds, I can see where the water is going. Either way is a trespass.

I steer toward the almonds, past a row of worker housing and a main gate. I enter an equipment yard where a Wonderful farmhand is standing next to a tractor. He eyes my car as if it's an alien landing. He doesn't wave me off or give chase. He knows what I don't know. This road ends abruptly at the rise of a second fence. With nowhere to turn, I turn back around and roll down my window. He's smiling but speaks only Spanish. He doesn't know what "pipeline" means. But if it's the "*tubo*" that I'm looking to follow, I must drive through the almond grove. A road will pick up and connect me to where the tube is going.

"Why is the tube here?"

"To carry water from someplace far away to another place far away," he says.

I thank him and follow the dirt road through the almonds, eyeing my rearview mirror to see if a Resnick truck is tailing me. I'm driving too fast for the ruts in the road. My head keeps hitting the sunroof. A minute later, I reconnect with the pipeline and pursue its length for a football field. Each section of pipe is forty feet long. I try to calculate how many hundreds of aluminum sections needed to be linked seamlessly, or at least watertight, to cover the distance of a mile, and then many miles. Just ahead I can see the last section of pipe throwing a cascade of white water into a main canal belonging to the Lost Hills Water District. I hop out of the car.

"RAIN FOR RENT" is tattooed across the pipes. If Resnick retains every drop, he might squeeze fifteen to twenty acre-feet of water a day out of both pipes. He needs one thousand acre-feet a day for 165 days—the length of nut-growing season—to hang a good crop across his acres in western Kern. This last-ditch water in Lost Hills won't even come close to making up the difference. But it's flowing to a place of dire thirst, and there's no denying his desperation. For as far as I can see, the water pouring into the canal runs blue through his orchards. Because the road ends here, there is no physical way to follow the flow. I take out the cell phone and swipe across Google Maps. The canal water moves on and on through miles of western Kern. This is one of the ways the nut king and the pomegranate princess are defying the California drought. This is how the land of Wonderful is keeping its trees from dying.

I call the manager of the Lost Hills Water District. He used to work for the Resnicks before Stewart put him in charge of the district. He's a decent guy making $216,000 a year who doesn't pretend that he isn't beholden to Wonderful. As the head of a quasi-public agency, he knows he can't completely blow off my questions. He doesn't feign surprise when I tell him about the pipeline, but he dismisses it as a private matter between private parties. It takes me visiting the irrigation district office during a public meeting—the secretary can't recall a journalist ever being there—for him to cough up more details. Yes, the pipeline belongs to Resnick. Yes, it's delivering water straight from the Dudley Ridge Water District in Kings County. What he doesn't cough up is that the water is coming from a variety of sources, including groundwater pumped in covert style from two counties away. Resnick is using every drop of it to irrigate his almonds and pistachios in Lost Hills.

I find a former partner of Resnick's. He doesn't know about the pipeline. What he knows is that Wonderful is buying 50,000 acre-feet of water a year in a series of hidden deals. The sellers include big farmers in the Tulare Lake basin who are pumping so much groundwater that the levee protecting Corcoran has sunk several feet. The J. G. Boswell Company, for one, has drilled more than fifty wells in the old lake bottom to extract and sell the water to Resnick and other parched farmers. Residents of Corcoran (not Boswell or Wonderful) are paying the $10 million in local taxes to fix the subsidence caused by the mining of

Resnick's secret pipeline

groundwater. Altogether, not counting the flow of water in the secret pipeline, Resnick has purchased 300,000 acre-feet from other farmers and water districts to cover his shortfall. This drought water has cost him more than $200 million.

I meet up with the Wonderful field man who first tipped me off to the pipeline. He says he doesn't feel sorry for Resnick. He got himself into this jam. "This is a company that runs its resources to the max," he tells me. "When Resnick plants, he plants his trees wall to wall. That's why he's in trouble."

"He left no space for drought?"

"He thought the water bank was going to save him forever. But the water that's left in the bank isn't real."

"So he makes a deal for private water?"

"Yep. That's why he built the pipeline. He needs every drop he can get."

"Whose water is it?"

"Don't you know? It's John Vidovich. Billionaire comes to the rescue of billionaire."

"But those two guys hate each other."

"Not anymore. They're drought's best buddies."

John Vidovich will tell you that he's the interloper who came over the other set of mountains, the Coast Ranges. His father, a Croatian of sturdy stock, grew grapes, cherries and apricots in the Santa Clara Valley back when Stanford University had a reason to be known as the Farm. He sold a chunk of land to the builders of Sunnyvale and then decided he could develop the rest himself. He plowed under the twenty acres of fruit trees where he was born and built the De Anza Shopping Center. He took other parcels of farmland and erected apartments and condos, office complexes and mobile home parks. He built the De Anza Racquet Club and the Cupertino Inn Hotel. His real estate empire grew big enough to allow him to bring aboard each of his four children. By the time he died an old man on his tractor at his home in the Cupertino hills, where he had planted grapes again and was making wine, the transformation of his valley by the silicon chip was complete.

John, the oldest son, had served in the military as an intelligence officer and graduated from Santa Clara law school. He had none of his father's sentimentality. He paved over the family's last orchard with some apartments and then went looking for another valley where he might build his own empire. That was how he happened upon the San Joaquin. "There's a lot of people who don't like me," he said after his father's death. "But nobody didn't like my dad."

It was a curious statement but true. The son, five foot six and thin, with closely cropped blond hair and blue eyes that fix on you with stone-cold coldness, isn't concerned about ingratiating himself. In a time span even shorter than Resnick's, the sixty-one-year-old Vidovich has bought up more than one hundred thousand acres of farmland scattered across the valley. He's planting ground that no one has ever planted before. If you study his moves, you can see a method to the acres he is accumulating. He's grabbing land where the groundwater is plenty or a river runs through it or the aqueduct spills its north-to-south flow. Don't let his boots, blue jeans and ball cap fool you, the old-timers say. He isn't farming dirt. He's farming water.

Back in the winter of 2010, Vidovich put up for sale half of the state water he drew from the Dudley Ridge Water District. This amounted to 14,000 acre-feet a year. Everyone knew where it was going. It was going to houses. California had passed a law intended to stop new towns from rising in the middle of nowhere. Developers now had to identify a source of water before a city or county would approve their projects. So off the developers went in search of farm water. Resnick himself had sold 7,000 acre-feet to a proposed new town in the fields of Madera. Vidovich didn't have to wait long for a buyer to come calling. The Mojave Water Agency, in the high desert, needed a backup supply. The communities of Barstow, Apple Valley and Victorville were growing by twenty-five hundred houses a year from all those exiles fleeing Los Angeles. The flows of the Mojave River had been exhausted. The state project water that the high desert counted on had been slashed by 20 percent—to keep fish in the faraway delta alive. Knowing that the full state water allotment was never coming back, Mojave jumped at Vidovich's offer. He went home with $74 million in his pocket.

The sale got under the skin of valley farmers. It was true that agriculture had been selling its state water to the cities for at least two decades, but those deals involved one water district selling its entitlement to another water district. This deal made headlines because it was engineered by one farmer—a poacher from the city, at that—for his benefit only. It didn't help that he had sold the water at an exorbitant price:

$5,321 an acre-foot. The growers didn't like the public finding out about such profit making. If farming went to hell, selling the water was something they might all do. And here was Vidovich giving away the game. To top it off, the "greedy SOB" (they never uttered his name) intended to keep farming his nut trees in Dudley Ridge. He only needed to find groundwater from another basin to replace the state water he had just sold.

Vidovich went on a shopping spree in the old Tulare Lake basin. He bought a stake in Westlake Farms, a fifty-thousand-acre spread owned by the Howe family. After three generations of growing cotton on the north end of the lakebed, the Howes had come upon hard times. To survive, they had idled thousands of acres and turned them into a massive dump for sludge—baked human excrement—trucked in from Southern California sewer farms. Vidovich had no interest in recycling waste. He wanted Westlake Farms because it gave him access to groundwater and Kings River flood flows. He then headed to the other side of the lake basin and grabbed twenty thousand acres of junk land—ground that not even Boswell would farm. He had no intention of farming it, either. But those twenty thousand acres outside Pixley in Tulare County came with an endowment: a little spit of earth that produced endless amounts of groundwater. Never mind that this was one of the most overdrafted basins in California or that the earth was sinking six inches a year. Vidovich dug seventeen new wells, several to the depth of fifteen hundred feet, and pumped groundwater into ditches and canals that flow miles across the flat lakebed.

Where did the water end up? Right there in the big canal and reservoir of the Dudley Ridge Water District. Because Vidovich still grows nuts in the district, he gets to use Dudley Ridge as a wheeling station. Not only is he able to irrigate his trees with an imported flow of groundwater, up to 40,000 acre-feet in some years; he can also mix this private water with his leftover state water and ship it to at least one stranded neighbor who will pay the price.

Who would have imagined Stewart Resnick and John Vidovich in cahoots? Not long ago, Vidovich was trying to grab water from Resnick, not give it. In 2008 he accused Resnick of using shell companies to monopolize control of the Kern Water Bank. A public resource had been privatized for the purpose of growing tens of thousands of acres of nuts, he charged. The matter was headed to court when Vidovich, suddenly contrite, paid a visit to Resnick. His ego had gotten the best of him, he conceded. What if he dropped his lawsuit and the two of them worked together to solve their water problems? That's all fine and good, Resnick replied, but what about the more than $1 million he had spent on lawyers' fees? Vidovich wrote out a check for the full amount, then went looking for the water to prop up Resnick's monopoly. He found it.

By car and foot, I trace the silver pipeline the other way, back to its source, as it creeps north through Wonderful pomegranate orchards. One mile, two miles, three miles and four—it keeps going until it reaches deep into Kings County and leads me back to one of the main canals in the Dudley Ridge Water District. A pump is shooting water out of the canal and into the "RAIN FOR RENT" pipes. The water is cold, clean and salty, though not too salty for a desperate man. Or at least that's the way Vidovich puts it when I finally reach him.

"This drought has brought Stewart to his knees, what can I say. We've had our battles in the past, and I don't agree with everything he's doing. But when your neighbor is going to lose his crop, you do what you can to help him."

I tell Vidovich this sounds almost charitable. "How much water are we talking about?"

"I'd rather not get too specific. It isn't a lot of water."

"What's the cost?"

"I'm not going to give you the numbers. Neighbors don't tell on neighbors."

Vidovich has more than one reason to be evasive. The farmers in Pixley already have sued him once for taking too much water out of their ground and moving it. The court settlement allows him to take the water to Dudley Ridge, but it can't go outside Kings County. Yet the Resnick pipeline is doing just that.

"Resnick picks up the water in Dudley Ridge," Vidovich says. "It's his pipe, not mine. Where he takes the water is none of my business."

"Come on. You know where he's taking it. He's taking it across Kings County into his orchards in Kern. That breaks your court agreement with the farmers. You can't be exporting groundwater from one basin to another."

"Whatever water he's taking, it's too little, too late."

I try again to pin him down, but he's the sort of man who likes to think of himself as wily. So I ask about the big picture: "What's all this say about Wonderful? Its future? The future of farming in Kern?"

"Let's call it what it is. It's gambling. Stewart gambled and won for many years. He gambled on the price of nuts going up. And he gambled on the water never going dry. He kept planting more and more trees. But he got too big. Too many pistachios. Too many almonds. Too many pomegranates. Like a lot of empires, it comes to an end."

"So what about you?" I ask. "What kind of empire are you trying to build?"

"I'm here to show the farmer that ag's footprint needs to get smaller."

I chew on his answer for a second. The calculation and hubris inside it. The truth a mercenary has landed on. "I get it," I finally say. "You're the one who leads the way on selling agricultural water to the cities. Fallowing the farm until the footprint gets smaller and smaller. Making hundreds of millions of dollars in the process?"

"It can't be farmed like it was," he says.

To grow an almond in Lost Hills, the farmer has to import water, men and bees. The water crosses the delta border in the north. The worker crosses the desert border in the south. The bee crosses the Rocky Mountain border in the east. Two million colonies—nearly sixty billion bees—are packed into the backs of semitrucks in Florida, Minnesota and North Dakota each winter and hauled to California to pollinate the valley's almond bloom. The beekeeper refers to it as "the world's biggest brothel for bees." The insects pick up all kinds of nasty things in their flights from field to field. The early death rate of bees has climbed to near 50 percent from "attrition," he says. The die-off used to be at 10 percent before the almonds took over. Is there a connection? No county in California relies more on Lorsban—Dow Chemical's insecticide tied to Parkinson's disease and lung cancer—than Kern County. With the rise of nuts and mandarins, the use of Lorsban here has climbed from 207,000 pounds to 285,000 pounds over the past decade. The beekeeper, in deference to the nut grower, doesn't want to talk about the links between pesticides and herbicides and the collapse of his bee colony. The neurologist calls the valley "Parkinson's Alley," but he doesn't want to talk about any link, either.

I'm thinking of the bees because they've made such a fine crop in this

The road through Wonderful

orchard along the main road to Lost Hills. Six hundred and forty acres doesn't look like six hundred and forty acres—a full square mile—until they start ripping out the trees on a spring day. The white flowers have set into nubs, and the nubs have become baby almonds covered in fuzz. Now it's the Bobcat's turn. Even as farmers across the valley continue to plant almonds in new ground, the biggest farmer of them all is in retreat, just as Gustavo had told me, tearing out as many as ten thousand acres. He doesn't have enough water here to cover the nuts to harvest. Since the middle of the drought, the price of almonds has dropped almost in half. Maybe when the floods return and the water bank fills up again, he'll plant the ground in pistachios. Or maybe it'll stay bare. For now, in a region of wall-to-wall plantings, one of the walls is crashing down. The way the Bobcat goes full steam, it takes but a few seconds of splendid violence to uproot a tree. The farmer isn't here to smell the cracking open of wood, the ripping open of warm, secret earth. No farmer ever is. The sentimental ones stay away. The bloodless ones stay away. On the day the trees fall quietly upon the orchard floor, no one is here but the Mexican on his tractor.

Fifteen

THE CANDY MAN

Jack Pandol Jr. stands in the silt of his vineyard on the east side of the valley and tries to figure out what damage the rain has done. He had almost made peace with this dry. It would end when it was ready to end. But a drought broken only for a moment by a freak summer storm, "a no-good rain," borders on the cruel. "The worst drought ever," he mutters, "and the sky decides to open up now?" It's late July, and the harvest of table grapes has leaped into full swing. So much fruit hangs on the vine that the whole place feels swollen. As soon as a grape starts to ripen, it's on a fast track to perish. Trouble in a vineyard begins with the microscopic, but it doesn't stay that way for very long. If moisture gets out of hand, the skin on a berry cracks open, and filaments of fungus rot the whole cluster in a hurry. Most table grape growers, attuned to the lurk of mold and mildew, harvest their grapes on the early side. Pandol, who may be the most picky table grape grower in California, which is to say the nation, wants to maximize flavor. He'll hold his fruit on the vine until it reaches peak taste and only then call in his picking crews. For a couple extra points on the sugar register, a measure known as Brix, he'll even risk a week of 105-degree weather. But a rainstorm in the middle of summer? It doesn't happen here.

He would curse the sky, but he knows it won't do any good. His father, Jack, a legend of Delano for the way he went after Cesar Chavez and his campesinos during the labor strikes and grape boycotts of the 1960s, farmed this stretch of valley for more than fifty years. He died in 2010, eulogized as one of the greatest grape growers of all time, a pathfinder who opened the market to Chile so that North Americans and South Americans could feast on one another's grapes in their opposite seasons. His father's father, Stjepe, left the vineyards of Brusje in Croatia, on the island of Hvar, more than a century ago and farmed this same dirt. The old man outlasted drought, flood and pests with little more than sulfur dust at his side. He used to tell Jack Jr., "Learn from your mistakes, but don't go to school all your life."

It's been seventy years since the Central Valley Project distributed its first imported flows to the east side. At age sixty-two, Pandol is a child of the System. He's never grown a grape without the Friant-Kern Canal as a presence slashing across the land. During this drought, the federal project has delivered either no snowmelt or very little snowmelt from the San Joaquin River fifty miles to the north. The federal canal is filled with pooled water nearly up to the brim, but it's there only to keep the structure from falling into a state of disrepair. Like so many other growers, Jack Jr. is pumping devilish amounts of water from below the ground. The two old wells on this vineyard went dry more than a year ago. He drilled a third well to a depth of 1,000 feet, and it's about to go dry, too. The bowls that retrieve the water were set at 350 feet deep when he dug the hole two years ago, and now they're at 900 feet. That's a monstrous plunge in the aquifer. "I can only afford to dig deeper because I'm growing a crop with good returns," he says. "But how much deeper?"

A dry summer is why a table grape grower can even attempt to grow "nature's candy" in this unfit ground. Every year, Pandol relies on the seasonal drought, from May to September, to visit the valley. The vineyard on its own is already a living, breathing place disposed to rot if not for the farmer's myriad interventions. Add in the emitters of drip irrigation, and it's about all the moisture a California grape can handle. Many of the circumventions Pandol employs during the growing season have to do with keeping the clusters free from mold and mildew. There's no fruit more bent and coddled by human hands than the table grape. What's done in the name of fighting fungus isn't any more of a stretch than what's done to pump up size, color and yield. Crews of workers thin the leaves to allow more air to flow through the berries. They apply sulfur dust and a steady dose of fungicides. But not one of these measures means a thing when a rain like this comes down. "All bets are off," he tells me.

Driving in from his Bakersfield home, he could see the damage to the vineyards all around him. The Flames ripened early this year and were a week shy of winding up their harvest when the storm hit. The loss wasn't great. The Thompsons, however, were just finding their right sugar when the rain cracked their skins and their sweet insides started to weep. Mildew set in as fast as the clouds came and went. The farmers watched five thousand acres rot on the vine.

"We need to get the air circulating," he says. "That's why we came in right after the rain and pulled off a lot of leaves. We clipped off berries. We dusted with sulfur and sprayed with fungicides." He feels the sun settle in on the back of his neck. He hopes it comes with a breeze. "I think we're gonna save it. We may lose twenty to twenty-five percent of the crop. But it won't be a wipeout."

What brings me to the east side of Tulare and Kern Counties isn't an absurd summer storm but table grape varieties that Pandol is growing with water from ground and canal. These eating grapes aren't Flames or Red Globes or Crimsons or any of the other usual varieties. They emerged from a test tube in a lab inside the old Delano farmhouse where his grandfather and grandmother used to live. He will tell you that they are like no other grapes anyone has ever eaten, and that may be true. One of the varieties is a hybrid of two distinct species—East Coast father, West Coast mother—and tastes like cotton candy. Fat, green and seedless, it actually goes by the name Cotton Candy and carries 30 percent more sugar than a conventional grape. With its northeastern lineage, it doesn't panic when it gets rained on. The other grape, Sweet Celebration, seedless and red, is a genetic freak of a different derivation. It was bred by combining the strongest traits inside a single species of grapes commonly found in the United States and Europe. Breeding, though, is only half the trick of altering the taste and durability of the table grape. The other half of the revolution that Pandol is introducing to these fields is the way he tends to his berries right up to the moment they're picked. All through spring and summer, he's been pumping calcium into the tissues of both varieties to boost their natural flavors and enhance their ability to ward off fungal disease.

"The biggest problem with this vineyard is water," he explains. "Not only the lack of it but the quality. It's high in sodium. So we use calcium in the drip irrigation system. I happen to believe that calcium is one of the most overlooked ingredients in growing good fruit. We've way overdone nitrogen. Nitrogen pumps up the fruit to unbelievable sizes because it blows it up with water. Nitrogen may be great for corn in the Midwest, but it kills the flavor of a grape in California. Calcium, by contrast, kicks out a grape that tastes sweet and smooth on the tongue. And it strengthens the cell walls so the skin doesn't break open and rot the whole vineyard."

Pandol is an average-sized guy with green eyes and blond hair that's begun receding since he hit middle age, like his dad's did. His build isn't quite as stocky, and he has only a hint of his old man's sweetly tough face. He says he more resembles the Zaninovich side of his mom's tribe, though who knows what a full-blooded Slav should look like given the roads that have crossed Croatia for twenty-five hundred years.

We're standing at the not-so-pretty edge of the dairy belt in Tulare County, where the Holsteins have more clout than people and much of the ground, middling at best, bristles with alfalfa, the biggest water hog of them all. More than a third of the county's cropland is planted to some kind of hay or corn to feed all those masticators. Alfalfa isn't harvested once but is mowed a half dozen times through the year, so it's pretty much growing all the time, which means it is drinking all the time. For each acre, each irrigation, it takes three acre-feet of water to grow table grapes, but it can take double that to grow alfalfa.

Table grapes are still being planted here, though more and more the money is coming from hedge funds and investor pools on the East Coast. Soil and water being what they are, Pandol decided he needed outside capital himself to convert alfalfa field to vineyard. He found one "very wealthy family" in Philadelphia (he won't say their name) to underwrite the cost of $40,000 an acre. A good chunk of his eighteen hundred acres scattered across Tulare and Kern Counties, he owns himself. But on this land, he's a tenant farmer sharing the crop with partners in the City of Brotherly Love.

He steps under the canopy of cane and leaves, a gable-roofed trellis system he borrowed from South African grape growers because it maximizes both sun and shade. His boots sink into the earth made spongy by all the compost he's spread. For too long, he says, grape farmers have treated soil like dirt. He's found over the years that the more fertile the earth—the more potent its microbial matter—the stronger and more flavorful his grapes turn out to be.

"Since we converted this ground three years ago, I've probably spread

Jack Pandol Jr. measures the sugar in his grapes.

fifteen tons of compost. This is the first year we're picking grapes, our first crop. The way it's looking, even with this rain, we're going to pull off something in the range of fifteen to eighteen hundred boxes an acre."

"How does that compare to the old days?"

"When I first got out of school, growing those old varieties with the old T-trellis system, watering by furrow instead of drip, we were probably averaging five to six hundred boxes of grapes an acre. We've tripled production. My dad was using five acre-feet of water for every acre. We're using three acre-feet."

His father was a big-hearted man who loved nothing more than cooking for large gatherings of people, feeding his famous mostaccioli with meaty Slav-style sauce to Richard Nixon and Ronald Reagan, among others. There was an art to cooking that his parents were determined to pass on to their kids. His older sister, Maria, became the food section columnist at the *Fresno Bee* and then worked in the test kitchens for Nestlé in Los Angeles. For Jack Jr., the family cooking gene morphed into a fascination with how science might join art to tease out different flavors in the vineyard. What if he could create shapes and flavors that had never existed before and let each cluster ripen to its fullest? Not the 16 or 18 on the Brix sugar scale that most grapes reach but 20 to 24 Brix.

"Farmers in California, my family included, have been going down one road for at least the last sixty years," he explains. "The way we breed fruit isn't for taste but for shipping. The way we grow fruit isn't for the tongue but for the eye. We harvest early so the fruit doesn't go soft by the time it reaches the market. What does it matter that it tastes like wet cardboard?"

Talk to most growers and supermarket buyers, and they'll tell you that the consumer wants fruit that's big and colorful. But Pandol says that's old-school. Foodies demand flavor. The lack of it is why so many people have stopped eating fruit, or why they buy it once a season but not twice. It's why tens of thousands of acres of peaches and plums, apricots and nectarines are being bulldozed across the valley. He yanks a few berries off a vine and hands them to me. They're swollen and colorful, like the grapes they sell at the supermarket. I bite down, and they're crunchy, too. But they don't taste like a supermarket grape. They taste like the sunbaked Thompsons my father and grandfather used to grow in our backyard. Sweet but not syrupy sweet. Then another flavor, one I'm not prepared for, takes over.

"Wow. Those are really good."

He smiles and nods. "We want you to say, 'Wow.' That's the response we're looking for. And if that sensation on your tongue triggers a recollection of you walking down the midway of the county fair as a kid and eating cotton candy, all the better."

The salesmanship comes second nature to a son whose dad used to travel the world promoting the family's grapes. In the decade since he introduced Cotton Candy, more than fifty thousand acres of his genetically flavored varieties have been planted in the San Joaquin Valley and around the world. Growers pay him a licensing fee and a 5 percent royalty on sales and must adhere to certain quality controls and acreage limits to keep the market from glutting up. From field to lab to licensing to the growing, it's a model his father would scarcely recognize: bending water to grow bent grapes. "All this genetic breeding aside, my father would probably say we're returning to the old way. To flavor. We've forgotten that what brings people back to fruit is taste, the memory of taste."

I first heard about "Junior's" experiments on the farm twenty-five years ago when I walked into a Perko's diner in Delano early one morning and got to chatting with some of the growers drinking coffee and eating eggs and cantaloupe. Sons of the desert, they were descended from men who had been putting grapes in the Delano soil since 1924, when Marin Caratan, a Slav from that same village of Hvar, leveled 160 acres by himself with a team of mules and founded Columbine Vineyards. Soon followed the other clans: Zaninovich, Jakovich, Radovich, Kovacavich, Pandol, Pavich, Caric, Divizich, Dulcich, Bozanich, Buksa and Tudor. They filled the pews and collection plates at St. Mary's Catholic Church and exercised such influence that when Cesar Chavez launched the farmworker movement here in the fall of 1965, it tore Delano in two, dividing east side from west side, growers from their Mexican and Filipino farmhands. Even as big-city monsignors marched alongside Chavez and his strikers, Father James Dillon, the parish priest at St. Mary's, had to declare himself neutral. "We've taken a stand that it's not our place to take sides," he told writer John Gregory Dunne, who had come to Delano in the summer of 1966 to tell the story of the California grape strike. "The rightness or wrongness of the strike is something I can't answer. I think it's an economic issue. It's not a moral issue."

Jack Pandol Sr. had a difficult time kneeling in the presence of such holy equivocation. On Sundays, he no longer drove in the direction of St. Mary's for Mass. He drove ten miles east of town to a little Catholic church in tiny Richgrove where, paradoxically, he worshipped with a parish of brown-skinned men and women who worked in the fields. Sitting in the Perko's in 1993, the growers had seen a quarter century pass by since Delano became one of America's civil rights datelines. The wounds of that battle were still evident in their pose. The strikes and boycotts had left them more scarred and distrustful than they naturally would have been, and this caginess had been passed down from father to son.

I told them I was looking to write a different story, one from inside the vineyards about how man and nature were going to greater lengths to out-trick each other. Growers were manipulating an ever-wider arsenal of petrochemicals, and the bugs were responding by creating superspecies impervious to the assaults. Where would it end? They seemed to be all ears—no cell phones glued on back then—as I shared my thesis: Next to siphoning the rivers, nothing had accounted for the growth of valley agriculture more than the rise of insecticides, herbicides and nitrogen fertilizers, by-products of chemical weapons labs idled after the Second World War. For half a century, these chemicals had brought higher yields, higher profits and lower supermarket prices. Farming by chemical calendar—herbicide this week, miticide next week—was simple and easy. In the face of nature's caprice, the applications were among the few things predictable about farming. Who knew, or cared to know, that these same chemicals were poisoning our drinking water and polluting our air?

They nodded their heads in consent. No grower had been a more strident devotee of chemical farming than Jack Pandol Sr. and his two younger brothers, Matt and Steve. They had built their table grape empire ("Three Brothers" was their label) on the trigger of a spray rig. To save on costs, they even bought their own chemical-distribution business. But beginning in the late 1980s, a change had come to Pandol Brothers that mystified them. Jack Jr., the middle son, the one educated at the ag school at UC Davis, had talked his dad and uncles into a crazy experiment. On three thousand acres of vines, the Pandols slashed pesticide use by 70 percent and switched from synthetic fertilizers to different blends of compost. On forty acres east of their packing plant, Junior was fermenting ten thousand tons of high-grade stuff. At his side was a ponytailed guru dressed in shorts, a T-shirt and sandals known as Amigo Bob. As part of their communing with the soil, Junior was even insisting that his office workers drive to the piles of compost and stick their hands in the 140-degree heat to feel its life. The growers around the table wrote Junior off as a little goofy. The hippies and the turkey shit, they figured, had gotten to his brain. Then each one of them paid a visit to the Pandol vineyards to take a look for himself. Spiders and lacewings, the good bugs, were devouring the bad bugs. A load of grapes was hanging on the vine. The Pandols had always grown a good-sized berry full of color. These grapes tasted even better.

And with that introduction, I drove out in the late summer of 1993 to meet Jack Jr. He had lived at home until he was almost thirty years old, and though he was now married and a young father, he was still careful not to say anything that might upset his dad and uncles. It had taken a great deal of persuasion to get them to agree to go "sustainable," he said. Whenever the counts of bad pests in the fields climbed, they began to panic. "We need to roll out the spray rigs," they'd tell him. "Let's wait a few days longer," he'd calmly reply. "Let's give the good insects a chance to catch up."

The rationale behind the conversion was deceptively simple. In fact, it was a throwback to Grandpa Stjepe. Healthy soil high in organic matter produced a healthy vine that warded off pests and disease. Of course, farming this way was a pain in the ass. When Junior unwisely cut back on one critical soil supplement, the vines got hit with mites. It took three chemical applications to wipe out the infestation. "But that's the way you learn," he said. As we stood in the middle of his compost yard, row after row of black mounds baking in the sun, he lifted a handful of humus to his nose. "It doesn't smell like manure at all," he said, sharing it with my nose. "It smells like good, rich garden soil."

My story about the Pandols jumping off the chemical treadmill ran on the front page of the *Los Angeles Times* in the summer of 1993. A few days later, Jack Jr. got a call from the secretary of the California Environmental Protection Agency. Would he like to come up to Sacramento and join the staff as undersecretary of the agency? He wasn't a politician or a bureaucrat. He wasn't even sure he was an environmentalist. But sharing a farmer's perspective inside the state capitol was an opportunity he couldn't pass up. He and his wife, Carolyn, and their two young children moved to Sacramento, where he spent the next three years at CalEPA. By the time he returned to Bakersfield, his father and uncles had abandoned sustainable farming and decided to split up the operation.

On 320 acres he had bought on his own, Jack Jr. returned to the family habit. He began growing the usual Red Globes, Autumn Royals and Crimsons with an emphasis on yield, size and color. "I was pumping more water, more citric acid, more nitrogen fertilizer to get that size," he said. "Got to get them bigger because that's what the consumers want." At the time, his son and daughter were playing junior league soccer and tennis. When it was the Pandols' turn to supply the team snacks, Jack went into the vineyard and picked grapes from his personal home supply, bunches ripened to full flavor.

"These kids and their parents start walking up to me. 'Wow, these grapes are so good. How come the stuff we buy in the grocery store doesn't taste like this?' At first I'm tone-deaf. I'm saying, 'You know, it's fresh. I picked it this morning.' But they're telling me, 'No, it's the flavor.' And that's when the lightbulb started to go on. Taste is important. People really care about taste. I had been indoctrinated so far in the other direction, I forgot the basic ingredient."

He decided to start from scratch and create new varieties that pushed flavor in a novel direction. He went looking for local investors and a top breeder to build a lab and develop a program. He teamed up with Sunridge Nurseries and David Cain, one of the most innovative fruit breeders in the country, and formed International Fruit Genetics. By the spring of 2001, Cain had developed thousands of crosses, each one genetically unique. On small test plots outside Delano and Arvin, Pandol grew the most promising offspring. Five years later, under the brand name Flavor Promise, he was picking the first varieties of Sweet Surrender, a black seedless grape that ripened early and tasted like a conventional grape, only far better. "It was more than sweet," he said. "It was sweet plus flavor."

His marketing wiz persuaded a small grocery chain in San Diego to take a chance on the grapes. Pandol labeled his bags the way vintners label their bottles of wine. The tag told a small story: "These are the best grapes you're ever gonna eat. Tell us what you think." He signed his name to the Flavor Promise pledge and provided his e-mail address so customers could respond. The chain agreed to take two boxes a day of Sweet Surrenders at each of its markets. Within three weeks, they were ordering full loads, running through fourteen boxes a day. "It blew their minds," Pandol said. "It blew our minds. 'Hey, we've got something here.' And that's when our breeding started to get creative. How do we find flavors never delivered by a grape before?"

The problem with seedless grapes is they have no seeds. Table grape growers in California, a fraternity of stressed and punctilious men, spend an inordinate amount of their days trying to make up for this fact. When breeders decided to remove the seed from the berry, which wasn't the first time man messed with the genus *Vitis,* they castrated an entire family of grapes. Without the seed, the vine no longer produced gibberellic acid that naturally thinned every bunch and sized and colored each berry. To replace the seed's function, grape growers apply a synthetic form of gibberellin—agriculture's version of the human growth hormone—in a series of methodical sprayings from spring to summer. Gibbing, they call it. They swear that a single small error in their gib coverage, one drop too heavy or too light, one day too soon or too late, is enough to change everything. Problem is, they won't know how badly they screwed up for another ninety days, when their mistakes stare up at them from the bottom of a clamshell box. "I deal in parts per million" is how the table grape grower describes his life.

The absence of seeds forces breeders such as Cain to reach across different species of grapes to develop new varieties. Unlike wild grapevines, cultivated grapevines carry "perfect flowers," meaning they have both male and female parts that allow for self-fertilization. A seedless grape is actually a fake. Rather than being completely barren, the grape hides tiny seeds that get arrested at an early stage of development, so small our teeth and tongues don't notice them. Through seeds, each berry conveys traits from both mother and father to its own offspring. Most grapevines grown in California and Europe belong to the species *Vitis vinifera,* a hardy type that produces a single crop of fruit each year and reaches peak production between the ages of five and twenty years. Plenty of recessive genes exist in the family to endow the children with infinite variations. This allows a breeder to play all sorts of fun genetic games, crossing a Cabernet Franc with a Sauvignon Blanc, for instance, and creating a Cabernet Sauvignon.

What if the goal, however, is to create a table grape that does a better job of resisting drought or mildew or, daresay, tastes like spun sugar with a hint of vanilla? What if the only way to steal such properties is to reach outside the species and hunt in the gene pool of a different species? Say a Concord grape from *Vitis labrusca,* a clan native to the Northeast with large seeds and tough skins but also flavors and aromas that can be almost exotic? This requires a different scale of rending, techniques known in the trade as hand emasculation and embryo rescue, that might make Luther Burbank, the father of California horticulture, wonder exactly what he set in motion more than a century ago when he bred the Santa Rosa plum, Elberta peach, plumcot (half plum, half apricot) and the eponymous Russet Burbank potato.

An amateur nurseryman from Massachusetts, Burbank followed his brother out to California and set up shop in Sebastopol on a fifteen-acre spread of gopher-riddled land. The genetic tampering that took place there—he had as many as three thousand experiments involving millions of plants at any one time—proved no less a factor in spreading agriculture across California than the railroad and irrigation. He was an odd strain himself. He stood five foot three with a long face and an emaciated body. Twice married, he produced no offspring of his own. A dignified man, he dressed in a black wool suit, bolo tie and short-brimmed top hat while at work, because he never knew when a curious visitor might interrupt his test trials. People regarded the horticulturalist as half Darwin, half Edison, and he became known far and wide, much to his disliking, as "the plant wizard." Over a half century of crossbreeding and hybridization, he created more than eight hundred strains and varieties of plants and watched his seeds and cuttings get cultivated by the state's largest growers, who often made fortunes and gave him little in return.

Burbank spent seventeen years perfecting a single flower, the Shasta daisy, which boasted so many extra copies of genes that it was impossible to separate what Burbank had done to it from the genetic havoc the flower created on its own. He died in 1926, four years before Edison talked Congress into allowing plant materials to be patented. In his influential text *New Creations in Fruits and Flowers,* Burbank advanced the proposition that California's botanical diversity, which allowed for such playful inventions as his freestone peach and white blackberry, was a function of plants adapting to take advantage of the region's "so many different climates, altitudes, moisture conditions and growing seasons."

Like all modern horticultural breeders, Cain owed no small debt to the wizard. In Burbank's spirit, Cain first sought to enliven the *Vitis vinifera* grape in 2003 when he crossed it with a species native to upstate New York, Massachusetts and the Mississippi Valley. He was deliberately pushing the envelope of genetic prodding degrees beyond Burbank's manipulations, though not quite as far as scientists in Oakland who were implanting a flounder gene into a tomato so it could better handle cold weather. Genetic engineering, the science of cutting and splicing genes, was not where Cain was headed.

To create his Cotton Candy berry, Cain reached out to the University of Arkansas, in Fayetteville, where the resident fruit breeder had been collecting different hybrids and species of grapes since 1964. Cain knew who his female was going to be. She was a Princess grape from California, a fat green berry with a nice crunch and the faint flavor of Old World Muscat. For its mate, he combed through the storehouse in Arkansas and chose grains of pollen with Concord grape lineage (think Welch's juice) plus five different wild species indigenous to North America. He waited for the spring blooming of the Princess vine and pulled its male parts off the flowers. This emasculation left its ovary, part of the pistil, without a sex partner. Cain then introduced the pollen shipped out from Arkansas—horticulture's version of a stud. The mating of the two, a dab of pollen applied with an artist's brush, produced hundreds of green berries.

With scalpel, tweezers and microscope, Cain cut into the tissue and excised the seeds that were the premature babies. He placed the seeds into petri dishes filled with seaweed extract and let them sit for two months, until they grew into a kind of callus. Inside each callus rested an embryo containing the combined DNA of its mother and father. Cain and his crew then delicately transferred each embryo into a sterile test tube filled with solutions of sugar, nitrogen, potassium, phosphorous and magnesium. Sealed shut, it became an artificial womb. After six weeks of feeding and stretching, the babies measured three inches long, with hairy roots on one end and faint leaves on the other. That winter, Cain and his crew pressed each spindly plant—ten thousand of them—into containers of potting soil and stuck them in a greenhouse.

By spring, each one had turned into a distinct vine. Each one, brother or sister to the other, shared the same mixed lineage and yet was completely unique in its own right. The vines were now big enough to be transplanted into real dirt on the eighty-acre vineyard where Pandol's grandparents had lived. It took a year or two, first leaf to second leaf, for the vines to produce enough fruit to distinguish the promising crosses from the mundane. The special ones, like Cotton Candy, were given a chance to produce real grapes in a real vineyard. The ordinary ones were yanked out.

"We're looking for thin but strong skins, hardy color, no discernible traces of seed, with a nice crunch," Cain explains from inside the lab. "The supermarkets don't like grapes that are reddish black. They want grapes that are either red or black. Of course, one of the main things we're now aiming for is flavor that dazzles. A good sugar-to-acid balance. You need acid to stop the sweetness from sitting heavy on the tongue."

Cotton Candy was standing in the middle of the test plot, row 48, vine 221, he recalls, when it began to fruit in 2005. He popped the first ripe berry into his mouth and wasn't sure what to make of the flavor. "I wasn't looking to create a grape that tasted like cotton candy. I kept saying it was burnt sugar, a caramel flavor. I wasn't sure how other people would react to it. One of the workers took some bunches home to his family, and his kids loved it. They said it tasted like cotton candy. That sounded as good a description as any."

I hop into Pandol's Toyota 4Runner and we land in a vineyard where the crosses are so fantastic they'll never go commercial. Here, a grape called Sweet Sapphire, a black seedless variety that looks like an amputated pinkie finger, dimple on its blunt end, is finding its last color and sugar.

"These are probably nineteen Brix. They're plenty good already. But we won't harvest for another week or so. They'll easily get to twenty-one Brix without losing any of their crunch."

He'd been watching Sweet Sapphire grow in a test plot for two years and dismissed it as a gimmick. The shape struck him as too grotesque for even a novelty grape. The more he kept popping the berries into his mouth, though, the more the flavor won him over.

"It's not like Cotton Candy. When you eat it, you know you're eating a grape," he says. "But it has a lot of flavor still." After that first harvest of Sweet Sapphire, Pandol received several e-mails from customers in Florida, singing the praises of "the black grape." He didn't know which black grape they were referring to. None of them, oddly, mentioned the most defining thing about the fruit, its shape. "It's really easy to grow, and we get big yields. And it's a tough grape. It travels well."

I pluck off a berry and roll it between my thumb and index finger. "Strange. Where does this elongation come from?"

"A gene from the Middle East."

I give it a bite. With Cotton Candy in my head, my tongue has a hard time dialing back. "That's a good grape."

"In another week," he vows, "that will be a very good grape."

We head seventy miles south across the Kern County line to his vineyard near Weedpatch. This is where my own grandfather's story in America began, where his uncle dropped him off in the summer of 1920 to work for Villa Kerkorian, the big shot who grew Thompson Seedless grapes on ranches up and down the valley before it all went south in the raisin glut of 1922. We are greeted by an expanse of uninterrupted vineyards, orchards and fields. From my grandfather's arrival to the present, the irrigated cropland in Kern County has jumped from 140,000 acres to 900,000 acres. Back then, 10 percent of the farmland

The test tube grape called Sweet Sapphire

was planted to permanent crops. It's now 60 percent. Somewhere along the way, I tell Pandol, drought stopped being a reason to fallow farmland.

We cross a vineyard that looks more perfect than the others. "Who owns that?" I ask.

"Deseret," he says. "The Mormon Church."

"I can't tell you how many Mormon acres I've crossed in this drought," I say.

"I had a Mormon classmate in college. He told me, 'We have a problem every Sunday. We tithe. What to do with all that money? So we buy, buy, buy.' It makes it hard for the regular farmer to compete. That's why I went to Philadelphia to find investors."

Half the farmers in the valley are being propped up by outside dollars, so no shame there. While the national media fixates on the woes of a parched California, farmers are teaming up with hedge funds and pension groups looking to make 20 and 30 percent on their money. Good luck getting it. They'll be lucky to clear 5 or 10 percent. But that's not the point. The investors are here in the first place, betting on California, because of the insane magnificence of our hydraulic system.

"It's magnificent until it isn't," Pandol says. He recalls his reading of Genesis, how Joseph had a vision that there would be seven years of drought, seven years of dearth. This gave him seven years to prepare for the hard times. He filled the granaries of Egypt with so much wheat it was like the sand of the sea. The seven years of famine came true but not in the land of Joseph's Egypt.

"We have a prophecy, too," he says. "It's called history. We've always had droughts and always will. But we pretend it's not going to happen again."

He then makes a concession that maybe only a Kern farmer who's also been undersecretary of the California EPA would make: "Across this whole southern valley, we've planted fencepost to fencepost. And there's just not enough groundwater to keep it all going."

The diverters of the Kern River had never gotten together and portioned out the water supply like they did next door in the Kings River basin. Instead, for the past half century, the development of Kern agriculture was allowed to outstrip the groundwater supply, and not by a little. Today, Kern County finds itself in a forever state of overdraft. Some years, the unsustainable pumping is near one million acre-feet. Pandol understands the need to finally regulate groundwater and limit pumping to levels that are considered "safe yields." But he's worried that once the new law goes into effect, the fallowing of farmland will find no end.

"You're talking about hundreds of thousands of acres in the valley that will have to be fallowed to achieve a sustainable aquifer," he says.

I don't tell him that the head honcho at the water agency in Bakersfield is citing a figure of 300,000 to 400,000 acres that will have to be idled in Kern County alone unless agriculture can find a way to undermine the law, which it's actively trying to do. Some big farmers are installing wells on third-rate land inside proposed "groundwater service areas" to establish a record of pumping. This way, before the teeth of the law bite down, they can transfer that "historical use" to their better ground inside the same area. By inflating their demands now, they can secure themselves a more ample "sustainable" supply in the future.

"The enviros could really give a rat's behind about us," Pandol says, suddenly sounding like his father. "They don't know what we do here and what it takes to do it. We've got eight to nine million irrigated acres in California. And more than half of those acres are planted to crops that can't be grown anywhere else but here. Is that not worth saving?"

We pull into his vineyard outside Lamont, where a crew of farmworkers, each one a veiled secret, are picking a seeded black grape called Sweet Jubilee. Sam's Club won't be ordering these. Neither will any of the other U.S. buyers who happily compete for Pandol's seedless varieties. The Sweet Jubilees are headed to Asia and Mexico, where people not only don't mind seeds in their grapes but prefer to chew them.

Pandol had hoped to give the bunches more time on the vine, to catch their full flavor. He now sees that the rain fell heavier on Lamont, so he's not sure how far the Sweet Jubilee can travel without succumbing to mold. He's going to send some berries back to the lab, where they'll be crushed inside a sterile petri jar and allowed to incubate for six days.

"The level of mold in the jar will tell us how long the grape will last in cold storage and shipping. That'll determine whether we sell these grapes to Mexico or if they can make the longer haul to Asia."

Just a dirt clod's throw beyond us sits the town of Arvin. You won't find any Di Giorgios there. The old man died in his pajamas at Casa Di Giorgio in February 1951. He had managed to fight off every attempt to unionize his farmworkers, including the one led by Caroline Decker, a petite twenty-one-year-old blonde, the child of Jewish Communists from New York, who had led six thousand field hands off the job in the summer of 1933, the largest strike in California history. Di Giorgio's four nephews took over the operation and fought Cesar Chavez in a campaign every bit as ugly. When their field hands voted to join the UFW in 1967, the Di Giorgios, half out of spite, transformed their fresh fruit company into a canner and distributor of fruit and vegetable juices and a wholesaler of Italian specialty meats. They fled farming, fled Arvin, blaming Chavez, the Catholic archbishops and the 160-acre law.

Jack Jr. was a sophomore at Delano High wrestling in the 138-pound division when the bad blood spilled over to his classmates. Protests divided white from brown. Freddy Chavez, Cesar's nephew, was student body president, and Maria Pandol was vice president. "Freddy got kicked out for protesting, and my sister ended up giving the speech at graduation," he recalls. "My sophomore year the Brown Berets drove in from who knows where and came on campus. It was pretty scary."

One day Jack Jr. was out in the field swamping grapes with his brother Jim when picketers pelted them with rocks and set afire the Styrofoam boxes used to pack the fruit. Jim was trying to take the boxes off the truck when the truck caught fire, too, and burned his hands. That night, their cold storage shed went up in flames. Their father knew damn well the union was behind it. The old soldier who'd fought the Japanese in the jungles of the Philippines during World War II went into full battle mode. He armed his two boys with shotguns and a spotlight and told them to patrol the ranch in the pickup truck. Then he hired a former Santa Clara County sheriff's deputy and Republican Party activist to break into the UFW's offices at Forty Acres. The files the man filched—financial records, lists of contributors, names and addresses of UFW members, detailed plans of union actions—set back the national grape boycott by six months.

"What the news media printed, what the public believed, was not true," Jack Jr. tells me. "It wasn't slavery all over again. It wasn't Jim Crow. On the other hand, we weren't always providing the best working conditions. And the wages could have been higher. There wasn't a counterbalance. The farmworker had no power."

On a summer day in 1970, the Pandols and twenty-seven other local growers signed contracts with the UFW. Jack Pandol Sr. blamed the beatniks, hippies and yippies, Marxists and the Leninists for his defeat and refused to attend the contract signing. He made his younger brother Steve go. In his office, he erected an exhibit to show off the crowbar he used on "The Day the Growers Stood the Line."

"The day your dad signed the contract . . . Talk about *Grapes of Wrath*."

"My dad hated Cesar Chavez until his dying day. He thought Chavez was a Communist, and he hated nothing more than a Commie. After we signed that three-year contract, the union never organized to get a renewal. They disappeared. That's how much the United Farm Workers cared about the workers."

It's the end of the day, and we're sampling grapes on his test plot between Delano and McFarland. He bought this 160-acre ranch when he was still in his thirties, when farmland sold for $2,500 an acre. There's a rustle a few rows away and out jumps a young Chinese man with a pruning shears draped over his shoulder. He's Dr. Yi Zhang, who grew up in Shanghai and earned his doctorate in viticulture at Ohio State. He's come to the valley to do postdoc work at Fresno State and figure out what practices in the field—irrigation, pruning, micronutrients—allow Cain's genetic crosses to achieve their optimum flavors. It helps that he's got a sommelier's degree on top of everything else. "Each of these factors can be manipulated," he says. "The trick is to determine which manipulation, if any, is responsible for a flavor evolving in the field."

He watches as Pandol and I grab flavors from the vines like the kids in *Willy Wonka*. "This one will really blow your mind," he says, tossing me a black grape that feels a little soft but tastes like something I can eat all day long. "Fabulous, huh? That's twenty-five or twenty-six Brix. It's too soft to pack and ship, but I'm hoping we can salvage the taste by backcrossing it into a grape with more durability."

He tosses me another. "I call it the Lollipop grape. It tastes like a kid's sucker."

"You can really tell the Concord in it, that's for sure," I say.

"When you breathe out, it's almost like perfume on your breath. It's too thin-skinned to go commercial. The minute it gets ripe, it splits and turns into a rotten mess. But I keep it here because I just love eating it."

We climb into his 4Runner and carve a path through layers of valley dust suspended in the air. We arrive back at his headquarters, a big white industrial complex skirted by vines and palm trees. Workers are stacking boxes of warm berries onto pallets and tying them down for a stay in cold storage. He throws a couple bags of Cotton Candy into my backseat and tells me to enjoy them. I tell him my acceptance of his gift counts as a crime of journalistic ethics, and he laughs in my face.

I leave Delano in the throes of harvest, wondering if agriculture is now doing to fruit what it has already done to soil, river, aquifer and man. I ponder Luther Burbank laid to rest under the big cedar of Lebanon at the Luther Burbank Home & Gardens in downtown Santa Rosa, only for the cedar to die of root rot. He had once crossed the California black walnut with the English walnut and created the Paradox walnut, which seemed not to know where to put its catapult energies. It threw out walnuts with thinner shells and bigger kernels but with branches and limbs that dwarfed every other walnut tree. The Paradox soared in its youth to sixty feet tall with a trunk that measured two feet wide, a true freak. So much vegetative growth weighed down its sprawling arms that they had to be propped up with metal crutches. The Paradox that the wizard planted in 1914 still graces the grounds of his old garden, a brittle giant with gorgeous gnarls and sweeps that can't stop itself from growing. Once Burbank realized that his Paradox was never going to be a prolific producer of nuts, he thought it might make fine wood for furniture, only to discover that its rapid cellular growth produced a wood too porous. What the Paradox finally became was a vigorous and disease-resistant rootstock that more fecund varieties of walnuts could be grafted onto. The Paradox is still grown commercially today, but it's hardly the same walnut tree that Burbank bred. A century of genetic mutations have appeared spontaneously in various orchards. At the same time, generations of breeders have continued their tinkering of Burbank's tinkering in the lab. Together, nature and science have forever splintered the Paradox's chromosomal makeup.

How fancy can the table grape get? How far can Jack Pandol Jr. take the sunrise and sprinkle it with dew? How much more can he push grapes to sugar before they become not "nature's candy" but confectioner's candy? I expect the obesity police will soon be on the prowl for his Gum Drops, Brix 26. He isn't taking taste back to memory, they'll say. He is using science to create new tastes that obliterate memory. He's now hired a molecular geneticist out of Cornell to identify exactly which genes in a given cultivar express the traits of mildew resistance or extra yield or that citrusy flavor on the back end. He believes the ability of molecular science to single out these markers will guarantee more precision when he tailors his next generation of flavored grapes.

As he powers forward in his vision, he seems not unlike the artificial intelligence boys in Silicon Valley moving forward in theirs, with a belief that the pursuit alone is cleansing. This is not to say that he hasn't given thought to its implications. Obesity and diabetes, if you don't count meth and opioids, are the two great robbers of life in this valley. But each harvest season, as Pandol samples his fruit and gains five pounds, he comforts himself with the knowledge that fresh fruit, for all its sugar, delivers healthy phenols for the heart. He reminds himself that candy has been stealing flavors from fruit since candy began, and when fruit turns around and does the same, it can be a slippery slope. Fruit isn't candy, he knows, nor should it try to be. But while he respects the line between the two, he isn't precisely sure where to draw it.

As I approach a stinky dairy outside McFarland, I reach into the bag of grapes, yank a Cotton Candy off the stem and pop it into my mouth. I pop another and another. The line, my tongue tells me, already has been crossed.

Sixteen

CITRUS HILLS

The first time I saw one of our rivers act like a river was when my buddy Chuck Shearn, in the summer of 1980, took me fishing on the east side along a stretch of the Kings far enough upstream that the snowmelt riffled over big boulders and knocked you off your feet if you got heedless. A ways down, the flow answered wholly to agriculture and the water became something else. Here it belonged only to the Kings. Spending an afternoon in its full presence, I didn't catch a thing except for a memory. The road was crooked past Centerville, where Mark Twain's nephew, a journalist grown tired of words, once tried to start a water war by blowing up a rival's brush-and-rock dam. Had Chuck and I ventured a little farther east, we would have come upon a gap in the two hills that separated Reedley from Sanger, two rivals in high school football, and landed in the thermal belt, where citrus groves were stitched into hillsides.

I once heard that more millionaires per capita lived in Exeter, the small east side town that belonged to the Emperor grape before it belonged to the navel orange, than any other place in America. I puzzled over how that was possible until I came to understand that 40 acres of oranges and lemons could send four kids to college and 80 acres of oranges and lemons, if the citrus crop failed in Florida, could make a man believe he was rich, and 160 acres could actually turn him into one of those millionaires in Exeter. On the west side, 160 acres was hardly enough to bury a man. And so the east side had its own economy of scale, where farms stayed small, and the children of the white growers went to school with the children of the Mexican farmworkers, and they built communities as close to the agrarian ideal as any in the valley. It helped that three rivers, the Kings, Kaweah and Tule, ran through the land, and the waters of the San Joaquin came in on the haunches of the federal canal. Even so, when drought stuck around, the east side was no more immune from hard times than the riverless west side.

The citrus belt sits above the valley floor on a ledge of granite that can hold only so much snowmelt. By gravity, most of the runoff flows down the slope and filters through the east side and settles in the center valley, thirty miles away. The aquifer's depth on the east side is so shallow—maybe eighty feet before a well driller strikes granite—that only a small quantity of water can be stored in its crevices. The pockets of water that exist inside the rock have become so depleted that some growers are lucky to extract one hundred gallons a minute with their pumps. Water that sat at twenty feet deep before the drought now sits at sixty feet deep. Sand Creek, for one, has been nothing but sand for the past three years. To reduce an orchard's thirst, some growers have pruned back their trees so severely that from roadside they appear to be shrubs. Others have ripped out their orchards altogether, replacing old trees with baby trees that drink a lot less water, at least for the time being.

Citrus groves along the San Joaquin Valley's east side

I've landed on a knoll the other side of Curtis Mountain, which isn't really a mountain, where the Munn family has been growing citrus since 1912. That was the year Stanley Munn rode up with a gang of tall, blond, square-jawed young men from Pasadena, sons of bankers, and transplanted the Southern California orange culture into the ground of Tulare County. They dug into hard mineral earth to find water. They found it at ten feet deep. They trucked in baby navels from the Teague Nursery, down near Los Angeles. They dropped sticks of Hercules dynamite into the hardpan to blow open enough earth to plant each tree. They mined sand from Sand Creek to fabricate their concrete irrigation pipes. They built sheds with no interior walls to live in and grew enough oats and grain to raise their Berkshire hogs. They waited four years for the trees to hang their first oranges and packed the fruit with Sunkist, which had followed in their tracks.

The photos of that conquering have been laid out on the coffee table in front of me by Reed Munn, born and raised in this citrus belt, who's proud to say that the water his father fed to those trees is the same water he's drunk all his life. As snowmelt percolates down the Sierra and through the rocks in his hillside, its picks up minerals and other stuff that he credits for giving the Munn family tree a jolt. "I'm six foot two," he tells me. "That's three inches taller than my father was. And I'm going on ninety-five years."

He's a handsome man with a full head of gray hair and blue eyes he took from his Scottish side. He can't explain how a native Californian came to talk in a Missouri drawl, other than he must have picked it up from neighbor kids when he was impressionable. To keep his memory intact, he splashes a little red wine into his daily glass of Pom juice. Before his wife, Ann, died a few years ago, he was able to fit into his wedding tux to celebrate their anniversary. They met at the University of California at Davis before the Second World War and raised three boys and two girls, who graduated from UC Davis, too. His second son, Dana, who's siting on one side of him, runs the Shafter-Wasco Irrigation District, one of the contractors of Friant-Kern water. His youngest son, Andrew, who's sitting on the other side, farms the forty acres at the bottom of the knoll and another forty acres a field away on the downslope of Curtis Mountain. Reed Munn has eight grandchildren, and not one is a farmer. Among them are an actress in New York, a financier in Connecticut, a biomedical engineer, a microbrewer, a high school teacher and a civil engineer. "You're looking at the last of the farming Munns," says Andrew, who at six foot five is Exhibit A for the wonders of the local water.

In a century scarred by seven droughts, the Munns have never lost a single citrus tree to thirst, though they've come close. One dry year, Reed had to walk buckets of water upslope to keep the alkali from poisoning the roots. Most years, though, he's been able to depend on the cracks in the earth to capture enough snowmelt to keep his aquifer going. The pumps drawing up that water cease only when they die. From the centrifugal era to the turbine era, he lines the driveway leading up to his redwood house with every spent pump. It's kind of a monument to the fallen. As another one goes kaput, he adds it to the memorial. The good pumps served him fifteen years. The oldest one, a jack pump, goes back to his father's time. Even in the worst drought, the jack pump was able to pull up water. In wet years, its nose for water tended to get it drowned. That was when the centrifugal pump came in handy. It moved a lot of water when the water was easy to fetch. The later turbine pumps didn't care if the water table was low or high; they kept working.

Reed considers himself lucky because a lot of growers along the citrus belt don't have groundwater to call on. They've got surface water from the Central Valley Project and nothing else. Son Andrew has the luxury of mixing fresh snowmelt from the San Joaquin River with the saltier water from the ground. The blend is easier on the trees. It also means less pumping, which lets the water table recharge in wetter years.

"There's a CVP turnout right where you drove in," Reed says. "No water has come out of it for two years. There's some politics involved in denying the east side that water. But there's some miscalculation on our part to add to the hurt."

"What do you mean?" I ask.

"So much of this citrus belt doesn't have groundwater. It's never had groundwater. But they put in trees because they thought they could always get federal water from the canal."

"You mean your neighbors?"

He nods. He doesn't want to come off sounding superior, because he considers the entire hillside, his family's eighty acres included, to be more or else an experiment, a gamble against the odds of drought, freeze and pestilence. "That's where it's going to come in rough for them this year. They've got the trees but no water."

"This is even worse than 1976," Dana says. "We're not built for dry on dry on dry. Another dry year and this will be the Cadillac desert."

Reed Munn can understand his father, Stanley, wanting to plant oranges a century ago on the easy hills that rolled out to the Sierra. It was one of the more gorgeous spots in all California, a huddle of knolls green in spring and bleached in summer where the only crop had been wheat thrown out as seed and dry-farmed. Stanley Munn, a child of Omaha, had wandered all over the country before arriving in Pasadena in 1909 to visit an aunt. In every direction, he could see emerald orchards painted gold with oranges. Here was the mythical Southern California Eden. Every Washington navel kissed by the sun was incomparably fat and juicy and traced its lineage to a couple of trees planted in the early 1870s by Eliza Tibbets, a settler of the Riverside Colony. She was a remarkable woman, an abolitionist and spiritualist from back east who had married three times and divorced twice, adopted a black child and marched with Frederick Douglass for a woman's right to vote before migrating to California with her newest husband, Luther. The Riverside Colony was, among other experiments, a farm looking to grow unique varieties of grains and citrus. Eliza had a friend in Washington, D.C., who ran the test gardens for the USDA and was growing a variety of orange discovered in Brazil. He sent a few of its cuttings out to California, and Eliza was able to keep them alive by irrigating with dishwater. She and Luther sold more cuttings to other growers for a dollar apiece, one year reaping twenty grand before Luther's eternal fights with neighbors over water consumed their fortune.

The couple died penniless even as the clones of their Washington navels planted tens of thousands of acres across Southern California, created the marketing machine called Sunkist, lured trainloads of East Coast émigrés dreaming of another kind of gold, and ensconced a new class of gentility, in their fine suits and gowns, who earned four times the income of the average American. Millionaires' Row in Pasadena wasn't named Orange Grove Boulevard for nothing. Mansions were set amid perfect lines of citrus with the San Gabriel Mountains as backdrop and a couple of palm trees thrown in for good measure.

This became the picture postcard that sold California to the world—the Golden State's "bourgeois utopia," in the words of historian Kevin Starr.

Stanley Munn was sent to Tulare County by clever businessmen in Pasadena who were looking to relocate that postcard image to Exeter and Orange Cove, Porterville and Strathmore. They knew already that the future of Los Angeles lay in paving over its orchards. The San Joaquin Valley did not furnish the soft ocean breezes and mild Mediterranean clime that made the Southern California orange second to none. But the Sierra did form a "thermal belt" like the one created by the San Gabriels to buffer against freeze, and three rivers and a half dozen creeks ran down the mountain and through the east side. More important, a culture of men and women who knew how to wrest crops from the alkali had already planted their heels in the ground. A pioneer named James William Center Pogue had been growing oranges and lemons since 1877 on the knoll outside the nearby town of Lemon Cove. By 1905, local citrus growers had dug a ditch and built a packinghouse next to the railroad and were selling their fruit as part of the Lemon Cove Association. "The four businessmen from Pasadena were named Coy, Katel, Hurrell and Dickey. Coy was my dad's uncle by marriage," Reed says. "They bought the Curtis Mountain Land and Cattle Company, which took in the mountain and a mile beyond it."

Their intention was to cover the hillside in oranges. They sent their sons and nephews to do the dirty work. Where soil ran salty and the aquifer thin, they planted olives as a backup crop. Some years the olives brought home more money than the citrus. Dozens of families came out from Ohio, Kentucky and Tennessee and grabbed their own forty acres on the hillside and plain below. When the Great Depression struck, they had no money to drill deeper wells. They just folded up and left the trees to wither. "It was tough ground. You only had so much groundwater," Reed says. "I wouldn't call it a land swindle exactly. A gamble, I'd say. These were people who were used to rainwater to raise their crops. They didn't realize until they were in too deep that California was a different animal."

The sky closed up in the early 1920s. Half the hillside turned barren. Dry farmers came in and planted grain again. The Munns survived because they had groundwater. Still, the price for oranges dropped so steeply that Stanley Munn couldn't cover his packing charges. If he was going to make it, he had to find a way to pack his fruit on his own. He took on a partner and they started a little packing shed. They delivered their oranges straight to the stores. To help his father, ten-year-old Reed drove a tractor and raised a Hampshire hog, feeding it grain and oats and table scraps until it got 180 pounds big. Then the worst drought of all—the one that began in 1929 and kept going until 1934—turned a bunch of orchards into dust. Truth is, these farms were barely scraping by when Mother Nature delivered a final blow. What the banks didn't take back was now in the hands of the county tax collector.

This time, the Freemasons decided to make noise. The main man leading the charge to find an outside source of water was Frank Mixter, a Spanish-American war vet who owned the drugstore in Exeter. Mixter wore rimless glasses and double-breasted suits and got himself elected to the state assembly and then the state senate at the same time he was rising to become the grand master of the Masonic Order in California. The U.S. Bureau of Reclamation was filled with civil and hydrological engineers who were Freemasons. They lent a patient ear to Senator Mixter as he helped advocate for a Central Valley Project to save the east side.

The imported flow of the San Joaquin River began arriving in 1949. Until this newest drought, the feds were able to keep the supply running. They delivered on average 80 percent of the contracted amount—39,200 acre-feet a year for Orange Cove—through the decades. For a long time, the water table was able to rebound and stabilize. Today, it's as badly depleted as it was in the 1920s. Some of this has to do with drought's return. Most of it, though, is a consequence of too much land planted in too much citrus, both inside and outside the irrigation district. Each year, from the perch on his knoll, Reed Munn can see the navels, lemons and mandarins extending out a little farther. They march up the hill and in the opposite direction across the valley floor, beyond the protection of the thermal belt. From Orange Cove to Terra Bella, tens of thousands of acres have been planted on the pledge of actual federal water guaranteed by contracts. Tens of thousands of additional acres have been planted on the promise of intermittent flood deliveries from the same Central Valley Project. In the latter event, the orchards are real, the water an illusion.

The situation, it would seem, cannot be sustained. In the living room of the Munn household, it frames a remarkable exchange between father and sons:

"I don't recognize these hills. I don't recognize this valley," Reed says. "They're planting citrus darn near down to Fresno. That's where the frost can get 'em. They're going to get smacked by the next freeze and then cry for relief."

"It's not the small guy overdeveloping the land," Andrew says. "It's the big ranchers and the moneymen from who knows where. They buy it, plant citrus and get some hired gun to farm it for them."

"I don't see neighbors anymore. I see investors. And they've got no faces," Reed says. "I bought this ranch from a Japanese family who was growing tomatoes on it. The father got into a car wreck and was killed. One of his sons became a pharmacist. The other son wanted to stay and honor his father, but his heart wasn't into farming. I had half the hill, and it made sense to buy the other half."

"I remember when we were growing Valencias, and all Dad could hope for was a freeze in Florida," Dana says. "Now everyone is pulling out Valencias as fast as they can and planting mandarins."

"My guess is the production out here has doubled since the last drought," Reed says. "They've put in these big pumps. If we don't get rain, they're going to pump out the rest of our aquifer in a year or two."

"We'd better get used to it," Andrew says. "There's going to be even more land consolidation with climate change. The small farmer who built these communities on the east side won't be able to ride out the variability. It'll require deeper pockets to go deeper in the ground. As much as I hate saying it, we're going to end up looking more like the west side."

The west side of the valley, he means. The giant Westlands Water District, seventy miles away. The true flat desert. To the east side citrus grower in these poetic hills, there would be no worse fate.

Twenty-five miles south of the Munns, deeper into the citrus belt, I come on a packing shed just beyond Woodlake; "A CITY WITH TRUE WESTERN HOSPITALITY," the sign says. This is where John Kirkpatrick, who's been growing citrus for seventy-five years, has set aside a special place in the cold storage room for the prize of his harvest: the citron. Its seeds have traveled across four thousand years and from a world away to find root in a small plot on his fifty-acre ranch up the hillside. The fruit, which looks like a large, bumpy lemon to those who don't know better, matures through summer and is ready to pick by August, a few weeks away. The harvest is as close to grabbing dollar bills off trees as a farmer can get, though Kirkpatrick isn't inclined to boast about it. The eighty-six-year-old Presbyterian, the nation's sole citron grower, is a modest man. And he's been sworn to secrecy by "the rabbis in New Jersey," as he affectionately calls his partners.

No fruit is more venerated by Orthodox Jews than the citron, known in Hebrew as the *ethrog*. Bronze coins from the Jewish uprising against Rome in the first century were embossed with an image of the tree. The perfumed fruit finds its way into the homes of devout Jews across the globe during Sukkoth, the feast that comes on the heels of Yom Kippur and marks the desert wandering of the Exodus. The million and a half citrons sold around the world aren't cherished for their flavor. In fact, they're rarely ever eaten. The fruit is one of the four species—along with the date palm's frond and the branches of the myrtle and willow—held in the hand and shaken in the air on each morning of the festival. The *ethrog* represents the "heart of man," and as a symbol of faith, repentance, healing and redemption, that heart must be free of any blemish or it never makes it out of the field.

From winter to summer, the fruit is fussed over by rabbis and other experts of kosher law dispatched to the orchards of Israel, Italy and Morocco. Kirkpatrick's three-acre plot on the outskirts of Exeter—soon to be a five-acre plot—is visited four times a year by one or another bearded man from back east draped in woolen prayer shawls. Eight out of ten of his citrons never pass muster. If Kirkpatrick or his son, Greg, don't see the blemish and cast aside the fruit, the rabbis will. Imperfection can be as tiny as a flyspeck. Of the twenty thousand pieces of fruit Kirkpatrick will box and send to market—a dozen wooden pallets—the beautiful ones with stems intact can fetch up to eighty dollars apiece. Once, and only once, he was graced with a specimen so perfect, at a moment of perfect demand, that it sold for two thousand dollars. "It's a load of diamonds," Kirkpatrick says outside the cold storage room ornamented by Hebrew scripture where this year's haul will soon come to chill. The old citrus farmer in his fedora and Levi's can see the math going through my head. In a good year, the multiplication works out to

John Kirkpatrick checks for flaws in his prized citrons.

more than a million dollars. Too bad it doesn't land in his bank account that way, he says. No fruit in the citrus belt, no fruit in the entire valley, for that matter, costs more to nurture. "Maybe only raising my children cost me more," he says.

He's not sure how, back in 1980, Yisroel Weisberger, an eighteen-year-old yeshiva student from Brooklyn, got his phone number. Weisberger was tired of buying imported *ethrogs* for twenty and thirty dollars apiece. His plan was to grow citrons in California and sell better fruit for less money in New York. If he mailed out a packet of rabbinically blessed seeds from Israel would Kirkpatrick consider planting them? "Sure, it sounds intriguing," the farmer said. Weisberger warned him that the citron was not an easy fruit to grow according to Orthodox Jewish standards. Kirkpatrick, a sturdy man with a wry wit, thought he had seen just about everything there was to see in farming. He'd been growing oranges and olives since he was eleven years old, the year his big brother went off to the Second World War. He had raised tomatoes, avocados, squash, freestone peaches and a dozen varieties of citrus, drawing his water straight from the Kaweah River by virtue of what farmers call pre-1914 irrigation rights, which essentially meant he owned a piece of the river. The citron, however, turned out to be an exercise in a particular kind of patience.

He cleared a plot of land where he'd been growing avocados and planted the seeds Weisberger sent him—seeds that traced back to ancient China. Eighty baby citrons sprouted. He watched them grow, though he wasn't sure what they were growing into. Tree or bush? They were covered with nasty thorns, and their branches had to be stretched and splayed onto a lattice. A rabbi drove up from Los Angeles with his seventy-two-page guidebook to show Kirkpatrick how. The lattice, the rabbi explained, was designed to keep the limbs from lashing out in a fit of wind and cutting nicks into the fruit's skin—blemishes that would not go unnoticed. A year later, when the bushes set their first fruit, Kirkpatrick wanted to celebrate with a harvest. He found himself strapped by kosher dictates. He couldn't sell a single piece of fruit, at least not to anyone celebrating Sukkoth. By rabbinical law, the citron had to come from wood that was at least three years old.

After that third year, Kirkpatrick formed a joint venture with Weisberger and his brother-in-law. He would grow the citrons, and they'd sell them at a premium. To protect the fruit, he built a retractable shading out of wood, metal and cloth to minimize the harshest rays of sunshine and ward off winter frost. For almost forty years now, they've been partners. One year, 1999, the trees took the brunt of a big freeze and literally burned to the ground. He had to wait until the following spring for the bush to push up green again. It then took another year for the fruit to return. "Thank goodness the three-year law doesn't apply to trees coming back from frost or we would have had to throw that crop away," he says.

The citron harvest is as fussy as harvests get. He and his son, Greg, along with one farmhand, Jesus Serrano, a Seventh-Day Adventist who's been with him for thirty-eight years, are the only ones trusted to select the perfect specimens: twice the size of an egg, narrow at the top and broad at the bottom, bumpy but not grotesquely so. They don't yank the citrons off the limb. They gingerly snip them off, taking care to keep the stem intact and place each one into its own cushioned holder in a box. This way, the sixteen citrons in each box never get close enough to scar each other. He'll watch, a pained expression on his face, as the Orthodox grader makes one final call inside the cold storage room. "Almost anything the good eye can see qualifies as a blemish," he says. "A tiny scarring from a bug called thrips or a blister." It softens the blow a bit to know that the culls will be sent to a craft distiller in Alameda,

St. George Spirits, where Kirkpatrick's citrons will infuse a high-end vodka.

Across from the cold storage room, the oldest citrus packing line still operating in Tulare County rests between harvests. Built in the 1930s, it once served the groves of Riverside and then followed the orange over the Tehachapi Mountains to Lindcove, where Kirkpatrick discovered it gathering rust in a warehouse "like an old Cadillac." Its belts and rollers pack two bins of fruit an hour compared to the big modern machines that pack fifty bins. It couldn't fit his philosophy better: keep things simple and small. He produces a steady stream of fruit throughout the year—lemons and citrons, pomegranates, tangelos and three varieties of mandarins. Fruit that ships well, he sells through Sunkist. Fruit that doesn't ship well but tastes like sugar, he sends to farmers' markets. He's forever toying with the mix, pulling out old varieties, planting new hybrids, seeing if he can catch the market at peak price. In the seventy-five years he's been growing citrus, he has never seen a lemon market like this one. From November to May, every lemon he picks puts forty cents into his pocket. "The beat goes on. Once we send off the citrons, it'll be pomegranates and then mandarins. No rest for the wicked."

I first met Kirkpatrick fifteen years ago at a book reading in Exeter. As I got to know him over the years, he struck me as a different breed of grower. His middle-of-the-road politics was refreshing to find in a place whose KKK roots still kept blacks out of Visalia. He didn't whine when his crop went south. Not even a freeze made him sour. He was a genuine family farmer who was living out a life on the soil that would have made the old Grangers proud. His wife, Shirley, grew up in west side farm country, and he brought her to the east side when they married, fifty-eight years ago. Even in harvest's frenzy, they'd sneak off and grab lunch together. "She's a partner in everything I do," he once told me. "Every decision we make here, we make together." Two of their children had careers that took them to other parts of California. Greg, the eldest, stayed and farmed with his parents and became a city councilman who dared to talk about sprawl and how the real estate developers were corrupting Visalia's general plan and paving over farmland.

As the drought dug in and the feds cut off water to the west side and the east side, I checked in with the Kirkpatricks to find out how the citrus belt was faring. Then I came up with the idea of taking a drive along the paved bank of the Friant-Kern Canal to glimpse drought's distress. I called up John wondering if he knew an easy way past the canal gates. It just so happened that the ditch tender for the irrigation districts was a buddy of his. He called back to say that his friend would open the gate and guide us down. "I told him you wanted to do some fishing," John said, snickering.

We're only a few minutes into our drive, the foothills straight ahead and the Sierra just beyond, when he hits the brakes on his Ford Explorer and pulls over to the side of the road. Out my window is a vast open field studded with abandoned wells and their little wooden pump houses beaten by a hundred years of weather. I can't see the St. John's or Kaweah Rivers, but John says they're close by. This is the ground that in a previous century brought about a war between the citrus growers on the hill and alfalfa growers on the plain. "You're looking at the Great Swamp that the Tulare Irrigation District and the Lindsay-Strathmore Irrigation District went to dynamite over," he says. He's shaking his head at the thought that men would fight for forty years, in and out of court, to possess such a forlorn spit of earth and at the audacity of the water mining that took place here. "They made peace only because they knew the Central Valley Project was coming. I hate to imagine all the water that got pumped out of here. It's dry as hell now."

By the time we reach the main gate of the Friant-Kern Canal, the ditch tender is waiting for us. The canal is not even two-thirds full, he says. If the molecules of water could tell their age, most would date their arrival to a snowfall four or five years ago. This being another "zero delivery" year, the canal has ceased to function as a giver of irrigation. It's nothing more than downstream storage to help out the dam. The quiet and still are not an illusion. The water is scarcely moving at all. In a wet year, the canal delivers 1.7 million acre-feet. In a dry year such as this one, it will be lucky to deliver 60,000 acre-feet. Unlike the aqueduct, which relies on hydraulics to send water downhill and then uphill, the Friant-Kern Canal drops a steady half foot every mile and works on gravity alone. The only pumps out here are metered and belong to the irrigation districts and a handful of municipal users for the purpose of taking that water. Those pumps are silent now.

Even at drought's worst, the farmer does manage to receive some unmetered water from a whole universe of cracks in the concrete. Untold acre-feet leak out from the canal's bottom and recharge the aquifer. The windfall delights the adjacent farmers. Since the drought hit and they began digging deeper beneath the earth for more groundwater, the farmers have created a giant sucking action. More canal water is being drawn through the cracks at the same time the ground beneath the canal collapses. The sinking proceeds at a record pace. The poor ditch tender isn't in a position to talk about it. I've done enough of my own digging to know that the Bureau of Reclamation has no idea the extent of the subsidence or what it's going to cost to repair the canal. The canal's capacity to deliver water along one twenty-five-mile stretch has been reduced by as much as 60 percent. Water that moved down the canal at 4,000 cubic feet per second is now moving at 1,650. This is an astonishing figure, though no one in an official position wants it attributed to them. The earth has sunk three feet, but it hasn't made the news. It will likely take a half billion dollars, if not more, to fix.

Like the subways back east, the canal shoots you through the entrails of a place. We pass rows of rotund citrus trees dusted white with a clay that reflects the heat of the sun and land upon a community of battered trailers and shrunken shacks. Welcome to Tooleville, John says, one of the poorest dots on the California map, a tiny rural settlement that once housed Dust Bowl Okies and now houses Dust Bowl Mexicans.

He stops the car, and we linger on the place: busted-out windows, bedsheets for curtains, shells of cars, old tires piled high, rusted mailboxes, snowflake lights never taken down since Christmas, Chihuahuas on the prowl. Where, I wonder, are the three hundred or so residents? "The parents are farmworkers," John says. "The kids are gang workers." It's not an easy thing to hear, especially from such a wise and tolerant man, and I tell him I've struggled myself trying to explain the stubbornness of such a scene. How is it that the Japanese, Hindus and Armenians were able to overcome discrimination and exploitation and move from picking crops to growing crops? Why is it that Mexican farmhands, for more than a century, have been so passive about the concept of owning the land? Might their proximity to the border explain it, a belief kept in the heart that they are here for only a short while and will be returning to the soil of home? Or is it that each new wave of Mexicans who cross the border undermines the bargaining position of the previous wave, so that they are never able to gain a real foothold? Or might the root cause be a peasant culture that has responded to Mexico's oppression and corruption by adopting a "live for today" strategy, a reflex only strengthened by the oppression on this side of the line?

Whatever gifts and deficits these residents may carry across the border, they also find themselves in a valley where the ladder is missing most of its middle rungs. We've designed a valley economy that provides no real competition to the farm. Each generation of farmer reaches deeper into the rural heart of Mexico for his labor. Once here, the picker, packer, pruner and irrigator occupy a firm but bottom rung on the ladder. No people work harder. But what happens to their children and grandchildren? If they reject the fields, as so many of them understandably do, what becomes of their lives? There is no other major industry here to realize their labor; there are few middle rungs to compete with the fields. Hammer-and-nail jobs offered by the building industry are just another bottom rung.

Whether the gaps in our ladder are by design to keep the worker captive to the fields, or simply a failure of imagination, I don't know; I've heard it explained both ways. What is clear is that we are telling children who come from homes where English is not spoken, where education has for generations been a proposition that ended in the fifth grade, that they must excel and go to college. They must take a leap from the bottom rung to the top rung with no station in between. I have taught children at Fresno State who've made such a leap. I have encountered many others in southeast Fresno, in some of the most impoverished neighborhoods in the nation, who might have become electricians or welders or plumbers if their junior highs and high schools had steered them that way. Instead, frustrated by the want of an option other than college, they drop out, join gangs and raise children out of wedlock.

John listens intently, though I'm not sure he's comfortable exploring the matter any further. Maybe he regards our conversation as having ventured a good distance beyond the canal and the subject of water. Maybe he's grown weary of high-minded arguments that reduce valley agriculture to a plantation caricature. He's quiet for a good half minute as we study Tooleville's existence.

"We've always had our Toolevilles and always will," he says finally. "But I used to think of the east side as the exception in the valley. We had real communities here, Mark, where whites, Mexicans and Asians integrated. Real honest-to-God American communities. But that has started to change the past few decades."

I wonder if he might be romanticizing the past. He doesn't think so.

"That climb up the ladder, sad enough, is not happening the way it should," he says. "The Japanese made it. The Hindus made it. Most of the Okies made it. A lot of Filipinos made it. But the Mexicans as a group are having a harder time. As we've brought in successive generations to work the fields, it's created this underclass."

A long time ago in the valley, an immigrant could sink to his hands and knees in the fields and earn enough money over four or five harvests to buy his own twenty acres—and a ditch full of snowmelt to keep it in water. My grandfather had done exactly that. But no matter how much you bust your ass in the fields today, no matter how committed you are to stacking dollar bills, it's virtually impossible for a farmworker to become a farmer. That chasm is a fact scorched into the ground. Even so, John does not blame the loss of community cohesiveness on economic disparity alone. The separateness he sees on the east side is equally a consequence of immigrants ghettoizing themselves, he believes. As much as some Mexican immigrants want to bust out of the barrio, many others are content to live among themselves. Their mostly undocumented status only serves to widen this chasm. "Something's been lost," he says.

No place is easy to pin down, and the valley may be more elusive than most. It took a Steinbeck and a McWilliams to capture one aspect. It took a Saroyan to capture another. The east side, the west side, the center valley—each has its own relationship to water. That relationship explains not only the type of agriculture practiced in each but the culture itself, why each one looks and smells and vibrates the way it does. The land blessed with river is one kind of place. The worker there is more likely to share in the spoils of irrigation. The land reliant on imported water and water mined from the ground is another kind of place. The way things work there bears more than a passing resemblance to the feudal system. The puzzle of the east side, what makes it such a challenge to unpack, is that it combines the two.

Tooleville is easy to grasp. It exists for a reason. Way back when, the

Where Tooleville ends at the Friant-Kern canal

migrant worker was locked out of towns and cities. Economics barred the "ditch bank" Okies. Hatred barred the blacks and Mexicans. Racist real estate codes were written in official language; redlining was written in the idiom of wink and nod. Migrants were given little choice but to seek out a patch of alkali in the country and plop down their shacks and trailers. For years, they fetched water by milk pail. Some still do. The codes were wiped clean of offending language years ago, but their effects still linger.

Just the other side of Tooleville, five minutes away, sits the immaculate little town of Exeter. The road sign from here to there would be truer if it marked the distance as one hundred miles. Years of community beautification have turned Exeter into a tourist gem. The restored brick buildings downtown have been painted with splendid murals. One of the larger murals, on the side of the old Mixter pharmacy, depicts the orange harvest as Norman Rockwell might have. A little white girl in a red dress is sitting in the orchard. She's put down her Raggedy Ann doll to clutch an orange bigger than the doll's face. A tall white man elegantly climbs the second rung of a ladder to fill up his canvas sack with fruit. Not a pant leg is smudged. Row after row of perfectly symmetrical trees extend from the flat foreground to the hills in the background. The scale of the farming is industrial, but the work is easygoing.

"I know it's an idealized scene from the 1940s or '50s, but where are the Mexicans?" I ask John. He says when he first set eyes upon it, he wondered the same thing. If I look carefully at the faces of workers, an argument can be made that one or two of them appear to be Mexican or perhaps Filipino. I know from my reading of *Factories in the Field* that it was on these same streets, during a carnival to celebrate the end of the 1929 harvest, that white farmworkers pushed Filipino field hands off the sidewalks and physically barred them from places of amusement. One of the molested Filipinos grabbed his bolo knife and stabbed a white man. A mob of whites was immediately organized. They beat and roused the Filipinos from the fields and drove them from their labor camps, burning their shacks and tents to the ground. The violence against Filipinos spread to Tulare and then to the Salinas Valley. When John says the Filipinos in the citrus belt "made it," he really means that they made it out of here alive. No Filipino works these fields today. No Filipino grows an orange.

We spend the rest of the afternoon navigating the canal's length, crossing from Tulare County to Kern County, threading through eight different irrigation and water districts, from Lewis Creek to Tea Pot Dome to Rag Gulch. Since the federal canal became a presence seven decades ago, the three counties where the flow goes have nearly doubled their cropland to 1.9 million acres. This growth has occurred both inside the irrigation districts served by the federal water and outside the districts in a no-man's-land without federal water. Nothing has been able to deter the farmers. Not the worst alkali and hardpan. Not the bitter thirst of drought. Consider the Kern-Tulare Water District as it sprawls across both counties. In the second year of this drought, the district was farming 16,776 acres of grapes, nuts and citrus. By the fourth year of drought, it is farming 18,017 acres of grapes, nuts and citrus. As the footprint of agriculture keeps extending outward, the canal water keeps getting spread over a wider and wider area. The groundwater replenishment that occurs because of these imported supplies does not last. As soon as the aquifer builds up, it becomes an excuse for growers to add more farmland and pump even more.

The Central Valley Project, built in the name of saving east side farmland, seems to have lost its way. It's been stretched to a point that can no longer be sustained. As John and I pass through orchards whose emerald leaves have turned a sickly yellow or whose sixty-year-old trunks are being ripped from the earth on account of drought, the irony is plain. This is the same ground that was imperiled by successive droughts in the 1920s and 1930s, the same ground that launched the cries of "Steal us a river!" and the building of the project. The land has landed in the same place where it started almost a century ago. Only now, there's no more water, near or far, to steal.

A dust devil rises in front of us, its swirl blowing the leaves of the orchard upward, like a gust lifting a woman's skirt. A citrus tree can take a lot, John says. Some of the trees we're passing are nearly one hundred years old and still producing tasty fruit. Sadly, by the looks of things, this orchard won't be able to ride out the drought.

"This is a guy on his uppers," John says. "He may lose his place."

"Uppers?"

"Yeah, he lost his lower teeth from grinding. Now all he's got left are the uppers."

For the most part, the ranches on either side of the canal are even smaller than I thought they'd be. Not even the big growers own big chunks of land in the citrus belt. A guy might be farming a thousand acres, but it's broken up into twenty acres here, forty acres there and eighty acres ten miles away, John says. Even Resnick grows his citrus on lots of smaller ranches. There's a good explanation for this. Forty acres of citrus can still sustain a family, and this is why so many of the original families have held on to the land. The wealthier growers who might have accumulated citrus empires were prevented from doing so by federal reclamation law. The 960-acre limit wasn't openly flouted in the citrus belt the way it was elsewhere. The law, however, doesn't apply anymore. When the water contracts recently came up for renewal, the east side irrigation districts borrowed enough money from Wells Fargo to pay off the federal government for the canal's original construction costs. In the process, the districts freed themselves from the dictates of acreage limits. There are no more obstacles left to slow the shift of small ranches becoming larger ranches, and the culture of the east side will go with it.

On the way back to his packing shed, I tell John what the Munns told me: He's now an endangered species standing the same doomed ground as the Tipton kangaroo rat.

"What's stopping these hedge funds and pension groups from

swooping in and buying this ranch and that ranch?" I ask him. "They can accumulate five thousand acres of citrus and get the federal water for cheap."

"They're doing it as we speak," he says. "They're spending millions of dollars taking out old varieties and planting new ones. The only way a small guy is going to hang on is if he's willing to do something crazy."

With another do-or-die harvest of citrons in front of him, he doesn't have to explain what "crazy" means.

It was J. G. Boswell who first told me the story of Otis Booth and his orchard perched on a rocky hillside in the far northern reach of the citrus belt. Booth was a cousin to Otis Chandler, the Stanford shotputting champion who became the publisher of the *Los Angeles Times*. As the great-grandsons of the epic bellower General Harrison Gray Otis, Booth and Chandler were both beneficiaries of the Owens River heist that created Los Angeles. The way the family trust fund worked, the Chandler kids had a lot more money and clout than the Booth kids. Otis Booth got his engineering degree from Caltech and an MBA from Stanford and then went to see his cousins about a possible role in the newspaper dynasty. They named him vice president of production, a fancy way of saying he was now in charge of procuring the paper that the news was printed on. He made a comfortable living and built a house in San Marino like the rest of them. By his mid-thirties, he had mastered the skills of fly-fishing, big-game hunting, saving money and investing money. He and his buddy Charlie Munger were making a tidy sum buying and selling condos on Orange Grove Boulevard in Pasadena when they heard about a prodigy from Omaha, Nebraska, named Warren Buffett. They were so beguiled by his skills that they kept shoveling money to him. Booth's early investments in Berkshire Hathaway were somewhere in the range of $1 million. Forty years on, he was worth nearly $3 billion.

Booth was no farmer, of course. He had inherited his first forty acres in Ivanhoe from his Grandma Farnsworth and hired a professional to plant the trees for him. That was back in 1955. He quickly discovered that selling oranges made for a decent return, but the real windfall was the open-ended tax write-offs that the federal government allowed for growing them. Everything from trees to tractors to Cadillacs (if a Cadillac is what you considered to be your tractor) was a deduction. The millionaires of Exeter, who reported yearly incomes of thirty and forty grand, were experts in tax avoidance. Booth, a tall man with shoulders beefed up from lifting weights with cousin Otis, drove up and down the citrus belt looking for more orchards to buy. Like fishing the White River in Colorado or hunting rare species in Africa or exploring the South Pole, collecting orange groves became one of his hobbies. He started on flat ground and ended up climbing the hill. He didn't stop until he owned ten thousand acres. In the citrus belt they called him "the king of the navels."

He'd been blessed with four children, three from his first marriage and one from his second, which allowed him some swing to get around reclamation law. He put enough 960-acre chunks in his name and the names of his wife, children, grandchildren and nephews that it almost covered the entire ten thousand acres. His daughter Loren from his first marriage was Daddy's girl. He could take her fishing and hunting, and she'd hold her own. She could get on a horse and fly. She majored in animal science at Cal Poly and met and married a Bakersfield potato farmer. She had bothered to learn enough agriculture to bug her father and his citrus consultant about what they were doing on her 960 acres. They tried to brush her off, but her questions only got more pointed once she graduated from the California Ag Leadership program. Why was her father allowing the company that sold him farm chemicals to instruct him on how much chemicals to use? Why didn't he have his own independent pest control adviser? Why was he allowing his packer to be his picker? There wasn't a single employee at Booth Ranches tasked with counting the oranges that went into each bin. Valencia trees loaded with fruit—fifty bins per acre—were packing out at twenty bins an acre. Something was amiss.

This was how she "pestered" her way into the fields and the front office. By the time she was done pestering, Booth Ranches was packing its own citrus in its own shed and selling oranges with its own marketing team under its own labels. Father and daughter were partners. Divorced from the potato farmer, Loren Booth moved to the cattle spread on top of the hill that overlooked the orchards. People who visited her mansion said it belonged on the cover of *Architectural Digest*. Her father came to trust her enough that he'd be away for weeks at a time at his home in Bel Air. He'd fly up in his Learjet 24 and stay long enough to approve some of her bigger decisions and then fly back. When he died, in 2008, she took the advice of old Charlie Munger, executor of his estate, and bought out all her siblings. Now she's one of the biggest citrus growers in California. "It's all me. Just me," she tells me on the phone. "I'm the only one drowning in a dry well."

The new headquarters for Booth Ranches looks nothing like an office. Crafted in the style of a grand Spanish-Mexican hacienda, it appears lifted from the old Californio days. Roses and fountains lead to a front door carved from a huge split of wood. I'm tempted to act the smart-ass and ask the secretary where the last vaqueros twirling their lassos are hiding. That's when, out of the corner of my eye, I catch the big framed photo hanging on the wall. It's a picture of a vaquero named Buddy Montes, who watches over a few hundred of Booth's cattle on the hilltop. Buddy is a Tejon Indian whose father was head cowboy at Tejon Ranch, the 270,000-acre spread in the mountains between here and Los Angeles. The ranch was once part of Chandler territory, and Otis Booth enjoyed going up there to hunt elk. That was how he met Buddy's father.

Among the decorative items sits an Old West safe and a beautifully restored saddle studded in silver. I'm about to feel its polish when I hear a jangling from down the tile-floored hallway. A woman in her late fifties, lean and strong, her brown-blond hair tied in a ponytail, is fast approaching. She's wearing jeans and cowboy boots outfitted with real silver spurs. Each drop of her boot sounds another jangle. "I got up early this morning and rode," Loren Booth says, explaining her getup. "I needed to escape."

She talks fast and chews off her words. Her father has left her quite a chore. He overplanted his oranges by more than three thousand acres. He stuck trees in ground with no groundwater and too little surface water from the federal project to cover the shortfall. It was trick enough to wiggle by in the years of decent snowmelt. In dry times, the system became a turnip with nothing left to squeeze. Her father's water broker, an engineer named Dennis Keller, was considered a savant in the wheeling of snowmelt from one region to the other. Keller would find a block of water that a faraway irrigation district was willing to sell and grab it for a price that Otis Booth, ranked 189 on Forbes list of the 400 richest Americans, didn't mind paying. The water, thus purchased, would be deposited in the aqueduct like money in a bank account and would make its journey from west side to east side via a little marvel called the Cross Valley Canal. A few days later, an equivalent amount of water would be available for withdrawal from a turnout on the Friant-Kern Canal. Traveling a go-between of ditches, pipes, pumps and drip lines, the water would scale the hillside to irrigate 1,538 acres of oranges that had no business being up there.

"In all the years of the Friant-Kern, we've never had a year of zero deliveries," she says. "Even in the worst drought back in 1976, we were able to get some federal water. But zero upon zero?"

She tours me around the kitchen, where she serves her staff a meal every Tuesday and Thursday, and then the sales office, where fruit brokers, ears glued to phones, wave hello. In her office, she fumbles around for a photo of her father and Otis Chandler on one of their hunting or fishing trips. "I had the weirdest upbringing. I mean, there we were living in San Marino with all these captains of industry and their socialite wives and pampered kids. But my dad was just about the most frugal person you could imagine. I never had a tennis or dance lesson. We didn't do anything. Now, when it came time for me to be presented

Loren Booth oversees the citrus packing line she designed herself.

to society, I was presented like all the others at the Pasadena Guild of Children's Hospital Debutante Ball. Oh, yes. At the Huntington Hotel. I was Otis Booth's daughter, even though he had divorced my mother when I was in the fifth or sixth grade and married a wealthy woman named Dody. Thank goodness I loved animals. He wasn't really a presence in my life until his last five years, when we began to redo our entire operation. We really got close. It was a lot of fun."

Even before this dry time, she could see the upside-down legacy her father had left her: too many oranges and not enough water. Back in 2009, she'd reduced his ten-thousand-acre footprint by selling off twenty-five hundred acres of marginal orchards in one district and another. A few months ago, she sold off four hundred acres located outside the reach of an irrigation district, an area dependent on a water table fast dwindling. She's pruned back some of her orchards so radically that the trees appear shrublike. With their canopies rendered practically fruitless, she can starve the trees of water and still be able to green them up when the drought ends, assuming it ends in the coming winter. But even with these measures, she still finds herself short of thousands of acre-feet to irrigate her trees on the hill.

After an exhaustive search, Dennis Keller located enough water from the open market to cover the cutbacks in the government supply. Problem is, the sellers are demanding up to $1,500 an acre-foot for this water, twice what it would cost in a non-drought year. She and her fellow growers here, members of the Hills Valley Irrigation District, aren't about to let water-rich farmers to the west and north prey on their desperation. They've decided to make do with half the water they truly need.

"We're looking at pushing out another three hundred and fifty to four hundred acres," she says with a groan. "No other choice. Maybe when the rain comes back, we can plant it again."

I assume she means the navels and mandarins up the hill that she and her father planted together. But she's actually talking about bulldozing another orchard on flatter ground miles away. This doesn't make sense, at least not to anyone making an unsentimental calculation of things. Why favor hilly ground where the aquifer is poor and government supplies run iffy, I ask her. If you need to tear out more orchards and reduce your footprint, doesn't it make sense to do that up here?

"You can look at Hills Valley and say, 'No way. No way should citrus trees be planted up here.' But this is virgin ground," she says firmly. "The soil is some of the most productive in the citrus belt. It grows beautiful fruit. These orchards back up against the mountain, so they're protected. We're sitting in the best of the thermal belt. This is the warmest ranch we farm."

She knows time isn't on the side of Hills Valley. The state's groundwater management plan, once it goes into effect, could very well declare the district's fragile water table off-limits to agriculture. She and the other growers on the hill would then have to shut down their pumps and rely on the government canal alone. This would make it near impossible, come the next drought, to find enough water to keep the trees alive. She may be a cattle rancher, too, but it would not be easy to see the orchard return to range.

A half mile up the hill, the road peters out and I can't tell where it picks up again. Inside the lush grove, her irrigation men are planting meters three feet into the earth, so they can constantly monitor the moisture content. The sensory sticks allow her to turn on the drip lines only when the trees are in an optimum phase of growth. If all goes according to plan, she might increase her yields and reduce her water use by as much as 30 percent. Maybe technology will get her through this drought with no more harm. Maybe it will allow these trees on the hilltop to survive the next one, and the next one. For the time being at least, the horizon is a billow of emerald green.

There is only one Mulholland left in the world who can trace his branch to the William who dried up Owens Valley and gave birth to modern-day Los Angeles. This last Mulholland, Tom Mulholland, happens to propagate and grow an aberrant variety of mandarin orange on fourteen hundred acres in the citrus belt. Like the Booths' saga, the Mulhollands' story traces a path of California. The orange did not vanish with the paving over of Los Angeles. Neither did the Holstein. They simply moved over the mountain from one valley to the next, following the waters of irrigation. Seeing how this was the road I was retracing, I couldn't very well leave the east side without knocking on the door of William Mulholland's only great-grandson. "I have three sisters and I have two daughters," he tells me on the phone. "There are no men left in the family. I'm the last of the Mulholland line."

Citrus brokers down in Los Angeles had warned me that Mulholland was unlike any other mandarin grower I would encounter, more hippie than rancher who even into his mid-sixties possessed a "wild energy" that was both gift and curse. He gyrated from nursery to orchard with a mind constantly overtaken by new ideas. Some of the ideas were brilliant and realizable, others pure duds. He might have become the richest citrus farmer in California, they said, had he been able to distinguish between the two. As it was, he was a wealthy man who had helped revolutionize the industry, pushing California citrus culture away from its roots in the Washington navel and toward varieties of mandarins whose sweet and tart delight the consumer. Before the Cutie, before the Halo, there was the Delite. It was propagated, watered, picked and marketed by Mulholland.

A few miles north of Orange Cove, four hundred feet above the valley floor, I pull up to his entrance gate, which is even more odd and arresting than he had described to me. It is a beautiful piece of metal artwork carved in ornate depictions of oaks and redwoods that he designed himself as a "tribute to two species of trees that have been nearly decimated as mankind took over California." The metal is painted a reddish wood color that only adds to its effect, and I am compelled to get out of the car and touch and study it as one might a piece of art. After a few minutes of communing with the gate, I glide down the long driveway—"MULHOLLAND HIGHWAY," the sign reads—toward a citrus estate not unlike the ones in the Pasadena picture postcards, circa 1905. The orchard isn't an orchard but a backyard. The hedges are tall, and the fountains are burbling. Grandkids are splashing in the swimming pool.

Tom is tall with broad shoulders, wire-rimmed glasses and a Mulholland balding head. He talks fast enough that I'll have to slow down my tape recorder to play him back. "I had ADHD before there was ADHD," he jokes. His father's recordings of Jimmy Smith riffing on his Hammond organ served as his "Ritalin" growing up. He takes me into a study where a big elongated banner hangs from the wall. It's the giant face of Great-grandpa William, of neither ill nor good humor, chomping on a cigar beneath his beautiful mustache. When the old man died, in the summer of 1935, his farm in the San Fernando Valley went to his son Perry, a tall man with a cruel bent who refused to sell out even as housing tracts and shopping malls surrounded him. Grandpa Perry held on until 1965, until L.A. sprawl made it all but impossible to farm grapefruits anymore. He sold the ranch to a Northridge developer, who anchored the land with a Kmart. What was left of the $2 million sale, a modest amount, went to Perry Mulholland's three children, including a son, Richard, who worked for Sperry Rand, the military contractor; and a daughter, Catherine, who wrote *William Mulholland and the Rise of Los Angeles* to set the record straight about her grandfather. He had no financial stake, she explained, in the land syndicate that turned stolen water into fabulous fortunes.

In the mid-1950s, Richard quit Sperry Rand and moved to Orange Cove with his wife, three daughters and his son, Tom, the one who's sitting across from me. Richard bought 240 acres along a funky road, drilled three wells and planted black-eyed peas and cotton as transition crops. A mathematician by training, he built a nursery and propagated his own citrus trees. By 1960, he was growing Valencias and holding off frost with wind machines and smudge pots. "My father came here because the San Fernando Valley was being encroached upon. He didn't want to farm behind a cyclone fence," Tom says. "He knew this was going to be one of the last places in California to turn urban. Because he didn't believe in borrowing money, all he could afford to buy was poverty ground. Two hundred and forty acres for two hundred dollars an acre." The University of California had a citrus field station not far away, and Tom's father started doing rootstock trials there. Tom was ten years old when he germinated his first orange seed in 1962. "You might say I'm the longest-running citrus propagator in the state of California."

Richard was both aloof and demanding. He taught his children that the San Joaquin Valley, for all its agricultural innovation, was a hidebound place where the southern plantation had been reborn. See it for what it is, he advised. He subscribed to the *Los Angeles Times* by mail, refused to buy a television set and filled the house with the sounds of jazz, the more improvisational the better. Each Sunday evening, the family sat down to eat at a formal table set with fine china and heavy silverware passed down through the generations. This upbringing allowed Tom to see the world in a more nuanced way. He became a committed environmentalist in college and ached to return to the ranch to pursue his passion of propagating and growing citrus. He married Jill Rosenberg, a Fresno girl, and they raised two daughters and built this house with extra-thick walls as insulation against the valley heat. He kept farming alongside his father until his father's death in 1992. The returns on his citrus were good enough that he was able to grab 400 acres in Dinuba and 150 acres in Farmersville to add to the home ranch.

Tom loved citrus for the same reason he loved jazz: He couldn't predict where it was going. Citrus was an oddity of creation. Each different fruit belonged to the same genus. The variants among them—orange, lemon, lime, grapefruit—were a product not of man's hybridization but nature's chaos. The Washington navel wasn't the Washington navel until some cosmic ray struck a branch of a tree in Brazil and created two or three buds that were different from all the other buds. The accidental fruit that grew from those buds—easier to peel, free of big seeds, sweeter than its predecessor—had come by way of mutation, what the farmer called a sport. Every so often over the centuries, if the right farmer was paying proper attention, he'd walk into his orchard and discover that one of his trees had decided to offer up something different. Often, the sport was a negation of the original, a fruit best left to rot, a branch wisely lopped off the next pruning. Now and then, though, the cosmic ray struck just right. This happened late in the last century in a field of mandarins in Morocco that belonged to the king. An aberration of a slightly different order, a chance seedling, was discovered, and from that seedling a tree was propagated. The blossomed fruit—few in seeds, easy to peel, a taste beyond other mandarins—became known as the W. Murcott. The budwood traveled across the ocean to North America and found its way to Riverside, California, and then to Tom Mulholland, who'd been preparing all his life for such a moment.

It was 1997, and he and his wife had divorced. He traveled to Morocco to see the king's orchards for himself. He tracked down the set of Murcott buds sent to the citrus experts at the University of California, Riverside, for propagation. Seeing that he was the first grower in line, the university gave him the buds, no strings attached. He promptly replicated them in his nursery. Right away, he knew he had found the "golden nugget." He pulled out 150 acres of Valencias and planted the Murcotts. The trees took to the hard ground like billy goats. The fruit, which he marketed as Delites, were delicious. The Cuties brand didn't exist yet. He was at least a year ahead of Resnick and his partner Berne Evans, who were just starting to plant their varieties of seedless mandarins.

"This is the first time I have something that's really good," he recalls. "I know it's going to be good, but sometimes people need validation.

'Do you believe in it, too?' I panic. I don't know marketing. I don't own a packinghouse. I'm a nurseryman and family farmer. My father drummed it in my head to never borrow money. So I go down to Los Angeles and see Berne Evans at his Sun Pacific office. He's one of the biggest growers in the state. He doesn't know me from a load of coal. I go in with a contract already written about marketing my variety, the Delite. 'Mr. Evans, would you like to join my organization?' He *ha, ha, ha*-ed me. He penetrated all my orifices, and I walked out with no deal."

By himself, knowing he had a head start, Tom took a shot. He began selling his Delites to Whole Foods and Trader Joe's. Walmart even gave him a spot in its produce aisle. Consumers loved his Murcott. He picked and sold the Delites from February to April. It was a short window, but it belonged to him. Then, just when it looked like he had snagged the prize, the Cutie came crashing through the door. Resnick and Evans were riding a rocket. Who cared that their brand was a fabrication? The Cutie wasn't one piece of fruit but three varieties of mandarins: the Clemenule, the Tango and the Murcott. Each variety had its own flavor and ripened at a different time. But by marketing all three as one brand, Resnick and Evans covered multiple seasons. They made consumers believe, through tens of millions of dollars in advertising, that a spring Cutie was the same fruit as a winter Cutie. If the November Cutie was drier, the shopper assumed it was happenstance. If the March Cutie was sweeter and juicier, the shopper figured it was the way the fruit was supposed to be. Who knew that one was a Clemenule and the other was a Murcott? Masquerading as one, Cuties could outlast any competitor. Suddenly, every citrus grower in the valley was planting different varieties of mandarins to sell into the Cuties line. As space in the produce aisle squeezed down, Mulholland tried to find new niches.

And then on Halloween Day 2011, the two big guys, Resnick and Evans, met at the Jonathan Club in Santa Monica to iron out a dispute. They were fifty-fifty partners in the mandarin deal. When one planted a new block of trees, the other had to plant a corresponding block. Evans had found out that Resnick was adding acres without his approval. Lunch had not yet arrived when Evans decided to broach the subject. Resnick cut him off: "Berne, I'm taking over this business. And I'm going to charge you six percent commission for selling your fruit."

Evans was a citrus man. He was the one who had come up with the idea of growing different mandarins. He had shared the idea with Resnick, who didn't know the difference between a Murcott and a Tango. He wasn't about to be turned into a common grower of fruit for Wonderful. Evans got up from his chair and thought about decking Resnick right there. Instead, he told him to go to hell and stalked out. By the time they were done fighting, three years later, Evans had paid the Resnicks $40 million to buy the Cuties label. The Resnicks ginned up a new brand, Halos.

A pair of heavyweights warring for market dominance left Mulholland too little space. His Delite could not survive on its own. He had to make a choice: join the Cuties family or join the Halos family. "They did three mandarins as one brand," he explains. "And I was being too honest. I was too small, and they were so big. Even at fourteen hundred acres, I couldn't compete. Not enough land. Not enough water. I had to pick a side, so I chose Resnick."

Then the drought arrived, and the feds slashed deliveries to nothing, and he cranked up the volume on his pumps, only to now watch fifteen of his wells go dry. Even his "wagon wheel" wells, workhorses extraordinaire, have stopped producing. These ingenious wells were dug in the 1960s and required a worker to enter a hole seventy feet deep until he hit a fissure of water in the rock. If the crew above him miscalculated the water's pressure and volume, the fissure could easily drown him. It wasn't so much an aquifer he was striking but a vein of water that extended across the granite shelf. A conventional pump—designed to suck water from a vertically deep aquifer, not a horizontally wide and shallow one—would have done little good down in the rock. But the wagon wheel well used holes bored laterally, like spokes, for hundreds of feet across the granite to reach a fissure of water. "My wagon wheels are studs. They never go dry. But they're going dry now," Tom tells me. "They're coughing up water for an hour or two and then nothing. It makes more sense just to shut them down."

To get his trees through the summer, he's negotiating with the water-rich families sixty-five miles to the west who raise row crops on the historic floodplain of the San Joaquin River. Back in the 1940s, when the river was dammed and the flow to their farms shut off, these families sold their old Henry Miller rights to the government. In return, they received first draw to the federal water imported from the delta. Even in the worst of dry times, the Sacramento water flows to them. The asking price for a chunk of this primo supply is $1,500 an acre-foot. This is the water that Loren Booth has passed up. This is the water that Mulholland cannot afford to pass up. "We all have our different calculations," he explains. "Mine tells me that I can sell my mandarins for a high enough price to make that high-dollar water pencil out."

Citrus growers are pushing out older trees to squeeze through the drought, but none of those trees are mandarins. The mandarin is the closest thing a grower has to a sure bet. If not for its rise over the past few decades, the citrus belt, too, might be part of the nut belt. But with the returns on the fruit every bit as lusty as those on almonds and pistachios, citrus still rules here. Not only can the mandarin cover the swindle of drought's high-priced water, but it uses 15 to 20 percent less water than the almond.

Mulholland sounds more like an environmentalist than a rancher as he pays through his nose for the water needed to survive this drought. "Maybe I'm just as guilty as the big guy," he says. "Manifest destiny teased us onto ground that maybe should have never been farmed. The tragedy of the commons—that's exactly what we're seeing out here. Reasonable people, for the most part, acting reasonably. But the cumulative effect of it is compromising the resource for everyone and every use."

I look him in the eye, wondering if he's being sincere or simply working me. He's glued to a barstool at the kitchen counter and gazes back at his daughter Heather, who's been sitting quietly for the past half hour in a big sofa chair. She knew all the way back in grammar school that she wanted to follow her father and grandfather into citrus. "My sixth-grade project was on insects beneficial to agriculture," she explains. Now a partner in the operation, she is a keeper, too, of the Mulholland story. There are moments when her father's mind grabs at errant thoughts and takes off, and she scoots to the edge of her seat and seems about to jump in to guide him back. Only she resists doing so. She knows this is the way her father, raised on the jazz of Charles Mingus, tells his stories, and she loves him for it. But now as he's finishing up, explaining how his dream, so close, got away, she has tears in her eyes.

"I should have borrowed money," he says. "I should have built my own packinghouse. But I wasn't taught by my dad to think that way. I was a one-man band. I was doing the fiddle and beating the drum. We gave it three years, and then we put the last Delite in the box.

"I had to pick a side. And that's the story. We're a grower of W. Murcotts, but it's hard to say that it's 'our' fruit anymore."

Seventeen

RAISINLAND

There's a stretch of Highway 99 in the center valley where the new plantings of almonds at last give way to the old plantings of vines. This is where Fowler and Selma, small towns that hitched their prosperity to the raisin more than a century ago, still live and die by the Thompson Seedless grape. Like the citrus belt, the farms here tend to be smaller by valley standards—60 acres, 80 acres, 120 acres. If you knock on the door of one of the ranch houses amid the vines, a real farmer is likely to answer. He'll tell you he can afford to keep the tradition of his father and grandfather because his loam is among the finest in the world and his water doesn't require the nth degree of extraction. The snowmelt moves in an earthen ditch that runs across his front or backyard, a flow pushed his way from the nearby Kings River. In the months when the ditch isn't running, he'll turn on one of his pumps and draw from an aquifer that, after a century and a half of growing Thompsons, still sits eighty feet below the ground.

This is the kind of agriculture that Nordhoff and Muir and all the other agrarian boosters envisioned for California back when the soil was being stolen by the goliaths of wheat. That a piece of it still exists after so many cycles of boom and bust and the ownership of land becoming concentrated into fewer hands is what brings me here, looking for a center. That center is not only the farmer and his relationship to water, a different relationship than Resnick's or Pandol's or Booth's, but his relationship to the workers who irrigate his vines and set down his grapes to cure into raisins. The land itself is the geographic center of the valley, which is why the recharge from the rivers moving east to west pools here and allows for a more sane life. That center, as it happens, also coheres the story of my own tribe, the Armenians, the original grape culture. Survivors of massacre, they're tough customers. How has drought left them?

The temptation is to think of this land as a relic, lovely and lost to time. It's true that the notion of picking clusters of grapes to cook under the sun goes back to California's very beginning. In 1852, a Hungarian named Haraszthy was farming in San Diego when he took the seeds of a Muscat of Alexandria sent over from Spain and planted them in his dirt. By design or sloth—who knows which—he allowed the grapes that grew from those seeds to bake into their essence. Shriveled up, they weren't pretty to look at, but the sugar had turned into a kind of caramel.

The Muscat found its way to the fabulous estate of Francis Eisen, the aristocratic Swede from San Francisco who'd become a gentleman farmer in Fresno. In the very hot summer of 1877, before Eisen could pick the crop and send it to his winery, a portion of his Muscats dried on the vine. His men removed their stems, packed them into boxes and sent the boxes to San Francisco. The fanciest grocers exhibited the raisins in their show windows as the new dried fruit of Peru. The seed gave a crunch and a slightly bitter flavor to complicate the sweet chew. No one considered this a problem until William Thompson and his son, George, farmers in Sutter County, grafted one of their backyard vines with an Old World Sultana from Smyrna and in 1875 began producing a new variety of seedless raisin, the Thompson.

No towns embraced the Thompson with more zealotry than Fresno, Fowler and Selma. Laced by the same stretch of 99, they fought for years over which one was really "the raisin capital of the world," until Selma finally settled it—presumptuously, I am told—by plastering the title on its highway welcome sign. Who would remember that up until that day Selma had sold itself to the world, complete with a stirring song by bandmaster Louis Everson, as "Selma, the Home of the Peach." The raisin villages would put aside their feuding each year to hold the Raisin Day Parade in downtown Fresno led by the Raisin Queen, a local beauty, and Hollywood cowboy Tom Mix, the Raisin King, riding his wonder horse, Tony, and followed by floats that were every bit as fancy as the ones in Pasadena on New Year's Day. They sponsored the Raisin Bowl, the biggest youth football championship game in the nation, and the Raisin Ambassadors, high school students sent abroad to promote the many different uses of the wrinkled grape. At some point in our collective fervor, the plantings of Thompsons covered 470 square miles of countryside. Lawyers and doctors found a vineyard to invest in. It was a crop that could be grown at an easy profit because of the easy reach of water in the center valley. And because raisins didn't rot, they could be stored for years by the ton. With each harvest, the tons kept growing.

The raisin glut made for wonderful theater. We had a Raisin Advisory Board, and its chairman was Sox Setrakian, a wily little Armenian with a booming tenor who used to travel to Munich and Athens, Paris and London, giving fiery speeches that would bring him to tears as he tried to sell the world on why it needed to buy more valley raisins. "I cry easily, but why blame me?" Setrakian said once. "The tears that I have shed have brought in dividends." Who knew of a more virtuous and conformable crop than the raisin? Raisins in cereal, raisins in bran muffins, raisins in salad, raisins in brandy, raisins in toothpaste. "Raisins everywhere, even in gravy" became a motto. Yet at the end of Setrakian's global touring, we still had 120,000 tons of raisins too many, a surplus so great that every raisin grower could fall asleep for a year and we'd still have enough crop to supply the globe all over again.

The raisin, its highs and lows, became the way we communed with one another and talked to God. The Armenians held their biggest shish kebab gathering of the year at the Fresno Fairgrounds on a Sunday in August to celebrate the "Blessing of the Grape." Old priests and young acolytes in gold-and-purple vestments waved incense and recited prayers from two thousand years ago over fat bunches of green Thompsons. In the pounding sun, we kids would slide down the grassy knoll of the fairgrounds on carpets of cardboard while our parents danced to the oud player's strained song: "It's a lie. It's a lie. The whole world is a lie." When the smoke of the picnic lamb had cleared, the grapes hit the dirt. For the next eighteen days, as they baked into brown, we said our prayers for no rain.

The summer of 2016, like every other summer in Fowler and Selma, finds the raisin farmer at his most sour, contemplating a question that has plagued the valley for more than a century: Can enough workers be rounded up to pick the crop? He knows from empirical evidence that few citizens of the United States are willing do the work. He knows that the salvation of farm and community lies on the other side of the border. When a grape grower plows under his father's vines and plants almonds, he doesn't speak of water or heartache or pests. The reason, he'll plainly tell you, is labor. A nut doesn't require a hand to pick it. Because a machine does all the work, nothing bleeds in an almond orchard. The grape harvest, on the other hand, bleeds everywhere. Man against sky, man against fruit, man against microbe, man against man. Artificial intelligence may soon change everything about us, the Thompson farmer says. It may turn us into the human equivalent of calves confined to boxes three feet by six feet whose bodies, never tested, become tender pieces of veal. It won't, however, change the relationship between him and his water and him and his farmworker. No machine will ever be programmed to pick bunches of grapes and lay them down on paper trays in rows between the vines.

Every day in August, in the still dark of morning, men and women from rural Mexico, curved blade in hand, fill up the vineyards on both sides of Highway 99. That they come without legal documents, with a smuggler's debt hanging over their heads, is the shame we try to bury. At Malloch Elementary, I threw touchdown passes to a new kid named Jorge Álvarez who showed up a month late for the sixth grade. He had a mustache and wore his jeans rolled up fifties-style. He knew enough words of English to understand my play calling. Streak left. Streak right. Man, he could fly. He was here and gone in a season.

The men and women who planted, irrigated, sprayed and picked our crops remained phantoms. The farmer himself didn't know them. He had hired a labor contractor as his go-between. On our way to Disneyland, we must have blinkered our eyes heading down 99. We didn't see the tumbleweeds along the roadside or the strip of parched earth that separated what remained of the desert from the perfect rows of irrigated agriculture. We didn't see our creation, much less the figures bent under the canopies of vine that our creation counted on. Then one day, they walked out of the fields and materialized in our streets with signs protesting their short-handled hoes and deplorable wages. Suddenly, you were either with Cesar Chavez or against him. My father, the lapsed grape grower, brought in the East L.A. band El Chicano to perform at his nightclub. My grandfather began writing poems about his "brown brothers and sisters under the sun." Such were our gestures.

Grandpa Arax used to tell me how brutally the sun in the San Joaquin

Valley beat down on a man who had lost his country. After his uncle had dropped him off in Weedpatch in the summer of 1920 to work for Villa Kerkorian, the harvest did not go according to plan. The raisin crop, only 65,000 tons a decade before, was nearing 200,000 tons. In two years' time, the price paid to the raisin grower had dropped from ninety-five dollars a ton to twenty dollars a ton. With too much crop and too little market, Kerkorian was feeding raisins to his hogs, horses and cattle. The paper millionaire tried everything to save his ranches from foreclosure. He went from service station to service station buying old crankcase oil and threw a barrel of it down a well, trying to convince the bank that his farm sat atop an undiscovered oil field. As the bank was holding its auction to sell off his farm equipment, Kerkorian flew into a rage, grabbed a hoe and severed the ear of the auctioneer. The bloodshed did not halt the sale.

My grandfather joined a legion of fruit tramps—Volga Germans, Japanese, Filipinos, Hindus, Mexicans, Swedes, white hoboes—who threw their lot to the fields. After three years of labor, he and his brother, Harry, saved enough money to rent the Golden Dawn, a beautiful piece of ground east of Fresno, just down the road from where the Chakurian family farmed. When Alma Chakurian, the oldest daughter, walked outside at the right time of night, she could hear the Araxes on their front porch eating watermelon and talking politics. Her family told her to stay away from that "bunch of Bolsheviks" occupying the Golden Dawn, but it was too late. Aram was already writing poems to her that had nothing to do with Lenin. He stole her off the farm, drove her to city hall in San Francisco and married her without a relative from either side present. It took him a couple of good crops to buy his own twenty acres west of Highway 99 with a front-yard ditch. This is where my father, Ara, was born on September 24, 1931, an eleven-pounder on the produce scale.

Good labor wasn't easy to find in the Depression years. My grandfather knew that only one country could still be counted on to send its most desperate to pick the crop. He found a crew of Mexicans to put down his Thompsons in late August and then hired them again in the fog of winter to prune and tie the vines. The Armenian farmer and the Mexican farmworker have been a duo since the early 1900s. Familiarity has bred its contempt. One of the first secret words an Armenian kid learns growing up here, after mastering the Armenian words for anatomical parts and bodily functions, is *Mexa-goat-see. Goat-see,* for short. The *see,* a linguistic accent, means that such a person is "from" such a place. *Ita-lat-see* for an Italian or *German-ah-tsee* for a German. The utterance of *Mexa-goat-see,* however, allows the *goat* to get stuck in the throat because it's there that contempt for the Mexican gets registered. The bigger the contempt, the more throaty the *goat.*

The word for shame in Armenian is *ah-mote.* When a farmer enters his vineyard during harvest, he sees Mexican men and women, and sometimes Mexican children, brought to their knees by the urgency of his crop. Whose *ah-mote* is this? The Mexican complicates how the farmer thinks of himself. He wants to think of himself as pious, honorable, churchgoing, civic-minded. The bent-down Mexican can drive the farmer to madness, to drink, to whoring, to collecting Ferraris, to the roulette table to gamble it all away. That's why the labor contractor came into existence. It's not as if the farmer can't find his workers on his own, though the contractor does find them more easily. It's not so much that the combination of paperwork and payroll is a pain in the ass, though it is. The presence of the contractor is really about the farmer and his need to be insulated from the farmworker on his hands and knees. It's about distancing himself from *ah-mote.*

On a Saturday morning, the car radio blasting the hot air of a cockeyed presidential campaign, I drive past the packinghouse where I boxed peaches and plums as a kid and come to a stop in a vineyard outside Selma, where the raisin harvest is about to begin. The thermometer has shot beyond one hundred degrees for fourteen straight days. Three farmworkers have died in this heat. The vines haven't drunk water for thirty days, but that is by design. The dry condition lets the farmer reconfigure the dirt rows between the vines, buiding a slight slope that angles toward the sun and allows water, in the event of a freak rain, to drain off the grapes baking on paper trays. Down the dirt road that runs through the vineyard, Honda Civics on their third owners line the path. I step out onto the fine powdery loam and pick a dusty row to walk. Not a worker can be seen. All is quiet.

A few yards inside, I hear the faint sounds of *banda* and follow the music to a cell phone in the back pocket of a skinny young man. He's

Pickers dump raisins into a bin before a rainstorm, near Caruthers

wearing worn cowboy boots, torn jeans, one long-sleeved shirt over another and a San Francisco 49ers cap splattered in grape juice mixed with dust. He parts the curtain of cane and leaf and steps completely inside the vine, hacking away at its purple bunches with one hand and letting the bunches plop into a plastic tub he holds with his other hand. It takes him forty-eight seconds to fill the tub. Then he bends over in the opposite direction and spills the fruit across a paper tray in the row's middle, in the full sun. This is the oven where the grapes will bake.

He says his name is Uriel, and he's twenty-one years old and a native of Guerrero, the Mexican state where his family has lived forever in poverty. Four years ago, after finishing the ninth grade, he decided to follow the trail that had sent his father and older brother north. He hired a coyote to get him past the border's barrier. The four-thousand-dollar fee was double the price from a few years ago, but there was no haggling. These weren't the coyotes of yesteryear. These smugglers were now at the command of drug lords; two commodities, laborer and heroin, crossed the border at once to satisfy America's twin lusts.

"I came for just a year and then the year turned into another year and another year and another year," Uriel says.

He shares an apartment in the citrus belt with three other farmworkers who are here alone, as well. He is able to work nearly year-round by picking oranges, olives, cherries and grapes. Skinny and small, he's the perfect size to move in and out of the vines without any stooping to slow him down. The drive to the vineyard takes him forty-five minutes in the dark, but he would have traveled even farther because this farmer pays by the piece. If he works through lunch, nine hours straight, he will make more than the minimum wage. He will make 260 trays, or $105. This is more than he would earn from an entire week's labor in Guerrero. In the best months here, he's able to send half his paycheck back home.

The next row over belongs to Ponciano, who crossed the border by himself when he was twelve and has worked the last eight years picking mandarins, blueberries, pears and apples. This is his first stab at raisin grapes, and he finds the work miserable. He'll be lucky at day's end to have made 200 trays, he says, $75. A handsome kid with seen-it-all eyes, Ponciano says he is looking for a wife to keep him here.

"I know there are better days coming soon," he says. "If I can help it, I will not go back."

He whistles to José, deeper in the vineyard, to join him on their break. But José had arrived from Mexico only a few days before and owes three thousand dollars to a friend who covered his border crossing. "My friend told me that the grapes turn into gold in California," José says. "I came to find out if that was true."

The sun isn't quite overhead but already feels like a furnace. There is one row where a grape picker has laid out the paper trays far in advance. This strategy strikes me as risky, for it has the potential to break a man's spirit, to underscore the quarter mile of row still to go. But as I watch the tiny figure covered in hoodie, hat and bandanna, I can see that it's ingenious. It allows the worker to build toward a trance of picking and filling and dumping that is never broken to put down one tray at a time. I walk over to introduce myself and only then do I see that this picker is a woman. Her name is Maria, and she has been working in the orchards and vineyards for eleven years. Her husband works beside her. Together they can make $175 a day. "I don't work as fast as I used to," she tells me. "I am thirty years old already."

She had awakened at three in the morning to fix lunch for herself and her husband and to cook the food the babysitter will serve at home to their three children. During the harvest, this routine never varies.

After work, she washes the stains off her hands and face and prepares dinner and gives the children a bath and tries to find a half hour to herself to think about something else. She thinks about her children, who were born here as U.S. citizens, and how they will learn English and go to college and never work a day in the fields.

"Will they allow us to stay?" she asks, her voice pleading.

His name had not come up, but she is speaking of the Republican candidate for president, Donald Trump, and all that he has unleashed in the country. He had held a rally in Fresno before the harvest, and growers cheered and waved "FARMERS FOR TRUMP" signs. Even some Mexican-Americans had climbed aboard. It makes no sense to her. An edict that sends the workers back to Mexico and a wall that keeps them from returning? Who will pick the fruits and vegetables? How will the cities, much less the farms, survive?

"The man has a rock for a heart," she says.

"Let them build a wall," Uriel shouts from his row. "We will be like Spider-Man and vault it."

"I'm afraid of heights," Ponciano says, laughing. "We will be like gophers and tunnel underneath."

"Don't they know that they can't keep us out," José says, his face to the sun. "We are Mexicans."

My visit is costing them time and money. I thank them for allowing me to share their rows and drive off. Crossing the Kings River, I ponder how the manipulation of water has compelled us to manipulate the movements of Mexicans. A piece of paper that says the migrant belongs here is hardly necessary as long as he or she is crossing for the purpose of leveling our land, planting our fields, harvesting our crops. I think back to 1994, to the aftermath of another election, when I walked into a coffee shop in Selma to meet with a bunch of growers. I wanted to hear their feelings about a controversial measure on the California ballot—Proposition 187—that was going to deny public schooling and other life-affirming benefits to undocumented residents. The measure had passed emphatically, and I was surprised to learn that many of the fruit farmers had voted for it, a vote that seemed to run opposite to their own self-interest, a vote that soon would be declared unconstitutional by a federal court.

At the counter sat the biggest fruit grower in the valley, a soft-spoken Lebanese-American named Ray Gerawan who knew my family and pulled me closer. Let me explain what seems like a paradox to you, he said. It isn't a paradox at all. The farmer and the Mexican are engaged in a centuries-long game. As rich as the farmer might be, his workers can still bring him to his knees if they realize their power. The farmer doesn't like feeling vulnerable. He supported the ballot measure because he knew that even if it went into effect, nothing would change. Law or not, the Mexicans would keep coming to his fields. And as long as they kept coming, he wanted them to always feel a little "iffy."

I drive east along Adams Avenue through the town of Fowler, 5,764 residents. I linger at old Parnagian Packing where I worked one summer tying rubber straps around boxes of fruit with a stapler-like gun called a palletizer. I repeated the action so many times during the day that I dreamed about it at night. There was no kind of overtime to cover those hours. A forklift driver broke my big toe, retiring me from agricultural duty at the age of nineteen. The Parnagians took their packing plant to the other side of 99. Hard to believe but they don't handle a single peach, plum or nectarine—the stone fruit that made them a fortune—anymore. On the land they're not turning into subdivisions, the next generation of Parnagians are growing and packing table grapes and Halos. I pass Simonian Fruit Company, Bedrosian's Champion Raisin and the high school with its flawless little football stadium carved out of vineyards. Last season, a quarterback named Kahaian threw TD after TD to a wide receiver named Jimenez.

I spot a big diesel land leveler, wheels churning on a metal track, bearing down on a first row of vines. I exit the car and walk across loam that feels like air, my boots sinking three inches with every step. A big black crow on a telephone wire bows to Mecca, its *caw-caw* audible because the tractor barely makes a sound as it begins to erase this farm on the corner of Adams and Leonard. The removal of a vineyard is a civilized act compared to the removal of an almond orchard. The tractor driver gently pushes with his front prong, and lifts out the trunk. The ground is so friable that the vine hardly registers a protest. Twisted wood, its mossy skin sloughing, falls to the middle of the row like a child being laid down in a crib. The neat line of doomed vines follows in a zipper. I can smell earth, feel its warmth clinging to roots.

In the center valley, 75,000 acres of Thompsons have been pulled out over the past decade. Only 170,000 acres of raisin grapes still remain in California.

In case I'm still wondering what follows the Thompson grape, the answer stares back at me from across the road. The farm belongs to the Gavroian family and used to be a vineyard, too. Way back when, we would gather here on foggy winter days (easier to hide from the federal revenue agents) and brew raisin moonshine in Khachig's old copper still. The vineyard is now an almond orchard on its third leaf. Almond trees grow like puppies. I walk across Adams and knock on the door of a farmer I interviewed fifteen or twenty years ago. I had called to warn him I would be in the neighborhood. Out comes Harry "Rusty" Rustigian, ninety-three years old, in work shirt and work pants and work boots. He invites me into his ranch house.

"What do you do?" he asks.

"I'm a writer," I say.

"I know that. But outside of that? That's all you do?"

He has me laughing already. He's laughing, too.

He hasn't changed much. He's still built like a bull, his hands the size of old-fashioned baseball mitts. They have the same texture, too. His wife, Virginia, guides us to the kitchen table. Rusty was born on these forty acres, she tells me. His bedroom in the old wood house—the house that burned down—was right where the kitchen now stands. Ninety-three years and Rusty has never left.

His father and mother had come from the same Armenian province on the vast Anatolian peninsula in what is now eastern Turkey. Their kin had lived there for centuries, side by side with the Turks, friend and foe. The "ian" on their last name was a way for the Turk to identify an Armenian. The "ian" means "the son of." Thus, Housepian is "the son of Joseph," and Topalian is "the son of the crippled one," and Medzorian is "the son of fat-ass." The Turks and Armenians once shared a sense of humor. In 1912, a Turkish neighbor told the Rustigians that bad times were coming for the Armenians. "Get your sons out as soon as you can," he warned. He didn't need to say more. The Rustigians had gotten lucky once already, outlasting the massacres of 1895. Rusty's father, a hard worker, landed in the United States in 1913. Drawn by the promise of the vineyard life, he settled in the rich loam of Fowler. This is where Rusty's father and mother met in 1921, a few years after the genocide.

"My mother had gone someplace in Fowler or Selma, and my father had seen her, and he told this fellow, 'If she'll marry me, I'll marry her right away.' This fellow told my mother, and I guess that's all it took. They got married right away."

There was no dawdling back then. When you go through the things his parents had gone through, you don't wait on life. And so life happened. Rusty was born in 1922, the first Rustigian raised outside historic Armenia. The planting of Muscats by his father was a transmission of culture. The Armenians had been grape people going back three thousand years. Rusty wonders if the Muscats were more than that, if his father was telling the Turks "nice try, but we're still here."

His parents didn't talk much about the past, but Rusty caught glimpses. His mother, stronger than strong, would sometimes cry for no reason. Once, he got her to tell him about the massacres. On the march across the desert, she had to eat grass and put her lips to the ground to drink what little water puddled in the hoofprints of horses. She kept on walking only to learn that her parents, three sisters and one brother had been murdered. "She told me she lived because her mother had given her some gold, and she had used this gold to buy herself out of harm's way. I might have asked another question or two, but she started to break down. She lived to ninety-three, but every time she talked about it, she had to stop."

His father, mostly a gentle man, could turn fierce out of nowhere. He reserved a special anger for the thugs from Sun-Maid. To stay in business, the co-op had to sign up 85 percent of the valley's raisin farmers. The Armenians weren't co-op people. They were obstinate people. The success of the signature drive was sold as a matter of economic life and death for every community in Fresno County. The vote count became front-page news. "SUN-MAID DRIVE LEAPS FORWARD—VICTORY IN SIGHT," the headline shouted. Wylie Giffen, Sun-Maid's leader, was one of the valley's most prominent men. "Call us a cartel if you want to, but we're a benevolent one," Giffen insisted. Though he publicly disavowed violence, Giffen set his Sun-Maid night riders loose to gather signatures by whatever means necessary. In Biola, a gang of Swedes tied independent raisin farmers to fig trees and horsewhipped them into signing contracts. It helped that the sheriff was in Giffen's corner, if not his pocket.

The Armenians were not going to be bullied, not after the Turks.

Rusty was ten or eleven when the Sun-Maid boys came calling. He and his little sister and mother were cutting nectarines to dry in the sun when five Model T Fords pulled up to their ranch. His father, out of nowhere, grabbed a huge wooden grape stake and told the Sun-Maid boys to move no closer. "My little sister was crying and my mother was shouting, 'No,' and all I could do was stand there," Rusty recalls. "My father told them, 'You come one step more, and I'll lay this grape stake over each of your heads.' He wasn't a big guy, but boy was he mighty. These guys looked at each other and turned around and walked back to their cars. Before they took off, one of them shouted, 'We'll be back!' My dad told them, 'Next time, there'll be a gun in your face.' "

To honor his father, Rusty stayed an independent raisin grower. It tugged at his heart in 1950 to pull out his dad's Muscats and plant Thompson Seedless. The Thompson grape made a good raisin and could always be sold to the wineries in years when the raisin went bust. He and Virginia raised two boys and a girl and built a nice brick house on these forty acres. With his oldest son, Dennis, beside him, Rusty did most of the tractor work and sulfuring, and most of the pruning, too. Water was never a problem. The bowls of his pump were set at thirty feet. In the good years—and there were plenty of them—they put away forty thousand dollars at each harvest's end.

After harvest last summer, Rusty lost his *hahvas,* the Armenian notion of life force, for farming. Raisin growers across Fresno and Madera were pulling out their Thompsons and planting varieties such as Selma Petes that dried on the vine and required no human labor to pick them. The fiberglass fingers of an AI machine shook off the raisins when they were good and sweet. But Rusty wasn't sure if he had the *hahvas* to try a new way of raisin farming. He told his son he had gotten too old to battle the ups and downs of a market made even more volatile by the supply of raisins from Turkey, of all places. His son told Rusty that he needed to make a clean break and pull out the vines and plant almonds. Because the profit margins on almonds made sense. Because nuts, unlike Thompsons, could be picked by machine. Because it was time, after a century, for a change.

A few weeks ago, Rusty stepped outside, hesitantly, as the Caterpillar D9 took to his field. Vine after vine, row after row, the big angled blade made easy work of it. "I didn't lose sleep," Rusty tells me, "but boy, it was hard on my heart. Because you think back to what you had to go through, what your father and mother had to go through, to keep it alive. The grape, you know, goes way back in our blood."

As the new trees went in, he started to laugh at the sound of it: Harry "Rusty" Rustigian, almond grower. For old times' sake, he kept one gnarled Thompson vine standing next to the water well.

I am sitting with Richard Hagopian, the oud master, in the middle of his forty acres of vineyard along an alluvial fan of the Kings River. Even here, he tells me, where the conditions could not be more perfect for an agrarian life, the days are numbered for the Thompson Seedless grape and small raisin farmers like him who live on their land. One of his wells is coughing up sand, and he's not sure how long the other well, which he reconditioned this year at a cost of twenty thousand dollars, is going to last. The water table has dropped thirty feet in the past two years alone. He wishes he could blame it all on this episode of drought; that way it would have a beginning point and an end point, too, and he could go back inside and pick up his oud, the Arab's big-bellied guitar, and play until it rained. But he motions to the hundreds of acres of new almond trees that envelop his vineyard like a siege. "It wasn't so long ago that this was all hog wallows," he says. "The excess water from the Kings would fill up over there and it would be ponds all year-round and recharge the aquifer. Now it's all under cultivation. Not so long ago, this whole area was Thompsons. Now it's all almonds except for me."

I used to think of the men I encountered at the Blessing of the Grape picnics as belonging to one of three categories: a raisin farmer in the present, a raisin farmer in the past, a raisin farmer in the future. I figured my father, once he had his fill of entertaining Fresnans at his nightclub, would stage his own return to the Thompson. His girdling knife, I reminded myself, was still stuffed away in a drawer in our garage. But who would have thought that the short, goateed bandleader strumming his oud in a corner of the fairgrounds was a raisin farmer, too.

The strings of the oud, if plucked just so, can steal your soul. Or at least that's what the old ladies sitting in their aluminum lawn chairs at the fairgrounds used to tell us kids. As we slid down the grassy knoll on our sheets of cardboard, they'd call us over to where they were huddled. Nylons rolled halfway down their calves, tongues tsk-tsking, they

Richard Hagopian in his Thompson Seedless vineyard outside Selma

would then fill our heads with the same admonition told a dozen ways: "When an ox dies, its skin is left behind. When a man dies, his name is left behind." Or "From mouth to mouth it goes, and on and on it grows." Or "It's better to lose your eye than to lose your name." One wrong move, they wanted us to know, and the past could brand you for life. A poor guy stole a crate of raisins during the Depression and forever lost his name. He was known all the rest of his days as the *chamich gogh,* the raisin stealer. Forty years later, one of the old ladies sitting in her lawn chair pointed to a teenager standing in the shish kebab line. "That's the *chamich gogh*'s grandson," she said. All the old ladies in their lawn chairs nodded their heads vigorously.

They kept at it, curse and gossip, in the 101-degree shade until the first pluck of strings on Hagopian's oud. *Ning, ning, ning, ning, ning, ning, ning . . . Ning, ning, ning, ning, ning, ning, ning.* They began to clap and stamp and implore the young ones to dance. My mother, Flora, and her sisters, Rosette and Jeanette, broken birds whose childhood in France had been stolen from them by the Nazis and the death of their mother, who had married men who couldn't figure out how to make them happy, didn't need coaxing. Already, they had made their way to the concrete floor under the pavilion top. Holding on to each other's pinkies, the three sisters, the priest's daughters, were skipping and kicking to some pattern from way back that I could not discern. They moved left and then right, arms up, arms down, dictated by the pulse of the oud. Others soon joined them, first women, then men, then the teenage girls, whose dancing was like a coming out. The line, now a circle, grew and grew and moved faster to keep up with Hagopian's playing. My mother, laughing with her whole face, urged me to join them. "Come on, come," she said. I stuck to where the old ladies were sitting and watched as the big gyrating wheel spun like one of those rides at the Fresno County Fair, taking my mom to a place before her marriage to Aram Arax's volcanic son. She looked to be something else to me, a bird in flight.

How Hagopian became an oud player who farmed raisins, or a raisin farmer who mastered the oud—he told it both ways—had nothing to do with the fate etched into our foreheads at birth. *Jagadakeer,* we called it. What is written, no one can change. Instead, the raisin and the oud had been handed down not by accident from his father, Khosroff, who died of lung cancer at forty-nine. Richard was seventeen and his sister was eleven, and their mother had no idea how to run the farm. He put aside college—forever, as it turned out—and took over the ranch.

Curses come in pairs. The year Richard's father died, 1954, visited an early heat wave on the Selma-Fowler area. For three straight days at the beginning of June, the temperature hit 112 degrees. The berries were so young on the vine they hadn't yet built up even a little sugar. Without sugar, there was no way they could take the heat. The whole crop burned. "When it is my turn, everything dries up" goes the Armenian proverb.

The vines, their fruit stolen, came back even stronger the next year. It was a lesson learned. To ride out the tough times, Hagopian needed to find a second way to make money. That's where the oud came in. At his father's insistence, he had taken violin lessons. In middle school, he had started to play the clarinet, an instrument central to Middle Eastern music. Then one day, he heard a recording by Udi Hrant, the blind Armenian oud master. His playing seemed to emanate from a trance. Over and over the boy spun the vinyl. He taught himself how to pluck the strings and began to land gigs up and down the valley. In the years to follow, he would study under Udi Hrant himself and travel to Philadelphia and Washington, D.C., Istanbul and Yerevan, to perform concerts and play festivals. A *New York Times* critic would call Richard Hagopian "one of America's foremost folk musicians."

He thought raisins and music would be enough to support his family. He had fallen in love with Geraldine Simonian, a carpenter's daughter from Yettem, the east side town the Armenians named after Eden. Blessed with three sons, they worried about finances. How would they ever manage to send them to college? To take advantage of Geraldine's Armenian cooking, they opened a Middle Eastern delicatessen and restaurant in downtown Visalia. They kept the place running for thirty-six years, until they both ran out of steam. A sixty-five-year-old man had no business juggling a restaurant, a vineyard and a band. They returned to Selma, to the ranch on Nebraska Avenue. He tore down the old house, built a new one and dug a well. He found water at twenty-nine feet. That was back in the year 2000. Today, the water table sits at ninety feet. After four years of drought, four years of no surface water deliveries from the Kings, four years of overpumping by agriculture, his old well has now run dry.

"If not for my Sikh neighbor right next door, my vines would have gone dry, too," he tells me as we climb into his truck. "He pumped water to me and only charged me for electricity."

Richard Hagopian, oud master

He pulls out of the driveway and aims his Chevy pickup down Nebraska. Time suddenly switches. It's 1936. That ranch over there belongs to a man named Kalustian. His ground is so lousy with alkali that he brings in thousands of tons of fresh dirt from elsewhere. When he puts in his end posts to configure his vineyard, water fills up each dug hole. That's how high, and perched, the aquifer is. It's World War II. A man in the city named Shekoyan wants to keep his sons out of the fighting. He buys this ranch foreclosed upon for only $750 an acre. The sons claim they are Thompson Seedless farmers, which is enough to keep them on the home front. The ground is so hot that the old man harvests back-to-back bumper crops and pays off the bank in two years. It's 1946, and Armenians occupy this whole area and then some. The Gamoians live on Nebraska, just down from the Hagopians. The Barigians live across from them. The Nalbandians live on Sunnyside Avenue. On Fowler Avenue are the Boyajians, the Moradians, the Arabians and the Housepians. Harry Khasigian, who has a skin disease and can't take the sun, farms his Thompsons on Mountain View Avenue wearing a huge sombrero right down to his eyes. Next to the corner of Fowler and Saginaw, the Arax family arrives.

"This is the original vines and original house that your family owned," Richard says, slowing down so I can take a closer look. "I think it was forty acres they had. As you can see, the vines are tired and weak."

"I never knew about this ranch. Are you sure?"

"Yeah. Aram Arax and his family. They weren't here long. Maybe a couple years."

"That sounds about right. My grandfather's story. Hit and run, hit and run. A few dollars in his front pocket. The *New Masses* in his back pocket. On to the next promised land."

Other families found their ways to stay. When raisins went bust again, some of them burned down their houses and claimed it was arson. They used the insurance money for a shot at another crop. At some point, enough houses belonging to "ian" families were catching fire that one or two of the insurance companies refused coverage to Armenians. With ten rows of vines between them, the families knew each other's business. They knew one farmer was spending so much time at the *bohz-ah-notes,* the whorehouse, that his crop came in light. His wife kicked him out of the master bedroom and the guest bedroom, too. He ended up sleeping in the tank house. At least it didn't end like the story of Khachadour Avedisian. Back in the Depression, he stabbed his wife thirty-seven times with a pocketknife as she was baking lavash bread in the kitchen. Her blood soaked into his underwear. He never gave a reason during the trial. The neighbors filled in their own reason. The wife had taken a lover. The wife had signed up for Americanization classes at Fowler High. He was sentenced to life in San Quentin prison.

And now down the road past the old cemetery, we've come to a rolling landscape of almonds that used to be grapes. "Resnick," the oud master says, his hand tracing the trees. "He's leased up all this ground and planted nuts. First-class. Look at those brand-new pumps and wells. They've got to reach five hundred feet deep, at least."

It wasn't long after these pumps went in that Hagopian's well went dry. Was it drought? Was it Resnick? He thinks both are to blame. "There's just too many straws in this ground," he says. "I don't care how many wet years you have. There's only so much that a well can give you. We've maximized our water, and gone beyond."

The well driller tells him that a new well on his farm, dug deep enough to compete, will cost at least one hundred thousand dollars. He's eighty years old with hardly a dark hair left in his goatee. One son is a pharmacist in Fresno. Another son, a graduate of Juilliard, owns a violin shop on Ninety-third Street in Manhattan. His oldest son, who took over the deli, died of kidney disease five years ago. The boys and their father once played as a band, Richard Hagopian & Sons. Now he listens to his grandsons who have formed their own Middle Eastern quintet. He's not sure how many crops he has left in him. Maybe not enough to pay for such a well. "I could go deeper, but how deep is deep enough? Who am I kidding? I'm never going to outlast a Resnick."

"The water goes," the Armenian proverb says. "The sand stays."

Eighteen

THE WHALE

The road from Raisinland to Westlands takes an hour. How far that hour takes you, from riverine to dry, is California's contradiction in microcosm. Only creeks cut a gouge on this side of the valley. They run down from the Coast Ranges, and when it rains they roar. They are silent now. I begin at the creek where Joaquín Murrieta, myth and man, met his end, a hail of bullets fired by gringo rangers and then a knife blade that sliced off his insolent head. It was put in a jar of gin and displayed up and down a California freshly stolen from Mexico, so that when the people met the pickled eyes of the bandit, they saw not only their own version of the man, thief or hero, but their own version of California, stealer or giver.

I follow Cantua Creek to the backyard of Bill Bettinsoli and his wife, Nella, who was born here in 1946 and has lived all her life at the butt of the creek. She was a Minnite, a name that used to mean something on the west side. Her father, Ralph, served as both principal and superintendent of the little Cantua Creek School. Her uncle and aunts lived here, too. "We had a Minnite compound, a Minnite commune," she tells me, shaking her head at the photos in her album. "We opened a restaurant and a grocery and a bar. We had a service station and a variety store, too. I grew up with all my cousins. What a life."

Back then, the land out here was owned by cotton ginner Anderson Clayton, whose thirty thousand acres went by the name Vista del Llano. German POWs lived in domed huts across the road and helped the Mexicans and white winos pick the cotton. "When the cotton machine replaced the picker, some of the tramps stayed out here and did odd jobs," she recalls. "There was Charlie White. They found him shot dead in the field. They said he did it to himself. I went with my cousins, and we saw him lying there. The constable said, Take a look, and it was Charlie, only he had a hole in his face." In the same field, during pheasant-hunting season, she and her cousins would crunch the ground with their feet, and the birds would get riled up and start running. "We'd shoot them like nothing and bring them home to our grandmother Nella. She cooked the pheasant meat in her spaghetti sauce and poured it on our polenta."

In the snap of thumb and finger, she says, the old generation died off, and the farmers began using machines to pick their tomatoes, too, and the workers dwindled. Cantua Creek became a place of only memories. All that's left of the Minnite bar, restaurant, market and general store is fallen rubble and roof piled in the dust on the corner. "Except for agriculture, this place is dead," she says. "People blame the delta smelt and shutting off the pumps. But it died long before that. The workers moved on, and so did the farmers. Their wives didn't want to live in the boonies anymore. But they kept their farmland. It's their sons and grandsons who are planting these nut trees. The ground keeps sinking. The road you drove in on used to be flat as a board. It's now up and down, up and down."

"Why did you and Bill stay?" I ask.

"The house and the quiet," she says. "And the garden."

"You ought to see my vegetables," he says, coming to life. "You won't believe what this dirt can grow."

"The Panoche loam," I say, half skeptical.

"Ain't nothing like it. Numero uno. The most fertile in the world. I got a friend from the city who comes out here just to smell it. He times his visits right after an irrigation. When he gets out of his car and breathes, he can't believe the aroma."

He takes me past the garage they're constructing and into a back forty acres, where on a small patch he's growing all the usual vegetables and then some. Parsley, Irish green, stands four feet tall. Where the soil is dry, it crunches beneath your feet like pieces of broken china. Where it's wet . . . well, look here, he says. He bends over and grabs the green top of a beet. He pulls and pulls, first with only his hands and then with a knee planted in the dirt to give him leverage. What he yanks out of the ground doesn't look like a beet. Dangling from locks, it looks like a human head colored purple.

"I've been on sandy loam," he says. "I've been on loam more clay. But nothing compares to the Panoche loam. It makes grown men dream crazy dreams."

In the spring of 1968, when I was still in grammar school and stuck in the chamber of unknowing, my father bought a piece of fig land in northwest Fresno and built a house out of adobe bricks in the style of the California missions. We moved from east Fresno, where my pals were Okies, Mexicans and blacks, to northwest Fresno, where I felt for the first time the strange and mannered presence of the South. Across the street sat a red brick Georgian mansion with white columns where Berson Frye, a son of New Orleans, and his wife, Ginger, a lady of Memphis, lived with their two teenage children. Mr. Frye sold California cotton around the world for a company headquartered in Louisiana. Mrs. Frye doted on her Irish setter and stayed active in numerous civic organizations, among them the Holiday Guild, the Junior League and the Cotton Wives Auxiliary. They took their southern serious. Around the house, Mr. Frye, a skinny man with hair the color of coal, wore a white panama hat, white T-shirt and white shorts, which showed off his deeply tanned legs. When he'd come outside to say hello to my father and me playing catch in the front yard, he almost always held a short glass of bourbon over two ice cubes in his hand. This struck me as different. My father owned a bar, but I never saw him fix a drink for himself at home.

On the side of town we came from, the neighbors didn't require outside help to run their households. Wives cleaned their kitchens and bathrooms and hung out the laundry to dry. Husbands mowed the lawn and weeded the flower beds. The Fryes had a Japanese gardener who tended to their immaculate yard twice a week. A black woman in a maid's outfit entered through the back door in the morning and exited out the back door in the late afternoon. This coming and going of cleaning ladies and ironing ladies and ladies to take care of the kids when they came down with German measles wasn't curious in the least in a part of town known as Fig Garden. What caught the attention of our neighbors was my spending Saturdays mowing and edging the lawn and washing Dad's Firebird Formula 400 and Mom's Gremlin. Mrs. Frye, a thin brunette with great charm, was so impressed by my labor that she walked over one afternoon and asked if I might be willing to wash and wax her Jaguar. I couldn't believe it when she picked up the car a few hours later and handed me a check for thirty dollars.

Not too long after, Mr. Frye invited me inside their house. The light was different from the light in our house. The vases were crystal and filled with fresh flowers, and the paintings on the wall were of duck hunts and the dam on the San Joaquin River that formed Millerton Lake. A billiard table occupied the middle of the den. It wasn't a seven-footer with fat, forgiving pockets and a metal slot for quarters, like the one my father had brought home from the bar. It was a perfect eight-footer with tight leather pockets and smooth felt and a slate top on which the shots ran true. Mr. Frye challenged me to a game of eight ball not knowing I was a little shark. "Schooled by a kid," he kept muttering.

Then he showed me the polished trunk where he kept his memorabilia from the South—the papers of ancestors who had owned plantations, and slaves, and had fought as heroes in the Civil War. A great-great-uncle on his dad's side, Stand Watie, was not only a Cherokee who had walked the Trail of Tears; he also was the last Confederate general to surrender. The blood drip of Indian, he said, explained his black hair, high cheekbones and the tan on his skin. He then led me to a glass-enclosed sunroom furnished in pink wicker. Mrs. Frye brought out a Roy Rogers for me, a splash of Cabin Still bourbon for him and a mint julep for herself. They talked about India, Egypt and Italy and all the other places cotton had taken them. The dense drawl of his voice was almost sleep-inducing until he broached the subject of race and I heard for the first time an adult in my world utter the N-word. It came out so blithely as he sat in his chair the color of Pepto-Bismol that I stuck around to hear it a second time, and then I thanked him for the game of pool and the Roy Rogers and walked back home.

I carried into high school only the faintest sense that the farmers on Fresno County's west side shared a secret the rest of us had to guess at. Among my classmates were children of the cotton growers and children of the tractor, pump and chemical company owners. Liz Willson was a few grades behind me. Her father, Melville E. Willson, had become one of the nation's largest distributors of agricultural fertilizers, pesticides and herbicides by serving California's cotton belt. If we were dumb to all the anhydrous ammonia he was dumping on the land, his TV and radio jingle innocently played over and over in our heads: "See the men who walk the furrows, who know the problems there. For a quick and sure solution, they're the ones who always care. It's the men who walk the furrows, who know the problems there. Where do growers find their answers? The Melville E. Willson Company, that's where." The sons and daughters of cotton knew how to keep the family secret, too. Now and then, I'd get a peek at something that hinted at their confederacy. They'd miss classes to go skiing at China Peak and return to school the next day with lift tickets attached to their blue jeans and raccoon tans on their faces. One girl's lawyer father was helping one boy's grower father evade what teeth were left in the 160-acre law. But not even our most radical teachers breathed a word about how the sun-blasted west side—and the 250 families that farmed there—benefited from one of the biggest gifts of public water that ever took place in the West.

In truth, the sons and daughters knew only a little more than we did about the functioning of the Westlands Water District, the six hundred thousand acres of irrigated agriculture carved in the shape of a whale, the largest water agency devoted to food production in the country. Their houses in Fig Garden sat fifty-five miles from their farms. Their lives were bordered by country clubs, not cotton fields. Their dads made the trip each morning in their Cadillacs or airplanes and returned at sundown, in time for martinis. Their moms organized a guild called Llanada, "the vast land," and planned their annual western barbecue to raise money for Valley Children's Hospital. Westlands was a federal reclamation project that had come to fruition in the 1960s. The government limited its subsidized water to 320 acres for each grower and his wife. The Bureau of Reclamation, the agency in charge of enforcing the acreage law, somehow failed to articulate a clear position on brothers, sisters, cousins, aunts, uncles and the children themselves. It got so silly that as soon as a baby was born and possessed a Social Security number, he or she became a farmer entitled to the water that came down the aqueduct. This was how the vast land became vaster. Because so many of the grower families were Catholic, the whole thing had an ecclesiastical cover.

By the 1970s, the cover had begun to be lifted. In the *Fresno Bee,* the same paper that carried the good deeds of the Cotton Wives Auxiliary on its Ladies Pages, reporter George Baker was writing stories about cotton growers visiting and revisiting the government trough. The federal water was costing them only $7.50 an acre-foot, and they didn't have to pay any interest for the canals and pipelines the government had built. The crop subsidy checks they deposited at the bank made Governor Ronald Reagan's screed against black welfare queens driving Cadillacs not only apocryphal but irrelevant. The entitlement program had been designed for the smaller farms of the American South and set a $55,000 ceiling on price supports for each cotton grower. Valley growers regarded the subsidy as nowhere near enough to cover the needs of their larger operations. This was how the names of friends, employees, lovers and Chinese cooks began to appear on the government rolls as co-owners of west side land. Each one was entitled to his or her own $55,000 check. Among the repeat collectors was U.S. District Court judge Robert Coyle, whose name would one day grace our new federal courthouse downtown.

A second federal program sought to reduce the nation's cotton surplus by paying farmers to idle a percentage of their acres. Growers were suddenly being paid *not* to grow cotton. They dealt with this existential dilemma the only way they knew how: They inflated the amount of farmland they were idling, adding thousands of acres of junk ground that had never been farmed before. The "set-aside" ground now eligible for cotton subsidies included airplane landing strips and the bottoms of canals and ditches. In some cases, valley growers kept their promise not to plant cotton on set-aside ground. But rather than fallow these acres, they secretly planted barley and wheat. They were harvesting a grain crop at the same time they were harvesting tens of thousands of dollars in cotton subsidies. When bad weather hit and yields went down, a third government program, Disaster Relief, came to the rescue. The same USDA that was paying farmers to idle land was guaranteeing them a considerable sum if they failed to realize 75 percent of their normal yield due to an act of God. "Normal yield" was a term that meant almost nothing out in the field, where yields varied year to year depending on water, chemicals and weather events short of God. The uncertainty of what constituted a "normal yield" gave growers so much wiggle room that in some years the disaster relief payments to the valley exceeded $15 million.

Among the long list of valley men abusing one farm subsidy program or another was Kenneth Frick, a big, burly grower who had left his cotton fields in Kern County to become the head of the nation's farm subsidy program. Even as Frick was going around the country railing against agricultural "welfare" on behalf of President Nixon, he was perfecting a scheme to collect more payments by putting his fields in the name of his teenage daughters and son. The Frick family was cashing government checks amounting to nearly $1 million to underwrite their cotton crop, and this didn't count the water subsidies they were receiving as customers of the Friant-Kern Canal.

The government accountability inspectors began leaking the sordid details to Baker and other reporters, and for a time it looked as if the bigger abusers might have to pay hefty fines or face prosecution by the Justice Department. Then the local politicians started pushing back, none more forcefully than our boy wonder, Bob Mathias, the Tulare congressman who had been declared the world's greatest athlete at the age of seventeen after winning the 1948 Olympic gold medal in the decathlon. Congressman Mathias argued that charges of fraud on the part of our farmers had no basis in fact because government probers lacked the qualifications to understand the technicalities of the farm program. In the end, ninety cotton growers were fined a total of $80,000. Congress pledged to enact reforms to free agriculture from the shackles of government largess, but the subsidy payments kept arriving in the mail. No zip code in America received more subsidy checks in larger amounts than 93711. That would be our neighbors in Fig Garden, 250 of them—farmers, corporations, partnerships and absentee landowners.

Fresno didn't keep a blue book the way Los Angeles and San Francisco did. Our promising teenage girls weren't summoned to a coming out at an annual cotillion ball. We didn't have blue bloods who married blue bloods and produced blue-eyed, blond-haired boys who stood six foot four. We imported people built low to the ground, all the better for picking field and vine. The valley was a place where you could stand five foot ten and feel like a giant. Cotton king Russell Giffen and his devoutly religious wife, Ruth; their four children, Patricia, Mike, Price and Carolyn; and their children's children were the nearest we had to patricians. We made a game of following their epic crops and epic griefs. They

Russell Giffen flanked by sons Mike and Price,
Firebaugh, 1950s

went off to Cal Berkeley, where the Giffen boys pledged to a fraternity and the Giffen girls pledged to a sorority and they rooted riotously for the Bears football team and no one cared that they left before obtaining degrees. Public events were held at their ranch beside the Kings River, where Russell kept his elegant American Saddlebred horses and Ruth kept her Catholic chapel. They served beans and barbecued tri-tip on plastic plates. When we needed guidance on where to donate our charitable contributions, we took a lead from the Giffens. It was Carolyn and older sister, Patty, who organized the Candlelight Guild, which raised hundreds of thousands of dollars for Valley Children's Hospital. It was Price who helped start Kelso Village for kids with "mental retardation."

When the stories in the *Bee* started to complicate our view of things, civic leaders and citizens alike rationalized the overreach of our farmers as something we might all do if given the opportunity. Their grab of land and water and the mess their petrochemicals were making of our air didn't register. If one of the growers was kind enough to acknowledge us in public, he was considered a "good guy." As long as he occasionally threw his attention our way, he was forever a "good guy." The good-guy stories told about the Giffens were said to be more deserving than the rest. At the public library downtown, Fresnans could trace Giffen altruism to at least the early 1900s, when a book about the pioneers of Fresno County was published; it offered the following anecdote about patriarch Wylie Giffen:

> The city of Fresno had tried to reimburse Mr. Giffen for his services as an arbitrator in a damage claim against the city. When the fifty-dollar check arrived at his residence, he attached it to a note to the mayor and mailed it back to city hall. "You can do anything you see fit with this check—either return it to the fund from which it was taken or use it in behalf of the playgrounds. Fresno has been good to me, and I would rather render any service that I can without pay."

Wylie was said to be a far-seeing man who somehow didn't see the raisin bust of 1922 barreling his way. He had grown up in nearby Fowler as the son of a Presbyterian minister and had become one of the most respected citizens in Fresno County. A bank president and the head of Sun-Maid raisins, he was farming ten thousand acres of vines when the price of raisins plummeted from 11 cents a pound to 2.5 cents. He tried everything within his considerable powers to fend off disaster not only for himself but for the industry. This was the same Giffen whose Sun-Maid night riders were horsewhipping raisin growers to sign contracts with his cooperative. He talked his fellow growers into investing $2.4 million in advertising and $3.5 million in a new Sun-Maid plant. But not even holding half the raisins in storage could keep the bottom from falling out. Vineyard land selling for $2,200 an acre suddenly wasn't worth $200 an acre.

Giffen lost his ten thousand acres, his president's chair at the Fidelity Trust and Savings Bank and his director's seat at Sun-Maid. The creditors even took his English Tudor manse and the fifty acres of estate that surrounded it. He was fifty-one years old, the father of three adult children, and there was nowhere else for him and his wife, May, to go but into the desert. He had purchased a few hundred acres where the valley began its climb to the Coast Ranges—land considered so worthless that the creditors let it be. In a half century's time, this squatters' prairie would become the most contested farmland in America, a target of acreage reformers and environmentalists who viewed it as a desecration of every ideal of reclamation pledged by the federal engineers. But back then, no person of sound mind considered it suitable for crops. Not even the Basque sheepmen who'd been grazing stock out there since the 1870s had any idea of the promise, and poison, the soil held. One visitor trekking across the west side on his way to Fresno proper described it as "the purest alkali land on which not even a mortgage or salt grass could be raised, and not unlike the country around the Dead Sea in Palestine, where the birds fly high in passing over it."

By 1923, Giffen had planted two wells in the sagebrush and was attempting to grow grapes and tree fruit. A group of investors all the way from Massachusetts—the Boston Land Company—heard about his experiment and decided to cultivate forty thousand acres of vines and orchards on the same ground. With the advent of the turbine pump, they were taken with the notion that the west side could one day rival the east side as a producer of fruit. But three years into the plantings, the leaves on the vines began to curl and brown. What berries hung in clusters were too small to be considered grapes. No matter how long the peaches and plums were kept on the tree, the sugar wouldn't come. The culprit, it was determined, was too much boron in the water. Giffen and another west side pioneer, W. J. Hotchkiss, tore out the vines and trees and planted cotton, which could stand up to salt and boron. The Boston Land Company did the same. This was how the plantation (the growers called it "the ranch") came to be on the soil of Fresno County.

Giffen's younger son, Russell, was a high school dropout and a billiards shark. He stood five foot seven is his size 5 shoes. He had a piercing gaze and a photographic memory and a deep need to redeem his father's failure. He bought 320 acres of ground in Arvin in 1923, married a local Catholic girl named Ruth Price and planted potatoes in the sandy loam. A freak Easter frost destroyed his entire crop, and he watched the equipment dealer repossess his every last tool. He and Ruth tied up their sixteen workhorses into one long wagon train and treaded from Arvin to Mendota, a 152-mile plod across farm and desert. He knocked on the door of his father, Wylie, who was more than happy to take them in. For the next seven years, he helped his father and older brother farm cotton and grain on the west side, until their disagreements over water started to turn heated. Russell thought his father was diminishing the quality of the cotton by planting too many acres served by too few wells. He believed that water, not ground, should determine how much seed a cotton farmer planted. Spend every last drop of water on the best dirt only, he urged, and watch the yields jump from one and a half bales an acre to two bales.

Wylie was too old to listen. It was 1933, and Russell struck out on his own again. His eye caught a section of west side land near Cantua Creek, and he went to see cotton ginner Anderson Clayton, looking for a loan to drill a well. "You got a good piece of dirt, but not a single asset," Ronald Jensen, the head of finance, told him. "I can't in good conscience sign Anderson Clayton's name to a loan. But I can sign my own name." With that, Jensen handed Russell a personal check for $2,500. Before he knew it, they were calling Russell Giffen the cotton king. He went from 640 acres that first year to 6,400 acres the second year to 20,000 acres the third year. Some of the ground he bought; much of it he leased from Southern Pacific and other absentee owners. By the time *Fortune* magazine caught up with him in 1949, he had sold his first cotton spread, 54,000 acres, to Anderson Clayton for a $7 million profit and was amassing a new operation double its size.

The beauty of growing cotton was that it required none of his own money. Most of the enterprise was financed by Anderson Clayton, on the condition that he gin and sell his fiber through them. The rest was backed by a bank or insurance company. His entire year's budget was borrowed money. Success or failure rode on a single cotton crop. He had to keep his pumps running night and day, year-round, because turning the power on and off could cause a well to shear in two. He planted safflower in March not because he gave a damn about safflower but because it gave him a reason to keep the pumps churning in an otherwise dead season. His power bill came out to $1 million a month (more than any other customer), and Pacific Gas & Electric let him pay in winter, when his cotton money came in. If he didn't pay by then, what could the utility say? Russell Giffen sat on PG&E's board of directors. Peerless Pump, run by his good friend Elmer Hansen, let him wait until December 31 to clear his debt. It was no small favor as he proceeded to drill 124 wells in and around Huron.

The town was a den of dope, prostitution, gambling and several other vices and well on its way to earning the title of "Knife-Fight City." Though Huron appeared to be lawless on its face, it was actually controlled with some thoughtfulness by the Fresno County Sheriff's Office.

The bagmen who collected payoffs from the pimps and bookies were deputies acting on the orders of Sheriff Melvin Wilmirth, who'd grown up in nearby Coalinga, the son of an oil-rig mechanic. The sheriff and the cotton king reached an immediate understanding. What took place in the pool halls, taverns and five-and-tens on main street—a neon-lit version of a Wild West town—was the sheriff's domain. What took place on the far side of the asphalt, where the cotton grew a half foot taller than it did in the South, was the province of Giffen. And so it stood for the next twenty-five years.

Each late September, the call rang out for the cotton pickers. Ten thousand migrants poured into the west side, dragging their twelve-foot-long sacks. Giffen set up his camps on the dirt of his fields. One camp was for white Okies, one for black Okies, one for Mexicans and one for German and Italian prisoners of war. The migrants lived in one-room cabins that Giffen bought for ten dollars apiece from the military. They picked up their provisions from the company store and cooked their meals on woodstoves. The tractor drivers and irrigators numbered in the hundreds and worked for Giffen year-round. They were treated better and given decent houses. A Chinese cook and his crew fed them two meals a day. Breakfast wasn't eaten until Mr. Giffen walked through the kitchen door and took a seat among them. He was friendly but never wasted a word. He knew each of their names and the ranches and tasks to which they were assigned.

Among the harvest gypsies were Albert and Lucille Bell, who had fled the dust and depression of Arkansas with forty-four jars of chopped cabbage pickled by Lucille. Their Model T Ford broke down so many times along Route 66 that she gave away forty-two of the jars to mechanics merciful enough to fix their jalopy for free. The Bells, she liked to say, had sauerkrauted their way to California. In the late summer of 1948, they led a caravan of "ditch bank" Okies to the Giffen camps on the outskirts of the west side. Seven Bell children, ages three to sixteen, piled out of the car. Seeing the size of their brood, the camp supervisor assigned them to a pair of one-room shacks situated side by side. Twelve-year-old Elvin Bell enrolled at the Cantua Creek School run by Ralph Minnite. The boy soon found himself receiving two educations, one at school and another at the camp. On weekend mornings, he'd walk the long path of outhouses and come upon one cotton picker and another lying in the dirt. They'd been beaten or stabbed, and their pockets emptied out. These were the winners of the previous night's dice games. He saw, too, the swift justice administered to families that tried to skip out on their debt to the company store. "Giffen had these double agents who lived among us in the camps," he would recall years later. "Their job was to spy on us and let the goons know if any debtor was packing up the car and leaving at night. They would run them down and beat the hell out of the husband. Then they'd slash the tires or torch the car. This served as a lesson not only to them but to all of us watching."

On school breaks, Bell and his siblings would awaken at dawn and grab their cotton sacks. Herb "Speedy" Newman, the labor contractor whose pockets were stuffed with Giffen cash, barked out instructions. He talked in Yiddish. He talked in rhyme. His mouth had no governor, which was probably how he got the nickname Speedy. Pulling in behind him, at six-thirty sharp, was a collection of old yellow buses he had bought from one of the school districts. Half the seats were already filled with winos picked up an hour earlier in downtown Fresno. As the kids lined up to get on the bus, Speedy would hand out pieces of candy. If he thought one or two of them were going places, he'd give them a wristwatch. He had an encyclopedic knowledge of world geography, but how he landed on Fresno County's west side and became a middleman to the cotton giants, he couldn't explain. The second they climbed aboard, their nostrils filled with the reek of Thunderbird. Bell never forgot one tramp named Star who would fall asleep on the ride to the fields and spill his rotgut all over the floor. "We'd hop off the bus with muscatel sticking to our shoes and pick cotton the whole day," he said. "If you owed a debt to the company store, you didn't get paid real money. We got paid pieces of paper. The paper was worth seven dollars and fifty cents at the company store. This was the new plantation. And we were the rented slaves."

Graduating from the eighth grade at Cantua Creek bestowed the following: a trip to a theme park in Southern California paid for by Giffen and other growers; one full day to recover from the sleepless night; and a short-handled hoe and a ten-foot cotton sack of their own. The fields called the next morning. Sugar beets in summer, cotton in fall. Plutarco

Flores, who had come from a little town outside El Paso in the summer of 1947, was fourteen years old and weighed 115 pounds. What choice did he have? His mother had died in childbirth, and his father had left him in the care of his maternal grandparents. He never saw a theme park again. He could separate a sugar beet from its stealing weed with one chop. That first season picking cotton, he averaged two hundred pounds a day. He felt good about his labors until he caught sight of the blond-haired, blue-eyed Mexicans from Monterrey. "They started a month before us, picking cotton in Texas. By the time they got to California, they were smoking. I mean, five hundred and six hundred pounds a day. We were rookies compared to those guys."

By 1949, Giffen was telling the reporter from *Fortune* that he couldn't wait for the day when he would put a match to the cabins and burn down every last camp. As he sat in his chintz-draped ranch office wearing a lightweight jacket and a matching fawn hat, he conceded, "There's no such thing as a good cotton camp," though his provided electric

Cotton pickers filling their sacks in the San Joaquin Valley

lighting, firewood and some running water. While he regarded the camps as a blight on the land, he wasn't going to replace the human cotton picker with a mechanical one until he was 100 percent sure it was as reliable as his crews. He was letting smaller cotton growers shoulder the burden of testing the machines. "What we are doing here is profiting on the trials and failures," he explained.

He had sunk close to $4.5 million in wells to irrigate his eighty-six thousand acres of cotton, wheat, barley and flax. He'd invested $2.5 million more in land, buildings and equipment. Not counting the seasonal pickers, he now employed 450 tractor drivers, irrigators, foremen and office assistants, whose wages ranged from eighty cents an hour to $11,000 a year. Each December, he ordered dozens of aluminum trash cans and stuffed them with toys he had bought from Arthur's Toys in Fresno. On Christmas morning, he delivered the cans and frozen turkeys to the doorsteps of his tractor drivers and irrigators. He handed out $500 bonuses to his best employees and was especially generous to a crew of Hindus who had once refused to cash their paychecks to help him through a rough patch. He could afford such giving, he told *Fortune,* because he was about to net, in one year's time, $3 million before taxes. When asked to name his biggest nemesis, he could come up with only one: Russian knapweed, a plant so virulent he couldn't eliminate it with a hoe. Only the most powerful herbicide would do.

Within a few years, the kinks in the mechanical cotton picker were smoothed out, and a single machine was now doing the work of many men, and the government was so bullish on cotton that it was paying Giffen even more to subsidize his crop. The Cadillac dealership in Fresno knew to have its latest fleet of navy blue models—Giffen Blue—on the lot when the cotton king came in for his yearly purchases. He didn't buy his suits and ties at Hodge & Sons or Roos/Atkins or any of the other haberdasheries in downtown Fresno. He drove to Los Angeles and was fitted and dressed by a tailor whose clientele included movie stars. He enjoyed a cigar but didn't drink when he traveled to Memphis or Dallas to get together with his southern pals at their annual cotton gatherings. They regarded him not as a Californian but as one of their own. That his kin had started out in Virginia was credentials enough. His and Ruth's white-columned house, with its sweeping grounds and horse pastures along the Kings River (he had moved the bank to bring the water closer), could have been transplanted from Georgia. Their black servants from the South were known to the Giffen children and twenty-one grandchildren by their first names. In recalling the outsize role that Emma and Henry, Hazel and Earl, and John and Smiley played in their lives, more than one Giffen would compare them to the black characters in *Gone with the Wind*.

Russell was no braggart, but he couldn't resist informing the southern cotton gang about the yields that came off his fields. As an upstart, California already was producing almost one million bales of cotton a year. This ranked fifth behind Texas, Mississippi, Arkansas and Alabama. But when it came to pounds of cotton picked per acre, no other state could compare with California. The west side growers took to their gins almost seven hundred pounds of fiber by the acre. This contrasted with the three hundred pounds an acre in the South. The quality of California fiber was so superior that it sold for a 15 percent premium.

Credit for the big yields went to the seeds, fertilizers, insecticides and herbicides sold in a flow as fantastic as the water by Melville E. Willson. He was one of the "Shirtsleeve Millionaires" featured in the September 1951 issue of *Life* magazine—the only one not dressed in shirtsleeves. Wearing a fancy suit, a white Stetson and two-tone shoes, he was standing in the weeds in front of one of his giant fertilizer billboards, chomping on a fat stogie. Credit also went to an agronomist named George Harrison, who manned the USDA field station near Bakersfield and developed the exceptional cotton plant known as Acala 4-42. Harrison had been born to a family of former slaves in a cotton field in Corpus Christi and studied agronomy at East Texas State before following the cotton trail west in 1934. When asked to account for California's record yields, Harrison pointed not to his own diligent work but to the Panoche loam that came washing down the flash-flood creeks of the Coast Ranges in thick, broad fans. The clay, sand and rock formed a slope that tilted west to east and dropped eight feet a mile. The gray-brown topsoil, a medium to heavy texture, measured six feet deep and deeper. When dry, it looked like any other desert dust. When water struck, it became something else.

The farmers talked about its supernatural properties as if they were practicing alchemy. The till passed through it with ease, which was a good thing, because they had to survey, scrape, fill and water—again and again—until the earth finally sank and settled into farmland. It held its moisture so well that all it took to make an entire season's cotton crop were three well-timed irrigations. In private, the growers joked that the most skilled among them wouldn't stand a chance in the less-forgiving soils on the east side. On the west side, the saddest sack could call himself a farmer. But be careful. As you moved eastward off Giffen slope and into the basin, a different loam met you in Mendota. This ground was heavier and beneath it sat a layer of clay not so easily penetrated. If a farmer applied too much irrigation, the water would back up on him. The topsoil would turn boggy and salty at once, for the land in the main was alkali.

The unruly development of Westlands, much like the story in the rest of the valley but only magnified, began on primo ground and ended on problem ground. The cotton and grain fields covered fifty thousand acres in 1929 and nearly five hundred thousand acres in 1948. Between Mendota and Huron, three hundred wells were sucking water from depths as low as twenty-five hundred feet. The tapping of the aquifer had accelerated to eight hundred thousand acre-feet of water a year, enough to fully satisfy the residential needs of Los Angeles—for two years. On some ranches, the water table was dropping forty feet from one growing season to the next. The earth was falling, too. The well casings on Giffen's ranch near Three Rocks were protruding eight feet above the ground.

The lobbying effort to bring in outside water and save the west side from the repercussions of runaway growth had begun in December 1942. "West Side Ranch Operators Seek Irrigation Water," the headline in the *Fresno Bee* read. "Land Owners Discuss Forming of Vast District to Get River Supply." The way Giffen and his fellow growers saw it, they were only attempting to pull off what the east side farmers had already done. Grabbing snowmelt from Northern California and moving it to their fields would boost the local economy. The fresher water would allow them to cultivate high-dollar vegetables and fruits. The story made no mention of their desperation, the millions of dollars a year they were spending on electrical power to chase a dwindling water table laced with ever-higher concentrations of boron and salts. It made no mention that there was no outlet, natural or man-made, for all the water they were pouring onto their crops. Agriculture on the west side was like a giant plant stuck in a clay pot, only this pot had no hole in its bottom. Irrigation mired and salted up their fields the same way it had mired and salted up the Fertile Crescent between the Tigris and Euphrates four thousand years before. As one west side rancher crudely put it to his neighbors, "We're shitting up our own bed. Even a puppy dog knows to do better."

In 1948, few causes tugged on the purse strings of Congress like the cause of reclamation. The budget for the Department of the Interior was increased to nearly $600 million, a jump of $120 million from the previous appropriation. While none of the money was headed to the valley's west side, the Interior Department did commit to a plan on paper. The Central Valley Project would extend its plumbing to the one thousand square miles of the west side, to the farmers who had already reclaimed large swaths of desert but just needed more water to complete the job. This second phase of the project, the so-called San Luis Unit, envisioned a giant canal, reservoir and pumping station that would siphon water from the delta and ship it south to their cotton and grain fields. Giffen was pleased by the pledge but disappointed that no money had been attached to it. He had journeyed to Washington, D.C., more than once in the mid- to late 1940s to testify before the Interior committees deliberating the contours of the project and had thought it had gone well. When asked to describe himself, the second-biggest cotton grower in America described himself as a plain old "family farmer." Not every face on the committee appeared amused.

Now it was the spring of 1952, and still no money for the waterworks had come. Giffen was sitting in his ranch office in Huron, trying to figure out the next move, when the phone rang. It was J. E. "Jack" O'Neill, who farmed up the road in Five Points. O'Neill had thought of a different strategy to secure public funding for the San Luis Unit and wanted to discuss the idea in person. The two titans had known each other for twenty years, beginning in the hardest days of the nation's Depression when both had wrested a fortune from the same ground. No one knew better than they did how fast the water table was receding and salt spreading out over the lower lands. If they didn't move quickly to secure a freshwater supply from the delta, their experiment on the plain would soon be over. The Panoche loam would return to sand and sagebrush.

Giffen hopped into his Cadillac and drove up Lassen Avenue to the ranch office where O'Neill directed his cotton and cattle empire. On the walls hung framed photos that told of a life of fulfillment. There was O'Neill with his prized stud War Dad; O'Neill posing beside an agricultural exhibit at the Fresno District Fair, where he served as director; O'Neill standing lumpy in the uniform of the Order of the Knights of St. Gregory, an honor bestowed on him by Pope Pius XII in a special Vatican ceremony. On this day, if habits held, O'Neill was dressed in western shirt, bolo tie and slacks. His thick gray hair was combed straight back with Brylcreem. He rose from his desk to greet Giffen, whom he considered not only a farming genius and a gentleman but a trusted friend. The regard was mutual.

O'Neill, raised on a small farm in Ontario, Canada, had lost his first wife young. He raised their daughter and two sons by himself until he met a horsewoman from Carmel and married her. Her name was Paloma, Pal for short, and she could shoot a rifle like Annie Oakley. From their first kiss on, she made it clear that she wasn't going to be living with a bunch of jackrabbits as neighbors. They bought a grand house in Fresno, and he divided his time between his five thousand acres on the west side and his three companies in town: Producers Cotton Oil, O'Neill Meats and television station KJEO. The call letters had been chosen for his initials. The station's first telecast a few months earlier had seized him with a case of stage fright. He had greeted viewers in a quavering voice. His good friend Governor Earl Warren, who was beside him for the occasion, came to his rescue.

O'Neill told Giffen that his idea was to play the state government off the federal government and get one or the other, or both, to commit to the San Luis project. The state was already talking about building a great canal along the Coast Ranges and sending delta water not only southward to Kern County but all the way over the mountain to Los Angeles. Why couldn't the same canal drop off some of that water to their farms as part of a joint state and federal effort? If the Reclamation Bureau feared losing the project to the state, O'Neill reasoned, it might move more quickly. And if the feds and state agreed to share the costs, it might win over the congressmen from the East and South who were opposing more reclamation for the West. Giffen thought it was a fine idea and offered to lead the campaign to persuade other growers of its wisdom.

They shared the idea with grower Frank Diener, who was O'Neill's neighbor and a fellow knight of St. Gregory. Diener thought the plan was the only sensible path forward, but he did have one concern: Water that came from a federal canal was water chained to the 160-acre rule. This might prove a sticking point for other west side growers. Let's get the canal built, O'Neill told him, and worry about acreage limitations later. The three men met with Gilbert Jertberg, a Fresno attorney and soon-to-be federal judge, and drew a boundary line to form a water district under California law. They weren't shy about the district they created. The first line took in four hundred thousand acres. The second line would add another two hundred thousand. The province they called the Westlands Water District began at one end of Fresno County and extended past the other end. No irrigation body in the United States was bigger. O'Neill hired a full-time lobbyist, a former Foreign Service officer who had served a stint in Iran, and moved him to Washington. On September 30, 1952, the Westlands board held its first official meeting and named Jack Rodner as director. Rodner had been the longtime head of the local office of the U.S. Bureau of Reclamation. "Go grab the government's guy if you want to grab the government's water" was probably not an adage that Westlands invented. But the district would employ it to ends never before achieved.

Next, they had to find themselves a new man to run for Congress. Oakley Hunter, the smug incumbent Republican, couldn't stand dealing with the federal bureaucrats. The growers might have agreed with him philosophically, but they were practical men. Water with strings attached was better than no water at all. The Twelfth Congressional District was Commie-baiting country. No pro-union Democrat stood a chance. The only Democrat the growers could find to run was a goofy-looking cotton picker from Texas who was selling tires in downtown Fresno. Bernice Frederic Sisk was his name. Everyone called him Tex. He was tall and lanky, with a pair of jug ears and a wide grin that showed the gap in his teeth. His drawl was so thick it was hard to understand him, and he was a union man to boot. But what he lacked in schooling, he made up for in cunning. They trotted him out in front of several local power brokers, including Gordon Nelson, the farm reporter for the *Fresno Bee,* and Nelson's editor, Diz Shelton, who came straight from his barstool at the Hi Life. They asked Sisk enough questions to determine that he could, and would, stick to a single issue: the need to build the San Luis Unit and save Fresno County from economic ruin. As to the matter of his name, Bernice wouldn't do. Neither would Tex. How about B. F. Sisk?

The signs went up and the cash poured in, the biggest checks signed by O'Neill, Giffen and fellow grower Jack Harris. In November 1954, B. F. Sisk, lifted by all those new Okie and Arkie voters, eked out an upset victory and was sworn into Congress. The Southern Democrats in charge of the House of Representatives greeted him as a long-lost cousin. When B.F. opened his mouth, they understood exactly what he meant. As he led the fight for the San Luis project, he never received a word of bad press in the *Bee*. How could he? Reporter Nelson was covering the water beat at the same time he was doing public relations for the Westlands Water District. Nelson called his little effort the "San Luis Boosters" and took a $600 contribution from the growers to get it rolling. By 1956, his man Sisk was sitting on the Interior committee chaired by Clair Engle, the cowboy congressman from Northern California. Engle might have been inclined to side against a reclamation project that was going to steal more water out of the northern rivers and ship it south to raise surplus cotton. But his father had been a Bakersfield rancher before moving the family to Shasta County, and the congressman kept a soft spot for row-crop farmers. Engle helped Sisk steer his legislation every step of the way.

It was now time for the growers to fly to Washington and testify before the committees and subcommittees hearing the bill that would authorize $193 million for the federal portion of the project. One by one, they told their sad story. They did not hide their desperation. Their pumping of the aquifer had reached one million acre-feet of water a year. This was a level of extraction that no other farmland in the world could claim, if you didn't count the fields nearby in Kern County. The congressmen who'd been around awhile had heard this story before. Drilling hundreds of new wells and watching the land sink was a drama that had played out two decades earlier on the valley's east side. There, the cry of "Dust Bowl" had given rise to the original Central Valley Project. Now the west side boys had created the same set of facts on the ground. They had chased agriculture so far into the horizon that they were contriving the same water scarcity and hitting up Congress with the same plea: "How can you let us lose all that we have built?"

———

Cotton planter on Giffen Ranch, west of Fresno County, 1949

Seated before the committee, Russell Giffen practically contorted himself into the shape of an agrarian populist. Cheap federal water, he vowed, would enable small farmers to gain a foothold on the west side and bring to an end vast holdings such as his. Under the present conditions, only a big farmer could afford the cost of drilling new wells and running day-and-night electricity. "We must begin to build a supplemental surface water system in what is now a deep-well area to make it possible to break up these large holdings into small economic farm units," he said. J. E. O'Neill, introduced by Congressman Engle as "one of the outstanding citizens of California," agreed that the nation must do its part to democratize farming on the west side. The cheap and clean waters from the north would "permit the small landowners on the west side, who presently lease their properties to these large farm operations, to farm that property themselves should they so desire."

The idea of a grand canal running down the west side wasn't new. Cattle King Miller and his fellow industrialists had brought out an engineer from India to build such a canal, only to settle for a ditch that irrigated their lands. Now, nearly a century later, Governor Pat Brown was assuring the congressmen that California was ready and able to contribute its 55 percent share of the project. He was endorsing a funding plan, first conceived by O'Neill, to combine taxpayer-backed bond moneys with millions of dollars from state oil revenues. "I have asked leaders of both the state senate and assembly to count noses to find out whether we have the votes to do this," Brown reported, "and they tell me we have the votes."

Even Paul Taylor, the liberal UC Berkeley economist, was supporting the project, albeit with a strong caveat that acreage limits had to be imposed. "The moral basis of the 160-acre limitation is to prevent unjust enrichment resulting from subsidies to irrigation provided by interest-free federal money," Taylor noted.

Congressman Sisk sensed that his moment had arrived. A man known for his butchery of the English language, he sounded almost poetic as he spoke of the transfiguration sure to take place in the settlements of Mendota, Huron and Five Points. He had seen a vision not unlike the one Brigham Young saw in the Great Salt Lake Desert. The population of the west side would quadruple with thousands of farmers living off the fat of the land and an equal number of rural folk and city folk calling the west side home. "In all," he pledged, there would be "87,500 people sharing the productivity and the bounty of the fertile lands blossoming with an ample supply of San Luis water." Not 88,000. Not 87,000. But 87,500 citizens.

The helicopter landed in the western hills above the San Joaquin Valley, and out of the dust walked President John Fitzgerald Kennedy. It was August 18, 1962, and the sun would not let go. In the hollow of the mountains, where California was about to build its newest reservoir, summer had baked the earth to a tan and shrunken form. The hills seemed to be covered in hide. Though not a drop of rain had fallen from the sky since March, no one in the assembled crowd, and certainly not the cotton kings, thought of this as drought. Going dry for eight months was California's condition, and here was the young president coming west to deliver California's fix. Though he was a son of Massachusetts, he knew that this was a place where "things do not happen but are made to happen." Looking down on the valley from the helicopter, he had seen nature's aridity and man's answer side by side. Desert and farm, salt and fruit. The difference was the reach of an irrigation canal.

President Kennedy and Governor Brown arrive by helicopter to break ground on the San Luis Project, 1962

Two Irish politicians at the peak of their power, JFK and Governor Pat Brown, were meeting outside Los Banos to build the nation's largest reservoir that didn't have a stream feeding it. Here, no dam would be stopping snowmelt inside a river canyon. Here, a different magnitude of capture would take place. More than 1.5 million acre-feet of federal water would be pumped out of the delta each year and lifted by hydraulics into the California Aqueduct. The aqueduct, built bigger than most western rivers, would then carry the water to a massive gouge cut into the hillside where the two men were standing. The San Luis Reservoir would store the water and make deliveries to three farming districts—Westlands the biggest—and a municipal district that took in the developing suburbs of what would become the Silicon Valley. The political genius of the aqueduct was that it would serve two masters. Working also on behalf of the State Water Project, it would take an additional 4 million acre-feet of water out of the delta and ship it even farther south—to the farms of Kings and Kern Counties and the housing tracts of Los Angeles and San Diego. No partnership between Washington, D.C., and a state government had ever tackled a project of such monument. By the force of the new reservoir and the aqueduct, the Central Valley Project and the State Water Project would join hands.

The protectors of the environment, such as they were in the early 1960s, didn't question what damage Westlands would do to the Trinity River or the delta below it. No court was asked to weigh the benefits of growing cotton and melons against the harm posed to salmon and steelhead trout by dam, lake, tunnel and pump. The Trinity shot out of the Klamath Mountains on the North Coast and gave life to one of the best salmon runs on the continent. For thousands of years, the Hoopa tribe piled sticks and stones to slow down the river so they could catch the giant Chinook. A concrete dam built by the Reclamation Bureau had now stopped the Trinity cold, creating Clair Engle Lake (ironically, named after the local congressman who gave away the river). The project was sold as a centerpiece of hydroelectric power but was really one giant diversion in the cause of faraway agriculture. A fourteen-mile-long tunnel carried the Trinity's flow from Engle Lake to the watershed of the Sacramento River. The Trinity found itself mingling in the strangeness of the delta. Now its flows would be called to an even more alien place: the San Luis Reservoir. From there, it would be packaged and delivered to the newly blessed land of Fresno County's west side.

It was true that half of Westlands boasted some of the finest loam in the world. It was also true that the other half hid nature's time bomb. The layer of clay, lodged a few yards below the surface, plugged up three hundred thousand acres of alkali ground. This was the land that could not fully drink water. Irrigation after irrigation, deadly salts were backing up into the root zone. The Bureau of Reclamation was now intending to deposit 1.2 million acre-feet of imported water on both the good and the bad ground of Westlands. The farmers and the politicians knew that an elaborate system of drainage would have to be erected alongside the elaborate system of irrigation to remove the polluted water from the least permeable ground. But the cost of such a system, and who would pay for it, were questions Congress did not fully answer in the San Luis Act. What damage the contaminated water might do to aquatic life when it was finally dumped into the ocean wasn't considered, either. No one knew how long it would take for the sump of Westlands, drainage system or not, to come up poisoned. Each year, 1.5 million tons of salt built up in the irrigated soil on its own. The extra water shipped in from the brackish delta would add another 1.5 million tons of salt. It was going to require the equivalent of forty railcars a day to remove all the salts from the newly irrigated lands.

None of those doubts would intrude on this day, the groundbreaking for the San Luis Reservoir. President Kennedy and Governor Brown stood beside each other in the shade of a speaker's platform festooned in red, white and blue bunting. Twelve thousand people had awakened early that morning and driven from miles around into the parched hills. The women wore fine summer dresses and white gloves. The men had put on slacks and short-sleeved white button-down shirts and straw hats. That the kids were dressed in their Sunday school clothes seemed appropriate for what they were about to witness: the miracle of man working through God in "giving rain and fruitful seasons." Kennedy was wearing an elegant dark suit and a blue tie with diagonal stripes. His hair was stuck at perfect. He seemed transfixed by the paradox of the valley. "We can see the greenest and most richest [*sic*] earth producing the greatest and richest crops in the country," he told the crowd. "And then a mile away we can see the same earth and see it brown and dusty and useless, and all because there's water in one place and there isn't in another."

Standing off to one side were the proud conquerors of the American desert: Stewart Udall, head of the Interior Department, and Floyd Dominy, who ran the department's Reclamation Bureau. The two men, one the son of Arizona, one the son of Nebraska, both raised in drought country, despised each other. Dominy, who ruled over reclamation by striking terror in the hearts of his bureaucrats, had found a different way to deal with the man above him. He ignored Udall. "Who does he think he is?" Dominy once said. "The Commissioner of Reclamation?" At the celebratory dinner in downtown Fresno the previous night, Dominy had run down the list of new irrigation projects his engineers were constructing, from California to Utah to Texas. Before a mission to the moon was even dreamed of, the idea of capturing western water behind massive dams had run deep in the American imagination. As long as Floyd Dominy stayed in charge, reclamation's passion would not wane.

Joining them in the shade of the platform was Congressman Sisk, who couldn't stop smiling, and Clair Engle, the Democrat from up north who was now Senator Engle, and his colleague Thomas Kuchel, the Republican senator from down south. "This is one state, not two," Senator Kuchel had said in support of the project. "What helps Northern California helps the south as well." It was a sentiment that rang almost true during reclamation's reign from the mid-1920s to the mid-1960s but would rarely ring true again as the politics of water began to splinter California into a state of three, if not more. At the other end of the platform, Joseph Jensen, chairman of the Metropolitan Water District of Los Angeles, pulled the cotton kings aside. "It's a great day for all of us," he confided. Russell Giffen and Frank Diener agreed, though they were too gentlemanly to remind Jensen that his MET had opposed the project until the governor pledged to deliver most of the water down the aqueduct to Los Angeles. The two farmers could only regret that J. E. O'Neill wasn't there to enjoy the victory. The man who had done more than anyone to bring water to the west side had died sixteen months earlier, at the age of sixty-nine. His twelve nephews had carried his casket to the Catholic cemetery on the outskirts of Fresno, and a dozen knights of St. Gregory in ostrich-feathered hats had saluted him with their swords.

Now, as the sun poured into the clearing, President Kennedy counted one, two, three, and he and Governor Brown pushed down on a pair of brass plungers, setting off sticks of dynamite packed into the hillside. Two clouds of smoke, four miles apart, billowed skyward, marking the future shoulders of the earthen dam. At that moment, a helicopter flew across the canyon trailing red smoke 320 feet above the floor to show everyone how high the dam would stand. The crowd let go an earnest cheer. "It is a pleasure for me to come out here and help blow up this valley in the cause of progress," the president quipped. It would take another six years for the aqueduct, reservoir and O'Neill forebay to be built and the first drops of the Trinity—one more river stolen—to irrigate the still-expanding fields of the west side. There, already lurking below ground, a massive pool of water was turning more toxic with each irrigation. Slowly, it was creeping toward the surface as the cotton crept toward the sun.

Nineteen

POISONED POND

The land began to fill with government water in 1967. Over the next decade, crop production in Westlands shot up from $48 million a year to $444 million. The growth was breathtaking, but farmers were only keeping to their end of the pledge. They took snowmelt and used it to grow cotton and then garlic, tomatoes, broccoli, lettuce and cantaloupes. No longer did they have to fallow whole sections of land. They had enough water to leach down the salts and make every square inch of the west side bloom. They planted cotton in spring and picked it in fall. They planted wheat and barley in fall and picked it in spring. Because urban water users weren't taking their full share of delta water in the first years, the farmers had extra supplies to grow fruits and vegetables throughout summer. With 1.5 million acre-feet of imported water at their disposal, no one needed to rely on the salty aquifer anymore. In 1966, before the feds came to the rescue, farmers in Westlands were mining almost one million acre-feet of water from the ground. By 1976, they were pumping less than a tenth of this amount. The plummeting water table was rising back up. The sinking land was sinking no more. Giants like Giffen stayed giants. Growers operating two-thousand-acre ranches doubled in size.

For nearly two centuries, the term "family farmer" had meant one thing in America: the resident yeoman plowing modest acres with his own hands. How to now characterize fathers, sons, brothers, sisters, nephews, nieces, cousins joining tractors and six-row pickers to farm tens of thousands of acres on Fresno County's west side? Many of them were genuine characters, American originals on a par with the moguls who had built Hollywood.

Atop the slope, Jack Stone, the new president of Westlands, was farming seven thousand acres of Panoche loam. His father, a civil engineer, had introduced him to the land in the 1920s when he was not yet ten. Driving his sleek Cadillac Phaeton, top down, L. M. Stone bounced along the dirt roads of the raw prairie like he was crossing some hard-to-fathom sea. Every half mile or so, he pointed to salt grass poking out of baked earth. "That's where the dirt is the most fertile," he told young Jack. Stone taught his own two sons, John and Bill, how to farm by ground and by airplane. On the latifundia of the west side, a farmer needed a man's eye and a bird's eye. John was trying to land on the ranch one June day in 1976 when he pulled up sharply to turn, stalled and crashed in a cotton field. Halfway to the hospital in Fresno, the ambulance broke down, and he died. At least a dozen west side ranchers or their help had perished or would perish in similar plane crashes. John was twenty-nine years old with a wife and one-year-old son. "He tried to make a fancy landing and fouled up," Jack Stone told a reporter years later. "It was tough, tough." Stone wore suspenders, had a mop of gray hair and was built like a bantamweight boxer. He formed eight separate ranches—each one in a different family member's name—to get around acreage limits and keep the largess flowing. In reality, he ran the entities as one. "By God," he shouted, "it's legal."

On the heavy ground of Mendota, the "cantaloupe capital of the world," Helen Stamoules was farming two thousand acres in honor of her late husband, Spero. He had grown up in a mountain village outside Athens, sailed to New York City in the early 1900s and took a job as a waiter at the Waldorf-Astoria. He instructed the breakfast crews to put aside the remains from cantaloupes so he could salvage their slimy seeds. He returned to Greece at the age of thirty-eight and met Helen in a village not far from his own. She was half his age and eager for an adventure, and they landed in Mendota in 1927. He bought one hundred acres of tumbleweeds and planted the seeds he had kept in a bag. By 1944, Spero's ice-packed cantaloupes were being transported across the country under the label S&S. The ice would melt and the melons would swell up. By the time they reached Chicago, they were full of sugar. A sentimental man, he got the idea of following the first rail shipment of melons back to New York City—to mark the full circle of his crop. Bounding across Grand Central Terminal, he suffered a massive heart attack and died at the age of fifty-five. Helen was still a young woman and could have sold the farm for clean and moved herself and baby daughter, Peggy, to Fresno. She chose to hang tough in Mendota and grow melons, cotton and alfalfa for the next thirty years.

Five miles to the west, Jess and Dick Telles, who'd grown up in an old Miller & Lux colony called Las Deltas, were fast becoming the new melon kings. The two brothers had taken twenty acres handed down from their Azorean Portuguese father and parlayed it into thirty-seven thousand acres on the west side and another seventeen thousand acres in Arizona. Their astonishing rise—they bought land from Giffen and were farming both sides of the Colorado River—was said to be a function of their differences. Jess was water; Dick was dirt. Jess was a Stanford-educated lawyer; Dick was a row-crop farmer who'd taught himself how to grow cotton, wheat, melons and lettuce. Their ground was so clean that other farmers took their unsuspecting bankers by the Telles ranch on Nees Avenue and pretended it was theirs. The bankers were only too eager to approve the loans. The brothers were able to amass their empire even as their wives turned against each other. Jess and his family lived in Los Banos, and Dick and his family lived in Dos Palos. It was just enough highway between them to keep the peace.

Then the split happened. Jess had three sons who were older than Dick's one son, and two of them were aching to get in. Who could blame them? Travelers Insurance and Anderson Clayton were underwriting the multimillion-dollar enterprise, and government water was cheap and easy, and the crop subsidy checks and kickbacks from cotton broker Heinz Molsen bought them second houses and airplanes, too, and allowed Jess and Dick to keep their girlfriends mostly off the books. In 1975, the two Telles brothers, to their lasting regret, sat down to divide the company in two. The land, the water, the farmhouses, the equipment, the packing sheds—there was no way to make it equal. When one asset turned out to be more valuable than another, the family rift grew to engulf the next generation, even as Jess and Dick still got together for lunch three times a week.

Some of the people they had listed as "owners" to evade the acreage law started asking questions. So, where's our share of the money? Where's our piece of the crop? Dick's wife had a sister who lived in Hawaii and was "farming" one of the 160-acre chunks. She had never set foot on the land. Give her a map and she couldn't point to within twenty miles of it. But Dick was using her identity and the identities of her children and her parents to draw more water and subsidy checks. Then she discovered that he was also using her name to secure millions of dollars in loans from Travelers Insurance. Fearing fraud of another sort, she hired an attorney. That was when her sister and the rest of the Telles family flew to Hawaii and showed up at her house. "Boy, my God, all hell broke loose," she told a reporter. "It was awful. They came over and my sister, my God, she beat me up. My father had to pull her off me. It was just terrible." Though she lived in Hawaii, she believed she had a rightful claim to the land. Dick told her that all she had done was sign her name to a few documents. He, on the other hand, had farmed the dirt with his own sweat. "You're never going to end up with this land," he told her. "I'll go to prison first."

On the other side of Mendota, the Ryan brothers, Mayo and Mike, were farming the ground their father had first plowed back in 1937. Forty seasons had passed, and the soil was turning more salty and waterlogged. The Ryans calculated that with the cleaner federal water coming down the pike it was as good a time as any to lease out the ranch. Their four thousand acres landed in the lap of Albert Britz, a complicated man carting a complicated story. His father had been a lumber magnate in Germany with an exclusive deal to supply railroad ties to the Weimar Republic. Between the First and the Second World Wars, hyperinflation made his contracts practically worthless. As Albert told it, the Britz family went from a mansion with butlers and maids to a dank cubbyhole. He was able to leave Germany before the Nazis began sending Jews to the death camps on the same rail lines his father had helped build. A chemistry whiz, Albert graduated from UC Berkeley and earned an advanced degree from Stanford, then spent the war years developing new types of munitions to bomb the Germans. That was where he met Helen Davis, a tall, big-boned Jewish girl whose talent at the piano confronted her with a choice: continue her artistic pursuits or help Albert mix his liquid fertilizer at the Oakland port and ship it in barrels to the farm belt? She chose Albert, who was brilliant, absentminded and crude and in need of her finishing touches to make him the man he might become. They landed in Five Points in 1952.

For the next forty years, Helen tried her best to conform Albert to social conventions, but the west side titan would not be tamed. He would show up to fancy affairs with a rope cinched around his pants. At the Kahala Hilton in Hawaii, he offended the chef by insisting that he cook him a "Wiener schnitzel" for dinner. For the next five nights, Albert ordered the same. He disappeared from the hotel one morning, and Helen couldn't find him. She was shouting so loud—"Albert, Albert!"—that she unnerved the famous dolphin swimming in the hotel's pool. They eventually located him on the country club's ninth fairway, where he had taken a seat under a palm tree, tee shots whizzing by, to read a biography of Dwight D. Eisenhower. His eccentricities crossed over into the uncouth. One afternoon, he and a farmer had agreed to meet at his house. The farmer arrived on time and knocked on the door. No answer. He heard Albert's exuberant voice inside and knocked again. Still no answer. He knocked a third time, then turned around to leave. Out then shuffled Albert, pants around his ankles. "Can't you hear that Helen and I are fucking. You know 'fucking'?" he said in his German accent, and then slammed the door.

On the far south end of the Westlands Water District, Leland McCarthy and his partner, Vernal Amaro, were farming five thousand acres of cotton, tomatoes, melons and iceberg lettuce. In 1970, they found themselves on the giving side of Prudential Insurance, which agreed to hand them a $50 million check each year for the next decade. It came with only one stipulation: Develop more farmland than you ever thought possible. Across the Tulare Lake basin, they converted 32,000 virgin acres into a vast planting of olives, wine grapes, almonds and the first pistachios and pomegranates (a variety called Wonderful) on the west side. Soon they were farming 90,000 acres of fruits and vegetables, from one end of California to the other. This didn't count the 40,000 acres of cotton and peanuts they were growing in Texas or the 20,000 acres of sugarcane they were raising in Louisiana or the 1 million acres of leased land in New South Wales, Australia, where they were grazing sixty-eight thousand head of cattle. They were taking care of themselves, too: $1,800 Tony Lama crocodile boots, nine-inch Cuban cigars, two King Airs and a $15 million Hawker Siddeley twelve-passenger jet with a pair of Rolls-Royce engines that could fly from West Coast to East Coast without needing to refuel.

McCarthy stood tall and lean with a slight paunch growing under his silver horseshoe belt buckle. In his white cowboy hat and full-length black leather jacket, he looked like he couldn't decide between the Marlboro man and an Irish mobster. He was laconic, though it may have been the shame of his eighth-grade education. Most every joke he told had masturbation as its punch line. Amaro, who'd been a football and baseball star at Selma High, was shorter and beefier and forever tanned. He was an inventor with three U.S. patents to his name. Two of his fabrications, the first mechanical wine-grape picker and the first mechanical pomegranate picker, were such monstrous contraptions that they had to be folded sideways and escorted from one ranch to another by two units of the California Highway Patrol.

If the two of them craved freshly caught salmon, they would fly up to the Pacific Northwest. If they craved $500-a-night girls, they'd fly themselves and their closest bankers, real estate agents and tractor salesmen to Lake Tahoe. They once drove to San Francisco in McCarthy's Rolls-Royce and made such a night of it that they lost the car. The hotel where they were staying tracked it down two years later. Prudential stayed oblivious to their excesses until they decided to maximize the subsidy payments on their cotton fields. They created eighteen separate entities, each one entitled to receive $50,000 from the USDA. The entities had their own colored binders: purple for Amaro Trust and orchid white for the McCarthy Brothers and pastel green for Berenda Vineyards. Their scheme wasn't quite as audacious as what the southern cotton boys had done with their Mississippi Christmas Tree, so named because of all the different ownership branches it sprouted. But the McCarthy-Amaro version caught the eye of Prudential's money managers just the same. Everything from their jets to their wrong colored wine (they had planted mostly white varietals) suddenly became a problem for the insurance company.

McCarthy made the trip back to Newark, New Jersey, to hear for himself the findings of the "Pru Review." As the money managers told him they had lost their appetite for agriculture and were pulling out—earth, well, pump and tractor—McCarthy grabbed a leather pouch from his jacket and pulled out a small iron statue of a skinny cowboy sitting on a stool. The cowboy was naked except for his Stetson hat and Tony Lama boots, and he was stroking his outsize penis. McCarthy put the statue on the conference table and walked out without saying a word. He and his partner, Amaro, were as good as broke. Their debt to Crocker Bank alone exceeded $50 million. Three years earlier, the ranch with the pomegranates had so impressed the elders of the Mormon Church that they offered $125 million to buy it. Prudential had said no to the deal. That same ranch would end up being sold to Stewart and Lynda Resnick at the bargain price of $30 million—and those Wonderful pomegranates would stamp their name on a new agricultural kingdom. What was left of McCarthy and Amaro agriculture became the biggest farm auction in the history of the San Joaquin Valley. It took up forty acres of an old military training base outside Lemoore Naval Air Station. The items included 150 tractors, 300 tillage implements, 100 pieces of heavy construction equipment, 5 cotton harvesters, 40 desks, 10 refrigerators, but no Rolls-Royce and no statuette of a self-pleasuring cowpoke.

No matter how much ground he covered, Russell Giffen could never cover enough. One day in the early 1970s, on his way to the family beach house in Santa Cruz, he instructed Henry, his chauffeur and butler, to make a slight detour through the west side. Henry knew what this meant. The boss wanted him to follow a route that took in a goodly portion of his 120,000 acres. In the back of the Cadillac sat Giffen's wife, Ruth, their granddaughter Marian, and Marian's best friend, Jennifer Baird. Somewhere in the middle of nowhere but cotton, Giffen told Henry to stop at the side of the road. Jennifer thought Mr. Giffen, who was dressed in a suit, might need to take a pee. She was sure this was the case as he walked fifteen or twenty rows deep into the field and turned his back to them. But then she saw him grab at a single plant that had grown taller than the cotton and was nearly as tall as him, and he kept yanking until he pulled the weed out of the ground. It was an impressive feat for a man nearly seventy years old. Then he walked back to the Cadillac, wiped the dirt from his hands, took his seat and off they went for a weekend of ocean and Henry's cheeseburgers and root beer floats served in the sand on silver platters.

During those chauffeured trips, Giffen never asked Henry to take him by Cantua Creek or El Porvenir, two colonies of old cotton pickers who had settled next to his fields. Ray Minnite, brother of the school principal, had opened his own café and shops along the main road connecting the two communities. He had invited the Catholic Church to build a parish there. Hundreds of Mexican farmworkers lived in cabins that Giffen chose not to burn down but to sell for a few dollars apiece. Minnite was delivering electricity to the shacks (by what source no one knew) and dirty water from the federal canal. When the farmworkers contracted worms, Fresno County was shamed into shutting the colonies down.

That was when Bard McAllister, a gray-bearded Quaker in a red beret, showed up with his band of peaceniks. The idea was to match government anti-poverty dollars with sweat. The peaceniks joined hands with the Mexicans and built a real community to replace the shantytown. They dug a well for drinking water, cleared fifty lots and erected stucco houses with front and backyards. El Porvenir it was christened: "The Future." They set aside ground for a community park and planted corn and blueberries on forty acres. The growers loaned them equipment and furnished irrigation water, but the crops were ravaged by worms. El Porvenir kept going. The farmworkers stayed on even as their houses began to sink from all the groundwater the Giffens were pumping to add more fields.

Three of Giffen's children had followed their father into row-crop farming. Giffens were hacking at every corner of Westlands, developing good land and land that was good for nothing but the subsidies. Mike, the older son, taller and more handsome than his father, had taken on too much farmland. He was operating five thousand acres inside Westlands and another three thousand acres in the next district over. The late 1970s turned out to be a lousy time to expand. Mike ran into cold weather, a dip in the cotton market and a strike at the tomato canneries. He would keep on farming but never fully recover. Russell's younger son, Price, taller and even more handsome than Mike, was raising cotton and tomatoes on eight thousand acres in Westlands and having his own tough go of it. He had gone broke a decade before and survived only because brother Mike—"Uncle Mike" to everyone on the west side—had been so generous with his farming equipment. Their little sister, Carolyn, the most like Russell when it came to grit, was farming the low ground along Highway 33 in Mendota. She had married Sumner Peck, a north valley boy she had met at Cal Berkeley. Sumner was shrewd and world-class smart, though his method of farming six thousand acres—getting up late, fixing himself a gourmet breakfast and then inching his sky-blue Cadillac two miles an hour along the roads where his crops grew—didn't always meet with Russell's approval.

The old man mostly kept his mouth shut. The starch had been taken out of him. He had expanded his own operations to include tens of thousands of acres along the Gila River in Arizona, only to see his grandson and namesake fall into the main canal and drown. Little Russell, son of Price, was five years old. Price and his wife, Joann, were inconsolable. Grandpa Russell didn't know what to say or do. They buried the boy in Phoenix and returned to Fresno and could not bring themselves to utter his name. For his younger brother, Chris, the day Russell drowned was his first memory. And that was how it began, a string of tragedies that made people in Fresno think of the Kennedys whenever they thought of the Giffens.

Ross Giffen, the cousin who was like a brother to Russell, was flying over the ranch to inspect for dry spots when his plane stalled and came crashing down. He died on the Panoche loam. Price and Joann's youngest daughter, Mandy, was born severely disabled and had to be institutionalized for the rest of her life. Mike's teenage daughter, Marian, went with her friends to a party at a Portuguese hall east of Fresno. Crossing the farm road, she was struck by a car and killed. Sumner Peck, overweight and relying on narcotics to ease a bad back, died of a heart attack in his early fifties. Carolyn, surrounded by her eight children, refused to let go of his body and insisted on burying him in the backyard of their new house in the fancy Sunnyside part of town. County ordinance prohibited home burial so she hired an attorney to take the matter to higher authorities in Sacramento. For several days, she waited on a decision. It got to the point that the wives and husbands of Westlands were swapping tales of Carolyn inviting them to the house for an old-fashioned and propping up Sumner's body at the table, with an old-fashioned for him, too. The truth was creepy enough. His embalmed body was lying in a casket on the back porch awaiting a special permit from the government. Permit granted, the cotton king's daughter built a mausoleum in her backyard, where she placed the remains of her husband.

Russell Giffen did not forget the words he had spoken to Congress in the 1950s. His 120,000 acres, he had testified, needed to be broken up and the water portioned out so that farmers smaller than he might be given a chance. The early 1970s seemed the right time to make good on his pledge. He had suffered a second heart attack and couldn't summon the same enthusiasm when another March told him it was time to plant cotton. As he considered how best to break up his massive holdings, he knew there was no fair way to divide the ranches among his four children and not have it turn into ugliness. He had seen jealousies over land destroy too many farming families to visit that upon his family. He owned fifty thousand acres outright and leased another seventy thousand acres. Had he wanted to play the reclamation game, the government was offering growers a ten-year grace period in which they could receive cheap federal water and not have to abide by acreage limits or break up their holdings. But Giffen didn't care to delay things. The day before Thanksgiving 1973, he summoned to his office his devoted right hand, Jack Woolf, whose attention to detail was nearly as prodigious as his. "I've thought about it, and now I'm sure. Let's sell it. Let's sell it all," he said. "I want two things. I want all the escrows to close on the same day. And I want all cash."

Woolf would recall the exact day he met Russell Giffen. It was June 4, 1946. Fresh from the battlefields of World War II, he had a job counting cottonseed for Anderson Clayton and was sent to Mendota to do an audit of Giffen, Inc. When the audit was over, Giffen pointed to a desk inside the office."We could use you here." Woolf signed up, and a few months later Giffen gave him a 5 percent interest in one of the ranches. Over the next three decades, Woolf put together every land deal at Giffen, Inc.

As he drove home that day with news that the company was liquidating, Woolf couldn't shake Giffen's words out of his head. "There'll be no gifts of land to my children or grandchildren," he had told him. "If they can afford to buy a section or two, they'll be paying fair market value. And if any of our top men want a piece, they'll have first dibs." Woolf knew what sections he'd pick if given a choice. He'd pick the ranches in Huron where the soil and groundwater were superior to all the rest. Huron was three-bales-to-an-acre cotton ground if there was such a place. To acquire those eight thousand acres, and the federal water that came with it, he and his wife, Bernice, would have to put up everything they owned as collateral. "Everything," he told her as he walked through the door that evening. "We'll do it," Bernice said. "Let's go." The next week, Woolf drove up to Sacramento on behalf of Giffen, Inc., to meet with the land men at the Bureau of Reclamation. He considered the company's breakup to be the greatest land reform in the history of California. One man was dividing up his 120,000-acre empire and selling it to two scores of men and their wives and children and grandchildren yet to take their first step.

The bureaucrats reminded Woolf that reclamation law prohibited the company from adding the value of the federal water to the sales price. At the same time, they weren't going to haggle with him over what was superior ground and what was middlin' ground. They agreed with Woolf that most of what Giffen farmed was good to excellent land. How about $600 an acre across the board? they suggested. Woolf drove home knowing that this was more than fair for Giffen and a steal for himself. The ground he had chosen in Huron was worth $1,200 an acre. He could finance his deal with a 100 percent loan from the bank. He'd be a rich man on paper before he ever planted a tomato or ginned a bale of cotton.

Woolf was able to negotiate a sale of Giffen, Inc.—land, leases, gins, cotton pickers, tractors, implements and wells—to multiple buyers, including himself, at $40 million. Giffen retired to his 12,000-acre ranch along the Kings River with at least $10 million added to his fortune. He was more proud of the fact that he had paid off every debt along the way, and this included wiping clean the considerable debt of his father, Wylie. He and longtime pal Melville E. Willson spent weekends riding their high-stepping American Saddlebreds across the Kings River. His third heart attack and the death of Ruth in 1978 stole from him, but not enough that he didn't find companionship again. In 1980, he married an old friend, Blanche O'Brien, who urged him to throw a Christmas party at the ranch. He hired a caterer and Les Brown and His Band of Renown and set up ballroom flooring under a giant tent on the rolling lawn. He put on a tuxedo and stood at the front door and greeted, one by one, the two thousand guests, most of whom he recalled by name. The black servants who had worked for him all those years weren't there to serve. He greeted them as guests, too, and they spent the evening in the kitchen playing cards. The night turned foggy, and by the time the last guest arrived, it was late and other guests were already leaving. He never made it to the party out back. He remained at the door the entire night. It was the last time most of them would see him alive.

In the late summer of 1983, a few months after Russell Giffen died, a federal biologist named Felix Smith leaked to the press a story that would call into question all the cotton king had built. Poisonous water was draining off west side farms and killing thousands of ducks and shorebirds at a nearby wildlife refuge. Horrible deaths they were. Beaks twisted into corkscrews. Gullets half-formed. Brains spilling out from skulls. Eyes missing. Wings that could not flap. Legs that could not stand.

The Kesterson National Wildlife Refuge was a place Giffen knew well. Every October, west side growers would bring their buddies and short-haired Labradors to hunt at their nearby duck clubs. They'd squat in the tule reeds at five-thirty a.m., a flask of Jack Daniel's in one pocket and shells in another, a twelve-gauge shotgun at the ready. If rain had come through, the ducks were usually plentiful, and they'd bag their legal six in a few hours. The farmers of Westlands, Giffen's daughter Carolyn among them, had surrounded Kesterson with hundreds of acres of ponds filled with salty runoff from their fields. The discharge, twice as brackish as the ocean, sat and stewed and slowly evaporated in the sun. A government plane flying overhead might have discerned a disaster in the making. From bird's eye, though, the wastewater looked nothing but beautiful. Ducks and geese on their migrations across the Pacific Flyway alighted to feed and swim and give birth.

At the U.S. Fish and Wildlife Service, a biologist told Smith that Kesterson was a place that eerily brought to life Rachel Carson's *Silent Spring*. Marshes were often alkaline, but this one didn't smell right. The odor had no olfactory reference. Stranger yet, no sounds could be heard. Not a croak, buzz or splash. Usually, cattails inhabiting a marsh never succumb to anything, but the tips of these cattails were singed. Floating on the water were mats of algae whose green was the only vivid thing. The stillness felt like death. Could salts alone have created such pestilence? The canker had crept by brackish water to two ranches on the fringe of the refuge. The Freitas family had been grazing cattle on their 5,500 acres for sixty years. In the previous two years, they had seen more cows turn frail and die than ever before. As agriculturalists, they were not pleased to point a finger at Westlands. At the same time, they had little doubt that something in the drainage ponds surrounding the marsh—and something in the marsh itself—was to blame.

Inside two Quonset huts on a dusty backlot at the UC Davis campus, the question of Kesterson took over. A team of Fish and Wildlife biologists kept a field station there and did work that not only challenged powerful forces in California but aggravated their own bosses back in Washington, D.C. Already, they had taken on the offshore oil drillers and the damage they were causing to the kelp forest and sea otters. They had tracked how urban runoff, shipping and dredging were putting more strain on a beleaguered San Francisco Bay. They had no qualms about going after Big Ag, too. But what made Kesterson such a challenge—and created such dissonance at the highest levels of the agency—was the reputation of the ponds. Up until that point, the ponds had been viewed as the reason waterfowl were returning to the west side in such abundance. With the flows of the San Joaquin River long dried up by Friant Dam, the tailwater from the farm fields was seen as a kind of poetic recompense. The same Central Valley Project that had stolen so much from the Pacific Flyway was now giving back to the birds. Yet a very different reality now stared back at two federal biologists as they paddled their canoe to the edge of the marsh at Kesterson. Felix Smith picked up a coot's egg and cupped it in his hand. Harry Ohlen-

The poisoned waters of Kesterson

dorf, chief of the Pacific field station and an expert on shorebirds, aimed his camera. At that moment, the bird inside was fighting to hatch. "Here were these birds hatching out," Ohlendorf told a reporter. "They had no eyes, no legs, no beaks. Some of them couldn't hatch because the deformities were so severe. Then there were also these embryos that just died before hatching."

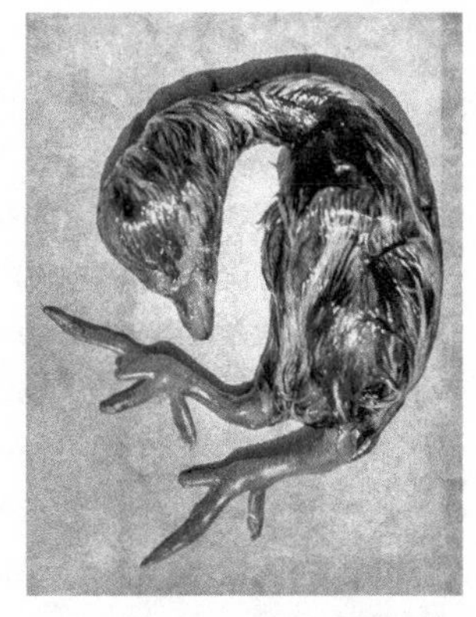
A deformed stillborn bird at Kesterson

A sampling of mosquito fish taken from the marsh showed a trace element that was natural to western soils: selenium. But the concentrations of selenium were so high that the literature did not offer up any precedence. Ohlendorf found a study from the 1930s on high levels of selenium in grain and how it had led to deformities in baby chickens in South Dakota. The selenium levels that had caused what the study called "monstrosities" in hatching chickens were ten times lower than the selenium levels found at Kesterson. The federal biologists shared their data with the U.S. Bureau of Reclamation, which oversaw the drainage canal in the San Luis Unit. The bureau could not come up with a single scientific reason to challenge the finding that selenium in the tailwater was the culprit.

The politics, though, were inconvenient. The bureau was looking to increase drainage—not reduce it—as part of its pledge to bloom agriculture in the Westlands Water District. Federal biologists began to sense that the bureau would prove no ally in the fight. They sat down with their in-house media team, prepared a press release and sent it up the chain of command at the Fish and Wildlife Service in Washington. The biologists waited and waited, not realizing that the resistance was imbedded inside their own agency, too. The press release never saw the light of day. Their regional director in California, Joe Blum, big, tall and blustery, told them to "tear it up" and forget it was ever written.

Felix Smith, raised on the tough side of San Francisco, had joined Fish and Wildlife in 1956. His career was full of commendations and scoldings for the same reason: he had never learned the art of compromise. He knew what a cover-up smelled like. He tore up the press release but only after making a half dozen copies. He wasn't about to let

Blum prevent him from meeting with a science reporter at the *Fresno Bee*. When the story came out linking the birds' deformities at Kesterson to the practice of irrigated agriculture, Smith and his colleagues were emboldened. At the very least, the McClatchy chain of newspapers stood behind them. What was taking place at Kesterson was a violation of the Migratory Bird Treaty Act, they charged, a crime now abetted by the Bureau of Reclamation's silence. Reporters and camera crews descended on the wildlife refuge and nearby farms. None was more obstinate than Lloyd Carter, a Fresno native who worked for United Press International. Carter not only taught himself the science of irrigation, drainage and selenium; he also examined the influence peddling of Westlands and the politicians in Sacramento and Washington who did the big farmers' bidding. Then he dug into the government bureaucrats who had fallen asleep on the job, allowing open abuses to the 160-acre law and the crop subsidy programs. Soon the story was airing on *60 Minutes*.

Two local politicians, Congressman Tony Coelho and state legislator Jim Costa, both Azorean Portuguese with family roots in dairy farming, seemed unable to grasp the severity of the situation. Even as Kesterson was being portrayed as the "Three Mile Island" of agriculture, they were urging the Interior Department to allow the tailwater to continue flowing into the marsh until more studies could be done. This was the compromise they were attempting to pull off when the House Subcommittee on Water and Power, under the chairmanship of Congressman George Miller from Contra Costa, convened a field hearing at the Los Banos fairgrounds in March 1985. No one in Congress knew more about California water and its manipulation than Miller, who relished playing the role of Big Ag's biggest foe. The environmentalists thought of him as a visionary, while the farmers considered him a Commie no different from his father, George Miller Sr., who had been a Bay Area union rep before becoming a state senator.

As Miller Jr. presided over the subcommittee hearing, an Interior Department official took over the microphone. The crowd quieted long enough to hear her announcement, which came straight from the desk of Interior Secretary Donald Hodel: The federal government was shutting down the drainage system in Westlands and stopping the toxic flow to Kesterson. The barnlike building erupted with the boos of farmers and the cheers of a scattering of environmentalists who had driven down from San Francisco. Sitting in the crowd was old Bernie Sisk, a.k.a. Tex, the tire salesman turned politician who had pushed the San Luis Act through Congress. During all the years he had advocated for the project, he told the subcommittee, he'd had no idea that the west side carried the poison of selenium. No farmer, bureaucrat or politician did. What was known to everyone at the time was the vexation of salt and the need for a drainage system that would transport the runoff from farm to ocean by way of a canal. So why had it not been built? What was a stunted canal that ended at Kesterson, only halfway to the San Francisco Bay, doing in its place?

When the state and federal governments drew up plans to irrigate the valley's west side in the early 1950s, a full drainage system was central to the project. Water engineers knew that every experiment in desert farming as far back as ancient Sumer had been doomed by the absence of a method to remove the toxic by-products of irrigation. Without an outlet, it took but a few centuries for Mesopotamia to turn from the Fertile Crescent to desert again. Ironically, the same partnership between the state and feds that was instrumental in building the San Luis Unit complicated matters when it came to the drain. The feds were looking to the state to take the lead on a master drain; the state was looking to the feds to supply the impetus. Both failed and then had the other to blame.

The bungle that led to Kesterson traced back to 1958 when a senator from New Mexico named Clinton P. Anderson refused to heed the warnings of California engineers. They had advised him that absolutely no water should be delivered to the San Joaquin Valley's west side unless and until a drainage system was in place. Senator Anderson, a Democrat, nodded his head and then proceeded to write an amendment to the act that all but guaranteed the delivery of water to Westlands before a drain could be built. His amendment, which came at the urging of Congressman Sisk, required only that the state or federal government make "provisions" for a drain. Neither party had to actually build it. Their mere words intending to build it were enough to secure congressional funding for the San Luis Unit.

California water bureaucrats had no problem pledging to build such a drain. In fact, the drain they pledged to build was a grand one. It would extend three hundred miles, from the far southern end of the valley to an outlet in the Sacramento–San Joaquin Delta. Salt, after all, afflicted the entire west side. But in 1960, when voters had handed Governor Pat Brown a victory by approving funds for the State Water Project, the revenue had added up to only $1.75 billion. The true cost of the state system was going to be nearly $4 billion. Among the works the state of California had to put on hold for a lack of funds was the drainage canal. On the federal side, the Bureau of Reclamation was a lot more skilled at making the desert bloom than in cleaning it up once it bloomed. At first, the bureau assured Congress that it could manage the contamination with an earthen canal that transported wastewater to the delta. The price tag? A paltry $20 million. On closer inspection, it became apparent that a canal made of dirt wouldn't be adequate. So the bureau and Westlands, in 1965, embraced a new $41 million plan that featured a main canal lined with concrete. The feds then waited for the state to pony up its share. By this time, the cost of building the state aqueduct had bled California dry. In March 1967, the state finally gave the federal government an honest answer: California could play no part in constructing a drain. This was how a drainage canal that began in Westlands and ended only ninety miles later in a wildlife refuge came to be.

But the original sin of drainage did not begin with Congress, the U.S. Bureau of Reclamation or the state of California. It began with the growers themselves, in particular Russell Giffen. Back in the 1960s, as Westlands negotiated its water deal with the feds, the growers weren't satisfied to exist as a 300,000-acre district that farmed only the most fertile soil. At Giffen's urging, Westlands kept adding tens of thousands of outside acres to its service area. This expansion took in poorer-class soils—those "unfit for agriculture"—in the lowest swales of the district. These lands were especially unfit because of the shallow clay layer that prevented water from percolating past the crop's root zone. It was only a matter of time before the poor soils, flooded with federal water, would turn into a salty bog. Westlands then extended its reach to the upper slope, annexing 200,000 acres known as West Plains, doubling the size of the intended district. This was where the Panoche loam ran thickest. This was where Giffen had turned prairie into his best cotton and tomato fields. The upper slope would never become boggy because it drained its tailwater onto the lower ground.

In a twist that no one in Westlands liked to talk about, the high ground developed by Russell Giffen and other growers was draining onto the low ground that belonged to his daughter Carolyn Peck. She was forced to install an underground system of drain tiles to collect the wastewater and dump it into the federal government's half-built canal. The runoff from her fields had become part of the flow that filled Kesterson and drew birds flying between Canada and Mexico down into the gorgeous blue of the valley. It was a blue that no migratory bird had seen here in decades, a place fetching enough to nest and lay eggs and watch those eggs hatch into grotesque versions of themselves.

Both expansions of Westlands (the lower-slope inferior soils and the upper-slope Panoche loam) had gone far beyond what Congress had approved in the original San Luis Act. Westlands directors and their friends in the Reclamation Bureau had found a way—illegally, some would argue—to nearly double the size of the district without a vetting by the American people. The bigger footprint took tens of millions of dollars from the drainage system and spent it instead on an expanded water-delivery system. It was the flows of this expanded water system that created the environmental disaster at Kesterson and shut down the drainage canal. Over the next two decades, tens of millions of dollars in government studies failed to find a solution to the contaminated soil. Then, in the mid-1990s, as growers began to feel the pain of federal water cuts, they went to court seeking relief for damage done to their land as a result of no drainage. Lawsuits pitting irrigation district against irrigation district, farmer against farmer, and farmer against the federal government tried to reconstruct entire legislative and bureaucratic histories in an effort to name a culprit.

In the end, what carried more weight was a fifty-mile field trip from the federal courthouse in downtown Fresno to a cotton patch on the low side of Westlands. Attorneys representing nearly two dozen farm families, including the Pecks and the O'Neills, boarded an old school bus with Judge Oliver Wanger and attorneys for the Bureau of Reclamation. It was the fall of 2002, and they rolled down Highway 33 past Mendota to where a cotton farmer named Ernie Carvalho was standing in the dirt next to a large backhoe. He was decked out in a pressed white shirt, pressed blue jeans, cowboy hat and cowboy boots. The judge and the attorneys stepped down from the bus and greeted Carvalho.

"Ernie, tell us what you're going to do," prompted William Smiland, an attorney for the growers.

"Well, I'm gonna to take this here backhoe, and I'm gonna dig a hole in the ground, and it'll show you what the drainage problem is."

Carvalho climbed onto the backhoe, fired up the engine and grabbed a scoop of earth no more than three feet deep. No sooner did he dig a shallow hole than it began to fill up with a nasty soup of water, mud and salts. Carvalho shut off the engine so his next words could be heard loud and clear. "Yup, that's it," he said. "That's the stuff that's killing my crops."

The settlement came very soon after that. Judge Wanger concluded that the Bureau of Reclamation had contractually obligated U.S. taxpayers to pay the costs of providing drainage to the Westlands Water District. As a point of law, it did not matter that the district's boundary line had taken in 300,000 acres of additional land without congressional approval. What prevailed was another logic: If you're going to dump more than one million acre-feet of imported water into a closed basin, you have to provide a way to drain it. The families who filed the lawsuit agreed to permanently fallow 32,400 acres of spoiled land in return for $140 million. The Pecks would retire 5,000 acres. The Woolfson family and its partnerships and trusts would retire 10,000 acres. Bill Jones, the California secretary of state who had recently lost his bid for governor, would fallow 1,000 acres.

I had been following the case from a distance when news of the settlement landed on my desk in late December 2002. As head of the *Los Angeles Times* bureau in the middle of California, I couldn't very well not write about it. Yet the story came with a hitch. My good friend Chuck Manock had married Carolyn Peck's youngest daughter, Katie. Chuck was a local attorney who had gone to work for his father, Kendall, a man who had devoted the better part of his practice to guaranteeing more water for Westlands. Chuck seemed poised to follow in his footsteps and was hoping I wouldn't pursue the story. At the very least, he didn't want me pestering his mother-in-law, who had claimed in a court document that the ponds had done more good than harm to Kesterson's waterfowl. "Don't take offense if she slams the door in your face," he said.

A week before Christmas, I walked down a quiet street in a lovely neighborhood of Fig Garden and knocked on Mrs. Peck's door. She was in her early seventies, a thin, sturdy woman with a long face creased by sun and a half century of smoking. She shook my hand and guided me through the kitchen and the butler's pantry and into a living area where the walls were covered in roses hand-painted by an artist she had flown in from New York. Her eight children were gathered around her, and she proceeded to command the room with a fierceness that caused several of them to pace about and take long drags off their own cigarettes. The oldest was in his fifties, the youngest in her thirties, and their silence and deference to her made me wonder about the silence and deference that her father, Russell, might have demanded of his children. The entire family seemed to be in a state of mourning, which struck me as odd because the federal government was about to hand them an $18 million check to retire five thousand acres of no-good ground.

"People hear about all these millions and think we're celebrating," she said. "But five generations of Giffens and Pecks have farmed the west side. This was some of the best ground anywhere. We built it with our own hands, and now we're losing our way of life." She wanted me to know that she and her late husband, Sumner, had not raised their children to be takers. Unlike the sons and daughters of other west side growers, they weren't sent off to Robert Louis Stevenson prep school in Pebble Beach to attend classes and play golf. They weren't given Porsche Turbos to gun down Spyglass Hill and crash into the sand dunes between the fourth green and the fifth tee. Her husband hadn't bought her a second house on the coast to live in or a boutique to run when she got bored. She and her children were dirt farmers. Because of the federal government's decades-long failure to provide them with a drain, she had watched the buildup of salt destroy their almond orchards and blight their cotton and melon fields. Now she would live to see entire stretches of the west side, where her father, Russell, and her father's father, Wylie, had produced such bounties, revert to desert. "What are we going to do?" she asked. "My sons are in their forties and fifties. We just can't up and leave and move to Oregon."

I had walked into a living room of Westlands when I was a kid and left with a story of cotton and slaves and plantations pillaged and a government that had stolen a way of life from the people. I walked out of another living room of Westlands thirty years later with the awareness that bitterness of that sort would never be put to rest.

Twenty

960-ACRE BABIES

From our last vineyard on the Madera side of the river to the Peacock Markets to the Ara's Apartments nightclub, my father never lost his farmer's nose. Three days out, he could smell the rain coming. My mother, who didn't have a farmer's nose, said she could feel it in her bones. Another summer has come and gone, and I don't smell or feel a thing. If this drought had been born a child, it would now be entering grammar school. My son Jake, who's turned eighteen, was a sixth grader the last time we drove up to Shaver Lake to play in the snow. Since my apricot trees first shed their babies three years ago, I haven't had enough fruit to cook even one batch of sun jam. Half the miles on my beat-up car are drought miles. My father's older brother, Navo, who grew his first crop of watermelons in the sandy loam of Manteca and stacked them in the bed of a Ford truck and drove the fruit to a storefront on Solano Avenue between Berkeley and Richmond and sold them in an afternoon (he was thirteen years old), asks me when I might be done chasing dust. I tell him that my wanderings south to Lost Hills, east to Orange Cove and up and down Highway 99 from Delano to Fowler are behind me. I don't bother to mention all the other places across the state that I've put into my notebook. He knows too well my persistence, having been on the receiving end of it more than once. Years ago, in my desire to solve my father's murder, I brought to his kitchen table a suspicion that he not only knew the men who had conspired to kill my father but had conspired with them. Not actively but tacitly, out of fear, out of weakness. Somehow, we forgave each other, and that years-long inquiry turned into others, and now this one.

I have been to the Imperial Valley and looked for the cut in the Colorado River bank where the farmers took their first diversion, causing the flood that created the lake called the Salton Sea. A century later, the sea is drying at the edges and blowing a toxic dust into the lungs of poor kids. I've touched the 155-mile-long pipeline that transports the Tuolumne River to San Francisco from the high mountain valley named Hetch Hetchy. I've gone to St. Helena, in the Napa Valley, and seen where a vineyard atop Howell Mountain slid into the main reservoir for the town's drinking water.

So many winemakers—mom-and-pop outfits, global corporations, venture capitalists who've grown weary of fly-fishing in Montana—have planted rows of Cabernet and Sauvignon Blanc on and around the mountain that it now carries its own appellation, a terroir of climate, elevation and rocky soil that creates tannin-rich reds with a wild, feral taste, they say. Who knows how much water the winemakers are siphoning from the Napa River's watershed? Certainly not the county of Napa, which is allowing millions of tons of dirt to be moved and streambeds to be altered in the name of "Wine Country living." From Imola to Calistoga, the vineyards, spas, restaurants, vacation rentals and tasting rooms keep going in. Danica Patrick, the NASCAR star, owns a winery on Howell Mountain. So does Gavin Newsom, California's next governor; and Louis Ciminelli, a building contractor who's facing corruption charges back home in Buffalo; and the Australian multinational Treasury Wine Estates, which enjoys a permit from St. Helena that grants unrestricted access to the city tap. "The same industrialization of agriculture that you see in the Central Valley is now happening here. It just looks prettier," Geoff Ellsworth, a St. Helena councilman, tells me. "All these people who made a ton of money in another life now want to make a Cabernet that scores one hundred points."

I tell Uncle Navo, who is growing blind and senile like my grandfather did, that I'm nearly finished with my peregrinations. All that's left for me to do is trace the northern water to its source, to the holiest place in all of California, Mount Shasta, and on the way back see the federal and state pumps planted like sequoias across from each other in the delta. I tell him this even as Westlands, modern-day Westlands, won't let me go. Bay Area environmentalists who have spent decades battling the big growers keep calling to admonish me. The changes that have come to Westlands since Carolyn Peck retired her land fifteen years ago hasn't changed the truth of farming there, they say. Pay no attention to the drip irrigation, the fallowed acres, the retired acres or the big-dollar crops that attempt to make west side farming sustainable. Yes, cotton is gone and so are the Giffens, but a reinvented Westlands is no more deserving of the north's water than the old Westlands was.

No one is more certain of this verdict than Patricia Schifferle, a fifth-generation Californian who grew up not far from where the crime against the northern rivers was committed. In the forty years since, she has papered Westlands with more requests for public records than any other citizen in the history of California's water districts. The documents she has managed to unearth have turned into front-page stories in the *New York Times* and lawsuits that continue to discomfort Westlands. "I know there's a war against science going on. But it's a fact that putting water on those soils creates a lasting problem of pollution," she tells me. "Every government scientist who has ever looked at Westlands has come to the same conclusion: We need to stop irrigating those lands." My buddy Brad Gleason, the nut grower who isn't shy about criticizing the men running Westlands, sees it differently. "Should Westlands be farming five hundred thousand acres? No. But what about two hundred and fifty thousand acres on the best land sitting on the best aquifer? Shouldn't that be the conversation we're having?"

I am tempted to leave it there and head to Mount Shasta, but drought's fifth year blows in the storm of a new candidate for president. He grasps, if nothing else, the banners hitched to the old cotton trailers. At a rally in downtown Fresno, he tells the delirious crowd holding "FARMERS FOR TRUMP" signs that the drought is a lie. It isn't the sky that has turned against them. It's the politicians, federal bureaucrats and judges. "There is no drought," he intones. Like "fake news" and "Mexican rapists" and "build the wall," it comes out of his mouth in a spittle that a parched people take to be rain. Mexicans who came here two and three generations ago stand up and cheer at the prospect that future Mexicans will be kept from joining them. Farmers whose livelihoods rely on the border crossings stand up and cheer, too. It makes no sense. It makes all the sense in the world.

Big growers from the west side, the east side and in between meet with the candidate at a private luncheon in a secret location in Tulare County set up by Congressman Devin Nunes. It costs $2,700 to get in the door and $25,000 to share a thought with the candidate. He isn't listening, however. He's too busy telling his own story of how he came to Fresno a decade earlier to take over a troubled golf course development called Running Horse but had to back out of the deal. He couldn't get any water because it was all going out to the ocean on account of a two-inch baitfish. The big growers, at that moment, smell a rat because Running Horse wasn't tied to the Central Valley Project or constricted in any way by the Endangered Species Act. The development, which is now an almond orchard, has all the water it needs from the Kings River. Before he leaves, he tells the growers that the pumps will be turned to full blast once again, and they'll be able to plant their crops like never before. No little fish will stand in his way. The growers write their checks big and small and drive home with their red "MAKE AMERICA GREAT AGAIN" caps.

No irrigation district in the nation plays politics with the same limbic instincts as Westlands. It boasts a half dozen lobbying firms under contract in Washington and Sacramento, a staff plucked from Congress and the Interior Department, and enough inside and outside lawyers to handle fourteen lawsuits at a time. Most of these energies are directed toward one aim: Keep the water flowing by eroding the Endangered Species Act and freeing the delta pumps from their federal shackles. The deputy general manager, Johnny Amaral, was the top aide to Congressman Nunes before he joined Westlands at a salary of $250,000 a year. His predecessor, Jason Peltier, was a high-ranking bureaucrat in the Interior Department whose perks at Westlands included a $1.4 million loan at an interest rate close to zero. He bought a riverfront estate on Millionaires' Row in Walnut Grove, which sits 150 miles north of Westlands' headquarters in Fresno. Peltier now owes the district $1.6 million for the loan even as he's bought himself a second house—in Pebble Beach. The Westlands board had been keeping the debt a secret. It came out in the newspapers at the same time that the Securities and Exchange Commission fined the district for lying about its financial well-being. Thomas Birmingham, Westlands' $400,000-a-year general manager, had signed off on what he called a "little Enron" accounting trick to hide revenue losses due to cuts in the water supply. His fine was $50,000.

A small group of Westlands farmers now wonder what other deceits might be going on in their name. As far as I can tell, only my pal Brad has confronted Birmingham and aired his concerns in public. In one respect, Brad says, Westlands is the nation's most capable agricultural water utility, with 111 full-time employees and an annual budget of $100 million. It spends more than $1 million a year on public relations and a similar amount on messaging done stealthily through front groups. In another respect, Westlands remains the same old club for men that it was in the 1970s, when no one breathed a word about what took place after the water was pumped and the cotton was baled. Because Westlands holds only "junior rights" to northern water—rights neither riparian nor "first in line, first in right"—its growers must stand at the back of the line during dry times. Just to be clear: They don't stand there wringing their hands. They're punching new holes in the salty earth and sucking out what's left of the aquifer. They're pumping 660,000 acre-feet of water per year—a level of extraction not seen since before the San Luis Unit was built. If Westlands were a city, this would be enough water to handle the needs of 6.6 million people.

And they're writing checks, handing over hundreds of thousands of dollars in campaign cash to the same congressmen and senators. Republican or Democrat, it doesn't matter. There's Kevin McCarthy, the onetime Bakersfield deli owner who now sits as the House majority leader, and Devin Nunes, Jim Costa and David Valadao, the good fellows of the Portuguese dairy mob, and Dianne Feinstein, the lukewarm liberal who hails from San Francisco. As long as they're pledging to build new dams, turn up the delta pumps and channel snowmelt to crops worth $1.5 billion a year, they can count on Westlands to be there. Senator Feinstein's relationship to the district is more ticklish than the others'. Back in 1994, she broke with tribal practice and met the growers on their own turf. At the time, it seemed a flirtation born of mutual insecurity. She was a first-term incumbent unsure about her chances of reelection; Westlands had just watched Congressman George Miller ram through a law—the Central Valley Project Improvement Act, he pointedly called it—that took 800,000 acre-feet of water from agriculture and returned it to the fish. Not just any fish but the Chinook salmon, whose last run on the San Joaquin River was a half century before. The meeting between Feinstein and Westlands went well enough that the growers, Republicans to a man, held a fund-raiser for the senator. Two decades later, their checks are still floating in.

Once again, the Republicans in the House of Representatives, urged on by leader McCarthy, are looking for ways to free up water stuck in the north. Some of the more liberty-loving growers in Westlands are demanding that Congress decree a special provision during drought, altogether waiving the Endangered Species Act as it pertains to the Central Valley Project. Senator Feinstein—who naturally regards this as an overreach—begins crafting her own bill in secret. It remains a secret from the public but not from the managers, attorneys and lobbyists of Westlands and the Metropolitan Water District of Southern California, whose edits mark the document up and down. When its contents are leaked, environmentalists feel betrayed. Feinstein is calling for more delta water to be shipped to valley agriculture and for new and bigger dams. San Franciscans throw a fit, and she pulls back the legislation.

At the behest of Representative Nunes, Representative Valadao introduces his own bill. He goes a step further than Feinstein in the way he weakens environmental restrictions and the way he hands over authorship to Westlands. As the bill is about to be considered, Valadao's legislative director writes frantic e-mails to Westlands General Manager Tom Birmingham and his main lobbyist, David Bernhardt. She needs the two skilled lawyers to provide her with a basic explanation of the bill's features. They are more than happy to oblige. "Thank you!! Saved the day again," she writes back. The Valadao bill then lands before the House Rules Committee, where Congresswoman Louise Slaughter of New York has little patience for amateurs. Here come California's water buffaloes at the eleventh hour again. No public hearing. No expert testimony. No analysis of the bill to determine if what they're proposing violates the law or not. "We didn't know until about three o'clock this afternoon that it was even here," she scolds them. "And we are supposed to do a sleight of hand and pull something off? I do not come here to do those kinds of tricks."

The legislation nonetheless makes it onto the House floor. There, Congressman Nunes imagines Communists at work again. "Listening to the rhetoric that is coming from the other side, I am reminded of the old saying about the Soviet Union: If you tell a lie long enough, eventually people will believe it," he says. "This is about San Francisco and Los Angeles getting all of their water, never giving up one drop. The poor people that they continue to make poor are my constituents because they have taken their water and dumped our water out into the ocean." Nunes, who calls global warming "nonsense," will be happy to know that mandatory conservation in urban California is about to reduce water consumption in both cities by 20 percent. The bill passes the House and moves on to the Senate, where Feinstein's ordeal remains fresh in everyone's mind. It ends up dying the same death that last year's model, authored by Nunes, did. Westlands is disappointed but by no means deterred. Senator Lisa Murkowski, a Republican from Alaska who heads the committee governing western reclamation, breaks bread with the growers and goes home with $100,000 in campaign cash. "You've got to give them an 'A' for effort," George Miller, now retired from Congress, tells the *New York Times*. "These boys are committed. They play at the highest level, and they never sleep—ever."

Drought-weary, Westlands farmers now wonder how best to spin their "narrative." They could assume the duty themselves if they weren't so neurotic about going public. Then again, who wants to hear another farmer whining about water? Back in 2009, during California's last dry spell, it had occurred to them that if the faces demanding more water for agriculture weren't the white faces of farmers but the brown faces of farmworkers, it might broaden the appeal. Thus was born the California Latino Water Coalition, the advocacy group funded by growers and fronted by comedian Paul Rodriguez. His appearances on Sean Hannity's Fox News show were anything but comedic. On the verge of tears, he told viewers that his own family farm was drying up because the federal government had turned off the pumps in the delta to save a two-inch fish. "It's really a sad situation that those of us who choose to farm, my mother and my family in the central San Joaquin, perhaps the most fertile soil in the world, are now just sitting there ready to go on welfare." Truth was, Rodriguez's forty acres were nowhere near the vicinity of Westlands, nowhere close to the aqueduct and its reduced flows. The Rodriguez farm sat in the cradle of the citrus belt on the other side of the valley where the federal water, in the summer of 2009, happened to be turned on full blast.

To be fair to the comedian, water in California is a subject that practically invites a person to lie. Who knows one system from the next, an aqueduct from a canal, a canal from a ditch? Water is a fungible thing. Steal a little here, give back a little there, no one notices. Now, one drought later, the Latino Water Coalition has spawned an offspring: El Agua Es Asunto de Todos—Water Is Everybody's Business. At a news conference in Fresno, a retired Mexican diplomat delivers El Agua's message: Drought has not merely fallowed farmland. It has robbed Latino farmworkers of jobs, shuttered Latino businesses and thrown Latino families out on the street. Ads and commercials then blanket Spanish-language radio, television, newspapers and social media. Neighborly Latinos sitting in their cars and standing on their doorsteps deliver a simple message: "*Sin agua, sin trabajo.*" No water, no work.

El Agua, it turns out, is less than frank about who is financing the campaign. The group claims to be funded by donations from local community leaders and family and friends. In reality, El Agua is another of the stealth projects bankrolled by Westlands. Michael Fenenbock and his wife, Daphne Weisbart, public relations experts fresh off a campaign to assist Israel's right-wing Likud government, hatched El Agua in their Manhattan and Fresno marketing offices. For two years of campaign work, Fenenbock and Weisbart pick up $1 million from Westlands and another $800,000 from the campaign coffers of Congressman Jim Costa. The story of Westlands and El Agua breaks on the front page of the *New York Times*. Westlands deputy general manager Amaral, who's learned well from Congressman Nunes, his close buddy, brands the story an insult. El Agua is no front for Westlands. "It's purely an educational initiative," he says, knowing that any political initiative would violate the law.

The story appears at a delicate time for Westlands. For a decade now, not counting the twenty years of quarrel that came before, they've been negotiating with the Interior Department to finally resolve the drainage problem. They're as close to a deal as they've ever been. The surest and most cost-effective fix—buying and fallowing the half of Westlands that should have never been farmed—turns out to be too contentious. So the two sides have settled on a middle course that leaves the drainage problem for future generations to solve. The deal appears to be this:

The federal government will be relieved of its burden—who knows the actual cost—to provide farmers with a drainage canal or any other solution. Westlands will now handle the salts and selenium within its borders in a way that does no further harm to wildlife. What drainage system will be built—and whether it will work or not—is up to Westlands to decide. In return, the federal government will forgive the $375 million debt that Westlands still owes it for building the San Luis Unit. The district will have to retire another 8,000 acres of contaminated ground, but it can continue to farm the remaining 200,000 acres of drainage-impacted farmland.

At 500,000 acres altogether, Westlands will remain the largest agricultural water district in the nation. It will be forever entitled to 75 percent of the federal water it has drawn by contract. In drought, the district will still be subject to the same severe cuts. Unless, of course, a new president succeeds in gutting the Endangered Species Act. Big farmers will no longer have to abide by acreage limits, as if they really ever did. They can keep on replacing seasonal crops with more permanent crops. They can keep on pumping vast quantities of groundwater whenever their imported supplies are restricted, at least until the state's new groundwater law says otherwise. The land can go on sinking.

Not all of the growers inside Westlands are pleased with the deal. The district will have to sell and service $185 million in bonds to reimburse farmers on the problem lands for their "loss of fertility" because of no drain. Growers on the good land who never needed a drainage canal will have to shoulder a portion of this debt. The farmers in the polluted areas—some of whom sit on the Westlands board and negotiated directly with the government for millions of dollars in payouts for themselves—will still be able to grow nuts. Their problem ground, it now appears, is no longer the problem it was. Because they're farming more salt-tolerant pistachios and irrigating with drip, the district lands impacted by drainage have suddenly dropped in half—to 100,000 acres. This naturally raises a question: If everything is so hunky-dory, why the need for such a generous payment to Westlands in the first place?

I've been warned that Jack Woolf has a legendary memory. Among the things he hasn't forgotten is a newspaper story I wrote fifteen years ago that mentioned him and his family in a not-so-kind light. He has no problem reciting the headline: "Some Farmers Growing Rich on Government Crop Subsidies." One line still irks him: "The Woolf family, which owns three vacation homes overlooking the Pacific in Santa Cruz, has received $1 million in subsidies for their crops in Fresno County." He considers the conflation a cheap shot. It took several months of persuasion on the part of his son Stuart, who now oversees the family's many agricultural enterprises, to get me past the secretary and into his father's office in new Fig Garden.

Jack (no one I know calls him Mr. Woolf) has managed to reach the age of ninety-eight in remarkably fit shape. When I shake his hand, I can't help but remark on his perfect posture. He says he has no choice but to consider the world from a ramrod-straight position. He was five foot five before he began to shrink. Being a small man came in handy in the trenches of the Second World War when he had to kill the enemy. In farming, he's counted on a nimble mind and an acid wit to last so long. Unlike so many agricultural giants who flew sky-high only to come crashing down in the auction yard, he built his empire steady-steady. As the biggest farmer in Westlands today, and scandal-free to boot, he's used to being fawned over. What people say they admire most about him is his devotion to his family. On his office wall hang the framed black-and-white portraits of each of his six children and twenty-four grandchildren.

"Is that how you keep all your ranches straight?" I ask, poking at him.

Every one of those kin, including the grandchild in Nicaragua procuring coffee and the grandchild in San Francisco saving the redwood forest, is "farming" his or her piece of the Woolf's west side. Back in the day, when evasions of the 160-acre law made newspaper headlines, this comment might have gotten me tossed out. But it's been years since acreage limits struck dread into the heart of Jack or any other Westlands farmer. In the early 1980s, lefty land reformers rallying under the banner of National Land for People went to war against not only the growers but also the reclamation bureaucrats who were ignoring the violations. Waving the 160-acre rule as if it meant something, the rural justice advocates looked as if they might actually change the "Big" in Big Ag. Then the attorneys, lobbyists and housewives of Westlands took to the halls of Congress and won a victory known here as "reclamation reform." "We got our ass kicked" was how George Ballis, the pro-labor photographer who headed National Land for People, described it.

No longer were growers in the Central Valley Project required to live in the vicinity of their ranches, a rule they had openly flouted. More pertinently, the land eligible for federal water was increased from 160 acres to 960 acres for each farmer. This is how the Woolfs, Jack and Bernice and their thirty heirs, have managed to stay within the letter of reclamation law. If there's a king of the west side still standing, it's Jack. A section here, a section there, his acres work out to forty square miles. What ground he and his children and grandchildren haven't fallowed because of drought, they've planted in almonds, pistachios, tomatoes, onions, garlic and wheat. Woolf Enterprises, at 25,000 acres, is a sprawling complex. It has a nut-processing plant and a tomato-processing plant. It has a well-drilling arm and a drip-irrigation arm. End to end, the drip lines would stretch for two million miles. No outsider would mistake Woolf's ranch for anything less than industrial agriculture at its most exalted. But talk to the Woolfs, and they'll argue all day long that it's just a family farm.

"A lotta land, a lotta family," Jack wisecracks. He smiles but it's gone before it registers. "Every one of them is a 'farmer.' "

Even if the Interior Department is now inclined to replace the 960-acre rule with no limits at all, Jack isn't about to change his opinion of the federal government. In this fifth year of drought, a solitary book sits on his immaculate desk. *Water for Sale: How Business and the Market Can Resolve the World's Water Crisis*. "It's not like it didn't rain this past winter," son Stuart explains. "We had two storms that sent a lot of water down the Sacramento River and into the delta. But instead of turning on the pumps and letting farmers grow food with that water, the biologists turned off the switch. The reason this time is they want to maintain turbidity in the upper delta. The smelt supposedly does better in turbid waters. Not as many of them get picked off by all those big bass that the state planted in the delta to make the fishermen happy."

Stuart, who warded off four years of liberal indoctrination at UC Berkeley with his own caustic tongue, can perform a comedic routine mocking the state and federal biologists who sit in mysterious offices in Sacramento, their names and faces unknown to the public, and make the daily call on whether to run the pumps or not using a metric that is an enigma to everyone but them. "You can see why, from our standpoint, this thing borders on the ridiculous. Each season, they come up with a different reason not to deliver the water they pledged to us by contract."

Jack Woolf and his many children
and grandchildren, every one a "960-acre farmer"

It was Stuart who suggested that his father give me a tour of the ranches. The way he planned it, I would be the one doing the driving from their office complex in northwest Fresno to their fields and orchards an hour away. "Look, we've already written his obituary," he tells me. " 'Jack Woolf, west side farmer, died at one hundred years old yesterday while driving out to the west side for the millionth time.' We didn't write it that a passenger other than my mother was beside him. So you'd better drive."

Out the door, Jack heads straight for his insect-splattered white Cadillac DeVille.

"I've never driven a DeVille," I say.

"Well, this won't be your first time," he deadpans.

He wants me to consider the odds. For the past fifty-five years, since moving to Fresno after his first job with Russell Giffen, he's driven to the west side three or four times a week, on average. That's close to ten thousand trips back and forth without an accident. The way he figures it, I'm in good hands. The way I figure it, he'll get us there safely or get us into a head-on collision, fifty-fifty odds.

"Relax," he says. "I made a bet with one of my grandsons. This is the one who's got dreadlocks running down to his ass. I told him if I make it to one hundred years old, I get to shave off his hair at my birthday party. I intend to be there with my shears in hand."

I fasten my seat belt and watch closely as he maneuvers out of the Woolf business compound and onto busy Herndon Avenue, a few blocks from my childhood home. As we cross Highway 99 and strip malls surrender to farmland, I switch on my tape recorder and fire away:

"You've been driving this road for more than a half century. Take me back to the 1960s. What was growing out here?"

"You'll need to talk louder," he shouts. "I can't hear out of my right ear."

He's nearly keeping to his lane as he explains the economics of federal water and why only the highest-value crops pencil out anymore. In 1963, the Interior Department set the price of water at $7.50 an acre-foot to irrigate Westlands' original 400,000 acres and $15 an acre-foot to irrigate the 200,000 upslope acres added on later. The farmers happily signed the original contract knowing there was no cheaper water to be had in the West. Only fifty cents from each acre-foot went into a kitty to build a drainage system. The rest of the water bill was supposed to pay back the federal government for Westlands' share of the San Luis Unit: the $190 million distribution system inside the district and the $500 million reservoir and aqueduct. A half century later, the farmers still owe the government half that money, at least until the drainage deal is signed. To speed up repayment, the cost of the federal water is now closer to $150 an acre-foot.

"It's still affordable," Jack says. "But even in years when it's raining and snowing, we never get our full allotment. The Endangered Species Act is in charge, and the farmer isn't on the list."

The new irrigation reality for Westlands is 50 percent of the contracted water in wet years and 0 percent in dry years. To supplement its dwindling groundwater and government supplies, Westlands must go looking for surface water to purchase on the open market. This search is made all the more urgent by another regulatory clock that's ticking. The state's groundwater law could eventually reduce the district's extraction by at least half. The hunt for river water takes west side nut farmers to the faraway Grange halls in Gridley and Orland, north of the delta. There, they thrash out deals with rice farmers who wade knee-deep in water even when the rest of the state is parched. Nut farmers, cash-rich, and rice farmers, cash-poor, shake hands and become partners. By the time the rice water glides down the Sacramento River and into the delta, siphons through pumps, lifts into the aqueduct and finally pours out the painted blue valves of Westlands, it will cost the Woolfs $650 an acre-foot. This is expensive water, but not too expensive for a farmer who's getting three and four dollars a pound for his nut crop. But what happens when the price of nuts drops to two dollars a pound or below? What happens when the rice guy realizes he can use the same market to sell his water to a housing developer for $2,000 an acre-foot?

"All hell breaks loose," Jack says. "Do the fish win then?"

Not all is aboveboard in Westlands' rummage for water. Drought has drawn farmers to the very edge of the Mendota Pool, a small federal reservoir filled with snowmelt shipped in from Sacramento. The pool doesn't sit within the boundaries of Westlands, but that matters little to Westlands farmers trying to get by in drought. At the lip of the pool, a good distance from their crops, they've installed dozens of pumps that whir and whine twenty-four hours a day. They are not only drawing groundwater, which remains free for the taking, but siphoning water out of the porous bottom of the federal pool itself, which is not. The agency that administers the Mendota Pool, the Bureau of Reclamation, is a party to the theft. The bureau lets farmers pump from below the reservoir, draw up its never-ending water and then dump it right back into the pool. This recycling is rewarded with official "credits" from the federal government. The credits then allow farmers in Westlands to draw federal water a second time—this time legitimately—out of the nearby California Aqueduct and send it via ditches to their crops.

The whole setup brings to mind a money-laundering scheme, except in this case it's ill-gotten water the farmers are washing. "I'm not going to tell you that my pumps aren't drawing from the Mendota Pool," one Westlands grower had told me. "I'd be lying. But we're desperate, you understand? We're hanging by a thread, and if the Bureau of Reclamation is going to let us get away with this, we're going to do it." Jack knows the farmers who are draining federal water and selling it back to the government for credits. Among the biggest pumpers listed in official reports is Don Peracchi, president of the Westlands board. Some pumpers are going one step further and selling the credits to other farmers for cash. Jack has seen for himself the wells that rim the pool, but he isn't dying to talk about the scheme.

"It's not something we partake in," he says, and leaves it at that.

No government agency, not the county or the state or the Reclamation Bureau, has ever calculated the full extent of the operation. But hydrologists and geologists say a staggering amount of water—actual groundwater and siphoned pool water—has been drawn from the earth to exploit the federal credit program. So much water, in fact, that during the 1992 drought the water table in Mendota plunged fifty feet in a single month. Salty water invaded the town's aquifer, corroded fire hydrants and violated state drinking water standards. Mendota (population 11,418), sometimes called Macheteville because of the hacked bodies that turn up in the fields, routinely ranks among the five poorest towns in the state.

The Reclamation Bureau has since placed a 40,000-acre-foot lid on the water pumped from the pool by growers. But Westlands keeps finding new and creative ways to make more water materialize during drought times. The district reaches outside its boundaries to fetch an astonishing amount of snowmelt each year through credits, exchanges and purchases. These transactions aren't easy to trace. Public water auctions are rare; buyers and sellers confer behind closed doors and stay mum about the deals. In the driest years, Westlands spends close to $450 million to acquire as much as 500,000 acre-feet of outside flow—an extraordinary amount that still doesn't quite compensate for the zero deliveries of federal water. These transactions include the straightforward and sensible purchases of water from rice growers in the Sacramento Valley but also schemes that are more byzantine and harmful to the environment.

Westlands growers, for instance, are purchasing large quantities of water from J. G. Boswell in the Tulare Lake basin. These sales, sanctioned by state and federal regulators, depend on groundwater being mined from twenty-five hundred feet beneath the old lake bottom. Problem is, the earth keeps sinking, and the poor residents of Corcoran must dig into their pockets to shore up the town's levee. At the same time, Westlands farmers are pumping degraded groundwater from their own aquifers and dumping it into the California Aqueduct. The credits they receive from the federal government for this tainted water then enables them to pull out an equal amount of cleaner water from a different section of the aqueduct. The credits are encouraging growers to deplete the aquifer and create more subsidence, but that's not the worst of it. By offering the aqueduct as a drain, state and federal regulators are allowing groundwater laced with arsenic, boron and selenium to contaminate drinking water. The pollutants flow down the aqueduct and wind up in Southern California, where most residents have no knowledge of the dumping, even though their monthly water bills reflect the increasing costs of treatment. The local agency that should be watching out for their interests, the Metropolitan Water District, has yet to tell Westlands, their hydraulic brother, to knock it off.

Jack's tour doesn't stop at the Mendota Pool and its garrote of pumps. He follows instead a southerly route past Kerman and hops onto the diagonal that is McMullin Grade. From here to the belly of the whale, we hardly cross a cotton field. The nuts and fruits we're driving through didn't exist two decades ago. Now there's 120,000 acres of almonds and pistachios planted in Westlands alone. Jack sees a glut on the horizon. "They're doing a great job of marketing them, but if we keep planting almonds and pistachios, no amount of hype is going to save us from too many," he says.

The Woolfs have devoted a quarter of their land, six thousand acres, to nuts. In years of water plenty, they grow nine thousand acres of tomatoes. This year, the aquifer exhausted, they've planted five thousand acres. The groundwater they're pumping must not only irrigate the tomatoes but flush down salts that accumulate on the soil like a light snow and steal fertility. "Our water supply is as tight as a drum," he confides. "We're having to dig more than two thousand feet deep. Odd enough, we found some pretty good water down there. It's salty but not too salty."

Across the plains of Westlands, nine hundred wells have been drilled below the clay layer since the district's inception. Forty-three of these wells belong to the Woolfs, who don't have to wait months for outsiders to dig their holes. They're among the few farmers whose irrigation side business can lay down miles of drip lines and drill wells two thousand feet deep in the same week, a $50 million asset, if Jack had to guess. "A farmer isn't a dirt farmer anymore," he says. "If he is, he won't last long. He has to either have a full-time job in the city, like my son the dentist, or he has to vertically integrate his operation. This is even more true in Westlands, where the challenges are bigger."

No one with the last name Giffen farms this ground anymore. Melons are still packed under the Telles label, but the Telles family isn't growing them. Dick Telles gambled on lettuce and strawberries in the Imperial and Salinas Valleys—crops he didn't know in soils he'd never farmed—and burned his last gallon of diesel in the 1980s. Albert and Helen Britz died in 1986 and left their three children a $23 million estate that included 19,000 acres of cropland and a chemical company with $229 million in annual sales. The Stamoules ranch, which widow Helen kept going until her death in 1992, has grown to 18,000 acres of melons, sweet corn, broccoli and nuts. Her only child, Peggy, married Tom Stefanopoulos, an electrical engineer from Greece who's become one of the more innovative, and pump-happy, farmers in the district. Their daughter works in the sales office, a son oversees irrigation and another son, an architect, designed the company's new $10 million headquarters in Mendota. It's quite a presence rising out of the flat fields: three stories tall and ultramodern, with hardwood and tile floors, lime-green office cubicles and a marble conference table of such mass that it took a score of men to carry it in.

Jack knows the stories buried in ditch and field, but he keeps mum as we pass green groves of mandarins and row after row of pistachios. The new Dust Bowl, as traveling journalists have dubbed it, doesn't seem so dusty. Jack rolls ahead toward Huron, where his main tomato man is waiting for us. The road slices through Helm (population 148) and Five Points (population 1,847), though no sign says you've arrived unless you count the sign that declares, "CONGRESS CREATED DUST BOWL." We come upon a field fenced off with metal sheeting topped with barbed wire. It could be one of the half dozen prisons shining their sickly glow that the state of California has plunked down in old cotton country as a way to diversify the economy and lock up drug offenders caught in the net of "Three Strikes and You're Out," the merciless law passed in the 1990s in the name of a murdered Fresno girl. But this glare comes from the sun bouncing off row after row of solar panels tilted toward the Pacific. A PG&E solar plant, Jack mutters. Twenty-four thousand acres of sun farms now add to the nuts, fruits, vegetables and grains of Westlands. "There's a place for solar in California, but not on ground this productive," he says.

We pull into Jack's town (population 6,941).

Welcome to Huron. The Meanest City in California. Now Maybe You'd Better Go Home.

Those were the words on the cover of a magazine called *West* back in the 1990s, when major newspapers still published Sunday magazines. The story was written and photographed by Richard Steven Street and remains one of my favorite portraits of rural California. It begins this way: "In Huron, at lettuce time, you're odd if you don't have a big lettuce knife stuffed into a stapled cardboard sheath stuck in your hip pocket. The lettuce knives are razor-sharp. It's common to see people clean their fingernails with those knives, or massage their temples, pick bits of dust off their arms or pop beer bottle caps. No wonder every fifth man you shake hands with has a scar between his left thumb and forefinger, and every 13th is missing a finger."

Farmers are wont to blame the town's poverty on the stinginess of the federal pumps. Truth is, Huron, wet or dry, has been the same poor for the past seventy-five years. I look for the El Rancho Bar, where the mural above the pool table was titled *Death of the Matador* and was pocked with bullet holes fired by a pair of assassins who one night administered a coup de grâce in front of 130 patrons. Not a one of them saw a thing. The old landmarks in *la ciudad de la puñalada,* the city of the stabbings, must have followed the way of cotton because the bar is gone, and so is the hotel that overlooked Needle Alley. The main street is wide, the pickings few. The mural that rival gang members painted on the community center wall in a show of peace—the one depicting Cesar Chavez and Mexican war hero Zapata—is gone, too. City officials made them whitewash it so the growers wouldn't take offense. The only icon permitted in Huron is a head of iceberg lettuce.

"If you had to guess, Jack, where do you think the unemployment rate stands today?"

"Unemployment?"

"Yeah."

"Well, it's a farm labor town."

He sidesteps the subject, and I would, too, if I were in the driver's seat. Since farmers began pulling wealth from this ground, three-quarters of a century ago, the jobless rate in Huron has never fallen below 30 percent. Most years, whether federal water flows or not, it's

40 percent. With more machines idling farmhands, it will soon be 50 percent. Thefts of a people's dignity never have been regarded as a crime here. Mexico's condition is Westlands' exoneration.

Yet if Huron remains one of the sorriest places in all of California, it must also be said that its gangs and drug dealing and idleness grow out of Latino rural cultures that crossed the border and transplanted themselves almost unadulterated here. Successive generations of the migrants have failed to take advantage of the fuller opportunities California affords—opportunities that other ethnic groups, scathed by their own histories, have managed to grasp. That noted, the structure of governance and power on the west side, and the complete dominance of its natural resources by a farming few, have made upward mobility a far trickier climb. Huron's residents draw the same surface water from the same aqueduct that the ranchers draw to feed their crops and cattle. Residents pay $90 a month for this privilege. But their dollars do not make the water fit to drink. The city's treatment plant is a half century old, and dilapidated. Arsenic, boron and cancer-causing trihalomethanes contaminate the supply, and Huron keeps getting slapped with "non-compliance orders" from the state. Westlands and the feds are still charging $300 an acre-foot for this water.

When a hard rain falls, the main road through town turns into a lake for several weeks. Residents have to find another way to and fro. For years, the state has been promising Huron a new road that isn't "subject to flooding." Until such a road is built, new businesses refuse to consider locating here. The small park where children play soccer is pocked with gopher holes. The coach tallies goals and twisted ankles. The nearest high school is an hour's bus drive away in Coalinga. Years back, Jack pledged to donate fifty acres of his land so that Huron might finally have a high school. The negotiations continue with his son Stuart.

Jack eases into the driveway of his ranch office and parks the car. We've made our destination without a scratch, it seems. He shuts off the engine and jerks his head my way.

"I told you I was deaf in my right ear."

"Yes, you did."

"What I didn't tell you is I had a cornea transplant in my right eye that didn't take. I'm half-blind."

He's still chuckling as he waves to Jesus Cuevas, the man revered as the west side's "tomato guru." Cuevas opens the doors of his Chevy Silverado, and we climb in. Machines twice the size of his truck, each one attended by a small crew, have begun to plug thirty million baby tomato vines into four-foot-wide beds whipped up to a fluff. These aren't the fussy Early Girls or Better Boys or Brandywines I grow in my backyard. These varieties, the N6366 and the CXD187, can endure the pounding of machine harvest and produce a paste that makes Heinz happy. In the old days, before he sent off three sons and a daughter to college, Cuevas was satisfied with a yield of thirty-five tons of tomatoes an acre. Thanks to drip irrigation lines buried in the beds, the new varieties can sip doses of water, nitrogen, phosphorous and potassium around the clock. These days, anything short of fifty-five tons an acre is considered a failure.

"We plant two crops of tomatoes," Cuevas explains. "What we plant in March, we harvest in July. Then we come back in and plant another crop in July that we harvest in fall. Every processing plant wants a different variety. Some want a tomato only for paste. Good sugar, good viscosity. Some want a tomato that peels easily. We have varieties that can do all three."

We exit the pickup, and I hustle to follow the transplant machine

Farmworker enjoying a beer after a long day's toil in Huron

and its crew of six. The beds are flawless. The furrows are flawless. The Panoche loam is so airy it makes me want to do a headfirst slide. The machine's tires tread along the furrow without disturbing the bed. Women covered with bandannas and long-sleeved shirts that billow in the wind perch atop the contraption, plopping each spindly plant, six inches tall, into a tiny hole dug by one mechanism. Another mechanism then pinches and presses the soil and sets the plant firmly into earth. Three other workers plodding behind the machine fill by human hand any vacant holes. In a ten-hour workday, each crew can cover twenty acres, an awe-inspiring amount.

With two fingers and his thumb, Jesus is making the sign of the cross. Every March, he explains, he starts over again like a baseball player. It doesn't matter that last season he led the league in home runs and made the All-Star team. This season, the tractor erased all the old marks from the ground. A new field stretches out before him. "It whispers to me not to worry. 'Relax. It's just like the old ground,'" he says. "But I don't listen to it. Each year is different. Mother Nature changes. It can be your best friend or your worst enemy. I can't fall asleep. Some nights I sleep maybe two hours. These tomatoes are my babies. I spoon-feed them like babies. If I do everything right and Mother Nature cooperates, maybe we'll hit seventy tons an acre."

I glance back to where the pickup is parked and see Jack take off down the planted row. For the first time, I really notice his age. His gait, each leg raised up high as if he were riding an invisible bicycle, is a plod. I think to myself: What San Francisco environmentalist coming upon this scene—an old man in cuffed slacks and a blue V-necked sweater, gray hair blowing in the desert wind—would recognize a farmer communing with his land? His Rockports sink deeper and deeper into the gray-brown loam. The old Giffen bean counter doesn't need a calculator. If all goes well, he's looking at a $22 million crop. The afternoon wind leans against his babies, gusts strong enough that I can see the purple fuzz under each little leaf. "They'll bend," Jack says, "but they won't break."

I offer to drive back home, even put down my foot, but Jack is no less determined to take the wheel than he was on the way here. We retrace irrigated earth that overlays what aeons ago was seabed. Clear-eyed farmers, among them his son Stuart, see the day soon approaching when restrictions on surface and groundwater will do what the federal government never had the gumption to do: limit Westlands to 250,000 acres of its finest loam. End-to-end pistachios, if that's what they want to grow here.

"Might not be a good thing," Jack says, "but I won't live to see it."

There's a lot I don't press Jack on. I don't tell him that I've been making my own trips to Westlands over the past few months. I've been to Cantua Creek and El Porvenir, the two tiny settlements that sprang from old cotton camps on Giffen's upper slope. I've seen where the earth in both communities has sunk and swayed from too many farmers' wells, where houses belonging to farmworkers have begun to sink, too, where families pay $120 a month for drinking water they cannot drink. I don't tell him that I've traced the worst of the pumping back to Farid and Darius Assemi, new growers in Westlands. I don't ask Jack why the vision of Giffen, O'Neill and Congressman Sisk—west side towns filled with 87,500 working people, schools, parks and prospering main streets—never came to be. He's not likely to share my theory that the very notion of community was doomed as soon as farmers decided that the west side wasn't a place where they could raise their families. Jack and Bernice at least tried. They lived in Huron until the early 1960s and might have stayed longer had there been a parochial school nearby that could have offered their children a decent education. Instead, the Woolfs and so many other farming families packed up and left the west side, moving to the exclusive neighborhoods of Fresno.

Among other comfortable things, this allowed them to treat the land in a way they might have thought twice about had they lived here. If the land were their home, they might not have farmed it with so many chemicals or tolerated drinking water no one could drink. If they lived on the land, they might have seen the value in devoting some of its acres to businesses, a school and parks. To not live here was to regard such uses as a waste of resources. It made sense to maximize the land's cultivation because the farm had become an abstraction distant from the hearth. The abstraction let the farmer regard the land as a thing apart from the community and himself. The abstraction then allowed for a magnitude of extraction—the draining of an aquifer as old as the Panoche hills—that had few parallels in human history.

His son Stuart, who bested his siblings and won his father's vote to take over Woolf Enterprises, lives with his family on the prettiest street in Fresno's Fig Garden. His workers live an hour away next to the crops in labor camps disguised as towns. He does not see their faces at the market; he's never watched his children play with their children on the soccer field. He does not know their names. He has given himself the distance—52.6 miles as the car drives, a million miles as the conscience flies—to think of them as strangers.

Jack talks about Russell Giffen as if the cotton king were a shadow still trailing him. It might be expected that he would resent such a presence and do what he could to erase it. Instead, Jack does the opposite. He pays tribute to the cotton king every chance he can. The way he tells the story, Giffen could do no wrong. He grabbed the loam and then grabbed the water. Out of dust he made fiber and food. A finer mentor he could not have imagined. For Jack, it isn't enough to own Giffen's dirt. He owns the Giffen beach houses overlooking the Pacific, too. He knows Giffen history better than the Giffens. He knows the year each of Russell's children was born. The ones who have died, he knows those dates, too. It is not by accident that one of his grandsons is named Wylie Woolf. Jack has chosen not to run from the shadow but to inhabit it. Maybe this is his way of acknowledging his own indebtedness: the Giffen land man who grabbed for himself some of the best pieces of Giffen land.

Considering the expanse we have just crossed, barren of farmhouses, barren of farm families, barren of community, it seems right to conclude that the lions of west side agriculture cooked up a story in the mid-1950s and sold it to the American people. They understood that the Reclamation Act of 1902 affirmed something deeply ingrained in the American soul. To foster family farming and develop rural communities where farmers and merchants and field hands shared a common bounty—these were ideals that connected back to Thomas Jefferson. And so when they found themselves in front of Congress asking for a project of unprecedented dimensions—the building of a reservoir where no river ran—they made a calculation and channeled the words the American people wished to hear, the agrarian ideals of Jefferson. Stillborn dream or living lie, the Westlands they ultimately built became an abomination of those words.

Out of respect for a man who will make his one hundredth birthday and live to shear the dreadlocks from his grandson's head, I don't try to corner Jack. I wouldn't be able to, anyhow. He sees the world the same way he's seen it since before I was born. Besides, we do agree on this much: A husband and wife and their thirty children and grandchildren can plow and plant an expanse of twenty-five thousand acres and be considered "family farmers." No disrespect to idealist George Ballis and his National Land for People, but the west side could never have flourished as a cradle of small farms. For all the wisdom of the law of 80 or 160 or 320 or 960 acres as it applied elsewhere, we had to be honest about its application out here. Even if the Bureau of Reclamation hadn't struck itself blind to the myriad contortions that farmers used to turn the law into a laughingstock, acreage limits would not have worked in Westlands. Not on land that has no river and is laced with salts. Not on land that holds its water at such depths that wells and pumps cost an arm and a leg. Not on land that had to be planted with such boom-and-bust crops that only a farmer backed by a generous bank could ride out the turns. Maybe if almonds and pistachios had been churning out the profits back then that they do today, the small guy could have occupied a modest piece of the west side. But who saw the nut coming?

Certainly not Berge Bulbulian, a small farmer who walked off his vineyard on the east side in the 1960s to fight alongside Ballis as second-in-command at National Land for People. In his living room a few months before his death, Berge tells me, "A small guy wouldn't last on the west side. There's no question. For all the reasons you cite. But that's not what drove me to fight." He listens patiently to my argument that 250,000 acres of Westlands, the very best land, still deserves the people's water, but he's not buying it. The U.S. taxpayer has spent close to $1 billion trying to wrest crops from a doomed land, he says. How much longer must we prop up an agriculture that has all the newest technologies at its disposal but whose bottom line will never be anything but feudal? "What drove me to fight was a belief all along that the west side should have never been irrigated," Berge says. "It should have never been farmed."

But it was, and it is, and now what?

Twenty-One

HOLY WATER

One winter day in 1998, a snow fell on the valley. Not a dusting, mind you, but an honest-to-goodness snow. My son Joseph was seven years old, about the same age I was when it last snowed in Fresno. We were driving east on Shaw Avenue, watching big fat flakes make it all the way to the ground, awestruck. Then a startle jumped his face. Standing before us, brushed by the same white, was the giant blue of the Sierra Nevada. He knew we lived in a valley in the midst of mountains, but they'd been hidden behind a veil of dust, smoke and smog for eight months. "Why are the mountains in the street?" he asked me. He was literally correct. In the center of the road in front of us, the Sierra shot out of the ground like a piece of urban landscape. There was a shopping mall to our right and an automobile dealership to our left and in between the looming mountains. The miles of city and suburbia that rolled out to flat farmland, and the miles of flat farmland that rolled out to foothills, did not exist in our window. Only the mountain that made our valley, that put water in our river and water in our ditch and water in the earth below, stared back at us.

I am thinking about that image now because right before me, rising straight out of the asphalt highway four hundred miles from home, is the conical peak of an ancient volcano that takes up the entirety of my view. Here I am, at last, in the embrace of Mount Shasta. How to tell you of its presence? It is not the mountain range of middle California but, rather, an eruption so severe that no other mountain dares stand next to it. It stands alone.

All great mountains deserve their own bard, and Mount Shasta has a beauty, a fabulous gadabout named Joaquin Miller who arrived, like the rest of them, in 1850 and ended up a killer of Indians and a savior of Indians, a plunderer of earth and a planter of tens of thousands of trees, a liar and a poet, which may be another way of saying he was no better or worse at heart than any other Californian, caught in a time and place that was one thing one minute and something near its opposite the next, giving a man no choice but to change with it. "There loomed Mount Shasta, with which my name, if remembered at all, will be remembered," Miller wrote. "As lone as God, and white as a winter moon." On another occasion, he remarked, "A great pyramid and shining shaft of snow, with a crown of clouds, pierced heaven."

Born Cincinnatus Hiner Miller, he was raised on his father's farm in Oregon and arrived here at the age of sixteen, drawn by the legend of bandit Joaquín Murrieta. He changed his name to Joaquin Miller, grew his curly hair long and dressed like a vaquero, with a sombrero, a red silken sash and high-top boots. A devout Quaker, he joined a posse of white men who cornered a party of Wintu below Mount Shasta. As a matter of veneration, the Wintu would not ascend the mountain past its timberline. This was where the Good Spirit dwelled inside a great wigwam with his people, the smoke and steam of their civilization venting from crater's top. In the massacre that ensued, Miller took an arrow to the side of his face that knocked out two of his teeth and left him with a scar that he covered up with a thick beard, or so went the tale he told. In his novels, short stories and poems, he recounted natives killed and natives sent to rot on a rancheria on the hot plain of the Sacramento Valley. "It is impossible," he confided, "to write with composure or evenness on this subject. One wants to rise up and crush things. . . . Ages may roll by. We may build a city over every dead tribe's bones. We may bury the last Indian deep as the eternal gulf. But these records will remain and will rise up in testimony against us to the last day of our race."

The first white man who climbed solo to the summit of Mount Shasta had heard his share of confessions no less cleansing. Reverend Israel Diehl came to California in 1853 on order of his Methodist superiors. Once here, he traveled more than three thousand miles by stagecoach, horseback and on foot to deliver what was said to be one thousand public lectures to the new sinners of California. His single topic was temperance. All his walking and preaching made him the perfect candidate to not only attempt his climb to the 14,180-foot summit on the beautiful and bright morning of October 9, 1855, but to write an account for *Hutchings' Illustrated California Magazine* that was filled with grizzly bears and falling lava rocks, red clay bluffs colored by the sweat of iron and snow-hidden gorges one hundred feet deep and three hundred feet wide. More than once, he believed he had scaled the summit only to find that it lay beyond: "I was both disappointed and pleased to see the table-land of snow from one-fourth to one-half mile in diameter, where it lay from one hundred to probably one thousand and more feet deep. . . . From this field, a few hundred feet from the summit, the Sacramento River takes its rise; running through the deep gorges, sometimes on top, then hidden, then appearing at the summit of hills, then concealed for miles, it breaks forth in magnificent springs and miniature rivers, with sulphur and soda springs intermixed."

I am standing at the base of the mountain on a late summer day as rivulets of snowmelt bleed out of rock and fill up a small pool whose waters will join other pools and form the river that more than any other river created California. I am joined by Buddhists and mystics and seekers of Mount Shasta's lizard people, clock people, spaceship people and the myth of Lemuria, the lost continent buried beneath the Pacific. As the legend goes, one of Earth's cataclysms struck and left only a single refuge, Mount Shasta. For centuries, the ancient Lemurians, a people seven feet tall, lived in a splendid golden city inside the mountain. Today's pilgrims are drawn by the mountain's vortical pull and the strange flying saucer cloud that hovers over the top of the crater. It is known as a lenticular cloud, and Mount Shasta is one of the few places in the world where it can be found in such dramatic form. What makes this cloud a phenomenon is a stream of air that condenses one edge and evaporates the other edge and travels at a speed of fifty to one hundred miles an hour. Yet the cloud itself doesn't move. Gravity and buoyancy fight to a draw. The cloud absorbs sunrise and sunset, projecting such spectacular glows that it's no wonder people ascribe otherworldliness to Mount Shasta.

Those who abandon their former lives and move here for good come to the mountain's base each day and reverently dip their jugs into some of the last pure water left in the West. I climb to a ledge above the pond and sink my cupped hands into the ice-cold snowmelt and take a sip and another delicious sip. The man in a brown gown standing next to me calls it "raw water" and explains that it takes a half century for snow on the shoulders of Mount Shasta to filter down through the volcanic aquifer and bleed out the base. If that is true, I'm drinking water nearly as old as I am, or far older if you consider the Pacific, whose moisture condensed into the storm that dropped the snow.

Where water is pure, the industrial water bottlers with global reach aren't far behind. Nestlé, Coca-Cola and Danone have made friends in the three little towns that form a half circle around the mountain. They've made enemies, too. Big-city exiles who have moved to the communities of Weed, McCloud and Mount Shasta—the imported environmentalists—are fighting to prevent the bottlers from mining the pristine water. The Wintu nation—what's left of it, anyway—fights beside them. Two dozen natural springs flow where the pine, fir, oak and dogwood make a forest. Already, one spring has been tapped by Crystal Geyser, which is part owned by Otsuka, the Japanese pharmaceutical giant. One million gallons a day are put into plastic bottles at the plant in Weed and shipped out across the planet. Crystal Geyser is now eyeing a second spring, and a Sacramento developer who has never bottled water before is scoping out a third.

Environmentalists who blocked Nestlé's water grab are now headed to court again to stop Crystal Geyser. The cause polarizes mountain people. For more than a century, their towns were company towns devoted to the wholesale harvesting of forest trees. The old lumber barons built the community's pitched-roof houses and high school. They built the swimming pool and theater. When Abner Weed gave you a job, it was considered a job for life. Then the sawmills shuttered and the economy withered. The county of Siskiyou and the city of Weed thought themselves improvident for not acting on the one exportable natural resource still ripe for the taking. Out-of-town businessmen blew in their ears. Water is a commodity. Water is a mutual fund. Water is jobs. But in the case of the one bottling plant up and running in Weed, Crystal Geyser pays not a dime to the city or the county for the water. The locals looking for the state government to intervene will be disappointed.

What is or is not a safe yield of the aquifer is not a question that California water engineers apply to Mount Shasta. By reckoning of the new groundwater law, Mount Shasta may be the most profuse water source in all the Far West, but it does not qualify, in the eyes of the state, as a defined groundwater basin. Its springs come from nowhere and everywhere. In other California locales, the extraction and sale of bottled water would require a modicum of government oversight and even constraint. The constraint might entail measuring the water table every so often or placing a ceiling on exports or setting a minimum flow in the riverbed to sustain fish and wildlife. But here at the headwaters, bottlers need only declare themselves a "mutual water company" to occupy a jurisdictional no-man's-land where the sole watchdog—the state's Public Utilities Commission—is no watchdog at all.

For the Wintu, the theft of their mountain's snowmelt began not with international water bottlers but with the raising of Shasta Dam in 1945. At a town park where the river's headwaters gush forth many miles above the dam, several Wintu gather for a rally. "WATER IS LIFE," one sign reads. Their official statement mixes legend and legal brief: "The Winnemem Wintu were born from the pristine water of Mount Shasta and regard this water as a sacred relative, a living being that is being exploited, desecrated and polluted when it is put in a plastic bottle and commoditized." Chief Caleen Sisk, a regal woman whose long braid of black hair spills from her tribal skullcap, speaks of another theft: Governor Brown's Twin Tunnels and legislation in Congress—introduced on behalf of the Westlands Water District—to raise Shasta Dam by 18.5 feet. "We have lived on the banks of the McCloud River for thousands of years, and our culture is centered on the protection and careful, sustainable use of its salmon," she says. "These projects would only push the remaining salmon runs toward extinction and inundate our ancestral and sacred homeland."

Sixty miles below the headwaters, the dam already stands 602 feet high. Its imposition on the river's canyon is cruel and brilliant at once. The lake forming the state's largest reservoir is low even by drought's stick, but not low enough to reveal the old copper mining town of Kennett, its bars, bordellos and other houses of worship buried underwater for three-quarters of a century now. I follow the path of the Sacramento River, twisted one way by snowmelt and another way by irrigation, for more than three hundred miles and arrive several hours later at the delta, a place that is hardly what it was when John Sutter stepped foot in the tules. Yet his wonder is not difficult to summon for a Fresno boy whose only river is a dead one. For all its impingements, for all the failures of the Delta Protection Act to keep real estate developers from ravaging its marsh, the Sacramento flows steady and high between wider banks. Even crippled by sprawl and drought, it scoots past farms and towns and beneath old metal bridges, and the light it captures and throws off and the air it grabs and cools makes the delta a very different place than my valley.

A northern contingent of environmentalists and bass fishermen who recite the "crimes against nature" perpetrated by the Westlands Water District tend to downplay the feats of engineering that have redone this landscape, too. We can start with Reuben Kercheval, who came West from Ohio in the 1850s to prospect for gold but found the swamp more to his suiting. His crew of Chinese, California natives and Kanakas swung shovels and trundled wheelbarrows to erect twelve miles of levee along his section of Grand Island. Described as lean of hip and wide of shoulders, Kercheval knew that his delta neighbors would need to match his levee with one of their own or else risk an even bigger flood the next time the Sacramento went high. "You can tell just how stingy or generous a man is by the height of his levee and the width of his base line," Kercheval is quoted as saying in Julian Dana's book *The Sacramento*. Kercheval's levee rose high and wide enough to allow him to plant hundreds of acres of pears, peaches and grapes, along with corn, potatoes and grain. The next spring, he watched the flood of 1861 overtake the river and carry his vines and trees into the sea.

Kercheval had the persistence of an ant. When his seventeen thousand acres of peatland dried out, he surrounded the farm with a levee so uniform that "a man could pace twenty-nine-and-a-half circuitous miles and return to his starting place without stepping from his dikes." He and his delta neighbors held a "Levee Day" celebration and delivered grand speeches and feasted on a grand meal made only from food grown on Grand Island, "a dinner fit for the gods." Then the snowmelt of 1876 found a weak spot in the levee and drowned the farmland again. Kercheval pledged to his wife, children and community that he would build a system of dikes to withstand the river even at its worst. That fall, he raised $150,000 and hired two hundred Chinese and forty Kanakas to construct a levee the likes of which had never been seen here: one hundred feet thick and twelve feet high, with a five-foot-wide crest. This time, the river appeared beaten. Kercheval harvested a record crop in 1877, and even the storied grouch of Grand Island, J. W. Brocas, smiled approvingly. Neither man yet knew of the flood of 1878, a rain that would not cease. The new levee was a beauty. It held and held until slickens from far-off gold mines came slamming down. Kercheval had planned for water, not tons and tons of mud and debris. His crop ruined again, the old swamplander died and left the farm to his sons. He never got to see the big clamshell dredgers, the tule breakers, scoop out the river's bottom and build new levees from the mud of the mines.

Had Kercheval listened to Will Green, who had survived the river's fits upstream, he might have saved himself a little grief. In his defense, it wasn't easy enduring one of Green's lectures. He made you pay attention to him twice, once at a public meeting and then again in the columns of his *Colusa Sun*. Green had migrated from Kentucky at the age of eighteen with a backwoods education, an unapologetic belief in slavery and a hunger for knowledge that kept his nose stuck in books. Not all of the books preached to his sentiments. After landing in San Francisco in the summer of 1850, Green piloted a small steamer into the delta islands and followed the river upstream. Past the city of Sacramento, he kept on going another sixty-five miles, until he found a spot where the wild oats grew taller than six feet and a sea of wildflowers waved in a gentle breeze. "I seemed to be reveling in a very Garden of Eden," he wrote. "A scene so enticing that it took away all the enchantment of the mines of gold." He and his fellow pioneers were then overtaken by a peculiar American impulse to name their place after the culture they were sending to the trash heap. Honor or insult, they christened it Colusa after the tribe of local Indians.

Their townsite endured a tortured relationship with the Sacramento River. Upstream, the river grabbed elevation from Red Bluff to move its heavy flow. Water coursed down the hill at almost 2 million gallons every second. The river's banks, owing to such power, sat three-quarters of a mile apart. Just below Will Green's Colusa, however, the hill gave way to flat valley, and the speed of the river slowed. Here, the banks narrowed considerably. Because the confined riverbed had trouble handling flows above 525,000 gallons a second, floodwaters routinely bled out into the adjoining sloughs. This was how nature designed it. It would have been fine except the farmers were now attempting to plant crops in the sloughs. Who could fault them? Irrigation was only a small ditch away, and the earth there was fertile. But the river's physical funnel—that pinch below Colusa—was going to drown these same crops in the very next flood. The only solution, townsfolk reasoned, was engineering. Common sense dictated that levees needed to be built, and they had to be strong enough to contain flows more than three times what the natural banks could confine. With the usual enthusiasm, citizens grabbed their shovels and scrapers and constructed levees capable of withstanding such flows. Miles and miles of sloughs were planted to crops. Then the same waters that would bedevil Kercheval showed Colusa's folly, too.

Civic-minded Will Green took it upon himself to become a student of the situation. He taught himself civil engineering and sized up the pinch in the river in all its convolutions. He surmised that sloughs and marshes outside town allowed the river to take a breath and let off a little steam. The solution to flooding wasn't building a superlevee. The solution was letting the river spread its wings. Not all the way, of course, but enough to slow its speed and reduce its volume.

Thanks to Green, the concept of a flood bypass—an alleyway beside a river off-limits to city building—was born in California. By giving the river some of its historic floodplain to roam, man could steal a good bit of its rampage. Living next to the Sacramento River afforded Green an angle of study, and he became much more than a swamplander, much more than a loudmouth for state's rights and slavery. He became a newspaper publisher, writer, state legislator, U.S. surveyor general for California, state treasurer and one of the fathers of Sacramento Valley irrigation. Because so few of his fellow legislators were willing to upset riparian landowners, the idea of a bypass was not quickly adopted. In fact, it took a new century, and many more floods, for Green's notions to be realized, in the formation of the sixty-thousand-acre Yolo Bypass.

Inside the delta's maze, a 738,000-acre estuary that drains 40 percent of California's landmass, it is best to second-guess your eyes. The narrow asphalt ribbon that shadows the river appears to be terra firma. It's actually a levee dug out from water on one side and piled high with old

The San Joaquin and Sacramento Rivers meet in the delta.

peat and mud on the other side. This was a trick of the Chinese, the Celestials, as they were called, who would stand waist-deep in malarial swamp and build a levee on Monday and a tiny wooden village on the same floating bank on Tuesday. They named their little hamlet Locke after the man who owned the land, but it was known far and wide as "California's Monte Carlo," a Wild West town erected of lumber and sticks, with five gambling halls, five brothels, a half dozen speakeasies and opium dens, a school, a temple, an herb shop and market, and a boardinghouse that filled with one thousand Chinese farmhands during harvesttime. Because of laws that discriminated against Asians, the houses behind Main Street were some of the only houses the Chinese were allowed to own in California. The places they had settled in before Locke had kept burning down. Was it the hot oil of their cooking or the match of racism? This was the question of the day.

Here in the delta, where Chinese workers had built the railroads and the levees, and the dirt they moved was said to be more dirt than it took to carve out the Panama Canal, a certain debt was owed them. At first, they were allowed to buy the houses but not the dirt the houses sat on. Finally, in 1977, the heirs of George Locke sold the town and its fourteen acres to Chinese investors from Hong Kong. On a late afternoon in 2016, it appears all but abandoned, one more sleepy historic place on the national registry, until the saloon doors on Al the Wop's tavern swing open and reveal travelers on a break from the scenic route drinking gin and eating steaks with garlic fries as the bartender recounts how the last fire in a century of fires sparked on easy tinder and swept through town. There are no Chinese to be found in Locke now, only the busts of Confucius and Sun Yat-sen, father of the Republic of China whose Kuomintang Party once had a chapter here.

Up the road, tucked into a sublime nook of river, hides the Hemly pear farm, first cultivated by a forty-niner who, lore has it, endured a drought so severe that one summer day he walked across the river and didn't get his feet wet. That was how dry and salty the delta could become on its own—before the river was dammed, before the towns and farms drew from its waters, before the hydraulic system connected north and south and sent snowmelt hurtling seven hundred miles downstate in a path the salmon and smelt did not swim.

I knock on the door of the Hemlys, one of the original delta families who have trusted me with their ancestor's diary, which sits atop my research pile back home. Six generations after great-great-great-grandpa Josiah Greene walked on the river, Doug and Cathy Hemly and their grown children are fighting the $20 billion Twin Tunnels that Governor Jerry Brown wants to bore beneath this same stretch of river. Replumbing the delta in the name of moving a more reliable supply of water north to south is a tune Cathy Hemly has heard before. "We're farmers. We understand the importance of water," she tells me. "Among my circle, I don't know of anyone who isn't in favor of exporting surplus water to farms and cities south of us. Problem is, how do you define 'surplus'? How do you define 'reliable'? It's one thing to export some of our water in wet years. But how do you send it in dry years and not do damage to the farms and cities here?"

Hemly isn't one of those environmentalists relitigating in her head the building of a Central Valley Project. She knows that the damming of river, the subduing of flood, is what allowed for their life here. Thanks to dependable releases from the Shasta Dam, their orchards have never gone without water. In the worst of drought, she's never seen the river go dry. "We're as dependent on the federal project as the farms in the San Joaquin Valley and the cities in Southern California are," she acknowledges. "We see the benefit. We know the deal. But more and more, the water left behind is salt water. The delta is a delicate balance between ocean and fresh water, and now the balance is being tilted."

She's a stylish woman in her late sixties who wears her hair in a pixie and a pink oxford shirt with sleeves rolled up. After each harvest, she travels to a different country with her husband or hikes the John Muir Trail with girlfriends, but she has found no place she'd rather come back to than here, the delta, to the lovely no-nonsense folk Victorian built out of redwood, where she knows every flower, bush and tree, and every mood of the Sacramento. "The river isn't some abstraction. It's our front yard. A Chinese elm and ten feet of green grass and then the river. This levee we're standing on is the same dirt my family has been standing on for more than one hundred and sixty-five years. Josiah Greene was an abolitionist in a redneck world. He was 'escaping his troubles' in Virginia. He came with his brother. They arrived on December 31, 1849. By the skin of their teeth, they were forty-niners."

The brothers thought they were coming to a place where rivers, like home, were reliable. But there's no average here. It rains. It floods. It doesn't rain. Drought comes. Everything depends on Sierra snowmelt. The seasons here aren't so much spring, summer, fall. They're the asparagus, cherry, pear, apple and grape. "We have one thousand, one hundred and eleven acres. A perfect lineup of ones. How did it happen? It was just one foot in front of the other, day by day, generation after generation. It's not sexy or glamorous. It's making your own luck. My children's children are growing up on this land now. My granddaughter Ria is fascinated by an almost English sense of history in the delta. The history of the West is a history of throwaway. We occupy a place and then give it up. Or our children give it up. But here is a real sense of home, and you don't give it up. You find a way to bend your dreams and ambitions to fit the land. And if you have to bend the land a little, that's okay, too. But you and the land fit together. It's the dirt that gives mortality a meaning."

We walk to Highway 160, a.k.a. River Road, a.k.a. her driveway. The river is low and, to my eyes, perfectly still. She sees motion. She hears the buzz of their little rust-colored pump sitting a few feet deep in the river, the vibration of irrigation. "We know where our water comes from. We are reminded of it every time we turn on the pump," Hemly

Cathy Hemly gazes out to the Sacramento River
from the steps of her house built in 1875.

says. "It isn't shipped here from some faraway river. During high water, when this island fills up with rain and seepage, we close the road and pump the water back into the river. You can see from here where the footprint of the tunnels will reach. The state engineers call it Intake Number Five. It starts here and extends to that clump of trees. It will take up that entire stretch of river bend. It'll be bigger than the river is wide, and there will be two more of those monsters. They call them intakes. We call them outtakes."

The tunneling project, known officially as the California WaterFix, would impound a portion of the river's flow and ship it around the rest of the delta. This would result in less salty, higher-quality irrigation water sent south to agricultural giants such as Boswell and Resnick and higher-quality drinking water for Southern California. More fish will be spared the fate of the federal and state pumps. "Or at least that's what they tell us," Hemly says. "That's what they promise. But without that fresh water flowing through the delta, what will happen to our ecosystem, our irrigation and drinking water?" We walk through crooked rows of Bartlett pear trees, planted a century ago with a horse-drawn plow driven by an ancestor who had no sense of straight, and stand at the river's edge. "From a taker's standpoint, it's perfectly logical. From a supplier's standpoint, it's a travesty."

On River Road in the opposite direction, I drive past Isleton on my way to Rio Vista. This is where, in the 1920s, the fruit tramps in my family, after picking grapes in Fresno, traveled like a caravan of gypsies to work in the canneries of "Row Vista" (spoken with the *R* rolled), slicing peaches into perfect quarters with hands they soaked at night in apple cider vinegar to get the soreness out. Right here, this spot, is where Uncle Harry, my grandfather's brother, before he killed the cop and was sent away to San Quentin, jumped off the metal drawbridge and swam across the Sacramento, more mighty than it is now, and duly impressed a Portuguese girl, whom he deflowered that night in a field behind the camp. He told me the story himself after he'd finally gotten out on parole and was dying of lung cancer, and my mother was fixing him *kheyma,* the Armenian delicacy of finely ground raw meat, bulgur, tomato sauce and paprika topped with fresh parsley and onions, in the kitchen of the adobe brick house my father built on fig ground, no more restrictive covenants barring us Fresno Indians from the fancy part of town, and she was working and reworking the meat with her thick hands, the only thing sturdy about her, so that when she finished, the *kheyma* didn't taste raw at all, and they ate it with lavash bread and Uncle Harry laughed and said that for every cell the lung cancer was eating, the *kheyma* was manufacturing two more, and my mom laughed with him, not knowing that the same cell was about to take her life, too.

The sun bounces off the Montezuma Hills as I glide across the reclamation districts of the delta, each one named after a number. What are they but islands lifted from marshlands where tules rotted long ago and formed a rich peat that still fouls the air with bad carbon? The map titled "The Irrigation Districts of California" that has guided me well for the past five years says I've landed on Sherman Island. The battered road meanders past wild artichokes. Inland sea surges to my right and vast field slouches to my left, and the water sits many feet higher than the field, and yet the field remains dry. The levee's crown, piled high with jagged rocks, measures six feet across. It keeps one realm of delta from intruding on the other realm. It also provides an excellent roost from which to watch my river, the San Joaquin, at last more than a trickle, roll in from the south. Wind whips over wide water, a battering force the engineers call fetch, and blows away peat and erodes island, hastening its sinking into sea. After too many floods and government rescues, the state has purchased the entirety of Sherman Island, as well as much of Twitchell Island next door. California is now handing this slice of delta back to the tules—in hopes of capturing carbon, stopping erosion and slowing subsidence. It is one of a score of action plans, some of them downright plausible, now being tried to "Save the Delta."

Here is where Sutter got lost in the sticks and the earnest taking of California began. I stand on the levee bank and watch the San Joaquin meet its bigger sibling and together push out past Pittsburg and into the bay and become one more pull of the Pacific. This ebb and flow, the daily exchange between salty ocean and freshwater delta, lies at the heart of our misunderstanding. The delta farmers, environmentalists and sports fishermen who live in the north want us to believe that the giant pumps of the Central Valley Project and the State Water Project, lined up warlike across from each other in the southwestern corner of the delta, stand alone as culprits. Their combined power, especially when activated at the wrong tidal hour, alters the currents and sends the salts flushing inward and the Chinook salmon and the delta smelt swimming toward their predators. The farmers to the south who rely on these pumps argue that a much longer list of actors is conspiring to salt up the delta and push the fish to the brink of extinction. Yet it is their pumps, alone, they say, that bear the blame and weight of mitigation.

It might be best to leave the misunderstanding right there, let each tribe preach its sermon, creed and rant to its own, for no book, long or short, could ever hope to bring peace to California's water wars. But I have learned something else in my trek north, something from the mouths of the top water directors and the biologists who work for the state and federal governments and don't often speak with such candor: The delta is not what it appears; or, rather, it is much more than it appears.

They tell the story of the demise of the salmon and the smelt as a kind of allegory:

It took a long time but the debris of gold mining finally cleared itself from the Sacramento River and its tributaries. The last plug of silt washed down in the late 1990s, after an epic flood. This was a good thing, it was thought. We had finally rid ourselves of the tailings, if not the legacy, of mining. Then we discovered that the scoured-out river channel scarcely carried any sediment or proper food for the fish. All the engineering that followed the gold rush—shoring and reshoring of levees, dredging of river bottom, separation of river from sloughs, building of dam—had transformed the Sacramento into a fire hose. Gone was the sediment that created turbidity, a stirring up that allowed an endangered species to hide from its predators. Gone, too, were the phytoplankton, zooplankton and aquatic bugs that turned a fingerling salmon into a plump juvenile.

Early on, the delta was a place bent to the demands of not only farms and towns but a significant maritime trade. A branch of the river was carved into a channel for ships that sailed in from everywhere. As the vessels discharged their ballast water, they impregnated the delta with dozens of foreign species, among these types of clams and plants whose capacity to reproduce was outdone only by their capacity to filter columns of water over and over, as many as thirteen times a day. Thanks in part to their tireless grazing, the river water became nearly sterile, a food desert. Of the 212 known invasive species, none posed a greater threat to salmon, smelt and steelhead trout than the bass. Like the Asian clam, the striped bass and the largemouth bass had no business being in the delta. These were fish common to the Atlantic Coast. They weren't borne by ballast. Striped bass came here in milk cans aboard transcontinental trains as early as 1879. The first planting of largemouth bass took place a decade later when the U.S. Fish Commission deposited 620 fingerlings into the Feather River. By 1995, a federal study would declare the delta conquered. "The depth and extent of biological invasions is greater than for any other aquatic ecosystem in North America. In some regions of the Bay, 100% of the common species are introduced communities."

Striped and largemouth bass are skilled hunters of shrimp, shad, fellow bass and, more important, smelt and salmon, but any notion of controlling them has been squelched by the bass anglers and bass sporting shops and associations. For decades, the bass lobby has acted as an indomitable force in the delta, even persuading the state Fish and Game department to propagate hundreds of thousands of striped and largemouth in Northern California hatcheries. Nearly two hundred million fry a year were found in the cooling water intakes at the PG&E

plants in Antioch and Pittsburg. The delta built an economy fueled in part by the region's status as a "world-class" bass fishery. In the fight over water, bass enthusiasts stand toe to toe with farmers in Westlands. Every day in delta country, it seems, is bass tourney day.

"When you put aside drought, which levels everything, the number one bad actor in the delta imperiling the salmon and smelt isn't the pumps. It's the bass," Kevin Clark, a state biologist with the Department of Water Resources, tells me. "The number two bad actor would be the destruction of habitat for the smelt and the salmon. When we lost the sloughs and the floodplain to agriculture, we lost areas rich in food and largely free from predators. The sloughs were literally breeding ground for fat and happy fish." Instead of letting young salmon and smelt hang out in the historic floodplain and join the river downstream, the fish are funneled into the river's watery slide and then into the mouths of the bass and shorebirds on the delta's south side. Ask Clark where the federal and state pumps rank on the list of culprits, and he'll tell you they're number three. Ask him how those pumps became the top villain in the eyes of federal scientists managing the water and endangered species, and he'll say it's all about the flick of a switch. The pumps, 34,500 horsepower each, are easy to vilify and easy to shut down. "Why do we make the pumps bear the burden of environmental mitigation? Because there is no switch to remove the bass or the Asian clams or the invasive weeds or all the other detriments," Clark says.

One of the biggest misconceptions about the federal and state pumps is that they draw endangered salmon and smelt into their swirl and chop them into pieces. The myth is so widely shared that I believed it myself for the longest time. But the risk the pumps pose isn't as giant Cuisinarts. Rather, it is the currents altered by their pumping that conspire to kill the fish. Revved up too high and at the wrong tidal hour, the pumps can reverse the internal flows of the delta and lure salmon and smelt from the safer north side to the still waters of the south side, where bass and shorebirds park themselves as if sitting down to a buffet. "The public would love us to rank the bad actors one to ten. But it isn't that easy," says Ted Sommer, a state biologist who's been working to save the salmon and smelt for more than thirty years. "Depending on the season and whether or not it's a wet or dry year, the list of actors changes. If it's wet, the effect of the pumps is trivial. If it's dry, the effect of the pumps can be significant."

The drought has placed so much extra stress on the delta's ecosystem that the numbers of smelt have fallen to record lows, and the fall and winter runs of the Chinook salmon hardly qualify as runs. Predation on the delta's south side, never a good thing, becomes a crisis in drought, and this is why the federal agencies focus so much of their concern on the pumps. How much to throttle them back each day is the call of the National Marine Fisheries Service and the U.S. Fish and Wildlife Service. From December through June, when fish are migrating, the federal agencies err on the side of extreme caution and restrict pumping. From summer to fall, the window for pumping water into the aqueduct and the San Luis Reservoir opens up, though it can close again if drought is too severe.

Saving endangered fish is a tricky science, pumps or no pumps. The delta smelt, a vital link in the aquatic life chain, is a terrible swimmer, lives for only a year and can't stand drought. Among its habits, it chases turbidity across the delta—for protection and food. This survival instinct turns deadly when government pumps create swirls of turbidity that coax the smelt down into the south delta killing fields. The eleven pumps that belong to the state government are housed at the four-story-tall Banks Pumping Plant. Turned on full blast, they draw 10,300 cubic feet of water each second from sea level and lift it 250 feet into the aqueduct's maw. The federal pumps, located two miles away at the Jones Pumping Plant, are not nearly as grand. Turned on full speed, they move 5,500 cubic feet of water each second. The difference in pumping power becomes real when the hours and days to pump get restricted. The extra horsepower of the state pumps means more water gets exported south. This is why in dry years, the farms and municipalities that drink from the State Water Project can still receive up to 30 percent of their contracted water. Meanwhile, the ranches in Westlands, drinking from the federal pumps, receive zero.

The well-being of smelt and salmon isn't the only factor that shackles the pumps. Even when the fish aren't migrating toward the south end, the pumps can be shut down. The agency shackling them in this instance isn't the National Marine Fisheries Service but the State Water Resources Control Board. The reason is salt. In drought, there's too little fresh water flowing down the river to push back on the Pacific tides.

Salt water sweeps across the delta's farms and towns and violates state drinking water standards. This isn't anything new, of course. Before the river was ever dammed, seawater intrusions happened on their own. Back in the early 1900s, sugar refineries in Crockett sent barges up the delta with test kits to figure out where the salt zone finally yielded to snowmelt. In some drought years, the barges had to travel thirty miles up the delta to find water fresh enough to process the sugar.

Salt might have been viewed as one of the plagues of nature that occasionally haunt a civilization established in the midst of an estuary six thousand years old. But once the federal and state governments decided to build the system and move the rain, mankind assumed the role of God and gave itself the duty to right the wrong of salt. The State Water Resources Control Board, as high and mighty as it sounds, is required by law to create conditions in the delta—including low salinity in drought—that are contrary to the delta's nature. Because exporting water to farms and cities concentrates more salinity in the estuary, the pumps must be shut down. In this way, the core function of the project—the act of moving the rain that turned us into God—turns on itself. God ties the hands of God.

No one wants a species to go extinct on his or her watch. When you plumb the waters of the delta smelt's favorite gathering spot and cannot find a single specimen of the genus *Hypomesus transpacificus*, you don't have the luxury of waiting on more science to give you all the reasons why. You reach for the things you can control and start fooling around with nature. The more stubborn the drought, the more desperate the fooling around. When fish migrate deep into the south delta badlands, they end up at the edge of two massive fish rescue operations, one run by the state and the other run by the feds. Here, a system of screens and funnels moves the fish into concrete holding tanks. Every two hours, the fish are lifted out of the tanks, counted and identified by species. Then they're loaded into an oxygenated tanker truck for a twenty-five-mile ride back to the more nurturing environs of the north delta. The migration by tanker happens twice a day. In wet years, fifteen million fish are saved this way. What's remarkable is that only 1 to 2 percent of the rescued fish turn out to be Chinook salmon, delta smelt or steelhead trout, the latter listed as a "threatened" species.

This suggests two possibilities: Either the bass and the birds are eating the endangered fish before they can be salvaged or only a small number of the species of greatest concern, drawn by the pumps, actually migrate down to the south delta. Each day, the agencies make their hard calls on the pumps. How much water gets exported to the rest of California is based on the number and types of fish that turn up in the rescue operations. The more endangered fish that are saved by the screens and holding tanks, the more the government feels compelled to throttle down the pumps. "This sounds counterintuitive, I know," Clark says. "Why should rescued salmon and smelt be viewed as a negative? It could be argued that the salvage operation is mitigation. If those fish are allowed to stay in the south delta, we know what happens. They're eaten. When the pumps are turned on, many are saved." In other words, what is God to do when his pumps that put the endangered species in harm's way are the same pumps that save them when they're put in harm's way?

The Chinook salmon stuck behind Shasta Dam need water below fifty-six degrees Fahrenheit to live. Cold water is hard to come by in drought. So federal agencies are now deciding to hold back summer and fall releases from the dam to keep the water cold. In doing so, they have relinquished their best tool downstream—a bigger pulse of water—to save the delta smelt. When the needs of one native fish collide against the needs of another native fish, both of them teetering on the brink of extinction, what is man playing God to do? Because he made this mess and now the better impulse in him must unmake it, he has to choose. He chooses the salmon.

Man's tinkering to undo his tinkering finds new realms.

In the south delta, state biologists are shocking the shallow waters with jolts of electricity, stunning bass to the surface and transporting them via tank and trailer to a reservoir six miles outside the delta, where they will never feast on smelt and salmon again. This doesn't please the bass anglers, who argue that striped bass populations themselves have plummeted in the delta, along with those of the salmon and smelt. The anglers, backed by Peter Moyle, a veteran fisheries scientist at UC Davis, believe that the federal and state pumps are a far bigger factor in the declines of native fish. Big farmers say it doesn't matter in the end if bass rank number one or number three on the list of culprits—good riddance. They're a junk fish whose sweet meat is so tainted with mercury that children and pregnant women shouldn't be eating them. At the same time, the growers are trying to force the California Fish and Game Commission to allow bass anglers to catch and keep more stripers, thinking it might allow the populations of salmon and smelt to recover and ultimately unshackle the government pumps. The commission so far has rejected their proposal by a 4–0 vote.

North of the delta, on the old floodplain of the Sacramento River, state biologists busy themselves with a different sort of meddle. They are attempting to manipulate the aquatic food chain to mimic conditions that existed before levees and dams were built, taking California backward a century, so to speak. The Department of Water Resources is working with rice farmers who are willing to run their ditch water and drain their tailwater down the Yolo Bypass. This is the old floodplain where, it turns out, even small puddles can create vibrant communities of phytoplankton and zooplankton that nourish the aquatic insects that feed the salmon and smelt.

The theory that loitering in the bypass can create large enough populations of hardy salmon and smelt to outlast their predators first occurred to Ted Sommer, the state biologist, two decades earlier. Each of his visits to the old floodplain showed its marvelous vascularity. All that rich aquatic life was ready to burst forth, if it could only drink a little water. Reconnecting the river to its plain was what newspaper editor Will Green had been harping about a century and a half ago: "Give the river room to breathe and spill out some of its water." Now rice farmers are directing river water into their canal systems and releasing it down the bypass. At first, Sommer wondered if the tailwater from rice fields carried some special ingredient that fattened the fish. But river water and groundwater, he found out, work, too. If the biologist gets his way, this demonstration project will turn into an official state program to release water down the bypass—twenty to thirty thousand acre-feet each year—where it can spread out, capture sunlight and grow fish. "So much of our focus has been on the south end of the delta—what's happening in the badlands," Sommer says. "This is about what's happening to the fish before they even hit the delta. Predation is one reality. Starvation is the other. If you're going to try to save a species, you have to find ways to deal with both."

I leave here fearing that the delta, a place every bit as stolen as Westlands, may be just as doomed. If not from the consequences of man's forever meddling then from the Big One, or the five-foot rise in sea level that will accompany climate change and mess up the delta's ebb and flow, or the next five-hundred-year flood that will breach the levees and drown everything from here to Sacramento. I recall the Wintu foretelling: *The white man makes too many demands of the earth. He stretches it too thin. Cracks will open up in the ground and swallow him up. The spirit of the land will strike back. First drought, then flood. When the Indians all die, then God will let the water come down from the north. Everyone will drown. The white people dig deep long tunnels. Eventually the water will come.*

I'm halfway home to Fresno, sailing along Highway 99, when I ring up the Oracle. I gave him the nickname many years ago, after he sequestered me in the back room of the Madera Irrigation District one sweltering summer afternoon and gave a marathon performance, four hours straight, about land and water and the booms and busts of agriculture stretching back to his grandfather, who grew up near the Leaning Tower of Pisa and arrived in the Italian-Swiss Colony of Madera in 1905.

"So you want to see something nuts?" the Oracle asks me. "Something that makes no sense?"

I'm no better than a smelt in the thrall of a giant pump. "I'll be there in a hour."

It's a few days shy of Thanksgiving, the afternoon sun still muscular in the sky. I pass the old Mission Bell winery and a gaudy mansion edged by cypress trees in the middle of farm country—a picture that no longer startles my eyes. This one measures twenty-eight thousand square feet and belongs to an Indian Sikh named Brar who operates thousands of acres of nuts, as well as hotels and a car dealership. His toys include a Gulfstream jet.

In the back of his own fancy farmhouse, the Oracle is waiting for me, and we hop into his GMC truck. A Muscat vineyardist since the age of seventeen, he is wearing a ball cap over his balding head, hiking boots and a white button-down long-sleeved shirt tucked tight into blue jeans. He stands five foot eight and has managed to make it to his mid-sixties without a pus gut, which is saying something around here. He talks fast in a high-pitched voice, and his hands never stop gesturing. Over the past few years, he's sold all his nut orchards and invested $20 million in commercial property in Idaho. As we head into the sun, he starts narrating the spread of farmland.

"When I was a kid, this was all open. You can understand the first expansion and maybe even the second expansion, but not the third and the fourth. When the expansions are happening in the middle of drought . . ." He doesn't finish his sentence. Between here and Chowchilla, inside the two irrigation districts, 225,000 acres are being farmed.

"How much of it deserves water?" I ask.

"Fifty thousand acres should have never been planted," he says.

We're crossing farmland of a different sort—acres that no irrigation district would annex because the soil sits heavy with salts. Here the nut trees and alfalfa drink from groundwater only. "There's a reason my grandfather and your grandfather never touched this land," he says. "It's the shits." In Australia, where he still grows wine grapes and almonds, this sort of ground would never be farmed. The government zones agricultural land no less than it zones commercial and residential property. Because water is scarce, Australia won't allow a farmer to plant grapes or fruit trees or alfalfa on poor soil. This was the concept that UC professor Sidney Harding tried, and failed, to impart here in the years before the Central Valley Project was hatched.

"Agriculture in the valley was unsustainable in the 1920s, and it's only gotten more unsustainable as we've made more money," the Oracle says. "We've dealt with agriculture the same way we've dealt with housing. We've given it over to a pattern of sprawl. We spread the resource of water farther and farther out until we became hooked on a deficit model."

I tell him he is speaking my language, and he feigns a flinch. Every time the farmers were about to confront the hard truth of scarcity, I say, society bailed them out. When crops grew beyond the capacity of our rivers, the government wouldn't tell them, "No more." Instead of letting farmers suffer the consequences of their overreach, the government came to the rescue. It stole them not one river but two. The Sacramento was boxed up and shipped here. The San Joaquin was boxed up and shipped to acres south. The growers then did what growers are fixed to do: They kept expanding. Madera County was no different from Fresno County or Tulare County or Kings County or Kern.

"The farmer cried wolf and got himself a new river and a couple of dams," he says. "When he went dry again, he figured, 'Why not cry wolf a second time?' He got himself a new project and an aqueduct. We bought some time. We saved ourselves for thirty or forty years. In that window, we doubled down again. We grew and grew, and now we're right back where we started, crying wolf again. Only this time, no one is listening."

He slows down in front of an almond grove and gestures to a well broken free of its moorings. Its motor tilts several feet into the air like a magician's cockeyed trick. "It's not the well that came up. It's the earth that sank down," he says. "In my time, we've gone from twenty-five-horsepower pumps to forty-horsepower to seventy-five-horsepower and now one hundred-fifty-horsepower. The earth keeps following in the other direction."

The reach of the Central Valley Project never made sense to him. The feds designated 1.1 million acres of farmland here in Madera and down in Tulare and Kern Counties to be served by the project, he points out. But they only had an average of 1.4 million acre-feet of water in any given year—a combination of Class I water and Class II flood flows—to distribute to the farmers. No crop could be grown on this amount alone. By drawing such a large footprint, the U.S. Bureau of Reclamation sent farmers the wrong message: Spread your federal water far and thin and pump the hell out of the groundwater to make up the difference. Had we limited the reach of the Central Valley Project to, say, 500,000 acres, it would have meant plenty of water for each acre farmed and some leftover for the fish. It would have put fewer demands on the aquifer. We could have created a very different kind of valley.

"We let agriculture grow too big. We overallocated the water," the Oracle says. "The problem has been coming for a long time, but we speeded it up when we should have slowed it down. Last year, the nurseries bred something like seventeen or eighteen million almond trees. Dave Wilson Nursery, by itself, did four million new trees. You're looking at 1.5 million acres of almonds in California in the next few years. The whole thing is built on a house of cards. When Trump is sworn in as president and starts a trade war, the almond grower won't know what to do."

We pass one farm with a sense of humor. A camel with a real hump paces the field. We pass a dairy feeding hay and water to thousands of

Holsteins, fouling the air and the aquifer at once. We skirt ten thousand acres of open, undulating ground that the Madera Irrigation District, in what can only be described as a boondoggle, bought for $37 million. The plan was to convert the old cattle ranch into a water bank not unlike the one Resnick controls down south in Kern, but the irrigation district was never able to secure the permits. To pay off the bonded debt, the district is now forced to raise its water rates on farmers and sell some of its precious river supply to developers. One of these developers is a billionaire Wall Street financier named Peter Castleman, who is now turning Madera farmland into a new town called Riverstone. A river devoted almost wholly to agriculture for more than a century is becoming a river of suburbia without a single raised voice from the county board of supervisors, much less the federal Bureau of Reclamation.

The Oracle would like to show me every acre of the three thousand acres of frail earth being turned into cropland during this drought alone. The old Daulton cattle ranch, for one, full of rocks and pebbles and sitting on a measly aquifer, will soon be sprouting nuts. But we're losing light, and he really wants me to see a ranch on Avenue 12 where the San Joaquin River, in flood years, carves a bypass. He takes a dirt road, and for a second we're lost in a swirl of dust. When the dust settles, there's a rusted barbed-wire fence on one side and thousands of young almond and pistachio trees looking about as forlorn as an orchard can look on the other side. Two thousand acres of old cattle ground—dirt that five generations of Madera farmers deemed unworthy of crops—now flows with water from three wells dug at least five hundred feet deep. The county permitted the wells even though the aquifer is one good drought away from being tapped out.

"Here's the madness I was talking about," he says, his face more bemused than pained. "Nuts and more nuts."

"This must have cost twelve grand an acre to develop," I say. "Who'd give them that kind of money on ground so lousy?"

"You'd be surprised how easy it is. You can talk about the farmer. You can talk about his greed. But equity is what created this sprawl."

"The banker, you mean?"

"That's who I'm talking about," he says. "I remember in 1971. The boom hit the grape business. All of a sudden, land took off, and everyone had instant equity. You'd go to the bank and say, 'Hey, I want to borrow against my ranch,' and they'd say, 'Sure, you want to plant another vineyard? You'd need some living expenses in the meantime?' Then you look up a few years later, and there's an oversupply of grapes. Suddenly, the banker isn't so friendly. The easy money ain't so easy anymore. You ride out the correction, and then some study shows that wine is good for the heart, and UC Davis ag comes out and says, 'You can't plant enough grapes.' And the Bank of America comes out and says, 'You can plant grapes on the rooftops.' "

He's on a roll, saying things farmers don't often say, and I stay out of his way.

"I've gone through three of these cycles, and none of them has been crazier than this one. In my grandfather's day, if you didn't have your land paid off, you couldn't add a single acre. Today, you can be carrying a debt of eight grand an acre, and they'll let you borrow twelve grand an acre to plant more almonds and pistachios. Equity and cheap interest rates means oversupply. And oversupply means a demand for water that cannot be met. The Federal Reserve can print all the phony money it wants. But it can't print water. We can put off the national debt, but we can't put off the day of reckoning out here."

"How ugly do you think it's going to get? With the new groundwater law and all?"

"Half of what we just drove through won't be here. The correction never happens on the front end. It happens on the bloody back end. That's why I sold my almond orchards. That's why I've taken my money to Boise. I'm telling my son, who's a grape grower, God bless him, to sit tight with the three hundred and thirty acres we already have. You don't want to be part of this bloodshed."

On the way back to his farmhouse, the Oracle and I kick around ideas that might bring a little sanity to the delirium, and maybe a small truce to the water wars. I write them down in my notebook like this:

1. Clear out manzanita and other brush in the Sierra. Harvest the smaller trees and prune the dead lower branches of the bigger ones. This will expand the mountain's capacity to hold snow and water and create new springs, not to mention reduce wildfires.

2. Stop building more dams upslope. Let's fund more water banks downslope in aquifers that can store one million acre-feet of water and more.

3. Restrict groundwater pumping to levels that are truly "safe yields." In Westlands, say good-bye to the days of pumping 700,000 acre-feet of groundwater to outlast drought. The safe yield is only 175,000 acre-feet. Westlands then sizes down from 500,000 acres to 250,000 acres.

4. Retire two million acres of irrigated farmland in the San Joaquin Valley. Reduce the "white areas" outside irrigation districts by half, if not more. Cropland in the valley slims down from six million acres to four million acres. Limit surface water imports to the highest-value crops on the best soils. Mega-dairies growing water-guzzling alfalfa should be given a check to relocate to states where cooler climes truly make for happy cows.

5. Build a scaled-down version of the Twin Tunnels. This will keep endangered fish out of the south delta. Spend more money on programs that send water into the Yolo Bypass to grow more salmon and smelt. Allow a just amount of snowmelt to follow its path to the ocean to lower salts in delta water.

6. Enhance water marketing by removing obstacles—physical and bureaucratic—that are complicating sales in the federal and state projects. This will encourage rice farmers up north to sell their excess water to farmers on the west side. Prohibit water transfers

The folly of an orchard planted too far from water's reach along Interstate 5

from farms to cities. Water set aside for irrigation districts and farming must continue to grow crops, not houses.

7. Draw a limit line around sprawling cities and create an agricultural preserve. Portland did it. Revise the tradition of "home rule" that allows counties, and not the state, to get the last word on new town growth. Protect the most productive farm region in the world. Suburban sprawl is a Ponzi scheme that costs cities more in services than it raises in revenues.

8. As climate change delivers more havoc, pass statewide bond measures to fund the building of ocean desalinization plants. This will free up water now shipped to Southern California and the Bay Area to be used inland where populations are growing.

9. Tax municipal water users $1 a month and assess a small fee on farm chemicals to fund the building and maintenance of water treatment plants. These plants will clean up the contaminated drinking water affecting hundreds of thousands of mostly poor Californians.

10. Continue statewide conservation measures that encourage residents to cut their water use. In this drought alone, the saved water adds up to 1.2 million acre-feet. This is more than the yield of the three new dam projects the hydraulic brotherhood is still pushing.

I read the list back to the Oracle. He thinks fallowing two million acres of farmland in the San Joaquin Valley might be going a bit too far, and he doesn't trust state bureaucrats or local politicians to mend the water markets or suburban sprawl. Other than that, he signs on. "I believe in capitalism, Mark," he says. "I believe in private property rights. But when it comes to water, a necessity of life, the system has to be tweaked. If we're going to keep growing food in this valley, we can't allow water to be sold to the highest bidder."

A harvest moon hangs orange in the sky over our old ranch by the river. There's enough light left and enough light gone that I can pretend it's 1955. My mother hasn't yet married my father, who's come back from his football scholarship at USC. My grandfather Aram, at the tail end of his peripatetic searching, has bought an eighty-acre ranch a little north of the San Joaquin. My grandmother is trying to turn one more broken-down farmhouse into a home. She and grandpa, who now live in old Fig Garden, are hoping to persuade my father to move out here and farm the ground. The earth isn't much. It's hardpan and hog wallow. The forty acres of vines are weak. The fig trees need a good pruning, and the peach and plum, if you want to do things right, ought to be pulled out. My dad is dating the "priest's daughter" from France, the same Flora Mekhitarian whose phone number he scrawled on the inside cover of the little green book on the Central Valley Project. There will be bickering over which Armenian church in Fresno will marry them, the right-wing one or the left-wing one, and my grandfather Mekhitarian, the firebrand anti-Communist preacher, will prevail.

It makes sense that my father, and not his older brother, is being groomed to run this ranch. He's a farmer in body and spirit who's enrolled in viticulture classes at Fresno State. He has given sweat and blood to this ground. He was discing the hardpan soil when the tractor got stuck in a low spot. Instead of hopping down from his seat and studying the situation, he decided to free the tractor by unhooking the disc. He grabbed the hitch pin that held the disc and yanked it out. The disc tongue, tension coiled, flew out and tore open his brow. A quarter inch lower and it would have taken his eye. A month later, he was pruning fig trees and piling the branches in a stack to burn. "It's too windy, Ara," my grandfather warned him. "We can burn it tomorrow." Grandpa disappeared into the barn, and Dad doused the pile with gasoline and struck a match and the fireball exploded back on him. A neighbor named Cobb saw him take off across the orchard, clothes aflame. He ran him down and made him roll in the dirt.

The third-degree burns, like the gash on Dad's brow, turned into scars I hardly noticed when I was growing up. I never recall him talking about the ranch. He'd take me to the river to launch golf balls, but we never crossed the bridge to the ground on the other side. With its quarter-mile entrance lined in pomegranate trees, that last ranch became a faraway picture to me. We had sold the eighty acres to a farmer, who sold it to a developer, who turned it into Rolling Hills Estates, so named after its hog wallow knolls. After my father was shot and killed, the river ranch became a way for us to imagine a different fate. Grandpa Arax told me one version of the story, and Grandma Arax told me another. "Your mother wanted to live in the city," Grandpa recalled.

"She told your father she wasn't going to live in a farmhouse full of rats. So we sold it." As Grandpa plunged deeper into senility, his accusations against my mother grew more shrill, even when he had forgotten her name and taken to calling her "the priest's daughter." "We would have saved your *fahder* had we kept that ranch by the river. He was farmer. Not a goddamn bartender. He'd get on that tractor and drive like hell. I'd say, 'Ara, what are you doing?' He'd say, 'I am enjoying.' But the priest's daughter refused to live there." In general, Grandma Arax did not give my mother much slack, either, but when it came to the last ranch, she blamed Grandpa. "Your grandfather was a gypsy. He did cuckoo things. He could never stay put. How many farms did he buy and sell? He should have guided that boy. He should have told Ara, 'The bar business is not your business.'"

I'm roving the streets of Rolling Hills Estates, trying to locate one pomegranate tree that bears the fruit of family history. Lovely houses sit on half-acre lots set off by sego palms and eucalyptuses and red, pink and white oleanders. Here's Pomegranate Road and Pomegranate Place and Pomegranate Court, but no pomegranate tree. I come upon a resident, who tells me that two of the three wells in the subdivision have run into sand. With only one well operating, homeowners are restricted to twice-weekly drip irrigation for their yards. "We're going dry," Julie Johnston says. "We're trying to find another strata worth digging for. Who knows how long the third well is going to last." Right behind her, on the other side of an olive grove, Riverstone rises as part of a new town of thirty thousand houses to be built over an aquifer that won't last itself. To secure the county's approval for the project, the developer has struck a deal across four county lines to import seven thousand acre-feet of water a year from a big farmer who has water challenges of his own. She's forgotten his name. "Stewart Resnick," I tell her.

I cross back over the river near the base of towering Friant Dam, where a year earlier I had stood with a team of federal and state biologists intent on restoring the long-gone spring run of Chinook salmon. They had spent the morning netting fifty-four thousand fingerlings out of the deep pool below the dam's face. The fish had been brought back to their ancestral home by order of a federal court. After an eighteen-year legal battle between local irrigation districts and the Natural

Fake water tower at Riverstone, a new town built on a depleted aquifer

Resources Defense Council in San Francisco, an environmental wrong had been righted. U.S. district court judge Lawrence Karlton found that Pat Brown, once as attorney general and a second time as governor, had flouted state law. Section 5937 of the California Fish and Game Code required dam operators—in this case, the U.S. Bureau of Reclamation—to release enough water to keep the fish alive. The ruling was sweet vindication for Jack Fraser, the state Fish and Game manager who had publicly challenged Brown in the 1950s to preserve a salmon run that history books describe this way: "The San Joaquin was a stream of pure icy water, and clear as a crystal. . . . Salmon ascended to the spawning grounds by the myriads, and when the run was on, the fish were hunted with spear, pitchfork, shovel, even with shotgun and revolver. It was recorded that restful sleep was disturbed because 'myriads of them can be heard nightly.'"

The fingerlings that had been placed into the pool of river two days earlier made no such noise. These weren't the wild Chinook salmon of my grandfather's day but a watered-down hatchery version. Yet once acquainted with this spot, they would acquire the ability to identify the chemical signature of the river in concentrations as low as one part per many trillions. If the experiment went well, they would link us to our prehistory, a living, leaping little dinosaur that would start in this pool and migrate out to the ocean and then return to this very spot in two or four or eight years. By the time the biologists are finished, it will have cost the federal and state governments $1.5 billion to revive the run.

This won't include the additional releases from the dam—184,000 acre-feet in dry years, 556,000 acre-feet in wet years—needed to restore the river's bone-dry stretches. Until then, the fish need a team of biologists to pull them out of the pool, put them in an oxygenated tank and truck them to another pool one hundred miles downstream.

"These are my babies," Elif Fehm-Sullivan, a scientist with National Marine Fisheries Service, told me as the crew loaded the fiberglass tank into a four-by-four truck. She lifted the hatch and let me take a peek inside. The fish, each one two and a half inches long and tagged with a code that said when and where it was planted, were doing backflips in the aerated water.

"Of the fifty-four thousand, how many will make it back here, you think?"

"If we're lucky, maybe seven or eight," she said.

It was at that point that I fully understood what we as a people had done. A river is a highly dynamic force that possesses incredible powers to heal itself. Like the salmon, it had been coded to find its way back. But our destruction of the San Joaquin—six dams upstream, a seventh dam right here, a flow devoted to agriculture with only a trickle left over for fish—was an incredible force of its own. No degree of noble gesture, certainly not $1.5 billion, would bring the old run back to life. In the 1940s, even before the last dam went in, the spring run had dwindled to fifty thousand or so salmon. We would be quite blessed now to see seven or eight fingerlings make their way back home.

It quit raining in my valley five years ago. The tule fog and frost quit, too. You might think this odd, but it isn't. Drought is California; flood is California. The lie is the normal. No society in history has gone to greater lengths to deny its fundamental nature than California. The Netherlands figured out long ago its arrangement with the sea. California, for a century and two-thirds now, keeps forgetting its arrangement with drought and flood. The repeat of each new cycle is greeted by the populace as a spectacle. Our staying dumb to our essential nature is such a shared trait that even among the most enlightened citizens of Los Angeles and San Francisco there exists a profound ignorance about where our water comes from. It comes from someplace else. The blankness runs deep and is self-justifying to the point that big-city residents feel something close to righteous indignation as they rip into the Fresno almond grower for drawing upon water swindled not from hundreds of miles away (like their water is) but from right beneath his feet. I've made the trek up and down the state three times and have yet to hear a politician, big-city or small-town, even come close to capturing the nuance of California water. Knowing how the subject has swallowed up eight or nine years on my clock, I can hardly blame them. Politicians have a much easier time pandering to the prejudices of their tribal backyard and listening to its local music. The north shouts water grab, the middle shouts we're feeding the world and the south shouts the greatness of its city.

What I have come to learn from the record of history is that every dry time turns to flood time soon enough. The rivers will jump their banks, and the delta will bust open its levees. Houses will drown, people too, and the journalists from the East Coast will parachute in to see apocalypse assume its opposite form. For a year or two, we'll debate the folly of building suburbs in a floodplain. Then the high water, listening to millennia, will give way to drought once more. California's back-and-forth, back-and-forth. It wouldn't be a disaster either way, just a matter of adjustments, if we weren't so insistent. But this is a place that earthquake and ice and volcano and ocean carved out and man decided to set hard lines to, declaring it one unified state even though it had a dozen or more states of nature residing within it.

Highest mountain, lowest desert—we've been trying for a century and two-thirds to reconcile the extremes of California. It would be too smug to call the effort hubris. The extremes gave rise to both the need and the ambition of a system. To enable our lesser lands—lesser only in God's shorting—a chance to be everything they might be, we dispatched the rain in our name. Together, the Central Valley Project and the State Water Project—the System—became the grandest hydraulic engineering feat known to man. California was a land whose magnitude could imagine such a thing. Here, a magnitude of geography met a magnitude of psychology to believe it could be possible. Here, we built a marvel of dams, aqueducts, canals and ditches that turned into a different gravity. The System became imbued with the force of nature itself. Its length and breadth became both its ambition and its flaw. Its movement created two if not three world-class cities and an agricultural colossus in the middle that outproduced every other farm region in the world. But like all great designs to remedy the slight of nature, its fabrication fell short.

We grew in wet years and kept growing in dry years. Whenever we found ourselves in the grips of one, we forgot about the other. If the other didn't exist in our heads, the other might never return. The boomers and farmers forgot worse than anybody. We can now see that the bulwark we put to the task wasn't enough to do all the things we believed we were entitled to do. The farmer wanted more than his 80 percent. The city wanted more than its 20 percent. Even in generous years of snowmelt, there wasn't anywhere near enough water to cover what the System promised us.

As an endeavor of grandiosity, the System was predicated on our notion of an average year of weather. All the presumptions of water capture and water delivery were based on "normal" rainfall and "normal" snowmelt. Year after year, the actual water captured and delivered fell short of the normal or far beyond it. Our System got it wrong the way all efforts designed to remedy nature's inconstancy get it wrong. The calculations of growth it relied on were premised on the lie of full delivery. The difference between what the System promised us and what it could actually supply was some two million acre-feet of water most years, a shortfall that didn't count drought. When the big flood came, it made us oblivious to scarcity all over again. We had so much water that we sprawled our cities and overplanted our crops. We had so little water that each region stole from the region just beyond it, so that Los Angeles stole from Owens, and Imperial stole from the Colorado, and San Francisco stole from Hetch Hetchy, and Bakersfield stole from Fresno, and Fresno stole from Sacramento, and Sacramento stole from Mount Shasta, where the System was born in a volcano's cistern, with water that dripped down from snows that had fallen a half century before.

We'd been shot out of Sutter's cannon. Ever since the poor captain weighed the nuggets discovered by Marshall and found out they were twenty-three-carat gold, we've been stuck in the same gear. Because our beginning was supercharged, we never had a chance to catch our breath and correct our excess. The fever never left our System. It followed us down the mountain to the valley. It became our System. We built a state capitol where two rowdy rivers met. We spent a century trying to conquer the Sacramento River. When we finished conquering it (or not), we killed the San Joaquin. Of all the crimes of the System, this is the one that cannot be forgiven. The farms of Tulare and Kern Counties had rivers of their own to exploit well enough. That they aspired beyond those rivers should not have been a price the San Joaquin had to pay.

The paradox of the Central Valley Project was that it was designed to save agriculture on one hand and exploit every drop of water on the other hand. The System pretended to draw lines on the land where water would go and not go. At the same time, it provided a method by which to exploit its buffer zones. Such a zone, anathema to the System's ideology, was promptly judged a wasted resource. To bloom every acre of land, every drop of river water had to be captured. The rivers, by force of pumps, ran backward before they ran empty, spilling their flow into a million and one ditches. A culture of importation took root. The demand for water became the demand for human labor, chemical, insect and fruit gene. The bee's journey and the migrant's journey were as serpentine and labyrinthine as the journey of the water. The lengths we went to put a nut inside a flower were no less, and no more, than the lengths we were now going to save a salmon.

I live in the city. I live in my head on the farm. The big, water-sucking corporate farmer is easy to paint from above. He becomes something more complicated, and compelling, on the ground. It makes sense to me that the middle of California looks different from the north or the south. It makes sense to me that the highest and best use of the land isn't suburbia. I know that almonds, pistachios, citrus and grapes are permanent crops that a farmer cannot fallow in dry times, but they're a lot less permanent than houses that sprawl across the desert. It may be perverse to think of it this way, but when water flows to nuts, fruits and vegetables instead of flowing to housing tracts, it not only feeds us but drives our cities—the enlightened ones anyway—to pursue a policy of infill, recharge and smarter growth. The farmer's almonds—and the gallon of water each nut drinks—are their own buffer. Can you imagine the mess California would be if it could call upon an unlimited supply of water?

If nothing else, drought imposes sobriety. Scarcity demands restraint. Given the seriousness of the drought before us—and the climate change we are about to face—one would think the question of slowing down growth might be broached. Instead, we ask communities that have existed for decades to cut their water consumption by a third so the savings can be banked, sold and shipped to some new town. Our rationing becomes a subsidy for the next developer. Likewise, we dodge the question of how long California can keep up its rate of growth. How many residents can we sustainably house? We already host the worst air in the nation and hold more people in poverty than any other state in the Union, even as we leapfrog Great Britain to become the fifth-largest economy in the world. Kudos to us for investing to build an economy not on fossil fuel but on green technology. But with growth as our guiding light, we now have arrived at forty million people. Can we sustain fifty million? Seventy-five million?

If we're going to find a way to save a robust form of agriculture in the middle, we have to be honest about what we're saving. The valley has become a fool of its own branding. We keep telling ourselves, and anyone who'll listen, that we feed the nation, that we produce a quarter, if not more, of the food in America's refrigerator and pantry, and this doesn't count what we're shipping to Asia, Europe, Mexico and Canada. We'd be more honest to say that we grow the nuts and fruits and vegetables that can't be grown elsewhere, or at least not with the quality and fecundity that we grow them here. Let the rest of America raise corn and soybeans, wheat, alfalfa and cotton. Let the Holsteins go to states where the water and soil aren't so valuable. We need to keep on growing our specialty crops. In the process, we should face the fact that we probably won't be saving California's small farmer. He's as endangered as the delta smelt. Instead, we'll be saving the custom grower who farms soil owned by insurance companies, investment groups and hedge funds. We will be saving family farmers whose families made enough wise decisions over the decades that they possess abundant land, abundant wells, abundant water and children still interested in growing fruits and nuts, if not an agrarian life. Will they find a way to pay the worker a wage that reflects the brutality and skill of his or her labor? Will they find a way to consume less water and spray fewer chemicals?

At night, the stacks of history on the picnic tables that crowd my office talk back to me. Father Serra wants to issue an apology on behalf of himself and the Franciscans. Chief Tenaya, more gracious than angry, says his curse against the white man has gone on long enough. Sutter remains a fusty fool forever aggrieved. Miller, the cattle king, is haunted by the entrails of the slaughtered. Muir wants to take me, and my fear of bears, nine thousand feet up into his granite temple. Luther Burbank, father of the Santa Rosa plum, offers a crossbreeding solution for the sudden drop in production of my apricot trees. J. G. Boswell wants to pour the two of us a shot of Jack Daniel's and chew the rag. We burned through Eden in the blink of an eye, he tells me. At the edge of a continent, there seemed no way back. He sees another end to the valley. It won't happen in my lifetime or even in the lifetime of my children. But it will happen soon enough and without the spilling of blood. The farmer, as it should be, will make the final call. The returns on his nuts and mandarins flattened out, he'll decide that the water is worth more than the land. In another sequel to *Chinatown,* he'll sell his share of the snowmelt to the city.

Agriculture's piece of the water pie will go from 80 percent to 70 percent almost without anyone noticing. It will stay at 60 percent and then at 50 percent, moving in a direction that California is all too familiar with. The farmland will not be erased, for there is simply too much of it. But the middle of the state will move closer and closer to the model of Los Angeles, the old suburb putrefying from the core so that the new suburb on the edge can rise and take its place. This will be accomplished through the clean efficiency of the water market. The farmer will do it to himself. Boswell's children and his children's children control 15 percent of the Kings River. The flow in an average year (we know there isn't such a thing) is 1.7 million acre-feet. That's a lot of housing tracts and mini-malls. Of course, the environmentalists, watching an even more debased form of ecological degradation rising in the valley, won't wish to recognize their hand in it. They'll blame the farmer's greed.

At night, when my fret gets the best of me, this is the future I imagine. And then in the morning, I look out the window and it is California again. I pick up the *New York Times* and read that we are defeating drought by every measure but precipitation. We've won back every job lost in the Great Recession and set a record for employment. We're creating nine thousand new jobs a week. No other state comes close. The drought and its Dust Bowl fearmongering have inspired no exodus. Even as our snowpack in the Sierra measures the puniest it's been since

California became California, our population grows faster than ever. Even as the earth keeps sinking, the farmers of Kern, Kings, Tulare, Fresno and Madera keep churning out crops of record value. The fig trees of Fig Garden may be gone, but there are six thousand acres of them, including a new variety with tiger stripes, now growing on the other side of the San Joaquin.

EPILOGUE
(FALL–WINTER 2017)

A pomegranate on the eve of harvest

Autumn arrives with the strangeness of clouds. The rain starts to fall, big, fat, slashing drops that feel like electricity on my open palm. It hardly ceases for the next five months. Drought turns to flood. The mudslides and the wildfires can't be far behind. The winter goes down as one of the wettest in recorded history. So much snowmelt comes down the mountain that it nearly takes out Oroville Dam. The dam ends up holding and the levees, too. All the new water pours into the delta, and what doesn't go out to sea fills up the aqueduct again. The State Water Project, for the first time in six years, delivers surplus flows. Tule fog sets down again in the valley. The great drought is officially over. California is free to return to its amnesia.

The Wonderful Company has enough water to irrigate its orchards in Lost Hills and park tens of thousands of acre-feet in the water bank. The Resnicks are growing again. From the east side of Tulare County to the west side of Fresno County, they're planting more nuts and Halos. Of the 22,000 acres they ripped out during the drought, 18,000 acres are being replanted to pistachios. On Sleepy Farm Road outside Paso Robles, the Resnicks are looking to add 380 acres of wine grapes and build a small reservoir to fill with groundwater. One of the neighbors watches in disgust as the bulldozers tear into the hillside. Thousands of California oaks are felled. Only after the media are alerted do Stewart and Lynda claim to have discovered the clear-cutting. Up and down the Central Coast, restaurants begin boycotting their Justin wines. "When we learned of the terrible situation, not to mention our poor reputation within the community, we were ashamed and are sorry," their official statement reads. "We were asleep at the wheel. We are horrified by the lack of regard for both neighbor and nature, and we hope that the community will accept our deepest and most sincere apologies and find it in their hearts to forgive us." They pledge to donate the 380 acres to charity.

I write an e-mail to the Wonderful PR team. A day later, I receive a call from Mr. Resnick. It's been more than a year since he gave me the cold shoulder at the pistachio conference. He tells me to meet him in Lost Hills.

He's dressed Italian chic in Loro Piana jeans and Hogan tennis shoes. "I would have worn my Levi's," he says, "but Lynda's here, and she thinks I dress like a bum." We're standing in the sun outside the plant's corporate office, a building whose clean lines and retro furniture wear the imprint of Lynda, too. He's surrounded by a half dozen of his top men and women, the same ones who've been artfully dodging me for the past three years. They greet me with smiles and handshakes. A van pulls up to the curb, and the door slides open. Resnick has saved the front seat for me. "You're the one who needs to see," he says.

We pull out of the parking lot, past palm trees and roses, and head up the thin ribbon of Highway 33 into the dust-swirling tunnel of nuts and fruits. The big goateed man behind the wheel is Bernard Puget, a Basque sheepman's son who oversees these orchards. As we hop down from the van to inspect pomegranates on the eve of harvest, Resnick motions to Bernard's belly. In his best nasal Borscht Belt accent, he takes a jab: "Bernard, what's happened? You get exempted from the company's wellness program?" Bernard has actually lost a few pounds. "I'm down, Stewart," he protests. "I'm down."

The leathery skin on the fruit has turned a nice orange-red. Each bush is saddled with more than a hundred pomegranates the size of softballs and baseballs. The softballs will go to market as whole fresh fruit or as seedpods in a package. The baseballs will be crushed into juice.

"These are loaded," Resnick says. "It sure looks heavier than last year."

Bernard smiles and nods to the others. "He's fishing right now. He thinks I've understated the crop."

Resnick grabs at a pomegranate that might win a blue ribbon at the fair and tries to twist it free. No luck. He yanks and pulls and it finally comes off, throwing him a foot backward. "You sure this isn't eighteen tons an acre?" he says, goading.

"It's loaded," Bernard says. "But for every good-sized fruit, there's a bunch that never sized up." Resnick gives him one of his looks. "What?" Bernard says. "You don't believe me?"

"No, I believe you," Resnick says. "It's going to be what it's going to be. We'll still make money."

We pile back into the van and head up the road. Then it hits me. This isn't any road. This is Twisselman. Bernard, hard to believe, is driving straight toward the aqueduct. The knoll begins to rise. I gaze out the passenger window looking for the glint of Resnick's secret pipeline. It should be right here, but I don't see it. It's gone. I glance back at Resnick. He's oblivious, or so it seems. Bernard's eyes are fixed straight ahead. He's trying to play dumb, but I can see the slyest of grins peeking out from under his mustache.

"It's gone," I say. "How come?"

"We don't need it anymore," he whispers.

Back at the plant, Lynda is meeting with Wonderful doctors, nurses and farmworkers. They're coming up with ideas that might lead to a bigger drop in the number of employees with diabetes. Stewart tries to interrupt, but she won't let him. He's not the boss in this room. "Thirty-five percent of our prediabetic population has gone into the healthy range,"

Aqueduct brimming with snowmelt, California replenished for now

she tells the team. "They're no longer in danger. Now they have to keep that up, right? So how do we do even better next year?"

Stewart guides me to the company café, and we grab our lunches from the buffet. He unfolds a twenty-dollar bill from a wad he keeps inside a bent paper clip, and we take a seat in the far corner. For a silent minute, we dig into our bowls. I feel his gaze going past me, hear his voice turning oddly sentimental.

"When I look around here at what we've built and then look back at my life in New Jersey, I think, 'How did it happen?' For one man and woman to build something like this would be almost impossible today."

One hundred and twenty thousand acres of nuts and fruits and berries in California and still counting. They had survived the drought. Did it teach him any lessons?

"Lessons?" he says, sounding perplexed. "Who knows when a five-year drought is coming? Who anticipates that you can't fill a water bank for six or seven years?"

"Come on," I say. "It's California."

"Sure. But you take some risks in business. And when you've been as lucky as we've been, you start to think you can ride out drought, too."

He did learn one lesson: You can plant only so many acres on ground that has no groundwater. From now on, they'll expand on land that offers a double protection against drought. "State or federal water isn't enough. We want good groundwater, too."

"You mean no more pipelines carrying water in the dead of night?"

"The pipeline . . ." He stammers a bit. "Look, I delegate a lot of things, obviously. I'm sure I knew we had a pipeline in there. But that's not an issue I deal with."

"How much water was it bringing in?"

"I don't even know what it was, to be honest with you."

I take a last bite of cauliflower rice. I know there's a more forceful way to ask the question, but to what end? This was the same distance—geographic, psychic—that allowed him and Lynda to clear-cut the oaks and to kill off the independent pistachio commission, to grab a water bank that belonged to the state and to pretend for thirty years that Lost Hills wasn't a place of dire need. It is the same distance that allows them to control more land and water—130 billion gallons a year—than any other man or woman in California and still believe it isn't enough.

"I know I can't do this forever," he says. "I'm eighty years old. Problem is, I feel like I'm fifty. I feel too good to give any of it up."

His oldest son is retired in Seattle. His second son is a psychiatrist. His daughter, who used to own a restaurant, is busy raising her only son. Lynda has a son who works as a musician and a son who suffered a birth trauma and lives in a care facility. Their four grandchildren have visited the orchards once or twice. Not a single one of them wants any part of Wonderful.

"Who gets the keys to the kingdom?"

"I don't know. All I know is, I don't want to split it up or sell it in some leveraged buyout. I want to know that what we built will continue into the future."

He takes a look at his watch. He's got another meeting to attend. As he walks away, I notice his $400 sneakers. They're dusty with San Joaquin dirt.

I retrace the road I came in on and cross old Tulare Lake, which rose by flood and sank by drought. Four tribes of Yokut lived along its shores. On the shallow bottom, the women fished for mussels and clams with their toes. The nets of the Chinese during the gold rush caught terrapin that was served as turtle soup in the fanciest restaurants in San Francisco. Then the men of cotton, driven out of the South by the boll weevil, put the five rivers into canals and dried up the lake. They made a new plantation here. Before he died at age eighty-six, J. G. Boswell told me what a fool he and his forebears had been for wasting water, sun and soil in California to raise fiber, of all things. Cotton still grows on the lake bottom, but less and less each year. Thousands of acres of pistachio trees now await the next flood. Boswell's pumps reach twenty-five hundred feet into the earth looking for water to grow crops, looking for water to sell. For now, they're selling it to farmers like Resnick who can pay the price.

The extraction of water beneath the lake bottom won't last forever. California's new law that aims to regulate groundwater pumping will go into full effect in a decade or two. Whether it ends up retiring a couple million acres of cropland remains to be seen. By then, Wonderful, if it still exists, will be a portfolio run by men even farther away than Beverly Hills. Some of the water stripped from the land and sold to developers will stay here, and some will go over the mountain. In my lifetime alone, California has gone from fourteen million people to forty million. Nothing will stop the houses. The wheat king begets the cattle king, and the cattle king begets the cotton king, and the cotton king begets the nut king and pomegranate princess. Like the waters of the lake, the indent of the Resnicks will recede from the land, too. The Yokut had a saying that when the farmer drained the last drops of snowmelt from Tulare Lake, the water would return. It would return as tule fog to remind the white man of his theft. The fog is our history.

ACKNOWLEDGMENTS

A book piles up its debt on the sly. Before you realize it, you owe the very capable research assistant at the downtown library your house. Of course the bank owns the greater portion of your house. And the research assistant wouldn't take the money anyway. She did it as a favor for the sake of the book. Because she still believes in the idea of such a thing.

I imagine this is why this page was invented long ago—to acknowledge debts that cannot be repaid. The author does this one of two ways: Having kept track of each obligation along the road, he lists in alphabetical order (so as to not rank or offend) every giver. For the first two years of this project, I honored such a list, and it grew and grew until it included two hundred and forty eight people. Then I lost the list, or maybe I tossed the list.

After 500 pages of storytelling, it occurs to me that the fewer names on this page the better. So here is my posse of ten:

Kris Dahl, my one and only literary agent who has never once treated me like the "mid-lister" I am.

Andrew Miller, my editor at Knopf, who harbored not a single East Coast cliche about California. He wanted a book about California as a native son saw it. *Let memory inform the idiosyncratic.*

Pete King, my dear friend and "the first reader" on each of my books, a task in which the reading is the least of it.

Kit Rachlis, one of the finest editors in the country, a mensch who edited the excerpt, "A Kingdom From Dust," that appeared in *California Sunday* and then gave the whole book a final close read.

Tom Willey, farmer and scholar who has enriched my life for the past twenty years, first with his one-of-a-kind organic leeks and then with his one-of-a-kind meditations on agriculture, science and history.

Jem Bluestein, musician and healer who read my earliest draft (far more sprawling) aloud to his wife and told me it did not act as a soporific.

Paul Gilmore, gifted local professor of water and power who assured me I wasn't being too facile with the history.

Joel Pickford, photographer, author, linguist and close buddy who agreed to curate the historical photos and shoot the present-day ones even though I handed him the chore thirty days before deadline.

And, finally, Joseph Arax and Jake Arax, my two sons who have lived amid my piles of drought and flood for the past five years. May they remember the lamb barbecues every Sunday and the fresh vegetables, fruits and eggs from our backyard garden in northwest Fresno.

BIBLIOGRAPHY

Books and Bound Journals

Arax, Mark. *West of the West.* New York: Public Affairs, 2009.

Arax, Mark, and Rick Wartzman. *The King of California.* New York: Public Affairs, 2003.

Beebe, Rose Marie, and Robert M. Senkewicz, eds. *Lands of Promise and Despair: Chronicles of Early California, 1535–1846.* Santa Clara and Berkeley, Calif.: Santa Clara University and Heyday Books, 2001.

Billington, David P., Donald C. Jackson, and Martin V. Melosi. *The History of Large Federal Dams: Planning, Design and Construction in the Era of Big Dams.* Denver: U.S. Department of the Interior, Bureau of Reclamation, 2005.

Boule, David. *The Orange and the Dream of California.* Santa Monica, Calif.: Angel City Press, 2013.

Brechin, Gray. *Imperial San Francisco: Urban Power, Earthly Ruin.* Berkeley: University of California Press, 2006.

Brewer, William H. *Up and Down California in 1860–1864.* Berkeley: University of California Press, 1966.

Bunnell, Lafayette H. *Discovery of the Yosemite.* New York: Fleming H. Revell Co., 1892.

Carle, David. *Introduction to Water in California.* Berkeley: University of California Press. 2009.

The Central Valley Project. Compiled by the Workers of the Writers' Program of the Works Projects Administration. Sacramento: California State Department of Education, 1942.

Cerve, W. S. *Lemuria: The Lost Continent of the Pacific.* San Jose, Calif.: Supreme Grand Lodge of Amorc, 1931.

Clemings, Russell. *Mirage: The False Promise of Desert Agriculture.* San Francisco: Sierra Club Books, 1996.

Dana, Julian. *The Sacramento: River of Gold.* New York: Farrar & Rinehart, Inc., 1939.

Daniel, Cletus E. *Bitter Harvest: A History of California Farmworkers, 1870–1941.* Ithaca, N.Y.: Cornell University Press, 1981.

de Roos, Robert. *The Thirsty Land: The Story of the Central Valley Project.* Washington, D.C.: BeardBooks, 1948.

Deverell, William, and Tom Sitton. *Water and Los Angeles.* Oakland: University of California Press, 2017.

DeVoto, Barnard. *The Year of Decision, 1846.* 1942. Reprint, New York: Truman Talley Books, 2000.

Didion, Joan. *The White Album.* New York: Simon & Schuster, 1979.

Diener, Mary Alice Ferry. *Westside Pioneer Farmers.* Fresno, Calif.: Pioneer Publishing, 1989.

Dillon, Richard. *Fool's Gold: A Biography of John Sutter.* New York: Coward-McCann, 1967.

Dunne, John Gregory. *Delano: The Story of the California Grape Strike.* New York: Farrar, Straus & Giroux, 1967.

Federal Writers Project of the Works Progress Administration. *San Francisco in the 1930s: The WPA Guide to the City by the Bay.* Berkeley: University of California Press, 2011.

Gottlieb, Robert. *A Life of Its Own: The Politics and Power of Water.* New York: Harcourt, Brace and Jovanovich, 1988.

Hackel, Steven. *Junípero Serra: California's Founding Father.* New York: Farrar, Straus and Giroux, 2014.

Hallowell, Joell, and Coke Hallowell, eds. *Take Me to the River: Fishing, Swimming and Dreaming on the San Joaquin.* Berkeley, Calif.: Heyday Books, 2010.

Harris, Tom. *Death in the Marsh.* Washington, D.C.: Island Press, 1991.

Hundley, Norris, Jr. *The Great Thirst. Californians and Water: A History.* Berkeley: University of California Press, 2001.

Hurtado, Albert L. *John Sutter: A Life on the North American Frontier.* Norman: University of Oklahoma Press, 2008.

Hutchings' Illustrated California Magazine. Volumes 1–5. Bound reprints from the University of Michigan Library, July 1856–June 1861.

Igler, David. *Industrial Cowboys: Miller & Lux and the Transformation of the Far West, 1850–1920.* Berkeley: University of California Press, 2001.

Ingram, B. Lynn, and Frances Malamud-Roam. *The West Without Water.* Berkeley: University of California Press, 2013.

Johnson, Stephen, Gerald Haslam, and Robert Dawson. *The Great Central Valley: California's Heartland.* Berkeley: University of California Press, 1993.

Karl, William L. *Water and Power.* Berkeley: University of California Press, 1982.

Kelley, Robert *Battling the Inland Sea.* Berkeley: University of California Press, 1989.

Kowalewski, Michael, ed. *Gold Rush: A Literary Exploration.* Berkeley, Calif.: Heyday Books, 1997.

Kramer, W. M. *San Francisco's Fighting Jew.* N.p.: California Historical Society, 1974.

Lund, Jay, Ellen Hanak, William Fleenor, Richard Howitt, Jeffrey Mount, and Peter Moyle. *Envisioning Futures for the Sacramento–San Joaquin Delta.* San Francisco: Public Policy Institute of California, 2007.

Maass, Arthur, and Raymond L. Anderson. *And the Desert Shall Rejoice.* Malabar, Fla.: Robert E. Krieger Publishing, 1986.

Madley, Benjamin. *An American Genocide.* New Haven, Conn.: Yale University Press, 2016.

McFarland, J. Randall. *Water for a Thirsty Land: The Consolidated Irrigation District and Its Canal Development History*. Selma, Calif.: Consolidated Irrigation District, 1996.

McWilliams, Carey. *Factories in the Fields*. Boston: Little, Brown and Company, 1939.

———. *Southern California Country: An Island on the Land*. New York: Duell, Sloan & Pearce, 1946.

Madgic, Bob. *The Sacramento: A Transcendent River*. Anderson, Calif.: River Bed Books, 2013.

Mount, Jeffrey F. *California Rivers and Streams. The Conflict Between Fluvial Process and Land Use*. Berkeley: University of California Press, 1995.

Muir, John. *His Life and Letters and Other Writings*. Edited by Terry Gifford. London: Baton Wicks, 1996.

———. *The Mountains of California*. New York: Dorset Press, 1894.

Nordhoff, Charles H. *California for Travelers and Settlers*. Berkeley, Calif.: Ten Speed Press, 1973.

O'Neill, Bill. *A Mountain Never Too High: The Story of J. E. O'Neill*. Fresno, Calif.: Valley Publishers, 1977.

Orfalea, Gregory. *Journey to the Sun: Junípero Serra's Dream and the Founding of California*. New York: Scribner, 2014.

Orsi, Richard J. *Sunset Limited: The Southern Pacific Railroad and the Development of the American West, 1850–1930*. Berkeley: University of California Press, 2005.

Orsi, Richard J., and Kevin Starr. *California History: The Magazine of the California Historical Society*. Four vols.: Summer and Fall 1997, Winter 1997 and 1999, Summer 2000, vol. 81, nos. 3–4. Berkeley: University of California Press, 2003.

Paterson, Alan M. *Land, Water and Power: A History of the Turlock Irrigation District, 1887–1987*. Spokane, Wash.: Arthur H. Clarke, 2004.

Pisani, Donald J. *From the Family Farm to Agribusiness: The Irrigation Crusade in California and the West, 1850–1931*. Berkeley: University of California Press, 1984.

Polley, Frank J. "Americans at the Battle of Cahuenga." *Annual Publication of the Historical Society of Southern California* 3, no. 2 (1894): 47–54.

Provost, James R. *Development of the Kings River*. [Fresno, Calif.]: self-published, 2014.

Reisner, Marc. *Cadillac Desert: The American West and Its Disappearing Water*. New York: Penguin Books, 1993.

Rose, Gene. *The San Joaquin: A River Betrayed*. Clovis, Calif.: Word Dancer Press, 1992.

Royce, Josiah. *California: A Study of American Character*. Berkeley, Calif.: Heyday Books, 2002.

Sackman, Douglas Cazaux. *Orange Empire: California and the Fruits of Eden*. Berkeley: University of California Press, 2005.

Sakayan, Doris. *Armenian Proverbs in English Translation*. Montreal, Quebec: Arod Books, 2009.

Saroyan, William. *My Name Is Aram*. New York: Harcourt, Brace and Company, 1937.

Sawyer, Charles, ed. *One Man Show: Henry Miller in the San Joaquin*. Los Banos, Calif.: Ralph Milliken Museum Society and Loose Change Publications, 2003.

Shoup, Laurence H. *Rulers and Rebels: A People's History of Early California, 1769–1901*. iUniverse, 2010.

Sisk, B. F. *The Memoir of Bernie Sisk: A Congressional Record*. Fresno, Calif.: Panorama West, 1980.

Starr, Kevin. *Inventing the Dream*. New York: Oxford University Press, 1985.

Stoll, Steven. *The Fruits of Natural Advantage: Making the Industrial Countryside in California*. Berkeley: University of California Press, 1998.

Street, Richard Steven. *Beasts of the Field: A Narrative History of California Farmworkers, 1769–1913*. Stanford, Calif.: Stanford University Press, 2004.

Thornton, Bruce. *Searching for Joaquín: Myth, Murieta, and History in California*. San Francisco: Encounter Books, 2003.

Treadwell, Edward F. *The Cattle King: A Biographical Account of Henry Miller of the Miller & Lux Cattle Empire*. Fresno, Calif.: Valley Publishers, 1931.

Vandor, Paul. *History of Fresno County*. Los Angeles: Historic Record Company, 1919.

Worster, Donald. *Rivers of Empire: Water, Aridity, and the Growth of the American West*. New York: Oxford University Press, 1985.

Zack, Richard. *Quest for Water: Tulare Irrigation District—Its History, People and Progression*. Carlsbad, Calif.: PartnerPress, 2016.

Reports, Articles, Oral Histories

Potential for Irrigation and Agriculture in California:

Committee on Rivers and Harbors, House of Representatives. *Reports on the Control of Floods in the River Systems of the Sacramento Valley and the Adjacent San Joaquin Valley*. Washington, D.C.: Government Printing Office, 1911.

History of Fresno County, California, with Illustrations, Descriptions of Its Scenery, Farms, Residences, Public Buildings. San Francisco: Wallace W. Elliott, 1882.

Mead, Elwood. *Report of Irrigation Investigations in California*. Washington, D.C.: U.S. Department of Agriculture, 1901.

Meteorological Department of the State Agricultural Society. "Brief Notes on Resources of State of California for the Year 1887," *Annual Meteorological Review of the State of California*, 1888.

Thickens, Virginia E. "Pioneer Agricultural Colonies of Fresno County." *California Historical Society Quarterly* 25, no. 1 (1946): 17–38.

Documentation That Early Agriculture in the San Joaquin Valley Was Expanding Too Rapidly and onto Inferior Soils and Causing Unsustainable Pumping of Groundwater:

Adams, Frank, David N. Morgan, and Walter E. Packard. "Economic Report of San Joaquin Valley Areas Being Considered for Water Supply Relief Under Proposed California State Water Plan." Berkeley, Calif.: U.S. Bureau of Reclamation, 1930.

Harding, Sidney T. *Ground Water Resources of the Southern San Joaquin Valley*. Sacramento: California State Department of Public Works, 1927.

Harding, Sidney T. *A Life in Western Water Development*. Edited by Gerald J. Giefer. Berkeley: Berkeley: Regional Oral History Office, Bancroft Library, University of California, 1967.

The Case to Build the Central Valley Project, First and Second Phases:

Adams, Frank, David N. Morgan, and Walter E. Packard "Economic Report of San Joaquin Valley Areas Being Considered for Water Supply Relief Under Proposed California State Water Plan." Berkeley, Calif.: U.S. Bureau of Reclamation, 1930.

Autobee, Robert. "Friant Division: Central Valley Project." *U.S. Bureau of Reclamation Historical Review,* 1994.

Central Valley Basin. A Comprehensive Departmental Report on the Development of the Water and Related Resources of the Central Valley Basin, and Comments from the State of California and Federal Agencies. Senate Document 113. Washington, D.C.: U.S. Department of the Interior, 1949.

Chatters, Ford A. *View from the Central Valley: The California Legislature, Water, Politics and the State Personnel Board.* Interviewed by Amelia R. Fry. Berkeley: Regional Oral History Office, Bancroft Library, University of California, 1976.

Marshall, Col. Robert Bradford. *Irrigation of Twelve Million Acres in the Valley of California.* Sacramento: California State Irrigation Association, 1919.

Montgomery, Mary, and Marion Clawson. *History of Legislation and Policy Formation of the Central Valley Project.* Berkeley, Calif.: U.S. Department of Agriculture, Bureau of Agricultural Economics, 1946.

Posz, Gary. *The Central Valley Project and the Role of Frank Mixter and the Freemasons.* Chronicles of the Hydraulic Brotherhood blog, 2015.

San Luis Unit, Central Valley Project: Hearing Before the Subcommittee on Irrigation and Reclamation of the Committee on Interior and Insular Affairs, U.S. Senate. March 16–18, 1959. Washington, D.C.: U.S. Government Printing Office, 1959.

Special Task Force Report on San Luis Unit, Central Valley Project. Washington, D.C.: U.S. Department of the Interior, U.S. Government Printing Office, 1978.

Stene, Eric. A. "Sacramento River Division: Central Valley Project." *U.S. Bureau of Reclamation Historical Review,* 1994.

Stene, Eric A. "Shasta Division: Central Valley Project." *U.S. Bureau of Reclamation Historical Review,* 1996.

Summary Report on the Water Resources of California and a Coordinated Plan for Their Development: A Report to the Legislature of 1927. Bulletin No. 12. Sacramento: California Department of Public Works. Sacramento, 1927.

Supplemental Report of Water Resources in California: A Report to the Legislature of 1925. Bulletin No. 9. Sacramento: California Department of Public Works, 1925.

Water Resources of California: A Report to the Legislature of 1923. Bulletin No. 4. Sacramento: California Department of Public Works. 1923.

Social and Economic Pros and Cons of the Central Valley Project, Including Enforcement of the 160-Acre Rule and Environmental Consequences of Exporting Water Out of the Delta:

Abel, Edson. "The Central Valley Project and the Farmers." *California Law Review* 38, no. 4 (October 1950): 653–65.

Clawson, Marion, et al. *The Effect of the Central Valley Project on the Agricultural and*

Industrial Economy and on the Social Character of California. Berkeley, Calif.: U.S. Department of Agriculture, Bureau of Agricultural Economics, 1945.

Frampton, Mary Louise. "The Enforcement of Federal Reclamation Law in the Westlands Water District: A Broken Promise." *U.C. Davis Law Review* 13, no. 89 (1979): 89–122.

Graham, Leland O. "The Central Valley Project: Resource Development of a Natural Basin." *California Law Review* 38, no. 4 (October 1950): 588–637.

Hanemann, Michael, and Caitlin Dyckman. "The San Francisco Bay-Delta: A Failure of Decision-Making Capacity." *Environmental Science and Policy* 12, no. 6 (October 2009): 710–25.

Factual Reports for the U.S. Bureau of Reclamation Designating Boundary Lines, Acreage and Soil Types for Irrigation Districts in the Central Valley Project:

Orange Cove Irrigation District, 1947.
Lindmore Irrigation District, 1948.
Tulare Irrigation District, 1949.
Chowchilla Water District, 1950.
Delano-Earlimart Irrigation District, 1950.
Exeter Irrigation District, 1950.
Lindsay-Strathmore Irrigation District, 1950.
Madera Irrigation District, 1950.
Shafter-Wasco Irrigation District, 1950.
Southern San Joaquin Municipal Utility District, 1950.
Terra Bella Irrigation District, 1950.
Porterville Irrigation District, 1952.
Arvin-Edison Water Storage District, 1954.
Lower Tule Irrigation District, 1955.
Pixley Irrigation District, 1958.

Statistics for Irrigated Acres and Crops in California (Statewide and County by County):

"Agricultural Developments in the Friant Region." Testimony of Professor W. Michael Hanemann, 2005.

Annual crop reports from Madera, Fresno, Tulare, Kings and Kern Counties, 1940–2017, at five-year intervals.

"California Harvested and Irrigated Acres, 1924–2012." Statistical analysis compiled at the author's request by the California Department of Agriculture, using the U.S. Census of Agriculture data.

California State Board of Agriculture. *Statistical Report for the Year 1920.* Sacramento: California State Printing Office, 1921.

Kern-Tulare Water District crop reports, 2011–2015.

Note: Yearly crop and acreage statistics can vary depending on which agency—local, state or federal—is compiling the data. The author consulted multiple sources for such estimates.

The Death of the San Joaquin River:

Bork, Karrigan, Joseph F. Krovoza, Jacob V. Katz, and Peter B. Moyle. "The Rebirth of California Fish & Game Code Section 5937: Water for Fish." *UC Davis Law Review* 45 (2012): 809–913.

E-mail correspondence with Bill Kier, retired California Fish and Game biologist and state senate principal consultant.

Firpo, Robert. "The Plain 'Dam!': Language of Fish & Game Code Section 5937—How California's Clearest Statute Has Been Diverted from Its Legislative Mandate." *Hastings West Northwest Journal of Environmental Law and Policy* 11, no. 2 (2005): 101–20.

State Water Rights Board Decision No. D 935, June 2, 1959.

The Monterey Agreement That Amended State Water Project Contracts, Allowed Big Ag to Grab the Kern Water Bank and Eased Farm-to-Urban Water Sales:

Internal documents and confidential memorandum of the Kern County Water Agency, 1994.

Keats, Adam, and Chelsea Tu. "Not All Water Stored Underground Is Groundwater: Aquifer Privatization and California's 2014 Groundwater Sustainable Management Act." *Golden Gate University Environmental Law Journal* 93 (2016): 93–108.

Testimonial of Tom Clark, former head of the Kern County Water Agency, and Gary Bucher, Clark's assistant, August 8, 2008.

"Water Paper" review of the Monterey Agreements. Kern County Water Agency, 1994.

Effects of the 2011–2016 Drought on Farms and Cities:

The author interviewed between 275 and 300 people across California, including farmers, farmworkers, irrigation district managers, state and federal water bureaucrats, government biologists, soil experts, water brokers, environmentalists and attorneys specializing in water law. The author recorded 130 hours of oral histories.

The author was also informed by the dispatches of journalists working for the *Sacramento Bee, Los Angeles Times, New York Times,* San Jose *Mercury News, San Francisco Chronicle,* Stockton *Record, Fresno Bee, Bakersfield Californian, The Atlantic, National Geographic* and *Mother Jones.* A special nod to the fine storytelling of Alexis Madrigal, Josh Harkinson, Bettina Boxall, Adam Nagourney, Lois Henry, Ryan Sabalow, Alan Heathcock, Tom Philpott, Dale Kasler, Phillip Reese, Diana Marcum, Yasha Levine and, last but not least, the late Mike Taugher, who is sorely missed by the dwindling band of California reporters who still call water their beat.

Note: Eight paragraphs in the book tracing the history of water and land development in the San Joaquin Valley appeared in slightly different form in *The King of California.*

INDEX

Page numbers followed by *f* indicate a figure.

ILLUSTRATION CREDITS

Photographs on pages 6, 14, 23, 47, 59, 61, 81, 85, 93, 101, 113, 197, 204, 218, 319, 324, 346, 356, 363, 371, 378, 384, 400, 408, 410, 471, 479, 495, 509, 513, 522 and 525 by Joel Pickford

31: San Diego History Center
68: United States Geological Survey
122: Carlton Watkins, UC Berkeley Bancroft Library
126: David Schmalz, Coast Weekly
135: Private collection, Germany
140: Gleason's Pictorial Drawing Room Companion, UC Berkeley Bancroft Library
157: Joseph Dixon, courtesy National Park Service
159: Society of California Pioneers
170: A. Rosenfield, San Francisco, UC Berkeley Bancroft Library
178: Lithograph by American Oleograph Co., 1875, Library of Congress Prints and Photographs Division
184: Glasshouse Images / Alamy Stock Photograph
211: Bradley & Rulofson, San Francisco, UC Berkeley Bancroft Library
228: Arax Family Collection
235: Michael J. Semas Collection
242: Harding Family collection
252: Mulholland-Scattergood Virtual Museum
261: Los Angeles Department of Water and Power Photograph Collection, Los Angeles County Library
273: San Francisco History Center, San Francisco Public Library
289: Loomis Dean, The LIFE Picture Collection, Getty Images
294: Loomis Dean, The LIFE Picture Collection, Getty Images
298: Trent Davis Bailey
303: Copyright © Bob Chamberlain, *Los Angeles Times.* Reprinted with permission.
312: Trent Davis Bailey
335: Photograph by Marina Zenovich
341: Trent Davis Bailey
420: Giffen Family Collection

426: Ernest Lowe
434: Giffen Family Collection
436: *The Fresno Bee*
452: Photograph by Trent F. Johnson
453: *The Fresno Bee*

A NOTE ABOUT THE AUTHOR

Mark Arax is an author and journalist whose writings on California and the West have received numerous awards for literary nonfiction. He is a former staffer at the *Los Angeles Times*, and his work has appeared in *The New York Times* and *The California Sunday Magazine*. His books include a memoir of his father's murder, a collection of essays about the West and the best-selling *The King of California*, which won a California Book Award, the William Saroyan Prize from Stanford University, and was named a top book of 2004 by the *Los Angeles Times* and the *San Francisco Chronicle*. He lives in Fresno, California.

A NOTE ON THE TYPE

This book was set in Minion, a typeface produced by the Adobe Corporation specifically for the Macintosh personal computer and released in 1990. Designed by Robert Slimbach, Minion combines the classic characteristics of old-style faces with the full complement of weights required for modern typesetting.

Composed by North Market Street Graphics,
Lancaster, Pennsylvania

Printed and bound by Berryville Graphics,
Berryville, Virginia

Designed by M. Kristen Bearse